Schooling and Society

RODMAN B. WEBB
ROBERT R. SHERMAN
UNIVERSITY OF FLORIDA

Schooling and Society

SECOND EDITION

MACMILLAN PUBLISHING COMPANY
NEW YORK
Collier Macmillan Publishers
LONDON

Macmillan Publishing Company
866 Third Avenue, New York, New York 10022

Collier Macmillan Canada, Inc.

LIBRARY OF CONGRESS CATALOGING-IN-PUBLICATION DATA

Webb, Rodman B., 1941–
  Schooling and society.

  Includes indexes.
   1. Education—United States. 2. Educational
sociology—United States. 3. United States—
Intellectual life. I. Sherman, Robert R.,
1930– . II. Title.
LA212.W37 1989   370′.973   88-1786
ISBN 0-02-424900-9

Printing: 1 2 3 4 5 6 7   Year: 9 0 1 2 3 4 5

*For Elise, Joy,
and James E. Wheeler*

Preface

Werner Stark, an eminent sociologist, once turned away a question about a book he had written by saying, "About books of mine that have been published I feel as Calvin felt about the dead: There is nothing more we can do for them; they have gone to their doom." Apparently, Stark never wrote a textbook, for this peculiar form of writing has a way of returning from "doom" to haunt the author. In fact, the week after the First Edition of *Schooling and Society* was published, Lloyd Chilton, our optimistic editor, suggested I get to work on the Second Edition. Of course, I did not act on that suggestion. I had other work to do and I had just spent four years in conversation with the book and was not eager to reopen that discussion.

I need not have worried. Snatching one's work back from doom can be enjoyable, or at least it was for me. The work was made lighter, better, and infinitely more pleasant because Robert Sherman agreed to join in revising the book. Together we clarified points students had found difficult, updated material that was no longer current, and added chapters on civic education, teachers' careers, race and education, and current reform literature. As a result, the Second Edition is substantially larger than the First.

The First Edition offered a heavily sociological analysis of education. The Second Edition retains that emphasis, but adds historical and philosophical material. We have tried to maintain a balance among theory, facts, and practice. The purpose of the Second Edition is the same as that of the First: to offer a critical analysis of schooling in America. As such, it remains well within the social foundations tradition, though, ironically, it represents a radical departure from what most social foundations textbooks offer today. This contention deserves elaboration.

Social foundations studies traditionally have aimed at developing critical-mindedness and social analysis among educators. The goal has been not merely to impart facts—although facts are certainly important—but to help teachers use facts in developing educational policies and determining classroom practices. Early textbooks (such as those written by Harold Rugg, George Counts, William Kilpatrick, and William O. Stanley) were manifestos in defense of critical-mindedness. With a confidence all too rare today, these authors declared that the problems facing education could be analyzed, understood, and ultimately solved. They were confident that teachers could be helped to identify pressing educational problems; to find, interpret, and constructively criticize information relevant to those problems; and to make warranted choices among alternative courses of action. They asserted that the goal of social foundations studies ultimately must be to inform educational practice.

These lofty goals are still the unifying theme of social foundations instruction. They dominate the literature in the field[1] and are written into the "standards for academic and professional instruction" of the American Educational Studies Association (AESA).[2]

Few current textbooks, however, offer social analysis as a unifying theme or present critical-mindedness as an educational objective. Typically, textbooks present a potpourri of facts loosely organized around topic areas. Students are left with the impression that social facts speak for themselves. However, as Dewey pointed out half a century ago, facts do nothing of the sort. The data of social science are meaningless until they are connected to human purposes and social consequences. If social facts are to be useful, Dewey claimed, they must be bound "together into an intelligible whole" and organized around "leading ideas." Such an integration is the product of social analysis and the goal of social foundations studies.

If we expect students to engage in social analysis, we must provide them with examples of how such work is done. The examples provided in this text are designed to provoke students' interest and to sharpen their analytical skills. Conclusions are not presented as more facts to be memorized. Students are shown in a step-by-step fashion how the authors use facts to arrive at warranted conclusions about the current policies and potential practices of American schooling. Students are encouraged to criticize the text's conclusions, to strike out on their own, and to engage in their own analysis. They are encouraged further to examine their own taken-for-granted assumptions regarding education. The text instigates both an outward analysis of social facts and an inward exploration of personal opinions.

This book is addressed to undergraduate and graduate students who have an interest in education. Most of these no doubt will be engaged in professional preparation in some field of education. But we have been presumptuous enough to believe that the book might also be of use to those who do not plan to settle

---

[1] Lane F. Birkel, "Foundations of Education for Undergraduates; When and Why?" *Kappa Delta Xi Record*, Vol. 10 (February 1974), pp. 88–89. Harry S. Broudy, "The Role of the Foundational Studies in the Preparation of Elementary Teachers." Paper presented to the Second Invitational Conference of Elementary Education, Banff, Alberta, on October 26, 1967. Freeman Butts, "Reconstruction in Foundations Studies," *Educational Theory*, Vol. 20 (Winter 1973), pp. 27–41. David Conrad et al., "Foundations of Education—the Restoration of Vision to Teacher Preparation," *Educational Theory*, Vol. 23 (Winter 1973), pp. 42–55. Robert Havighurst, "Sociology in the Contemporary Educational Crisis," *Journal of Research and Development in Education*, Vol. 9 (Fall, 1975), pp. 13–22. T. Howell and Nobuo Shimahara, "Educational Foundations: Contributions at the Undergardaute Level," *The Record*, Vol. 71 (December 1969), pp. 207–216. John Lipkin, "On the Nature and Purpose of Educational Foundations Studies," *Journal of Teacher Education*, Vol. 21 (1970), pp. 486–488. Mary Anne Raywid, "Social Foundations Revisited," *Educational Studies*, Vol. 3 (1972), pp. 71–83. Wayne Urban, "Social Foundations and the Disciplines," *The Record*, Vol. 72 (December 1969), pp. 199–205. Janice Weaver, "Some Additional Questions for the Foundations of Education," Proceedings of the Third Annual Meeting of the *Educational Studies Association*, 1971, pp. 163–170.

[2] See *Educational Studies*, Vol. 8 (Winter, 1977–1978), pp. 329–342.

in the education profession. For this reason, the text does not presuppose much knowledge about education beyond that formidable body of information one gathers while attending school. The book also assumes that students are blissfully ignorant of educational jargon. Wherever possible we have tried not to disturb this ignorance, believing, as we do, that most of education's professional dialect provides more clutter than clarity.

Although we have worked to write clearly and to present ideas in an orderly, comprehensible manner, we have not attempted to impose an artificial simplicity on complex matters. Talking down to students is offensive in itself and invites into the profession individuals who may be ill suited for its difficult tasks. At the same time, it deprives dedicated, capable students of the analytical experiences they need if they are to develop their own critical skills.

Section I of the text deals with the place that individuals hold within society. In this section we explore the nature of human nature and the tension that exists between social order and individual autonomy. We try to make clear that the conflict teachers feel between clamping down and loosening up, between meeting standardized objectives and meeting individual needs, and between teaching facts and encouraging imagination is rooted in a fundamental tension between social order and individual autonomy. Human beings are born into an ordered society and are socialized to accept that order. Schooling is a part of the socialization process. Yet, the imposition of order need not crush human freedom; indeed, order can enhance freedom. The challenge for every democratic society is to find a productive balance between order and freedom; that is, to build institutional structures in which and through which individual autonomy can be encouraged and maintained. Except for the family, no institution has more of an effect on the development of personal autonomy than does the school.

Section II extends the discussion begun in Section I by examining education in the context of American society. American values are explored and the tenets of democracy are given special emphasis. The development of civic education is traced in Chapter 7. Chapter 8 raises the question of educational aims and suggests that new aims are needed to prepare individuals for the fast-paced changes of modern life.

Section III focuses on the backgrounds and careers of teachers. The problems facing the teaching profession are discussed at length, not because we wish to discourage anyone from entering this vital profession, but rather because those who plan to teach should know what to expect. Also, we have found that people who are presently teaching are relieved to know that problems they believed unique to them are, in fact, shared by others. Although we discuss the problems facing teachers, we do not ignore the rewards of teaching.

Section IV examines the school as a social system. The methods employed in this section are sociological and are introduced in Chapter 11. The school is examined in Chapter 12, using the model of the total institution. In Chapter 13, we point out that different groups of children often experience schools in very different ways. In Chapter 14, we look at how teachers experience their jobs. The benefits and limitations of bureaucracy are examined in Chapter 15. The last chapter in this section revisits the issue of educational aims. Its purpose is not merely to reiterate the aims set out in Chapter 8, but to see whether there is research to suggest that the aims we propose can, in fact, be achieved in American schools.

Section V examines the issues of class and race in American society. Special attention is paid to the relationship that exists between social status and equal educational opportunity. We are aware that *Schooling and Society*, Second Edition, gives greater attention to these issues than do most other texts. The issues of race and class do not get the public attention they once had. However mute the press and politicians may have become on these issues, the fact remains that teachers face the consequences of social stratification every day. We point out that the common school in America—where individuals from different backgrounds are educated together—is presently being threatened by the urbanization of poverty and a growing social class segregation.

The last section, Section VI, reviews the current crop of reform proposals. We point out that different reform reports serve the interests of different constituencies. Such reports are proliferating today because there is a growing perception that the quality of education is declining and because the debate over educational aims increasingly is being carried on by many constituencies and especially at the national level. The last chapter reviews research on school improvement and suggests what might be done to "make schools work."

Anyone familiar with the work of Peter Berger and James Wheeler will recognize their influence on our thinking. We share with Berger the belief that sociology and philosophy can be liberating, that these disciplines reveal both the limits and possibilities of human freedom, that human beings are creators of the social world that, paradoxically, creates them, that modernity provides unprecedented opportunity for freedom and alienation, and that mediating institutions can nurture autonomy and provide a cushion against alienation. We share with Wheeler a faith in reason and commitment to the possibility of community and democracy, and we are indebted to him for introducing us to pragmatism and especially to the work of George Herbert Mead and John Dewey. We have not tried to write a book that would please Berger and Wheeler, for it would be impossible to satisfy two such original and, in many ways, divergent scholars. Still, we hope that both would find what we have done here generally consistent with their conception of philosophy and social science.

We owe an enormous debt of gratitude to the many colleagues at the University of Florida and elsewhere who have been kind enough to read and comment on the book: Alden Carlson, State University of New York–Cortland; Harold Cadmus; Robert Curran, The University of Florida; George J. Harrison, Kent State University; John Laska, The University of Texas–Austin; Hal Lewis, The University of Florida; Rao H. Lindsay, The University of Maryland–College Park; Richard Renner, The University of Florida; Fred Schultz; Robert Soar, The University of Florida; Colin Turnbull, George Washington University; Mary Yeazell, West Virginia University; Amos Hatch, The University of Tennessee; Patricia Sikes, Open University; Ivor Goodson, The University of Western Ontario; Stephen Ball, The University of London; and Betsy West, Witchita State University. We are especially indebted to Len Roberts, Troy State University; Jeff Roth, The University of Florida; and Robert Morrison, The University of Florida.

R.B.W.
R.R.S.

Contents

SECTION III

The Teaching Profession: Ideals and Realities   *191*

CHAPTER 9

Teacher Backgrounds: What Teachers Bring with Them to the School   *193*

CHAPTER 10

Teachers' Careers   *223*

SECTION IV

The School as a Social System: Institutionalizing Educational Aims   261

CHAPTER 11

Studying Institutions: Bureaucracy and Education   263

CHAPTER 18

Equal Educational Opportunity and the Ideology of Stratification   428

CHAPTER 19

Social Class and Child Rearing: What Children Bring with Them to School   449

CHAPTER 20

Schooling and the Stigma of Poverty   *471*

CHAPTER 21

Education and the American Meritocracy   *490*

CHAPTER 22

Race, Poverty, Democracy, and the Common School   *512*

SECTION **VI**

*Improving Schools: Balancing Quality
and Equality*   *555*

CHAPTER 23

*Revising Education: Multiple Calls for
Educational Change*   *557*

CHAPTER 24
Making Schools Work   *588*

Culture and the Individual: A Question of Balance

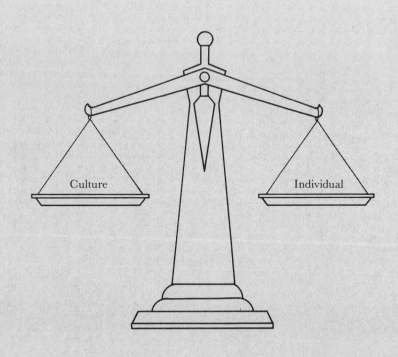

CHAPTER 1

Discovering Schooling: An Introduction

The activities of teaching encourage us to see education in the narrowest, most microscopic terms. A teacher's attention is drawn not just to the class or to an individual student but to very narrow portions of students' lives and talents. The everyday events of classroom life put small but important questions at the forefront of a teacher's attention:

- Can Nancy spell *chrysanthemum*?
- What might be done to help Jeff become more aggressive?
- Is Jean behaving better today than yesterday?
- Has Toby forgiven his brother for not taking him camping?
- Does Wendy really understand the theory of evolution?

These are not cosmic issues, but they have their importance. Everything obvious in the everyday events of teaching focuses the teacher's attention on the small details of student growth and development, and this is appropriate. Life, after all, is made up of details. The small events within the vision of a teacher, however, are tied to larger forces that lie behind the scenes or beyond the walls of the classroom. These forces connect the events of the classroom to structured arrangements in the school, the family, the community, and the society.

This book is about these larger forces. It is not about the details of teaching but the social system that makes teaching situations what they are. It is a story of connections, and its intent is to expand the vision of teachers beyond the details of their daily routines. The purpose of this text is not to survey the landscape of human events but to *understand* the larger scene in terms of the meaning it holds for teaching. Its purpose is not to turn the teacher's attention away from students but to supply the information and outlook needed to appreciate more deeply what transpires within the school.

Personal Trouble and Social Issues

We are all apt to view education as something that transpires between teacher and student. When a problem crops up, we are likely to define it in personal terms: Johnny suffers an inadequacy in reading or Sally has a behavior problem. There are perfectly obvious reasons for this view. If Johnny can't read, then something must be done to help him with *his* problem. It may soothe Johnny's feelings to know that his trouble is widespread, that an estimated 20 percent of today's high school graduates have deficiencies in reading and/or mathematics.[1] But to overcome Johnny's problem will require focused and persistent work with Johnny himself. It is *his* problem in the important sense that teachers can only guide, encourage, coach, and coax him along. They can (indeed, they must) insist that he stay on task, but they cannot learn to read for him.

C. Wright Mills, an American sociologist, makes a useful distinction between what he calls "personal troubles" and "structural issues." The activities of teaching encourage us to see most problems as personal troubles. These have to do with the character or skills of the individual. "The resolution of troubles properly lie[s] within the individual as a biographical entity and the . . . social setting that is directly open to his personal experience."[2]

Structural issues are problems of another sort. These are of a public nature and pertain to troubles in the social structure, in institutions or the economy, and in cherished values or public attitudes.

Personal problems overlap other areas. For example, if Johnny was black and living in an earlier time, "compulsory ignorance" laws in many states would have forbidden his learning to read.[3] Under these conditions, Mills would call Johnny's illiteracy a social, or structural, issue rather than a personal problem.

But let's keep the example current and assume that Johnny is attending one of four Kansas City high schools where a quarter of the tenth graders scored at or below the sixth percentile on the Comprehensive Test of Basic Skills.[4] (Many scored below the fifth percentile—the score that students are likely to achieve if they blindly guess their way through the test.) In Johnny's school (and, sadly, hundreds of other schools like it across the country), the problem of poor reading is a social issue. There is something in the social milieu of the school and/or surrounding community that works against Johnny's learning to read. The trouble does not lie in flaws in Johnny's character, or the limits of his intelligence, or perhaps even his will. It exists somewhere in the larger social system.

Seeing Johnny's reading problem as a social issue rather than as a personal trouble will, of course, not make it go away. But it should influence how we deal with the issue. Certainly, teachers will have to work long and hard with Johnny, and in that sense the problem remains his own. But it is also important

---

[1] Carnegie Council on Policy Studies in Higher Education, *Giving Youth a Better Chance* (San Francisco: Jossey-Bass, Inc., Publishers, 1979), p. 2.

[2] C. Wright Mills, *The Sociological Imagination* (New York: Oxford University Press, Inc., 1975), p. 8. Available in paperback.

[3] Meyer Weinberg, *A Chance to Learn: The History of Race and Education in the United States* (New York: Cambridge University Press, 1977), p. 13. Available in paperback.

[4] Daniel V. Levine, Cris Kukuk, and Jeanie Kenny Meyer, "Poverty in Big Cities," in *Educational Environments and Effects*, ed. Herbert J. Walberg (Berkeley, CA: McCutchan Publishing Corporation, 1979), p. 333.

that we make changes in the school system that is serving its students so poorly. It is easier, of course, to focus on Johnny's deficiencies, to view the problem as peculiar to him. But to do so diminishes the likelihood that remedial efforts will succeed. Rather, it guarantees that a long succession of students like Johnny will follow in his footsteps.

Consider another example. If a handful of entering freshmen cannot write well enough to do college work, they have "personal troubles." But if 20 to 30 percent of the entering class is unable to write a coherent sentence, then we ought to start looking for other explanations. Something vital in the educational system has collapsed.

We needn't look far. If students are to learn how to write, it is essential that they write early and throughout their school careers. Their papers must be read, corrected, commented upon, and handed back quickly. Records must be kept so that the teacher and, just as importantly, the student, can keep tabs on progress. A bit of arithmetic will reveal one part of the larger problem. Let's say the average English teacher teaches five periods a day (some teach six) and that he or she has twenty-five students in each class (though some have as many as thirty-five or more). If each student writes a short paper only once a week and if it takes the teacher just eight minutes to correct each one, the teacher will have to spend the equivalent of seventy-four work days a year just correcting papers. Looked at in this way, the writing problems of college freshmen are not mere personal troubles but have their origin in the school system itself. Such problems will not be solved by remedial-writing clinics at the college level but by changing the workload of English teachers in the high schools.

Unhappily, examples such as these could be multiplied indefinitely. But we

Some personal troubles are also social issues.   *Source:* National Education Association, Joe Di Dio.

need not wash the whole window to see through to the point. Social factors operate in classrooms, and if teachers are to be of optimal help to their students, they must understand how these forces work; they need what the European sociologist Karl Mannheim called social awareness.

By social awareness, Mannheim did not mean the "mere acquisition of rational knowledge," though some of this won't hurt. He meant instead *"the readiness to see the whole situation* in which one finds oneself, and not only to orient one's actions on immediate tasks and purposes but to base them on a more comprehensive vision"[5] (emphasis added).

The Readiness to See

It is worth pausing here to ponder what Mannheim meant by the phrase "the readiness to see." Mannheim believed, as most sociologists do, that people generally live their lives by habit. They tend to have routine ways of doing things and habitual ways of seeing and defining the world. These habits of thought, which Mannheim called ideologies, have immense power because they are shared with others and are built into the structural assumptions of institutions. For this reason, few people stray very far from the "official definitions" of reality.

When Mannheim talks about a readiness to see beyond the matters at hand, a preparedness to see the whole situation, he means that teachers must occasionally put aside their habitual ways of thinking and hold in abeyance their taken-for-granted assumptions about the social world. They must be willing to suspend "those interpretations of situations which are not the outcome of concrete experiences but are a kind of distorted knowledge of them which serves to *cover up the real situation* and works upon the individual like a compulsion"[6] (emphasis added). This isn't easy. Habits are strong and usually work below the level of conscious awareness.[7] To suspend our belief—if only momentarily—can be an uncomfortable, even terrifying, experience. But it can also be a source of useful knowledge and personal exhilaration. In any case, it is difficult to become aware of the multiple forces that bear upon our thoughts and actions and those of our students unless we are "ready to see."

The task, then, is to pull back the ideological tarpaulin human beings spread across their lives and view the naked reality that lies beneath it. If we are to understand what is really going on, we must *dis-cover* the schools and the world around them. Thus, the title of this chapter, "Discovering Schools," and indeed the aim of the whole book, implies discovery both in the sense that (1) one comes to know something new by (2) *dis-covering*, or uncovering, what is taken for granted about it. To accomplish this task, it is necessary to subject ourselves to surprises. When we look behind the scenes of our institutions or peer through the everyday interpretations of events, we are likely to be surprised, even astonished, by what we see. Thus, when Mannheim suggests that teachers have a readiness to see, he is, in fact, referring to a willingness to be shocked.

---

[5] Karl Mannheim, "Education, Sociology and the Problem of Social Awareness," in *From Karl Mannheim,* ed. Kurt Wolff (New York: Oxford University Press, Inc., 1971), p. 374.

[6] Karl Mannheim, "Educating for Democracy," in *From Karl Mannheim,* p. cxv.

[7] Philosophers say that habits work prereflectively. For a useful account of the prereflective powers of habit, see Victor Kestenbaum, *The Phenomenological Sense of John Dewey: Habit and Meaning* (Atlantic Highlands, NJ: Humanities Press, Inc., 1977).

The Tools and the Task

The tools we will be using in this text are largely drawn from sociology, history, and, less obviously (but no less importantly), philosophy. A debunking tendency exists in all these disciplines. None of them accepts the world as it appears or takes at face value the official definitions of reality. For example, a social scientist might be interested in such questions as:

- Do schools equalize opportunity, or is their function or effect to inhibit the chances of the poor?
- Is the purpose of schooling to encourage students to think for themselves, or to think as others do?
- Do special education classes and vocational education programs serve the needs of students, or do they serve as a convenient dumping ground for students whom teachers find difficult to manage?
- Are teachers motivated by a desire to help young people, or are they in teaching for the rewards of money and long vacations?

Even to ask such questions means that we are not sure of the answers. Such queries challenge official dogma, unmask vested interests, offend deeply held beliefs, and upset myths and stereotypes. They are about as welcome to true believers as a Sunday sermon is to a disbeliever.

If the questions of social science are so potentially threatening and if its findings are so frequently painful, why do people bother with such work? Max Weber, a German sociologist of great insight but precarious mental health, answered that question with chilling clarity: because, he said, "I want to see how much I can stand."[8] But most social scientists use their discipline for more practical purposes.

Few social scientists are perennial malcontents or professional Peeping Toms. The purpose of social science is not to declare the emperor naked for the sheer fun of watching him blush, nor is it to debunk institutions merely to expose the pretensions and pratfalls of stodgy officials.

The driving aim of social science is to understand what makes society tick. As Peter Berger has said of the discipline of sociology,

> It presupposes a certain awareness that human events have different levels of meaning, some of which are hidden from the consciousness of everyday life. It may even presuppose a measure of suspicion about the way in which human events are officially interpreted by the authorities, be they political, juridical or religious in character.[9]

But for all the snooping and mistrust, for all the curiosity, hard work, and discipline necessary for social science, its fundamental objective is to understand.

Understanding, one might think, needs no justification beyond itself. The desire to understand, many optimistically contend, is a natural urge in human

---

[8] Quoted in Peter Berger, "Sociology and Freedom," in *Facing Up to Modernity: Excursions in Society, Politics, and Religion,* ed. Peter Berger (New York: Basic Books, 1977), p. xiv.

[9] Peter Berger, *Invitation to Sociology: A Humanistic Perspective* (New York: Doubleday & Co., Inc., Anchor Books, 1963), p. 29.

beings. Yet ignorance does have its social uses. Giving ourselves blindly to conformity frees us from the agony of ambiguity and the necessity of choice. When we subject our taken-for-granted world to sociological analysis, we are putting this world at risk. Taboos may appear less forbidding, customs less compelling, social reality suddenly precarious, and much of the social enterprise downright comical. But if understanding has its dangers, it also has its uses. To live in society is to be subject to many forces of which we are seldom aware. As Reece McGee has said:

> Freedom consists in knowing what these forces are and how they work so that we have the option of saying no to the impact of their operation. For example, if we grow up in a racist society, we will be racists unless we know what racism is and how it works and then choose to refuse its impact. In order to do so, however, we must recognize that it is there in the first place. People often are puppets, blindly danced by strings of which they are unaware and over which they are not free to exercise control. A major function of sociology is that it permits us to recognize the forces operative on us and to untie the puppet strings which bind us, thereby giving us the option to be free.[10]

How can we be sure that social science will lead us to freedom rather than to cynicism and despair? Of course, there are no guarantees in this or any other human enterprise, but the chances of avoiding disenchantment are greatest if we nurture in ourselves a commitment to humanity, a capacity for compassion, and, perhaps above all, a deep and abiding love of laughter.

One further thing needs to be said about the burning desire of social scientists to know the hows, whys, and whats of human behavior. The understanding they seek is a special kind. It is disciplined, objective, and scientific. This is not to say that there are not other kinds of understanding. The physicist who defines water in terms of its molecular makeup (H_2O) would be foolish to deny a poet's romantic description of the sea. The social scientist's observations of a wedding will no doubt be different from those of a religious official conducting the service, the lovers who are getting married, or the insurance salesman who inevitably lurks nearby. There is no need to argue the relative merits of these "angles of vision." The world is large and can be looked at in many ways. Each vision has its merits; it would be an ugly fantasy to imagine a world without poets, religious leaders, scientists, and perhaps even insurance salesmen.

The Uses of Social Science

The uses to which we will put social science will be circumscribed by our central concern—education. Although this will put boundaries on our inquiry, we will find ourselves working in ever-widening contexts. As Mannheim observed,

> It is impossible to think of a teacher who does not, day by day, meet with behavior difficulties in the child which, properly observed, are but symptoms of conflicts within the family, [and] in the community.[11]

---

10 Reece McGee, *Points of Departure: Basic Concepts in Sociology*, 2d ed. (Hinsdale, IL: Dryden Press, 1975), pp. x–xi.
11 Karl Mannheim, "Education Sociology and the Problem of Social Awareness," in *From Karl Mannheim*, p. 371.

When we trace private troubles to their public source, we are compelled to confront larger institutions, such as the school, family, community, subcultures, and society at large. We are forced to question the makeup of human nature and ponder the connections that exist between individuals and society. The aim in this endeavor will be to increase our knowledge so that we can improve our teaching practice.

But the need for what Mannheim called a "more comprehensive vision" does not begin only with the vocational interest of improving our performance as teachers. We are confronted not only with problems of "how to do it" but also with the prior and more troublesome question of what it is we are supposed to do.

In a simpler time, there was seldom any question of what should be done. As long as the future could be trusted to replicate the past, the overall prescription for education was "more of the same."[12] Teachers did not need to ponder the purposes of education, because purpose already was built into their ideologies, into the structure of the school, and into the expectations of the general public. The system worked like a giant machine, predictably and without need of ideas. Under conditions such as these, teachers could be blind to society; indeed, they often were expected to be.

As history began to move at a faster pace, society soon outstripped its traditions. Science and technology produced an industrial environment that our traditional beliefs, morals, and religions were ill equipped to interpret and regulate. This situation demanded that education rethink its aims. Teachers were no longer preparing their students for a known world, but for a future more complex and precarious than had ever existed before. At the end of World War II, Mannheim declared, "From now on, the aim of the school is not to impart ready-made knowledge but to enable us to learn more efficiently from life itself."[13]

Americans such as John Dewey had been saying the same thing since the beginning of the century. Educators would have to become aware of their purposes, more conscious of their connections with society, and more thoughtful about the future. We now live in a world where ideas—ideals—can make a difference. The education we provide for our children reflects the kind of society in which we want to live. If we fail to understand that connection, we fail to appreciate the moral purpose of education.

However, it is difficult to crack tradition or to contemplate the direction education should take. In 1970, Charles Silberman said,

> What is mostly wrong with the public schools is not due to venality or indifference or stupidity, but to mindlessness. . . . It simply never occurs to more than a handful to ask *why* they are doing what they are doing—to think seriously or deeply about the purpose or consequences of education.[14]

[12] The philosopher Alfred North Whitehead has said: "The history of human thought in the past is a pitiful tale of self-satisfaction with a supposed adequacy of knowledge in respect to factors of human existence. We now know that in the past such self-satisfaction was a delusion." "Immortality," in *The Philosophy of Alfred North Whitehead*, ed. P. A. Schilpp (Chicago: Northwestern University Press, 1941), p. 683.

[13] Karl Mannheim, "Education, Sociology and the Problem of Social Awareness," in *From Karl Mannheim*, p. 368.

[14] Charles Silberman, *Crisis in the Classroom* (New York: Random House, Inc., 1970), pp. 10–11. Available in paperback.

Social science can help us think about the purposes and practices of education. That is its contribution. It will not create a different world, for the business of social science is to see the world as it really is. Social science promises only to take those who are ready to see deeper into the world they already are aware of. It will help them see the world from a new angle of vision and with a deeper appreciation and understanding of what lies before them.

Social science will not tell you what to do. It will not provide easy recipes for change or prescriptions for the future. It can only guide your attention to new facets of the social world, inform your judgment, and help you think more clearly.

Used wisely, social science can provide what Mills called

> a quality of mind that will help [people] to use information and to develop reason in order to achieve lucid summations of what is going on in the world and of what may be happening within themselves. . . . By such means the personal uneasiness of individuals is focused upon explicit troubles and the indifference of publics is transformed into involvement with public issues.[15]

These are qualities that can serve an educator well.

Suggested Readings

The view of social science expressed in this chapter is developed more fully in the sociological literature. Readers are referred to the following:

BERGER, PETER L. *Invitation to Sociology: A Humanistic Perspective.* Garden City, NY: Anchor Books, Doubleday & Company, Inc., 1963.

LYND, ROBERT S. *Knowledge for What? The Place of Social Science in American Culture.* Princeton, NJ: Princeton University Press, 1939.

MANNHEIM, KARL. "Education, Sociology and the Problem of Social Awareness." In *From Karl Mannheim,* edited by Kurt H. Wolff, pp. 367–384. New York: Oxford University Press, 1971.

MILLS, C. WRIGHT. *The Sociological Imagination.* New York: Oxford University Press, 1975.

NATANSON, MAURICE, ed. *Phenomenology and Social Sciences,* Vol. I. Evanston, IL: Northwestern University Press, 1973.

SCHUTZ, ALFRED. *Collected Papers,* Vol. I: *The Problem of Social Reality,* edited by Maurice Natanson. The Hague: Martinus Nijhoff, 1971.

WEBB, RODMAN B. "The Recovery of Experience in Sociology." In *The Presence of the Past: John Dewey and Alfred Schutz on the Genesis and Organization of Experience,* pp. 99–109. Gainesville, FL: The University Presses of Florida, 1976.

WEBER, MAX. "Science as a Vocation." In *From Max Weber: Essays in Sociology,* translated and edited by H. H. Gerth and C. Wright Mills, pp. 129–156. New York: Oxford University Press, 1958.

[15] C. Wright Mills, *The Sociological Imagination,* p. 5.

CHAPTER 2

Identity and the Social Order

René Dubos, a microbiologist and sensitive social critic, began his book *So Human an Animal* with these words, "Each human being is unique, unprecedented and unrepeatable."[1] Dubos is no doubt correct, but his observation brings with it an important question: How is it that large numbers of unique, unprecedented, and unrepeatable human beings can live together in relative harmony? Or, to put it another way, how can individual diversity and social order coexist?

This question is not new, but it has been asked with new intensity in modern times. Life today, despite its many rewards, puts an enormous strain on individuals. It is difficult to feel a close connection with the immensely powerful institutions of society. We find them difficult to understand, hard to relate to, and almost impossible to influence. These powerful institutions (corporations, government agencies, unions, organized professions, and educational establishments) have been called *megastructures*.[2]

Megastructures are run by persons who seem remote and impersonal—without humor, imagination, or courage. Face-to-face interactions with such people are usually superficial. We feel little or no bond with the individual who processes our health insurance, the highway toll taker who collects our change, the registrar who sends our grades, or the infirmary nurse who dispenses medicines. Our interest in such people typically begins and ends with the narrow duties they perform for us. We expect them to be efficient, are pleased when they are polite, but would be downright shocked if they were warm, caring, or intimate. Such qualities are not often found in the megastructures of society.

When megastructures deal with us smoothly, we have the feeling of being processed, but when the bureaucratic machinery fails, we feel as if we are being chewed up, pushed around, or ignored. It is little wonder that the megastructures of society do not provide genuine meaning for our lives or identity for our being.

There is another aspect to our experience of megastructures that has signif-

---

[1] René Dubos, *So Human an Animal* (New York: Charles Scribner's Sons, 1968), p. vii.
[2] This term is borrowed from Peter Berger. See his "In Praise of Particularity" in *Facing Up to Modernity: Excursions in Society, Politics, and Religion* (New York: Basic Books, 1977), pp. 130–141. For the idea of *megastructure* in education, see Clark Kerr, *The Uses of the University* (Cambridge: Harvard University Press, 1963), especially Chapter 1, "The Idea of a Multiversity."

icance for modern life. As individuals find their way through and between giant institutions, they are likely to find areas of unprecedented freedom. For example, university students are driven to distraction by the tedious and impersonal rituals of registration. They are frustrated because they are treated like numbers and because the institution fails to give them personal attention. Yet the same students may find a jubilant sense of freedom when left alone by the university to experiment with different life-styles, identities, political beliefs, religious preferences, and sexual experiences. Such a phenomenon is not peculiar to university students. Most adult members of modern society are left pretty much alone to create their own meanings and identities in the intimate circle of their personal lives.

This is a great paradox of modern existence. On the one hand, individuals are set free to create a meaningful world within the *private sphere*. Here individuals are neither hampered nor helped by institutions. They are treated to a bewildering variety of possibilities. On the other hand, the public work of the society is carried on within the impersonal megastructures of the *public sphere*. Here the individual must work with impersonal efficiency. Activity within this bureaucratic order is unlikely to supply a sense of belonging or meaning.

The division between the public life and private life of an individual presents many problems. Individuals are expected to "get it together" in their private sphere. There, with help from family and selected friends, individuals create identity and meaning that enable them to survive in the impersonal world of the public sphere. But the private sphere is precarious because it does not have institutional support. Therefore, life in the private sphere is always vulnerable. The carefully constructed meaning and identity of the private sphere are badly disrupted if a lover leaves, a friend dies, a child rebels, or a spouse undergoes a change in personality. When such changes occur, an individual may no longer be able to endure the impersonality of the public sphere. Such disruptions are difficult for individuals, but they also present problems for society. Megastructures cannot be run by individuals who are in a perpetual state of personal crisis.

Individuals have to learn to keep the public and private spheres of their lives in a delicate balance. The public sphere has given us a degree of efficiency the world has never known. It has allowed us unprecedented freedom. But it has loosened the social ties among us, depersonalized our interactions, and deprived us of strongly felt, shared meanings. We are less sure of who we are, what we are about, and where we are going. This form of uncertainty is often called *alienation*.

The private sphere enables us to combat the alienating pressures of modern society. However, the private sphere has few institutional supports. It runs the risk of being overrun with the concerns of the public sphere despite our efforts not to bring problems at work home with us. The problems presented by the separation of public and private life will be better understood if we look more closely at the question of alienation.

Five Forms of Alienation

Alienation refers to an individual's feeling of separation from some portion of society. It is essentially a sociological term, but it is widely used in everyday English. Its popularity is perhaps a crude sign of its validity. Alienation apparently plays a part (if we are lucky, only a small part) in all of our lives. But the popularization of the term has brought difficulty, for even social scientists use the term to describe a wide variety of experiences. We will define five of the more common meanings of *alienation*. Some of these deal with an individual's experience in the public sphere, others with that experience in the private sphere.

Each of the following descriptions includes a definition of a special kind of alienation and a discussion of how individuals normally deal with it. These definitions are not exhaustive.[3] There are other definitions that are not discussed here. Also, it should be kept in mind that the types of alienation discussed are not mutually exclusive. There is nothing in the construction of individuals or society that prevents us from experiencing more than one form of alienation.

Alienation as Powerlessness

Alienation as powerlessness comes about when individuals sense their inability to participate in decisions that directly affect their lives. Modernity has created two conditions that heighten the feeling of powerlessness. First, modern society has created megastructures so enormous that the average citizen has little or no control over them. Second, modern society creates a personality structure that has a low tolerance for the impersonality and powerlessness experienced in the public sphere. This second point needs elaboration. In modern life, vast portions of individual lives are unstructured by society and unmonitored by institutions. Important parts of human existence, such as the creation of meaning, identity, and purpose, are left to individuals to construct for themselves in the private sphere. One result of this has been to heighten the individual's sense of dignity, rights, and self-importance. In the private sphere, most of us learn from childhood that we are (or can become) special beings, capable and worthy of love and significant enough to be included in decisions that directly affect our lives. On the other hand, the public sphere often violates these assumptions. Megastructures are not personalistic. They do not treat individuals as being in any way special, are not guided by the rhetoric of love, and carefully guard the right to make institutional decisions.

These two conditions—megastructures and our heightened sense of individual worth—intensify the feeling of powerlessness in modern society. Everyone feels powerless some of the time and some individuals feel powerless all of the time. Of course, individuals cope with powerlessness in a variety of ways. The coping strategies listed here are but a few of the most common ones found in the United States.

1. One way to cope with powerlessness is to retreat into apathy. This is perhaps most apparent in political life. Recent political elections excite the voting interests of just over half of the number of eligible voters. Over 40 percent of people eligible to vote do not do so. A major reason for not voting is said to be the feeling of powerlessness. Many believe that "my vote won't make any difference." There is a disturbing but accurate logic to such belief. As popula-

---

[3] The five headings used here are the ones used by Melvin Seeman in his article "On the Meaning of Alienation," *American Sociological Review*, Vol. 24, No. 6 (December 1959), pp. 783–791. There are some differences between Seeman's discussion of these forms of alienation and the definitions presented here.

TABLE 2-1.   Rising Expressions of Powerlessness

Question: "Now I want to read you some things that some people have told us they have felt from time to time. Do you tend to feel or not feel (Read Each Item)?"

	"Tend to Feel"								
	1980	*1977*	*1976*	*1975*	*1973*	*1972*	*1971*	*1968*	*1966*
	%	%	%	%	%	%	%	%	%
The rich get richer and the poor get poorer	78	77	77	79	76	66	62	54	45
What you think doesn't count very much any more	64	61	64	60	61	50	44	42	37
The people running the country don't really care what happens to you	50	60	61	63	55	45	41	36	26
You are left out of things going on around you	48	35	42	32	29	24	20	12	9

SOURCE: Louis Harris, *The ABC News-Harris Survey.* New York: The Chicago Tribune-New York News Syndicate, 6/2/80 and 12/8/77. Data from 1966–76 were published in slightly different form in *Public Opinion,* May/June, 1978, p. 23. These copyrighted data are printed with permission of the American Enterprise Institute.

tion grows, every vote becomes a smaller fraction of the total. Government becomes more and more external and claims less and less of an individual's interest or allegiance. Polls by Louis Harris show that in 1966, 37 percent of adult Americans agreed with the statement, "What you think doesn't count very much any more." (See Table 2-1.) That percentage had grown to 64 by 1980. In 1966, 26 percent of adult Americans agreed with the statement, "The people running the country don't really care what happens to you." By 1980, that percentage had risen to 50.

Political apathy is only an example of a much wider disengagement from institutions in the public sphere. College students, especially in large universities, are not likely to feel a strong allegiance to their schools. Some workers are similarly detached from their jobs. At least part of this trend toward detachment is traceable to the feeling, as institutions get larger, that individuals have little or no control over what happens to them in the public sphere. Apathy is an acceptance of their powerlessness.

2. Individuals tolerate powerlessness and apathy in the public domain by retreating to the private sphere, where they have more control over their lives. Thus, apathy in the public sphere results in even greater importance being assigned to private life. This may further escalate the sense of powerlessness.

3. Another method of dealing with powerlessness in the public sphere is to organize competing structures that challenge the authority of public institutions. Unions are organized to counter the power that businesses have over employees. Government watchdog agencies are designed to safeguard the public from the excesses of business. Public interest groups (Ralph Nader organizations, Common Cause, environmental groups, and so on) are established to counter the power of both business and government. These counterstructures themselves must be massive if they are to be effective. Their size, however,

makes it equally difficult for individuals to participate meaningfully in their governance. Counterstructures run the risk of becoming part of society's mega-structures and can heighten, rather than alleviate, the feeling of powerlessness that pervades modern society.

Alienation as Meaninglessness

The megastructures of modern society are vast and beyond an individual's abil-ity to experience them in a total way. We understand institutions only as ab-stractions.[4] We cannot directly experience the totality of the federal govern-ment, General Motors, or the state university system. We do not experience or understand such institutions as richly or fully as we do, say, the family, the church, or some voluntary organization.

Abstract institutions present individuals with special difficulties. Because we do not experience them fully, we cannot get a clear idea of how or why they function as they do. For example, if we work for General Motors or for the Los Angeles school system, it is difficult to feel a deep connection or unity with the goals of the institution. Indeed, it is hard to tell what those goals might be.

Modern life demands that we spend much of our time working in or dealing with megastructures. This experience is often frustrating and seldom provides us with a sense of community or shared meaning. Yet a sense of meaning, community, and purpose are essential to human life. How, then, do individuals cope with the meaninglessness of the public sphere? The answer has already been suggested. They withdraw into the private sphere, where meaning and community can be constructed in a concrete rather than abstract fashion.

Alienation as Normlessness

Despite the abstract nature of modern megastructures, society manages to pro-vide its citizens with general goals to work toward. For example, American society is success oriented. Individuals are expected to strive for high grades, high salary, more power, and so on. Society also defines the acceptable means for achieving these goals. A student is expected to earn good grades but is warned against getting straight A's by cheating. People in business are expected to improve their financial situations but not through embezzlement. Socially prescribed goals and socially accepted means for achieving those goals are called *norms.*

Some individuals may accept the goals society offers but find themselves un-able to achieve them through prescribed means. When the means-goals coor-dination is seen as unrealistic, normlessness results. Under such conditions in-dividuals are likely to find their own methods for achieving social goals. Cheating may become standard practice in a class where students see no other way to get acceptable grades. An individual who feels unable to achieve a share of the good life through work may try to get it by breaking the law.

Here we find a form of alienation that drives individuals more deeply into

---

[4] The conception that public institutions are essentially abstract has a long history in sociological thought. Georg Simmel, Emile Durkheim, Karl Marx, and Max Weber all gave this idea consid-erable attention. It has been dealt with in a fascinating book by Anton Zijderveld, *The Abstract Society* (New York: Doubleday & Co., Inc., 1970). Available in paperback.

the private sphere. In this case, individuals withdraw to the private realm in order to find support for their antisocial activity. Crime is easier on the conscience when it is legitimated by a peer group.

Alienation as Isolation

The forms of alienation discussed so far represent a separation of individuals from the larger society. We turn now to a more radical and all-encompassing form of alienation, that of individual isolation, where a person rejects the desirability of any active participation in society. The individual rejects the goals of society, the means of achieving those goals, and even the meanings supplied by the social order. Such individuals isolate themselves almost totally from society and, quite literally, live in worlds of their own. Although other forms of alienation may lead to mental disturbance, alienation as isolation can lead to outright insanity.

Gregory Bateson's theory of schizophrenia provides an example of alienation as isolation and the environment in which it grows. Bateson began his discussion of schizophrenia by referring to a situation he had observed in a mental hospital. A schizophrenic boy was being visited by his mother. When the child saw her, he put an arm around her shoulder and squeezed her affectionately. The mother recoiled slightly and the child immediately dropped his arm. It was clear to him that his mother was made uncomfortable by his show of affection. However, as the child withdrew, the mother sent a new and contradictory message. "Don't you love me any more?" she asked. She chastised the child for his inability to show his feelings.[5]

The boy was caught in what Bateson called a *double-bind*. To show his mother affection was to offend her. Her displeasure could be read in her body language and would result in some disconnected punishment in the future. To accommodate to her feelings, however, and to repress his desire to show affection was to risk punishment of a different kind. The mother denied the message sent by her body language and reproached the child for not showing affection. His desire not to offend was given new meaning when the mother asked, "Don't you love me any more?" The child was caught in a contradiction. Any action he took would offend his mother. He was unable to express his dilemma and was forced to grapple with it internally. Bateson was, of course, not suggesting that individuals are catapulted into schizophrenia by a single event. However, when life is full of such events, an individual is flooded with feelings of helplessness, fear, exasperation, and rage. Mental isolation becomes a way of dealing with such feelings and the situations that cause them.

Bateson's breakthrough theory of schizophrenia examined the extreme mental isolation of his patients. He believes schizophrenics have found a method for dealing with the massive contradictions they face in family life. They shield themselves from these contradictions by withdrawing into the isolation of their own totally private world—a world that makes sense only to them. This is not a private sphere peopled by family and friends. It is a world of almost complete isolation, a world of insanity.

---

[5] Gregory Bateson, *Steps to an Ecology of Mind* (New York: Ballantine Books, Inc., 1972), pp. 201–227.

Alienation as Self-Estrangement

The fifth and last form of alienation, *self-estrangement,* is common in America. Self-estranged individuals find little or no intrinsic satisfaction in the roles they play or the work they do. Activity has no intrinsic purpose but is carried out to achieve external rewards, such as pleasing others or making money. You may know people who play at being college students yet gain little or no satisfaction from academic life. They persist only to please their peers or parents, or perhaps in the misguided hope that a college diploma will bring a high-paying job. In a similar fashion, some individuals endure bland jobs although they offer little satisfaction beyond that of a paycheck.

How do self-estranged individuals endure playing roles they neither believe nor enjoy? David Riesman describes such people as *other directed.* In his book, *The Lonely Crowd,*[6] he explains that other-directed individuals are motivated by an intense desire to please others. They define themselves in terms of what others think of them. Pleasure is nothing more or less than social approval. It is difficult, however, to fulfill the conflicting expectations of different groups. To accomplish this feat, other-directed individuals adopt a radarlike personality, sensitive to all signs of social approval and disapproval. Other-directed individuals are trained from childhood to be "popular," "nice," "well adjusted," "friendly," "in with the group," and above all, noncontroversial. They are likely to be careful consumers and buy clothes, homes, cars, and other accessories that will impress their friends. Other-directed people are expert at self-manipulation, changing in chameleon fashion to ensure that they get along well with their peers. The vast and growing literature of self-adjustment testifies to the other-directed Americans' desire to please and appease. Newsstands and bookstores are filled with self-help texts that promise happiness through good grooming, elegant parties, well-cooked meals, interesting conversation, exciting sexuality, cult religion, or the newest fad in psychotherapy. Everything from mouthwash to kitchen wax is sold by advertising that warns against offending the expectations of others.

Riesman's *The Lonely Crowd* examines the broad sweep of American history in search of what he calls the American character. His view is wide and inclusive, not minute and detailed. Another sociologist, Erving Goffman, has devoted his professional life to a microscopic examination of American behavior in face-to-face interactions. Goffman's work is very different from Riesman's, although his analysis of social interaction supports the idea of other directedness. In such works as *The Presentation of Self in Everyday Life* and *Relations in Public,*[7] Goffman concludes that most face-to-face relations are explained by what he calls *impression management.* He finds Americans continually reading others to ensure that they present the proper image. People do not struggle to communicate who they are but rather who they think they are expected to be. Full attention is given to manufacturing social harmony and avoiding social discomfort. Few fears are greater than that of feeling out of place or being judged negatively by our peers. Thus, individuals become expert at manipulat-

---

[6] David Riesman, Nathan Glazer, and Reuel Denney, *The Lonely Crowd* (New York: Doubleday & Co., Inc., 1950). Available in paperback.

[7] Erving Goffman, *The Presentation of Self in Everyday Life* (New York: Doubleday & Co., Inc., 1959); *Relations in Public: Microstudies of the Public Order* (New York: Basic Books, 1971 [1957]). Both are available in paperback.

ing facial expression, eye contact, tone of voice, body posture, hand gestures, and verbal messages. They carefully regulate social space to avoid the appearance of being too intimate or too aloof.

Goffman offers another option, although many would find it no more inviting than the first. He believes that the ideas of selfhood we manufacture in the private sphere are often different from the images projected by our public roles. For example, the role of cashier in a college cafeteria may demand that you charge a student three cents for the pat of butter he or she has hidden on the food tray. Yet to rummage through the student's meal in search of a three-cent item, even when you are sure it is there, may project so offensive an image of yourself that you may choose to ignore the petty thievery.

But let us add another dimension to this drama. Imagine that your boss signals that the next two customers have hidden pats of butter under their bread. You can ignore your role no longer without offending your boss. Yet you cannot perform your role without projecting an image of yourself that you do not much like. How do you handle such a situation? Very probably you will employ what Goffman calls *role distance*.[8] You will do what is expected, but you will whisper to the customers. "The boss says I have to charge you three cents for that lousy pat of butter. You'd think with food as bad as this, they would give it away." You play your expected role, but you have tried not to be associated with it.

Role distance is a process of cynical detachment from the role we play. When employing role distance, we do not play our role to the hilt, with total commitment, the way a football hero is expected to put his whole being into his performance. Instead, we protect a sense of who we are through small acts of resistance against our role situations. Another example: A student teacher may be required to stop children who are running in the hallways of the school and remind them of the dangers of such behavior. But the student teacher may feel awkward in this role. His discomfort is magnified when he realizes that his friend and fellow student teacher, Bob, is nearby watching his performance. He continues to play the role expected of him and tells the youngsters in a stern and thoroughly official voice, "Go back and walk!" He then turns to Bob and winks, as if to say, "That isn't the real me talking." He has slipped out of the definition of him provided by the role of student teacher, and, at least for Bob, has projected another image of who he truly is.

The Social Goals of Education

A discussion of the social goals of education can seem abstract unless it is dealt with in the context of actual social issues. The discussion of identity in modern society provides an excellent context for the discussion of the social aims of education. What role should education play in binding individuals to their society? Should education concern itself with the problem of alienation? If so, how might this concern be handled? There are essentially three possibilities, which will be discussed under the headings: "Education as Cultural Transmission," "Education as Individual Growth," and "Education as Democratic Process." Numerous variations can be played on these themes. The aim here, how-

[8] Erving Goffman, *Encounters* (Indianapolis: Bobbs-Merrill Co., 1961), pp. 85–152. Available in paperback.

ever, is simply to show how dissimilar assumptions about the nature of education can turn schools and societies in very different directions. In order to clarify issues and avoid abstractions, each perspective will be examined through the ideas of one or another prominent educational thinker.

Education as Cultural Transmission

Emile Durkheim (1858–1917) is remembered primarily as a founding father of sociology. He held the first university chair of sociology, which was created especially for him at the Sorbonne in France. Less well remembered is Durkheim's deep interest in education. He taught courses in pedagogy throughout his career and wrote extensively on the role of education in society.

In order to understand Durkheim's work, it is necessary to understand something of his time. France was in a period of political upheaval and social disharmony throughout Durkheim's life. The discord of the age culminated in what is called the Dreyfus affair. The case had to do with an army officer, Alfred Dreyfus, wrongly accused and convicted of revealing military secrets.

In more stable times the case probably would not have aroused widespread social concern, but the political climate of the day was such that the Dreyfus affair consolidated public opinion behind two ideological forces, the left and the right. The left was Republican (meaning it supported the revolutionary ideals that forged the French Republic) and anticlerical (meaning it desired to eliminate the close relationship between the French government and the Catholic Church). The right represented a conservative resistance to change. Not incidentally, the right also was highly suspicious of intellectuals, who, it claimed, corrupted youth by spreading false and immoral ideas through their teachings and writings. Anti-Semitism, anti-German feeling, and opposition to the military also inflamed the conflict.

Durkheim was politically active on the side of Dreyfus, the left, and the intellectual community. When the conflict ended in 1905, the left succeeded in separating church and state in France. These events did not bring social harmony, however. Many worried that the suspension of religious instruction in public schools would eventually lead to moral decay. Durkheim was asked to head a commission investigating the feasibility of nonreligious, moral education. He was well suited for the task. The major focus of his work had been to investigate the essential elements of social cohesion.

The basic question of Durkheim's sociology was simply this: What accounts for social order? Durkheim's answer to this question is found in what he called *collective consciousness.* According to Durkheim, society consists of a collection of ideas, sentiments, and habits that its members hold in common. This collective consciousness is the glue that binds society together. Although carried in the minds of individuals, it is not an individual creation. Individuals assimilate consciousness from society. Thus, the fundamental characteristic of collective consciousness is its externality. It exists apart from us and cannot be understood by simply looking inside ourselves. It existed before we were born and it will live on, with only slight alteration, after we die. As Durkheim put it, "We are immersed in an atmosphere of collective ideas and sentiments which we cannot voluntarily modify."[9]

---

[9] Emile Durkheim, *Education and Sociology,* trans. and introd. Sherwood D. Fox (Glencoe, IL: The Free Press, 1956 [1922]), p. 95.

We best understand the coercive nature of collective consciousness if we think of it as an object or thing rather than as ideas or states of mind. Like physical objects, Durkheim explained, collective consciousness resists our attempts to create, destroy, or transform it. Society can change individuals much more readily than individuals can change society.

Such ideas are repugnant to people who put individuals rather than society at the center of their thinking. Durkheim, however, saw society as paramount. In his view, society leaves its imprint on all individuals, and this imprint accounts for what is best within us. Human beings cannot long endure chaos in their own thinking or in the social order. Society gives us the order we must have if we are to live peaceably and remain sane. There is no such thing as physical or psychological self-sufficiency. Human beings develop in and are enriched by a social order. As Durkheim put it:

> Someone who does not live exclusively of, and for, himself, who offers and gives himself, who merges with the environing world and allows it to permeate his life—such a person certainly lives a richer and more vigorous life than the solitary egotist who bottles himself up and alienates himself from men and things.[10]

Individuals are free to reject what society offers, but they do so at a terrible cost. They cut themselves off from order, predictability, and a sense of belonging. Without the support of collective consciousness, individuals lose a grip on reality itself. They experience disorder and isolation, a state that we have called *alienation* but that Durkheim referred to as *anomie*.

Social ties can be broken through individual rebellion or through social decay, but in each case individuals are put under a tremendous strain. Some individuals prefer death to a life deprived of social meaning and human connection. Durkheim discovered that suicide rates climbed when social ties were loosened by urbanization, divorce, and religions that promote self-reliance. Suicide rates go up during periods of acute social readjustment and subside during periods of national unity.[11]

Durkheim believed that social order is essential to individual well-being and that order is possible only when individuals share a core of common beliefs. Thus, it is easy to see why Durkheim valued education. He saw education as an agency that promotes social cohesion. For Durkheim, the aim of education is to make the collective consciousness of society part of the consciousness of every child. This does not mean that all children will be exactly alike but that they will be enough alike to ensure cooperation and rational communication. Durkheim explained it this way:

> Society can survive only if there exists among its members a significant degree of homogeneity; education perpetuates and reinforces this homogeneity by fixing in the child, from the beginning, the essential similarities collective life demands.[12]

Durkheim felt that the essential ingredients of collective consciousness were not self-evident in a complex society. They could be discovered only through careful study. He was not willing to leave it to teachers to promote their per-

---

[10] Emile Durkheim, *Moral Education,* trans. Everett Wilson and Herman Schnurer (New York: The Free Press, 1973 [1925]), p. 73. Available in paperback.

[11] See Emile Durkheim, *Suicide,* trans. John A. Spaulding and George Simpson (Glencoe, IL: The Free Press, 1951 [1897]).

[12] Emile Durkheim, *Education and Sociology,* p. 70.

sonal version of collective consciousness. It was, rather, the state's responsibility "to remind the teacher consistently of the ideas, the sentiments that must be impressed upon the child to adjust him to the milieu in which he must live." To do otherwise would, in Durkheim's view, leave education to the private whims of individual teachers.

> The whole nation would be divided and would break down into an incoherent multitude of little fragments in conflict with one another. One could not contradict more completely the fundamental ends of all education.[13]

Society and social order were the dominant themes of Durkheim's sociology. When he was commissioned to study the problems of secular moral education, he looked to society to provide moral guidance for human behavior. In Durkheim's view, to act in the collective interest (according to collective consciousness) is to act morally. Moral life is essentially social. Schools promote morality, not as something religious, but as a secular and social entity. Children should experience the positive effects of moral existence in school. Durkheim insisted that he was not promoting indoctrination and that students would not be asked to accept blindly social morality. In his view, morality (that is, social life) is the only rational choice, and he believed that students could be educated to understand the rational basis of morality. They would thereafter choose to behave in a moral manner. Durkheim saw such a choice to be liberating rather than enslaving.

We have asked the question, What role should education play in binding individuals to their society? It is clear that Durkheim's whole sociological and educational theory is aimed at strengthening the social ties among individuals. Conscious conformity, in Durkheim's view, is essential to social progress and individual happiness. Education is the best way to build the collective consciousness into individuals and thereby prepare them for social life. Schools can quell the impulses of individuals to go their own ways and do their own things. True freedom, Durkheim believed, is found in thoughtful compliance with the will of the group. The individual is not to be the central concern of educators. The focus of education, rather, is to be on successfully transmitting culture.

Education as Individual Growth

Emile Durkheim's reasoning begins with the group and moves to the individual. In his view, individual troubles are diminished when there are strong ties to society. Our next theorist, Carl Rogers, moves in the opposite direction. His reasoning begins with the individual and moves outward to society. Durkheim put education in the service of society, arguing that this function is best for the individual. Rogers reverses this outlook by putting education in the service of the individual, arguing that, in the long run, this is best for society.

Carl Rogers (1902–1987) is an American psychologist who has had a major influence in his own field and in education. One could view his entire psychological theory as an attempt to solve the problems of alienation and other directedness in modern society. He sees human interaction in this age as emotionless and inauthentic. Individuals have become overly sensitive to the

---

[13] Ibid., p. 79.

judgments of others and typically live in a state of vulnerability. To protect themselves, Rogers believes, they hide behind false fronts, deny their real beings, and wall themselves off from their emotions. Their efforts to conceal themselves are so great that they sometimes lose sight of who they really are. You will remember that this form of alienation was called self-estrangement.

One consequence of self-estrangement, according to Rogers, is that individuals lose the capacity to fashion their own values. Individuals merely adopt the values presented by society. This is not necessarily a conscious process. Most people are not even aware of the values they inherit from the world around them. Such values may be contradictory or may not square with their personal experience. Under such conditions, Rogers says, values become rigid and are not easily changed.

Rogers places the locus of "true morality" in the individual and not in society. Individuals know best what values are proper for them and can be trusted to adopt productive values if they are freed from social restraint. Rogers does say that individuals may benefit from the advice of others and the wisdom of tradition, but he warns that the individual must take such evidence "for what it is—outside evidence—that is not as significant as [our] own reactions."[14]

Rogers's ideal is to live in a world where individuals freely choose and create the value structures that make most sense to them. It is clear that this ideal is Durkheim's most dreaded nightmare. Rogers would liberate individuals from the damaging constraints of society; whereas Durkheim would liberate them from the chaos of their private lives.

Society, in Rogers's scheme, is a potential enemy of the whole and healthy person. It encourages individuals to play roles and to lose touch with themselves and their feelings. Rogers believes the inner life (emotions and intuitions) are the "organismic base for an organized valuing process within the human individual."[15] Here again Rogers is at odds with Durkheim. The French sociologist believed that moral values were essentially social and rational; Rogers sees them as individual and emotional. Feelings and intuition, he contends, are often wiser than the mind or society.

Rogers believes that conformity and role playing can detach individuals from their emotions. The object of his therapy and the aim of his educational strategy are to put individuals back in touch with their emotional lives and the "potential wisdom of [their] own functioning."[16] Rogers's educational aim is not designed to create a new individual; its aim is to help the individual regain the self it lost through socialization. The idea is that there is a "real self" waiting to be released from behind the false fronts and social roles society presses upon it. This "real self" is born with us but gets misplaced as we grow up. Rogers wants his students and patients to return to the uninhibited freedom of their childhood selves. Well-adjusted, healthy human beings are those who have regained contact with the honest feelings of the "genuine self" they were born with.

How are individuals to be reunited with their "real selves"? Rogers believes this is possible only in an atmosphere of trust and "unconditional positive regard." Here individuals are given the experience of being accepted for what

---

[14] Carl R. Rogers, *Freedom to Learn: A View of What Education Might Become* (Columbus, OH: Merrill Publishing Company, 1969), p. 249.

[15] Ibid., p. 251.

[16] Ibid., p. 247.

they are and not for the images they create through impression management. Rogers suggests that a trusting educational atmosphere can be created if teachers present themselves to students without fronts or façades. They must be "genuine" and resist the tendency to present themselves to students as roles rather than real people. The aim of the teacher must not be to instill learning or to be judgmental but rather to help students explore their own feelings and pursue their own interests. For this reason, Rogers prefers the term *facilitator* to *teacher*. He insists that he is not interested in teaching anybody anything but is rather concerned with helping individuals learn what they want to know. Whatever name we apply to teachers, however, Rogers sees their goal as freeing students from alienating social restraints. Pupils must first be trusted and then set free to learn what is important to them.

You will remember that this chapter began with the question, How can individual diversity and social order coexist? If we asked this question of Rogers, we might put it another way: How is society possible when individuals are governed only by personal feelings and intuition? Durkheim saw collective consciousness as the glue that holds society together. Rogers looks elsewhere for social ties. According to his theory, human bonds are organic, not social. He means that our capacity for harmonious living is born with us, but it can be damaged or destroyed through socialization. If people can regain selfhood through therapy or education, they will regain their natural ability to associate lovingly with others. The possibility of community grows, in Rogers's view, as individuals are freed from collective consciousness. The self-actualized individual finds something noble in the "real self" that allows a more perfect union with others.

Rogers goes so far as to contend that people who have undergone successful therapy, no matter what their background or culture, come to share a "commonality of value direction" that promotes social harmony.[17] Individuals who have undergone therapy cast away their social pretensions and emerge from behind their social masks. They become nonjudgmental and more tolerant of human diversity. They are less driven by the expectations of others and more accepting of their own desires. They are more able to tolerate change and more open to inner experience. And finally, according to Rogers, they are more capable of deep relationships with others.

Education as Democratic Process

The problem of alienation has led us into a consideration of individual freedom and social order. Durkheim claimed individual freedom was best realized through social constraint. Rogers believes the best social order comes about when individuals are freed from social constraint. We turn now to the ideas of John Dewey (1859–1952). It is tempting to view his position as a compromise between the extremes represented by Durkheim and Rogers, but such would fail to grasp the radical nature of Dewey's proposals. It is important to keep in mind that Dewey did not seek a position that would satisfy the claims of these extremes. He offered a very different conception of the individual's place in the social order.

John Dewey was a philosopher whose wide-ranging interests took him into

[17] Ibid., p. 253.

studies of science, psychology, ethics, religion, politics, social science, and, of course, education. For Dewey, philosophy was a practical affair. It was a method for clarifying problems and was useful only if it suggested methods for dealing with social and personal difficulties.[18]

Dewey saw the lack of connection between the individual and society as a major problem of modernization. Philosophy, he thought, could be used to clarify the nature of the problem, to evaluate the usefulness of proposed solutions, and to suggest directions for the future. The experience of alienation is, in Dewey's view, individually painful and socially damaging. The difficulties of alienation encourage people to consider extreme solutions. Some submit totally to the will of the group, as Durkheim suggests. Others resist society completely and beat a hasty retreat into privatism, as Rogers suggests. Dewey sees both these positions as products of the problem of alienation, not as solutions to it. Thoughtless obedience to the will of others produces only the "other-directed" personality described by David Riesman and the impression management described by Erving Goffman. Running after the "real-self," which Rogers speaks of, is to chase after something that does not exist. The idea that there is no such thing as a native self (a self we are born with) needs explaining.

Dewey believed that the individual is not a product of nature (as Rogers would have us believe) but a product of society. "Everything which is distinctly human is learned, not native," Dewey said.[19] It would be impossible to conceive of an individual totally isolated from others. Conversely, society cannot exist without individuals. Each is essential to the existence and continual development of the other. The problem in Durkheim's and Rogers's solutions to alienation is that they see the self and society as separate and hostile. The only possible solution under such a conception is to assign dominance or victory to one side or the other. And this is, of course, what Rogers and Durkheim have done. But if we view the individual and society as organically connected, as Dewey has done, new solutions present themselves.

Dewey did not look for a way to give dominance to individuals or to society. Instead he sought to exploit their interdependence. He wanted to allow all the freedom necessary to create and maintain individuality. But at the same time, he wanted to maintain enough restraint to make social order possible. As he put it, "To learn to be human is to develop through the give and take of communication an effective sense of being an individually distinctive member of the community."[20] One can be *individually distinctive* only as a member of a group. The aim is not to free individuals *from* society but to create freedom *in* society.

Communities, institutions, and other social organizations can become inflexible and thereby limit freedom and innovation. Individual personality can also become rigid and intolerant of change. The challenge, therefore, is to find a process that allows both order and innovation in individuals and society alike. Dewey finds this process in human intelligence.

Like personality or selfhood, Dewey believed intelligence is largely a social product. He did not see it as a native capacity but rather as a habit of mind that must be learned in interaction with others. Intelligence involves powers of

---

[18] John Dewey, *Democracy and Education* (New York: The Free Press, 1966 [1916]), chap. 24. Available in paperback.

[19] John Dewey, *The Public and Its Problems* (Chicago: The Swallow Press, Inc., 1957 [1927]), p. 154. Available in paperback.

[20] Ibid.

Dewey sought a balance between the individual and society.   *Source:* National Education Association, Joe Di Dio.

observation that allow individuals to recognize and define problems. It involves reasoning and judgment. It demands that we learn from experience and put what is learned in our stock of knowledge where it can be called on when needed in the future. Most important, intelligence allows us to examine our habits and social customs to determine whether they still serve useful purposes. When they do not, intelligence gives us a means for changing them. However, when habit and custom do prove worthwhile, intelligence gives us a reason to support them.

It is little wonder that Dewey saw intelligence as the "key to freedom."[21] Intelligence offers us "freedom from control by routine, prejudice, dogma, unexamined tradition [and] sheer self-interest." It represents the "will to inquire, to examine, to discriminate, to draw conclusions on the basis of evidence after taking pains to gather all available evidence."[22] Intelligence allows individuals to be unique and not "imitators or parasites of others" because it gives individuals power to see the world for what it is and to reflect upon what it might become.[23] It gives people the power to recognize choice when it exists and the wisdom to choose wisely.

[21] John Dewey, *Human Nature and Conduct* (New York: Random House, Inc., Modern Library, 1930 [1922]), p. 304.
[22] John Dewey, *Theory of Valuation* (Chicago: University of Chicago Press, 1939), p. 31. Available in paperback.
[23] John Dewey, *Philosophy and Civilization* (New York: G. P. Putnam's Sons, Capricorn Books, 1963 [1931]), p. 298.

Dewey believed institutions could be constructed in ways that would help develop human intelligence and distinctive individuality. One way to do this is to allow "all those who are affected by social institutions [to] have a share in producing and managing them."[24] Individuals should not be placed into fixed subordination through hard and fast roles, lines of absolute authority, or fixed social classes. They must be given the opportunity to express their opinions and to persuade others through reason. In face-to-face interaction, especially, they will find opportunities for personal communication. If institutions could be so fashioned, Dewey believed, we might at last become tolerant of one another. We might learn to have a "sympathetic regard for the intelligence and personality of others, even if they hold views opposed to ours."[25]

Dewey believed that communities and societies are not simply collections of individuals. They produce a collective wisdom that is more than the sum of its parts. This wisdom is composed of a common purpose or set of values that binds individuals together. But common values and goals must be flexible so that they can be modified to fit the shifting conditions of modern life. It is essential, therefore, that individuals be aware of the common values of society (Durkheim's collective consciousness) and that they take part in their creation, maintenance, and reconstruction. However, one value would not change. Dewey believed the best society is maintained when there is a common commitment to intelligence as a way of developing social aims and planning for the future. Dewey called this value *social intelligence*. By this, he did not mean the sum of individuals acting intelligently; rather, he thought of "the social" as a context in which individual intelligence was shaped and directed.[26] Social intelligence is the social organization of intelligence, which works to improve the quality of individual thought. Such an organization would free individuals from the temptation to follow blindly the dictates of social institutions. It would allow individuals to take part in social life, to help maintain it, and, when necessary, to help modify it.

The alert reader will have already realized that Dewey's idea of individual and social intelligence carries within it the ideals of democracy. Dewey does not see democracy simply as a convenient way to solve problems or pass laws. Democracy is, rather, a means of enhancing intelligence and enriching community life. It is a method of bringing individuals in closer communion with society. The individual is not forced to accept external values or to create a wholly private morality. Instead, the individual is given the means to participate in the continued construction and reconstruction of community norms.

Like Durkheim and Rogers, Dewey believed education is vital to the success of his program. The aim of a democratic education is to provide the best possible opportunity for the development of individual and social intelligence. Education will help individuals gain a sympathetic regard for others. He believed it is silly to teach children to accept uncritically the views of teachers, accept passively the rules of school, and grind out thoughtlessly assignments that have no purpose or meaning. Students trained in this way will be unintelligent and ill prepared for democratic life.

Dewey proposed, instead, that students be given the opportunity to learn by

---

[24] John Dewey, *Intelligence in the Modern World*, ed. Joseph Ratner (New York: Random House, Inc., Modern Library, 1939), p. 401.

[25] John Dewey and James Tufts, *Ethics*, rev. ed. (New York: Holt, Rinehart & Winston, 1932 [1908]), p. 365.

[26] John Dewey, "The Inclusive Philosophic Idea," in *Philosophy and Civilization*, pp. 77–92.

doing. By this he meant that students should grapple with problems that excite their interest. Their activities should increasingly challenge their present abilities. They should have an escalating involvement in the governance of the classroom and the school. They should be encouraged to develop a sympathetic understanding of the views of others.

Summary

This chapter began with one of life's most fundamental questions, How can unique individuals possibly live together in an orderly way? In premodern society, where communities were small and human contact frequent, unity was seldom a problem. There were shared meanings and people knew where they stood in society. In modern society this is not the case. An individual is no longer a single entity, acting in essentially the same way in every segment of life. We are now many entities: student, Red Cross volunteer, Methodist, part-time worker, student teacher, second vice-president of the campus Young Republicans, occasional counselee at the campus mental health center, and so on. Each activity calls for a different way of behaving and draws on different portions of our personality. It is difficult to keep these segments of life in coordination.

It is also difficult to find meaning or identity within the giant megastructures of society. We manage these difficulties by dividing our lives into two spheres, one public and the other private. Although this is helpful, it is also troublesome. The private sphere is a precarious entity, without institutional support. The reality, meaning, and sense of selfhood manufactured in this domain are threatened when the private sphere is thrown into turmoil.

The segmentation of modern life puts individuals in a constant threat of alienation. Five forms of alienation were discussed: powerlessness, meaninglessness, normlessness, isolation, and self-estrangement. The purpose of this discussion was to give a deeper understanding of the complexities of modern society and the problems it presents in bringing individuals into a meaningful unity with society. It also set the stage for a discussion of the social aims of education.

Modern life provides us with many benefits and many problems. It is the job of education to pass on to future generations all that is best in society. But schools must also prepare children for the problems they will face in adult life. One problem that they will certainly face is alienation. We therefore examined the ideas of three thinkers—Emile Durkheim, Carl Rogers, and John Dewey— to see how they viewed the role of education in binding individuals to society. Durkheim wanted to build the individual through the creation of a strong social order based on collective consciousness. Rogers wants to build a social order through individual liberation. Dewey wanted to build individuals and society through a careful application of intelligence and democracy. Whatever view we accept (or whatever new view we might develop) will aim education in a different direction.

How can an individual decide among the social theories and educational aims of Durkheim, Rogers, and Dewey? One method, of course, is to choose the one that "feels" right. Another method is to examine what we know about human nature to see whether our educational aims fit this knowledge. This examination will be the next topic on the agenda.

Suggested Readings

Discussions of the public sphere and private sphere in society date far back into the sociological literature. Some of the most useful current discussions of this issue have been carried on by Peter Berger. For a brief discussion see "Toward a Critique of Modernity," in Peter Berger, ed., *Facing Up to Modernity* (New York: Basic Books, 1977). Berger's student, Anton Zijderveld, has elaborated some of the problems of modern life in his book, *The Abstract Society* (New York: Doubleday & Co., Inc., Anchor Books, 1970). For a philosopher's view, see John Dewey, *Individualism Old and New* (New York: Capricorn Books, 1962 [1929]) and *The Public and Its Problems* (Chicago: Swallow Press, 1957 [1927]).

The topic of alienation has a vast literature. For a useful introduction to the concept see Melvin Seeman, "On the Meaning of Alienation," *American Sociological Review*, Vol. 24 (1959), pp. 683 ff.

The issue of alienation has special relevance for the young and their schooling experiences. Students wishing to explore this issue are advised to look at the following:

BECKER, ERNEST. *Beyond Alienation.* New York: George Braziller, 1967. This is a provocative inquiry into the state of education, its relationship to youth, and the future of the society.

GOODMAN, PAUL. *Growing Up Absurd.* New York: Random House, Inc., Vintage Books, 1962. Something of a classic, this book anticipated the disaffection of youth in the 1960s and 1970s. The analyses that Goodman sets out here are as applicable today as they were twenty-five years ago.

LARKIN, RALPH W. *Suburban Youth in Cultural Crisis.* New York: Oxford University Press, 1979. In this portrayal of middle-class youth in affluent society, Larkin concludes that the protective environment of suburbia has left the young bored, without community, and alienated.

MUSGROVE, F. *Youth and the Social Order.* Bloomington, IN: Indiana University Press, 1965. Musgrove gives a historical account of the relationship between youth and social order. The book is heavy going in spots, but its historical insights provide a useful backdrop against which to view modern society.

The view that schooling should transmit culture is discussed by Emile Durkheim in *Moral Education* (New York: The Free Press, 1973 [1925]). See also Durkheim's *Education and Sociology* (New York: The Free Press, 1956 [1922]). More recently, those who would have schools transmit the culture have emphasized the importance of the liberal arts in education. According to this view, schools should systematically expose young minds to the cultural wisdom of the ages and to the mental discipline that liberal arts study requires. Perhaps the most influential advocates for the liberal arts tradition in American education are Robert M. Hutchins and Mortimer J. Adler. Hutchins's most important writings include *Higher Learning in America* (New Haven: Yale University Press, 1936); *The University of Utopia* (Chicago: University of Chicago Press, 1953); and *The Learning Society* (New York: Frederick A. Praeger, 1968). Adler is noted in education primarily for his *How to Read a Book: The Art of Getting a Liberal Education* (New York: Simon and Schuster, 1940) and his leadership of the Paideia Group: see *The Paideia Proposal: An Educational Manifesto* (New York: Macmillan Publishing Co., 1982) and *Paideia Problems and Possibilities* (New York: Macmillan Publishing Co., 1983). For a while, the liberal arts tradition in education fell on hard times, but it has rebounded today, no doubt spurred by the "back to basics" movement. The liberal arts have been defended recently by Adler's Paideia proposals and by Eva T. H. Brann, *Paradoxes of Education in a Republic* (Chicago: University of Chicago Press, 1979). A critique of the liberal arts tradition is found in Frantz Fanon, *The Wretched of the Earth* (New York: Grove Press, 1965).

John Dewey's philosophy of education is most thoroughly expressed in *Democracy and Education* (New York: The Free Press, 1966 [1916]). *Experience and Education* (New York: Collier Books, 1938) is a brief overview of Dewey's educational thought. Also useful is Dewey's *How We Think* (Boston: D. C. Heath and Co., 1933).
Dewey was a leader in what came to be called *progressive education* in the United States. Other writings in the progressive tradition include

BODE, BOYD. *How We Learn*. Boston: D. C. Heath and Co., 1940.
CHILDS, JOHN. *Education and the Philosophy of Experimentalism*. New York: The Century Co., 1931.
———. *Education and Morals*. New York: Appleton-Century-Crofts, 1950.
COUNTS, GEORGE. *Dare the Schools Build a New Social Order*. Carbondale, IL: Southern Illinois University Press, 1978 [1932].
RUGG, HAROLD. *American Life and the School Curriculum*. Boston: Ginn, 1936.

Progressive education in the United States is related to the American philosophy of "pragmatism." Some useful interpretations of pragmatism are

CHILDS, JOHN L. *American Pragmatism and Education*. New York: Henry Holt and Co., 1956.
COVITZ, MILTON, and GAIL KENNEDY, eds. *The American Pragmatists*. New York: Meridan Books, 1960. This is an anthology of writings by major American pragmatists.
RUCKER, DARNELL. *The Chicago Pragmatists*. Minneapolis: University of Minnesota Press, 1969. This book traces the development of pragmatic thought in various departments at the University of Chicago.
WIENER, PHILIP P. *Evolution and the Founders of Pragmatism*. Cambridge: Harvard University Press, 1949. This book traces pragmatism from evolutionary thought.

Those who see the purpose of education as being individual growth and self-actualization draw heavily from the literature of perceptual psychology. Some examples are

ALLPORT, GORDON. *Becoming*. New Haven: Yale University Press, 1955.
MASLOW, ABRAHAM. *Toward a Psychology of Being*. New York: D. Van Nostrand Co., Inc., 1968.
ROGERS, CARL. *On Becoming a Person*. Boston: Houghton-Mifflin Co., 1961.

Perceptual psychology was brought to education by Arthur W. Combs and Donald Snygg, *Individual Behavior*, rev. ed. (New York: Harper & Row, Publishers, 1959). The most recent version of that work is by Arthur W. Combs, Anne C. Richards, and Fred Richards, *Perceptual Psychology* (New York: Harper & Row, Publishers, 1976). See also Arthur W. Combs and Donald L. Avila, *Helping Relationships*, 3d ed. (Newton, MA: Allyn and Bacon, 1985) and Carl Rogers, *Freedom to Learn* (Columbus, OH: Merrill Co., 1969).

CHAPTER 3

The Question of Human Nature

Introduction

Why Worry about Human Nature?

The theories of Durkheim, Rogers, and Dewey are miles apart. You may have found it surprising that intelligent people can disagree so profoundly on such basic questions. An explanation of these differences is found in the ideas concerning human nature that these men put forward. This point can be clarified if we look at just one component of the human nature question, the idea of freedom. Durkheim seeks to limit individual freedom; Rogers seeks to maximize it; Dewey believes freedom is best achieved in a democratic setting. Durkheim's school of thought is suspicious of human freedom, believing that human beings must be protected from their own capacity for evil. Durkheim stops just short of saying human beings are essentially bad, but he does say human beings must keep their "natural inclinations" in check. This may amount to the same thing.

Rogers emphasizes the natural goodness of human beings. He acknowledges the existence of evil but claims it is the result of social restraint, not human nature. Society is hostile to individuals, and the aim of education (and psychotherapy) is to aid the good individuals to defeat the evil in society.

Dewey takes a third position. He claims human beings are not good or evil but self-constructing. They are capable of intelligence and can work *together* to develop this capacity. The more successful they are in this endeavor, the more good will result. If they fail, there will be little to protect them from the damaging (evil) consequences of their blind (unintelligent) activity. It is important to remember that Dewey saw intelligence as the ability to assess problems accurately and to solve them successfully.

The point being made here is that Durkheim, Rogers, and Dewey arrive at different conclusions because they begin with very different ideas about the essence of human nature. Their theories, though carefully reasoned, are basically projections of their underlying assumptions about human nature. This phenomenon is not restricted to the work of these three thinkers. Scratch the surface of any theory of human behavior (and this includes all theories of education), and you will find a set of assumptions about human nature. If we fail to understand these assumptions, we fail to fully grasp the theory itself.

What are we talking about when we discuss human nature? Human nature refers to our ideas about what human beings are like—our assumptions about their abilities, characteristics, and place in the universe. These assumptions answer such questions as: Are human beings free or determined, good or evil, cooperative or competitive, selfish or altruistic?

The assumptions we hold about human nature have far-reaching consequences. Popular conceptions of human nature form the foundations of governments, the aims of education, conceptions of justice, interpretations of the present, designs for the future, attitudes toward elites, beliefs about poverty—in short, all the elements vital to social living. To a greater extent than we usually realize, our ideas about human nature are self-fulfilling. Human beings often become what they collectively believe themselves to be. This process gives us reason for hope, especially in these trying times, but it also gives us cause for concern. Conceptions of human nature that degrade and repress human beings have a self-fulfilling power we dare not ignore. Richard Means makes this point when he writes, "If the fascist and totalitarian revolutions have taught us nothing else, [it is] that the views of the nature of man, the reigning metaphors of social interpretation, cannot be taken lightly."[1] He goes on to say that we must continually cross swords with dangerous views of human nature because, if they go unchallenged, they may soon become rationalizations for cruelty, bigotry, warfare, and totalitarianism.

Digging Out Our Assumptions about Human Nature

It is often difficult to know what assumptions about human nature motivate a theory of behavior, a government policy, or a teaching method. Such assumptions are often silent partners in human activity and difficult to identify. All citizens, especially educators, must learn to recognize these assumptions even when they are well hidden in a theory, policy, or prescription for action.

This skill is not easily mastered. One place to start is by looking into your own assumptions. Even this can be difficult to do. Someone with insight once said, "We cannot determine who discovered water, but we can be sure that it was not the fish." The point of this observation is that we are often least conscious of the things we know best. Your ideas about human nature are very much a part of you and are therefore difficult to detect.

Rather than looking inward to discover our beliefs about human nature, we will look outward to other cultures. The advantages to this approach is that everything in another culture seems new and exotic to us. Yet, as we view the strange routines of others, we can gather a new understanding of our own habits of thought and action. The *surprises* we encounter in looking at another culture can give us insight into some of the things we most take for granted in our own culture.

Some warnings are in order. As you study the two cultures we are about to sketch here, try not to judge them according to your own moral standards. Instead, take each surprise or shock as evidence that some of your ideas or

[1] Richard L. Means, *The Ethical Imperative* (New York: Doubleday & Co., Inc., 1969), p. 76.

assumptions have been offended. Ask yourself what those ideas or assumptions might be. The advantage of looking at other cultures is that you gain a means of looking more deeply into yourself.

There is another advantage in viewing other cultures. As we study differences among peoples, we come to realize how alike they and we are. It is at this point that we begin to find some empirical grounds for understanding human nature.

Even so, you will find it difficult to resist making comparisons between the cultures we are about to examine and your own American background. But you must try to put off this activity until you have tried to understand the cultures on their terms, according to their internal standards. When you do make comparisons, however, do so in both directions. That is, look for similarities as well as dissimilarities. There is something to be learned from both.

Assumptions are unstated beliefs that "fill a gap" in an argument; they are the bases or warrants for thinking as we do. Their function is to complete an argument or, at least, to ground or anchor it in some other belief or evidence. While the term *assumption*, like most words, has many meanings, the ones that we are concerned with here are its uses as a *premise* to a conclusion, or a given point of view (in deductive reasoning), or as a *presupposition,* which must be true if a statement or a belief is to be considered sensible. Our concern, in fact, is even more with the latter kind of assumption. For example, "the students in Miss Bailey's mathematics class outperformed all other students in the city," assumes that there is a Miss Bailey who teaches mathematics and probably assumes that "outperformed all other students in the city" is to be restricted (context) to mathematics and does not refer to any or all types of performance.

The word *probably* in the statement indicates that, in finding an assumption, we are not concerned with logical necessity, with the idea that the assumption is the only one that can support the argument. Such claims for logical necessity can be made, but they turn out to be trivial, usually a restatement—though perhaps in different words—of the conclusion. Rather, what we look for in assumptions are the ideas that can be employed to "fill the gap" in an argument—and they can be many. Our task is to find the assumption that the believer, or the one who asserts a claim, will recognize and come to agree is the basis for his or her belief. Someone who has written about assumption-finding has said, "The moral is: Be careful in your assumption-finding. Do not ascribe to a position an assumption which can easily and plausibly be replaced by one which is more likely to be true."[2]

Some rough guides can be proposed for assumption-finding. They are especially pertinent to the premise (deductive) type of assumption, but they are useful in probing for presuppositions as well. Criteria for claiming that an assumption is made are that the assumption would contribute to making a conclusion more acceptable: it fills a gap in an argument, making it valid (deduction) or more probable (induction); it completes an explanation; it predicts something that would not occur if the assumption were false; or experts in the field would not accept the position (conclusion, argument, belief) if the assumption was not first believed to be true.

---

[2] Robert H. Ennis, "Assumption-Finding," in *Language and Concepts in Education*, ed. B. Othanel Smith and Robert H. Ennis (Chicago: Rand McNally & Company, 1961), p. 166. Our discussion of assumption-finding is based in Ennis's work; see ibid., Chapter 11.

Two Cultures

Having said these things, let us turn to a view of two cultures, with the aim, later, of noticing their assumptions. Both cultures are described by the anthropologist Colin Turnbull, who studied two different kinds of primitive people in central Africa.

The BaMbuti

In the Ituri Forest, in the northeast corner of the Belgian Congo (now Zaire) live the Pygmies. *BaMbuti* is the general term for all Pygmies who live in the rain forest. They have been known for thousands of years. Aristotle (384–322 B.C.) believed they were real, not a fable, living in the land "from which flows the Nile." Europeans had seen them primarily outside the forest, in modern villages or on plantations, where they appeared to be submissive, indeed almost slaves, and were thought to have no culture of their own.

Colin Turnbull first visited the BaMbuti in the forest in 1951 and returned in 1954. He found that when left to themselves, or when in the forest, the Pygmies' lives were as full and as satisfying as they were empty and meaningless when in the modern world. The change was dramatic. With all of its problems, hardships, and tragedies, the forest nevertheless made life more than just worth living; it was a wonderful place, full of joy and happiness.

The BaMbuti feared nothing except what was *not* in the forest. Turnbull's Pygmy companion said, "When we are Children of the Forest, what need have we to be afraid of it? We are only afraid of that which is outside of the forest." Old Moke, an elder, explained,

> The forest is a father and mother to us, and like a father or mother it gives us everything we need—food, clothing, shelter, warmth . . . and affection. Normally everything goes well, because the forest is good to its children, but when things go wrong there must be a reason.[3]

When in the forest, the Pygmies are occupied with building their huts and with hunting. The women build the huts but not because there is a division of labor by sex; there is no discrimination among the Pygmies. Men will pick mushrooms and berries for food and will tend children. Women usually build the huts (though bachelors have to build their own) while men are at the hunt, which they must do every day. If building materials are left over after building her own hut, a woman will let others use them. Sometimes they will even go into the forest to gather more materials for those who have been lazy.

Men do the hunting and make the nets for hunting, though a woman sometimes will make a net as a gift for a new couple. Groups of at least six or seven families, each with its own net, live together as a hunting group. The families extend their nets end to end so game cannot escape. If the Pygmies were to hunt individually, game could go around or through a gap in the nets. When game is caught, it is divided among all the families; everyone has a share.

---

[3] This account of the BaMbuti is drawn from Colin M. Turnbull, *The Forest People* (New York: Simon and Schuster, Inc., 1961). The quotes here are from pp. 74 and 92.

The responsibilities of child rearing are not determined by sex or, indeed, by actual parentage. All adults act as parents and grandparents; all discipline and care for the children. The child knows its real mother and father, but it also learns that it belongs to the whole group. Until adulthood, life is one long frolic for children, but the shift to adulthood, to hunting in the case of boys, is subtle and hardly noticed. Adult activities are learned from early life by observation and imitation. When in the village, the Pygmies will participate in village ceremonies to initiate boys into adulthood, though they do not take it seriously. Although he may be an adult in the village, the Pygmy is still a child when he returns to the forest. Turnbull observed that after the ceremony, the Pygmy boys went back to live with their mothers when in the forest.

Cooperation is the dominant relationship among the BaMbuti. Women work together for companionship. The men hunt together and for the group as a whole. Everyone gets a share, and by and large they stick to the rules. This is not to say that the rules are formal. Pygmy life has few rules. There is a general pattern of behavior, but great latitude is given and taken. There is an apparent lack of organization or, as Turnbull says, a certain amount of perpetual disorder. There are no chiefs, councils, judges, juries, or courts. The Pygmies dislike and avoid personal authority. The maintenance of law is a cooperative matter. The more serious crimes, such as theft, are dealt with by a cooperative thrashing by everyone who cares to join in.

Incest is the greatest shame. The violator is driven into the forest to live alone, which, of course, means certain death. But animosities do not linger. Violators almost always are allowed back into camp, where all is forgiven. Disputes are settled, not in reference to right or wrong, but with the aim of restoring peace to the community. The Pygmy will fight only with words. If a hunting group oversteps its bounds, there is no trouble as long as there is plenty of food. If they do meet, those not on their own land will run away and leave whatever they have taken. "That is the only way we ever fight—we are not villagers."

The Pygmies are not self-conscious about showing emotion. Their wailing for the ill is copied from other tribes and does not seem to be serious. They distinguish between being "dead" (that is, ill, with the hope of recovery) and "dead forever," for which they show real, uncontrollable grief, even the men, and friends as well as relatives. Turnbull noticed a different sound in the latter kind of grief. A Pygmy who is too old for the exertion will cry to himself, unashamed. Ancestors are as important as the living, and only those who are initiated into adulthood will join them when they themselves are "dead forever."

The only time the Pygmies are quiet is when they are on the hunt. They have a saying that "a noisy camp is a hungry camp." They distinguish between forest people and others by the way they walk. A Pygmy runs silently and swiftly, without slipping, tripping, or falling, in order to capture food or to escape a charging buffalo or a sleeping leopard.

But when not on the hunt, when busy with other things, the Pygmies are noisy. Quiet is a danger signal in Pygmy camps; something must not be going right. They usually are talking, shouting, and laughing with each other. They will laugh until tears come to their eyes, hold on to one another, slap their sides, snap their fingers, and go into contortions; and when they are too weak to stand, they will sit or roll on the ground and laugh still louder. They joke about themselves as well as each other. But, when they choose, humor can be a severe punishment. Although he or she will laugh at everyone and everything else, nothing upsets a Pygmy more than being laughed at himself or herself.

Singing also is important in BaMbuti life. It took Turnbull some time to realize how important it was. At first, it seemed to be just a beautiful sound. And it was everywhere. The Pygmies sang whenever they were in the mood. Singing, it turns out, is not concerned with ritual or magic. Rather, it expresses the sense or emotion of companionship between the Pygmy and the forest. To the noisy Pygmy, music is not noise but rejoicing. Moke, an old man, explained,

> Normally everything goes well in our world. . . . [But] when something big goes wrong, like illness or bad hunting or death, it must be because the forest is sleeping and not looking after its children. So what do we do? We wake it up. We wake it up by singing to it, and we do this because we want it to awaken happy. Then everything will be well and good again. So when our world is going well then also we sing to the forest because we want it to share our happiness.[4]

Whenever the Pygmy plans a return to the village, outside the forest, one may observe depression, wailing children, and bad-tempered adults. Only the youth are cheerful at the prospect of village enjoyments. The Pygmies are said to steal and to cheat and deceive the villagers. In return, the villagers try to gain the Pygmies' favor for the meat and honey they bring from the forest. The villagers treat the Pygmies as slaves and believe they are right in imposing their beliefs and practices on a people without a culture. In a sense, each regards the other as a convenience.

The villagers try to control the Pygmies through the adulthood initiation ceremony, but the Pygmies delight in making fun of the villagers by breaking all their taboos. They think the villagers are too superstitious. But Turnbull found there was more to it than this. The Pygmies behaved as they did not only because the village restrictions were meaningless, but because they belonged to a hostile world. Some chiefs in the village complained, "How can we control them? It is their forest, and they can hide from us whenever they want to. They are worthless people. They only come to the village when they want to steal."

A well-meaning government administrator hoped to "liberate" the BaMbuti from their "subjugation" to the villagers by settling them on their own plantations. He cleared part of the forest and hoped the Pygmies would cultivate crops that the government could collect and market. It was a disaster. The Pygmies cannot stand direct sunlight and become ill when they are not in the shade of the forest. They also were more exposed to village diseases. The idea was that the Pygmies would be more independent if they did not have to rely on the villagers for food. But, in point of fact, this misread the Pygmies' relationship to the villagers. They were not dependent on the villagers for anything except metal for knives and spear blades, but the settlement plan did not aim to teach them metalworking. The Pygmies pointed out that the more the forest was cut down for roads, mines, plantations, and villages, the more it would have to be cut down to make plantations to feed the laborers. The whole enterprise "was not a happy outlook for them."

Toward the end of his stay, Turnbull toured the forest for a last time. At one outpost, his Pygmy companion saw a great black mass in the distant haze.

---

[4] Ibid., pp. 92–93.

Turnbull explained it was the mountains, about a day's drive beyond the last of the trees, but the Pygmy could not imagine it. "No trees? No trees at all?" The Pygmy wondered if it was good country and what the villagers were like. On the way to the mountains, the Pygmy tasted and smelled the grass and pronounced it "bad grass"; and the mud was "bad mud." Sniffing the air, he said it too was "bad air." "It was altogether a very bad country."

In the Ishango National Park, patrolled by European officials, Turnbull and the Pygmy were not allowed to live together in the guest house or even to eat together in their dining room. It was the first time the Pygmy had faced race discrimination. Some days earlier, in a village, a wounded Pygmy had been brought in, and though he did not want the white man's medicine, the resident missionary was asked why he had not visited the Pygmy. "Why should I pray for him?" the missionary said. "He is not [our religion]." The remark was meant for Pygmy ears; perhaps it would scare them into conversion. But at the end of the stay, Turnbull's Pygmy companion was asked what he thought of the religion, and he replied, "It is the biggest falsehood I know."

Turnbull and the Pygmy met other missionaries, who gave a better idea of what their religion stood for. As they were leaving the mountains to re-enter the forest, they turned for a last look at the beautiful scene. The Pygmy shook his head and clucked in amazement. At last he said, "The Pere Longo was right; this God must be the same as our God in the forest. It must be one God."

The Ik

The anthropologist Colin Turnbull was anxious to get back into the field. It was 1966 and some years since he had been to Africa. His studies there had fascinated him and had interested Americans as well. His book about *The Forest People* had been well received by anthropologists and laymen alike. Its popularity was a tribute to Turnbull's skill as a scientist and writer, but it was no less a tribute to the noble people he studied. Theirs was a gentle society brimming with kindness and cooperation. One could not read about them without coming away inspired by the possibilities alive in the human spirit.

Turnbull's next visit to Africa was to be devoted to the study of a small and isolated group of hunters who lived in the mountains that separate Uganda from Kenya, just south of Sudan. So little was known of these people that most outsiders did not know their correct name. They called themselves the Ik (pronounced *eek*).

Anthropologists learn to anticipate culture shock with some excitement. They know that its presence announces that they are about to learn something new: not simply a new language or odd customs but new ways of thinking and seeing. Turnbull's shock, however, was more than he had bargained for.[5]

He had met two young Iks at an outpost some distance from their mountain villages. He was happy to have his first meeting with the Ik on neutral ground and quickly employed them to teach him their language and to serve as guides on his first venture into Ik territory. The young men had been attending a missionary school and had adopted (or been assigned) the Christian names

---

[5] Read Turnbull's chilling account of the Ik in *The Mountain People* (New York: Simon & Schuster, Inc., 1972).

Peter and Thomas. Turnbull found communication with the two difficult, but he persevered and before long had mastered a 400-word vocabulary.

On Turnbull's first visit to an Ik village, Peter and Thomas led him along a narrow footpath that twisted its way across the rim of a mountain range. At one point, Turnbull lost his footing and stumbled toward a cliff. As he arched back in an effort to avoid falling into the ravine, he caught sight of his guides. They stood some distance away, smiling. They made no effort to help and laughed as Turnbull scrambled to the relative safety of the footpath. As the threesome pushed on toward Ik territory, Turnbull felt strangely alienated from his companions. Why had they not run to assist him, and why had they found his brush with death a source of humor?

Arriving at an Ik village, Turnbull learned that it was Thomas's home, to which he was now returning after two years' absence. The young man did not run to greet old friends or rejoin his parents beside the village stockade. Instead, Thomas sat by himself on a mountain ledge and surveyed the land below. Turnbull thought that Thomas was enjoying a view remembered from childhood but later learned that his vigil had no aesthetic motive. Thomas was looking for food. When Turnbull asked what kind of game could be found in the region, Thomas did not bother to answer. After a long silence, Peter replied, "Other Ik," and laughed heartily at his improbable joke. Turnbull saw he had a lot to learn about Ik humor.

Conversations with the villagers brought news that Thomas's mother had fallen ill. Turnbull relayed the information to her son, but Thomas showed no interest. It was getting late, he said, and suggested they move on. The three men walked around the stockade of bundled sticks that surrounded the village and made their way to the mountain footpath. As Thomas passed the portion of the stockade wall that separated him from his mother, he shouted his first message in two years. "Give me food," he yelled. "There is no food," came the reply. Thomas showed no emotion as he walked away.

At first Turnbull attributed the behavior of his guides to some flaw in their character. Rather than seeing them as typical Ik, he suspected that they were deviants from a culture he did not yet understand. There were signs that other Ik were more humane. There was the old man, Atum, who bargained shrewdly but showed a deep concern for his ailing wife. Turnbull provided food and medicine, and Atum brought the daily reports of her failing health. And there was Kauar, a middle-aged, lanky, angular man, who ran once a week to collect Turnbull's mail from a government outpost, a two-day trip away. He ran with loping strides and would appear at Turnbull's hut, mail in hand, asking if he had made good time. He would sit in smiling silence as Turnbull read his mail from home and would drink dark tea with Turnbull in the late afternoon. Kauar would count the spoonfuls of sugar Turnbull added to his tea and took care never to take more than his host. He would sometimes save the biscuits Turnbull offered and share them with the children of the village. In fact, Kauar was the only adult Turnbull ever saw playing with Ik children. The anthropologist would watch man and children frolic as the setting sun cast long shadows on the stockade wall.

Turnbull gradually came to realize that Peter and Thomas were not deviant Ik. Their behavior accurately reflected the norms of their culture. Atum's concern for his dying wife turned out to be a ploy to get food. His wife was sick, but Atum never shared his bounty with her. "Why waste food on the dying?"

he asked Turnbull. He ate the food himself and sold the medicine at a nearby police outpost. When his wife finally died of neglect, he buried her in the compound so that Turnbull would not get news of her death. For weeks thereafter, he continued to report his wife's failing health and would gratefully receive supplies to help her. The ruse might have continued, but another villager could not resist telling Turnbull he was being taken. Honesty did not motivate this disclosure. The villager just wanted to watch Turnbull's pained reaction. Few things brought the Ik as much pleasure as the discomfort of another human being. Atum, for his part, showed no embarrassment when accused. He said he had forgotten to tell Turnbull about his wife's death and skillfully moved the conversation to other matters.

The kindnesses of Kauar were genuine, however, and Turnbull came to see that he, not Peter and Thomas, was the deviant in Ik society. Unfortunately, Turnbull's friendship with Kauar was short-lived. The tall and friendly native had set out to get Turnbull's mail one day but failed to return from the trip. The day after his expected return, word came to the village that Kauar had been found on the mountain trail. The excursion had proven too much for his frail body, and he had died a mile from the village, alone on the mountain trail.

The news caused no commotion, although a few people did visit the body to see if Kauar had been carrying anything of value. The only sadness that his wife displayed came when she learned that his few possessions had been stolen before she could find the body. Kauar's son had been playing in the village when the message came of his father's death. Someone called out the news, but the boy showed no interest and went on with his game. No one brought Kauar's body back to the village. His naked corpse was thrown into the bushes and left for the buzzards.

With Kauar's death, Turnbull began to understand the extent of hunger among the Ik, for it was starvation that had brought his friend down. The Ik had been a hunting people, but they had been ordered by the Ugandan government to stop hunting and take up farming. The Ik tried to till the rocky, unyielding soil, but it was of little use. Drought was a frequent companion, and the Ik could make little grow. They hunted when they could, harvested what they could, and as time went on, slowly gave themselves up to starvation. The old (those over thirty) were the first to die. They were the least able to fend for themselves and could eat only when food was plentiful and close at hand. The children were the next. Turnbull began to recognize the signs of starvation only when it first hit children. The elderly had suffered out of Turnbull's view. They had spent most of their time in the compound, and he had not yet been allowed behind its walls. The third victims in the cycle of starvation were adults.

With time, Turnbull began to see that the Iks' entire social system was designed to deal with the constant presence of hunger. The system did not guarantee survival but made it more likely for a strong and selfish few.

The old starved because no one would feed them. The emotional bonds that had once held the Ik together had been severed. Social obligations became an encumbrance that threatened survival. No one felt responsibility for others; everyone's full attention turned inward. Love was a luxury they could not longer afford, a folly that brought death closer to the door. This emotional transformation of the culture was not an immediate or conscious process, but within a generation or two it had been achieved. Only the old remembered a past when things were profoundly different. Everyone else saw only the present and accepted it as it was.

Turnbull searched for the signs of human connection that anthropologists expect in every culture. He found few. Families existed, but more as a relic of the past than as a viable institution of the present. Husbands and wives lived together in small huts behind the impenetrable walls of the compound. Inside, other walls circled each hut. Entrances were small and close to the ground, making them difficult to pass through. Booby traps made them dangerous. Human bonds had been replaced by barricades, and family life, such as it was, went on inside a walled fortress. The outside walls of the compound protected the Ik from other tribes. The inside walls of the compound protected them from each other.

Marriage was dying out. Turnbull saw no signs of affection between adults, and flirtations were more commercial than romantic. Sexuality had become little more than a business transaction which helped some women obtain food and live another day. Adultery was commonplace and did not initiate jealousy.

Families cared for their children until they were three or four years of age. At that time the young were expelled from the family hut and expected to fend for themselves. Infants were tolerated but not loved. There was no sign of affection and little sign of parental concern about a child's well-being. It was not extraordinary for adults to watch with gleeful anticipation as a small child crawled toward a campfire. Everyone would laugh as the youngster's hand plunged into the hot coals. On one occasion parents abandoned their sick daughter in a barricaded hut, promising a quick return; they came back a week later to dispose of the body.

Turnbull found the closest thing to Ik cooperation and friendship among the children. It grew not from kindness but necessity. Pushed out of the home at three or four years of age, a child entered the first of two bands of youngsters. The junior band was made up of three- to seven-year-olds. The senior band consisted of children between eight and twelve. The groups scoured the countryside for figs, berries, and small animals. They would ward off bigger children who attempted to steal what little food they could find. Sometimes the children would attack the elderly and take whatever food they might have. It was considered something of a sport to watch a grandmother drop some morsel into her mouth, then swoop down and attack her before she had time to swallow. When successful, the children took great pride in their achievement, laughing with communal glee as they emptied the mouth of the helpless and crying grandmother.

When a child grew big enough to challenge the other members of the junior band, he or she was expelled and forced to join the older group. When they outgrew the senior group, they entered the solitary life of the adult. Young girls were treated as equals in the younger group because they were about the same size as the boys. Later, when they entered the senior band, they had a relative disadvantage in size, but the burgeoning sexual interest of the older males gave young girls a new bargaining power. An attractive girl could trade sex for food; less desirable girls starved.

Turnbull ends his book on the Ik by commenting on the extreme individualism of the culture. No one took responsibility or even interest in the survival of others. Every old custom, ritual, and belief had either been abandoned or transformed in the interests of individual survival. The older Iks suffered starvation and remorse for a past that seemed far away. The new generation suffered no such sorrow. Dispassion was their defense against the harsh realities of hunger.

Lessons from Two Cultures

The Dangers of Ethnocentrism

The ability to get inside a culture and understand it on its own terms—to grasp its own meanings—is called *cultural relativity*.[6] The tendency to judge other cultures according to the standards of one's own is called *ethnocentrism*. The narrow perspective of ethnocentrism makes social science impossible. If you view the Ik or the BaMbuti ethnocentrically, you are not likely to learn the lessons they offer.

Where would an ethnocentric explanation of the Ik or BaMbuti lead us? It could lead to the conviction that human beings differ from one another racially, nationally, or ethnically, and that some groups possess a natural or genetic superiority over others. According to such a view, the Ik are of inferior stock, genetically inclined to self-destruction. The BaMbuti according to the same ethnocentric logic, are a superior, though simple, group. And Americans, the argument might then go on, are superior to both. Carriers of ethnocentrism always seem to place themselves at the top of the cultural and genetic heap.

Ethnocentric ideas are as old as recorded history, but they became particularly popular during the industrialization and imperialism of the nineteenth century. They were given pseudo-scientific justification when the discoveries of Darwin were perverted to legitimize some of the seamier aspects of human behavior. This distortion, known as Social Darwinism, claimed that all life is a struggle for survival. Only the fittest are destined to survive the rigors of human history. The lesser forms of life merely follow behind their superiors or die away. As an articulate Social Darwinist explained:

> Vice is its own curse. If we let nature alone, she cures vice by the most frightful penalties. It may shock you to hear me say it, but when you get over the shock, it will do you good to think of it: a drunkard in the gutter is just where he ought to be. Nature is working away at him to get him out of the way, just as she sets up her processes of disillusion to remove whatever is a failure in its line.[7]

The author of this statement, William Graham Sumner, would not have found much to complain about in the behavior of the Ik. Their starvation would simply be seen as a part of nature's plan to eradicate "inferior" forms of human life. Social Darwinists would have explained that the Stone Age conditions of the BaMbuti resulted from their unwillingness to compete. They sacrificed material improvement for social harmony.

---

[6] For a discussion of the sociological concept of "relativity," see Peter L. Berger and Hansried Kellner, *Sociology Reinterpreted* (New York: Anchor Press, 1981), Chapter 3, ". . . The Problem of Relativity." Available in paperback.

[7] William Graham Sumner, "The Forgotten Man," in *Selected Essays of William Graham Sumner*, ed. Stow Persons (Englewood Cliffs, NJ: Prentice-Hall, 1963), p. 122. Available in paperback.

It is an easy tendency to describe the behavior of the BaMbuti and Ik as belonging to a lower order of human life. But the assumption that certain groups are simply better than others can justify all manner of behavior. Indeed, it has been used to justify racism, slavery, and imperialism; it has also been used to explain laissez-faire capitalism, the existence of social classes, and the inevitability of poverty. The line of reasoning in all these cases is that some individuals or groups are in some way inferior and that their place in society is a reflection of the will of nature. It should be pointed out that such explanations are particularly useful to people who hold privileged positions in the world. It serves to justify their status and rid them of the responsibility to aid those less fortunate than themselves. Such ideas are very much alive in the world today. They reached their zenith in the tragic events that followed the rise of Hitler or Stalin.

Anthropology and other social sciences provide no substantial evidence to support the ethnocentric idea that some groups are genetically or culturally superior to others. Although it is true that there are indeed differences among individuals, these differences are often as great within any one group as they are among groups. When we examine racial groups in search of significant differences, we find these are few and superficial: eye color, skin color, the shape of the nose or eyes, the texture of the hair, and so on. In fact, most anthropologists consider race an arbitrary and unrealistic vantage point from which to study human variability.[8]

Ethnocentrism does not help us account for the behavior of the BaMbuti or Ik. Let us look at another age-old idea—the notion that human nature is a fixed entity—and see whether it can unravel the mysteries of human behavior.

Two Rigid Conceptions of Human Nature: Good vs. Evil

We have all heard the expression, "You can't change human nature." It expresses the idea that all human beings share a set of fixed attributes that cannot be eliminated or modified. There are many different ideas about what these attributes might be, but they generally fall under one of two headings: Human beings are basically good, or human beings are basically evil. Both ideas have been around for a long time and have had a significant influence on determining how human beings govern themselves.

Looking at the BaMbuti, we might conclude that Rogers was right when he claimed that human beings are inherently good, loving, and cooperative creatures. But the behavior of the Ik seriously challenges any such heartwarming assumption. How nice it would be if our drive toward goodness were as biologically determined as our drive to breathe. But if we have learned anything from the Ik, the Nazi experience, the Ku Klux Klan, or terrorist bombings (the list is endless), it must be that there is little fixed in human nature that will protect us from the horrors of human cruelty. Rogers's notion that human beings are basically noble and good is probably misguided.

---

[8] See Ashley Montagu, *The Idea of Race* (Lincoln: University of Nebraska Press, 1965), three brief and lucid lectures; and Ashley Montagu, *Man's Most Dangerous Myth: The Fallacy of Race,* 5th ed. (New York: Oxford University Press, 1974), which covers most of the topics about race, e.g., origin of the concept, biological facts, social factors, a parallel with antifeminism, eugenics and genetics, and the meaning of "equal opportunity."

Do we conclude, then, that human beings are by nature selfish and destructive? If left to their own devices, can we expect human desire and passion to lead to evil as Durkheim suggests? This is a popular belief in America, and it holds that only the restraints of civil society cause bad people to behave like good ones. The proponents of such a view would point out that the destructive behavior of the Ik began at just the time when cultural restraints were diminishing. In turn, they would ascribe the more humane behavior of the BaMbuti to their strong social ties.

The Lazy Fallacy

Both these views of human nature (that we are naturally good or naturally evil) are flawed and for the same reason. Each explains some aspect of human nature by asserting, in effect, that it causes itself. The optimistic view that humans are basically good contends that we love and cooperate because we are loving and cooperative creatures. The pessimistic view contends that we are evil and selfish because of evil and selfish tendencies. This kind of thinking is circular. We might as well say that apples fall because of their inherent "fallingness." Yet, as every grade school student knows, gravity brings apples down, not some mysterious force in the nature of apples.

John Dewey termed this form of circular thinking the *lazy fallacy*.[9] He pointed out that when we say human beings love because of their loving natures, we have said nothing at all. We have merely reproduced in causal terms the very behavior for which we want to account. The consequence of this thinking is that it stops inquiry into the social conditions that promote or retard loving behavior. We do not seek its social origins. In that sense, we are lazy.

Why are lazy fallacies so prevalent? They are probably common because they can be used to "prove" anything. The inevitability of war, peace, prosperity, poverty, communism, capitalism, religion, and so on, can be "proven" by the assertion that they are inherent in the human condition. Like a taxicab, the lazy-fallacy argument will take you anywhere you want to go—anywhere, that is, short of understanding.

When we rid ourselves of the idea that human beings are inherently good or evil, we find our thinking about human behavior getting clearer. We see that such prized attributes as love, compassion, cooperation, meaningful sexuality, and purposeful work are not fixed in our nature. They are responses to the conditions of daily life, and, if we desire these attributes, we must pay close attention to the conditions that nurture them. The Ik's inability to change from hunting to farming, though it was ordered by the government, demonstrates this point. Similarly, hate and greed prosper in certain social arrangements, and, if we hope to retard their development, we must modify the conditions that encourage them. This insight has special significance for teachers, for it focuses their attention on the environment of the classroom, school, and community, rather than on some hypothetical natural force that lurks deep within the child.

[9] John Dewey, *The Public and Its Problems* (Chicago: The Swallow Press, Inc., 1957 [1927]), pp. 9–10. Available in paperback.

The Open Encounter

We have dismissed two popular views of human nature: (1) the ethnocentric view that some people are naturally superior to others and (2) the lazy-fallacy assumption that we are all either good or evil. Are we now forced to conclude that there is no such thing as human nature? Not at all. We must look elsewhere for a conception of human nature that satisfies the canons of logic and is broad enough to account for the behavior of such different people as the BaMbuti, the Ik, and ourselves. We turn now to just such a view of human nature.[10]

Human beings occupy a unique position in the world. Unlike other animals, they are born relatively free of coercive instincts. The term *instinct* refers to a pattern of behavior that is unlearned and genetically determined. Eagles are born with an instinct for hunting, wolves are born knowing how to fight (and more importantly, how to end a fight), and geese come into the world knowing how to perform elaborate courtship dances. Such information is not taught; it is simply there in the genetic makeup of the animal. Many instincts, such as the ones just described, show up in the adult behavior of animals even when they have been separated from their species since birth. For example, goslings, born in an incubator and raised in the isolation of a laboratory, will automatically and accurately carry out elaborate courtship dances when they grow to adulthood, even though they have never seen such rituals performed. They are biologically prewired to carry out this behavior.

Human beings are born with few, if any, such instincts.[11] Their behavior is not determined by innate biological instructions. This is one of the most exciting facts of human life, for within this fact we find the seeds of human freedom. Other animals inherit a closed world. The social organization of ants or bees, for example, is wholly determined by their instincts. The actions of each insect are little more than a predetermined response to specific environmental stimuli. Human beings, on the other hand, are *world-open*. Their social organization is the product of choice, culture, and custom, not instinct. Children learn how to behave from adults; they do not inherit their behavior genetically.

Human beings build their own world and pass that world on to their children. Whereas other animals inherit a world through genetics, human beings learn a world from adults and the continuing experience of the environment. At this point, we begin to sense the ambiguity that characterizes the gift of world-openness. The remarkable plasticity of human nature allows infants to learn whatever is presented to them. They do not spring from the womb with a complete set of moral precepts. Justice, morality, love, responsibility, and cooperation are human inventions; unfortunately, so are hate, greed, disunity, irresponsibility, and violence. One set of lessons is learned just as readily as the other.

[10] The following view of human nature is informed by John Dewey's important work, *Human Nature and Conduct* (New York: Henry Holt and Co., 1922).

[11] Ethologists (people who study patterns of animal behavior), such as Konrad Lorenz and others, disagree strongly with this view. They assert that human beings are more creatures of instinct than reason. Lorenz would concede, however, that human beings are able to use their intelligence to direct their instincts into socially useful and morally acceptable channels. He does not say that we are slaves to our instincts. See Konrad Lorenz, *On Aggression* (New York: Harcourt Brace Jovanovich, 1963). Sociologist E. O. Wilson makes a similar point in his important book, *Sociobiology* (Cambridge: Harvard University Press, 1975).

Human beings have remarkable freedom in their behavior, but, as Erich Fromm pointed out, choice can be agonizing.[12] When possibilities are infinite, they can overrun our ability to handle them. Intelligent action becomes impossible. An example may make this point clearer. Biologists have pointed out that schools of fish confuse their predators, because each fish is camouflaged by the others around it. The predator cannot focus attention on any one fish for long enough to chase it down. The predator darts haphazardly from one target to another and is soon exhausted by the chase. Analogously, humans can be confused by infinite choice. Nature has left us open to the world, but it is necessary for us to narrow our options and avoid the chaos of infinite choice.

Like the predator in the preceding example, human beings can have so many options that they become unable to function. As every parent knows, toddlers in a room full of inviting toys often become frustrated. They cannot play with any item for very long because other toys excite their interest. Such problems can be suffered by adults as well. Some restriction is essential before human beings are able to take advantage of their freedom to choose their behavior. This narrowing of options is accomplished through culture—the attitudes, values, customs, and habits we learn as children from adults. We will discuss culture in the next chapter. Suffice it for now to say that culture accomplishes for human beings what instinct does for other animals. It narrows our choices. In doing so, it allows us to use our intelligence.

Too much freedom, then, is as enslaving as too little. Human intelligence is as much hindered by too many options as by too few. It is a paradoxical truth that the processes that restrict our choices within wide but manageable limits are the same processes that make choice possible. Or, to put it another way, out of the measure of restriction comes a measure of freedom. We could view much of human history as a struggle over just this issue; how much restriction (or how much freedom) is too much?

Another point needs to be made before we leave this topic. Human beings do not live without restrictions. But they are distinguished from other animals in the nature of these restrictions. Unlike other animals, humans play a part in creating the limitations that guide them. Other animals cannot influence their instincts, but human beings can and do influence their culture.

Conclusion: Human Nature and Education

This chapter began with the assertion that Durkheim, Rogers, and Dewey came to different conclusions about education because they began with different assumptions about human nature. It was further suggested that one's ideas about education spring from what one thinks people are like, what they are capable of doing, how they can relate to one another, and so on. But thoughts on these topics are so taken for granted that they are seldom given conscious attention.

One method for establishing our taken-for-granted assumptions is to take a look at people who do not share these ideas. For that reason we examined two cultures, the Ik and the BaMbuti. The idea was to shock you (or at least to surprise you a bit) because each shock is a sign that a taken-for-granted assumption has been violated. Each surprise acts something like a metal detector.

[12] Erich Fromm, *Escape from Freedom* (New York: Avon Books, 1965 [1941]).

It makes you aware of things you cannot see (in this case, ideas about human nature) and tells you where to dig to find them. Perhaps you were surprised by the BaMbuti's innocence, kindness, unselfishness, unity, and lack of competition, envy, violence, crime, or deviance. The Ik may have shocked you with their extreme individualism, selfishness, cruelty, generational warfare, and their lack of family bonds or social unity. If you follow your feelings of shock back into your taken-for-granted beliefs, you are likely to discover what you believe about human nature.

Do you believe that human beings are good or evil? Should society emphasize conformity or creativity? Should we promote freedom or constraint? What are the sources of human values? Do values grow from the individual, from society, or from some other source? What about identity? Does it grow within the individual, within the social order, or somewhere else? Answer these questions, and you begin to discover the foundation of your ideas on education.

The descriptions of the Ik and the BaMbuti served a second purpose. They set the stage for a discussion of the lazy-fallacy thinking of Durkheim and Rogers. They also make a case for a world-open conception of human nature.

One thing must be made clear at this point. Not everyone will accept the world-open conception of human nature. It is presented here because it is compatible with available evidence from the social sciences and the values of American democracy. Thoughtful and informed people (Carl Rogers and Emil Durkheim, to name just two) would take exception to these ideas. You may choose to look elsewhere for ideas on human nature that are more compatible with your own. Your aim, of course, must be to work out a model of human nature that finds support in evidence from the social sciences, is clear, and can guide you in the formation of educational aims. Having another model (such as the one presented here) to argue with should help you clarify your thinking.

The world-open view of human nature is compatible with the educational aims of John Dewey. It gives substance to many of the assertions spelled out in the last chapter. You will remember that Dewey insisted that selfhood and intelligence are not simply born within us, nor are they given to us by society. Rather, Dewey claimed, they develop in the interaction of the individual with other human beings.

The world-open position encourages teachers to focus attention on the interaction of children with their environment. It discourages lazy-fallacy thinking. An example of lazy-fallacy thinking in education is found in such statements as these:

> I caught some boys fighting at recess and read them the riot act. But I know that's a waste of time. Boys will be boys and sometimes they just have to fight it out.

> I never take my eye off students during a test. If I do, they cheat. I guess I understand; it's just human nature.

Sometimes in education assumptions about human nature are debated in more abstract form, in discussions of whether heredity or environment, nature or nurture, contributes most to educational development.[13] The error in this thinking rests on the assumption that fighting or cheating (or anything else,

---

[13] A recent outbreak of this debate can be found in Arthur R. Jensen, "How Much Can We Boost IQ and Scholastic Achievement?" *Harvard Educational Review*, Vol. 39, No. 1 (Winter 1969), pp. 1–123; for a discussion of Jensen's views, see the following issue, No. 2 (Spring 1969), pp. 273–356.

Teachers' assumptions about human nature influence their educational theories and classroom practices. *Source:* National Education Association, Joe Di Dio.

for that matter) is built into human behavior and therefore beyond one's control. The danger of lazy-fallacy thinking is that it stops a teacher from investigating the environmental circumstances that encourage certain behavior. In effect, the behavior is accepted as inevitable, and no effort is made to examine its root causes or to change the conditions that foster the behavior. When this failure of effort occurs, a teacher loses the chance to see whether individual competition, grading practices, irrelevant subject matter, and so on, make cheating more likely. Similarly, if teachers believe that children are inherently violent, they will not investigate the conditions in the school and community that make violence more likely. For this reason, John Dewey has said that "native ability" (that is, human nature) is important only in the sense that it marks individual limits. How one student's ability compares with others is irrelevant to the teacher's work; and except in extreme cases, ability is more varied and has more potential than we yet know how to develop. What education should do is to provide opportunities for each and every child to develop through activities that have personal and cultural meaning.[14]

You can see from this explanation that lazy-fallacy thinking has a strong conservative bias. It is conservative because it takes teachers' attention away from the way schools operate. It accepts the status quo and does not encourage thoughtful questioning of prevailing habits, customs, or institutions.

Dewey believed intelligence could help end the blind acceptance of the way

---

[14] John Dewey, *Democracy and Education* (New York: The Free Press, 1966 [1916]), pp. 74, 172. Available in paperback.

things are. He did not believe, however, that intelligence leads inevitably to upheaval. Rather it helps us support that which is most useful and to modify that which is not. Intelligence grows when we employ our minds to meet and solve problems and use what is learned (including errors) to grapple with new problems. In a world of rapid change, where we have no idea what new dangers lie ahead, intelligence is our best hope for survival. Educational strategies that promote intelligence must be sought, and those that inhibit intelligence must be avoided.

Suggested Readings

This chapter invites you to examine your ideas regarding human nature. Since the beginning of recorded time, human beings have pondered what they are about. According to Sir Thomas Browne, "Man is a noble animal." Francis Church, however, insists that he is a "mere insect." Seneca called him a "reasoning animal," and Montaigne claimed he was "certainly stark mad." Louis Untermeyer claimed human beings were "great and strong and wise"; whereas Rudyard Kipling insisted they were "small potatoes." Such diversity of opinion makes the point that the definition of human nature is still an open matter. But our views of human nature have consequences, as we shall see in the next chapter.

Those interested in further exploring the question of human nature are invited to read any of the following:

MATSON, FLOYD W. *The Idea of Man.* New York: Delacorte Press, 1976. This is a perfect book for the beginning student of human nature. Matson reviews various conceptions of human nature and shows the consequences of each for social practice. After laying out the competing conceptions of human nature, Matson makes a strong case for a humanistic conception of humankind. Ashley Montagu said of the work, "it is the best, most readable, and heartening [book] of its kind. It inspires enthusiasm."

MEAD, GEORGE HERBERT. *Mind, Self, and Society.* Chicago: University of Chicago Press, 1934. Mead is a formidable author but the rewards he offers are well worth the work it takes to understand him.

PFUETZE, PAUL. *Self, Society and Existence: Human Nature and Dialogue in the Thought of George Herbert Mead and Martin Buber.* New York: Harper Torch Books, 1961. Though the book is heavy going, it usefully explicates the views of two important social philosophers.

STEVENSON, LESLIE. *Seven Theories of Human Nature.* London: Oxford University Press, 1974. Stevenson discusses, generally, rival theories and the criticism of theories, and then presents an analysis of the theories of Plato, Christianity, Marx, Freud, Sartre, Skinner, and Lorenz.

Students interested in how the social conception of human nature presented in this chapter coincides with the question of religion are invited to explore the following:

BERGER, PETER L. *A Rumor of Angels.* Garden City, NY: Anchor Books, Doubleday and Company, Inc., 1970; *The Sacred Canopy: Elements of a Sociological Theory of Religion.* Garden City, NY: Anchor Books, Doubleday and Company, Inc., 1967. Berger writes in a concise and lucid style, a talent all too rare among sociologists.

LUCKMANN, THOMAS. *The Invisible Religion.* New York: The Macmillan Company, 1967. Luckmann, like Berger, explores the relationship between individuals and society. He ponders the contribution of religion to individual meaning and social purpose.

Those wishing to explore notions of human nature that differ from the views presented in this chapter are referred to the following:

LORENZ, KONRAD. *On Aggression.* New York: Harcourt Brace Jovanovich, 1966. Lorenz believes that human behavior is largely controlled by instincts that work below the level of conscious awareness and often beyond the control of human will. Lorenz's work opened the way for a new field of investigation, sociobiology.

SKINNER, B. F. *Beyond Freedom and Dignity.* New York: Alfred A. Knopf, Inc., 1971. As one might assume from the title, this book presents a view of human nature that many Americans find difficult to accept. Though Skinner is not the most radical of the behaviorists, he is perhaps the most articulate and provocative of this group. His work has had a powerful impact on education, leading to the use of teaching machines, operant conditioning, and programmed learning. Though there is much in Skinner's behaviorism that is compatible with Dewey's view of human nature, they part company on the question of human freedom. Skinner has written, "I deny that freedom exists at all. I must deny it—or my program would be absurd. You can't have a science about a subject matter which hops capriciously about."

WILSON, E. O. *Sociobiology, the New Synthesis.* Cambridge: Harvard University Press, 1975.

A tribe of primitive people, with characteristics similar to the BaMbuti, was discovered in the Philippines in the early 1970s. John Nance's, *The Gentle Tasaday* (New York: Harcourt Brace Jovanovich, Inc., 1975), is a sensitive and moving account of those people. Unfortunately, recent information suggests that the discovery was a hoax. Nance has returned to the Philippines to check the report for *National Geographic Magazine.* See *St. Petersburg Times* (April 13, 1986), p. 2A.

Colin Turnbull's book, *The Mountain People,* initiated a vigorous debate among anthropologists. At times the debate dealt with questions of ethics and methodology. At other times, and more subtly, it revolved around the question of human nature. Too frequently it degenerated into ad hominem assaults on personalities. Although this is regrettable, it serves to point out that the issue of human nature is difficult to discuss even for those trained to study human behavior. For an example of this debate, see Fredrik Bart's "On Responsibility and Humanity: Calling a Colleague to Account," *Current Anthropology,* Vol. 15, pp. 99–102. See also the exchange of letters reprinted in *Current Anthropology,* Vol. 16 (1975), pp. 343–358.

The diversity of human culture is explored thoughtfully and with grace by Ruth Benedict in her now classic book *Patterns of Culture* (Boston: Houghton-Mifflin Company, 1934).

CHAPTER 4

Culture and the Individual: The Vital Connection

Humans as World Builders

Human beings are world-building creatures, and culture is the world they build. Social scientists have defined culture in literally hundreds of ways, but most of these definitions stay rather close to one put forward a hundred years ago by E. B. Tylor. He defined culture as, "That complex whole which includes knowledge, belief, art, law, morals, customs, and any other capabilities and habits acquired by man as a member of society."[1] In short, culture includes all the things that human beings produce in order to deal with their social and physical environment. Some of these products are material (such as tools) and others are not (such as beliefs). But all cultural products serve the function of ordering our experience, making sense out of it, and giving it meaning.

Just as there is little that is fixed in the nature of human beings, there is little fixed in the nature of culture. The culture of one people may look very different from the culture of another. It displays different behaviors and shares different meanings. This difference is an important concept for teachers to understand. We cannot make sense out of an individual's behavior until we know something of that person's culture. A perfectly normal, well-adapted, and successful Ik or BaMbuti would seem abnormal, maladapted, and unsuccessful in an American school.

Cultures solve the common problems of human beings, but they solve them in different ways. In this limited sense, all cultures are alike. Each provides its people with a means of communication (*language*). Each determines who wields power and under what circumstances power can be used (*status*). Each provides for the regulation of reproduction (*family*) and supplies a system of rules (*government*). These rules may be written (*laws*) or unwritten (*custom*), but they are always present.

---

[1] Edward B. Tylor, *Primitive Culture: Researches into the Development of Mythology, Philosophy, Religion, Language, Art, and Custom* (New York: Brentano's, 1924 [1865]), p. 1.

Cultures supply human beings with an explanation of their relationship to nature *(magic, myth, religion,* and *science)*. They provide their people with some conception of time *(temporality)*. They supply a system by which significant lessons of the culture *(history)* can be given a physical representation and stored and passed on to future generations. This representation usually comes in the form of dance, song, poetry, architecture, handicrafts, story, design, or painting *(art)*. What makes cultures similar is the problems they solve, not the methods they devise to solve them.

Ordering Behavior

Every culture provides its people with rules of conduct. These rules guide individual behavior by defining what is real and what is not, what is right and what is wrong, how things should be done, and what is of value. The rules of a culture include its knowledge, beliefs, technology, values, and norms. Let us deal with them one at a time.

Knowledge is that which can be shown to be "correct"—verified or "warranted" by experience or association—either by science (found in highly developed cultures) or by less rigorous means (everyday experience and common sense, for example, found in all cultures). The important point is that knowledge must have some verification or evidence beyond faith or opinion. The knowledge that corn will not grow if there has been no rain is an empirical fact; the idea that it does not rain because the rain god is displeased is an opinion (in fact, a myth) because it has not been proven by experience. The latter idea therefore would not be included in what we call knowledge.

Beliefs are ideas about the world that have not been empirically verified. There are two types of beliefs: those that can be verified but have not yet been tested and those that can never be verified. A teacher can hold a belief that a boy cannot read because he has a sight problem and needs glasses. This is a testable assumption, and a good teacher will take steps to test this belief. Once the assumption is tested and verified, the teacher can work from knowledge and not simply from belief. But if a teacher believes that a student cannot read because he or she is possessed by demons, science is incapable of proving or disproving this belief. What about the student who has a "bad attitude?" Can this belief be verified? If not, what results might come from a teacher's continuing to hold it?

Technology is the application of knowledge and belief in order to change things. We usually think of changes in the physical environment when we think of technology; steel, chrome, and plastic, for example, are changed by the powers of technology into automobiles and appliances. But technology spreads its influence over more than our physical environment. For example, our knowledge and beliefs are locked together in the methods of educators to form what could be called a technology of teaching.[2] There is obviously a lot of room for beliefs in education. It would be difficult to prove scientifically that democracy is a favorable form of government or that the rights of individuals should be protected. Yet, such beliefs play an important role in the educational enter-

---

[2] For an example see B. F. Skinner, *The Technology of Teaching* (New York: Appleton-Century-Crofts, 1968).

prise. There is also room for science in education. The use of verified facts would, surely, help us to attain our educational aims.

Values move us out of the realm of what exists or is thought to exist (what is) and into the realm of preference (what should be). A value is a belief that defines what is personally or socially desirable. Values do not exist in isolation. We do not simply value something; we value it in relation to, or in competition with, something else. We may value the looks of people we love (even if they are not handsome), but we do not value their looks as much as we value their personalities. Value, therefore, is not a quality that resides in a thing; it is an attribute we assign in comparison to other things. On the other hand, values can be either *intrinsic,* having worth for themselves, or *instrumental,* leading to other things of value. Values are the relatively enduring standards that guide our attitudes toward objects and actions.

Norms were discussed in Chapter 2. They refer to a culture's rules of conduct. Norms spell out the expected behaviors of specific people in specific situations. They are closely related to values but are more prescriptive than values. Norms define the goals of culture and the accepted behaviors for reaching these goals. Americans, for example, put a high value on money. Norms define the goal of making money, and they also set out the acceptable methods by which money can be acquired. It is acceptable to work for money, inherit it, or win it in a sweepstakes, but the norms of the culture warn us against making our fortune by selling heroin or robbing banks.

Cultural Universals

Ralph Linton (1893–1953) was an anthropologist who is best remembered for his book *The Study of Man.*[3] Although written in 1936, the book's insights remain fresh today. Culture, according to Linton, provides a design for living. It defines what is real, what is good, and what individuals are expected to do. Linton contended that culture can be divided into three categories: *universals, specialties,* and *alternatives.*

Within any culture there exist ideas, norms, values, beliefs, habits, and conditioned emotional responses that are held by all its sane, adult members. Linton called these widely held ideas and values *universals.* He contended that each culture has its own set of these commonly held assumptions about the world. You will remember that Durkheim called these shared assumptions our *collective consciousness.*

Cultural Specialties

There is more to a culture than the knowledge and beliefs that its members hold in common. Many cultural activities are carried on by only small portions of the population. Yet the products of these activities are understood and valued by everyone. Linton referred to such portions of the culture as *specialties.* They grow from the need to divide tasks and knowledge among the members of society. The distinguishing characteristic of cultural specialties is that although only a portion of the population possesses the specialized knowledge, most members of the society know how to contact specialists, what the function

---

[3] Ralph Linton, *The Study of Man* (New York: Appleton-Century-Crofts, 1936).

of a specialist is, and what the effect of the specialist's activity should be. For example, few parents know how to teach mathematics to their children, but they know how to enroll them in schools, how teachers are expected to act, and whether their children can add and subtract at the end of the year.

The universals and specialties of a culture make up its *core*. They form a solid and well-integrated center of gravity that holds individuals together in an efficient unit.

Cultural Alternatives

Some traits of individuals are peculiar to a group and are *not* shared by the culture at large. This is a broad category and includes such things as the unique habits of a family, the diverse doctrines of individual religions, the ideologies of competing political organizations, and widely differing theories of education. In every case, individuals are offered a choice of behaviors and ideas. Linton refers to these choices as *alternatives*.

Alternatives come into being when there are competing ways to arrive at similar goals. They can be grouped together according to the end they seek to achieve. For example, members of the culture are offered alternatives in the area of religion, political philosophy, sexual identities, club memberships, and so on. Within each group, there is usually a tension among the alternatives offered by the culture. The intensity of this tension depends on the social significance of the ends being sought. Intensity is not likely to be generated in a discussion about alternative deodorants or alternative versions of a nursery rhyme, but discussions about alternative sexual practices, abortion, religious beliefs, or political ideologies can get quite intense. When alternatives are socially significant, they compete for a place in the core of the culture. Groups adhering to a particular set of beliefs are likely to proselytize in an effort to get new members. They may argue with (or at least be suspicious of) people who hold ideas different from their own.

The zone of cultural alternatives plays a significant part in social change. New ideas can be tried out in this zone before they pass into the core of the culture. Universals and specialties can be eased out of the cultural core and

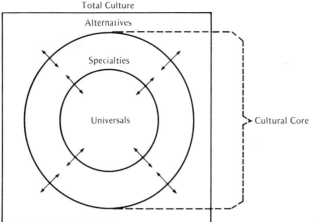

Figure 4-1   Ralph Linton's view of culture.

become alternatives. They may remain as alternatives, or they may eventually be forgotten and pass out of the culture completely. Unlike the core of the culture (universals and specialties), which is rather stable and integrated, the zone of alternatives is continually changing.

Figure 4-1 illustrates Linton's three-part view of culture. Universals and specialties make up the core of the culture. The alternatives drift outside the core and compete for entrance into the core. The three elements—alternatives, specialties, and universals—in combination, make up the total culture. The core of the culture is integrated and relatively stable, whereas the zone of alternatives is in continual flux.

Individual Peculiarities

Outside the realm of culture, but nevertheless important to it, is an area Linton calls *individual peculiarities*. These peculiarities are the ideas and behaviors that exist in an individual but have not been adopted by others. They would include an individual's secret love of peanut butter and olive sandwiches, an unknown craftman's unique style, or even Einstein's unpublished theory of relativity.

Obviously many individual peculiarities are of little significance to a culture. Some are very important, however, because they provide the spark for cultural innovation. What is taken today as knowledge—for instance, that the earth revolves around the sun, or (to take a school example) that girls are quite as able to do mathematics as boys—at one time were extreme peculiarities and even idiosyncrasies. In fact, individual peculiarities often are thought to be a threat to established knowledge or conventional belief. Nevertheless, the clash of individual peculiarities with a culture is a necessary element in revising that culture.

Education and the Cultural Core

Schools are concerned mainly with transmitting the core of the culture to students. Much of this is done consciously and with careful planning. Other portions of the cultural core are so taken for granted that they get passed along unconsciously during the normal operations of the school. A teacher may not assign girls in a class to sweep the floors and clean the wash basins in order not to enforce sexual stereotypes, yet that lesson may come through to children if it is reinforced on many levels of the culture.

Educators who go beyond the cultural core for course material may find themselves embroiled in controversy. The tension that exists between socially significant alternatives is found in classrooms, just as it can be found in the culture at large. Some teachers, taking advantage of this fact, bring up controversial topics in order to promote class discussion. They are sometimes surprised to find how quickly such a debate can spread beyond the classroom into the community.

Parents are often angered to find their children are being taught (or perhaps only introduced to) controversial cultural alternatives. Citizens may protest when they find that a teacher has invited a John Birch Society member or a homosexual to discuss his or her views with a high school class. Linton's insights do not tell us whether or not it is good educational practice to discuss controversial topics. Such questions are better answered by theories of education and democracy. But Linton's classification does give us a way to anticipate what issues are likely to invite controversy.

Teachers may attempt to avoid controversy by trying to discuss all sides of an issue. This may not work in every case. For example, Florida law mandates that high schools offer a course entitled Americanism vs. Communism. The same law specifically prohibits teachers or textual material from presenting communism as preferable to free enterprise economics. It is against the law to give both sides of this issue in Florida. Here is the full text of that law:

> *TEACHING ANTICOMMUNISM IN THE SCHOOLS*
> *STATE OF FLORIDA*
>
> 233.064 Americanism vs. Communism; required high school course.
> (1) The legislature of the state hereby finds it to be a fact that
>   (a) The political ideology commonly known and referred to as Communism is in conflict with and contrary to the principles of constitutional government of the United States as epitomized in its National Constitution,
>   (b) The successful exploitation and manipulation of youth and student groups throughout the world today are a major challenge which the free world forces must meet and defeat, and
>   (c) The best method of meeting this challenge is to have the youth of the state and nation thoroughly and completely informed as to the evils, dangers and fallacies of Communism by giving them a thorough understanding of the entire communist movement, including its history, doctrines, objectives and techniques.
> (2) The public high schools shall teach a complete course of not less than thirty hours, to all students enrolled in said public high schools entitled "Americanism vs. Communism."
> (3) The course shall provide adequate instruction in the history, doctrines, objectives and techniques of Communism and shall be for the primary purpose of instilling in the minds of the students a greater appreciation of democratic processes, freedom under the law, and the will to preserve that freedom.
> (4) The course shall be one of orientation in comparative governments and shall emphasize the free-enterprise–competitive economy of the United States as the one which produces higher wages, higher standards of living, greater personal freedom and liberty than any other system of economics on earth.
> (5) The course shall lay particular emphasis upon the dangers of Communism, the ways to fight Communism, the evils of Communism, the fallacies of Communism, and the false doctrines of Communism.
> (6) The state Textbook Council and the Department of Education shall take such action as may be necessary and appropriate to prescribe a suitable textbook and instructional material as provided by state law, using as one of their guides the official reports of the House Committee on Un-American Activities and the Senate Internal Security Subcommittee of the United States Congress.
> (7) No teacher or textual material assigned to this course shall present communism as preferable to the system of constitutional government and the free-enterprise–competitive economy indigenous to the United States.[4]

Idealizing Core Values

Traditionally, schools have concentrated so much on transmitting the core values of the culture that they have presented cultural ideals as if they were estab-

---

[4] *Official Florida Statutes*, 1979, published by the state of Florida, Tallahassee, p. 1164.

lished reality. This custom can be seen most clearly if we take a look at the past. Ruth Miller Elson concluded a study of nineteenth-century textbooks by saying the world they presented was

> a fantasy made up by adults as a guide for their children. . . . It is an ideal world, peopled by ideal villains as well as ideal heroes. Nature is perfectly if sometimes inscrutably planned by God for the good of man, with progress as its first and inevitable law. Nothing can hinder this march toward material and moral perfection, a movement particularly visible in the United States. Individuals are to be understood in terms of easily discernible, inherent characteristics of their race and nationality as much as in terms of their individual character. Virtue is always rewarded, vice punished. And one can achieve virtue and avoid vice by following a few simple rules.[5]

When the core values of a culture are taught uncritically, we run the risk of ethnocentrism. When American values are presented as if they are inherently superior (because they are American), we transmit an inaccurate picture of ourselves. We retard our ability to evaluate our culture and hence our ability to improve it. Nevertheless, education today is not as one-sided as it once was in these matters. There is a slow but perceptible movement in education to promote warranted and thoughtful criticism of our core values. Such criticism is not only compatible with democracy; it is an essential ingredient of the democratic spirit.

The Social Functions of Norms

We have said that norms are rules for conduct. They can exist as universals, specialties, or alternatives. We usually take them for granted, but when we stop and examine them, they sometimes seem arbitrary or even foolish. When we scratch beneath the surface of a norm, however, we find that it serves—or has served—some social function or purpose. This is not to say that all norms are desirable or that they necessarily serve moral or useful purposes. It merely suggests that norms do not grow in a vacuum. They take shape in the context of social problems. They may serve to avoid conflict, justify authority, or alleviate some threat to the social order. The functions served by cultural norms and values may be quite removed from the behaviors they regulate.

An example may clarify this point. American high schools usually have programs of competitive athletics. These serve to promote physical development, coordination, and health. It is often claimed that participation in competitive sports builds character, but competitive athletics serve a broader function than the individualistic ones just mentioned. They help to mend the splits that can develop among cliques of students or between students and teachers. They serve to unify the school against others. Schools possess an elaborate apparatus to promote group solidarity (a "we" feeling) against their competition. Cheerleaders, booster clubs, and pep rallies function to build enthusiasm for the coming game. Sports commentators and Monday morning quarterbacks serve to explain the win or the loss. Orchestrated cheers and spontaneous outbursts on the day of the game not only encourage the team, but they also amount to

---

[5] Ruth Miller Elson, *Guardians of Tradition* (Lincoln: University of Nebraska Press, 1964), p. 337. Available in paperback.

public declarations of commitment to the school. The wearing of a school letter is not only evidence that individuals fought for their team, but also that they cared enough about the school to do battle in its name. A varsity letter is part of the uniform of commitment to the school. The function of solidarity is further served by the fact that athletes frequently give their varsity letters to a person they especially care for. Thus, this symbol of commitment to the school is given wider circulation.

In summary, the norms and values that surround school athletics cannot be explained simply on the grounds of physical development or character building. They function to unify potentially conflicting groups and thereby to avoid potential conflict. Whatever other benefits may come from them, competitive athletics help to smooth the operation of the school and to make the jobs of teachers and administrators appreciably easier.

Manifest and Latent Functions

It is not always easy to discover the function of a norm. A contemporary sociologist, Robert Merton, has pointed out that norms can serve both *manifest* and *latent functions*.[6] Manifest functions are conscious and intentional, whereas latent functions are unconscious and unintentional. A parent may strike a child in order to achieve the manifest function of getting the child to behave, but such a punishment can also serve the latent function of justifying violence in the mind of the youngster. A guidance counselor may have the manifest function of helping students solve problems but may serve the latent function of freeing teachers from troublesome students. A school may have the manifest function of providing students with an equal opportunity to be educated but serve the latent function of convincing impoverished children that they cannot make it in a middle-class society. The discovery of manifest and latent functions should sensitize teachers to the fact that what they set out to accomplish is not necessarily what they end up accomplishing.

Enforcing Cultural Norms

Socialization (or *internalization*, as it is sometimes called) is the process by which we learn our culture. Most of us learn its lessons so well that deviation from its norms seldom occurs to us. If you are a female, you do not whisper reminders to yourself to behave like a woman. Your womanly behavior is part of your womanly self. You *are* a woman. Part of this fact no doubt is biological, but we know from the study of other cultures that females go about being women in very different ways. Much of female behavior is not biological at all; it is learned. The same obviously can be said for male behavior.

Most of what we take for granted in everyday life can be translated into what Robert and Helen Lynd have labeled *of course statements*. These habits of acting and feeling and speaking occur so naturally to an individual that an answer to any question concerning them will include the words "of course."[7] "Are schools supposed to teach children to read?" "Of course!" The most powerful force

---

[6] Robert Merton, *Social Theory and Social Structure* (New York: The Free Press, 1957).

[7] Robert S. Lynd and Helen Merrell Lynd, *Middletown in Transition* (New York: Harcourt, Brace and Company, 1937), p. 402.

encouraging obedience to norms is that we take them for granted. They become internalized into our makeup and unconsciously guide our thinking and behavior. They represent not only the core of the culture but also the core of our personality.

Not all norms are absorbed so completely that they become an unquestioned part of our makeup. Many norms are not fully accepted; others compete as alternatives for our attention. Socialization is an imperfect process, and deviance is always a human possibility. Cultures deal with deviance by providing a system of rewards or punishments, or, as social scientists prefer to say, a *system of sanctions*. In addition, norms usually give a range of acceptable behavior so that individuals have some leeway, or room for innovation, in their conformity.

The Infant, the Language, and the Culture

Because we cannot get inside the minds of infants, we cannot be sure what the culture looks like from their point of view. It is probably stretching reality to say that infants have a point of view. Theirs is a micro-world of bodily comforts and discomforts and very little else. They are blissfully unaware of the culture that surrounds them. It is an external force, separate from them, and they are born with no sense of its immense coercive power.

Infants are drawn into the culture slowly, largely through the acquisition of language. It can literally be said that language gives children a world. It identifies objects and distinguishes them from other shapes in the environment. It allows children to keep objects in mind and to refer to them even when they are not physically present. Language also allows objects to be brought together by type and referred to as a group. The child soon learns that the word *chair* can refer to many objects of a similar type. The word *teacher* not only refers to one person but also to a type of person who is expected to act in typical ways with children. The process of categorizing objects, behaviors, and ideas into groups is called *typification*.

Language makes it possible for children to hold events and meanings in mind and to refer to them at a later time. The fact that we can remember little, if anything, before we acquired language is probably traceable to the fact that we had no language with which to pack away the early events of our lives. As John Dewey has pointed out, the ability to remember events allows us to imagine events that have not yet occurred.[8] The skill of anticipating the future by remembering and critically evaluating what happened in the past is the basis of human intelligence. In short, language allows us to think abstractly, learn from our experiences, and anticipate our futures. It is the cultural foundation of human intelligence. A culture, largely through its language, orders the micro-world of its new citizens by giving it meaning. With time, the experiences of children extend into the macro-world of the adult culture.

Language and the Self

Some of the first words a child is likely to learn are the names of people around him. As he begins to learn the names of separate people, he becomes able to identify their attitudes and behaviors as being typical of them. The child begins to understand how others see the world, how they evaluate it. Over time, he

---

[8] John Dewey, *Democracy and Education* (New York: The Free Press, 1966 [1916]), p. 38. Available in paperback.

The self is social. Children find themselves in the social world.   *Source:* National Education Association, Joe Di Dio.

begins to see how they view him and how they evaluate his behavior. According to George Herbert Mead (1863–1931), a philosopher whose work has significantly influenced sociology, the ability to view ourselves from the point of view of others (or as he put it, *to take the role of others)* is essential to the creation of selfhood. We discover ourselves in the attitudes of others. The origins of the self are social. The self is not born with us but develops through interaction with others.[9]

Mead theorized that child's play is not simply an entertaining pastime but one essential to the process of seeing the world as others see it. Whereas play is common among other animals, it seems that only human beings play games that require them to take the role of others. This gives children practice in organizing (typifying) the behavior and attitudes of a mother, father, doctor, or teacher so that these people can be better understood.

Socialization and the Generalized Other

The first roles played by children have specific reference to important people in their lives. Mead called these people *significant others.* The process of typification (that is, ordering things by type) allows the child to expand these roles

[9] George Herbert Mead, *Mind, Self, and Society* (Chicago: University of Chicago Press, 1934). Available in paperback.

beyond specific individuals into general categories of people. A child "playing mommy" may not be referring any longer to her mother but to mothers in general. In other words, the child is forming a general idea of how mothers act and is slipping into that role as she plays house with her friends.

Over time, the general roles of mother, father, doctor, teacher, and so on, get further generalized until they form a common set of expectations as to how all people in the community are expected to act. Mead calls this more general role *the generalized other*. It is a corporate role that refers to no one in particular but to everyone (at least, everyone in the child's world) in general. It is a generalized expectation as to how individuals are supposed to behave. It represents the values, beliefs, and norms of the community.

The child does not play the role of the generalized other as he might play the role of a father. The generalized other has a broader function. It represents the corporate voice of the community in the mind of the child. It forms what is commonly called conscience. The internalization of the generalized other is an important step in socialization. It is as if the community has a representative in the mind of the child who comments on the child's behavior and argues with his or her urges to deviate from community norms. If there were no voice of a generalized other within us, society would be impossible. If the voice of the generalized other becomes too strong, it can drown out spontaneity and creativity. When this submergence happens on a large scale, individuality shrinks, and social change becomes exceedingly slow, if not impossible.

Culture as Tyranny and Opportunity

It is possible to take either a pessimistic or an optimistic point of view about the relationship between individuals and culture. We can see culture as an imposing force that squeezes all that is unique and creative out of individuals, or we can see culture as an instrument that makes thought and creativity possible. Evidence exists to support either point of view. But if each view is partially true, each is also partially false. What is needed is a position that extracts the truth and discards the error of both positions.

Humans are double beings. One part of us is internal, unique, creative, and essentially private. I alone can experience my thoughts. I alone can feel my feelings. My ideas and feelings are unique to me. When I describe my ideas and feelings to others, they can experience these only as abstractions. A second part of us is external, conforming, and essentially public. This is the portion of ourselves that plays roles and speaks in harmony with the voice of the generalized other. Some cultures give a greater emphasis to the other side, but it is wrong to consider an individual as being totally creative or totally conforming, as being completely unique or simply a mirror image of others.

The development of personality involves a conversation, an interaction, between an individual and society. Personal development is characterized by a struggle between an individual's need for self-expression and society's capacity for control. The individual grows under the influence of society, but the influence is not one-sided. As humans grow, they modify their social environment. The process is reciprocal. As cultures change, so do individuals; and as individuals change, so does the culture.

Externalization, Objectivation, and Internalization

Culture is a human product, yet, as we have seen, it has a powerful influence on making human beings what they are. This is the paradox of culture: It is a human product that recreates its creators. Culture creates individuals, and individuals create culture. To understand how this is possible, we must understand three important aspects of human activity: externalization, objectivation, and internalization.[10]

Let us begin with an example. It is clear that table manners are not supplied by human biology, and there is no reason to believe that they are given to us by God. Manners were invented by a great many people over a long period of time, and their exact history is largely lost. But let us say for simplicity's sake that manners were invented by one person in a short time. Then we can imagine that at one moment table manners did not exist and that at the next moment they did. They began as an idea in one human mind and were then shared by others. This process is called *externalization*. It is a process by which individual peculiarities come into being and are shared with others. Externalization is possible because human beings are able to have ideas. They are able to reorder what is known and give it new shape. Human beings do more than learn. They use what is learned to create something new. Externalization is the voice of invention.

Now imagine the inventor of manners scurrying around the countryside, convincing other people of the worth of the exotic idea. As more and more people adopt this notion, they put pressure on others to do the same. They begin to make value judgments about people who do not "eat properly." Table manners become an alternative in the culture. As this change happens, it becomes possible to talk about table manners as if they are an object. People begin to speak about table manners as if they are a thing with a reality separate from themselves. Sociologists call this process *objectivation*. The invention now seems to have a life of its own. It exists as a force in the culture separate from any particular individual—including its inventor.

Now imagine further that a mother and father decide to conform to the alternative norm of table manners. The decision is made consciously and freely, but they decide that their children must also use table manners. If we watch the children being taught how to "eat properly," we are not likely to believe that they chose to use table manners as consciously or as freely as their parents did. When the children are young, the parents are likely to give them a great deal of latitude in this area. Poor table manners will be accepted and may even be seen as endearing. (Many a family album contains pictures of an angelic child with dinner spread across the face.) But, as the children grow older, the parents become less tolerant of poor manners. (Few family albums contain pictures of a teenager casually rubbing mashed potatoes into his or her hair.) The parents begin to exert gentle (or perhaps not so gentle) pressure on children to conform to the objectivated standards of table manners. Children usually succumb to these pressures. Let us imagine, however, that the children of this fictitious family are intelligent beyond their years and aware of the social pro-

---

[10] These concepts are derived from many sources in the social sciences, but their interaction has been most thoroughly explored by Peter Berger and Thomas Luckmann, in *The Social Construction of Reality* (New York: Doubleday & Company, Inc., 1967). Available in paperback.

cesses they are living through. As the children stop eating with their fingers, we might ask them, "Why do you use a fork now when you didn't last month?" The answer might be, "We don't like to use forks; they aren't as much fun as eating with our hands, and we have a hard time with them. But we use a fork because if we don't, our parents withdraw affection, and we want them to like us." The children are conforming to an objectivated idea that is separate from them, one they experience as an external reality with coercive force. They use table manners to draw praise and to avoid pain.

If we return to the imaginary children later in their lives and ask the same question, the answer might be quite different: "Of course we use a fork; what do you think we are—slobs?" Notice that the children are no longer referring to some exterior force. The compulsion to eat with a fork comes from within. They now speak with the voice of the generalized other and take the norms of the culture so much for granted that they are surprised, even shocked, by our question. This process is called *internalization*. Of course, they eat with a fork; doesn't everybody? The norm of table manners has become so thoroughly a part of them (that is, internalized) that the sight of extreme violations of the norm (watching people eat raw slabs of meat with their hands) may disgust them and even make them physically ill.

Habit

When cultural norms are internalized, they become habits. No thought is necessary for their function. It is when norms come into conflict with new situations, or with each other, that thinking becomes necessary. The concepts of externalization, objectivation, and internalization might be thought to exist on a continuum, with thought being required for the function of the first two but not for the last. The psychologist William James has said that habit is "the enormous flywheel of society," and John Dewey also takes habit to be central to the human community.[11] They mean that internalized norms are the basis for all behavior. This does not mean that humans simply follow ruts (some of them do, but they encounter trouble); rather, they have integrated norms so well into their behavior that they do not need to think before they act. A baseball player who thinks about catching a fly ball will not do it well; a typist who thinks about the keyboard will make errors; and a teacher who is not sure of his subject, and thus is always worrying about it, will not teach well. These skills (norms) have to become habits.

On the other hand, when norms encounter problems, that is the time to think, to externalize the difficulty and objectivize the problem. Through this process, norms are reconstructed and become internalized again. A teacher who does not wonder why children misbehave in the classroom and does not try to construct a new norm or rule in light of what she finds is left with only the force of authority to make the children behave. The children will not internalize the behavior. Thus, more graphic than a continuum is the idea that norms function in a cycle, first being thought out (externalized, objectivized)

[11] William James, *The Principles of Psychology* (New York: H. Holt and Co., 1890), Chapter 4; John Dewey, *Democracy and Education*, pp. 46–49 and *Human Nature and Conduct* (New York: Random House, Inc., 1930 [1922]), Part 1.

and then internalized (habit); being thought out again when problems develop, and again being internalized; and so on.

Summary

The three-part character of this model of socialization and cultural change leads us to the conclusion that human beings are neither a product nor a producer of their social setting; they are rather both. The ability to have ideas and the desire for new experiences find expression in human externalization. Without externalization, human beings would not be able to create culture. We would have no structure of meaning to guide our lives and would suffer continued alienation.

Objectivation brings a measure of stability to human existence. It establishes our history and provides continuity. It makes us able to refer to such things as table manners, civil liberties, or honesty as if they are physical objects with coercive power. It allows us to talk about "the government" or "our university" as if they are stable entities, when, in fact, the people who make up their personnel change frequently.

Internalization allows us to bring the culture into ourselves in the form of a generalized other. It makes it possible to take things for granted so that we do not have to redefine reality at every turn. It gives us recipes for the solution of recurring problems. We internalize these recipes as habits and are able to carry them out with very little thought. Internalization leaves our minds free to consider other matters, such as the creation of new ideas or new solutions to unusual problems. Habits economize our everyday activities, but they also provide a background against which new ideas can take shape.

When individuals are confronted with new problems that cannot be solved by routine solutions, they must suspend habits to stop and think. They must reflect upon the problem at hand, re-examine their habits, reorder their ways of doing things, and try new alternatives. They use what they know to help them form new ideas. At this point, we are back again to the process of externalization. Our new ideas become objectivated and then internalized.

The rhythm of this interaction continues throughout our lives. The process is as old as human history and takes place in every culture. Only the pace changes, for some cultures undergo very little change, whereas others, like our own, undergo continual change.

Suggested Readings

The three-part model of socialization and cultural change presented in this chapter is explored in greater detail by Peter Berger and Thomas Luckmann in *The Social Construction of Reality* (New York: Doubleday and Co., Inc., 1967). Their analysis borrows heavily from the work of George Herbert Mead (see the suggested readings for Chapter 3). Other books that extend the analysis presented here include

GERTH, HANS and C. WRIGHT MILLS. *Character and Social Structure: The Psychology of Social Institutions.* New York: Harcourt Brace Jovanovich, 1964.
HOLZNER, BURKHARD. *Reality Construction in Society.* Cambridge, MA: Schenkman Publishing Co., 1968.

STRAUSS, ANSELM L. *Mirrors and Masks: The Search for Identity.* San Francisco: The Sociology Press, 1969.

A number of books, some of which focus directly on education, analyze the power that culture has to inhibit the full development of individuals. For example,

GOODMAN, PAUL. *New Reformation: Notes of a Neolithic Conservative.* New York: Random House, 1969. This is the last of a long series of books in which Goodman calls for a better balance between individual uniqueness and cultural necessity.

HENRY, JULES. *Culture Against Man.* New York: Vintage Books, 1965. Henry skillfully analyzes contemporary America and provides his readers with an understanding of the interconnections among institutions, values, and the American character.

MEAD, MARGARET. *Culture and Commitment: A Study of the Generation Gap.* New York: Natural History Press, 1970. Mead contends that the tradition by which the old pass the culture on to the young is now out of date. She contends that the fast-changing nature of modern-day culture is understood only by those not fully socialized into yesterday's society. Thus, the young, more than ever before, have something to teach older generations. She is not suggesting that the traditional processes of socialization be reversed but that the one-way direction of socialization be modified.

PETTITT, GEORGE A. *Prisoners of Culture.* New York: Charles Scribner's Sons, 1970. Pettitt brings his anthropological skills to this indictment of the educational system.

Summary of Section I

Taken together, the first four chapters give a perspective on culture and the individual, or what, for simplicity's sake, we might call the facts of life. The following facts of life have been addressed:

- Human beings are born with fewer instinctual instructions for living their lives than other animals.
- Human beings are autonomous decision makers. Other people can influence us, but ultimately we must make our own choices in life.
- Human beings are inextricably interconnected. Every decision we make affects other people.
- Human beings are born world-open, but culture provides guidelines for individual behavior that narrow our options.
- Human beings begin learning their culture from the moment of birth and continue the learning process throughout their lives.
- Human beings are both products and producers of culture. Other animals cannot voluntarily change their instincts, but humans can change their culture.
- The process of cultural change and transmission is carried out through externalization, objectivation, and internalization.
- Cultures are made up of universals, specialties, and alternatives.
- When the individual and the culture are out of balance, human beings can become estranged from the culture and themselves—isolated, aimless, normless—and sense that their lives lack meaning. Such individuals are alienated and are likely to retreat into privatism.

Several conclusions can be drawn from these facts of life.

- Much of what we learn from culture becomes taken for granted and sinks below the level of conscious reflection. One purpose of social science, indeed a purpose of all democratic schooling, is to make our taken-for-granted assumptions retrievable, understandable, and, when necessary, changeable.
- The common assumption that individuals and their cultures are in neces-

sary opposition is simplistic. Human beings need culture in order to become fully human. Similarly, cultures can be improved through invention and innovation.

- Education is a central function of every culture.
- When cultures are simple (when the future closely replicates the past), education takes place informally. Children learn by taking part in adult activities.
- When cultures become complex (when work becomes specialized and cultural change speeds up), simple imitation no longer prepares children for the future. Cultures then establish formal schools.
- The term *education* refers to everything an individual learns in the course of living. *Schooling* refers to what goes on in the formal structure of the school.
- Schools reflect their culture, but they do not exactly replicate them. Schools always are controlled environments designed to significantly improve upon the outside culture.

From the first four chapters, we have learned how education and schooling are possible and why they are essential. *No work is more fundamental to the long-term well-being of a culture than education.* We also have learned that all education (schooling included) must strike a balance between the interests of the individual and the needs of the culture, the requirements of freedom and the necessity of order. The job of the professional educator is to mediate between these interests.

Theories of cultural purpose and human nature are central to the aims of education. We have reviewed several educational aims in Section I: Durkheim suggested that the goal of education was cultural transmission; Rogers, that the goal was individual growth; and Dewey, that the goal was individual and cultural improvement through democratic processes. Durkheim and Rogers were criticized for having a one-sided view of human nature and the aims of education. Dewey's goal of creative intelligence (or what Jefferson called informed discretion) avoids self-absorption and blind conformity. Reviewing the human nature assumptions of Durkheim, Rogers, and Dewey showed how our beliefs about human nature ultimately affect our educational aims and practices.

Chapter Four spelled out the vital connection between culture and individuals and showed how cultures are built and changed. Within every culture there are *universal, specialist,* and *alternative* norms. Schools function, in great part, to pass on the universal and specialist norms of the culture. Public schools usually avoid dealing directly with alternative norms and can expect trouble from parents when one alternative norm is presented as desirable and another as undesirable.

Outside the core, specialist and alternative norms form an area of "individual peculiarities," or what might better be called the area of imagination. It is here where criticism, invention, creativity, externalization, and cultural change begin. An important task of education is to see to it that the *objectivated* norms of the culture are *internalized* by students while nurturing the possibility of imagination, *externalization,* and change.

Throughout these chapters, we have been confronted by paradox: Language limits our thinking but also makes thinking possible; culture creates human beings, but human beings create culture; education passes on the known but invites exploration into the unknown; imagination is the creator of knowledge, but imagination would be impossible without the benefit of past knowledge. If we ask how it is that human beings know more today than they did a decade ago, or a century ago, or ten centuries ago, the answer is inevitably shrouded in paradox. Knowledge has progressed because people who lived in relatively closed cultural systems used cultural knowledge to expand the frontiers of their culture and moved into open spaces where the imagination could see other possibilities.

The analysis presented here is fundamentally optimistic. Individuals can learn their culture through education and schooling. With hard work, respect for knowledge, attention to detail, healthy skepticism, and imagination they can explore new territories and make mistakes. If they possess creative intelligence, they can learn from their mistakes and create new knowledge. New knowledge competes for a place in the culture and, if it stands the test, ultimately it is integrated into the stock of cultural knowledge. The most useful knowledge is that which sparks the imagination of others and furthers the creation of new knowledge.

The paradoxes alluded to earlier all play a part in the adventure of education. Teaching is a process of imposing discipline and liberating the imagination. It respects the culture and the individual. It passes on knowledge so individuals can internalize and then surpass what teachers have presented. It entails attention to the present, but it puts human beings in touch with the past and in greater control of the future.

Education and American Society: A Question of Aims and Values

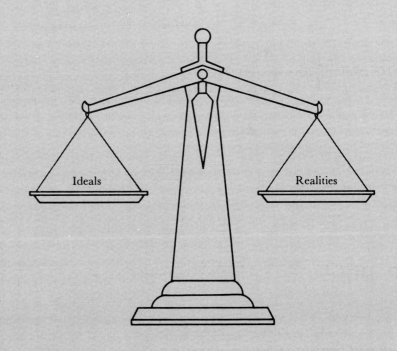

CHAPTER 5

Some American Values

Introduction

We cannot discuss what the average American believes, values, or does without allowing for a great deal of distortion. After all, there is no such thing as the "average American." The term refers to a fictitious character, or what sociologists call an *ideal type*. It is an abstraction that represents no one in particular but everyone in general. The ideal type of the "average American" is what someone would look like if he or she held all the beliefs and attitudes of the cultural core and behaved accordingly.

This chapter deals with some of the beliefs and attitudes of the cultural core. The discussion is not by any means inclusive. Because we must deal in generalizations, there will be many exceptions. A successful generalization does not eliminate all errors or account for all exceptions; it merely overpowers them by asserting what is, for the most part, true.

The cultural core, as was indicated in Chapter 4, is the cement that holds society together. The major problem of any culture is how to get its members to conform to its core values and beliefs. This problem is solved most effectively when the objectivated values and beliefs of the culture are internalized by its members. If society is to run smoothly, its members must not merely conform to its core values, but they must also want to conform. External forces of the culture must become internal compulsions of the individual. The core beliefs and values must become taken for granted. They must be felt and acted upon so naturally that they take on the quality of what the Lynds call of course statements.[1]

Our focus here is on a few of the most significant values and beliefs of America's cultural core. We will briefly discuss how these core values and beliefs are transmitted to the young. The examples used are meant only to be illustrative. They do not explain in full how an objectivated value is internalized by a youngster. The examples, however, show how certain values and beliefs

---

[1] Discussed in Chapter 4. Robert S. Lynd and Helen Merrell Lynd, *Middletown in Transition* (New York: Harcourt, Brace and Company, 1937).

are carried by the institutions of the culture and are woven into the experience of the child. We will find, again and again, that the school serves as a *carrier* (though certainly not the only one) of core values.[2] Sometimes this transmission is accomplished by the overt lessons of the school. In such cases, the transmission of the value is a *manifest function* of schooling. In other cases core values are less obvious and make up what is called the hidden curriculum of the school: The transmission of values is then a *latent function* of schooling.[3]

Striving and Success

Few values are so indelibly imprinted on the American mind as the value of striving. Americans are expected to throw themselves into their work, not necessarily because work itself is valued, but rather because work is a means to success.

The values of ambition and success would be impossible in a world where people do not believe they are rewarded on the basis of merit. If the values of ambition and success are to take hold, there must be a deep faith that one's status is not fixed, that opportunity is not limited, and that success is not accidental. Americans possess this faith in great measure, and although it is not altogether warranted, it is not wholly unwarranted either.[4] Schools have long played an important part in the transmission of this faith to our children. One textbook, published in 1852, quoted Henry Ward Beecher's observation: "I never knew an early-rising, hard-working, prudent man, careful of his earnings, and strictly honest, who complained of bad luck." Another text of that era stated,

> Many complain of Providence when the fault is all their own. If they would only labor and think, what wealth and eminence would be their lot instead of poverty and disgrace. . . . Remember that all the ignorance, degradation and misery in the world is the result of indolence and vice.[5]

The message that children must be ambitious and successful is not found only in the blatant lessons of early school texts. These values are also carried by the demands of athletic competition, graded work, and other means. Americans treasure a number of clichés that express their reverence for success:

Nothing succeeds like success.
Nobody loves a loser.

---

[2] The term *carrier* is Peter Berger's. For a lengthy discussion of how institutions carry a culture's taken-for-granted assumptions, see Peter Berger, Brigitte Berger, and Hansfried Kellner, *The Homeless Mind* (New York: Random House, Inc., Vintage Books, 1974), p. 16. Available in paperback.

[3] *Manifest* and *latent* functions were discussed in Chapter 4. For the idea of "hidden curriculum," see G. R. Snyder, *The Hidden Curriculum* (New York: Alfred A. Knopf, Co., 1970), and M. W. Apple, *Ideology and Curriculum* (London: Routledge & Kegan Paul, 1979).

[4] We will discuss in Chapter 21 the degree to which this faith is warranted.

[5] Both are quoted in Ruth Miller Elson, *Guardians of Tradition* (Lincoln: University of Nebraska Press, 1964), p. 254. This sentiment also can be found in the *McGuffey's Readers,* which date from as early as 1836: see *McGuffey's Fifth Eclectic Reader* (New York: New American Library, 1962 [1879 edition]); and in *Noah Webster's American Spelling Book* (New York: Teachers College, 1962), which was published in its first version in 1783. See also *The New-England Primer* (New York: Teachers College, 1962 [c. 1687]).

Anybody can be president.
There are no dead-end jobs, only dead-end people.
Anyone can move from rags to riches.
Start at the bottom and work your way up to the top.
The sky is the limit.
There is always room at the top.

Not everyone shares the American compulsion to strive, but those who do not must come to terms with its dictates. They have to explain to others—even to themselves—why they have chosen not to enter the race in pursuit of what William James called the "bitch goddess Success."[6] Such people have clichés to help them express what is clearly a minority view:

Money isn't everything.
The best things in life are free.
Take time to smell the roses.

To be a "self-made man" is an embarrassment in some cultures because such a designation reveals an individual's "poor heritage," but in America individuals who have pulled themselves up by their bootstraps advertise this fact with great pride.[7] Americans love success stories, especially when they are about themselves. The American compulsion to succeed, however, is not explained simply by a desire for money and what it can buy. Once the values of striving have become internalized, it is seldom possible to turn them off when we reach the top. Many wealthy Americans continue to strive long after earning more money than they could reasonably spend in a lifetime.

Why is this? Probably because money carries meaning about a person's worth. The origins of this idea began with the Calvinistic notion of predestination. This idea was brought to New England by the Puritans and lives on in muted form in our present value structure. It was Calvin's doctrine that all human beings are predestined to enter heaven or hell and that nothing can be done to reverse this destiny. Such notions were psychologically difficult to maintain. Even among disciplined Puritans the idea of predestination produced anxiety. People wanted assurance that they were among the chosen, and over the years, Calvinism was given an interesting twist. Worldly success came to be seen as a sign of divine election, a sign from God that a person is destined for heaven. Needless to say, this provided a powerful incentive to get ahead.

Americans still seek the assurance of acquisitions and salary to prove their worth to others and to themselves. Salary still records our progress. Although it no longer proves we are heaven bound, it does suggest that we are somehow better, brighter, and more deserving here on earth than those less fortunate than ourselves. Children learn at an early age that success is an important value that will bring many rewards. Parents are pleased when their children walk at an early age, talk before their peers, are better looking than other children on the block, write their names before others can manage the task, get into the

---

[6] *The Letters of William James*, ed. Henry James (Boston: Atlantic Monthly Press, 1920), Vol. 2, p. 253. James went on to say, "That—with the squalid cash interpretation put on the word success—is our national disease."

[7] Seymour Lipset, "Constant Values in American Society," *Children* (Washington, DC: United States Department of Health, Education and Welfare, Social Security Administration, Children's Bureau, November–December, 1959).

top reading group or accelerated classes, earn good grades, perform well in athletics, win awards, graduate at the top of their class, go to college, and so on. The point is not simply that adult Americans are concerned with their children's progress; they see progress as essentially competitive and quantifiable. The numerical measures of salary and grades carry messages of individual worth.

These ideas are embedded in the structure of our schools. We do not advertise the importance of an education by extolling the excitement of learning. Education is not seen as an end in itself but rather as a means to something else, something grander—namely, success. We sell an education to the young by advertising the dollar difference it will make in their lives. We do not boast of the other differences that knowledge can make. Such things are not as highly valued as money.

Activity

Visitors to our shores are usually impressed by the bustle of American life. We are a busy people who take pride in getting the job done. Harold Laski, an Englishman, overstated it when he said that Americans do not know how to be happy unless they are doing something, but his error was one of exaggeration and not one of fact.[8] Americans work hard and play hard, and it is often difficult to distinguish between the two activities.

There is something purifying in the American work ethic. Although many Americans would describe themselves as "naturally lazy," they see hard work as overcoming this innate character flaw. The discomfort of this self-improvement is lessened substantially by the belief that hard work pays off. As early as 1790, school texts were promising riches to the individual "who rises early and is industrious." One text warned that "poverty is the fruit of idleness."[9] There was obviously a great utility in hard work for a growing nation. If people on the frontier did not work, they literally did not eat. The work ethic may have grown out of the Puritan tradition and the frontier experience, but it persists today, even as affluence has made leisure more possible. The work ethic follows us into vacations and retirement, when individuals are often compulsively active. Labor-saving devices in the home do not seem to have freed homemakers from the drudgery of house cleaning so much as they have allowed more time to get things even cleaner. Some observers have been unkind enough to suggest that the work ethic has invaded even our sex lives.[10]

The message one might draw from the bustle of American life is that Americans are never satisfied with the ways things are. Believing in progress, we think that things can be better if we will only work hard enough. Progress in America has always meant "more": more income, more growth, more education.[11] And more, in turn, has meant "bigger is better": bigger cars, bigger sports stadiums, bigger schools.

---

[8] Harold J. Laski, *The American Democracy* (New York: The Viking Press, 1948), p. 15.

[9] Elson, *Guardians of Tradition*, pp. 252–253.

[10] Lionel S. Lewis and Dennis Brisset, "Sex as Work: A Study of Avocational Counseling," *Social Problems*, Vol. 15, No. 1 (Summer 1967), pp. 8–18.

[11] In education, the idea that "more is better" is detected by Andrew M. Greeley, "No School Before Labor Day," nationally syndicated newspaper column, *Gainesuille Sun* (August 28, 1979).

Relationship with Nature

When European settlers first landed on the American shore, many were appalled by what they saw. Although some spoke grandly of the land's natural beauty, others saw only a "hideous and desolate wilderness, full of wild beasts and wild men."[12] No one could avoid seeing nature, beautiful or hideous, as an adversary. The wilderness was a resource that early settlers believed God had provided especially for them, but had to be tamed. Forests had to be cut, stumps pulled, and boulders dug from the ground before crops could be planted. Cold winters and long, hot summers did not simply bring discomfort; they threatened life itself.

Once conquered, of course, nature gave to some the means for a comfortable existence, even for great wealth. No doubt taming the wilderness was a source of great pride for early settlers. Their success reinforced a psychology of exploitation regarding nature. The land and its resources were there for the taking. As Andrew Jackson put it in his second inaugural address:

> What good man would prefer a country covered with forests, and ranged by a few thousand savages to our extensive republic, studded with cities, towns and prosperous farms, embellished with all the improvements which art can devise or industry execute.[13]

Two myths were born in the early years of our nation. By *myth*, we mean a belief held uncritically. In a narrow context or perspective, a myth may appear to be true, but in a larger context, especially over time, its truth may be uncertain but undetected because of a lack of critical attitude.[14] One myth was that nature could be conquered and bent totally to the will of Americans. The second was the myth of superabundance, which asserted that in nature "there would always be more where that came from." These myths die hard, and despite much evidence of their shortcomings, they are still powerful today.

Competition

Because Americans measure success in material terms, there is competition to keep up with or beat out the people next door. Competition is an important American value; it exerts a continual pressure on individuals to do better than the next person. We find competition in every area of our lives: in sports, business, fund-raising campaigns—even in romance and religion. We find it especially in schooling, where children are compared with each other more than they are with their own abilities and effort. This tendency in school often contradicts the equally important value of cooperation, which is the means by

---

[12] These are the words of Nathaniel Morton, a resident of Plymouth Colony, quoted in Russell B. Nye, *This Almost Chosen People* (East Lansing: Michigan State University Press, 1966), p. 258. Spelling has been modernized for easier reading. See also Peter N. Carroll, *Puritanism and the Wilderness* (New York: Columbia University Press, 1969).

[13] Quoted in Nye, *This Almost Chosen People*, p. 276.

[14] The historian Carl L. Becker says a myth is "a once valid but now discarded version of the human story": "Everyman His Own Historian," in Robert R. Sherman, ed., *Understanding History of Education* (Cambridge, MA: Schenkman Publishing Co., 1984), p. 88.

which sociability is achieved. The conflict between competition and cooperation, and individualism and sociability, especially in school, will be mentioned again.

Individualism

The ideal of rugged individualism is deeply embedded in American culture. Early in the colonial experience, Americans developed an interest in what came to be called the inalienable rights of individual citizens. The idea of such rights was not unique to the American continent, but Americans did with it what no other people had done before: they built the idea of inalienable rights into a system of government. At the foundation of the American system of government are the ideals of the essential dignity of the individual, the fundamental equality of each person before the law, and the inalienable rights of freedom and justice. The American proposition was as bold as it was simple: people can be trusted to govern themselves. It was a revolutionary idea that had never before been put into practice.

The idea of individualism is a part of American law as well as of American values. The American creed of individual rights is written into the Declaration of Independence, the Preamble to the Constitution, the Bill of Rights, and the constitutions of several states. In addition to these are elaborate laws that protect many areas of individual life. Bankruptcy provisions and laws forbidding imprisonment for debt allow individuals to fail and try again. Each person is protected against unwarranted search and seizure, arbitrary imprisonment, slander, and bondage. We even have laws forbidding suicide. These freedoms have not been shared by all citizens equally (as we shall see in later chapters), but there has been a persistent pressure throughout our history to extend these rights to all Americans.

Independence and Individualism

Closely allied with the idea of individualism is the value of independence. It is not difficult to see the origins of this value. On the frontier, where families lived miles apart, nearly everything that was to be done had to be done alone. People learned to depend on themselves and to dislike the meddling interference of others. The land was open, opportunity unlimited, and few rules regulated anyone's behavior. About 70 percent of the population was self-employed as compared with 5 percent today.[15]

The historian Frederick Jackson Turner discussed the importance of the frontier experience in shaping the values of independence and "rugged" individualism. The frontier provided opportunities for those who were alienated from society to make it on their own terms. But Turner pointed out that, by 1900, most of the American frontier had disappeared. The independence of the farmer now had to conform to specific demands of urban life and industry.[16] Individualism looked somewhat different in this new setting.

---

[15] T. B. Bottomore, *Classes in Modern Society* (New York: Random House, Inc., 1966).
[16] Frederick Jackson Turner, "Contributions of the West to American Democracy," *Atlantic Monthly* (January 1903), pp. 83–96.

Much of the ethic of rugged individualism translated early into the values of capitalism. Americans still maintain the ideal that individuals should be free of meddlesome regulations, free to "take a stab at it" and "make a killing," free to innovate, take risks, and reap bountiful rewards for their ingenuity. But there are differences between the individualism of the frontier and the independence of laissez-faire capitalism. Organization is the backbone of industrial expansion. Rugged individuals are no longer independent persons making unilateral decisions. They are members of an organizational team, following directives from the administration above. In short, individualism, in its transformed state, is reserved more for those who run businesses than for those who work in them.[17]

There is another difference between workers in industry and the rugged individualists of the frontier: the question concerning self-interest. On the frontier, individuals did whatever they felt would maximize personal rewards. In business, however, there are restrictions on such behavior. Workers are expected to take jobs that offer the most money, but once hired, they must submit to restrictions of the profit motive. For example, one does not sell company secrets to the competition simply because the price is right. The worker is now a team member and is expected to behave accordingly.

The conception of independence has taken new shape for workers in the twentieth century: Workers cannot do as they please at work, although increasingly they can control their leisure time in the private sphere. Work is increasingly a means to an end (financial freedom) rather than an end in itself. Americans have put an ever higher value on financial independence. Parents prepare their children, through education, to move up the social ladder. Grandparents take pride in the newfound ability to provide for themselves after retirement. The ideal of independence has come to mean financial independence. Other kinds of independence—for example, social isolation—we shall come to see, are more problematical.

Ambition, Independence, and Competition in School

Schools are not separate from the culture, and therefore it is not surprising that they carry within them the culture's core values. A careful viewing of schools reveals that they do a great deal to encourage the values of individualism, striving, and competition.

Children are taught at an early age to be responsible for their own work. A child who does well in arithmetic is taught to take pride in this success and to feel no obligation to the child in the next row for whom mathematics remains a mystery. Learning is seen as an individual effort, not as a team effort. Occasionally, as a change of pace, students are allowed to tutor other students. But such diversions seldom change the unmistakable message of the classroom: Look out for number one. The lesson of self-reliance is reinforced by competition. Failures are made conspicuous and humiliating through ability grouping, grad-

---

[17] John Dewey, in *Individualism Old and New* (New York: Minton, Balch and Co., 1930), argues that only through association and cooperation can individuals any longer have an effect on the course of life. Available in paperback.

ing on a curve, and public games of academic skill such as arithmetic bingo. Jules Henry, an anthropologist who has carefully studied American classrooms, has examined a game called "spelling baseball."[18] The game follows the playground process for choosing baseball teams. Two captains are chosen to stand before the group. They take turns picking the best people—those who will help the team win. No doubt you remember this process from your childhood. To be picked first was public testimony to your skill. To be picked last was a declaration of your failure as a ball player. If you visit playgrounds today, you will see the same process in action. Children struggle to avoid being chosen last. They maneuver to get the captain's attention, scream reminders ("How about me? How about me?"), or try to cajole a captain with a pleading look ("Please, don't pick me last.")

Jules Henry watched the sides as they were chosen and watched the "spelling baseball" game begin. Teams took turns at bat. Each word read by a teacher represented a pitched ball. If it was spelled correctly, it was a base hit. If it was misspelled, it was an out. The game did more than bring life to the drudgery of a routine spelling lesson: It made every failure conspicuous. A general lack of spelling skill meant a child was chosen last. He had to stand by while the numbers of unchosen children slowly diminished around him and he was left standing alone. Once brought onto a team, the child suffered again if he misspelled a word. With three players on base and an opportunity to win close at hand, the team groaned when they realized the poor speller was at bat. They groaned again when the word was tossed by the teacher and panic crossed the batter's face. Befuddled, the boy misspelled the word, and the team groaned once more. Any possible chance of spelling the word correctly was lost in the terror of the moment. Henry points out the multiple levels of competition in such games. "Each child competes with every other to get the words right; each child competes with all for status and approval among his peers; each child competes with other children for the approval of the teacher; and finally, each competes as a member of a team."[19]

It may be that competition is inevitable in education. As Melford Spiro has pointed out, as long as teachers publicly inform children that their behavior is "good" or "bad," they motivate other children to do better. When we say to a child, "You are doing a fine job," our compliment ends with the unspoken phrase "in comparison to others."[20] The fact that the teacher never adds this phrase is not important. The children hear it clearly all the same.

The message of competition is carried in our grading systems. Grades not only indicate the degree to which a student has mastered a subject and school rules, but they also indicate how one student's mastery compares with that of other students. Grades are made a more potent force because they are often accompanied by rewards and punishments. As we said before, some students come to view grades as an indication of self-worth.

The competitive spirit permeates many aspects of school life beyond academics. Sporting events are an obvious example. More subtle, however, are

[18] Jules Henry, *Culture Against Man* (New York: Random House, Inc., Vintage Books, 1965), p. 300. Available in paperback.

[19] Ibid.

[20] Melford E. Spiro, *Children of the Kibbutz* (New York: Schocken Books, Inc., 1965), p. 401. Available in paperback.

such activities as Halloween parades (where prizes are given to students for the best costumes), homecoming-queen contests, class competitions to sell the most tickets to the PTA supper, boy-versus-girl playground games, tryouts for cheerleading and school plays, and a host of other events. All of these revolve around the competitive ethic.

Although it is true that some degree of competition is built into the socialization process of all human beings, the extent to which people choose to capitalize on this potential varies greatly from one culture to the next. The stress placed on competition in American schools is an indication of the place competition holds in the culture at large.

Some cultures have tried to reduce the emphasis on competition and replace it with a spirit of cooperation. Bruno Bettelheim[21] and Melford Spiro[22] concluded that the relative lack of individualistic competition on the Israeli kibbutz lessened the punishing aspects of the school experience. Other studies found the kibbutz children preferred games of cooperation over those that stressed competition. Bettelheim points out that the cooperative ethic operates in the kibbutz because there is a deep ideological commitment to conformity, mutual assistance, and the right of the group to shape individual behavior. There is reason to question whether such ideas could prosper in a culture such as ours, which emphasizes individual striving, competition, and independence. Nevertheless, there is reason to suspect that a lessening of competition in American classrooms could have beneficial effects.

Another society that minimizes competition is that of Communist China. We still do not know much about the culture that China has fashioned since its 1949 revolution, but we do know that the Chinese have paid a heavy price in human life and individual freedom for this cultural transformation. Recent visits to China by Americans have produced a great deal of interest and more than a little cultural shock. Shirley MacLaine, an activist actress, led a group of Americans to visit China. She related the cultural shock that the group experienced when they observed a large Chinese nursery school.

> Outside, one section of the school was in recess, and almost 100 children were engaged in a game of tug of war. Some of our American women started choosing sides and shouting encouragement. As if to answer us, the children stopped in the middle of the pulling and chanted to each other, "Friendship first! Competition second! We learn from you. You learn from us. We learn from each other!"
>
> The children continued chanting as the teacher looked on. . . . Suddenly Margaret [one of the American visitors] leaped into the fray; she chose a side, picked up the end of the rope, and pulled with all her might until all the children fell down. The other American women laughed and applauded, but I noticed that the children were confused and the teacher looked mystified.
>
> The children got up, and the teacher started shifting the players, so that some of the stronger children would balance out the sides. She blew a whistle and they started again. This time, Unita [another American] jumped in, added her 200 pounds to one end of the rope, and managed to topple as many children as Margaret had.
>
> The class was now completely disrupted, the teacher was annoyed, the children were looking at us as if we were violent and aggressive strangers who had come

---

[21] Bruno Bettelheim, *The Children of the Dream* (New York: Macmillan Publishing Co., Inc., 1969). Available in paperback.
[22] Melford Spiro, *Children of the Kibbutz.*

to play a game to which we did not know the rules. If the lesson of the game really was to make competition secondary to friendship, we had made a mess of the lesson. I suggested that it was time to leave.[23]

MacLaine relates the confusion that passed over the American party. They spent long hours discussing what they had seen. For many, the idea of a game without competition seemed pointless and somehow damaging. One woman insisted that the Chinese children looked freakish. Other women in the delegation found the experience edifying and hopeful. You will have to decide for yourself which interpretation makes more sense.

Conformity

For a nation that prides itself on individualism and human freedom, Americans tolerate a surprising amount of conformity. While conformity may be increasing, it is certainly not a new phenomenon. The Frenchman Alexis de Tocqueville warned of a driving force toward sameness as early as 1835: "I know of no country in which there is so little independence of mind and real freedom of discussion as in America."[24] More than 100 years later, the Englishman Harold Laski also commented on our astonishing uniformity of values.[25]

Conformity must be distinguished from obedience. While *conformity* has a broad meaning, we can, for our purposes, define it as a willingness to go along with others who have no special authority to compel us to do so. Conformity is a voluntary act. *Obedience*, on the other hand, means complying with authority. Stanley Milgram makes this distinction with the example of a military recruit. When a recruit complies with the orders of his commanding officers, he does so out of obedience. When he acts and talks like other recruits, he does so out of conformity.[26]

Social scientists have conducted many laboratory experiments to show that Americans are influenced by the urge to conform. The most well known of these was done by S. E. Asch.[27] Subjects in his experiments were shown four lines and asked to judge which two were the same size. They were tested in small groups, but only one of the subjects was the focus of the study. The others were associates of the examiner, who, unknown to the subject, had been instructed to give incorrect answers. The subject was asked to judge which two lines were the same size after the other participants had given the same incorrect answer. Under normal circumstances this was an easy task. Individuals could be expected to make errors only 1 percent of the time, but under the pressure of group opinion, the error rate rose to over 36 percent. The Asch experiments revealed the power of group opinion in America.

Why do Americans conform so willingly to the wishes of the group? Part of the reason, no doubt, lies in our history. A young nation could not endure the

---

[23] Shirley MacLaine, *You Can Get There from Here* (New York: W. W. Norton & Co., Inc., 1975), pp. 143–144.

[24] Alexis de Tocqueville, *Democracy in America*, 2 vols. (New York: Random House, Inc., 1945 [1835]), I, p. 273. Available in paperback.

[25] Harold Laski, *The American Democracy*, pp. 49–51.

[26] Stanley Milgram, *Obedience to Authority* (New York: Harper Colophon Books, 1975), p. 113. Available in paperback.

[27] Solomon E. Asch, "Opinions and Social Pressure," *Scientific American*, Vol. 193 (November 1955), pp. 31–35.

tensions caused by competing regional interests and divergent immigrant backgrounds. Unity was accomplished through the common experiences of the frontier, industrial work, and public schooling. Together, such experiences built into Americans the idea that, in most cases at least, the majority is right. De Tocqueville remarked in the 1830s that the power of the majority in America surpassed the power of kings in Europe. The authority of kings, he pointed out, was limited to physical coercion. Individuals had to act as the king directed, yet they retained their will. "But the majority [in America]," de Tocqueville said, "possesses a power that is physical and moral at the same time, which acts upon the will as much as it acts upon the actions and represses not only all contest, but all controversy." [28]

Modernization brought new pressures for conformity. Americans are (and always have been) highly mobile people. About 20 percent of the population moves each year. If people are to fit into new homes, new communities, new jobs, and even new social classes and religions, they must be highly adaptable. The strain of entering the unknown is lessened considerably if a person is able and willing to adapt immediately to new surroundings.

Even when Americans are settled comfortably into a steady job and a home just off Main Street, they are subject to what might be called *psychological mobility*. As we learned in Chapter 2, modern life is segmented into the public and the private spheres, and the individual must play numerous formal roles. The attitudes and behaviors appropriate at a meeting of the Chamber of Commerce are not necessarily appropriate at a poker game with the boys, a meeting with a marriage counselor, the Christmas party at the office, or a second honeymoon weekend. This need to commute back and forth between very different worlds at a moment's notice is called *psychological mobility*. It is not easily accomplished and creates many uncertainties. Each move demands a different way of behaving, thinking, talking, and defining the world. The strains are greatly reduced, however, if an individual develops an "other-directed," conforming personality structure that is highly sensitive to the expectations of others. [29]

Schools offer children their first dramatic introduction to this world of conflicting roles. A child is expected to play the role of the student, but other expectations exist and must be met. There are the expectations of parents and the demands of the peer group. Sometimes these expectations are contradictory and must be juggled with great skill. Each role must be played, but none can be played to the exclusion of any other. These conditions, though not intentionally created by the school, nevertheless educate students in the crafty skills of the other-direct personality. [30]

Obedience

Obedience, as we have noted, is submission to authority. It differs from conformity in important ways. It assumes a hierarchy of authority—meaning an

---

[28] De Tocqueville, *Democracy in America*, I, p. 273.

[29] The term *other-directed* comes from David Riesman, *The Lonely Crowd: A Study of the Changing American Character* (New Haven: Yale University Press, 1964 [1950]), pp. 19–25.

[30] For a more complete discussion of role problems in school settings, see Rodman B. Webb, "Youth Life-Worlds and the American Culture" in *Feeling, Valuing and the Art of Growing* (Washington, DC: Association for Supervision and Curriculum Development, 1971), pp. 29–52.

ascending series of people with rank having the right to tell others what to do. Obedience is a conscious act for which a subject claims little or no responsibility. Conformity, however, though often unconscious, is defended as being responsible behavior; that is, it involves the feeling of responsibility. Subjects in the Asch experiments (asked to judge the length of lines) denied or played down the power of the group, insisting they had come to their own decisions free of peer-group influence. Asked to discuss an act of obedience, a person explains, "I was only doing what I was told." Or, the manager of the complaint department of a downtown store states, "I'm sorry, that is just the policy. There is nothing I can do to help you." There are more chilling examples, however, and they often confuse obedience with conformity, authority, or responsibility. William Calley, the convicted murderer of women and children at Mylai, Vietnam, said at his trial, "I felt then and still do that I acted as I was directed, and I carried out the orders that I was given, and I do not feel wrong in doing so, sir."[31]

Yale psychologist Stanley Milgram points out that every time parents tell their children to (or not to) do something, they are sending two messages. The first carries a specific order. The second is a silent message that states, "You should always do what I tell you." On one level, the child is learning specific actions that parents want him or her to perform or avoid. On another level, the child is learning a broader fact of life: Children must follow orders. When the child goes to school, a similar message is heard in the directives of teachers and, finally, of all people in authority. Such messages are often subtle, but they are sometimes made explicit, as can be seen in Frederick Wiseman's now classic documentary film *High School*. In one sequence of the film, a student has been assigned detention study hall for an offense the student insists he did not commit. The teacher has sent the student to the official disciplinarian, the dean of boys. The dean tells him, "First of all, you showed poor judgment. When you are being addressed by someone older than you or in a seat of authority, it's your job to respect and listen . . . we are out to establish that you can be a man and that you can follow orders." The student protests, insisting that being a man entails doing what he thinks is right: "You have to stand for something," the student explains. The dean of boys pushes on, "I think your principles aren't involved here. I think it's a question of proving yourself to be a man. I think it's a question here of how do we follow rules and regulations." The student, defeated, accepts the punishment under protest and retreats.

A typical child is a subordinate for ten to fifteen years in a school's clearly delineated system of authority. Obedience is rewarded, and one of the most potent rewards is advancement up the authority ladder. Those who follow rules loyally are likely to advance to positions where they will be able to give orders to others. This not only rewards the behavior of obedience, it also perpetuates the authority system.

---

[31] Richard Hammer, *The Court-Martial of Lieutenant Calley* (New York: Coward, McCann & Geoghegan, Inc., 1971), p. 257. The feeling that conformity is freely chosen is equivalent to the belief by "brainwashed" soldiers that they have adopted their own views and, in teaching, by students that have developed their own ideas rather than having been "indoctrinated." See Edgar H. Schein, *Coercive Persuasion* (New York: W. W. Norton, 1961); and Thomas F. Green, *The Activities of Teaching* (New York: McGraw-Hill, Inc., 1971), pp. 29–33 (" 'Teaching' and 'Indoctrinating' ").

The Milgram Experiment

Milgram undertook experiments to determine the degree to which Americans are willing to submit to authority. He put advertisements in local papers, explaining that a study was being conducted and that subjects were needed. Individuals were paid $4.50 an hour to participate. Upon entering a special laboratory designed for the experiment, subjects were told that the study investigated the effects of punishment (the use of mild electrical shocks) on learning. Two people were interviewed at a time. They drew lots to decide which person would play the role of teacher and which the role of learner. It was explained that the teacher would read a series of word pairs to the learner, for example,

1. Red/sky.
2. Fast/car.
3. Blue/moon.
4. Ink/blot.

Later in the testing sequence the teacher would read a series of words, for example,

Red sky.
Red herring.
Red China.
Red ink.

The learner would be asked which of these word pairs corresponded to a pair he or she had heard earlier (in this case, red sky). The learner would indicate the answer by pushing a button. If the response was correct, the learner would be given another question. If it was wrong, the learner would be administered a shock before moving on to the next question. The shock would be increased by 15 volts after each wrong answer.

After the learner and teacher had been introduced to the experiment, they were taken into an adjacent room where the learner was strapped into a chair and an electrode was attached to his or her wrist. An ointment was put under the electrode, and the subjects were told this was to make sure the learner was not burned or blistered by the shock. The teacher was given a sample shock (45 volts) in order to understand what the learner was experiencing. The teacher and the experimenter left the learner strapped in the chair and went again into the other room. Here the teacher was introduced to the shock generator.

Across the front of the generator was a panel of 30 switches. Below each switch was the indication of voltage. The total voltage ranged from 15 to 450 volts. There were also labels below every four switches indicating the severity of the shock. These designations read Light Shock, Moderate Shock, Strong Shock, Very Strong Shock, Intense Shock, Extreme-Intensity Shock, and Danger: Severe Shock. Two additional switches on the high end of the scale were simply marked XXX.

After all these preparations were completed, the experiment began. The learner in the adjacent room was asked questions by microphone and pushed buttons to indicate his answer. The buttons lit lights in front of the teacher. When a wrong answer was given, a shock was administered.

The experiment was rigged. The teacher was never told that the learner was really cooperating with the experimenter and was not receiving shocks in the other room. The actual purpose of the experiment was to see how far a person would go in administering shocks to a stranger simply because he or she was told to do so.

How high up the voltage scale would you be willing to go in such a situation? Would you begin at all? Would you go as far as Moderate Shock? Further? How much further? Four hundred fifty volts? Psychiatrists who were asked this question gave an average answer of just over 120 volts (between Moderate and Strong Shock). College students surveyed gave an average answer of just over 135 volts (Strong Shock). What is your estimate of your own behavior?

The results of this study show that 65 percent of the subjects went easily to the end of the board. Without protest, many gave a full 450 volts to the learner. Disturbed by his findings, Milgram made various changes in the experiment. He instructed the "learner" to yell out in pain after 120 volts, to scream in agony after 270 volts, to fall silent at 330 volts. Still, over 60 percent of the subjects proceeded to give shocks all the way up the scale. In further experiments, the learner was moved into the same room where the "teacher" could observe his pain (though, of course, the "learner" was only acting). Forty percent of the subjects went all the way to 450 volts. Milgram put in another variation. The "learner" told the "teacher" and experimenter that he had a history of heart trouble. The "learner" was put back in the adjoining room but again was instructed to call out after 150 volts, to protest as the shocks escalated, and finally to fall silent. Again, over 60 percent of the subjects administered maximum voltage.

Milgram observed the experiment through a two-way mirror. It was clear to him that the subjects ("teachers") were under a tremendous strain, especially when they knew the learner had a heart condition. They did not believe what they were doing was proper, but they felt obliged to follow orders. Some people dropped out of the experiment, but most went along. Those who stayed with the experiment invariably made it clear that they were not responsible for what was happening. This dialogue was typical:

SUBJECT. I can't stand it. I'm not going to kill that man in there. You hear him hollering?

EXPERIMENTER. As I told you before, the shocks may be painful, but—

SUBJECT. But he's hollering. He can't stand it. What's going to happen to him?

EXPERIMENTER. (his voice is patient, matter-of-fact): The experiment requires that you continue, Teacher.

SUBJECT. Aaah, but, unh, I'm not going to get that man sick in there . . . know what I mean?

EXPERIMENTER. Whether the learner likes it or not, we must go on, through all the word pairs.

SUBJECT. I refuse to take the responsibility. He's in there hollering!

EXPERIMENTER. It's absolutely essential that you continue, Teacher.

SUBJECT (indicating the unused questions). There's too many left here: I mean, geez, if he gets them wrong, there's too many of them left. I mean who's going to take the responsibility if anything happens to that gentleman?

EXPERIMENTER. I'm responsible for anything that happens to him. Continue, please.

SUBJECT. All right. (Consults list of words) The next one's "Slow—walk, truck, dance, music." Answer please. (A buzzing sound indicates the learner has signaled his answer.) Wrong. A hundred and ninety-five volts. "Dance."

LEARNER (yelling). Let me out of here. My heart's bothering me! (Teacher looks at experimenter.)

EXPERIMENTER. Continue, please.

LEARNER (screaming). Let me out of here, you have no right to keep me here. Let me out of here, let me out, my heart's bothering me, let me out! (Subject shakes head, pats the table nervously.)

SUBJECT. You see, he's hollering. Hear that? Gee, I don't know.

EXPERIMENTER. The experiment requires . . .

SUBJECT (interrupting). I know it does, sir, but I mean—hunh! He don't know what he's getting in for. He's up to 195 volts! (Experiment continues, through 210 volts, 225 volts, 240 volts, 255 volts, 270 volts, 285 volts, 350 volts.)[32]

The Meaning of Milgram's Findings

Everything about this experiment is disturbing. Milgram gives evidence that most of us believe we would not go along with such an experiment, that we would protest its inhumanity. Yet his findings indicate that most of us would do as we are told. Facing this fact, we get a tinge of what it must have been like for subjects when they were told, at the end of the experiment, what it was all about. They learned a cruel lesson about themselves. They were willing to administer life-threatening shocks to innocent strangers, simply because they were told to do so. Whether or not Milgram should have conducted these experiments at all has been a subject of great debate.[33]

It would be easy to become enraged or disheartened by Milgram's findings and then let the matter drop. These pessimistic and defeatist responses are of little help, however, because they do no more than simply accept such obedience-oriented behavior as inevitable. It would be wiser for us to try to understand the dynamics of obedience. We are most likely to accomplish this if we try to look inside the subject and catch a glimpse of how he or she defines the experimental situation.

Human behavior is always contextual: It is regulated by the situations we are in. We will do things in a football stadium that we would never think of doing in a church. The subjects in Milgram's study entered a novel situation that they had to work to comprehend. Some meanings of the situation were assumed by the subject before the experiment began. The subject assumed that someone would be in charge and that such a person would know what he or she was doing and would do only what was ethical. These assumptions were confirmed when the experimenter played the role of a competent authority: He acted the way we might expect an official to act.

Another factor that defined the situation for the subjects was that they came of their own free will. By doing so, they entered into an implied contract with the experimenter. They silently promised to cooperate. The assumption that there would be someone in charge was reinforced by their agreement to co-

---

[32] Stanley Milgram, *Obedience to Authority*, pp. 73–74.
[33] For a philosophical analysis of Milgram's experiment, see E. D. Watt, *Authority* (New York: St. Martin's Press, 1982), pp. 22–25.

operate. It was also assumed that experiments would be moral and would serve a productive end. This assumption may seem unwarranted in light of what we know about the experiment. But such assumptions pervade our culture. We take it for granted that scientists know what they are doing, that they are working to better the human situation, and that they can be trusted to act morally. These assumptions have been recently questioned, but they are still a powerful part of the American scene.

When the experiment got under way, all these assumptions were at work. New elements appeared, however, when the learner cried out in pain. The subject experienced conflicting forces. On the one hand, he or she assumed the experimenter's competence, essential morality, and worthwhile aims. Added to these assumptions was the subject's voluntary promise to cooperate, reluctance to disrupt the experiment, and, not insignificantly, willingness to obey the dictates of authority. On the other side of the issue were the screams from the adjacent room. As we read about this experiment, it is difficult to understand why the pain of a fellow human being did not dominate the situation. Why wasn't the subject drawn to this immediately? Why didn't the subject stop the experiment?

The fact of the matter is that individuals do not see everything in a situation at once. As you read this page, for example, you are not aware (at least until now) of the position of your feet or the rhythm of your breathing. This paragraph is relevant to the task at hand—your feet or your breathing patterns are not. Every situation is structured by a system of relevance by which we determine what is important to the situation and what is not.[34] Values and taken-for-granted assumptions of the culture have a great deal to do with our structures of relevance. When we apply these considerations to the subjects of the experiment, we see that the learner's cries were not defined as relevant to the experimental situation.

It is clear from the discussions Milgram recorded between the experimenter and the subjects that the cries were not totally ignored. They battled for prominence in the minds of the subjects. This is the equivalent of alternative values battling for center stage or to enter the cultural core. Such a battle causes stress. Milgram believed that many of the actions of the subjects were designed to relieve this stress. Some individuals looked away from the learner, as if they were physically pushing him or her out of their minds. Others tried to distract themselves by denying personal responsibility ("You're responsible for this. I'm not responsible for what's happening."). Some relieved their stress by protesting. This gave them the feeling that they were doing something on behalf of the learner, but it also served to reinforce the assumptions of the experimenter's competence and authority. In most cases, subjects went right back to administering shocks after their protests. Another group shortened the duration of the shocks in an effort to minimize the learner's pain and perhaps their own. One of the most fascinating aspects of the experiment was that many subjects tried to subvert the experiment in subtle ways. They would emphasize the correct answer when reading the questions. For these people, we can say that their drive to cooperate did not spring from loyalty to the experiment but rather

---

[34] For a technical examination of relevance structures, see Rodman B. Webb, *The Presence of the Past* (Gainesville: University Presses of Florida, 1976).

from a reluctance to disobey. They willingly tried to corrupt the experiment, yet they could not bring themselves to say no to authority.

Obedience and Education

As soon as we bring children together in large groups, rules become necessary. Enforcement of rules brings authority into play. It would be difficult to imagine a classroom with fifteen or more children without rules and without authority. And, as we enforce those rules, we are bringing home the message, "You should do what I tell you," or, more generally, "You should do what people in authority tell you to do."

The problem is not with authority itself; it is rather with the questions of when, under what conditions, and to what degree authority is appropriate. Certainly, there are conditions under which authority is legitimate and highly desirable. We profit greatly from being able to appeal to courts to settle our differences. We want some responsible surgeon in charge in an operating room. It makes sense that the police should have the authority to ticket speeding motorists. But there are also situations in which authority is not legitimate. The massacre at Mylai, Vietnam, where American soldiers, under orders from an officer, murdered women, old men, and children is just one ugly example of this.

The question for educators is not simply one of supporting authority or doing away with it. It is rather a question of helping students to distinguish between what is legitimate authority and what is not. Do we give students an opportunity to learn such lessons? Do we tolerate reasonable and intelligent dissent in our schools? If the Milgram experiments are a fair measure, it would seem we do not. Most of his subjects were unable to examine their own system of relevance and rearrange it on the basis of the evidence at hand. Perhaps this failure should not surprise us. They had had little practice in such activities.

Democracy

All the values discussed so far can be put to positive or negative uses. No value yields wholly positive results. Striving and the urge for success have brought prosperity—but at the price of materialism. Competition has greatly improved the human condition, although it has loosened the bonds of community. Individualism has furthered efficiency but has left people lonely and without communal purpose. Respect for authority has allowed us to organize ourselves into complex and efficient bureaucratic structures, but it carries with it a potential threat to liberty. If we look only to the positive side of these issues, we grow euphoric over our accomplishments. If we look to the negative, we grow depressed by our failings. Neither state of mind is particularly useful.

One factor, more than any other, accounts for what we have achieved as a nation and explains why our failures have not, as yet, brought us down. That factor is our continued faith in democracy. George Counts, a progressive educator whose ideas had a significant impact upon schools during the first half of this century, began a book on education by saying, "The highest and most characteristic ethical expression of the genius of the American people is the ideal of democracy."[35] But what is democracy?

Some have said that democracy is simply a form of government, a method of organizing ourselves into a manageable unit. Such a view holds that democracy is not an ideal or a vision. It supplies no image of what is to be done and is simply a process for ending disputes through majority rule. This is a narrow view of democracy, as has been pointed out by Robert Sherman, a philosopher of education at the University of Florida. He holds that democracy is both an *ideal* and a *method*. By an ideal, he does not mean that democracy contains a fixed conception of a perfect world for which we should strive. The ideal of democracy is not so static. It is rather a regulative force that guides the direction in which democracy moves. As Sherman puts it, "Democracy needs the regulation or sense of direction that ideals provide, as well as the freedom of speculation and experimentation that is the process of life."[36]

No ideal is as central to the democratic faith as the ideal of *openness*. Sherman explains that "Openness implies that democracy must be protected as a continuing process." Actions that close down the democratic process or exclude individuals from taking part in it run counter to this ideal. For example, we could not hold a referendum in which the majority voted to restrict the rights of a minority, nor could a majority claim to have found "the truth" and pass laws against change in order to protect its discovery. Such actions would violate the democratic ideal of openness.

To remain open, a democracy must allow the free expression of ideas. Faith in the free expression of ideas does not mean that all ideas are good or equally appealing. It means that in order to discover what is good, we have to consider all kinds of ideas, some proving better than others. Because democracy is an experiment, just as life is an experiment, we must remain open to new ideas. It is not difficult to entertain ideas that confirm our prejudices. The real test of democracy is whether we can allow and even listen to ideas we dislike.

The ideal of openness is linked inextricably to the ideal of *reason*. This is not a belief that human beings will always be reasonable. Experience tells us this is not the case. The ideal more modestly asserts that people can be reasonable, that reason is the best hope for improving the human condition, and that reason is more likely when conditions in the environment encourage its development. Democracy, it can be argued, is the environment in which reason is most likely to flourish.

Democracy brings reason to bear on common problems. It puts matters of public policy up for public discussion, where they are most likely to be illuminated by evidence and enriched through an open sharing of ideas. Conclusions, when they are finally reached, are always tentative. They can be changed in the light of experience or newly discovered evidence. Thus, the mind of a democrat is never fully closed. Things are taken as true only until further notice, until new evidence renders old decisions obsolete.

The acceptance of democracy implies an acceptance of opposition or *conflict*. The process of debate is not necessarily calm. The conflict characteristic of

---

[35] George S. Counts, *Social Foundations of Education* (New York: Charles Scribner's Sons, 1934), p. 9.

[36] Robert R. Sherman, *Democracy, Stoicism and Education: An Essay in the History of Freedom and Reason* (Gainesville: University Presses of Florida, 1973), p. 8.

democracy is only a surface turbulence and does not extend to the depths of the culture. Beneath the surface, there is an essential stability born of our agreement to disagree, discuss, and compromise. Thus, it would be an error to assume that conflicts in a democratic state are necessarily a sign of chaos. They are more often a sign that readjustments are taking place. There is no doubt that totalitarian organizations can manufacture a surface calm, but this calm often masks extreme conflict deep within the system.

Democracy necessitates *compromise,* for how else can we solve problems that involve diverse interests? As Sherman points out, compromise is our only alternative to force and all the tragedies that follow from its use. If we are to come to a unified policy, there must be "reasonable discussion and mutual concession"[37] between people who have diverse personal preferences.

Unfortunately, some view compromise as selling out one's principles. When corrupted, it can be exactly that. But it is an error to mistake the corruption for the principle. Sherman explains this point:

> This is not to say that compromise is a vulgar condescension from truth, as it is commonly suggested today, or that it stands for an acceptance of less than the best. Until compromises are made, until decisions and concessions have taken place between men who have competing ideas of the good, the best goals for democracy are unknown. It is more to the point to say that a compromise is a gain, for its use carries a society further toward progress, at the same time bringing about respect for democratic values, than can any principle of an absolute sort. Similarly, compromises cannot be forced; they are not ends in themselves. T. V. Smith has said that the limits of compromise are necessity, peace and progress. To the usual meanings of these terms may be added the democratic conviction that compromises are necessary because truth is never final and the good is never absolute, and therefore a method that maintains democratic openness is necessary.[38]

It is the ideal and method of democracy that has safeguarded many American values from turning sour. While we may be shocked by the results of the Milgram experiments or dismayed by the blind ambition that instigates government corruption, we find strength in the fact that democracy allows us to learn from our mistakes. Reform is an assumption of the democratic process. We can make changes, strive to do better, and when necessary, we can "throw the bums out" and start again. Some measure of the American desire to learn from the past and to improve the future is found in our national compulsion to study our tragedies. Whatever the public problem—be it war in southeast Asia, racism in our cities, corruption in government—the issue is subjected to intense public scrutiny. We are a curious people, and few things attract our attention more completely than signs of our own failings. This tendency is not the result of a morbid fascination with our decay. It grows rather from a desire to know what went wrong and to do better next time.

The abilities to reason, to remain open to competing ideas, to engage in discussion and to form compromises are not easily attained. They take practice, especially in a culture that encourages conformity, obedience, and the development of other-directed individuals. What do schools do (and what can they do) to promote the skills necessary for democracy? We will look into this question in later chapters.

---

[37] Ibid., p. 32.
[38] Ibid.

Competing Values

Values are reflections of the lives we lead. Because our lives involve others, our values sometimes come into conflict, as we have noted in the discussion of democracy. Then we have to find ways to adjust our different interests so that we can get along with each other. This is one of the functions, Sherman said, of democracy. Also, because there is change in our lives and in the environment, our own values may change as well. This is true particularly to the degree that our values are specific, such as our taste for a brand of peanut butter or a style of writing. As we learn more, we modify our values. The more general, or significant, or "ultimate" our values are—such as honesty, or openness, or even democracy itself—the less likely they are to change directly through environmental circumstance, though their character and meaning surely will be transformed.

It often seems that half of the people want what the other half resist. (Most elections, for example, are won by slim pluralities, not by overwhelming mandates.) Thus, at one time competition in society and schooling may be favored, while at another time cooperation will be in vogue. At one time, individualism and independence will be popular; at another time, social concern and interdependence will be reinforced. It may appear from this that Americans cannot make up their minds and that they swing in contradiction. But there is a simpler explanation. Part of it is, as we have noted already, that democracy encourages a plurality of values; those that are taken as best at any time are the ones that gain the most agreement through rational persuasion and compromise.

Another part of the explanation is that if one value seems to dominate another at a particular time, it may be a reflection that an earlier overemphasis is undergoing correction. This is the view that the sociologist Amitai Etzioni takes of the current scene in America, particularly of the now-popular belief that we must avoid "big government" and instead let the individual stand alone.[39] Etzioni points out that big government grew for the same reason that we now want to avoid it—to protect individuals. But it is equally extreme to expect the individual to stand alone. What we need are ideas and practices that will avoid both extremes.

We have noted that none of the values discussed in this chapter is all good or all bad. Individualism can foster creativity, but it can lead to selfishness as well. Cooperation can enhance effectiveness, but it also can lead to conformity. Striving and ambition can be useful motivations, but they can lead just as readily to ruthlessness. Openness certainly is essential in a democratic society, but it permits triviality and tawdriness as well as refinement and character. The aim is to avoid the one and enhance the other through a delicate balance.

How do we know, at any time, which values to protect and which to avoid? Time and circumstances give the clue. Etzioni believes—and we do too—that equally as threatening today as too-powerful institutions is excessive individu-

---

[39] Amitai Etzioni, *An Immodest Agenda: Rebuilding America Before the 21st Century* (New York: McGraw-Hill, 1983), p. xii.

alism.[40] The fundamental problem in American society and education—and we might extend this to the world of nations—is individual isolation. Individuals are not well served by being urged further to go it alone, no more than they are now well served by total and excessively bureaucratic institutions. What is needed instead, according to Etzioni, is to refashion the ideas of "mutuality" and "civility," or "an enhanced commitment to others and to shared concerns."[41]

We will comment on these ideas again later, but right here, in discussing competing values, we want to press the importance of civility. By *civility*, Etzioni means "in the service of shared concerns."[42] That is, civil duties are obligations one has to and with others; they are the duties of being citizens. "Civic education," we will come to see in a later chapter, is a concern to develop the sensibilities and skills necessary to carry on these duties. But *civility* has a simpler meaning (though not unrelated to this one), which implies that one can get along with others. The dictionary defines it as "forbearance from roughness or unpleasantness." The synonym would be *courtesy*.

This sense of civility should be added to the conception of democracy outlined in the previous section. If compromise is necessary to shape public policy in a democratic society, civility or tolerance—of different ideas, and styles, and interests—is a means for protecting those opportunities. In a word, we tolerate competing values, and protect the good they might do us, because we are civil. To be sure, civility has to be learned. Many of us are not civil toward each other now; we often bully or ignore each other. And a person who has only a single interest is not likely to be tolerant of, or civil toward, others or of any interruption of his or her own interest. Intolerant single-mindedness, we believe, disrupts democracy. But worse, single issues simply are not realistic. Most of us, in fact, have a multiplicity of interests and values, and they often rub against each other. If we are to pursue those interests and resolve their conflicts without doing violence to each other, civility, compromise, and democracy will need to be employed. The "genius of American politics," Daniel Boorstin has said, is that it keeps the future open.[43]

Emerging Values

In the previous chapter, we described Ralph Linton's ideas of cultural *universals* and *specialties*, which comprise the cultural *core;* cultural *alternatives;* and *individual peculiarities*. Alternatives vie to enter the core, to become part of the cultural norm. We even argued that individual peculiarities are important and must be protected, though they are outside the culture, because they provide the spark for cultural innovation. All of this is to say that cultural values are not static, that they are forever being made and remade, though, to be sure, some cultures move more quickly at this than others. But to say that something is a

[40] Ibid., Chapter 1.
[41] Ibid., p. 26; see Chapters 2 and 3.
[42] Ibid.
[43] Daniel J. Boorstin, *The Genius of American Politics* (Chicago: University of Chicago Press, 1953).

culture is to say both that it has stability and, because that stability is "relative" (to circumstances), that it can change.

We also have seen that values compete with each other for dominance. (To say it correctly, and not anthropomorphically, *humans* compete with each other for the dominance of their values and interests.) Thus, at one time, competition or cooperation, individualism or interdependence, ambition or altruism, democracy or authoritarianism, or some degree of one or the other of these will be in ascendance. We have seen further that Etzioni believes that the great need today is to avoid the extremes of excessive individualism and isolation, on the one hand, and total and paternalistic institutions, on the other, and fashion instead a new conception of community through enhanced mutuality and civility.

This is to say that cooperation, a commitment to others and to shared concerns, needs to come back into style. Still another way to explain it, perhaps, is to say that the cultural core has shrunk too greatly, so that now it excludes too many individuals and their values. There is less common-sense, taken-for-granted agreement on things. Emerging values, outside the core, reflect this situation. Emerging values aim to restore the core to its former influence. For example, at this time, one might say that this is the aim of conservative attitudes in America. Such impulses, Etzioni says, have a point: "we must concern ourselves more with the family, school, neighborhood, nation, and character."[44] But we must be sure, too, that whatever we propose to do will in fact alleviate problems, not exacerbate them, and we must persuade others to try those solutions rather than impose the solutions on them.

This is not the place to make specific proposals to alleviate societal problems. Our purpose, rather, is to discuss the role of schooling in formulating solutions to whatever problems might lie ahead. But it is part of our task to notice changes in American culture that will affect that purpose. In addition to a revitalized community—to a reconstructed sense of individualism, to enhanced mutuality and civility—more recently, other values have come to the fore in America to compete for core status.

We cannot canvass them all; a few will be suggestive. Certainly one that stands out—and it is as different as night from day from earlier assumptions and attitudes about our relationship with nature—is the need for the conservation of natural resources. Certainly, this is not a new concern. But, with dwindling resources and more people claiming them, and with what we have come to know about interdependence in nature, it has assumed an urgency. Related to this is the idea of "ecology," that events must be viewed in a system rather than as isolated entities and that each is interdependent upon others. This idea now is being extended from the natural sciences into the social and human sciences.[45] But wherever used, the connotation is that everything is related and that adjustments must seek a balance rather than a one-sided commitment.

Furthermore, the American style of life is changing. We still may be affluent, but we are more aware of those who do not have our luck, and we are aware

---

[44] Etzioni, *An Immodest Agenda*, p. xii.

[45] Gregory Bateson, *Steps to an Ecology of Mind* (New York: Ballantine Books, 1972); and Robert N. Bellah et al., *Habits of the Heart: Individualism and Commitment in American Life* (Berkeley: University of California Press, 1985), pp. 283–286.

that our continued well-being is dependent, in some measure, on their good will. So we are more willing—or should be—to negotiate and compromise with other peoples for what we and they both need. There even is some evidence that we may be willing to live on a more modest scale. We drive smaller cars, use less energy, and even are going back to smaller schools. Small has become beautiful.[46]

The moral equivalent of these impulses is equality. Equality has become a more attractive alternative, even if it is not yet a universal principle. We not only have to conserve, share, and cooperate; we are more aware of the needs of those who, until now, have not had an equal chance: women, blacks, the handicapped, and third-world peoples.

Finally, we have a new sense of financial interdependence, especially among nations. If our dollar is strong, it means that others are weak; if their currency is to be stronger, we might have to get by on less. Even the President, who does not shy from touting our greatness, is reluctant to support domestic industries through import tariffs, because he knows that we will be as much hurt by them as will the countries who ship us goods.

None of this is to say that all of our problems are being worked out and that we are about to enter utopia. There is much more to do. Pessimism and loss of confidence have to be addressed (though those are not addressed directly but are outcomes from solving, or failing to solve, concrete problems), and credibility—who to believe and follow—still perplexes us.[47] Our purpose simply is to point out that different values have emerged in our recent experience and are available as cultural alternatives. Whether they will become part of our cultural core, as specialities or universals, will depend on how we work for them. As our conception is that democracy requires education for its continued development and functioning, emerging values, like any values, must become embodied in schooling if they are to have a chance of success. What are the values that should animate American schooling? We will turn to that question in a later chapter.

Suggested Readings

Many writers have analyzed American civilization in great detail. See, for example,

DE TOCQUEVILLE, ALEXIS. *Democracy in America.* New York: Random House, Inc., Vintage Books, 1945 [1835].

FROMM, ERICH. *Escape from Freedom.* New York: Holt, Rinehart & Winston, Inc., 1941.

GORER, GEOFFREY. *The American People.* New York: W. W. Norton, 1964.

HORNEY, KAREN. *The Neurotic Personality of Our Time.* New York: W. W. Norton, 1937.

KLUCKHOHN, CLYDE. "The Evolution of Contemporary American Values," *Daedalus.* (Spring 1958), pp. 78–109.

LIPSET, SEYMOUR. "Constant Values in American Society," *Children.* Washington, DC: U.S. Department of Health, Education and Welfare, Social Security Administration, Children's Bureau, November–December 1959.

MEAD, MARGARET. *And Keep Your Powder Dry.* New York: William Morrow & Company Inc.: Quill Paperbacks, 1965.

---

[46] Ernst F. Schumacher, *Small Is Beautiful: Economics As If People Mattered* (New York: Harper & Row, 1973). Available in paperback.

[47] Harry S. Broudy, *Truth and Credibility: The Citizen's Dilemma* (New York: Longman, Inc., 1981).

MYRDAL, GUNNER. *An American Dilemma.* New York: Harper & Row, Publishers, Inc., 1962 [1944].

NYE, RUSSELL B. *This Almost Chosen People.* East Lansing: Michigan State University Press, 1966.

REISMAN, DAVID, NATHAN GLAZER, and REUEL DENNEY. *The Lonely Crowd: A Study of the Changing American Character.* New Haven: Yale University Press, 1964 [1950].

RUESCH, JURGEN, and GREGORY BATESON. *Communication: The Social Matrix of Psychiatry.* New York: W. W. Norton, 1958.

Sweeping studies of American cultural values, or what is commonly called the American character, were in vogue during World War II and into the 1950s. As social scientists became more aware of the cultural diversity of American society, they began to study individual communities, subcultures, and social strata. Although this work lacked the breadth of cultural analysis, it added depth and detail to our understanding of society.

DOLLARD, JOHN. *Caste and Class in a Southern Town.* New York: Harper & Row, Publishers, Inc., 1937. This was one of the earliest studies to show the link between race and class.

HOLLINGSHEAD, AUGUST. *Elmtown's Youth and Elmtown Revisited.* New York: John Wiley & Sons, Inc., 1975. This study of adolescence in a Midwestern town emphasizes the influence of class. Hollingshead added two chapters to his 1949 study after revisiting Elmtown in 1973. The new edition is disappointing and does not live up to the high standard set by the earlier study.

LYND, ROBERT, and HELEN LYND. *Middletown.* New York: Harcourt Brace Jovanovich, 1929; *Middletown in Transition.* New York: Harcourt Brace Jovanovich, 1937. These are among the earliest and most impressive of the community studies.

MILLS, C. WRIGHT. *White Collar.* New York: Oxford University Press, 1951. Mills's hard-hitting analysis of the middle class is somewhat dated, but much of it still rings true today.

This chapter includes material on other cultures with the intent of instigating thought rather than spelling out details. Students who want to know more about child rearing on the kibbutz would find these works helpful:

BETTELHEIM, BRUNO. *Children of the Dream.* New York: The Macmillan Co., 1969. This book is an explication of child rearing on the kibbutz.

SPIRO, MELFORD. *Children of the Kibbutz.* New York: Schocken, 1965. This is a detailed and interesting study of the socialization process.

Much has been learned about life, culture, and education in the People's Republic of China since the establishment of diplomatic relations with the United States. Students wishing to keep up to date with the growing knowledge in this field will want to familiarize themselves with the journal *Chinese Education.* Also,

GEMBERG, RUTH. *Red and Expert: Education in the People's Republic of China.* New York: Schocken Books, 1977. Based on research and extensive travel in the People's Republic of China, the author describes the schools' emphasis on sharing and teamwork rather than competition in the early grades. The author describes the history of education in China, emphasizing the effects of the communist and cultural revolutions.

HU, SHI MING. *Toward a New World Outlook: A Documentary History of Education in the People's Republic of China, 1949–1976.* New York: A. M. S. Press, 1976. This volume includes official documents, edicts, regulations, and constitutional mandates dealing with education in the People's Republic of China.

Many excellent books have been written on the topic of democracy:

ALMOND, GABRIEL A., and SIDNEY VERBA. *The Civic Culture: Political Attitudes and Democracy in Five Nations.* Boston: Little, Brown & Company, 1965. Political scientists survey five cultures in an effort to uncover the essential ingredients of democratic government.

FRANKEL, CHARLES. *The Democratic Prospect.* New York: Harper & Row, Publishers, Inc., 1964.

HALLOWELL, JOHN H. *The Moral Foundations of Democracy.* Chicago: University of Chicago Press, 1954.

HAMILTON, ALEXANDER, JAMES MADISON, and JOHN JAY. *The Federalist Papers.* New York: The New American Library, 1961 [1787–1788]. Some founding fathers outline the case for democratic government, leading up to our Constitution of 1789.

MAYO, HENRY B. *Introduction to Democratic Theory.* New York: Oxford University Press, 1960.

MERRIAM, CHARLES E. *What Is Democracy?* Chicago: University of Chicago Press, 1941.

NUNN, CLYDE, HARRY J. CROCKETT, and J. ALLEN WILLIAMS. *Tolerance for Nonconformity: A National Survey of Americans' Changing Commitment to Civil Liberties.* San Francisco: Jossey-Bass Publishers, 1978. This update of an earlier study (S. A. Stouffer, *Communism, Conformity, and Civil Liberties.* Garden City, NY: Doubleday, 1955) gives evidence that Americans are expanding their tolerance for nonconformity and their commitment to civil liberties. It is an important, and in many ways a heartening, study.

THORSON, THOMAS L. *The Logic of Democracy.* New York: Holt, Rinehart and Winston, 1962.

There has always been a strong connection between America's conception of democracy and the purported purposes of education.

CURTI, MERLE. *The Social Ideas of American Educators.* Totowa, NJ: Littlefield, Adams & Co., 1966 [1935]. This important work examines the social philosophies of prominent educators in American history.

DEWEY, JOHN. *Democracy and Education.* New York: The Free Press, 1966 [1916]. The rise of pragmatism in the first half of the twentieth century clarified the necessary connection between democratic thought and educational practice. No one was more articulate on these matters than John Dewey.

SHERMAN, ROBERT R. *Democracy, Stoicism and Education: An Essay on the History of Freedom and Reason.* Gainesville: University Presses of Florida, 1973. As American pragmatism became less of a force in America, educators began to pay less attention to the necessary unity between democracy and education. Sherman's concisely written monograph reminds us that democratic government is impossible without a democratic conception of education.

The history of American textbooks is, in effect, a history of the social aims of American education.

ELSON, RUTH MILLER. *Guardians of Tradition: American School Books in the 19th Century.* Lincoln: University of Nebraska Press, 1964. This study of schoolbooks is, in fact, a study of our national values.

FITZGERALD, FRANCES. *America Revised: History Schoolbooks in the Twentieth Century.* Boston: Little, Brown and Company, 1979. This is a penetrating and provocative account of history textbooks and the forces that shaped them in the twentieth century. It is probably the best book of its kind to date.

CHAPTER 6

The American Family and Education

Studying the Family

It is difficult, even for social scientists, to view the family with cool detachment. Most of us have deeply felt convictions about what families are and should be. Beneath these conscious convictions lie assumptions that are so much a part of our thinking that we cannot easily get a view of them. As Brigitte and Peter Berger have put it,

> The family is an essential component of almost everyone's taken-for-granted world. It is all the more necessary to gain some distance from this taken-for-granted perspective if one is to understand what the institution is all about. Familiarity breeds not so much contempt as blindness.[1]

An example will help make the Bergers' point. Engaged people usually see themselves as unique, see their love as exceptional, and talk at length about how they are different from other couples in love. They speak of past romances when they played games and pretended to be what they were not. They comment on friends who are still caught up in such tactics. At times, they speak as if love, commitment, romance (perhaps even sex) were their personal inventions. Such couples are blind to the fact that other people say similar things. They are unaware that they are following a script, written and directed by society. Certainly, they ad-lib lines, vary the tempo of the performance, build intrigue, and adjust the props. Despite all of this, the pattern from one couple to the next remains remarkably similar.

The couple is acting in harmony with other social patterns as well. For ex-

---

[1] Peter Berger and Brigitte Berger, *Sociology: A Biographical Approach,* 2d ed. (New York: Basic Books, Inc., Publishers, 1975), p. 86.

ample, their ages probably are close to those of other engaged couples (men about twenty-four and women about twenty-one).[2] The man is usually a bit older than his chosen mate, and he is a bit taller. In all likelihood, they are of the same race, social class, and political persuasion.[3] They may not be of the same religion, but their denominations are likely to be closely related (Fundamentalist Protestants, for example), and they share the same degree of commitment to their chosen faiths (regular church attendance, for example). Their parents are in the same income bracket and have similar possessions and perhaps a similar kind of education.

The point here is simply that there is more to the engagement than meets the eye—certainly more than meets the eyes of the couple in love, and maybe this is just as well. No doubt something essential would be lost if marriage proposals included all the social factors just discussed:

> Darling, will you be my wife? Life without you would not be life at all. I have loved you ever since I realized your looks would not embarrass me in public and since I found that you were so solidly middle class. You are so marvelously Protestant, so profoundly Caucasian, and so admirably disinterested in politics. I swell with pride to know that you are four inches shorter than I am (two inches when you wear heels), that you can carry on light cocktail party conversations, and that you don't slurp your soup. I adore hearing people say, "Aren't they a cute couple" and feel the warm flush of security when my father winks knowingly and says, "You've got quite a catch there, take good care of her!" I appreciate your humanitarian concern for others (you're a teacher), your straight teeth (six years of orthodonture), and the fact that you haven't slept around a lot (serial monogamy is not moral laxity, as far as I'm concerned!).

By now, the reader may believe that social scientists are heartless folk, who take pleasure in debunking the dreams of people in love, but this is not the case. After all, social scientists fall in love, too. But a degree of scientific detachment allows them to step back from their taken-for-granted assumptions. From that perspective, they see that there is much more to marriage than romance and more to the family than what is seen in everyday life. If we are to understand what families are and how they work, we must look behind the scenes. That is the task of this chapter. We will look at the functions of family life, the historical roots of the American family, recent changes in family structure, and relationships between the family and education in the United States.

What Are Families For?

What functions do families fulfill in society? These vary from culture to culture and from one historical period to another, but certain basics are nearly universal. In most societies, families are *primary regulatory agencies*. They provide a model (a *micro-world*) of the larger society (the *macro-world*). Primary socializa-

---

[2] Mary Jo Bane, *Here to Stay: American Families in the Twentieth Century* (New York: Basic Books, Inc., Publishers, 1976), p. 23; and "Marital Status and Living Arrangements, March, 1978," *Population Characteristics*, Series P-20, No. 338 (May 1979).

[3] William J. Goode, *World Revolution and Family Patterns* (New York: The Free Press, 1963), p. 23; and Charles B. Nam, "Family Patterns and Educational Attainment," *Sociology of Education*, Vol. 38, No. 5 (Fall 1965), pp. 393–403.

tion of the young is carried on in this micro-world. Here children are taught the habits and attitudes necessary for harmonious life in the culture.

Few institutions rival the power of the family in the socialization process. It is society's most basic educational institution. Children are born to families, and, for an important period of their lives, the family is the only world they know. Gradually, children are introduced to the macro-world, but parents monitor this exploration. They try to regulate and define what children see and experience in the world outside. Parents, of course, can teach only what they know. They pass on their views of the world, share what they have experienced, and explain things as they understand them. Thus, the family is a basically conservative institution that instills the assets, but also the liabilities, of parents into the character and aspirations of children. These primary impressions are lasting and very difficult to modify—a fact of immense significance to education.

The family serves other functions as well. As you might have gathered from our earlier discussion of romance, the family plays an important role in mate selection. Parents may not choose the mates of their offspring (though this is done in some cultures), but they do significantly influence the taste of their children. The family defines and tries to police the boundaries within which mate selection can take place. The family also helps regulate (with varying success) the sexual practices of individuals. The most obvious and universal of such regulations is the incest taboo. Almost every culture forbids sexual relations between parents and children, brothers and sisters, and, somewhat less rigorously, between variously defined kin groups. The family regulates the sexual activities of husbands and wives. In the United States, despite the sexual revolution, adultery is still frowned upon. There are also regulations regarding the sexual behavior of offspring, although these rules are undergoing rapid change. Despite the increased frequency of sexual experience before marriage, there is still a rather strong taboo in Western societies against indiscriminate or recreational sex.

The family regulates the ownership and transmission of property. Every society has a way to decide who has claim to what and who will inherit that claim when an individual dies. The family is an integral part of this process. The rights of family members are usually defined by laws that spell out procedures regarding inheritance, alimony, and communal property. But the assumptions that undergird these laws are transmitted within the family setting. In a society that puts high value on personal ownership, the family socializes youngsters to see ownership as a fundamental right. This lesson is learned at an early age. Bring together a group of American children, for example, and you will soon hear the phrase, "Give me that, it's mine!" Adults may intervene, suggesting that "it's nice to share," but even this message underlines the significance of personal ownership. Sharing is a friendly concession by a property owner and not a right to be demanded by others.

The functions of the family discussed here (primary socialization, mate selection, regulation of sexual practices, and transmission of property) are nearly universal in nature. They apply, in varying degrees, to all families in all societies. However, our central concern is with the modern American family and its significance to education. In order to understand the unique functions of family life in modern America, we will have to look briefly at its premodern European roots.

The History of the American Family

The Premodern Family

It is difficult for anyone brought up in the present age to appreciate fully the family arrangements of earlier times.[4] During the sixteenth and seventeenth centuries quite different patterns existed in European families than those that exist in America today. For example, there was little or no pretense that family life rested on a foundation of love. Romance, in fact, is a rather modern invention. In earlier times, economic considerations were the central concern. Marriages were often arranged by families, and there was usually an exchange of material goods. An engagement announced the union of blood lines and dollar signs rather than the mutual devotion of individuals. Marriage partners were tied together out of a sense of duty to the family and community rather than by strings of romance, emotion, and sexuality.

Children were almost an inevitable consequence of marriage in an age before birth control. They were usually welcomed but for reasons more economic than emotional. Children were needed for their labor on farms and in cottage industries. They were living insurance policies against the day when old age or ill health made parents unable to work. When children were not needed for work around the home, they could be sold to someone else or rented out as apprentices or indentured servants.

Such conditions did not promote strong emotional relationships between parents and their children. To dearly love a child was to risk almost certain disappointment, for many children died in infancy or left home at an early age. There was little evidence of bereavement when a child died and much evidence of emotional restraint. Historical records show many incidents of parents forgetting their children's names or losing count of how many children were in the family.

The family was not the private, isolated institution it is today. In many cases, people lived in small, rural communities and worked land owned in common with others. Work was public and communication widespread. Every person had a personal stake in the attitudes and behaviors of others and paid close attention to what others were doing. Any violation of community norms was known quickly by everyone, and punishment could be swift and, when necessary, final.

The American Family: Early Patterns

The patterns of European family life were already changing when the colonization of America began. Conceptions of romantic love were spreading, and the bonds between husband and wife and between parent and child were becoming stronger and more emotional. These trends intensified in colonial America. Separated from European traditions, set out on a cold and distant shore, colonial families enjoyed a new intimacy, but marriage was still not the

---

[4] Much of the material in this section is borrowed from Edward Shorter's intriguing book, *The Making of the Modern Family* (New York: Basic Books, Inc., Publishers, 1975).

romantic institution it is today. One hopeful suitor, an eighteenth-century evangelist named George Whitfield, assured his prospective in-laws. "I am free from that foolish passion which the world calls love."[5]

Not all people were so restrained. Letters and diaries of the time reveal strong emotional bonds in many colonial marriages.[6] Just as in Europe, however, economic forces helped bring people together, get them married, and hold them in place. Dowries were a dying tradition and few marriages were arranged, but children were expected to ask permission to marry. One young man wrote his parents,

> I never shall think I am at liberty to dispose of myself without [your] consent . . . and if I should ever be so mad as to do it, though you should forgive me, I should never forgive myself.[7]

Historical evidence such as this shows that, though young people enjoyed a new freedom to choose their mates, they were expected to receive parental blessings. The fact that young men (such as the one just quoted) felt they must reassure their parents about this matter is evidence that the practice was no longer being taken for granted. Increasingly, young people were making up their own minds and following their own sentiments.

The relationships between parents and their children were still enormously affected by economic considerations. Child labor was essential, especially among poorer families. For this reason, families tended to be large, the average size being five or six during the colonial period.[8] Children were, at least in part, an economic commodity. If a family could not afford to feed an infant, they might abandon it on the doorstep of an orphanage or near the home of a wealthy family. If the labor of older children was no longer needed around the farm or family business, they could be rented out as day laborers or servants. Luckier children left home for apprenticeships, where they learned a trade. Economic considerations did not make love impossible, of course, but they did temper sentimentality. Parents fostered independence in their children and learned to hold their own emotions in check.

As in Europe, the frequency of childhood deaths worked to cool emotional relationships between parent and child. About 25 percent of all children died in infancy and another 25 percent died before the age of eighteen.[9] The chances

---

[5] Philip Greven, *The Protestant Temperament* (New York: Alfred A. Knopf, Inc., 1977), p. 138. Available in paperback.

[6] For example, see Edmund S. Morgan, *The Puritan Family* (New York: Harper and Row, Publishers, 1944). Morgan gives numerous examples of love and affection in Puritan marriages. He points out that the Puritans were not the ascetics they are often believed to be. Their marriages included both laughter and love. However, marriage partners were chosen on rational and spiritual grounds, and the affections of everyday life were tolerated only so long as they did not interfere with the Puritans' more heavenly goals.

[7] Greven, *The Protestant Temperament*, p. 188.

[8] The size of families varied geographically. In 1703, the average New York household contained 5.4 people, but in Massachusetts the number was 7.2. The 1790 census put the average United States household at 5.8 persons. By 1930, that number had dropped to 4.1. See Mary Jo Bane, *Here to Stay: American Families in the Twentieth Century*, p. 39.

[9] Cotton Mather, a Puritan clergyman not remembered for lighthearted optimism, warned children of their impending doom. He asked the young people of his congregation to look at one another and ponder the terrible truth that half of them would be dead before they turned eighteen. See Mary Cable, *The Little Darlings* (New York: Charles Scribner's Sons, 1975), p. 141.

Jonathan Edwards, another New England clergyman, warned the children of his congrega-

were no better than fifty-fifty that a child would live to maturity. Parents who made an emotional investment in their children were running the risk of bitter grief. Adults knew with relative certainty that the majority of their children would be taken from them either by early death or work away from home.

Religion served to slacken further the bonds of love between parent and child. Cotton Mather, a Puritan clergyman, explained to his congregation that God was not much interested in little children. "Their bodyes are too weak to labour, and their minds to study are too shallow . . . even the first seven years are spent in pastimes and God looks not much at it."[10] Parents were warned, however, that children must be taught at an early age to submit absolutely to authority. As one clergyman put it, children were "a blessing great, but dangerous."[11]

An article in a colonial magazine claimed that only an infant's small size and weakness protected parents from a child's rage. If children were given "the strength of manhood," they would "take your life."[12] Such grim warnings hardly encouraged parental love.

Not surprisingly, such an image of children led to harsh child-rearing practices, designed to break the will of the young. "Let every parent make it his inflexible determination, that he will be obeyed—*invariably* obeyed," was typical parenting advice during the colonial period.[13] Some parents must have been lax, however, for Puritan ministers frequently warned against treating children too tenderly. One minister went so far as to suggest that the high rate of infant mortality was the result of the "immoderate love" weak parents lavished upon their children. "Sinful tenderness and indulgence," he claimed, "is the ruin of many children."[14] Love was an acceptable emotion, but parents were warned that it must be tempered by another important emotion—fear. As one clergyman put it, children must learn to be afraid of their parents so that they would later fear God.

Parents of more moderate religious beliefs allowed themselves more affectionate relationships with their children. They emphasized love and duty rather than love and fear. Affluent families had the least restrictions on parent–child affection. Self-assured and financially self-sustaining, these families were seldom attracted to evangelical religion. Freed from economic and religious restraints and unbothered by what others thought of them, affluent families indulged their offspring. The result was a much higher degree of affection and, from the point of view of strict Puritans, many more spoiled children.

The most affluent families in early American history existed in tight private spheres, quite independent of the surrounding community. Other social classes were not so independent. Intricate social relationships tied them firmly to the outside community. Some of these relationships may have been more emotion-

tion, "God is angry with you every day. . . . How dreadful to have God angry with you. How dreadful will it be in Hell among the devils and know that you must be there to all Eternity. . . . You won't play together any more but will be damned together, will cry out with weeping and wailing and gnashing of teeth together." Quoted in Cable, ibid., p. 48.

[10] Ibid., p. 6.

[11] Greven, *The Protestant Temperament*, p. 188.

[12] Ibid., p. 29.

[13] Ibid., p. 33.

[14] Ibid., p. 34.

ally satisfying than associations within the household. For most American families, it was not easy to determine where the influence of the community ended and where the domain of the family began. When children misbehaved, for example, parents were admonished from the pulpit for not doing their duty. Even neighbors would be chastised for not preventing the rebellious behavior of the children next door.[15] If parents had difficulty with their children, they could depend on assistance from local magistrates. The law of one colony allowed town officials to administer whippings (ten straps per offense) to disobedient children. Another colony prescribed the death penalty for stubborn and rebellious youngsters. There is no evidence that this penalty was ever put to use, but its very existence gave community support to parental authority. Facts such as these dramatized the strong connection between family life and the macro-world. At least among poor and middle-income families, there was not the intense personal and private conception of family life that we know today.

Changing Patterns in the American Family

The New Emotionalism

Economic security, less intense religious beliefs, improved health, and growing industrialization have changed American families considerably since colonial times. Today, marriage is an intense emotional undertaking. People get married expecting that the union will fulfill their deepest and most intimate needs. The family unit has become an emotional oasis in an increasingly impersonal world. In Chapter 2, it was pointed out that the family is the focal point of the private sphere. It has become strictly segregated from the megastructure of public life.[16]

The idea that the family is fundamentally an extension of society (an idea popular during the colonial period) has given way to the notion that family life is fundamentally different from public life. Within its intimate domain, individuals seek protection from a world they see as competitive, dollar-driven, and impersonal. They find refuge in a private sphere where collective interests are paramount and individuals are treated according to who they really are, rather than the narrow roles they play. The family is the major primary group of individuals. It serves as a buffer against the turbulence of modern life. This new function has intensified emotional relationships among family members.[17]

Egoism

Greater emotionalism has led to egoism, a concern for oneself or one's family rather than for others. Individuals and families today have the resources to retreat into themselves and care only for their own interests. *Privatism* is the

---

[15] Thomas Jefferson Wertenbaker, *The Puritan Oligarchy* (New York: Grosset and Dunlap, Inc., 1947), p. 177. Available in paperback.

[16] This idea is discussed by Robert N. Bellah et al., *Habits of the Heart: Individualism and Commitment in American Life* (Berkeley: University of California Press, 1985), Chapter 4, especially pp. 88–89.

[17] For an interesting exploration of this idea, see Richard Sennett, *Families Against the City: Middle Class Homes of Industrial Chicago, 1872–1890* (Cambridge: Harvard University Press, 1970).

word coined to describe this phenomenon. The larger sphere of the extended family or the community thus has to care for itself. But, in fact, it will not be cared for as long as no one in particular has the responsibility. If there is anything still useful in contact with a larger community, it will not be successful as long as increasing numbers of individuals and families retreat from the public sphere. While there is point and purpose to the family acting as mediator between individuals and the community, as we shall see, a one-sidedness in favor of privatism is no better than an overemphasis on group control.[18] We will come to see that, in the coming years, egoism is one of the issues that American education must face. Greater emotionalism and egoism, in fact, characterize most of the other changes in the American family that we discuss. Like those other changes, the good that the changes effect must be balanced by minimizing the difficulties that the changes pose for society and education.

Equalization of Roles

The romanticizing of marriage has helped equalize the roles of husband and wife. Both partners now have an equal claim to happiness, emotional security, personal fulfillment, and sexual gratification. Decisions tend to be made democratically; the interests and concerns of both parties are considered. Household work still is divided according to sex, but there is increasing resistance to such practices—especially among younger couples and in families where women work outside the home.

Shrinking Family Functions

The increased emotional significance of the family has been accompanied by a shrinkage of its formal functions. Once a unit of production, the family is now a unit of consumption. Family members no longer share common tasks; children do not see their parents at work and are less likely to follow their footsteps into the family business. Vocational training and general education have become the function of school systems. Education has expanded its curricula to include matters previously handled in the home: values, sex education, home economics, and instruction in manners and dress and grooming, to name but a few. Schools sometimes feed children breakfast and lunch, provide guidance and mental health services, refer children to doctors, and even offer evening courses in child rearing for parents.

Other family functions have been taken over by corporations and bureaucracies. Fast-food chains have changed the nature of the dinner hour; nursing homes have considerably replaced family care for the elderly; hospitals have become sterile locations for birth and death; production is carried on in factories rather than in the home or on the family farm; and charity—once personal and direct—is now organized and faceless. All these changes have left the family with fewer social roles and have contributed to its isolation.

The family changes discussed so far (increased emotionalism, privatism, and shrinking functions) are tied to other trends (such as increased divorce rates,

[18] See Amitai Etzioni, *An Immodest Agenda: Rebuilding America Before the 21st Century* (New York: McGraw-Hill, 1983), Chapters 1 and 5.

growing numbers of working mothers, new roles for fathers, and the advent of television).

Divorce

As families have lost many economic functions and have become privatized and separated from the outside community, they have had to rely on the bonds of love and romance to hold together. But these bonds, too, are subject to severe strain, as can be seen from the nation's high rate of divorce. Recent data indicate that a woman born between 1940 and 1944 has a 30 to 40 percent chance of being divorced at least once in her lifetime. The risk is even greater among younger women.[19]

Government statistics show that, in 1960, there were 35 divorced persons for every 1000 who were married. In 1986, these figures had jumped to 133 per 1000, and they still are climbing. Although divorce rates have been rising for some time, dramatic increases are a recent phenomenon, as Figure 6-1 shows. There was a 112 percent increase in the divorce-to-marriage ratio in the decade between 1970 and 1980. In the previous decade, 1960–1970, there was only a 34 percent increase. Moreover, divorce affects some groups more than others. The ratio for men is lower than that for women: 106 compared with 157 in 1986; a difference that is due largely to the fact that more divorced men remarry than do divorced women. In other words, divorced women are more likely to live alone. Blacks have a much higher divorce rate than whites: 248 compared to 124 in 1986; and black women have the highest rate of all: 332. Neither does divorce respect age. About 70 out of every 1000 marriages among persons 65 years of age and older ended in divorce, a figure that is twice as high as that for *all* ages in 1960. Statistics show that the divorce rate (both sexes) is highest for persons 35 to 44 years of age; it is highest for men ages 30 to 34 and for women (177) 35 to 44 years old.[20] Clearly, divorce is a problem that affects all groups but some more seriously than others.

What strains provoke divorce? This is a complicated question, but some generalizations are possible. Poverty and the strain of unemployment make divorce more likely.[21] Teenage marriages are also subject to high divorce rates.[22] Many factors enter in here: the strain of premarital pregnancy, economic problems, isolation from peer groups, and the quick emotional shifts of adolescent life. Another factor in rising divorce rates is the recent liberalization of divorce laws. In most states, divorce has become a rather simple matter, at least when both parties favor the action. It is difficult to detect if easier divorce laws cause higher divorce rates or if they simply reflect changing attitudes. Clearly, divorce no longer holds the stigma it once did. A 1976 Roper poll revealed that 60 percent

[19] Arthur Norton and Paul Glick, "Marital Instability: Past, Present and Future," *Journal of Social Issues,* Vol. 32 (1976), pp. 5–20.

[20] Data are taken from the U. S. Bureau of the Census, Current Population Reports, Series P-20, No. 418, *Marital Status and Living Arrangements: March, 1987* (Washington, DC: U. S. Government Printing Office, 1987), p. 7.

[21] Phillips Cutright, "Income and Family Events: Marital Stability," *Journal of Marriage and the Family,* Vol. 33 (1971), pp. 291–306; and Isabell Sawhill et al., *Income Transfers and Family Structures* (Washington, DC: The Urban Institute, 1975).

[22] James Weed, "Age at Marriage as a Factor in State Divorce Rate Differentials," *Demography,* Vol. 11 (1974), pp. 361–375.

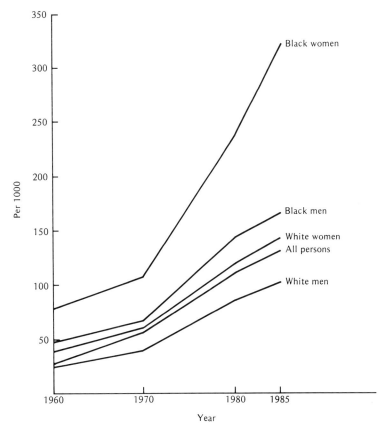

Figure 6-1   Divorced persons per 1000 married persons with spouse present; 1960–1983. (*Source:* Data from U.S. Bureau of the Census, Current Population Reports, Series P-20, N. 389, *Marital Status and Living Arrangements: March, 1983* [Washington, DC: U.S. Government Printing Office, 1984].)

of Americans saw divorce as an acceptable answer to an unhappy marriage.[23] As divorce becomes more common, is easier to obtain, and is given social approval, it is reasonable to assume that a lower threshold of marital strain will incite even more divorce.

Other factors are at work as well. Women today have more education, are accepted in the job market, have more employment experience, and are more capable of supporting themselves than ever before. In short, women today have more options; they no longer have to be tied to the home. One of these options is divorce.

---

[23] Quoted in George Levinger and Oliver Moles, "In Conclusion: Threads in the Fabric," *Journal of Social Issues,* Vol. 32, No. 1 (1976), p. 198.

Elizabeth Douvan found that 80 percent of Americans agreed that divorce is a good solution to marital problems, at least under some conditions. See her "Marriage Role: 1957–1976" presented at the American Psychological Association meeting in Toronto, 1978, p. 5. Available from the Institute for Social Research, University of Michigan, Ann Arbor, Michigan 48106.

The greatest single cause of divorce is probably the enormously high expectations couples have for marriage. They expect the institution to give them happiness, warmth, emotional and economic security, sexual fulfillment, honest and open communication, and profound personal satisfaction. When any of these expectations is unfulfilled (as is inevitable at times), the reason to remain married is severely strained.

Social Consequences of Divorce

The causes of divorce do not begin and end with the personalities of the couple, and the consequences of divorce do not stop at their doorstep. Divorce may be a personal problem, but it has severe public consequences.

Divorced individuals must adjust to loneliness, changing economic conditions, new relationships with old friends, and emotional trauma. Such conditions, no doubt, bring pain to all people involved, including children. Does this pain have lasting social or psychological effects on the young? The answer is not clear. Early studies found high correlations between paternal absence and low school achievement, psychological disorder, and delinquency in children. This research has been criticized recently, however, because it often failed to take into account important factors, such as poverty or the state of family life before divorce.[24] Still, no one doubts that children are better off when they live with happily married parents.

The issue is complicated. Divorce by itself may not cause problems for children. If the divorce is amicable, if it is explained to children, if parents do not use the children to punish one another, if they share child-rearing responsibilities, the chance of lasting harm is minimized. If, on the other hand, the divorce devastates the parents, if it throws the family into poverty (or deeper into poverty) and brings continued turmoil into the emotional life of children, the chance for lasting damage is great. Current estimates suggest that 23–35 percent of children under eighteen will experience a divorce of their parents or will be affected by annulments or long-term separation.[25] In the years from 1972 to 1986, the number of families maintained by women increased by over 60 percent, to a total of 10.5 million. One of every six families in 1986 was maintained by a woman. Three out of five of these women were in the labor force and had, on the average, fewer years of schooling than wives and were concentrated in lower-skilled, lower-paying jobs. Women maintaining families are far more likely to be unemployed than husbands or wives, and their median family income is less than half that of married couples. They are 5 times as likely to be in poverty than are married couples; 1 in every 3 such families, nearly 3.5 million, were in poverty in 1984, compared with 1 out of every 16 married-couple families.[26] Clearly, for many children, divorce is just the begin-

---

[24] Mary M. Thomes, "Children with Absent Fathers," *Journal of Marriage and the Family*, Vol. 30 (1968), pp. 89–96; and Elizabeth Herzog and Cecelia Sudia, "Children in Fatherless Families," *Review of Child Development Research*, Vol. 3 (Chicago: University of Chicago Press, 1973), pp. 141–232.

[25] If we add to these percentages children who suffer the loss of a parent through death or are born to unwed mothers, we find 34–46 percent of American children will experience family disruption before they reach nineteen.

[26] Data are taken from the U.S. Department of Commerce, Bureau of the Census, *Current Population Reports*, and Special Study Series P-23, No. 146 (Washington, DC: U.S. Government Printing Office, 1986), pp. 28–36.

ning of problems in their lives. They must deal with separation from fathers or mothers, poor diet, inadequate housing, insufficient health care, and more. These conditions are bound to have personal and social consequences. It can be seen from these facts that divorce is not simply a problem for families. The repercussions of divorce are often felt in schools, businesses, and the community.

Women Who Work Outside the Home

The term *working women* is misleading because it refers only to women with paying jobs. This definition tells us something about American values. We tend not to value work that does not bring in a paycheck. Can this be true? Do Americans assign low status to such important work as child care and homemaking? The sad answer is yes. Ask a homemaker what she does, and you are likely to get the self-depreciating answer, "I am just a housewife."

More evidence for the low status of child care and homemaking is found in the third edition of the *Dictionary of Occupational Titles* (1965). This is a government publication that rates jobs according to their complexity and required skill. On a descending scale, in which the highest figure (878) represented the lowest possible rating and the simplest work, the rating assigned to the jobs "Homemaker," "Foster Mother," "Child Care Attendant," and "Nursery School Teacher" was a dismal 878. Look at a few of the jobs given higher ratings (lower numbers) of difficulty: "Delivery Boy" (868), "Striptease Artist" (848), "Hotel Clerk" (868), "Barber" (371), and "Dog Trainer" (228). Happily, the government has deleted age and sex references from the titles and descriptions in the fourth edition (1977) of the *Dictionary,* and it "hides" the ratings in a complex coding system. But the fact remains that women-dominated jobs traditionally have received low status in our culture.

More and more women are seeking employment outside the home (see Figure 6-2). By 1982, 53 percent of all women over 16 years old were working or looking for work. These figures have increased from 33 percent in 1950. Younger women especially feel the pressure. Nearly half of the increase in the female labor force since 1970 has been among women age 25 to 34.[27] Some of this increase, no doubt, is related to the devaluation of homemaking, just discussed, and to the more recent tendency for women to put off child rearing until an older age; but most women take paying jobs for another reason; they need the money. Nearly two-thirds of all women in the civilian labor force in March 1984 were either single (25 percent), divorced (11 percent), widowed (5 percent), separated (4 percent), or had husbands whose 1983 incomes were less than $15,000 (19 percent).[28] We have noted already that in 1982, one of every six families was headed by a woman and that three out of five of these women worked outside the home. In other words, 10 percent of all families (up from 8.5 percent just three years earlier) are headed by women who have to work to support their children.

What kinds of jobs do employed women hold? There have been some shifts in recent years, but certain patterns persist. Women tend to be nurses rather

---

[27] Ibid., pp. 2–3.
[28] "Facts on Women Workers," Government Document (Washington, DC: U.S. Department of Labor, Office of the Secretary, Women's Bureau, 1984), No. 20, p. 2.

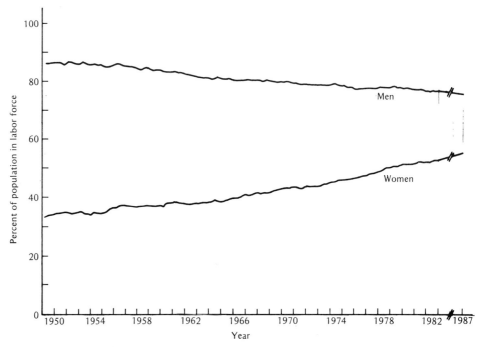

Figure 6-2   Labor force participation rates by sex, 1950–1982. (*Source:* Data from U.S. Department of Labor, Bureau of Labor Statistics, Bulletin 2168, *Women at Work: A Chartbook* [Washington, DC: U.S. Government Printing Office, 1983].)

than doctors, teachers rather than principals, and secretaries rather than executives. Progress has been made in most of the categories of women's employment, but women still are a long way from occupational equality. Women are concentrated in low-paying, service occupations. They hold 70.9 percent of all clerical jobs (1983) but only 40.9 percent of managerial and professional positions. Forty-eight percent of all professional jobs are held by women, but this percentage is abnormally high because traditionally female occupations such as elementary school teaching and nursing are included in the statistics. In 1986, only 24.9 percent of lawyers and judges, 26.9 percent of physicians and osteopaths, and 6.3 percent of engineers were women.[29] (See Table 6-1 for further data.[30])

No wonder some women resent the slogan, "You've come a long way, baby." They point out that they are not babies (though some people insist on treating them as such) and that they have not come far enough. In 1983, the average working woman who had four or more years of college education earned an income only slightly higher than men who had only one to three years of high

[29] Data are taken from U.S. Bureau of the Census, *Statistical Abstract of the United States: 1985*, 5th ed. (Washington: U.S. Government Printing Office, 1984), pp. 402–403.

[30] The data in note 29 and Table 6-1 are not the same. The data in note 29 are for 1983, and the occupation categories have been changed slightly since 1981.

TABLE 6-1.   Employment of Women in Selected Occupations, 1950, 1970, 1981, and 1986 (Numbers in thousands)

	Women			
	Percentage of All Workers in Occupation			
Occupation	*1950*	*1970*	*1981*	*1986*
Professional-technical	40.1	40.0	44.7	—
Accountants	14.9	25.3	38.5	45.5
Engineers	1.2	1.6	4.3	6.3
Lawyers-judges	4.1	4.7	14.0	24.9
Physicians-osteopaths	6.5	8.9	13.8	26.9
Registered nurses	97.8	97.4	96.8	92.1
Teachers, except college and university	74.5	70.4	70.6	71.0
Teachers, college and university (including presidents)	22.8	28.3	35.3	27.5
Managerial-administrative, except farm	13.8	16.6	27.4	38.8
Bank officials-financial managers	11.7	17.6	37.4	37.9
Buyers-purchasing agents	9.4	20.8	35.0	32.7
Food service workers	27.1	33.7	40.5	57.5
Sales managers-department heads; retail trade	24.6	24.1	40.4	40.9
Sales	34.5	39.4	45.4	40.9
Sales representatives (including whole-sale)	5.2	7.2	—	17.0
Sales clerks, retail	48.9	64.8	71.3	71.1
Clerical	62.2	73.6	80.5	—
Bank tellers	45.2	86.1	93.7	90.6
Bookkeepers	77.7	82.1	91.2	90.4
Cashiers	81.3	84.0	86.4	79.4
Office machine operators	81.1	73.5	73.7	55.0
Secretaries-typists	94.6	96.6	98.6	98.3
Craft	3.1	4.9	6.3	—
Carpenters	0.4	1.3	1.9	1.1
Bakers	12.2	29.4	—	26.1
Decorators-window dressers	32.6	58.3	—	—
Tailors	19.8	31.4	—	—

SOURCE: The 1950 and 1970 figures are from U.S. Department of Labor, Bureau of Labor Statistics, Bulletin 2080, *Perspectives on Working Women: A Databook* (Washington, DC: U.S. Government Printing Office, 1980), p. 10. The 1981 figures are from U.S. Department of Labor Bureau of Labor Statistics, Report 673, *The Females-Male Earning Gap: A Review of Employment and Earning Issues* (Washington, DC: U.S. Government Printing Office, September, 1982), p. 9. The 1986 figures are from Earl F. Mellor, "Weekly Earnings in 1986: A Look at More than 200 Occupations," *Monthly Labor Review* (June 1987), pp. 41–46.

school education: $14,679 to $12,117 respectively.[31] For the last 30 years, the average income for working women has hovered around 6 dollars for every 10 dollars earned by men, or 60 percent of men's earnings (see Table 6-2), though very recent data suggest that women's income may be—slowly—on the rise.[32]

[31] "Facts on Women Workers," p. 3.
[32] Peter Francese, "Women's Income Gains on Men's," *Gainesville Sun* (November 11, 1985), describing a March 1985 survey by the Census Bureau.

TABLE 6-2.   Median Annual Earnings of Year-Round,
Full-Time Workers, 14 Years and Over, by Sex,
1955–1985

Year	Annual Earnings		Women's Earnings as Percentage of Men's
	Women	Men	
1955	$ 2,719	$ 4,252	63.9
1957	3,008	4,713	63.8
1959	3,193	5,209	61.3
1961	3,351	5,644	59.4
1963	3,561	5,978	59.6
1965	3,823	6,375	60.0
1967	4,150	7,182	57.8
1969	4,977	8,227	60.5
1971	5,593	9,399	59.5
1973	6,335	11,186	56.6
1975	7,504	12,758	58.8
1977	8,618	14,626	58.9
1979	10,151	17,014	59.7
1981	12,001	20,260	59.2
1983	13,915	21,881	63.6
1985	15,624	24,196	64.6

SOURCE: *Perspectives on Working Women: A Databook,* p. 52. The 1979
and 1981 data are from *The Female-Male Earning Gap,* p. 9. (See
Table 6-1 for full citations.) The 1983 and 1985 data are from *Statistical
Abstract of the United States,* 1986 (p. 419) and 1987 (p. 403).

Note: Data for 1955 and 1965 are for wage and salary workers only
and exclude self-employed persons. Data from 1979 to 1985 are
for persons 15 years and over.

The earnings gap is explainable partially by the jobs women hold and by their
relative lack of work experience, but even when these factors are taken into
account, significant earning differences persist.

The changing status of women in society is an important topic, and we shall
look at it again later. For now, we limit ourselves to questions of direct relevance to education. What are the effects of working mothers on children and
on family stability?

Responding to the second question first, we may recall that 10 percent of all
families are headed by women who work, usually without a husband in the
home. Moreover, the marriages of women who work are somewhat less stable
than the marriages of those who stay at home.[33] Many factors enter into this
finding. Most working women are poor, and poverty has its own disruptive
effects on marriage. The added income from a working wife does not necessarily end financial crises of the family. Usually, she is poorly paid, and her
earnings are eroded by the cost of child care, transportation, clothes for work,
and taxes. Her energy is drained by her job and the extra burden of evening
shopping, cooking, child care, and housework. Even if these tasks are shared
by the husband (though often they are not), everyone is so tired by the end of
the day that minor disturbances can quickly flare into major disruptions. All of

[33] Bane, *Here to Stay,* p. 28.

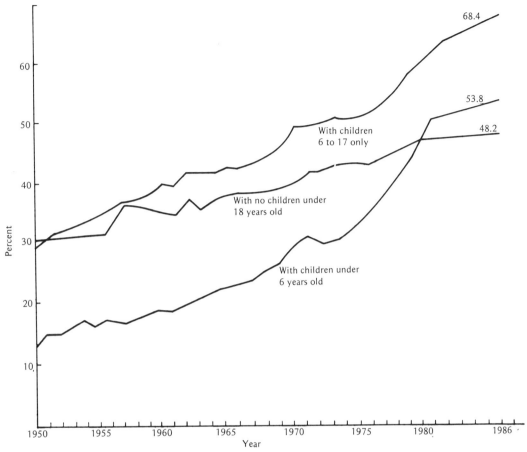

Figure 6-3 Labor force participation rates of married women with children present in the home, 1950–1986. (*Source:* U.S. Department of Labor, Bureau of Labor Statistics, Bulletin 2209, *Families at Work: The Jobs and the Pay* [Washington, DC: U.S. Government Printing Office, 1983], p. 3 and *Statistical Abstract of the United States*, 1987. [Washington, DC: U.S. Department of Commerce, Bureau of the Census, 1987], p. 383.)

this aside, however, the mere change in family routines brought by a working woman may cause conflict in some homes.

In 1986, 68.4 percent of all women with children over 6 and under 18 were employed or seeking work. Among women with children under six (children who we might think are most in need of parental care), 53.8 percent were in the work force. These numbers have risen dramatically from preceding years, as can be seen in Figure 6-3.

Are children adversely affected when their mothers work outside the home? No clear-cut answers exist at present. Some investigators have found quite negative results when studying families with working mothers. However, most of these studies have been challenged. Early research showed that children of working mothers had a higher chance of being disruptive, dependent, and even delinquent. But it is not at all clear that maternal employment caused these problems. If a child is having difficulties, these problems may be exaggerated by a mother's daytime absence. Similarly, if a family is having trouble, its problems may be accentuated when the mother enters the work force.

Recent studies have determined that children and families are adversely affected by mothers who are unhappy in their work, but this is true also for mothers who are unhappy in homemaking. Further research indicates that children will suffer if they are given inadequate substitute care while their mothers are away. However, when a mother is happy in her work, when the family is stable, and when the children receive good substitute care, children do not appear to be adversely affected by working mothers.[34]

The issue is far from closed, and more research is needed. Although it can be said that maternal employment, by itself, does not damage children, it must also be emphasized that damage is still possible when children are young, when there is trouble in the family, when the mother is unhappy in her work, and when substitute child care is inadequate. All of these conditions are most prevalent among the poor, and poor women are the ones most likely to have to work outside the home.

Fathering

Beyond the obvious functions of procreation and financial support, what are fathers for? That seems an odd question, but ponder it. The role of the father has been dramatically altered by modernization. He no longer teaches his children to hunt, plant corn, or run the family business. Most children never see their fathers at work and have only the sketchiest notion of what they do. The father plays a reduced role in transmitting cultural values to his children because he knows (and his children perhaps know even better) that many of today's values may not fit tomorrow's world. Those values that seem enduring are being passed on by other agencies, such as the school.

Where does all this change leave the father? The traditional role of the busy breadwinner, the aloof but not unkind disciplinarian, seems ill suited to the new emotionalism of family life. Many men are buffeted by the demands (real and imagined) of their jobs, and they have little time for parenting. Others find themselves sadly lacking in the tender patience that parenting requires. As a consequence, fathers typically spend very little time communicating with their children.

In one small study, researchers asked fathers to estimate the time they spent interacting with their newborn children. On the average, fathers said they spent fifteen minutes per day in such activities. When actual behavior was recorded, however, the researchers found that the fathers were in error. The actual time they spend interacting with their infant children was thirty-eight seconds per

[34] Alison Clarke-Stewart, *Child Care in the Family* (New York: Academic Press, Inc., 1977), pp. 34–35, 48; Helen L. Bee, "The Effects of Maternal Employment on the Development of the Child," in *Social Issues in Developmental Psychology,* ed. Helen L. Bee (New York: Harper and Row, Publishers, 1974), pp. 97–106, available in paperback; J. P. Kagan, B. Kearsley, and P. Zelazio, "The Effects of Infant Day Care on Psychological Development," *Evaluation Quarterly,* Vol. 1, No. 1 (1977), pp. 143–158.

day![35] Are men capable of warm parenting behavior? Research indicates that they are but that they do not have much opportunity to develop these skills. As children, boys are discouraged from practicing child-care skills because such behavior has been seen as effeminate. Until very recently, fathers were not allowed to participate in the birth of their children. They did not benefit from the usual instruction given to mothers by hospital officials, grandparents, and friends.[36]

There is evidence that fathers contribute to the psychological well-being of their children, but the dynamics of this contribution are not well understood. In general, children benefit from fathers who are guiding but not domineering and who are interested in and interact with their children. A rigid, unloving, insecure, and punitive father will probably do his children more harm than good.[37]

Television: The Child's Companion

Television is very much a part of our lives (and especially the lives of our children), and its influence is vast, though not fully understood. With the possible exception of the automobile, no other invention has so radically altered the lives of Americans. Consider the following facts:

- Virtually every home in America has at least one television set. Fifty-five percent of all homes have two or more sets. More homes in the United States have television sets than have indoor plumbing.[38]
- The typical television set is in use more than 7 hours a day. The average viewing time per week for all persons, children and adults, is 31 hours, 28 minutes. The highest use, more than 42 hours per week, is by women over 55.[39]
- Children are heavy users of television. The average American child spends nearly 4 hours a day watching television.[40] Some estimates put the figure for school children as high as 5.5 to 6 hours a day by age twelve.[41]
- Television viewing is particularly prevalent among young children, perhaps because parents find it a convenient baby-sitting device. Preschoolers spend between one-quarter and one-third of their waking hours before a television set.[42] That can amount to nearly 30 hours a week, or three-quarters of the time most adults spend at work.

[35] F. Rebelsky and C. Hanks, "Fathers' Verbal Interaction with Infants in the First Three Months of Life," *Child Development*, Vol. 42 (1971), pp. 63–68.

[36] Ross Parke and D. B. Sawin, "Father-Infant Interaction in the Newborn Period: A Re-evaluation of Some Current Myths," in *Contemporary Readings in Child Psychology*, eds. M. E. Hetherington and R. D. Parke (New York: McGraw-Hill Book Company, 1977), pp. 290–295.

[37] Julius Segal and Herbert Yahraes, *A Child's Journey* (New York: McGraw-Hill Book Company, 1978), p. 129. See also Michael Lamb, "Fathers: Forgotten Contributors to Child Development," *Human Development*, Vol. 18 (1975), pp. 245–266.

[38] *The World Almanac & Book of Facts, 1987* (New York: Newspaper Enterprise Association, Inc., 1986), p. 372.

[39] *Broadcasting/Cablecasting Yearbook 1984*, p. A-2; *World Almanac, 1987*, pp. 147–372.

[40] *World Almanac, 1987*, p. 372.

[41] J. Lyle and H. R. Hoffman, "Children's Use of Television and Other Media," in *Television and Social Behavior*, Vol. 4, *Television in Day-to-Day Life: Patterns of Use*, eds. E. A. Rubinstein, G. A. Comstock, and J. P. Murray (Washington, DC: U.S. Government Printing Office, 1972).

[42] Ibid.; also, *World Almanac, 1987*, p. 372.

- Low-income children watch more television than moderate-income and high-income youngsters. Black children watch more television than do white children.[43]
- Estimates indicate that children spend more time watching television than they do participating in any other single activity except sleep. A child who watches only 2 hours of television a day by age eighteen will have spent more time before a television set than in school.[44]
- Television programming is saturated with violence. One study examined the leading characters in network dramas and found that two out of three characters were involved in violence and about one half committed acts of violence themselves. Children particularly are subjected to violence, not only because they watch so much television, but also because programs designed for children, especially cartoons, contain three times the violence found in adult shows.[45]
- There is growing and convincing—some say compelling—evidence that exposure to television violence increases aggressive behavior in children.[46] Action for Children's Television, a citizen's action group, reviewed 146 articles representing 50 studies involving 10,000 children and adolescents from all walks of life and found that every study confirmed the antisocial effects of television violence.[47]
- Children are vulnerable targets for television advertisers. The average child is exposed to over 25,000 commercials a year. Many of these are designed for young audiences in order to sell sugar-laden junk foods that offer little or no nutritional value. The more they view television, the more favorable children are to advertising. As parents know from taking their children to the supermarket, young children interpret advertising to be "informational," and do not realize until they are older the persuasive intent of the advertising.[48]

---

[43] B. S. Greenberg, "Viewing and Listening Parameters Among British Youngsters," in *Children and Television,* ed. R. Brown (Beverly Hills, CA: Sage Publishing Co., 1976); B. S. Greenberg and J. R. Dominick, "Television Behavior Among Disadvantaged Children," in *Use of the Mass Media by Urban Poor,* eds. B. S. Greenberg and B. Dervin (New York: Frederick A. Praeger, Inc., 1970).

[44] This calculation assumes a six-hour school day, a 180-day school year, twelve years of schooling, and sixteen years of television watching.

[45] George Gerbner, "Violence and Television Drama: Trends and Symbolic Functions," in *Television and Social Behavior: Media Content and Control,* eds. George Comstock and Eli Rubinstein (Washington, DC: U.S. Government Printing Office, 1972), pp. 28–187. See also L. Rowell Huesmann and Leonard D. Eron, "The Development of Aggression in American Children as a Consequence of Television Violence Viewing," in *Television and the Aggressive Child: A Cross-National Comparison,* eds. L. Rowell Huesmann and Leonard D. Eron (Hillsdale, NJ: Lawrence Erlbaum Associates, 1986), Chapter 3.

[46] Ibid.; L. R. Huesmann and L. D. Eron, "Factors Influencing the Effect of Television Violence on Children," in *Learning from Television: Psychological and Educational Research,* ed. Michael A. Howe (New York: Academic Press, Inc., 1983), Chapter 7.

[47] Action for Children's Television, 46 Austin Street, Newtonville, MA 02106. See Robert M. Liebert, Joyce N. Sprafkin, and Emily S. Davidson, *The Early Window: Effects of Television on Children and Youth,* 2d ed. (New York: Pergamon Press, 1982), Chapters 3–5.

[48] Kenneth Keniston and the Carnegie Foundation on *Children, All Our Children: The American Family Under Pressure* (New York: Harcourt Brace Jovanovich, Inc., 1977), pp. 51–59; available in paperback. P. G. Christenson and Donald F. Roberts, "The Role of Television in the Formation of Children's Social Attitudes," in Howe, *Learning from Television,* Chapter 4. Liebert, Sprafkin, and Davidson, *The Early Window,* Chapter 6.

Moderate television viewing can expand the experience of children.   (*Source:* National Education Association, Joe Di Dio.)

• There is evidence that television contributes to sex and race stereotyping and can lead to other kinds of antisocial behavior.[49] As with advertising, these effects seem to increase with the amount of television viewed.

   Clearly, television is a powerful medium and like most powerful things it has potential for both good and evil. On the positive side, television has immensely expanded our experience. It brings political candidates, news events, national celebrations, sports—all things triumphant and tragic—into our living rooms. On the negative side, many believe television constricts our ability to experience. On the one hand, it overloads us with trivial choices. On the other hand, it is a passive medium that asks nothing of us and often substitutes violence and bland comedy for substance. Many teachers feel that television builds in students an expectation that they must be entertained. Students speak of boredom and complain that classes, books, and assignments are not interesting enough. Some of these complaints are, no doubt, warranted, but some may come from the misguided idea that "interest" is an objective quality having little to do with the subjective state of the person. Rather than say, "I am not interested in that," many students contend, "That is not interesting!" But interest is not a one-sided commodity. It grows in a transaction between the mind of the student and some portion of the world. Many teachers suspect that television so overloads students' minds with whiz-bam action and sight-gag comedy that they have little chance to develop a capacity to be interested in everyday life.

---

[49] Christenson and Roberts, "The Role of Television in the Formation of Children's Social Attitudes"; David H. B. Nias, "The Effects of Televised Sex and Pornography," in Howe, *Learning from Television,* Chapter 8; Liebert, Sprafkin, and Davidson, *The Early Window,* Chapter 7.

In comparison to the accelerated action of television, the slower pace of the real world seems dull and uninviting.

Many studies have confirmed the negative effects of television violence on the young, but another line of argument focuses on the behaviors that television prevents. Time spent before the television set is not spent in family communication, on reading, playing games, doing homework, or pursuing hobbies. It can be argued that watching television does not necessarily prevent these activities. Children do homework in front of the television, people talk about their day, eat dinner, and so on. However, the quality of these experiences is severely hindered by the background noise of the electronic performance and its magnetic pull on people's attention.

Television can be a useful educational tool. Even its critics acknowledge that we cannot "undiscover" it and go back to the way life used to be. It is here for good or ill, so we will have to manage it better. What can parents and the school do? It has been pointed out that the influence of television is greater when its message is confirmed by other social agents or when the effort of other institutions is on the wane.[50] So parents and the school must reinforce those values communicated through television that are wholesome. For example, research does *not* support the belief that violence on television is popular or that degrading sex and pornography are attractive to the great majority of television viewers.[51] The attractive messages of television can be combined with other prosocial teaching. In the end, it may be the regular work of the school that keeps the television message in perspective, for it has been said that it may be more feasible to improve children's "information-processing skills," critical intelligence, than it is to regulate the television message.[52]

The Dilemma of the Modern Family

The history of the American family has many dimensions. On the one hand, the family has turned more and more into itself. It has become the emotional nucleus of the private sphere and has helped to shield its members from the alienation of the public world. As this has happened, the family has lost many of its former functions. On the other hand, more and more family members have moved into the public sphere for longer portions of the day. Fathers work outside the home, children attend schools for expanding segments of their lives, wives are in the work force in increasing numbers. Young children of working mothers are sent to baby-sitters or day-care centers. Some children are left alone. So at the same time that the family has become privatized and separated from the wider society, its members spend less and less time with one another. Children's time is taken up with after-school activities, homework, dating, and the rest. Parents give time to commuting to and from work, going to meetings, keeping up the house, entertaining, and so on. And nearly everyone watches television. This leaves little time for the communal activities of family life, including child rearing. It makes it difficult for families to perform their primary functions: to reduce the alienation of the public sphere, provide emotional sta-

---

[50] Christenson and Roberts, ibid, pp. 94–95.
[51] Nias, "The Effects of Televised Sex and Pornography," p. 189.
[52] Christenson and Roberts, "The Role of Television in the Formation of Children's Social Attitudes," p. 96.

bility and moral commitment, and give individuals a place where they can "let down their hair," think out loud, and be themselves.

The Meaning of Family: A Summary

One might think that, before we can talk meaningfully about the family or outline its functions, we need to define what a family is. But this is not necessarily so. The belief reflects the assumption that knowledge is derived from definitions, when the reverse is more likely the case. That is, until there is inquiry, leading to the clarification of ideas and then to knowledge—as we have done in the discussion of the family—the meaning or definition of a word or practice is unknown. This is to say that words are not defined in the abstract; their meanings come from their uses.

So it is with the "family." We can see in the history of the family that the concept has changed. There is the "nuclear" family (father and mother and children) and the "extended" family (father and mother and children and relatives), the single-parent family, and, more common today, the "blended" family (previously divorced fathers and mothers living together with children from other marriages and sometimes from their own). What do we mean when we talk about the family in this chapter?

Etzioni believes that the number of parents who are in the home, whether they both work, and similiar things are not the essential issues. He envisions an "essential family" that, in order to carry on the educational mission of the family, has two features: *basic parenting,* or active and involved parents with time, energy, and commitment during the formative years of childhood, certainly to the age of six but preferably through adolescence; and a *mutually supportive educational coalition* among the adults in the home to promote academic achievement and to provide emotional support.[53] Any adults who perform these functions with children in the home constitute a family. We make a point of this idea to show that primary adults in the home, whoever they may be, must support and prepare children for schoolwork, and that role is related to what we have said above about the primary functions of families today. On the other hand, schools also must support the family. Let us see what they can do.

The Response of Schools to the Changing Family

How have schools responded to the changes in family life? One response has already been mentioned. Schools have expanded their curricula to include work formerly done in the family setting. They have attempted to overpower real and imagined deficiencies in the family by providing such remedies as compensatory education, values clarification, and counseling services. John Goodlad has given a long list of what we expect schools to do.[54] The tasks are numerous.

---

[53] Etzioni, *An Immodest Agenda,* Chapter 5. Brigitte and Peter L. Berger support the "bourgeois" family (often against the "bohemian") in *The War Over the Family: Capturing the Middle Ground* (Garden City, NY: Anchor Press/Doubleday, 1983).

[54] John Goodlad, *What Schools Are For* (Bloomington, IN: Phi Delta Kappa Educational Foundation, 1979).

In short, the schools have become educational *and* social service agencies. All of this has been expensive, and schools have increased in size in an effort to be more cost effective. As a result, schools have become bigger and school personnel more specialized. The interaction between the school and the community has become increasingly formal and bureaucratic. In short, schools have become more like megastructures and less like families.

New Directions in Education

Virtually all school systems have expanded during the last few decades. Some systems, however, have begun to question the wisdom of their present practices. They have examined their operations and realized how little communication exists between parents and the school. They realize that if parents become separated from the activities of the school, they are separated from the school life of their children. Rather than supporting the family, schools have unwittingly driven a wedge between the experiences of parents and the lives of their children.

Some school systems have developed programs designed to close the gaps between the school and the family and the parent and the child. Parents-as-Partners programs have begun in numerous cities and towns across America, from Jacksonville, Florida, to Yakima, Washington. Often beginning as programs for low-income families, these programs have expanded to reach all homes. School personnel go out into the community for home visits. They explain school programs, discuss student progress, and invite parent involvement in the classroom. School officials go on television and radio to discuss school policies and educational innovations. Some schools are providing home-learning activities designed for parents to do with their children.

These programs have interesting objectives. Realizing that parents are children's first and most influential teachers, the programs attempt to utilize parents in the education of children. Educational programs are explained to parents so that they will support school efforts through home activities. When this manifest function is accomplished, at least two latent functions follow. First, parents spend more time in educational activities with their children. Family communication is enhanced, and parents better grasp what is going on in the school life of their children. Second, schools that invite parent participation soon find parents offering assistance and advice to teachers. As schools incorporate parents' ideas and listen to their concerns, the parent–school relationship becomes less formal and less alienating. Parents become more approachable and schools less aloof. When such programs are run successfully, the educational system becomes more attuned to the values and concerns of the people it serves.

Hazards of Ignoring Family Problems

When there are problems in the family, they are often reflected in the behavior of children. Educators, facing these troublesome behaviors, have tried to solve the behavior problem in the school. A number of difficulties result. Knowingly or not, schools are treating symptoms rather than causes. They are treating the behavior of the child without paying attention to the family problems that initiated these behaviors.

Such services (whether they be group counseling, drug education, sex education, or instruction in middle-class values) are too often initiated without family consultation or involvement. An extreme case will make the point. A small-city school assigned a number of "troubled children" to sensitivity-training classes. Parents were not informed, school officials explained, because sensitivity-training was easily misunderstood and could cause parents undue worry. If parents became upset, the effectiveness of the program would be diminished. Parents, of course, found out about the sensitivity training and were angered that they had not been informed that their children were having trouble in school. They were further offended because their children were given "psychological treatment" without parental consent. In other words, the effect was exactly what the school officials had hoped to avoid by not informing the parents!

This example has many interesting facets, just one of which will be emphasized here. School officials tried to solve student problems without consulting parents. In doing so, they elevated themselves to the position of experts who knew "what is best" for their students. They left parents out of the diagnosis of the problem and did not invite parents to take part in its solution. Such actions widened the gap between parents and the school. By not allowing parents to share in their children's problems, school officials further disconnected parents from the lives of their children.

The irony of this behavior is that by leaving parents out of their children's problems, educators have increased the chances of school failure. If problems start in the home, the chances are great that they will have to be solved there. Chances are slim that schools can solve home-based problems without parental involvement. We have used an extreme example here to emphasize the need for parent–school interaction. We do not mean to suggest, however, that this cooperation is necessary only in extreme cases. What has been said here about sensitivity training could just as well be said about reading or mathematics programs. Parents who understand what is going on in the school will be in a better position to help their children.

Schools as Mediating Institutions

Many sociologists have studied the importance of the primary group in the lives of individuals. Charles Cooley (1864–1929) described primary groups as

> those characterized by face-to-face association and cooperation. They are primary in several senses, but chiefly in that they are fundamental in the forming of the social nature and ideals of the individual.[55]

Cooley was convinced that institutions need the guidance of ideals that grow in face-to-face interaction. "Where do we get those notions of love, freedom, justice and the like which we are ever applying to social institutions?" he asked in *Social Organization.* "Not from abstract philosophy, surely, but from the actual life of simple and wide-spread forms of society like the family or the play group."[56] When primary groups break down and can no longer generate and perpetuate social ideals, society is "diseased at its source."[57] For this reason,

[55] Charles Horton Cooley, *Social Organization* (New York: Schocken Books, Inc., 1962), p. 23. Available in paperback.
[56] Ibid., p. 32.
[57] Ibid., p. 49.

Cooley claimed, primary groups must be "watched and cherished with a very special care."[58] Without them, institutions lose their humane, moral purpose and become dedicated only to self-preservation and expansion. Individuals lose their connection with society and their sense of meaning, purpose, and identity. As we have discussed in previous chapters, these trends are underway in modern society.

What can education do to guard the family (the most significant primary group in our society) against the encroachments of impersonal institutions? For one thing, schools can work to diminish their own impersonality. They can encourage parental involvement and heighten the interaction between parent and child. Rather than becoming another institution of the megastructure, schools can become "mediating institutions." These institutions, Peter Berger explains, stand "between the individual in his private life and the large institutions of public life."[59] What would a school do if it acted as a mediating institution? Such answers have already been suggested in the Parent-as-Partners programs just discussed. A list of specific activities would probably be misleading, for appropriate activities will vary with shifting conditions. More important to note here are the principles that undergird the school as a mediating institution:

- Such schools recognize that parents are a child's most powerful teachers and usually the best judges of a child's needs.
- Such schools recognize the family as a vital institution, are sensitive to the pressures upon families, and work to alleviate these pressures. They are especially careful not to add unnecessarily to the pressures of family life.
- Such schools work to keep families informed about school activities and actively solicit parental involvement.
- Educators in such schools test their ideas through open discussion with parents. They resist the temptation to see themselves as expert professionals and to view parents as ignorant laypersons. They remain willing to hear other points of view and to modify their policies accordingly.
- Such schools do not simply blame parents for nonparticipation; they actually seek ways to integrate parents into school activities.[60] This sometimes involves training parents in new skills; it sometimes calls for changes in routine school practices. It always involves allowing parents to have a voice in the policies and practices that affect the lives of family members.

None of these principles is particularly new or innovative. They are simply democratic. Schools have slipped away from these essentials of democracy, not through conscious planning but rather through rapid growth. Much is heard nowadays of the back-to-basics movement. If schools are to move in this direction, a sensible place to begin is to return to the fundamentals of democratic participation.

---

[58] Ibid., p. 33.

[59] Peter L. Berger and Richard John Neuhaus, *To Empower People: The Role of Mediating Structures in Public Policy* (Washington, DC: American Enterprise Institute for Public Policy Research, 1977), p. 2. Available in paperback.

[60] For a book-length discussion of parent involvement, see Ira Gordon and William Breivogel, *Building Effective Home–School Relationships* (Boston: Allyn & Bacon, Inc., 1976).

Summary

The American family has evolved from a public institution, well integrated into the community, into a private institution, clearly separate from the outside world. Its evolution has been marked by an increasingly romantic relationship between husband and wife and an increasingly love-oriented relationship between parent and child. As the family developed emotional significance, it lost many of its former functions. Families are no longer the nation's basic unit of production but rather its basic unit of consumption. Children have become a financial liability rather than a financial asset. It costs the average middle-income family more than $85,000 to raise and provide a college education for one child.[61]

Schools have taken over the education of children (and much of the socialization function as well), doctors have increasing responsibility for health care, and entertainment industries have now replaced family fun. These developments have contributed to the isolation of families from the public sphere and have reduced the confidence of parents in their own abilities to raise children. Experts are called on to monitor the progress of a child, diagnose his or her problems, and suggest solutions. This monitoring is done, in many cases, without meaningful consultation with parents. The family is assumed to be incompetent, the expert all-knowing. Many experts in the helping professions are not accountable to parents but rather to their agency superiors. Thus, the family has been weakened even as it has taken on increased emotional significance for its members.

Worry that the family is no longer functional in America is probably mistaken. The family plays a vital role in the private sphere and, for most Americans, still provides a matrix for the development, redevelopment, and maintenance of personal identity and meaning. Soaring divorce statistics stand as testimony to the high expectations we have for marriage and do not necessarily indicate that the institution has become obsolete. In fact, after a period of lessened popularity, interest in marriage has rebounded. However, the rising divorce rate does indicate that the family is having difficulty in doing all that is expected of it. Economic strains, the increased incidence of working mothers, the limited opportunity for family interaction, and the shrinking role of the father in child rearing all challenge the viability of the family unit.

School personnel must understand the problems facing the American family. It is easy to use these problems as an argument for extending the influence of what are called the "helping" professions—education, social services, health care—but, in the long run, such tactics will only further debilitate the family.[62] The wiser course for the helping professions, especially education, will be to strengthen the family rather than feed on its weaknesses. This can be done by sharing with parents knowledge, decision-making power, and the responsibility for educating children. The helping professions must see parents in a new light, as potentially capable, caring, and knowledgeable—as unrealized potential—rather than as perpetually incompetent, apathetic, and ignorant.

[61] Thomas J. Espenshade, "Raising a Child Can Now Cost $85,000," *Intercom* (September 1980), p. 1. Population Reference Bureau, Inc. 1754 N Street, N.W., Washington, DC 20036.

[62] See Gilbert Steiner, *The Futility of Family Policy* (New Haven: Yale University Press, 1981).

Suggested Readings

The family is a fundamental institution in society. The study of its historical development is a fascinating undertaking.

GREVEN, PHILIP. *The Protestant Temperament.* New York: New American Library, 1977. This is an elegant account of family life in Puritan America.

HANDLIN, OSCAR, and MARY F. HANDLIN. *Facing Life: Youth and Family in American History.* Boston: Little, Brown & Company, 1971. More readable but less convincing than Greven and Shorter's works, this book nevertheless contains interesting ideas.

SHORTER, EDWARD. *The Making of the Modern Family.* New York: Basic Books, Inc., Publishers, 1975. One of the most substantial and significant works in the field, the book is indispensable for anyone who wants to understand the development of the modern family in Western culture.

An important component of family history is the history of childhood.

ARIÈS, PHILIPPE. *Centuries of Childhood.* New York: Alfred A. Knopf, Inc., 1962. Now a classic, this book surveys the history of child rearing over several centuries.

HUNT, DAVID. *Parents and Children in History.* New York: Basic Books, Inc., Publishers, 1970. The author compares Ariès's approach to childhood with the psychohistorical analysis of Erik Erikson.

Modern interpretations of family life in America include

BANE, MARY JO. *Here to Stay: American Families in the 20th Century.* New York: Basic Books, Inc., Publishers, 1978. Bane amasses overwhelming evidence that family life, though changing, is alive and well in America.

LASCH, CHRISTOPHER. *Heaven in a Heartless World: The Family Besieged.* New York: Basic Books, Inc., Publishers, 1979. This is a less hopeful but no less convincing analysis of family life today.

The influence of television and its effects on the young are causes of growing concern.

ADLER, RICHARD, et al. *The Effects of Television Advertising on Children.* Lexington, MA: Lexington Books, 1980.

BROWN, RAY, ed. *Children and Television.* Beverly Hills, CA: Sage Publications, Inc., 1976.

JOHNSON, NICHOLAS. *How to Talk Back to Your Television Set.* Boston: Little, Brown & Company, 1967.

LIEBERT, ROBERT M., JOHN M. NEALE, and EMILY S. DAVIDSON. *The Early Window: Effects of Television on Children and Youth.* New York: Pergamon Press, Inc., 1975.

WINICK, MARIANN P., and CHARLES WINICK. *The Television Experience.* Beverly Hills, CA: Sage Publications, Inc., 1977.

WINN, MARIE. *The Plug-In Drug.* New York: The Viking Press, 1977.

Methods for improving the family–school relationship are topics that now interests social scientists and educators alike.

DOUGLAS, I. W. *The Home and School.* London: MacGibbon and Kee, 1964. This study of a national sample of 5000 children in England found that parent interest and involvement with their primary-school-aged children accounted for four times as much of the variation in children's scores on intelligence and achievement tests as did measures of school quality.

GORDON, IRA, and WILLIAM BREIVOGEL. *Building Effective Home–School Relationships.* Boston: Allyn & Bacon, Inc., 1976. This book describes a model, called follow-through, designed to bridge the gap between the home and classroom.

LEICHTER, HOPE JENSEN, ed. *The Family as Educator.* New York: Teachers College, Columbia University Press, 1974. This book presents perspectives from the social sciences.

LIGHTFOOT, SARA LAWRENCE. *Worlds Apart: Relationships Between Families and Schools.* New York: Basic Books, Inc., Publishers, 1978. This is an account of the present barriers between families and schools that, according to the author, are often erected by educators. Professor Lightfoot proposes that schools and parents must build a positive alliance.

CHAPTER 7

Civic Education

The topic of this chapter is civic education, or the education of citizens for citizenship. We will begin with our colonial and revolutionary periods and show that from the very beginning education has had that aim. At times, the aim has been approached indirectly, through the teaching of reading and spelling and through history and literature. Thus, we will trace the impulse for civic education through early schoolbooks, some of which are still in use.

Civic education is a part of moral education, which often has been based on religion. Yet in the United States, the relationship between religion and government (of which schooling is a part) has been carefully structured to assure that neither dominates the other. We will describe this relationship as it has evolved historically and examine the present status of religion in education.

Finally, we will outline the shape that civic and moral education might take in the future. The chapter is ambitious in that we want to show some of the history of American education, discuss the place of religion in education, and describe the view that civic and moral education are primary aims in education. The discussion is lengthy but, we hope, clear and persuasive.

The Political Connection

The subject matter of civic education is political. That is, education not only reflects the political character of a society but has political aims as well. Thomas Jefferson made the connection for the new American society when he said that a civilized nation cannot expect to remain both free and ignorant.[1] Since Jefferson's time, we have used education to support our political way of life.

Education thus has a direct connection with politics. This connection can be traced from the beginning of Western thought. The important purpose of political theory is to initiate the citizen into the life of the community, and government exists, at least in part, to perform this task. It does so through educational activities, an important one of which is schooling.

[1] Letter to Colonel Charles Yancy (January 6, 1816) in John Bartlett, *Familiar Quotations*, 14th ed., ed. Emily Morison Beck (Boston: Little, Brown and Company, 1968), p. 473a.

The subject matter of civic education is political. (*Source:* National Education Association, Joe Di Dio.)

The English political philosopher Sir Ernest Barker makes the point clearly when he says that "the theory of education is essentially a part of political theory."[2] As evidence, he notes that the Greek educational tradition involves more than the psychology of learning and teaching (though that is important). The theory of education essentially is social, or political, theory; it involves the purposes, character, and needs of society and methods by which the young can be trained to achieve those things.

Thus, because the primary purpose of education is political, it is also moral. Education has the moral aim of producing citizens who will identify with, support, and improve the community.

A Definition of Civic Education

One writer has said that "Civic education now carries so many definitions that it has no useful meaning."[3] The term is imprecise because it covers so much territory. The study of civic education leads in many different directions: into such topics as political socialization, moral and spiritual values, values educa-

[2] Ernest Barker, *Church, State and Education* (Ann Arbor: University of Michigan Press, 1957), p. 192.
[3] James M. Banner, Jr., "Thinking About Civic Education," in *Civic Learning for Teachers: Capstone for Educational Reform,* ed. Alan H. Jones (Ann Arbor, MI: Prakken Publications, 1985), pp. 25–26.

tion, national values (see Chapter 5), and the aims of education (see Chapter 8). So vast a topic may appear to have no set boundary and, thus, no terrain of its own.

However, the problem of imprecision is not solved by abandoning the label and idea of civic education. It is solved by making its definition more precise. *Civic* comes from a Latin word meaning "belonging to citizens."[4] Its early use referred to a civic crown, a garland of oak leaves and acorns, given as a prize to someone who had saved the life of a fellow citizen in war. The term thus emphasizes the *responsibility* and *service* that a citizen has toward others, which is to say to the community.

The word *civic* has been used historically to indicate the rights and obligations of *citizenship,* in contrast to private concerns, for example. Civil rights are those that one has by virtue of being a citizen of a political community. Whatever rights and duties one may have in the private sphere, say as a member of a family or a church, usually depend on other things.

Political and Civic Education in Our Early History

Early Americans were not as confused about civic education as we seem to be today. Those who had very different political inclinations, such as Thomas Jefferson and James Madison, on one side, and Alexander Hamilton and Noah Webster, on another, nevertheless agreed that the ultimate good of education was its moral and civic outcomes. The French social philosopher, Alexis de Tocqueville, studying America in the 1830s, observed that

> In the United States politics are the end and aim of education . . .[and] the in-struction of the people powerfully contributes to the support of the democratic republic. . . . Every citizen receives the [elements] . . . of knowledge; [but] he is taught, moreover, the doctrines and evidences of his religion, the history of his country, and the leading features of its Constitution. . . . If you question an American . . . respecting his own country . . . his thoughts [will be clear and precise]. He will inform you what his rights are and by what means he exercises them; he will be able to point out the customs which obtain in the political world.[5]

Since that time, we have become less certain about the virtue and character of civic education. There are many reasons for this, which we will notice in our discussion. The concern for civic education seems to become urgent whenever we perceive our society to be in crisis. It was urgent to Thomas Jefferson and Noah Webster, trying to begin a new nation, and to the early promoters of public schooling. Once established, though, civic education may be taken for granted, by which we mean not that it is wholly forgotten but that citizenship is accomplished as a matter of course and does not require special attention. Thus, in times of crisis, a clear vision of civic education is not available, and the effort to promote it has to begin anew. That is where we seem to be today.

---

[4] See *The Oxford English Dictionary* (1970 edition). The OED is an authoritative source to begin a search for the meaning of an idea. Here, we find not just the meaning of a word but its origin, history, and uses. A good dictionary gives insight into the history of ideas.

[5] Alexis de Tocqueville, *Democracy in America,* 2 vols. (New York: Random House, Inc., 1945 [1835]), Vol. 1, pp. 327–330. Available in paperback.

R. Freeman Butts, an educational historian, has been a leading promoter of civic education for American schools for the last fifteen years. Butts believes that we should not try to solve all urgent social, economic, and intellectual problems through civic education but should focus on the political. Political education should be interpreted broadly and should go beyond simply presenting information to students.[6] Rather, civic education should include political values and concepts as well as political knowledge and participation. Moreover, it should engage controversial political issues and develop and use political analysis and participatory skills. Butts says,

> The goal of civic education for American schools is to . . . motivate . . . and enable [students] to play their parts as informed, responsible, committed, and effective members of a modern democratic political system. This . . . should include . . . three basic aspects: political values, political knowledge, and the skills of political participation needed for making deliberate choices among real alternatives.[7]

Butts's idea is not different from the characteristics of good citizenship listed by the National Assessment of Educational Progress. A good citizen is one who

- Understands the structure and function of government;
- Shows concern for the dignity and well-being of other people;
- Supports justice and rights for all;
- Understands national and world problems;
- Deals rationally with public issues and decisions;
- Participates in democratic civic improvement.[8]

Butts says that the ideas and concepts that form the common core of American citizenship are justice, freedom, equality, diversity, authority, privacy, due process, participation, personal obligation for the public good, and international human rights.[9] The program for civic education is to instill an understanding of and working appreciation for these central ideas. The question is how to accomplish this aim.

Early Schoolbooks

In the early years of our country, the most widely read books were not written by intellectuals but were schoolbooks written by printers, journalists, teachers, ministers, and future lawyers. Though perhaps ill-qualified to do so, the authors of early schoolbooks defined our national past and, in so doing, helped to shape the nation's future. Early textbooks were more interested in instilling "civic virtue" than in promoting learning and more interested in developing moral character than in providing technical training.[10] In modern terms, their aim was civic education.

---

[6] R. Freeman Butts, *The Revival of Civic Learning: A Rationale for Citizenship Education in American Schools* (Bloomington, IN: Phi Delta Kappa Educational Foundation, 1980), pp. 122–123.

[7] Ibid., p. 123.

[8] Catherine Cornbleth, "Citizenship Education," in *Encyclopedia of Educational Research*, 5th ed. (New York: The Free Press, 1982), Vol. I, pp. 259–265.

[9] Butts, *The Revival of Civic Learning*, Chapter 5.

[10] Ruth Miller Elson, *Guardians of Tradition: American Schoolbooks of the Nineteenth Century* (Lincoln: University of Nebraska Press, 1964), pp. vii, 1, 8.

The New England Primer

The New England Primer was not the first schoolbook in America. That distinction probably belongs to the hornbook, which was not a book at all, but a wooden tablet or paddle. On the paddle was mounted a sheet of paper with the alphabet, vowels, syllables, and some religious material such as the Lord's Prayer. The "book" was covered with a thin layer of animal horn to keep it from becoming soiled.

The New England Primer was the most successful early schoolbook; it was printed between 1687 and 1886 and sold at least 3 million copies. It has been called "The Little Bible of New England."[11] There is no doubt it began as a Bible. Paul Leicester Ford comments that uniting alphabet instruction with religious creed is as old as printed books, but early primers were not schoolbooks but *primary* manuals of church service. When reading instruction was added to the manuals, the books came to be called *primers*. The New England Puritans believed that men and women had a direct relationship to God and needed no intermediary. Thus, all people had to think, read, and reason for themselves. But this presented a danger, for if all people reason for themselves, none may think alike. Extreme individualism (or what today we call privatism) and heresy might result from too much independent thought. So, though it may appear contradictory, children were taught what to believe. This was the function of *The New England Primer*.[12]

Though the primers varied widely, depending on where and by whom they were printed, certain characteristics tended to mark the primer. They began with letters of the alphabet, followed by instruction (actually, repetitions) in vowels, consonants, double letters, capital letters, and italic letters. These were followed by lessons on syllables, which began with simple combinations and progressed by degrees to simple words and finally to words of six syllables. After that there was usually a series of moral and instructive sentences from the Bible. Every primer also contained the Lord's Prayer and the Apostles' Creed.

The New England Primer was famous for its series of rhymes and pictures designed to carry an alphabetical and moral lesson. Perhaps you have seen an example such as the one shown in Figure 7-1. These lessons are interesting to the modern-day educator and historian, not only because of their religious content but because they use pictures to present the lessons. The use of pictures was an innovation coming from the theory of the Czechoslovakian educator, John Amos Comenius (1592–1670).

A common belief is that the primers represented primarily a religious and dogmatic point of view. That is probably true, but the primers did change over the years. Those changes reflected changes in religious dogma and also new views of how children learn. In some periods, the primers took on an evangelical flavor and at others they became more secular. Children had difficulty with early primers, so changes were welcome. One of the things contained in *The New England Primer* was the Westminster Assembly's "Shorter Catechism," which

---

[11] Paul Leicester Ford, ed. *The New England Primer* (New York: Teachers College Press, 1962 [1727 ed.]), p. 1. Available in paperback.

[12] Ibid., pp. 4, 8; Clifton Johnson, *Old-Time Schools and School Books* (Gloucester, MA: Peter Smith, 1963 [1904]), pp. 69–70.

In Adam's Fall
We finned all.

Thy Life to mend,
God's Book attend.

The Cat doth play,
And after flay.

A Dog will bite
A Thief at Night.

The Eagle's Flight
Is out of Sight.

The idle Fool
Is whipt at School

Figure 7-1   A page from *The New England Primer.*

ran to 107 questions, the rote answers to which ranged from 8 to 100 words each![13] Children as young as four or five were expected to recite the catechism with "absolute . . . correctness."[14] For many it was a harrowing experience. Even Cotton Mather acknowledged that the Shorter Catechism was difficult for young children, and he preferred John Cotton's "Spiritual Milk for American Babes," a briefer catechism that was widely printed in the primers after 1690.

The point is that the primers were not static, but changed with circumstances, and there were many motives behind these changes. The primers became more secularized (more "civic" and less religious) as the colonies grew and the population became more diverse. Also, the primers attempted to keep up with advanced thinking about the instruction of youth. The primers also changed when the colonies won independence from England. A new civic morality had to be emphasized. Whereas the early primers opened with a picture of George II or George III, after the Declaration of Independence the picture of patriots such as John Hancock and Samuel Adams took their place. At the end of the Revolution, the standard portrait was of Washington.[15]

The move away from religion as an explicit support for morality started after the War of Independence and was clearly present by 1800. The religious emphasis was replaced by "civic" sanction. Good behavior was rewarded and bad behavior punished, not by the intervention of God but by the workings of the marketplace. Children were no longer taught with letters so they could read the Bible, but so they could prosper economically:

---

[13] Nevertheless, it was an improvement on another catechism that had 1200 questions and answers. See Ford, *The New England Primer,* pp. 37–44.
[14] Ibid., p. 39.
[15] Ibid., pp. 47, 49.

He who ne'er learns his A. B. C.
Forever will a blockhead be.
But he who learns his letters fair
Shall have a coach to take the air.[16]

"Success" had become the moral measure of one's life.

Webster's Speller

Noah Webster (1758–1843) was contemporary with the American Revolution and its political and military heroes. He was trained as a lawyer; became a schoolmaster; lectured Jefferson, Hamilton, and Madison on politics; edited newspapers; wrote a "History of Epidemics"; promoted copyright law and the census; and even revised the Bible. He also produced a new version of *The New England Primer.* The historian Henry Steele Commager has called him, not unkindly, "a cultural busybody."[17]

Webster's idea was to build the new American society by promoting nationalism through language reform. America had separated from Great Britain to become a polyglot of traditions, languages and dialects, religious beliefs, and political interests. It no longer could depend on the usual supports for nationalism: monarchy, state religion, and historical tradition. Moreover, after the Revolution, Americans began to quarrel among themselves. Differences in background, class, and religion had to be harmonized. Unity had to be found in diversity and a "national character" had to be formed.[18] The new nation needed a common language and a distinctively American literature. Webster spent his life promoting these ends.

Webster had wanted to call his first book *The American Spelling Book,* but the president of Yale College overruled him and gave the book the ponderous title, *A Grammatical Institute of the English Language.* Fortunately, the book survived its title and became an immediate best seller, in 1783. In 1807, Webster estimated that it was selling 200,000 copies a year, and by 1837 he estimated that the total sales had reached 15 million copies. As late as 1880, 100 years after its first edition, the speller still sold at the rate of 1 million copies a year, and it still is in print today. To date it has sold between 70 and 100 million copies.[19]

The book changed names three times, from the original *Institute,* to Webster's favored *American Spelling Book,* and finally, *The Elementary Spelling Book.* But its common name soon became, and remains today, the Blue-Back Speller because of the blue covers in which it was bound. Webster earned less than a penny a copy for each speller, but the proceeds were enough to support him and his family for the rest of his life. The income left him free to pursue his other interests and to compile his famous dictionary.[20]

The aim of the speller was not simply to teach reading but to promote moral

---

[16] Ibid., p. 47.
[17] Henry Steele Commager, "Schoolmaster of America," in *Noah Webster's American Spelling Book* (New York: Teachers College Press, 1962 [1831 ed.]), p. 4. Available in paperback.
[18] E. Jennifer Monaghan, *A Common Heritage: Noah Webster's Blue-Back Speller* (Hampden, CT: Archon Books, 1983), pp. 13, 234, n. 15.
[19] Ibid., pp. 11; 232, n. 1. Also, Lawrence A. Cremin, "Preface," in *Noah Webster's American Spelling Book.*
[20] Johnson, *Old-Time Schools and School Books,* pp. 168–169. For a different opinion, see Richard J. Moss, *Noah Webster* (Boston: Twayne Publishers, 1984), pp. 25–26.

education. Webster wanted to instill in students "some just ideas of religion, morals, and domestic economy."[21] The speller did not teach values overtly or in a heavy-handed way but through "the first rudiments of the language." It included lessons in the alphabet, sounds and syllables, pronunciation, and reading; however, everything was aimed at morality. The speller gave "advice"; reprinted fables with their morals; and had a "moral catechism" emphasizing the virtues of humility, justice, gratitude, charity, industry, and cheerfulness and condeming laziness, revenge, and greed. The important thing is that instruction in language was *combined* with its moral aim. The goal of the speller was "to teach children to read, and to know their duties."[22] Rules of pronunciation were combined with lessons in manners, morals, rules, and social precepts.

The average person today is familiar with Noah Webster through the dictionaries that still bear his name. Webster worked for twenty-five years to produce his *American Dictionary of the English Language,* which came into print in 1828. Like the spelling book, the project had a nationalistic aim. "Let us seize the present moment," Webster said, "and establish a *national language,* . . . as well as a national government. . . . A *national language* is a band of national union."[23] Webster wanted to simplify the language and free it from some of its European origins. He set out to demolish the "odious distinctions of provincial dialects" and make learning the American language easy for both native youth and foreigners through accurate and uniform pronunciation. He attempted to simplify and Americanize spelling. In this effort, he leaned on Benjamin Franklin, who shared his interest in making spelling easier and uniform. For example, Webster proposed such words as "hed" and "nabor," but he was not successful in getting their adoption, for the new spellings, though simpler, were too unconventional. But Webster was able to make some changes that have come to distinguish American from British English, such as reversing the *er* in *center* and *theater,* dropping the *u* in such words as *honor* and *labor,* and the *k* from such words as *public.*[24]

It was apparent in Webster's speller that students were to be drilled in the national virtues, not that they should learn to think for themselves. Webster was intent on teaching children but was less concerned about whether children understood what they read. Drill was the important thing. After the introduction of McGuffey's readers, with their better literary content and their attempt in increasing understanding, the spellers became spellers in the narrower sense of the word. When that occurred, the power of the speller as an instrument of moral instruction began to wane.[25]

McGuffey's Readers

In 1836, seven years before Noah Webster's death, William Holmes McGuffey, a minister and professor at Miami University of Ohio, published his first "graded,

---

[21] *Noah Webster's American Spelling Book* [1803], p. 18.
[22] Ibid., p. 55.
[23] Noah Webster, "The Reform of Spelling," reprinted in *Old South Leaflets,* Vol. VII (Boston: Directors of Old South Work, 1896 [1789]), pp. 396, 389. Emphasis in original.
[24] Ibid. See also Monaghan, *A Common Heritage,* p. 200.
[25] For use of the spellers in spelling bees, see Edward Eggleston, *The Hoosier Schoolmaster* (New York: Grosset & Dunlap, 1899 [1871]). Available in paperback.

eclectic reader." He thus continued a tradition that had begun with *The New England Primer* and was to run into the twentieth century. Other schoolbooks were available, but *The New England Primer,* Webster's spellers, and McGuffey's readers dominated American education for more than two centuries.

Webster's spellers and McGuffey's readers were alike in some respects. Their aims were to build a nation of one people, and they emphasized moral training. Both Webster and McGuffey were social and pedagogical conservatives. Webster's spellers changed hardly at all over his lifetime and, though McGuffey's readers changed in some ways, as we shall see, that is not because of his influence. One McGuffey scholar has said that no experience after he introduced his readers significantly changed his life or ideas. "With a single-minded determination and commitment, he spent his life striving to pass on his convictions to the next generation."[26]

But this is not to say that Webster's spellers and McGuffey's readers were essentially the same. Had they been, there would be no way to account for why the readers supplanted the spellers. McGuffey replaced Webster because his books improved reading instruction. McGuffey realized, as Webster did not, that children should understand what they read. His text also was an advance in intellectual and literary quality.

At first, McGuffey was an experimenter. He compiled the contents of his readers by gathering neighborhood children into age groups and trying out the lessons on them. The lessons were his own writings, magazine clippings, literary selections from the Bible and other works, and "borrowings" from other schoolbooks. (Though this was a standard practice of the day, McGuffy was accused of plagiarism and rewrote some material because of it.[27]) Thus the books were called "graded, eclectic readers." The "grade" indicated students' interest, ability, and comprehension levels. The series contained six readers, each aimed at a different ability level. "Eclectic," of course, refers to the books' contents, which were compiled from many sources.

Because the readers bear McGuffey's name, anyone may think that he compiled them all and that his sentiments can be found in the entire series. But McGuffey was the author of only the first four readers. His brother compiled the fifth and sixth readers, and McGuffey himself was not responsible for the readers after 1857. His name was added to the headline of the readers only in 1857, probably to ensure sales. The readers changed by 1879, emphasizing more the secular, middle-class values, and less the Presbyterian principles of McGuffey. Nevertheless, their moral tone remained.

The readers sold 120 million copies between 1836 and 1920, and still sold at the rate of 30,000 copies a year in 1960.[28] Henry Ford, the industrialist, reprinted the readers in 1928, emphasizing the "profound respect" his generation had for the moral principles they stressed. Industry, thrift, obedience, and patriotism are some of those principles. For having set all this in motion, McGuffey earned only $1000 from the sale of his books.

The reader is still printed. The 1879 edition of the fifth reader is a good one to examine. It contains fifty pages of introductory matter that emphasizes

[26] John H. Westerhoff, III, *McGuffey and His Readers: Piety, Morality, and Education in Nineteenth-Century America* (Nashville: Abingdon, 1978), p. 49.

[27] Ibid., pp. 45, 54–55.

[28] Ibid., pp. 14–15.

that this is an *advanced reader:* articulation, inflection, accent, emphasis, modulation, poetic pauses, and exercises. The remainder of the book is selections (117 in number) in prose and poetry. Some of the authors are Louisa May Alcott, Dickens, Hawthorne, Longfellow, Shakespeare, Tennyson, and Thoreau. It also includes selections from the Bible. The authors of the selections are identified, and definitions, pronunciations, and other useful instruction are given.

Henry Steele Commager, who wrote a Foreword to a recent reprinting of the fifth and sixth readers (1879 editions), characterizes their morality as certainly religious but more Protestant and Puritan than anything else. At the same time, the morality was materialistic and worldly. Good would be rewarded and error punished but in this world and by a gain or loss of personal and economic advantage. The values were middle class, conventional, and egalitarian, and, it was claimed, they applied to everyone in equal measure. Individual acts always had civic and moral consequences, which were always for the best because they were "deserved." The readers also reflected a distrust of governmental power that is characteristic of *both* Puritanism *and* Jeffersonianism.[29]

Finally, the readers are romantic. They take no notice of current events. Commager notes that the fifth reader, published in 1879, had only one selection about the Civil War and that was "a masterpiece of impartiality."[30] The readers certainly were noncontroversial, and this, no doubt, increased sales. They ignored anything that would challenge the taken-for-granted values of federalism, patriotism, Protestant religion, and middle-class morality.[31]

The McGuffey readers had a great attraction, and it will pay to determine what that attraction was and still is. Their contribution to education is paradoxical if not ironic. They conceived education to be primarily moral and only secondarily intellectual; the aim of education was to train character. In this, they echoed the sentiments of Noah Webster who had said,

> The great art to correcting mankind . . . consists in prepossessing the mind with good principles. . . . The *virtues* of men are of more consequence to society than their abilities, and for this reason the *heart* should be cultivated with more assiduity than the *head.*[32]

On the other hand, their literary content assured that some individuals, at least, received an intellectual education. (Most children, if they were in school at all, did not go beyond the fourth—intermediate—reader.) Hamlin Garland, writing about "school life" in the Midwest (the "middle border") in the 1870s, recalls,

> I wish to acknowledge my deep obligation to Professor McGuffey . . . for the dignity and literary grace of his selections. From the pages of his readers I learned to know and love [poetry]. I got my first taste of Shakespeare from the selected scenes which I read in these books.[33]

[29] Henry Steele Commager, "Foreword," in *McGuffey's Fifth Eclectic Reader* [1879 edition] (New York: New American Library, 1962), pp. v–xiv. Available in paperback.
[30] Ibid., p. xi.
[31] Richard D. Mosier, *Making the American Mind: Social and Moral Ideas in the McGuffey Readers* (New York: King's Crown Press, 1947), pp. 154–159.
[32] Noah Webster, *On Being American: Selected Writings, 1783–1828*, ed. Homer D. Babbidge, Jr. (New York: Frederick A. Praeger, 1967), pp. 83–86.
[33] Hamlin Garland, *A Son of the Middle Border* (New York: Macmillan, 1923 [1914]), p. 112.

The testimony continues to this day. Paul Woodring is "not quite so sure" that modern educators are correct when they scoff at the claim that our grandfathers got a better education than we do. The readers

> had the great virtue of introducing great literature. . . . My father, whose only formal schooling was in a one-room, country school could, and often did, quote long passages from poems and orations that he could only have learned from the *McGuffey Readers*. His pleasure in such literature was obvious and for this McGuffey deserves credit.[34]

Given this sentiment, it is not surprising that McGuffey is "dusted off" from time to time and reintroduced into the school. The company that still publishes the reader reports that it receives requests for the books from "hundreds of private school teachers, mostly in rural areas." The principal of a Christian school near Orlando, Florida, says, "it teaches old traditional principles that mean something." Another says that its stories "give children a sense of history and tradition."[35]

Almost anything can be made out of the McGuffey readers. Those who support them because of their stress on reading skills (or "basic skills") will find that they support literary and intellectual culture as well. Some want to use them because they introduce "phonetic reading," a method that is regaining favor today. Those who turn to the readers for patriotic reasons will find that they are more cosmopolitan than chauvinistic. The readers were unambiguous in their support of middle-class ideals, including competition and acquisition, but they also denounced war (while at the same time seeming to celebrate it in their selections) and inhumanity (especially, and unlikely at the time, ill treatment of the Indians and intolerance toward Catholics). From all of this, what can we take from the readers for civic education today? Well, as Gerald Grant says,

> We cannot . . . put McGuffey's Readers back on the shelves. But we need to reinvent a modern equivalent for McGuffey's Reader, a provisional morality that expresses some of the common beliefs of a democratic pluralist society . . . some salient or core beliefs to which all subscribe.[36]

Henry Steele Commager remarks that the striking thing about the readers is that they did not condescend to immaturity or try to be entertaining. They assumed that students would understand what they presented or that teachers would explain it to them. They did not protect children from the harsh experiences of what it means to be grown up. The great achievement of the readers, Commager says, is that they gave schoolchildren of the mid-nineteenth century something we lack so conspicuously today, that has been squeezed out of the study of literature and history at the elementary level, "a common body of allusion and a common frame of reference, . . . a sense of common experience and a common possession."[37] That is to say, of course, that it provided a civic education.

---

[34] Paul Woodring, *The Persistent Problems of Education* (Bloomington, IN: Phi Delta Kappa Educational Foundation, 1983), pp. 117–118.
[35] Associated Press report (December 30, 1985).
[36] Gerald Grant, "The Character of Education and the Education of Character," *Daedalus* (Summer 1981), pp. 147–148.
[37] Commager, *McGuffey's Fifth Eclectic Reader*, pp. x, xii.

Other Influences

To be sure, these texts are not the only influences that sought to shape the American moral character. The primers, spellers, and readers certainly aimed to develop moral, or civic, character. But other contributors shared that aim.

The Revolutionary War patriots were single-minded in their belief that education was the handmaiden of civic virtue—and political stability. Benjamin Franklin and Thomas Jefferson each advocated specific educational plans for their colonies (and later states), though they did not gain widespread adoption.[38] Another patriot, Benjamin Rush, proposed a plan for free schools in Philadelphia. The aim of republican education, Rush believed, was to "establish a government to protect the rights of property, and to establish schools which should encourage the virtue of its care."[39]

Rush was a medical doctor and educator who introduced clinical practice into medical education, wrote the first book on mental disease, advocated improved housing for mental patients, and for a short time, was Surgeon General for the Continental Army. But his interests extended well beyond medicine. He had signed the Declaration of Independence and served in the Continental Congress. He also advocated higher education for women; the abolition of slavery, the death penalty, and the use of alcohol; and he even proposed a federal office of peace, to counteract the War Department and the allure of military splendor! In Rush's plan, the secretary of this department was to supervise the schools in the United States and "be made responsible for the talents, principles, and morals of all his schoolmasters."[40]

The Northwest Ordinance

In 1787, in one of the last acts under the Articles of Confederation (prior, that is, to the new Constitution of 1789), Congress adopted what came to be called "The Northwest Ordinance" that established government in the territory northwest of the Ohio River. The first sentence of the ordinance declared, "Religion, morality, and knowledge, being necessary to good government and the happiness of mankind, schools and the means of education shall forever be encouraged."[41] It is not clear that the ordinance had *public* schools in mind, though a previous, and related, ordinance (of 1785) had used just that term. What came to be the practice was that in each township one section (640 acres) of land, and sometimes more, was reserved for public schools. This land was granted by the federal government to the states on their admission to the union.

---

[38] See *Benjamin Franklin on Education*, ed. John H. Best (New York: Teachers College Press, 1962); *Crusade Against Ignorance: Thomas Jefferson on Education*, ed. Gordon C. Lee (New York: Teachers College Press, 1961). Both available in paperback.

[39] Abraham Blinderman, *Three Early Champions of Education: Benjamin Franklin, Benjamin Rush, and Noah Webster* (Bloomington, IN: Phi Delta Kappa Educational Foundation, Fast back #74, 1976), p. 18. See also, *The Selected Writings of Benjamin Rush*, ed. Dagobert D. Runes (New York: Philosophical Library, 1947).

[40] Runes, *The Selected Writings of Benjamin Rush*, pp. 19–23.

[41] See Edward A. Krug, *Salient Dates in American Education: 1635–1964* (New York: Harper & Row, 1966), pp. 30–32, for a sketch of the ordinance.

The "school" land was used in many ways. Sometimes, it was sold and the money soon spent; at other times, the land was reserved for future schools or became the site of a school itself. In addition to representing (once again) the belief that education and government are entwined, the Northwest Ordinance was the forerunner of what has come to be general federal aid to education. And because it mentions religion (and morality), it also is at the heart of the debate over the role of religion in education in the United States. That issue will be seen again.

Up to this time, "public" or "free" education—that is, education supported by general taxation—generally was available, if at all, only for the poor. Most parents paid for their children's education, and those who did not were often required to take a pauper's oath. That requirement, no doubt, is one reason why even the poor did not readily send their children to school. The philosophy behind the Ordinance of 1787, however, was new and sprang primarily from a commitment to civic education. If education is the basis of orderly government, all children, rich and poor, must take part in it together. (There were exceptions to this rule, of course; slave children and Indians were excluded.) Thus, the extension of public education to include all children began early in our national history. The person who became the symbol of this effort is Horace Mann in Massachusetts.

Horace Mann's Influence

Earlier advocates, Jefferson and Rush notably, had spoken of education for the "common" man. Perhaps the fact that public education first was available for the poor gave the word *common* the connotation it still holds, that of ordinary, average, or, indeed, low quality. But to the early promoters of public education, the term *common man* meant every man (not yet every woman!) or all men considered equally. The popular phrase *common schools* meant schools for all, irrespective of wealth or status and supported by taxation. In this meaning, the word was parallel to *commonwealth,* which some states, significantly Massachusetts, had affixed to their names. A "commonwealth" existed for the well-being of all, and common schools were to bring that well-being into existence.

Horace Mann was an unlikely promoter of common schools. Initially, he was more interested in politics than education. Though he had taught for two years at Brown University in Rhode Island, he left that post to become a prosperous lawyer and member of the Massachusetts legislature. But, evidently, his general interest in humanitarian reform—his sympathy for oppressed immigrants, prisoners, and the temperance movement—convinced him that education was the best means to overcome social ills. He wrote to a friend,

> My lawbooks are for sale. My office is "to let"! The bar is no longer my forum. My jurisdiction is changed. I have abandoned jurisprudence, and betaken myself to the larger sphere of mind and morals.[42]

Mann was named the first secretary of the Massachusetts State Board of Education in 1837. He spent the next twelve years in that effort, before resign-

---

[42] Quoted in Lawrence A. Cremin, "Horace Mann's Legacy," in *The Republic and the School: Horace Mann on the Education of Free Men,* ed. Lawrence A. Cremin (New York: Teachers College Press, 1957), p. 3. Available in paperback.

ing to represent the state in Congress, where he battled for the abolition of slavery. He spent the last six years of his life as president of the newly founded Antioch College in Ohio, which was nonsectarian, coeducational, and free of racial discrimination.

The State Board of Education had not been given any direct power over education in Massachusetts; real power was in the hands of local districts. The quality of education throughout the state was uneven; there were complaints about incompetent teaching and unruly students; political and sectarian bickering were leading to fragmented schools; and many people could not see the benefit of tax-supported schools. Mann's job was to study the situation and inform the legislature about educational needs. He did so with such fervor that he has become known as the father of the common school (though others—James Carter in Massachusetts, Henry Barnard in Connecticut, Calvin Stowe in Ohio, John Pierce in Michigan—worked in the same field).

Mann's promotion of education came in yearly reports to the legislature. His first report, in 1837, was a discussion of how public apathy and governmental neglect had hurt public education. The report set the agenda for improving schools in the commonwealth. His last report in 1848 was a wide-ranging summary of issues presented in the earlier reports. It stands as Mann's "credo of public education."[43] Of interest to us here is Mann's view of moral and civic education. The ten other reports discussed such things as the teaching of reading and writing; the importance of free public libraries to schools and education; the necessary qualifications of teachers; the relations between students and teachers; the problem of discipline in democratic schools; and the need for health and physical education. Mann's ideas are remarkably prescient and pertinent even today. It has been said that it is his "timeliness, perhaps, more than anything else that establishes the contemporary value of Mann's legacy."[44]

Mann appeared to believe that all the ills in society—poverty, discord, crime, ill health—could be solved by education.[45] He did not suggest that information by itself would solve these problems. Education, he insisted, must shape values as well as intellect.[46] Although he believed that democratic values were rooted in Christianity, Mann opposed sectarian teaching in the schools because it would be divisive. What he wanted was high-quality schools where all parents would be eager to send their children.

Establishing high-quality, noncontroversial schools is difficult, especially when the community is diverse. There probably was less diversity in Mann's time than there is now; nevertheless, there were significant differences even then, especially in political and religious opinion. To overcome the problem of diversity, Mann focused on common values; he believed there were some religious and democratic values with which all could agree. Kindness, generosity, charity, love, and tolerance are examples. In addition, the study of the national and state constitutions, the division of government into three branches, the manner of electing and appointing officials, the use of courts for redress of grievances, and the change of laws and rulers by the ballot rather than rebellion "should be taught to all . . . children until they are understood."[47]

---

[43] Ibid., p. 79.
[44] Ibid., p. 28.
[45] See the Eleventh Annual Report (1847); ibid., p. 78.
[46] Ninth Annual Report (1845); ibid., p. 57.
[47] Twelfth Annual Report (1848); ibid., p. 79.

For Mann, the value of any study (whatever subject) ultimately rested in the contribution it made to moral and civic virtue. Mann advocated studies in reading, writing, spelling, arithmetic, grammar, and geography. The subjects were important in themselves, but they were also instruments of morality and necessary to commerce. To this rather standard curriculum, Mann added human physiology (health) and vocal music, for they too contributed to the well-being of society. Vocal music was an aesthetic and intellectual subject, and, in Mann's view, it could promote health by increasing the action of the lungs and stimulating the circulation. Its value didn't stop there; vocal music, said Mann, could even reduce deaths from tuberculosis![48] This may seem farfetched; but Mann made such claims in order to sell public schools to taxpayers. The claims were consistent with his belief that the larger worth of any subject is found in the contribution it makes to some social interest. In the days before radio and television, vocal music also could be a necessary social grace. Moral or civic education, it seems, is simply regular teaching and learning taken with some larger social interest in mind.

For Mann, the larger interest was social not only in value but in method. He believed that only through the interaction of individuals is anything learned and truth determined. This accounts for Mann's keen promotion of a single, common school for all people and his hard work to keep divisiveness out of the schools. He may have had his blind spots—he did not consider "whose brand of republicanism would be taught" in the schools[49]—but Mann saw the large social and moral concerns that still trouble us. What is more, he helped to establish the American faith that schools could have a hand in resolving these concerns.

There may be a question as to whether Mann would "indoctrinate" students by giving one view and discouraging the discussion of controversial topics. Mann was not alone in this respect. We have seen that Webster's speller and McGuffey's readers did not encourage controversy. Mann instructed teachers to use "discretion," especially in political and religious controversy. Whenever a controversial subject came up in the text, the teacher was told to

> either . . . read it without comment or remark; or, at most, . . . only to say that the passage is the subject of disputation, and that the schoolroom is neither the tribunal to adjudicate, nor the forum to discuss it.[50]

But to be fair, Mann was more interested in avoiding controversy than in promoting a single point of view. He worried, "If parents find that their children are indoctrinated into what they call . . . heresies, will they not withdraw from the school . . . and . . . resist all appropriations to support a school?"[51] Moreover, Mann believed that there was much on which citizens agreed and that they could not discuss disagreements intelligently until they were "thoroughly versed" in the matters about which there was no dispute. This is to say there are fundamentals in the history of culture that are the core of civic education. We have noted these to be the values worked out in the history of the republic

---

[48] Eighth Annual Report (1844); ibid., p. 56.
[49] Cremin, "Horace Mann's Legacy," in ibid., pp. 13–14.
[50] Twelfth Annual Report (1848); in ibid., p. 97. For a helpful analysis of the idea of "indoctrination," see Thomas F. Green, *The Activities of Teaching* (New York: McGraw-Hill Book Company, 1971), pp. 29–33.
[51] Twelfth Annual Report (1848); in Cremin, *The Republic and the School*, p. 95.

and the reasons, as well as the ways, by which our political system operates. If teachers explain

> the principle contained in the book; showing its connection with life, with action, with duty; making it the nucleus around which to gather all related facts and . . . principles;—it is this, and this only, which can be appropriately called teaching,

all will be well.[52]

Civic Education in Popular Culture

Mann suggests that the school can cure all our social ills, but history has shown that is not the case. Civic education can succeed only when many institutions work in concert to promote social order and rational discourse. Thus, the study of education always involves more than what goes on in schools. As Bernard Bailyn put it, the history of education is "not only . . . formal pedagogy but . . . the entire process by which a culture transmits itself across the generations."[53] Thus, as important as schools, curricula, and instructional methods is the work of other social agencies, such as newspapers, libraries and museums, legislation, recreation, business, and today, of course, radio and television. Each teaches social and moral lessons.

The civic lessons taught in nineteenth century schools were also being taught in the popular culture. For example, Henry Steele Commager observes that McGuffey's readers were a rural phenomenon and that their urban counterparts were the Horatio Alger stories.[54] Alger was a newspaperman and minister who, in the 1860s, went to New York to pursue a literary career. He wrote several books before striking the formula that was to make him famous—all his books are substantially alike. After visiting a home for foundlings and runaway boys, the focus for the rest of his life became the story of "rags to riches," of how honesty, perseverance, hard labor, and a bit of luck would lead to success. No description is more graphic of Alger's beliefs than the titles of his books: *Ragged Dick, or Street Life in New York; Struggling Upward; Brave and Bold; Risen from the Ranks; Sink or Swim;* and *Luck and Pluck.*[55] Like Webster's speller and the McGuffey readers, the Alger stories sold millions of copies and were published well into the twentieth century. The historians Samuel Eliot Morison and Henry Steele Commager judge that Alger influenced American culture more than any author other than Mark Twain.[56]

We are not without similar materials today. For example, the *Reader's Digest,* founded in 1921, today claims to be the "world's most read magazine," with more than 28 million copies sold monthly throughout the world. The magazine seems to deal only in facts and to accept ideas from many sources, but, as one critic puts it, the *Digest* "clearly is a political project."[57] A former chairman of the *Digest* board of directors agrees:

---

52 Quoted in Maxine Greene, *The Public School and the Private Vision: A Search for America in Education and Literature* (New York: Random House, Inc., 1965), p. 54.

53 Bernard Bailyn, *Education in the Forming of American Society* (New York: W. W. Norton & Company, Inc., 1972 [1960]), p. 14. Available in paperback.

54 Commager, *McGuffey's Fifth Eclectic Reader,* pp. viii–ix.

55 See Gary Scharnhorst, *Horatio Alger, Jr.* (Boston: Twayne Publishers, 1980), "Notes and References," pp. 146–150, for a list of Alger's books.

56 Ibid., Preface.

57 Ariel Dorfman, *The Empire's Old Clothes: What the Lone Ranger, Babar, and Other Innocent Heroes Do to Our Minds* (New York: Pantheon Books, 1983), pp. 135, 138, 153.

> Our basic thrust is our belief that people want to be better each day than they were the day before. It's a puritan philosophy, if you like, and we believe in a work ethic, and the perfectability of man . . . which will help you to be a better person.[58]

A recent copy of the *Reader's Digest* (June 1986) has articles on "Using the Old [L. L.] Bean" (business), "Simple Ways to Improve the Universe," and "The World's Worst Decisions," as well as the regular features, "It Pays to Enrich Your Word Power," "Points to Ponder," "All in a Day's Work," and "Life's Like That." The *Digest's* method is indirect, and much of its message is conveyed with humor, but the message is never far below the surface. It is the same message contained more formally in the primer, the speller, and the reader: that we live in the best of all possible worlds; we can perfect the world by perfecting ourselves; and hard work in the forge of competition is the best means to self-perfection. The *Digest* goes beyond our early textbooks by teaching these values not only to America but to the world.

Our aim in this chapter is not to give a complete history of the many efforts at civic education in the United States, but to note what is characteristic about the concern, which seems to be omnipresent. There have been other efforts at civic education: programs to "Americanize" immigrants who came to this country in the nineteenth and early twentieth centuries, and a self-conscious effort to promote "character education" in the schools. We have seen the motivations before: political stability, a shift from religious to state support for morality, an equating of virtue with good citizenship, and an overriding concern with semi-mechanical virtues, such as regularity, punctuality, neatness, and work habits, instead of the development of skills or intellect. As a result of these concerns, particularly in the early twentieth century, school organization changed. Homerooms and homeroom teachers were added in secondary schools, behavior ratings were given on report cards, and student government was instituted in secondary and higher education.[59] In short, character education programs were designed to help students adjust to the social order of the day.

Civic Education and the Development of the Intellect

Not all civic education neglects the teaching of knowledge and development of intellectual skills. Some educators, notably Robert Hutchins and Mortimer Adler, make no distinction between education in general and moral or civic education. That is, intellectual skills of inquiry, analysis, and judgment serve moral as well as logical ends. The aim of education for these educators is to bring the student into contact with the wisdom of the ages and develop the ability to think or reason. Civic virtue should follow, for virtue grows in the garden of reason.

Hutchins and Adler popularized the "great ideas" or "great books" approach to education. This approach began in higher education, moved to adult education (library discussion groups), and now is being tried in elementary and secondary schools. There are as many lists of "great books," perhaps, as there are those who do the listing. Our discussion here is about the approach devel-

---

[58] Samuel A. Schreiner, Jr., *The Condensed World of the Reader's Digest* (New York: Stein & Day, 1977), p. 77; quoted in ibid., p. 158.

[59] Stephen M. Yulish, *The Search for a Civic Religion: A History of the Character Education Movement in America, 1890–1935* (Washington, DC: University Press of America, 1980).

oped by Hutchins and Adler at the University of Chicago in the 1930s. Their idea is based on the belief that "the central problems of life are always the same, whether in modern America or in ancient Rome."[60] The important problems are the enduring moral or civic problems of good and evil, love and hate, war and peace, happiness and duty, and liberty and security. Authors from ancient to modern times have debated these problems repeatedly. The function of the "great books" curriculum is to present each problem "with an analysis of the greatest thinking about it . . . , to present the problem—not the solution—to the intelligent reader in terms set forth by the leading minds of all time."[61]

Many of the "great books" were difficult for the ordinary person to obtain, so in 1952, the Encyclopaedia Britannica published a 54-volume set of *Great Books of the Western World*. The collection is seven feet long and includes 443 works by seventy-four authors. A *Syntopicon*, or reference/index, catalogs the great books into 102 basic ideas, further elaborated into 2987 topics, which contain 163,000 "exact references" to passages in the *Great Books*.[62] Sales of the *Great Books* began slowly, and reached 40,000 sets by 1960. Study of the "great books" became as popular as Webster's speller and McGuffey's readers were in their times. The chairman of the board of Encyclopaedia Britannica concluded that "Americans . . . want their children to grow up in the company of great literature, great philosophy, great science."[63]

Eva T. H. Brann's *Paradoxes of Education in a Republic* is a recent, good example of the "great books" genre. The perennial "paradoxes" have to do with *utility, tradition,* and *rationality.* In summary, education is an end in itself, says Brann, yet it is used also as a means to other ends. Recent education seems to reject tradition as the basis for civic learning. And the dilemma of rationality is seen in the public commitment to reason as a means of knowledge and truth, but its use is for personal advantage. These paradoxes or dilemmas cannot be resolved through administrative or curricula innovations but will be resolved, if at all, by rethinking our civic culture.[64]

The uniqueness of Brann's argument is that she turns to the "great books" of our own civic experience and tradition: Jefferson and Madison, Alexander Hamilton and John Adams, our own Constitution and the debates it raised in the *Federalist Papers*. On the other hand, Brann is fully within the "great books" tradition, for "the course of education is the course of learning to read, and to have an education is to know how to read."[65] The important object is to resolve the dilemmas of education in a *republic*, emphasizing the *public* and *political* (persuasion) senses of the idea. What may appear to be a return to "classical" learning (though they are the classics of our own experience) is no less an effort at civic education.

The same might be said for the most recent revival of "great books" learn-

---

[60] William Benton, "Introduction" to Mortimer J. Adler, *Great Ideas from the Great Books* (New York: Washington Square Press, Inc., 1961), p. vi.

[61] Ibid., p. viii.

[62] Ibid., p. vii.

[63] Ibid., p. viii. See also Mortimer J. Adler, *How to Read a Book: The Art of Getting a Liberal Education* (New York: Simon & Schuster, Inc., 1940).

[64] Eva T. H. Brann, *Paradoxes of Education in a Republic* (Chicago: University of Chicago Press, 1979).

[65] Ibid., p. 16.

ing. Mortimer Adler has published *The Paideia Proposal* for elementary and secondary education. It is vintage "great books" advocacy. The object of education is intellectual development, from which students will develop moral and civic virtue. A democratic society must provide equal educational opportunity not only in quantity, the same number of years in school, but also by giving students, "with no exceptions," the same quality of education. In practice, this means that public schooling must have the same objectives and "the same course of study for all."[66]

"Basic" schooling must focus on the acquisition of organized knowledge through didactic instruction and will engage the learning of language, literature, fine arts, mathematics, natural science, history, geography, and social studies. A second kind of learning will develop "intellectual skills"—reading, writing, speaking, calculating, problem solving, and critical judgment, among others—through coaching, exercises, and supervised practice. The highest kind of learning, in advanced high school, college and university work, may be called enlarged understanding of ideas and values and is accomplished through Socratic questioning and active participation in discussion of books and the arts and involvement in artistic activities. (See Chapter 23 for a further discussion of *The Paideia Proposal*.)

Whatever one may think of the Paideia curriculum,[67] our point is to note that while it appears to be purely intellectual in character, Adler's larger aim is civic education, the development of informed and critical citizens. A virtue of the plan is that, unlike much modern schooling, all learning is united in behalf of civic education; one study, and each level of study, depends on another. That is to say that civic education is dependent on informed knowledge and intellectual skill. Virtue cannot stand alone. That is a good point to ponder.

Religion in Education

Most Americans believe that moral values need the support of religion. Gallup polls have shown that 95 percent of Americans believe in God, 90 percent pray, 70 percent are church members, 60 percent say that religion can answer all or most of today's problems, and 48 percent believe that the influence of religion is increasing in American life. Only 9 percent of Americans express no religious preference whatsoever.[68]

Religious belief, indeed, is part of our tradition. Every schoolchild knows that the Puritans came to this country for religious freedom. An early Massachusetts law (1647) required towns to provide teachers or pay to send children to districts where they could be educated, because, it proclaimed, Satan would benefit from the ignorance in children who could not read and follow the Scriptures. That legislation has been called the "Old Deluder Satan Law" ever

---

[66] Mortimer J. Adler, *The Paideia Proposal: An Educational Manifesto* (New York: Macmillan Publishing Co., Inc., 1982), pp. 4, 15, and generally Chapter 4. See also Mortimer J. Adler, *Paideia Problems and Possibilities* (New York: Macmillan Publishing Company, 1983) and *The Paideia Program: An Educational Syllabus* (New York: Macmillan Publishing Company, 1984). All three books are available in paperback.

[67] See *Harvard Educational Review*, Vol. 53, No. 4 (November 1983), for critical reviews and analyses.

[68] *Religion in American Life, 50 Years: 1935–1985*, Gallup Report No. 236 (May 1985).

since. We have seen also that the Northwest Ordinance of 1787 listed "religion, morality, and knowledge [as] necessary to good government and the happiness of mankind." The Founding Fathers of the republic believed in God and, with the possible exception of Jefferson and Madison, thought that both religion and education were needed to support republican government.

A recent study of the matter reaffirms these beliefs. James Reichley, in *Religion in American Public Life,* analyzes the role religion now plays in public life and suggests practical strategies for expanding that role in the future. Religion and politics are closely entwined, he believes, not only in our history but in the very idea of political democracy. His effort is to find "a common cultural denominator in which both are rooted."[69] Reichley's question is: Can secular value systems provide a sufficient moral basis to maintain the cohesion and vitality of a free society?

Dispensing with egoism, authoritarianism, monism, idealism, and personalism as insufficient for the task, Reichley distinguishes between *civil humanism* and *theist humanism* as supports for democratic politics. The term *humanism* does not have a good reputation among some people today, so if we (and Reichley) are to use it, the term must be defined carefully. By *humanism* Reichley means that "the individual person is a primary source of human value" and that values must not be merely imposed from on high as is the case with authoritarianism. He says further that "a truly human personality requires cultivation by society" and that a healthy society cannot be sustained by egoism and personalism.[70] *Civil humanism* derives values from "the self and society in combination." *Theist humanism* draws on those sources but adds a transcendent source. *Transcendence* is the belief that some purpose outside human experience directs that experience. According to Reichley, democracy cannot flourish without the support that comes from transcendent religious values. As he puts it, "Only theist humanism is fully congruent with values of both personal freedom and social responsibility."[71]

Early Views on Religion and Education

Reichley's argument is wide ranging (he examines the "Intentions of the Founders," "Interpreting the First Amendment," and "The Churches and Political Action"), but it is not new. Alexis de Tocqueville made the point more succinctly only fifty years after our independence. "By the side of every religion is to be found a political opinion, which is connected with it by affinity." America, de Tocqueville thought, could be described as "a democratic and republican religion."[72] He was certain that Americans thought that religion was indispensable to democracy; they "show by their practice that they feel the high necessity of imparting morality to democratic communities by means of religion."[73] "Despotism may govern without faith, but liberty cannot."[74] De Tocqueville thus believed religion should be

---

[69] A. James Reichley, *Religion in American Public Life* (Washington, DC: The Brookings Institution, 1985), p. 4.
[70] Ibid., p. 41.
[71] Ibid., p. 349.
[72] De Tocqueville, *Democracy in America*, Vol. 1, pp. 310–311.
[73] Ibid., Vol. 2, pp. 152–153.
[74] Ibid., Vol. 1, p. 318.

the unceasing object of the legislators of democracies and of all the virtuous and enlightened men who live there to raise the souls of their fellow citizens and keep them lifted up towards heaven."[75]

We have seen that Americans decided early in their experience to cultivate virtue through education and had free public education by de Tocqueville's time. So we may believe that the primary purpose of that education was to promote religion. Undoubtedly, this was true in some cases. But it also has been said that the Old Deluder Satan Law, for example, has deluded generations of historians who believed this simple story.[76] Samuel Eliot Morison contends that the motive of the early education laws in Massachusetts was not to impose the Puritan creed on all children. Morison is worth quoting in full on this point:

> When a small, homogeneous group of men in a colonial legislature declares that education is of singular benefit to the commonwealth, and that it fits children for future service in church or state; and when they enforce these injunctions by suitable administrative regulations, pains, and penalties. . . , it may be supposed without undue charity that they mean what they say, and that education was conceived of as a training for citizenship and service in a civilized state, rather than as a vehicle for sectarian propaganda, or "caste" dominance.[77]

Another historian, Clifford Shipton, challenges the "popular misconception" that interest in civic education grew only when the influence of the clergy declined. He notes that "New England legislatures and town-meetings frequently described their educational legislation as aimed to forward 'good literature' and other secular ends," and that even some ministers considered the religious goal to be secondary to literacy and morality.[78]

Our earlier discussion of schoolbooks provides further evidence of the point. *The New England Primer,* which appears to be a religious book, also served moral and sectarian aims. It was alternately evangelized and secularized throughout its history. Noah Webster would not use the Bible as a schoolbook because he thought reading and spelling should be learned from books designed expressly for that purpose.[79] The McGuffey readers were advertised in 1837 as being "neither sectarian nor sectional." Although, at the beginning, they had a strong Calvinist flavor, by 1879 that had disappeared and the middle-class values of patriotism, civic responsibility, assimilation of newcomers, occupational training, and producing an educated citizenry replaced any emphasis on salvation, righteousness, and piety. McGuffey was accused of eliminating religion from the readers (we must remember that he had nothing to do with them after 1857) to satisfy Catholics, but it is more likely that he represents the end of an

---

[75] Ibid., Vol. 2, p. 154.

[76] Edward A. Krug, *Salient Dates in American Education,* pp. 9–10.

[77] Samuel Eliot Morison, *The Intellectual Life of Colonial New England,* 2d ed. (New York: New York University Press, 1956 [1936]), p. 67.

[78] Clifford K. Shipton, "Secondary Education in the Puritan Colonies," *The New England Quarterly,* 7 (December 1934), pp. 646–647.

[79] Moss, *Noah Webster,* p. 42. Webster was criticized for his view and changed it. In later life, he came to believe that religion, not education, was the only salvation for humankind. Ibid., pp. 37–38.

era, a transition in the history of religion and education.[80] Other scholars have noted the periodic rise and wane of religious content in early schoolbooks.[81]

All of this is to say that equally as influential as religion in shaping the moral and civic character of Americans have been frontier conditions of life, the need for useful production, the development of a new nation, and, not of least importance, the identification of religion itself as morality. All of these contribute to the conclusion that national identity (and education) is the "civic religion" in America. Americans have been and are a religious people, but religion has been expressed publicly through moral rather than religious institutions. Education is one of those institutions.

The Public School Era

Something else must be considered. Americans have had multiple motives (values) when considering the role that religion should play in public life. They generally have avoided easy, either/or, inflexible answers. Though

> we are religious people whose institutions presuppose a Supreme Being, [that] is not to say, however, that religion has been so identified with our history and government that religious freedom is not likewise as strongly imbedded in our public and private life.[82]

The First Amendment to the United States Constitution (the first ten amendments are called, significantly, the Bill of Rights) declares that "Congress shall make no law respecting an establishment of religion, or prohibiting the free exercise thereof." These clauses, scholars note, run in counter directions: the "establishment" clause intends to keep religion out of government affairs, while the "free exercise" clause aims to keep government out of religious affairs. The pursuit of either goal can subvert the other one in some situations.[83] What is called for is a balance.

As much as he was an advocate of religion in public life, de Tocqueville also recognized this other tendency. De Tocqueville had observed that the spirit of religion and freedom in France "march[ed] in opposite directions," but in America they were united; and he sought to discover why. He found that the clergy in America "all attributed the peaceful dominion of religion . . . mainly to the separation of church and state."[84] He concluded that religions should "confine themselves within their own precincts," for if they go beyond religious matters, they run the risk of losing followers.[85] Thus, one may wonder how religion can play a role, yet not intrude, in public affairs. De Tocqueville admits it is not easy.

---

[80] Westerhoff, *McGuffey and His Readers,* pp. 18–23.

[81] Oscar Tinglestad, "The Religious Element in American School Readers up to 1830: A Bibliographical and Statistical Study" (Doctoral dissertation, University of Chicago, 1925), cited in Monaghan, *A Common Heritage,* pp. 264–265, n. 88; Mosier, *Making the American Mind,* pp. 172–173.

[82] U.S. Supreme Court Justice Tom Clark, in *School District of Abington Township v. Schempp,* 1963, quoted in William D. Valente, *Law in the Schools* (Columbus, OH: Merrill Publishing Company, 1980), pp. 124–125.

[83] Valente, ibid., p. 109.

[84] De Tocqueville, *Democracy in America,* Vol. 1, p. 319.

[85] Ibid., Vol. 2, p. 24.

> I am no believer in the prosperity any more than in the durability of official philosophies; and as to state religions, I have always held that if they be sometimes of momentary service to the interests of political power, they always sooner or later become fatal to the church.
>
> . . . The sole effectual means which governments can employ in order to have [religious values] duly respected is always to act as if they believed in [them] themselves; and I think that it is only by scrupulous conformity to religious morality in great affairs that they can hope to teach the community at large to know, to love, and to observe it in the lesser concerns of life.[86]

Let us take stock. De Tocqueville believed that although religious sects may differ in their forms of worship, they all "preach the same moral law in the name of God."[87] What is important about religion *for public affairs* is not particular beliefs but general morality. "Natural religion," that is, the moral essence of all religions, can and must influence public institutions, including education. The same belief led Horace Mann to put the Bible into every classroom while arguing against sectarian instruction.[88] De Tocqueville thought that religion and government had to be separated. If democratic government is to shape the morals of its people, it must do so, not through direct instruction, not by telling citizens what to believe and how to act but by information and example. We will come to see that this is also a modern conception of civic education.

Horace Mann worked these ideas into the fabric of common schooling. You may recall that he wanted schools to serve all children, irrespective of their parents' wealth, social status, religious or political beliefs, and occupation. Like the Founding Fathers before him, and Webster and McGuffey with their schoolbooks, Mann saw education to be the promoter of national identity, cultural unity, and civic morality. When he became secretary of the Massachusetts State Board of Education, the schools were torn by political and religious factionalism. Some towns, he decried, had even voted to exclude the Bible from the schools in order to avoid divisiveness. Mann restored the Bible to the classroom but also argued that religious belief was a matter of individual and family concern. Government could help in the "independent formation of [religious] belief," but it should not prescribe, coerce, or enforce it. All, Mann observed, are taxed for the support of public schools, but they are taxed as a defense against dishonesty, fraud, and violence, on the same principle that they are taxed for national defense, and not as a means of making citizens "vote with this or that political party . . . or making [them] join this or that denomination."[89]

Rather, according to Mann, religious education should enable the child "to judge for himself, according to the dictates of his own reason and conscience, what his religious obligations are, and whither they lead."[90] In his view, religious instruction was intellectual rather than evangelical. If government, then, is to protect religious freedom, specifically in education,

> it must abstain from subjugating . . . its children to any legal standard of religious faith, with as great fidelity as it abstains from controlling the opinions of men.

---

[86] Ibid., Vol. 2, p. 156.
[87] Ibid., Vol. 1, p. 134.
[88] Mann, Twelfth Annual Report (1848), in Cremin, *The Republic and the School*, pp. 101–112.
[89] Ibid., p. 103.
[90] Ibid., p. 104.

. . . The sovereign antidote . . . is, Free Schools for all, and the right of every parent to determine the religious education of his children. . . . It is a system . . . which leaves open all other means of instruction—the pulpits, the Sunday schools, the Bible classes, the catechisms, of all denominations—to be employed according to the preferences of individual parents.[91]

It is an odd coincidence that, at the same time, some religious influences themselves helped to secularize the schools. One was the opposition of Catholics to the public school, where the Protestant Bible and prayers were employed. After being unsuccessful in 1840 in New York state in getting a share of the common school fund for their own schools, Catholics began to expand their system, which enrolled nearly 6 million elementary and secondary students at its height in the 1960s (12 percent of total enrollments) and still enrolls 3 million students (6.5 percent of total enrollment).[92] In order to make public schools more congenial to Catholics, the religious slant had to be muted. Catholic concern about "irreligion" in the public schools is of more recent origin. Lawrence Cremin makes the point that Catholics have perceived the public school as "blatantly Protestant in the nineteenth century and dangerously secular in the twentieth."[93]

Separation of Church and State

Separation of religious and public affairs (church and state) is as much a part of our heritage as religious belief. In politics, two persons, Thomas Jefferson and James Madison, did more to promote that policy than, perhaps, anyone else. Jefferson wrote the "Virginia Act for Establishing Religious Freedom." While Jefferson was absent in France as ambassador, Madison addressed "A Memorial and Remonstrance" to the General Assembly (legislature) of Virginia and succeeded in getting the act passed into law in 1786.[94] The act quickly became a model for church–state relations, enumerated in the First Amendment to the Constitution, quoted earlier, and in many state constitutions that have similar principles.

The phrase, "wall between church and state" will not be found in the First Amendment. It comes from Jefferson and was used years later in a U.S. Supreme Court opinion.[95] The idea is not antagonistic to religion. It merely contends, as one historian puts it, that in a democracy, the individual "transcends

[91] Ibid., pp. 110–111.

[92] See Neil G. McCluskey, S.J. ed., *Catholic Education in America: A Documentary History* (New York: Teachers College Press, 1964), "Introduction," pp. 1–44; *Statistical Abstract of the United States, 1986*, U. S. Department of Commerce, Bureau of the Census (Washington, DC: U. S. Government Printing Office, 1985), p. 144, no. 293; Neil G. McCluskey, S.J., *Catholic Education Faces Its Future* (New York: Doubleday and Company, 1968), p. 45.

[93] Lawrence Cremin, "Preface" to McCluskey, *Catholic Education in America*, p. vii. The Sunday school movement, which taught literacy to poor working-class children, also reinforced the idea of schooling as a secular activity. For one example of Sunday schools, see Addie Grace Wardle, *History of the Sunday School Movement in the Methodist Episcopal Church* (New York: The Methodist Book Concern, 1918).

[94] William Lee Miller, *The First Liberty: Religion and the American Republic* (New York: Alfred Knopf, 1986), Appendix.

[95] *Everson* v. *Board of Education* (1947), in David Fellman, ed., *The Supreme Court and Education* (New York: Teachers College Press, 1960), pp. 9–30. Available in paperback.

every social order, most especially in his most fundamental convictions" and in the need for, and benefit to, society of uncoerced consent of the governed.[96]

If, as it has been said, the church–state provisions of the First Amendment run in counter directions, there comes a time, inevitably, when the question of which direction is to be followed in a specific instance will have to be judged. In our system of government, the courts have been established to make these judgments. Thus, we should know something about the way courts operate if we are to understand the conflicts and judgments about the role of religion, particularly in education.

How Courts Operate

Alleged violations of the United States Constitution are heard in federal courts; complaints about violations of state constitutions and laws are heard in state courts. The federal Supreme Court is given final appeal jurisdiction (over federal cases) by the Constitution, and Congress has enacted two intermediate levels of federal courts: district courts, where most cases originate, and circuit courts of appeal. Courts do not roam the country looking for trouble. Complaints are brought by individuals or government agencies (the plaintiff), who allege a violation by a second party (the defendant) of a constitutional provision or law. The plaintiff must have what is called standing; that is, the plaintiff must be able to show jeopardy to some tangible right or interest of his or her own, not someone else's. Complaints must be concrete, not abstract. The federal Supreme Court may not agree to hear a case. Because of limited time and the volume of complaints, that court hears only about 1 percent of the appeals addressed to it; it tries to hear those cases in which major principles are to be determined.

Strictly speaking, each case is judged on its own merits, though a court may be guided by past rulings. Until 1868, the federal Constitution governed relations only between the federal government and individuals, and state constitutions and laws could authorize more strict or lenient relations. Then, as a result of the Civil War, the Fourteenth Amendment to the Constitution was enacted, making the provisions of the federal Constitution binding on all the states. In this way, the First Amendment has come to be applied to public school activities in various states.[97]

The issue of religion in government is vast. Our concern is with religious practices in the public schools that are intended to support moral and civic education. Even in that arena the issues are more varied than we can manage here. We will have to focus on those matters that are most characteristic of the whole controversy, primarily prayer and religious exercises in the public schools, and pass over others.[98]

We have said that the "establishment" and "free exercise" clauses of the First Amendment, relating to religion in public life, may be seen to run in opposite directions. It is inevitable that at some time or another judgments will have to

---

[96] Miller, *The First Liberty*, p. 59.

[97] *Cantwell* v. *Connecticut* (1940), cited in Valente, *Law in the Schools*, p. 109.

[98] A related matter today, with implications for schooling, is the "creation science" discussion. See David A. Hamilton, "Creation Science in the Public Schools," in Thomas N. Jones and Darel P. Semler, eds., *School Law Update—1982* (Topeka, KS: National Organization on Legal Problems of Education, 1983), pp. 24–35.

be made about which sentiment will prevail in a particular case. Does the action "establish" religion, or is it merely the "free exercise" of religion? Robert O'Reilly and Edward Green have noted that there must be "an aspect of fair play" in such judgments. In the short term, the idea of the separation of church and state may not satisfy everyone, but in the long run it will provide a fair distribution of dissatisfaction. "The American system provides the opportunity for challenge on both sides of the several church–state questions and does not foreordain the winner. Totally, it is a picture of the fair play that is central within a political system of checks and balances."[99]

In 1973, after years of considering such cases, the United States Supreme Court formulated a test for determining the degree to which religion and government (schooling) can cooperate. Any rule or practice that a school intends to follow must (1) have a nonreligious purpose; (2) its primary effect must neither advance nor inhibit religion; and (3) it must not create excessive entanglement of government with religion.[100] This test does not disallow schools from teaching the literary, historical, or cultural significance of religion or prevent students from praying while in school. It does prevent schools from sponsoring religious activities.

We will look at some specific cases in a moment, but for now we can say that, in general and if permitted by state constitutions,[101] public schools *may* release students to participate in religious instruction off school grounds (but not on the grounds); they may provide transportation to religious schools and provide books and diagnostic services (if conducted on a religiously neutral site); and they may even reimburse religious schools for administering and scoring state-required tests in secular subjects and for the cost of keeping and reporting secular educational data. The state *may not* furnish support for religious schools; furnish instructional materials and equipment, other than books, to religious schools; provide religious instruction on school grounds; require school prayer or Bible reading, or that children salute the flag; or require that all students attend public schools.[102]

Religion and Education in the Courts

Several examples are worth looking at in detail. The state may require children to attend school, but it cannot require attendance at only public schools. A 1922 Oregon law required all children from ages eight to sixteen to attend public schools. The stated goal of the law was to promote civic education and foster an identification with the community. However, anti-Catholic motives also may have been at work. The U.S. Supreme Court declared in 1925, in *Pierce* v. *Society of Sisters,* that the Oregon law infringed on the constitutional rights of parents and those who operated private schools. It said that the school may not

---

[99] Robert C. O'Reilly and Edward T. Green, *School Law for the Practitioner* (Westport, CT: Greenwood Press, 1983), pp. 208–210.

[100] *Lemon* v. *Kurtzman* (1973), in Perry A. Zirkel, ed., *A Digest of Supreme Court Decisions Affecting Education* (Bloomington, IN: Phi Delta Kappa, 1978), p. 25; this is called the Lemon test. See Zirkel for a sketch of other cases as well.

[101] Some state constitutions are stricter than the federal Constitution on this and other matters.

[102] See Floyd G. Delton, *School Officials and the Courts: Update 1981* (Arlington, VA: Educational Research Service, Inc., 1981), pp. 30–31.

standardize its children by forcing them to accept instruction from public teachers only. The child is not the mere creature of the State; those who nurture him and direct his destiny have the right, coupled with the high duty, to recognize and prepare him for additional obligations.[103]

The *Pierce* decision was important for both religious and secular reasons. One observer has noted that to the extent private education is less available, parents with a great concern for religion will turn their attention to the role of religion in the public schools.[104] In other words, parents' right to educate children in schools of their own choosing can act as a safety valve against a too intimate involvement of religion in public schooling.

The point we are making is that the separation of church and state can work to the benefit of both religion and government. The case of *West Virginia State Board of Education* v. *Barnett* (1943) provides another example of the point. In 1940, the Supreme Court ruled that "the promotion of national cohesion" in public schools through a compulsory flag salute is more important than even religious freedom. Children could be required to pledge allegiance, "honoring the Nation represented by the Flag," even though it may violate a tenet of their religious faith. In 1943, the question came up again in West Virginia. Some parents argued that a state law requiring the salute violated their religious scruple to "not make . . . any graven image." The Supreme Court observed that "struggles to coerce uniformity of sentiment" are as old as time and have been urged by good as well as evil persons. When moderate methods to attain unity fail, more severe methods are urged; and as pressure for unity becomes greater, "strife becomes more bitter as to whose unity it shall be." "It seems trite but necessary to say that the First Amendment to our Constitution was designed to avoid these ends by avoiding these beginnings." The court noted that the case was more difficult because the flag was our own. It must have been difficult also because the nation was in the midst of a world war. Nevertheless, the court believed that "freedom to differ is not limited to things that do not matter much. . . . The test of its substance is the right to differ as to things that touch the heart of the existing order."[105] The court reversed its earlier opinion and ruled that the requirement to salute the flag was an unwarranted infringement on religious liberty.

In spite of the tradition of the separation of church and state, 69 percent of Americans favor an amendment to the Constitution that would permit prayer in the schools.[106] Undoubtedly, this is a response to a belief that the Supreme Court has "forbidden" prayer in the schools, though the court has held only that "official" prayers, or prayers and religious practices approved by school or government officials, violate the First Amendment provisions for the separation of church and state.

In the 1950s, the New York State Board of Regents wrote the following prayer that they proposed should be recited in the public schools:

[103] Fellman, *The Supreme Court and Education*, pp. 1–3.
[104] Robert M. O'Neil, *Classrooms in the Crossfire: The Rights and Interests of Students, Parents, Teachers, Administrators, Librarians, and the Community* (Bloomington: Indiana University Press, 1981), p. 72.
[105] Fellman, *The Supreme Court and Education*, pp. 31–44.
[106] "Prayer in Public Schools," Gallup Report No. 229 (October 1984), p. 7.

Almighty God, we acknowledge our dependence upon Thee, and we beg Thy blessings upon us, our parents, our teachers and our country.

The prayer was thought to be "nondenominational"; indeed, it has been said to be "rather innocuous."[107] However, religious belief is anything but innocuous. The Regents' Prayer was too general for some parents; it violated their belief in a personal and intimate relation with God. They thought, as well, that the prayer violated the First Amendment, though its advocates claimed that the aim of the prayer was not to enhance religion, but to serve such secular purposes as quieting active youngsters before they began their lessons! The Supreme Court (in *Engle* v. *Vitale*, 1962) determined that the prayer was unconstitutional, that it was "composed by government officials as part of a governmental program to further religious beliefs," and that "in this country it is no part of the business of government to compose official prayers for any group."[108]

There is a practical and prudent aspect to the question. Americans have become more pluralistic in their religious beliefs and affiliations. What used to be thought (though mistakenly, we believe) to be a religiously unified nation has become amazingly diverse. By one count, there are at least 157 distinguishable religious groups in the United States, including Buddhists, Muslims, and members of the Baha'i faith, in addition to Christian and Jewish groups.[109] Sixty percent of all Americans, nearly 141 million people, belong to some religious group, and of the whole population, whether or not they identify with a group or church, 57 percent of Americans claim to be Protestant, 28 percent Catholic, 2 percent Jewish, and 4 percent claim other religions; 9 percent have no religious preference[110] (see Figure 7-2). By the First Amendment, all of these people have the individual right to determine their own religious beliefs and practices. Their beliefs represent significant philosophical differences.[111] Is it possible to write a prayer that all would find meaningful and useful and that none would find offensive?

Even if it were possible, the Supreme Court has held, as we have seen, that it is "no business of government" to write prayers. The call for an amendment to the Constitution to allow school prayer is designed to get around the First Amendment. But unless there is an outright repeal of the First Amendment, or at least that portion relating to church and state, it is inevitable that some practice would bring the two amendments (the First Amendment and the proposed school prayer amendment) into conflict. That conflict would have to be resolved by the Supreme Court, and that would bring us right back to where we started: to the conflict between the free exercise of religion and the prohibition against state religion.[112]

---

[107] O'Neil, *Classrooms in the Crossfire*, p. 74.

[108] Fellman, *The Supreme Court and Education*, pp. 67–76.

[109] *The World Almanac and Book of Facts, 1986* (New York: Newspaper Enterprise Association, Inc., 1985), pp. 335–336.

[110] Ibid.; *Religion in American Life, 50 Years: 1935–1985*, Gallup Report No. 236, p. 27.

[111] See "Major Christian Denominations: How Do They Differ?" *World Almanac, 1986*, pp. 342–343.

[112] There also is sentiment for an amendment, not to authorize prayer, but to restrict the federal court system from ruling on such matters. This could mean that conflicts would go unresolved.

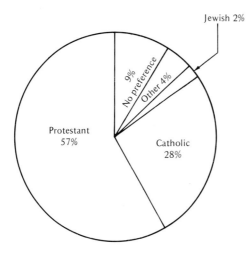

Jewish 2%

No preference 9%

Other 4%

Protestant
57%

Catholic
28%

Figure 7-2   Religious affiliation in the
United States.   (*Source:* Data from
"Religion in American Life; 1935–1985,"
Gallup Report No. 236 [May 1985],
p. 27.)

Summary

Both religious and nonreligious people support the separation of church and
state. Our tradition has religious roots, but it has other roots as well. Americans
have grounded their morality in religion, but religious freedom also has a firm
place in our tradition. Thus, for public purposes at least, religion has been
identified more with morality than with any particular faith. Frontier conditions, industrial development, immigration, nationalism, and pluralism have all
contributed to making the public (in contrast to the private) interest in religion
one that emphasizes civic morality rather than sectarian belief. We have argued
that the promotion of civic virtue and public morality is an important goal of
public education.

Some will say that the Supreme Court has not given guidelines to show educators how they can teach *about* religion and promote civic morality without
relying on religious faith.[113] We disagree. Whereas it is not easy for schools to
promote morality and citizenship without simultaneously promoting religion, it
is both possible and desirable to do so. The analyses of Jefferson, Madison,
Horace Mann, and de Tocqueville make just this point. And the Supreme Court
decision in *Lemon* v. *Kurtzman* (1971) provides a "test" to be used in determining whether religion or government has crossed the boundary.

Finally, consistent with the thrust of our book, if religion is to be helpful in
education, then it, too, should be a matter of critical inquiry. Critical inquiry,
we believe, is the means by which any subject must be judged for its inclusion
in the curriculum.

Moral Education in Practice

John Dewey said nearly a century ago that "It is a commonplace to say that the
development of character is the [aim] of all schoolwork." We have tried to show
that this certainly has been the case in American education and that it still is a

[113] Valente, *Law in the Schools*, p. 110, n. 6.

primary aim of education. But, as Dewey went on to say, it is easy to state an educational aim; "the difficulty lies in the execution of the idea."[114] Our task in this section is to suggest how civic education, the development of "character," might be accomplished in schooling.

Our recommendations for civic education are consistent with our analysis of human nature and the social order, American culture, and the aims and values of American society and schooling. This analysis has not been unambiguous. That is, we have reviewed a number of different interpretations of these matters but have argued in favor of social democracy, the importance of the individual, and the development of critical intelligence through education.

Our historical review of civic education suggested that morality, or "character," cannot be shaped directly; that is, no one simply can be talked into being a moral person. The word *moralizing* refers to such efforts, but they are seldom successful. What John Dewey says about education in general, that we never educate directly but only through an intermediate activity, is especially true of moral education.[115]

The development of moral skills does not demand a different kind of instruction from the development of intellectual skills or the study of subject matter. The content, context, and method of instruction all determine what is finally learned. John Dewey makes the point well:

> Moral education in school is practically hopeless when we set up the development of character as a supreme end, and at the same time treat the acquiring of knowledge and the development of understanding . . . as [if they had] nothing to do with character.[116]

Despite Dewey's warning, there is still a tendency to think of moral education as a special and separate subject matter. McGuffey, Webster, and Horace Mann did not make this mistake. They saw a direct connection between literacy and civic morality.

Neither is moral education achieved by learning a set of rules or duties. This is another way of saying that we do not educate directly. But, more important, it takes account of the fact that in our society there are many claims to what is right and wrong. The aim of moral education is not simply to sanction one claim and shun the others but to develop habits of mind and skills by which individuals make decisions for themselves and with others. This is what Daniel Boorstin means when he says that *The Genius of American Politics* lies in the fact that we have no fixed truths or what he calls graven images. The important values in our way of life are the democratic *procedures* we use to determine what is to be done or valued in any particular case.[117] Moral education must be consistent with this tradition. Indeed, if moral education were a matter of simply following rules, there would be no need for critical intelligence. We would all simply follow "the rules." Democracy demands that we do more than follow rules; we must also formulate and improve them. Moral education must prepare us for this task.

[114] John Dewey, *Moral Principles in Education* (Carbondale: Southern Illinois University Press, 1975 [1909]), p. 49. Available in paperback.

[115] John Dewey, *Democracy and Education* (New York: The Free Press, 1966 [1916]), p. 19. Available in paperback.

[116] Ibid., p. 354.

[117] Daniel J. Boorstin, *The Genius of American Politics* (Chicago: University of Chicago Press, 1953).

Numerous approaches to moral education have been tried in the schools.[118] We will emphasize only two of the most popular approaches here. The first is *values clarification,* and the second is Lawrence Kohlberg's idea of *cognitive/moral development.*

Values Clarification

"Values clarification" originates in the work of Louis E. Raths, Merrill Harmin, and Sidney B. Simon. They believe that children's problems do not always have emotional causes but spring instead from value conflicts. Children see apathy, confusion, and irrationality all around them, and they notice people who live without a consistent set of standards. Values clarification is not concerned with *what* values a person holds. Raths, Harmin, and Simon contend that our efforts to teach values have an "air of indoctrination [about them]. The idea of free inquiry, thoughtfulness, reason seems to be lost."[119] Values clarification, therefore, is interested in the *process* we use to determine what we value.

Determining values entails "how a person has decided to use his life."[120] Values (guides to behavior) are highly personal and change as we change and mature. Thus, proponents of values clarification focus on the process of valuing rather than on the particular values a student holds. Raths, Harmin, and Simon believe that values involve *choosing, prizing,* and *acting,* in the following ways:

Choosing 1. freely
          2. from alternatives
          3. after consideration of the consequences
Prizing   4. cherishing, or being happy with the choice
          5. affirming the choice publicly
Acting   6. doing something with the choice
          7. repeatedly, in a pattern of life.[121]

For values clarification, moral education involves encouraging, assisting, and providing opportunities for students to understand and act on their own choices.[122]

The description of the valuing process, just noted, suggests that values clarification is democratic. Values are chosen freely, from among different pref-

---

[118] See Larry C. Jensen and Richard S. Knight, *Moral Education: Historical Perspectives* (Washington, DC: University Press of America, Inc., 1981), especially Chapter 12, for contemporary approaches to moral education. Also, Barry Chazan, *Contemporary Approaches to Moral Education: Analyzing Alternative Theories* (New York: Teachers College Press, 1985); Richard H. Hersh, John P. Miller, and Glen D. Fielding, *Models of Moral Education: An Appraisal* (New York: Longman, Inc., 1980); both available in paperback.

[119] Louis E. Raths, Merrill Harmin, and Sidney B. Simon, *Values in Teaching: Working with Values in the Classroom* (Columbus, OH: Merrill Publishing Co., 1966), p. 41.

[120] Ibid., p. 6.

[121] Ibid., p. 30; see generally pp. 27–30.

[122] Ibid., Chapters 4–7. See also, Sidney B. Simon, Leland W. Howe, and Howard Kirschenbaum, *Values Clarification: A Handbook of Practical Strategies for Teachers and Students* (New York: Hart Publishing Company, Inc., 1972); and Sidney B. Simon and Jay Clark, *Beginning Values Clarification: A Guidebook for the Use of Values Clarification in the Classroom* (San Diego: Pennant Press, 1975).

erences and are publicly affirmed. The approach also appears to emphasize critical intelligence. Raths, Harmin, and Simon note that "we apply critical thinking techniques to matters that are largely in the affective domain."[123] And the *process* of valuing is emphasized because the authors do not want to impose values or indoctrinate students. This is all to the good.

One can wonder, though, whether values clarification is sufficient for moral education. A general criticism of the two approaches to moral education will be given after we discuss Kohlberg's theory, but for now we will note that values clarification is excessively individualistic (a topic discussed in Chapter 5) and supposes erroneously that a method can be divorced from both its subject matter and its civic outcomes.

We do not want to assert that social life is the only concern of moral education; there must be a concern and respect for the individual as well. But values clarification, in our view, is insufficiently concerned with social life. Raths, Harmin, and Simon say that "it is entirely possible that children will choose not to develop values. It is the teacher's responsibility to support this choice also."[124] This may not be good advice, for moral character and social democracy cannot exist in a values vacuum. However, our worry is not that children will shun values; children have values long before they come to school. The threat is that a purely individual choice of values might imperil someone else's choice. Morality arises in conflict. When there is a disagreement over values, how are individuals to know how to behave? Values clarification does not help them resolve their dilemma. Its advocates say only that someone with clear values will have "more consideration for his fellow human beings" and will be "someone who can be counted on."[125] The advice to leave the child alone also is difficult to square with Raths, Harmin, and Simon's contention that values "should work as effectively as possible to relate one to his world in a satisfying and intelligent way."[126] Because part of that world involves other human beings, morality always has a social dimension. The concern for civic education is about the social aspects of morality, about the relationship between the individual and society.

The problem for values clarification may come in its divorce of the process of valuing from the values themselves (products). We can understand the motive. Values clarification wants to avoid indoctrination and emphasize instead clarification and personal consistency. Clarity is important, but it is not enough. We need to ask what ends or values the methods of values clarification are to serve. Raths, Harmin, and Simon say that "there is an assumption" in their work "that humans *can* arrive at values by an intelligent process of choosing, prizing, and behaving."[127] Of course they can, and they often do. But what if they don't? Sidney Simon says, "When people learn the process, my faith and dream is, that they will be able to negotiate the future."[128] Concerning values, the historian Frederick Jackson Turner used to lecture, "The question is not whether you have a Philosophy . . . but whether the philosophy you have is

---

[123] Raths, Harmin, and Simon, *Values in Teaching*, pp. 8–9.
[124] Ibid., p. 47.
[125] Simon and Clark, *Beginning Values Clarification*, p. 18.
[126] Raths, Harmin, and Simon, *Values in Teaching*, p. 28.
[127] Ibid., p. 10.
[128] Simon and Clark, *Beginning Values Clarification*, p. 22.

good for anything."[129] Our point is that content, as well as process or method, is vital to moral education. We will return to the point later when we ask how we can make the best use of our history and tradition.

Kohlberg's Stages of Moral Development

Lawrence Kohlberg's theory of moral development is similar to values clarification in some ways. It functions in a democratic context and emphasizes, not the choices that are made, but the pattern of reasoning used in making choices. His emphasis is on the moral *judgment* process. Kohlberg, a psychologist, aims to show that the development of morality is directly related to cognitive development and also to social development. Thus, his theory is called cognitive/ moral development. Moral judgment or thinking involves an awareness of conflicts and issues, weighing conflicting values, and choosing an action for oneself.

Kohlberg interviewed children of various ages. He posed moral dilemmas and recorded and analyzed the children's responses. The dilemmas posed conflicts, usually between two equally good or bad alternatives, from which a choice had to be made. The archetypical dilemma is about a woman who was near death from cancer. One drug, recently discovered, might save her, but the druggist was charging $2000, ten times more than the cost of the drug. The husband tried everywhere to borrow the money, but, being unsuccessful, he asked the druggist to lower the price or to let him pay for it later. When the druggist refused, the husband broke into the store and stole the drug. Two questions were asked of the children: "Should the husband have done that?" and "Why?"[130]

Kohlberg found that responses to the dilemmas could be classified into levels and stages of development. A description of the levels and stages is given in Table 7-1.

Kohlberg contends that there are six stages of moral development. A stage is an idealized construction representing the ways that thought is organized in different periods of individual development. Each stage implies a structure or pattern of thought that guides an individual's response to a moral dilemma. The words Kohlberg uses to describe the levels or stages of moral development are instructive. Moral development seems to progress from an *egocentric* orientation, through a *societal* stage, and on to a *universal* perspective. And because most adult moral reasoning is at stages 3 and 4, it has been called *conventional*, while stages 1 and 2 are *preconventional* and stages 5 and 6 are *postconventional*.

Kohlberg believes that moral dilemmas may be answered from the perspective of any one of the stages.[131] But moral decisions should be made at the highest level of reasoning possible. To say that one stage is "higher" than another indicates that it is a more comprehensive way to organize facts, interests, and possibilities. It takes more interests into account; thus, it is more socially adaptive.[132]

[129] Carl L. Becker, "Wisconsin Historian," in Houston Peterson, ed., *Great Teachers: Portrayed by Those Who Studied under Them* (New York: Vintage Books, 1946), p. 245.

[130] Lawrence Kohlberg, "Stage and Sequence: The Cognitive-Developmental Approach to Socialization," in David A. Goslin, ed., *Handbook of Socialization Theory and Research* (Chicago: Rand McNally and Company, 1969), p. 379.

[131] See ibid., pp. 379–380, Table 6.5.

[132] Hersh, Miller, and Fielding, *Models of Moral Education*, p. 121.

TABLE 7-1. Kohlberg's States of Moral Development

Level	Stage	Orientation	Description
I Egoistic (Preconventional)	1	Obedience and punishment	Deference to authority. Obey in order to avoid punishments.
	2	Naive ego	Satisfying one's own needs (and occasionally others' needs).
II Societal (Conventional)	3	Good boy	Seek approval or to please others.
	4	Maintain authority and social order	Respect for law; doing one's duty.
III Universal (Postconventional)	5	Contractual/legal	Mutual or common agreement. Interest in human welfare.
	6	Conscience or principle	Act on universal and consistent principles. Concern for conscience and mutual respect and trust.

SOURCE: Lawrence Kohlberg, "Stage and Sequence: The Cognitive-Developmental Approach to Socialization," in *Handbook of Socialization Theory and Research,* ed. David A. Goslin (Chicago: Rand McNally and Company, 1969), p. 376, Table 6.2; Richard H. Hersch, John P. Miller, and Glen D. Fielding, *Models of Moral Education: An Appraisal* (New York: Longman, Inc., 1980), pp. 124–126, Table 7.1.

Cultural and environmental factors and innate capabilities may make some children reach a stage earlier or later than others. But all will go through the same steps, Kohlberg believes, regardless of their environment or teaching.[133] This is not to say that one can reach a higher level of thinking without a rich environment or sophisticated teaching, but only that the same structures of thought can be found in all societies. Kohlberg later revised his theory, acknowledging that a sixth stage of cognitive/moral development could not be found in longitudinal studies. The sixth stage seems to be a theoretical construction drawn from the experience of very special thinkers. Because so few people reach this stage, it might be best to see it as an advanced substage of stage 5.[134]

Kohlberg's theory of moral development has a number of beneficial characteristics. In his view, (1) moral thinking, like all other thinking, is closely related to cognitive ability. Individuals are not born moral; they learn how to be moral. How well this lesson is learned (how far along Kohlberg's continuum they progress) depends on the quality of their education. Moral education is more than learning rules; (2) it is a guided interaction between the individual and the environment. This student–environment interaction presents individuals with dilemmas and an array of possible choices. The choices students make structure their thinking and influence their later choices. Kohlberg (3) does not separate affective development from cognitive development. (This dichotomy

---

[133] Kohlberg, "Stage and Sequence," p. 357.

[134] Lawrence Kohlberg, "Revisions in the Theory and Practice of Moral Development," in William Damon, ed. *Moral Development: New Directions for Child Development* (San Francisco: Jossey-Bass, Inc., 1978), p. 86.

is common in discussions of moral education.) Like Dewey, he sees unity where others find division. Kohlberg's theory *unifies* the individual and society, cognitive and moral development, and affective and cognitive thought. As we have noted already, Kohlberg's theory of moral development (4) is (or intends to be) democratic. It is more concerned with the process of moral development (thinking, judgment) than with particular values to be held.

Kohlberg's stages should not be interpreted rigidly. Students do not move in lockstep fashion through the stages of moral development. Not all children are at stage 2 by age eight or stage 4 in mid-adolescence. Most adults do not advance beyond stage 4.[135] The teacher's job is to help students develop through as many stages as possible. Of course, development levels have to be considered; the only place to begin moral education is where the student is at the moment. But the development of moral judgment is a long-term affair. The aim is to develop an overall pattern of response to moral dilemmas, so students can improve the quality of their moral reasoning. Higher stage moral reasoning cannot be imposed on the student. Again, the idea is to *develop* rather than impose moral judgment. In stating moral dilemmas, the teacher should use the soundest reasoning that students can understand and encourage them to make decisions at the highest level of reasoning possible.[136]

According to Kohlberg, moral development involves awareness, weighing competing values, and making a choice for action. Teachers can provide opportunities for students to think through experience in increasingly complex ways. Good teachers pose moral dilemmas, ask questions, highlight different stage arguments, clarify and summarize those arguments, and promote role taking.[137] Role taking is very important in Kohlberg's theory. In fact, it may be a "precondition" for the development of morality.[138] Seeing things as others do inevitably challenges our own ideas, and through such challenges is morality developed. Kohlberg's dilemmas serve the same function.

Literacy and Moral Education

Values clarification and Kohlberg's cognitive/moral development theory are not without critics. Ideas have consequences. One critic, Christina Hoff Sommers, points out that a focus on methods of clarifying values and making moral decisions leaves out the substance or content of morality. Students do not become acquainted with moral traditions; in fact, tradition seems inherently to be suspect and to be avoided. Summers quoted Sidney Simon, a promoter of values clarification who says that "While the study of our cultural heritage can be defended on other grounds, we would not expect it to be sufficient for value education."[139]

---

[135] Hersh, Miller, and Fielding, *Models of Moral Education*, pp. 127–130.

[136] Ibid., pp. 121, 154.

[137] Ibid., p. 135. See also, Ronald E. Galbraith and Thomas M. Jones, *Moral Reasoning: A Teaching Handbook for Adapting Kohlberg to the Classroom* (Minneapolis: Greenhaven Press, Inc., 1976).

[138] James M. Giarelli, "A Comparative Analysis of the Conceptions of Development in Dewey, Piaget, and Kohlberg and Their Implications for Educational Theory and Practice" (doctoral dissertation, University of Florida, 1977), p. 124. Role taking is a way to consider *the generalized other*, discussed in Chapter 4. See George Herbert Mead, *Mind, Self, and Society* (Chicago: University of Chicago Press, 1934); available in paperback.

[139] Christina Hoff Sommers, "Ethics Without Virtue: Moral Education in America," *The American Scholar*, Vol. 53, No. 3 (Summer 1984), p. 382.

A single-minded emphasis on methods no doubt promotes tolerance for the beliefs of others. But, if that is the only virtue consciously promoted, it can inhibit other virtues, such as moral indignation (the feeling that something is not right), which Sommers believes is equally necessary for moral development. The result can be a kind of "no-fault history" or "moral agnosticism." It also can teach the wrong moral lesson, that ethics is simply a matter of knowing our own values.[140] What is needed *for* moral education, according to Sommers, is not values clarification but "some straightforward courses in moral philosophy and a sound . . . introduction to the Western moral tradition," from which one should learn that "there is an important distinction between moral and nonmoral decisions."[141] Values clarification "blurs" this distinction. Sommers does not think we can teach morality directly in values clarification classes but only indirectly as students grapple with the lessons of philosophy, history, and literature.[142]

Kohlberg is not unsympathetic to this criticism. Reflecting on his theory, Kohlberg has said,

> Some years of active involvement with the practice of moral education have led me to realize that my notion that moral stages were *the* basis for moral education, rather than a partial guide to the moral educator, was mistaken. . . . Although the moral stage concept is valuable for research purposes, however, it is not a sufficient guide to the moral educator, who deals with concrete morality in a school world in which value content as well as structure, behavior as well as reasoning, must be dealt with. In this context the educator must be a socializer, teaching value content and behavior, not merely a Socratic facilitator of development.[143]

It is not Kohlberg's aim to isolate moral education from the extended work of the school.

> If brief periods of classroom discussion can have a substantial effect on moral development, a pervasive, enduring and psychologically sound concern for the school's influence upon moral development should have much deeper effects. Such a concern would pervade the curriculum areas of social studies, law education, philosophy and sex education, rather than representing a new curriculum area. More deeply, it would affect the social atmosphere and justice structure of the school.[144]

Sommer's criticism is that values clarification and Kohlberg's development theory are examples of moral "form without substance." Her criticism is just the tip of the iceberg, for a more widespread criticism is that all of education, particularly teacher education, has become too "formal." If this criticism has merit, it has implications for moral education as well as other school activities. In fact, the point of the criticism is that education cannot properly be divorced from its moral substance, which is our cultural traditions.

---

[140] Ibid., pp. 387–388.

[141] Ibid., pp. 387, 383.

[142] Richard Mitchell makes the same point about consumer education: "The consumer who is duped by misleading advertising does not need consumer education; he needs to know how to read." Richard Mitchell, *The Graves of Academe* (Boston: Little, Brown and Company, 1981), p. 157.

[143] Kohlberg, "Revisions," p. 84; Kohlberg's emphasis. Although her criticism is more recent than Kohlberg's revision, Sommers does not mention it.

[144] Moshe Blatt and Lawrence Kohlberg, "The Effects of Classroom Moral Discussion on Children's Levels of Moral Judgment," *Journal of Moral Education*, Vol. 4 (1975), p. 153; quoted in Hersh, Miller, and Fielding, *Models of Moral Education*, p. 134.

For example, a leading critic, E. D. Hirsch, Jr., believes that formalism dominates in schools of education.[145] *Formalism* is the belief that teaching can be reduced to a technology; that is to say, that research can tell us what the most effective teaching methods are in any given situation and teachers can learn these techniques. In the learning arena, formalism is the belief that reading and writing are skills that, once learned, can be applied equally well in all situations. Reading and writing skills certainly are important, but Hirsch believes that they should not be overestimated. Equally important is the cultural part of language instruction, which used to get equal attention with skill development, as we have seen particularly in McGuffey's books, but which now seems to be crowded out of consideration by technique.

Hirsch uses the idea of "cultural literacy" to denote the knowledge (or content) on which "linguistic literacy" (skill) depends. Reading is not the mere decoding of words; it is making sense of ideas. Hirsch points out that we cannot make sense of ideas without first having a body of cultural knowledge. To be "literate" is to *know* something and be able to *use* what we know to help us learn more. Thus, we teach children to read by giving them books with familiar content and we help them improve their reading skills by broadening and deepening their knowledge of content. Content is the "tacitly shared background" that students used to hold in common.[146] We have seen in this and other chapters that we can no longer assume that students share a common stock of cultural knowledge. Hirsch argues that the decline in literacy in the United States is directly related to the fragmentation of our culture.[147] Thus, we cannot stop the literacy decline simply by teaching reading skills. We must also provide a stock of cultural knowledge. What is needed, for both a more literate and moral culture, is a reconstruction of what was called in Chapter 4 the cultural core.

Hirsch says provocatively that cultural literacy is a political, not a technical, matter. It requires not only political will (we must want literacy), but, more important, it involves the political process of working out the concrete values that best represent our culture.[148] These values should become the aim and focus of the school curriculum. They are the content of moral education. In coming to grips with this matter, there is, of course, a potential for running roughshod over minority views. Democracy demands that we not make this mistake. We may have drifted into formalism as a way to avoid this risk. It is significant that nearly all programs of moral education in our society try to avoid indoctrination and imposition. But, according to Hirsch, the proper way to avoid cultural imperialism is not to give in to formalism but to develop more heterogeneous values and traditions through political discussion, argument, and compromise.[149]

To take stock, what this all implies is that the content and methods of moral education should not be separated. They are two sides of the same concern. The content of moral education is our tradition and is embodied in such school

[145] E.D. Hirsch, Jr., " 'English' and the Perils of Formalism," *The American Scholar*, Vol. 53, No. 3 (Summer 1984), pp. 369–379.

[146] E.D. Hirsch, Jr., "Cultural Literacy," *The American Scholar*, Vol. 52, No. 2 (Spring 1983), p. 165. Hirsch has expanded this argument in *Cultural Literacy: What Every American Needs to Know* (New York: Houghton Mifflin Company, 1987).

[147] Ibid., p. 168.

[148] Ibid., pp. 162, 167.

[149] Hirsch, " 'English' and the Perils of Formalism," p. 376.

studies as history, literature, the arts, and even the story of science. Thus, we do not need a special study for moral education. Of course, this content has to be clarified and refocused whenever tradition, by which we mean "common agreement," breaks down. Teaching about a common culture—teaching moral education—should employ the same methods that are used in formulating that culture itself. In general, they are the methods of "critical thinking," which we discuss throughout this book. Thus, moral education is shown in yet another way to be civic or political education. A one-sided attention to either content or method in moral education—indeed, in education in general—produces formalism, on the one hand, and "moral agnosticism," on the other. The aim is to avoid both errors. It is sad to say that the formalism of method today has infected nearly every school subject that in the past contributed to moral education. History is a prime example.[150] Moral education needs to recover a sense of wholeness, a unity of content and method, and the ability to work through regular school subjects.

John Dewey's Conception of Moral Education

We can put these matters into theoretical and educational focus by referring again to John Dewey. Dewey points out that moral education does not require a separate study or the indoctrination of specific beliefs. Social life is the context of morality. To act morally entails going beyond one's own concerns and considering the interests of other people. Moral education should be judged by whether it develops an interest in community welfare.[151] The community is the arena of moral choice. As we have seen, the development of moral or civic character is an overriding aim of education, though we often overlook that fact because of attention given to subject matter and teaching methods. Dewey believes that the primary aim of schooling is participation in social life.[152] That aim is accomplished, of course, through subject matter, learning activities, and participation in the school culture. The problem of moral education is to relate what is learned to action.[153] The actions we wish to promote are determined by the aims we hold for education. Moral education thus develops insight, direction, and social concern.

What needs to be developed through education, according to Dewey, is not specific moral virtues but a general moral spirit or the habits of social imagination and intelligence.[154] Specific virtues, such as "good citizenship" or "discipline," are only shorthand ways of speaking about a whole system of general relations. Dewey says that it is a dangerous superstition

> to suppose that there is some one particular study or mode of treatment which can make the child a good citizen; to suppose, in other words, that a good citizen

---

[150] Joseph A. Diorio, "The Decline of History as a Tool of Moral Training," *History of Education Quarterly*, Vol. 25, Nos. 1–2 (Spring–Summer 1985), pp. 71–101; Frances FitzGerald, *America Revised: History Schoolbooks in the Twentieth Century* (Boston: Little, Brown and Company, 1979); Morris Janowitz, *The Reconstruction of Patriotism: Education for Civic Consciousness* (Chicago: University of Chicago Press, 1983), pp. 23, 168.

[151] Dewey, *Moral Principles in Education*, p. 17.

[152] Ibid., p. 11.

[153] Dewey, *Democracy and Education*, pp. 356, 360.

[154] Dewey, *Moral Principles in Education*, pp. 21, 40.

is anything more than a thoroughly efficient and serviceable member of society, one with all his powers of body and mind under control.[155]

Any study can contribute to moral education if it helps students to understand better their social environment. Although community welfare is the ultimate aim of education, the moral standard for judging school influences on individuals is whether their own interests are treated as important, whether schoolwork helps them to form good judgments, and whether they develop a sensitivity and responsiveness toward experience.[156] The only restraint of any worth in schooling, Dewey believes, is that which comes through concentrating one's powers on a worthwhile end. In all, to maintain a capacity for education, which these standards imply, is the essence of morality.[157] This is why Dewey believes that the only legitimate, general aim of education is continued education.[158]

Dewey believed that "moral principles are real in the same sense in which other forces are real; . . . they are inherent in community life, and in the working structure of the individual."[159] What is required in education is a faith that teaching moral principles can be as effective as, say, teaching reading and writing. Another educational philosopher has said that

> The fading of ideals is sad evidence of the defeat of human endeavour. . . . At the dawn of . . . civilisation, men started with the full ideals which should inspire education, . . . [but] gradually our ideals have sunk to square with our practice.
> But when ideals have sunk to the level of practice, the result is stagnation.[160]

In other words, "moral education is impossible apart from the habitual vision of greatness."[161]

All of this is to say that moral principles are ideals; they are not "utopian" but give specific direction and aim to our actions. To teach morals or civic consciousness is to elaborate the visions to which humankind has been attached and to show the function that vision has had and can have in life. In this sense, religion as well as any other subject can be taught in education, not as doctrine but as the record of human aspirations. Dewey also wrote about religion, making a distinction between religion and "the religious" and concluding, "Any activity pursued in behalf of an ideal end against obstacles and in spite of threats of personal loss because of conviction of its general and enduring value is religious in quality."[162]

There are other aspirations, to be sure. One set of them is embodied in our political documents, such as the Declaration of Independence and the Constitution. However, moral education requires no special subject matter or method, though it does require special attention. The potential for moral education is everywhere. Morality—and moral education—is simply the habits of critical intelligence and social sensitivity applied to individual conduct. Its content is the

---

[155] Ibid., p. 9.
[156] Ibid., pp. 53–57.
[157] Ibid., p. 54; Dewey, *Democracy and Education*, p. 360.
[158] Dewey, *Democracy and Education*, p. 109.
[159] Dewey, *Moral Principles in Education*, p. 58.
[160] Alfred North Whitehead, *The Aims of Education* (New York: The Free Press, 1967 [1929]), p. 29. Available in paperback.
[161] Ibid., p. 69.
[162] John Dewey, *A Common Faith* (New Haven: Yale University Press, 1934), p. 27; available in paperback. See also, Michael Eldridge, "Philosophy as Religion: A Study in Critical Devotion" (Doctoral dissertation, University of Florida, 1985).

record of human activity, which may be organized for educational purposes into what conventionally we call subjects or subject matter.

Institutional Supports for Moral Education

Of course the school cannot do the work of moral and civic education by itself. It must have the support of other social institutions. Two of these are the home or family and the political system. One pair of sociologists, Brigitte and Peter Berger, in fact, believe that the school is really the supporting institution to the family rather than vice versa. "The family, today as always, remains the institution in which at any rate the very great majority of individuals learn whatever they will ever learn about morality."[163] All the school can do is reinforce those values. This assumes, of course, that family values are individually and socially healthy. For example, the Bergers acknowledge that "youth culture," which arises because the school cannot provide the emotional and moral support given up by the family, should not be idealized, because it weakens individual autonomy.[164] As with education, other institutions, such as churches, legislatures, and courts, can reinforce only the values that are set in motion in the home.

The Bergers also believe that the importance of the family as the source of morality is endangered by the decline of religion. They observe that "the family alone, in the absence of a religious world view giving ultimate legitimacy to moral actions, cannot reestablish the civil virtues presupposed by a democratic polity."[165] They refer to such basic moral ideas as the sanctity of human rights, the willing assent to legal norms, and the belief that contractual agreements must be honored. We have seen this idea before. It is not necessarily an argument for partisan or sectarian religious instruction. At the least, it returns us to a consideration of religion as an ideal and as morality. We have attempted to show that this sense of religion is consistent with our democratic history and theory and can be a source of insight for education.

Another sociologist, Morris Janowitz, informs us of the contribution of national service to civic education. Janowitz believes that, especially recently, individual *rights* have been emphasized in society and education without corollary concern for *obligations*. Thus, the fundamental issue of citizenship and civic education is to restore a balance between rights and obligations. What is needed is "the reconstruction of patriotism." By *patriotism*, Janowitz emphasizes "the sentiment of belonging."[166] But although citizenship, even in democracy, involves such a sentiment, especially an attachment to a territory and society, it does not imply necessarily xenophobia, militarism, or blind and mechanical nationalism. In order to avoid these connotations, Janowitz prefers the phrase *civic consciousness*.

Civic consciousness cannot be achieved today by returning to the old formats; the matter is not that easy. Janowitz believes that we must accept alternative definitions of citizenship, which is to say that there is more than one way to express civic loyalty. But all forms of civic education in a democracy should expose students to the central and enduring political traditions of the nation,

---

[163] Brigitte Berger and Peter L. Berger, *The War over the Family: Capturing the Middle Ground* (Garden City, NY: Doubleday Co., Anchor Press, 1983), p. 176. Available in paperback.

[164] Ibid., pp. 159–160.

[165] Ibid., p. 177.

[166] Janowitz, *The Reconstruction of Patriotism*, p. 8.

teach essential knowledge about the organization and operation of governmental institutions, and fashion the identity and moral sentiments necessary to effective citizenship.[167]

Though the school is "the central agency of civic education," it has a limited role. Janowitz says that "democratic states are not particularly effective in civic education."[168] By this, he means that there is a great tolerance in democratic society for diversity of opinion; democracies are not quick to use coercion. In a democracy, Janowitz claims, the greatest contribution schooling can make is to teach basic literacy, for literacy and civic education are inseparable. Like Hirsch, Janowitz argues against the

> almost universal assumption . . . that students must first learn basic academic skills—especially reading and writing. Once they learn these skills, they are prepared to take part in . . . civic education. . . .
>
> I questioned whether this academic priority was [adequate]. Superficially, it seemed plausible. . . . [But] the reverse approach made better sense to me . . . : to develop civic attitudes and a sense of group affiliation, which would stimulate the mastery of conventional academic skills.[169]

Two ideas, according to Janowitz, have contributed more than any others to civic education in our culture: mass education and the "citizen soldier." The latter symbolizes the idea of obligatory service, which has a moral rather than a mercenary incentive.[170] The idea had its beginning, and perhaps its greatest effect, in our Revolutionary War period. Now, at the same time that schooling has drifted away from civic education, the idea of national service also has diminished. Military conscription ended in 1973. So neither national service nor education presently is designed to promote effectively civic education.

Janowitz believes we need to return to the idea of national service. He believes that "there can be no reconstruction of patriotism without a system of national service."[171] But the idea Janowitz presents is much broader than military service. He suggests that "national and community work" be required of all citizens. Janowitz models his idea after the Civilian Conservation Corps (CCC) of the 1930s and the more recent Job Corps and VISTA (Volunteers in Service to America) programs. The aim of national service is not to develop mechanical loyalty to the country or even to get important work done, such as rebuilding decaying neighborhoods or cleaning up the environment. National service would supply the context in which the work of schooling could have focus. Janowitz observes that "a cognitive, rational approach is not enough to 'move' participants in civic education. A democratic society requires . . . content capable of stimulating students to a sense of pride and self-esteem."[172] That is the important idea behind national service.

It might be some time before the idea of national service is restored in our society. Meanwhile, the idea could be encouraged within schooling itself by making experience and activity, rather than just study, an important element of moral and civic education.

---

[167] Ibid., pp. 12, 194.
[168] Ibid., p. 194.
[169] Ibid., p. 168. See also pp. 23, 25.
[170] Ibid., p. 32.
[171] Ibid., p. 194. See generally Chapter 7.
[172] Ibid., p. 105.

Summary

The thesis of this chapter is that an important aim of education is civic or political in nature, to prepare students for citizenship. Citizenship involves both the *rights* and the *obligations* of individuals in society. In the early years of our colonial and national experience, obligations seemed to be emphasized. School books, while they taught reading, writing, and even arithmetic, emphasized the even more important ends of loyalty, patriotism, and duty. Influences outside the school also supported these goals.

Religion has played an important role in American education. Whereas at first the aim may have been to advance sectarian belief, later (especially after the Revolution) public education worked to advance civic morality. To be sure, the civic morality taught in schools had a Protestant slant. Because of this, many who believed in other religions set up schools of their own. This was true particularly of Roman Catholics. Horace Mann was alert to the threat that sectarian religion and partisan politics posed for the common school. These concerns and others—frontier conditions, industrialism, immigration, nationalism, and pluralism—contributed to making the schools more "secular." Slowly the public's interest in religion began to manifest itself, not in the support of particular sectarian beliefs but rather in support of civic education.

In American life, the judiciary functions to resolve disputes between individuals and between an individual and society. Seldom is the issue clear or simple. Tough moral issues have to steer a course between competing values. The moral dilemma for religion and education is posed in the First Amendment to our Constitution, between the "establishment" and "free exercise of religion" clauses. The state (society) must show an important public purpose for injecting religion into public life, or the individual is to be left free to decide these matters.

Today the argument is made that civic education emphasizes the individual rights over national duty and obligation. In other words, the pendulum has swung from duty and obligation (in the time of *The New England Primer*, Webster's speller, and McGuffey's readers) to individual rights (in our own time). Thus, some critics argue that current programs of civic and moral education are one-sided and insufficient, emphasizing a "formalism," or a process, and neglecting affirmative content or values. What is needed in moral education, the critics say, is a return to a common body of knowledge and values from which individuals can find direction and a sense of community.

Yet, a common body of knowledge cannot simply be imposed on individuals. That is not the way of democracy. Nor can civic or moral education be taught directly. The need for a common body of knowledge returns us to political concern. Such knowledge, or rather the values that knowledge embodies, makes up the aims or ideals that we agree should be the objects of our political life and education. At the heart of civic education is our commitment to democratic discourse. Whatever our views, we must communicate and be civil with each other if we are to live and learn together. That has been the aim of American politics and education.

Much of the discussion in this chapter has been historical. In addition to our concern with civic and moral education, we have given a sketch of some aspects of our history of education. Although we cannot simply repeat the past, the enduring values of our society are embodied in our history and traditions. Civic education must take account of that past. The debate over civic and moral education is a debate over the meaning of our traditions. In order to join that debate, we must develop intellectual skill and social sensitivity. What John Dewey said in 1927 is reaffirmed by modern studies of education: "The essential need [for civic education] is the improvement of the methods and conditions of debate, discussion and persuasion."[173] If schooling would make these considerations more central in its work, we could trust that all would be well with civic and moral education.

Suggested Readings

The voluminous references in this chapter themselves suggest abundant further reading. We can add a few others and reiterate some of the more pertinent references to the general topic of civic education that should be considered in their totality and in detail.

Much of the information in this chapter is historical. Students could benefit from reading comprehensive accounts of the history or development of education in the United States.

BUTTS, R. FREEMAN, and LAWRENCE A. CREMIN. *A History of Education in American Culture.* New York: Holt, Rinehart and Winston, 1953.

CHURCH, ROBERT L., and MICHAEL W. SEDLAK. *Education in the United States: An Interpretive History.* New York: The Free Press, 1976.

CHURCH, ROBERT L. and MICHAEL W. SEDLAK. *Education in the United States: An Interpretive History.* New York: The Free Press, 1976.

CURTI, MERLE. *The Social Ideas of American Educators,* rev. ed. Totowa, NJ: Littlefield, Adams & Company, 1959 [1935]; available in paperback. Curti traced the ideas of influential educators and movements from colonial times to the mid-twentieth century, with an eye to revealing their social origins and social implications. The story of education, he tells us, is the story of politics.

POTTER, ROBERT E. *The Stream of American Education.* New York: American Book Company, 1967.

There is a wealth of reading, much of it new, on the relation between religion and government and education.

LEVY, LEONARD W. *The Establishment Clause: Religion and the First Amendment.* New York: Macmillan Publishing Company, 1986. A premier constitutional historian interprets the establishment clause as functioning to depoliticize religion and thus to maintain civility among all religious views.

MICHAELSEN, ROBERT. *Piety in the Public School: Trends and Issues in the Relationship Between Religion and the Public School in the United States.* New York: The Macmillan Company, 1970.

MILLER, WILLIAM LEE. *The First Liberty: Religion and the American Republic.* New York: Alfred Knopf, 1986. This book argues for strict neutrality.

REICHLEY, A. JAMES. *Religion in American Public Life.* Washington, DC: The Brookings Institution, 1985. Reichley argues in favor of the public accommodation of religion.

Several works by Neil McCluskey, a Catholic priest, set forth the Catholic view about religion, education, and morals.

[173] John Dewey, *The Public and Its Problems* (New York: Henry Holt and Company, 1927), p. 208.

McCluskey, Neil G., S.J., ed. *Catholic Education in America: A Documentary History.* New York: Teachers College Press, 1964. The introduction by McCluskey, pp. 1–44, is an insightful interpretation.

McCluskey, Neil G., S.J. *Public Schools and Moral Education: The Influence of Horace Mann, William Torrey Harris, and John Dewey.* New York: Columbia University Press, 1958. In 1958, McCluskey predicted what appears to some to have happened today: that, because of the influence of Mann, Harris, and Dewey, who defined morals independent of religion in the common, public schools, schools have become ever more secular and alienating to increasing numbers of parents who want some religious element in their childrens' education.

Several histories of schoolbooks have been cited in this and previous chapters. The study of history in schools perhaps has borne much of the burden of moral and civic education in our culture. There is a fear that that source is no longer useful today.

Black, Hillel. *The American Schoolbook.* New York: William Morrow & Company, Inc., 1967. This is an examination of how textbooks are written and sold, who decides what goes into them, and how they are selected for school use.

FitzGerald, Frances. *America Revised: History Schoolbooks in the Twentieth Century.* Boston: Little, Brown and Company, 1979. The rewriting of American history to suit pedagogical fads and political interest groups (not to mention sales) has led to the emasculation of history as a moral educator.

Several sociological studies should be recommended (in fact, reiterated) because of their implications for, and in some instances direct discussion of, civic education.

Bellah, Robert N., et al. *Habits of the Heart: Individualism and Commitment in American Life.* Berkeley: University of California Press, 1985; available in paperback. Part II, "Public Life," and the Conclusion, "Transforming American Culture," have suggestions for civic education.

Berger, Brigitte, and Peter L. Berger. *The War over the Family: Capturing the Middle Ground.* Garden City, NY: Doubleday Co. Anchor Press, 1983; available in paperback.

Janowitz, Morris. *The Reconstruction of Patriotism: Education for Civic Consciousness.* Chicago: University of Chicago Press, 1983; available in paperback.

John Dewey wrote nearly a thousand articles and books in his lifetime. It is fair to say that nearly all of them, except perhaps those on purely technical matters, had civic and moral implications. The following book summarizes well his concern for civic culture.

Dewey, John, *The Public and Its Problems.* New York: Henry Holt and Company, 1927; available in paperback.

CHAPTER 8

Educational Aims for American Society

Americans generally have been an optimistic people, which may reflect the abundance of this country and the opportunities we have had for change. We traditionally have seen the present to be an improvement over the past, and we look forward to an ever brighter future. Opinion polls show that 84 percent of Americans are satisfied with their personal lives (see Figure 8-1). We think we are better off than just a year ago (see Figure 8-2) and that we will be even better off in the future (see Figure 8-3).

This reservoir of optimism may account not only for the "anything's possible" mentality of industrialism but also for the relative stability of our political system. An enduring confidence in the ability of the system to solve long-term

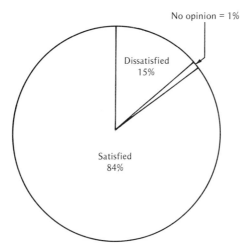

Figure 8-1   Satisfaction with personal lives.   (*Source:* Data from Gallup Report No. 246 [March 1986], p. 4.)

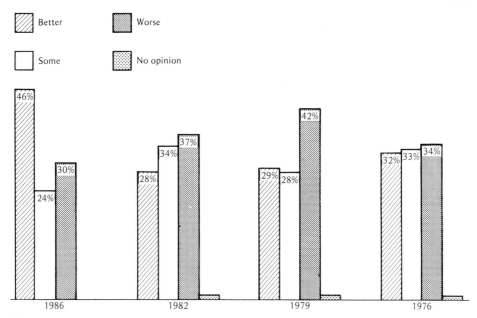

Figure 8-2   Are you better or worse off than a year ago?   (*Source:* Data from "Outlook Toward Personal Life," Gallup Report No. 246 [March 1986], pp. 8–9.)

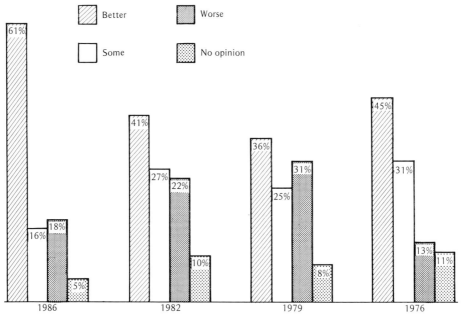

Figure 8-3   Looking ahead, do you think you will be financially better or worse off?   (*Source:* Data from "Outlook Toward Personal Life," Gallup Report No. 246 [March 1986], pp. 6–7.)

problems is essential to democracy.[1] Without this confidence it is unlikely that our government could have survived such grave challenges as economic depression, inflation, war, McCarthyism, the Civil Rights struggle, Watergate, and Irangate. Optimism has provided government with the margin of error needed to ensure political stability.

Changes in Confidence

Is the traditional American confidence waning? The answer, no doubt, depends on what we are concerned with at the moment and the general condition of society when we take its pulse. Americans seem to distinguish between confidence in their personal lives and in their public institutions. In a sense, this is paradoxical, for it implies that our personal and public lives have little to do with each other. It may carry over from our idea of individualism. And it may pose one of the crucial problems of the time, that of "privatism," which was mentioned previously and will be discussed again. In any case, until very recently, confidence in our institutions has decreased perceptibly as confidence in our personal lives has grown.

Table 8-1 shows information about our confidence in institutions. Some of the institutions are political or governmental, while others have to do with industry, information, and religion. They all have a powerful impact on our lives. The table shows a decline in confidence in almost all institutions in the ten years from 1973 to 1983. These were the years of Vietnam, Watergate, energy shortages, and environmental pollution.

Part of a loss of confidence in institutions may reflect the fact that some problems, such as inflation, energy shortages and costs, and environmental concerns, are stubbornly resistant to traditional solutions. In a sense, these are "new" problems and call for new solutions. But other problems may have been with us for a long time. "Traditional" problems such as war and international tensions and problems of the elderly appear today in the new clothing of nuclear weapons and an aging society.

More recent Gallup polls show that confidence in public institutions again is on the rise. Those figures are shown in the column for 1985 in Table 8-1. Confidence in the U.S. Supreme Court, Congress, public schools, and the military has increased sharply since 1983, while there has been a smaller increase for the other institutions. Notice also that in 1985, newspapers have a lower confidence rating than Congress and organized labor has a lower rating than television. That is, the relative standing of some of the institutions has changed. It is too early to determine, though, whether the rise of confidence in institutions is the beginning of a trend. That no doubt will depend on whether the institutions deal effectively with the problems we have.

Confidence in institutions relates to confidence in our leaders. Table 8-2 shows the degree to which we believe certain leaders are honest and abide by ethical standards. It is ironic that political leaders and lawyers, business executives, and labor leaders, to whom we look for much of our leadership in actually solving problems, do not stand high in the eyes of the American public.

---

[1] Gabriel A. Almond and Sidney Verba, *The Civic Culture: Political Attitudes and Democracy in Five Nations* (Princeton, NJ: Princeton University Press, 1963). Available in paperback.

TABLE 8-1.   Confidence in Institutions (percent answering "a great deal"; "quite a lot")

	1985	1983	1981	1979	1977	1975	1973
Church/religion	66	62	64	65	64	68	66
Military	61	53	50	54	57	58	NA
Banks/banking	51	51	46	60	NA	NA	NA
Supreme Court	55	42	46	45	46	49	44
Public schools	48	39	42	53	54	NA	58
Newspapers	35	38	35	51	NA	NA	39
Congress	39	28	29	34	40	40	42
Big business	31	28	20	32	33	34	26
Organized labor	28	26	28	36	39	38	30
Television	29	25	25	38	NA	NA	37

SOURCE: Data (1973–1983) from Gallup Report No. 217 (October 1983), pp. 4, 5–14. Data for the 1985 figures are from George Gallup, Jr., *The Gallup Poll: Public Opinion 1985* (Wilmington: Scholarly Resources, Inc., 1986), pp. 162–168.

NA = not asked

Though the data in Tables 8-1 and 8-2 are not exactly alike, there is a suggestion that, except for clergymen, American confidence in its leaders is lower than in its institutions.

One of the elements sure to affect our faith in institutions is the nature of the problems we face. Table 8-3 gives a list of some of those problems and the importance (percentage) that Americans assign to them. Other surveys have

TABLE 8-2.   Confidence in Honesty and Ethical Standards of Selected Leaders, 1985 (percent answering)

	"Very High"; "High"	"Average"	"Low"; "Very Low"
Clergy	67	26	4
Medical doctors	58	33	8
College teachers	54	35	5
Policemen	47	41	10
Bankers	37	51	9
TV reporters/commentators	33	48	15
Newspaper reporters	29	52	16
Lawyers	27	40	30
Business executives	23	54	18
U.S. Senators	23	53	21
Congressional representatives	20	49	27
Local politicians	18	53	24
State politicians	15	55	24
Labor union leaders	13	35	45
Insurance salesmen	10	49	38
Car salesmen	5	32	59

SOURCE: Data from George Gallup, Jr., *The Gallup Poll: Public Opinion 1985* (Wilmington: Scholarly Resources, Inc., 1986), pp. 191–193.

The figures do not add to 100 percent because "no opinion" has been dropped.

TABLE 8-3. The Most Important Problems Facing the Country Today

	Percent
War/international tension	27
Unemployment	20
Excess government spending/the deficit	18
Cost of living/taxes	11
The economy (in general)	6
Poverty	6
Crime	4
Drug abuse	2
Moral decline	2
Problems of the elderly	2
All others	14
No opinion	3

SOURCE: Data from "Most Important Problems," Gallup Report No. 235 (April 1985), pp. 19–21. See also, George Gallup, Jr., *The Gallup Poll: Public Opinion 1985* (Wilmington: Scholarly Resources, Inc., 1986), p. 253.

cited depletion of natural resources; increasing population and overcrowding; decline in the quality of education; people caring only about themselves, persons taking the law into their own hands, and loss of neighborliness; deterioration of family life and decline in religion; and a widening gap between "haves" and "have nots" as problems that pose a serious threat to the nation as we approach the twenty-first century.[2]

Another measure of confidence, or lack of it, is whether we think we can manage the problems in our future. The question, Do you think that for people like yourself the world ten years from now will be better, worse, or about the same as it is today? received a "flat-line" response from Americans in 1985, nearly one-third citing each of the possible answers (see Figure 8-4). Americans were more confident when rating "confidence in America to deal with world problems"; war and international tensions no doubt were foremost in mind but energy, terrorism, and balance of trade probably were in mind as well: 68 percent had considerable or great confidence, but 31 percent still had little, very little, or no confidence (see Figure 8-5). Sixty percent say that confidence has remained the same, while it has gone up for 16 percent and down for 22 percent.[3]

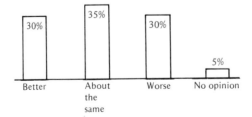

Figure 8-4 Will the world in ten years be a better place than it is today? (*Source:* Data from George Gallup, Jr., *The Gallup Poll: Public Opinion 1985* [Wilmington: Scholarly Resources, Inc., 1986], p. 31.)

[2] See *Roper Reports*, 80–84 (March 1980).
[3] George Gallup, Jr., *The Gallup Poll: Public Opinion 1985* (Wilmington: Scholarly Resources, Inc., 1986), p. 132.

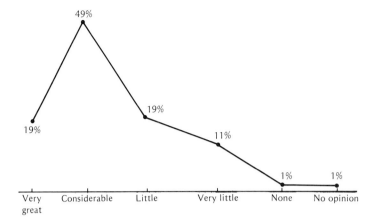

Figure 8-5 Confidence in America to deal with world problems (May 1985). (*Source:* Data from George Gallup, Jr., *The Gallup Poll: Public Opinion 1985* [Wilmington: Scholarly Resources, Inc., 1986], pp. 130–132.)

Human Problems

The striking thing about our problems is that they are human rather than technological problems; they are not likely to be solved by advanced technology or new equipment. They are people problems, and their solution will inevitably entail dramatic changes in human behavior. If we are to stop warring with our neighbors, depleting our resources, polluting our environment, overpopulating our fragile planet, destroying the family unit, and disrupting the sense of community, we must find new ways to act and interact.

The Tragedy of the Commons

A clearer sense of the difficulties we face can be gained through an examination of what biologist Garrett Hardin has called the "tragedy of the commons." Imagine a pasture (commons) owned by a community of herdsmen. The pasture is open to all for the grazing of cattle. The herd grows, and the herdsmen prosper, but the day comes when the number of cattle begins to overburden the resources of the commons. The grass is eaten faster than nature can replenish it. The cattle grow thin and the herdsmen, unable to sell their stock as profitably as before, begin to lose money. The herdsmen, like all of us, are independent human beings. They make their own decisions and look out for their own interests. What will the herdsmen do? Hardin spells out the tragedy: "As a rational being, each herdsman seeks to maximize his gain. Explicitly or implicitly, more or less consciously, he asks 'What is the utility *to me* of adding one more animal to my herd?' "[4] (Hardin's emphasis).

This grim calculus of personal interest has both a positive and a negative component. On the positive side, the herdsman gains the benefit of one more animal. This addition increases his profits. But, of course, the addition of an-

[4] Garrett Hardin, "The Tragedy of the Commons," *Science*, Vol. 126 (December 1968), pp. 1243–1248. For a full account of the significance of the "tragedy of the commons" for education, see Mary and Harry Bredemeier's excellent text *Social Forces in Education* (Sherman Oaks, CA: Alfred Publishing Co., Inc., 1978).

other animal will do even more damage to the commons. This is the negative component. However, the negative effects of overgrazing are shared by all the herdsmen equally. In other words, the person who adds an animal gets all the benefits from that animal, but the costs, the harm done to the pasture and the herd, are borne by the other herdsmen as well. Where does this situation lead? Ultimately to tragedy. Each profit-maximizing herdsman will see the utility of adding another animal to the herd—and another and another—until finally the pasture will support no cattle at all.

The tragedy of the commons has relevance for the American situation. The energy shortage is a case in point. Americans' demand for energy exceeds our petroleum and other resources. Most people agree that we must cut our energy consumption, and we have begun to do this. There are many ways to cut our consumption. We can walk or ride bicycles to nearby destinations; we can take public transportation to more distant points. We can join car pools and drive within the speed limit. If all of us did our part, the energy shortage would be more manageable.

But voluntary controls, such as those mentioned, do not seem to work. Rather, our individual choices seem to be governed by the logic of the commons. Every action we are urged to take (walking, bicycling, joining car pools, using public transportation, driving within the speed limit) entails some measure of personal inconvenience. It takes more effort; we have to wait for public transportation, coordinate our departure with others, and take more time to get where we want to go. This inconvenience, though perhaps not large, is direct and immediately felt, whereas the benefits of self-sacrifice are remote by comparison. The sacrifices will benefit society as a whole and may even help us personally in some small way, but the benefits are not clearly apparent to us. Unhappily, but not surprisingly, individuals do not choose to be inconvenienced unless there is a discernible payoff for them. The price of inconvenience is too high; the apparent benefits of conservation are too low. Worse, other individuals continue to guzzle gas while the socially minded conserve. Before long, conservers realize that their conservation only makes more fuel available for those who will waste it. Their good sense and good will merely subsidize the extravagance of others. With this in mind, some conservers go back to guzzling gas.[5]

The mentality of the commons is found in many areas of our lives. In the area of inflation, it operates as businesses raise their prices and profits and labor calls for higher wages. It operates when people litter rather than seek out nearby trash cans. It explains why some students steal books from the library, default on student loans, cheat on tests, and misuse food stamps.

Why Don't People Cooperate?

The answer to the tragedy of the commons, of course, is cooperation. If the herdsmen would agree to stem their personal greed, everyone would be better off. But cooperation is not easy to come by. Cooperation assumes that we know how our actions will affect others and that we care. Let us look at these issues one at a time.

---

[5] For many poignant examples of this problem, see Thomas Schelling, "On the Ecology of Micromotives," *The Public Interest* (Fall 1971), pp. 61–98.

ADEQUATE KNOWLEDGE.   We can imagine that the herdsmen ultimately will come to their senses and see that their actions are self-defeating. At this point, if it is not too late, rules will be set limiting the use of the commons, and some system will be developed to enforce these rules. This is not unusual behavior for human beings—even selfish ones. We limit the access to intersections by using traffic lights, to parking spaces by using decals and parking meters, and to service at restaurants by requiring reservations and waiting our turn. If selfish behavior is tolerated in such circumstances, we all suffer.

But this insight is not always available to us. It is difficult for some to see the connection between last year's extravagant use of gas and this year's shortage. (Indeed, a majority of Americans see the energy shortage as nothing more than an oil-company hoax.) It is hard to understand the relationship between the overeating of affluent nations and the starvation of poor ones. And what farmer (or home gardener), fighting pests with DDT, could have imagined that his action would destroy life in the ecosystem in far-off Alaska? The effects of our actions are often invisible, and because we cannot see them, we are not moved to change our ways.

ADEQUATE CARING.   The second assumption of cooperation is that once we know the consequences of our actions, we will care enough to do something about them. The problem of adequate knowledge has to do with gathering and communicating adequate information. The problem of caring has to do with what people value and see as rewarding. As we learned in Chapter 4, values are a matter of cultural definition. If we are to avert the tragedy of the com-

Citizens must cooperate to avoid the "tragedy of the commons."   (*Source:* National Education Association, Joe Di Dio.)

mons, we must learn to value cooperation at least as much as we value individualism, personal profit, and competition.

This is a big order. Although large portions of American life are governed by cooperative values, the idea persists that competitiveness is our major motivation. A closer inspection would reveal that cooperation is essential to all human groups. As David and Roger Johnson point out, no family, group, or institution can function without it.

> Without high levels of cooperation there would be no coordination of behavior on highways or sidewalks, in stores, in organizations, or anywhere else. No two individuals could communicate or interact without cooperating to form a common language and agreeable norms of behavior. Stores would not exist, exchange of goods and services would not take place, entertainment would not be possible, occupations would not be available, education would be unheard of, nothing but complete anarchy would exist without cooperation. Even in fighting wars and conducting competitive activities there are vast underpinnings of cooperative agreements concerning the way in which the competition or conflict will be conducted and the ways in which antagonists can express their hostility toward each other. *There can be no competition without underlying cooperation.* Competition is a very, very small part of interacting with other individuals in our society and probably not a very important type of human interaction.[6] [Our emphasis.]

Sadly, child rearing and schooling put a great emphasis on competition rather than on cooperative skills. Thus, competition becomes a dominating value. This priority not only jeopardizes the cooperative underpinnings of society but also makes it difficult to expand our cooperative efforts when faced with new problems. Our institutions, especially those in the public sphere, stress competition. It must be remembered that these institutions were developed at a time when our resources seemed unlimited, our population was small, and territorial and industrial expansion was booming. The competitive ethic spurred this expansion. Americans were taught that the best way to help others was to pursue their own self-interests, which in turn would create jobs and a high standard of living for others.

The conditions that engendered these values have changed, but the values live on. Like the herdsmen, we are taxing the ability of the environment to support us. Energy, clean air and water, open space, and easy access to beauty are suddenly in short supply. Our ability to produce goods has outdistanced our ability to fashion humane values, cooperative social systems, and reward structures that are in the public interest. Our social advancement has not kept pace with technological progress. As Mose Allison observed, "Things are getting better and better. It's people I'm worried about."[7]

Allison has good reason to worry. Cooperation demands full knowledge of how our actions affect others, an appreciation of our interdependence, and a willingness to pursue common goals. All of this suggests a heightened involvement with others in our communities, institutions, and professions. Yet, as we

---

[6] David W. Johnson and Roger T. Johnson, "Instructional Goal Structure: Cooperative, Competitive, or Individualistic," *Review of Educational Research*, Vol. 44 (1974), pp. 213–240.

[7] Quoted in Samuel Bowles and Herbert Gintis, *Schooling in Capitalist America: Educational Reform and the Contradictions of Economic Life* (New York: Basic Books, Inc., 1976), p. 276. Available in paperback. In the nineteenth century, Ralph Waldo Emerson said it this way: "Things are in the saddle, and ride mankind" (*Poems*, "Ode Inscribed to W. H. Channing" [1847]).

saw in Chapter 2, modern society has alienated many people from these aspects of life. More and more Americans are retreating to the private sphere. This fact brings us to the last roadblock to cooperative existence, the new privatism.

The New Privatism

In 1976, the Survey Research Center at the University of Michigan interviewed 2,000 adult men and women concerning their feelings of well-being and distress. The study was unique because it almost exactly replicated a survey conducted twenty years earlier, allowing researchers to study changes in attitudes over time. Data analysis revealed an overall stability in Americans' general happiness, feelings of well-being, and confidence in their ability to handle the stress of everyday life. However, there were troublesome shifts in other areas. The anxiety level of Americans had increased in the twenty years. This was true at all age levels, but it was especially prevalent among the young. Fifty-two percent of Americans between the ages of twenty-one and twenty-nine indicated that they worried a lot or always, up from 32 percent in 1957 (see Figure 8-6). Americans below fifty years of age reported more anxiety symptoms, such as insomnia, nervousness, headaches, loss of appetite, and upset stomach.

The 1976 survey has not been updated, but other data suggest that Americans, especially young people, are becoming increasingly alienated from society. A larger proportion of young men in America, 15 to 24 years old, commit suicide than do youth in two-thirds of the other countries surveyed; the rate is nearly 20 cases per 100,000 population.[8] (Israel and Ireland, among fifteen nations, have the lowest rate of suicide for both males and females. These also are nations where family life seems to be the most intact.) The rate of suicide for white men, 15 to 24 years of age, has nearly tripled in the last 40 years; out-of-wedlock births among white women in the United States have increased sevenfold in the last 45 years; and, although recent statistics on the use of illicit drugs shows a yearly decline from 1979 to 1985, nearly half of all U.S. high

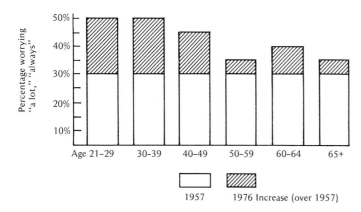

Figure 8-6   Extent of worrying among age groups in 1957 and 1976. (*Source: ISR Newsletter,* Institute for Social Research, University of Michigan, Winter 1979. The figure is based on data from research conducted by Elizabeth Douvan, Joseph Veroff, and Richard Kulka. Reprinted by permission.)

[8] *Information Please Almanac, 1986* (Boston: Houghton-Mifflin Co., 1986), p. 133. Based on data from *Statistical Abstract of the United States,* 1985. The figures are the latest available.

school seniors used some form of illicit drug in 1985.[9] One pair of interpreters of these statistics see them as implying that young people are "increasingly fleeing from reality."[10]

All of this points to an increased privatism in American life. People are not just withdrawing into the private sphere to find identity and meaning for their lives (see Chapter 2); they are disappearing into themselves. The evidence indicates that Americans are experiencing increased difficulty integrating into society. More and more citizens are seeing social structures as their problem and personal authenticity as their only viable solution. Social roles no longer provide automatic coping mechanisms for life's problems. This is especially true for the young. Deprived of several mechanisms for coping with stress, Americans have experienced increased anxiety. They also report increased confidence that they can face their problems on their own, but there is reason to doubt that this confidence is justified. If we are to avoid the extremes of oppressive social structures, on the one hand, and privatism, on the other, we must pursue flexibility through the aims and process of education.

National Problems and Educational Aims

You may think that we have left the topic of education to pursue issues that have nothing to do with the activities of teaching. After all, educators are charged with conveying information, developing skills, and facilitating physical and emotional growth. What do national problems have to do with these person-to-person responsibilities?

The connection is not remote. To make the point, let us look again at the responsibilities just mentioned. When we say that teachers must provide information and skills to their students, what are we implying? Certainly, we are not saying that any old information should be taught or that one skill is as desirable as another. We have something different in mind, namely, that education should prepare individuals for life in society. The information, skills, and habits we wish to instill in students are those that will help them become active and useful members of society.

What knowledge, abilities, and dispositions are needed for good citizenship? When societies are not changing rapidly, this question is easy to answer. Education simply continues to do what it has done traditionally. Educators do not have to make choices, at least not consciously. But the situation is very different when society is changing quickly. Under these conditions, education must prepare people for an uncertain future. This is a tricky business. If this preparation is to be done well, teachers must have a clear understanding of the kinds of problems the nation is likely to face in the future. We must make careful

---

[9] Edward A. Wynne and Mary Hess, "Long-Term Trends in Youth Conduct and the Revival of Traditional Value Patterns," *Educational Evaluation and Policy Analysis*, Vol. 8, No. 3 (Fall 1986), pp. 294–308. See also, Lloyd D. Johnston, Jerald G. Bachman, and Patrick M. O'Malley, *Monitoring the Future: Questionnaire Responses from the Nation's High School Seniors* (annual volumes, 1975–1984) (Ann Arbor: Institute for Social Research, University of Michigan); and Angus Campbell, *The Sense of Well-Being in America: Recent Patterns and Trends* (New York: McGraw-Hill Book Co., 1981).

[10] Wynne and Hess, ibid., p. 304.

judgments about the skills and dispositions most likely to be helpful in tomorrow's world. Educators cannot make such judgments alone, but they, of all persons, must have clear aims so that people outside the field can understand what teachers are trying to do and can help with ideas of their own.

What Are Educational Aims?

It is one thing to say that education should prepare people for an unknown future and quite another to do it. A first step is to define our goals in a way that can guide teaching practice. An educational aim is an indication of what we want education to accomplish.

Educational aims have some essential ingredients. They must be compatible with human nature, and they must fit the conditions of society. They must be flexible, so they can be changed when conditions change. They must help teachers decide what to do, suggest methods for doing it, and supply a way to measure whether the methods are working. Let us look at these matters one at a time.

It should be clear by now why this book began with a discussion of human nature. If we are to fashion useful educational aims, we must know something about the potential and limitations of human beings. Educational aims must take into account the human need for order as well as the human ability to create. Educational aims must promote a relationship between the individual and society that is within human possibility and in keeping with the best of our cultural heritage and aspirations. It should also be clear by now why so much space has been devoted to a clarification of American values, traditions, and problems. Educational aims must address national problems and take account of our cultural inheritance.

Educational aims need to be flexible; they are not to be seen as a list of fixed rules to be blindly obeyed. Aims must change as conditions change and we gain new knowledge. While aims must be flexible enough to allow for any needed modification, they also must be sufficiently enduring and clear to give educators guidance. Aims are useful only to the degree that they help us discover the means and methods for achieving our goals. They also give continuity to the educational process. With the guidance of aims, teaching becomes more than a sequence of random events; it becomes a progressive process that moves a student toward a clear goal. In short, aims provide direction.

Lastly, aims help educators judge whether their methods are working. Without clear goals, it is impossible for a teacher to know if a teaching technique, class arrangement, or curriculum is moving students in the desired direction. Without clear aims, teachers are likely to drift from one educational fad to another. Each fad (teaching machines, open classrooms, mini courses, token economies, and the rest) seems inviting and for the moment becomes widely adopted. Once tried, the new techniques disappoint teachers because they have not produced miracles. So new fads replace the old and the cycle starts again.

Teachers are especially susceptible to fads for two reasons. First, they often are frustrated because they cannot determine whether their students are making progress, so they grasp at any straw. Second, they cannot see progress because they do not have clear objectives. Unless we know where it is we want to go, it is impossible to know whether we are getting there. Clearer aims are the remedy for the waste of educational fads.

Some Options for Education

Everyone wants education to make a difference in the lives of students. Ultimately, we hope education will prepare them for the future. The disagreement comes when we clarify our aims and specify just what skills, knowledge, dispositions, and habits are to be promoted. We saw this disagreement in Chapter 2 when we looked at the educational aims of cultural transmission (Durkheim), individual growth (Rogers), and democratic process (Dewey). These men wanted education to produce very different types of human beings. Let us look again at these types, but this time from another angle. We will use the analytic typologies of W. I. Thomas, a pioneering American sociologist (1863–1947).

Thomas contended that personalities are developed in the give-and-take struggle between the individual and society.

> Personal evolution is always a struggle between the individual and society—a struggle for self-expression on the part of the individual, for his subjection on the part of society—and it is in the total course of this struggle that the personality . . . manifests and constructs itself.[11]

People develop different personalities depending upon the outcome of this struggle. According to Thomas, if society dominates (as Durkheim hoped it would), a Philistine is produced. If the individual dominates (as Rogers wanted), a Bohemian is produced. And if a creative harmony is established between the individual and society (as Dewey sought), a creative person results.

Let us examine these three personality types more closely. Remember that they are "ideal types," abstractions constructed to show what the personalities look like in pure form. In real life, no one possesses all the characteristics of one type. Rather, we are a combination of ingredients. We need to remember also that the words are being used descriptively; no good or bad connotation necessarily is intended (though we have to reckon with such connotations, for they come with experience). By looking at these types in pure form, we are better able to judge their worth as educational aims.

The Philistine

According to Thomas, the Philistine is the personality type developed when cultural transmission is total and society overpowers individual imagination.[12] As Thomas put it, Philistines choose "security" at the cost of new experience and individuality.[13] They walk the comforting, well-worn paths cut by society and do not wander off into uncharted regions.

---

11 W. I. Thomas, "Social Personality: Organization of Attitudes," in *W. I. Thomas on Social Organization and Social Personality*, ed. Morris Janowitz (Chicago: University of Chicago Press, 1966), p. 35. Available in paperback.

12 The word *Philistine* referred originally to a people who occupied the southern seacoast of Palestine and harassed the Israelites; thus, the word implies the enemy. It was used later by German students to refer to someone who was not a university student, implying someone deficient in liberal culture and enlightenment, whose chief interests are material and commonplace things. (See *Oxford English Dictionary*.)

13 W. I. Thomas, "Analytical Types: Philistine, Bohemian and Creative Man," in *W. I. Thomas on Social Organization and Social Personality*, p. 172.

We all know people who fit the Philistine mold and well may recognize some Philistinism in ourselves. Perhaps, we get the clearest example of this type from literature. In 1922, five years after Thomas described the Philistine, Sinclair Lewis drew a detailed portrait of such an individual in his novel, *Babbitt*. It is a compelling, pathetic story of a successful realtor in a mid-sized American city. One critic, H. L. Mencken, saw the book as more than a character sketch of one person. It was, for Mencken, a penetrating analysis of American society.

> In brief, Babbitt is seen as no more than a single member of the society he lives in. . . . His every act is related to the phenomena of that society. It is not what he feels and aspires to that moves him primarily; it is what folks about him will think of him. His politics is communal politics, mob politics, herd politics; his religion is a public rite wholly without subjective significance; his relations to his wife and his children are formalized and standardized; even his debaucheries are the orthodox debaucheries of a sound business man. The salient thing about him, in truth, is his complete lack of originality—and that is precisely the salient mark of every American of his class. What he feels and thinks is what it is proper to feel and think.[14]

The other-directed conformity of Babbitt wins him a place in the mainstream of his community. Here he is swept along by the currents of public opinion. Asked to give a speech to the local realty board, Babbitt spells out the characteristics of a good citizen. His emphasis is on conformity.

> "Here's the specifications of the Standardized American citizen! Here's the new generation of Americans: Fellows with hair on their chests and smiles in their eyes and adding machines in their offices. We're not doing any boasting, but we like ourselves first-rate, and if you don't like us, look out—better get under cover before the cyclone hits town."[15]

Babbitt's tribal solidarity with "the boys"; his "he-man,"[16] "go-getting," "glad-handing" extroversion; his financial standing and respected place in the community hierarchy bring him happiness—most of the time. But, as Thomas points out, there is inevitably a struggle between the individual and society. Although Babbitt's socialization is nearly total, it cannot extinguish the suspicion that there are other possibilities open to his life. At the beginning of the novel, we find Babbitt boasting,

> "When I was a young man, I made up my mind what I wanted to do and stuck to it through thick and thin, and that's why I'm where I am today."

At the end of the book he confesses to his son (and to himself),

> "Now, for Heaven's sake don't repeat this to your mother, or she'd remove what little hair I've got left, but, practically, I've never done a single thing I've wanted to in my whole life! I don't know's I've accomplished anything except just get along."[17]

---

[14] H. L. Mencken, in *H. L. Mencken's "Smart Set" Criticisms*, ed. William Nolte (Ithaca, N.Y.: Cornell University Press, 1968), pp. 284–285. Originally printed in *Smart Set* magazine (October 1922).

[15] Sinclair Lewis, *Babbitt* (New York: Harcourt, Brace and Company, 1922), p. 183. Available in paperback.

[16] Gertrude Stein once commented that the term *he-man* is a vulgar redundancy.

[17] Lewis, *Babbitt*, pp. 17, 401.

Conformity, as an abstract term, is a dirty word in America. No one reading *Babbitt* would mistake the title character for a cultural hero. We sometimes recognize our own Philistine tendencies and are bothered by them. It is not surprising therefore that no popular philosophy of education touts blind conformity as a worthwhile aim. As long as we stay in the realm of abstraction, all educators support independent thinking. But when we get down to specifics, that is another matter. At this level, conformity is a popular educational goal. We find it most stridently supported whenever cultural values have been challenged. Look, for example, at some comments of Max Rafferty, who, as superintendent of public instruction in California in the 1960s, had more teachers and students under his leadership than any educator in America.

ON STUDENT DRESS.

A school is not a freak show, nor is it a place to indulge distracting whims and crotchets.

It just doesn't make any sense at all to invest all this money on beauty and then uglify the whole scene with hillbilly beards, beat-up guitars and clothes which look as though they could stand up in a corner all by themselves.

ON DISCIPLINE.

Too many instructors compromise themselves and their careers in the hopeless attempt to convince some freckled-faced urchin . . . that he must discipline himself when all he really needs is a session after school with the ruler.

ON A COURT DECISION MAKING THE FLAG SALUTE VOLUNTARY.

Certainly if my son can now decline to salute the Colors merely because he decides he doesn't want to, he can also refuse to do certain other things for the same reason—things like bearing arms in his country's defense, paying his taxes to support policies he disapproves of, or . . . keeping his mouth shut in school so that the teacher can get the lesson taught.

For the logical implication of this flag-salute decision is that every man—indeed every child—now is to be the sole arbiter of his own conduct. He is to be ruled only by his own conscience in relation to organized society and to his fellowman, regardless of the wishes of the majority and the laws of the land.

Such a doctrine, if upheld, spells chaos for the nation and a death blow to the concept of responsible citizenship . . . which schools are rightly charged with the duty of passing from one generation to the next.

ON LOVE OF COUNTRY.

The child should be taught first to love his country so that later on in his schooling he will have a motive strong enough to spur him to understand her.[18]

The Case against Philistine Aims

We can reject the Philistine philosophy as a useful aim for education. The problems we face demand creativity and flexibility, which Philistines lack. The Philistine's desire for security and acceptance is achieved at the cost of individuality and creative intelligence. We dare not diminish these latter capacities at a time when the human intellect is our best hope for survival.

---

[18] Quoted in William O'Neal, *Readin', Ritin' and Rafferty* (Berkeley, CA: The Glendessary Press, 1969), pp. 21, 22, 19–20, 37.

It is true that Philistines are capable of cooperative behavior, which is a talent needed in the future, but Philistines are not innovative problem solvers. They have an allegiance to "the way things are" that blinds them to other possibilities. This allegiance can grow so strong that they begin to see institutions, roles, and values not as human products but as the creation of divine or natural laws. This view of the world is called *reification*, which means simply that human beings forget that they are the producers of culture and that they can change it if need be. As Peter Berger points out, "The reified word is, by definition, a dehumanized world."[19] It is a world where reform is not just unnecessary; it is impossible. In such a world, individuals relinquish their claim to the authorship of human events and thus lose control of them.

As we have seen, the urgent problems in our future are human problems. Their solution depends on our ability to take control of human events. Clearly, this control cannot be learned if students are taught to reify the social world, to see it as inevitable and unchangeable. Education must help students become aware of their creative powers and help them to control and direct those powers through intelligence and cooperative democracy. Some persons say that the development of creative powers is best accomplished by freeing human beings from social restraint. Thomas is not so sure.

The Bohemian

In Thomas's view, Bohemians are individuals who cannot fit into any social frame.[20] They spend their lives struggling to slip out of the definitions and restrictions society offers. They are reluctant to adjust to any social situation, and they resist falling into any predictable patterns or social routines. They are, therefore, unpredictable. Their personalities are in flux, and they are continually on the move. When defined in this way, nonconformity would appeal to few educators as an educational aim. Although some educators (Rogers, for example) want to free students from social restrictions, their goal is not simply to produce nonconformity. But let us look at a school designed to free students from arbitrary social restraint and see what really happens when such aims are put into practice.

A group of Oregon parents and teachers were appalled by the public schools in their community. They saw them as authoritarian, mind molding, and unimaginative. Frustrated and angry, they decided to start a "free school," where

[19] Peter Berger and Thomas Luckmann, *The Social Construction of Reality* (New York: Doubleday & Co., Inc., Anchor Books, 1967), p. 89. Available in paperback. In Chapter 2, we introduced the concept of objectivation, which is the process by which human inventions (manners, for example) take on thinglike qualities. We speak of good manners as if they are *things* rather than *ideas*. They exist outside of ourselves and have coercive force. Wherever objectivation exists, reification is near at hand. Once we see human inventions as objects with coercive power, it is a small step to assume that the objects are not human products at all but are products of some greater power over which we have no control. The great challenge of education is to help students understand and participate in their culture without reifying it. Such an aim would mean that education would respect both the human need for stability and the human capacity for intelligent originality.

[20] The reference is to gypsies from Bohemia. It implies a vagabond, adventurer, or person of irregular life or habits; that is, one who generally despises conventionalities. (See *Oxford English Dictionary.*)

children would not be dominated by adults. Jane Goldman, a teacher in the school, described its philosophy:

> We began meeting before the school opened to discuss the philosophy of the school. Noble-sounding ideas were the order of the day: we would provide an atmosphere where children could explore the world as their needs and desires dictated; we would remain subtly in the background while our children played and learned according to their own natural rhythms.[21]

Of course, the assumption was that the "natural rhythms" of the children would guide them to honesty, cooperation, and learning. There were no preestablished rules or structures because that would be "laying our trip on our children."[22] If rules were really necessary, they would "emerge organically," or at least that is what was hoped. Goldman describes what actually happened:

> The first week of the school was delightful and we were all proud of ourselves. . . . By the second week, all hell broke loose. By 10:00 A.M. each day the school looked as if a herd of elephants had stamped through. The paints were all over the floor; books were written in with magic markers; the brand-new microscope lay disassembled on the table; oil paints had been thrown in the fish bowl. . . . Our casualties included one black eye, one busted lip, a hamster lost in the supply room. . . . It's not that teachers weren't aware of the need for some sort of order. When we told the kids to pick up their mess, they'd screech, "Shut up. This is a free school and I don't hafta do anything I don't wanna. You told me so on the first day."
>
> Chaos, destruction, and physical injury weren't the only problems. We had hoped to change basic attitudes in our school simply by allowing children to interact in a free environment. Yet racism and sexism were as rampant in our school as in any public school.[23]

The Case against Bohemian Aims

Why did this experiment fail? Probably because it neglected some elementary facts of human nature. It assumed children would naturally explore and learn from the environment. It assumed that order and mutual respect would emerge spontaneously if children were left alone. These assumptions are not in keeping with the facts of human nature. The ability to learn, to cooperate with others, to seek long-term goals rather than immediate stimulation are intricate and delicate. If we wish to nurture them in children, we must construct environments that promote their growth. They will not develop spontaneously in the midst of chaos.

Another problem with Bohemian aims is their negativism. Such aims frequently are constructed by defining what one is against and promoting its opposite. If public education is restrictive, free schools will be liberating. If public education treats children as incapable of doing anything for themselves, free schools will allow children to do everything on their own. But Goldman concluded that education must have more positive aims.

---

[21] The Bay Area Radical Teachers' Organizing Committee, "Education and Corporate Capitalism," *Socialist Revolution,* Vol. 2, No. 2 (March–April 1972), p. 115.

[22] Ibid., p. 117.

[23] Ibid., pp. 115–116.

> Free school people need to be more conscious of where they came from and where
> they want to go. They need to band together not only because of the things they
> hate, but because they share certain values. This means knowing what sorts of
> human beings they want to create. It means giving up the notion that children
> will just naturally change for the better.[24]

What other options are available besides Philistine and Bohemian aims for
education? Thomas offers the ideal of creative individuality.

The Creative Individual

Creative individuals resist the normlessness of the Bohemian and the mainstream conformity of the Philistine. They satisfy their desires for new experiences by developing their capacities for critical thinking. This capacity to think
critically allows them to take part in society and to help renovate outmoded
norms and social values. They see routine, taken-for-granted situations in new
ways and offer new visions of the world.

Creative individuals are not interested in change merely for the sake of change.
They are not hell raisers, although Thomas admits that they share some Bohemian characteristics. They disorganize established systems, violate norms, and—
like Bohemians—are regarded as disorderly, especially by the Philistine. But
creative disorderliness "is expressed in the setting and solution of problems, in
the creation of new values," whereas Bohemian disorder is "merely negative—
destructive of existing systems." Creative individuals, according to Thomas, do
not try to escape their world. They seek, rather, to improve it. Their innovations are "regulated by plans of productive activity." In other words, they are
conscious of their aims. They know where they want to go and are careful
about how they will get there. With this sense of purpose, they not only know
what society stands to gain through the changes they propose, but they also are
aware of what society stands to lose.[25] Thomas offers Charles Darwin as an
example of a creative individual. He was not a rebellious person; he was simply
engrossed in the pursuit of knowledge. Yet, he was worried about the social
effects of his findings.

> In common with his naturalist friends he had long realized that something terrible
> was about to happen to the Old Testament, but when he finally had the proof
> that species were not immutable, he wrote to his friends that it was "like confess-
> ing murder," and in spite of his appreciation of the scientific world he felt deeply
> to the end of his life the censure of the religious-primary group which accused
> him of a determination to "hunt God out of the world."[26]

The Case for Creative Individualism

Earlier in this chapter, we listed the characteristics of good educational aims.
We stated that aims must be compatible with human nature. The aim of creative individualism is unique in that it recognizes the need for both cultural

---

[24] Ibid., p. 117.
[25] W. I. Thomas, "Social Personality," in *W. I. Thomas on Social Organization and Social Personality*,
pp. 172–173. See also p. 29.
[26] Ibid., p. 173.

order and individual freedom. It recognizes that we are products of our culture and yet that we are its creators and recreators. Creative individualism attempts to strike a balance in the struggle between the individual and society.

Another characteristic of worthy educational aims is that they prepare students for future life. This preparation is difficult when tomorrow's problems are unknown. Creative intelligence is the best preparation for an unknown future, for it enables people to assess problems as they arise and to invent appropriate solutions. Creative individualism has another strong point. It is consistent with the tradition of democratic thought. It does not call for the creation of a new ideal; it demands rather that we reacquaint ourselves with our past hopes and fashion them into articulate aims for the future.

In addition, workable aims must provide teachers with a means of directing and judging educational practice. They must help us to find what we should do and determine whether we are doing it adequately. As the text proceeds, we will apply the creative-individual model to judge what schools do and should do.

Finally, we argued earlier that problems the nation will face in the future will call for heightened cooperation among individuals. Will the aim of creative individualism make this possible? It will do so only if educators promote cooperation as a conscious aim. Creative individualism certainly makes cooperative behavior more possible but does not guarantee it. Therefore, as the book proceeds, we will pay special attention to the ways in which educators can help develop cooperative skills in themselves and others.

Summary

Americans are traditionally an optimistic people. Recently this optimism has been eroded by inflation and the onslaught of problems that defy traditional solutions. Although faith in our institutions is still high, there has been a dramatic decline in confidence in institutional leadership. The problems Americans are most worried about are people problems. Their solution calls for an increased appreciation of human independence and a new willingness to cooperate. Cooperation necessitates not only adequate knowledge but a value structure that promotes adequate caring for the well-being of others. Recent studies indicate that Americans are becoming increasingly self-oriented and find it difficult to fit comfortably into social roles. Privatism is especially prevalent among the young.

Cooperation will not just happen; it must be encouraged. Part of this encouragement must be done by educators. Teachers must clarify their aims and invite discussion of them with students, parents, and other members of the community. Worthwhile educational aims must address the probable future needs of the nation and world community. They must be compatible with human nature and flexible enough to change as conditions change. They must be explicit enough to inform the practice of teaching.

The personality types offered by W. I. Thomas give us a clear view of the options open to education. Thomas describes the Philistine, Bohemian, and creative individual as ideal types. As such, they give us a larger-than-life view of the kinds of people society can create. By seeing these types in pure form, we are better able to describe what it is we hope education will accomplish.

The Philistine is a total conformist and the Bohemian is a dedicated nonconformist. Thomas's third type, the creative individual, strikes a balance between these two extremes. A careful look at most educational strategies reveals that they promote, directly or inadvertently, consciously or unconsciously, the development of one of these three ideal types. When we view educational strategies with an eye to their explicit or implied purposes, it becomes easier to choose what methods are most desirable. Furthermore, if we have a clear idea of what we want education to accomplish, we will be better prepared to select intelligently appropriate educational policies, methods, and materials. Without the guidance of educational aims, school policies become random, teacher behaviors whimsical, and educational outcomes inadvertent.

Suggested Readings

The problems discussed in this chapter—confidence in the future and in the nation's leadership, privatism, and the breaking of community bonds—are receiving the attention of social scientists.

BELLAH, ROBERT N., et al. *Habits of the Heart: Individualism and Commitment in American Life*. Berkeley: University of California Press, 1985. This recent study shows how our traditions of individualism and public commitment often conflict and argues that they must be reassessed if we are to remain a democratic people.

LASCH, CHRISTOPHER. *The Culture of Narcissism: American Life in an Age of Diminishing Expectations*. New York: W. W. Norton, 1979. This hard-hitting, sometimes despairing account of the American condition quickly made its way to the nation's bestseller list. The book convinced President Carter that there was a national crisis of confidence and he addressed the nation on the topic in 1979.

LUCKMANN, BENITA. "The Small Life-Worlds of Moderate Man," *Social Research*, Vol. 37 (Winter 1970), pp. 580–596. This is a short and convincing account of the price we pay for modernity.

WYNNE, EDWARD A. "The Declining Character of American Youth," *American Educator* (Winter 1979), pp. 29–31. A brief account of youth's increasing disaffection from society.

ZIJDERVELD, ANTON C. *The Abstract Society: A Cultural Analysis of Our Time*. New York: Doubleday & Co., Inc., 1970. Zijderveld, a Dutch sociologist, suggests that the modern age has shattered the tightly structured societies of previous times.

The issues involved in the "tragedy of the commons" are explored in the following sources:

BREDEMEIER, MARY, and HARRY BREDEMEIER. *Social Forces in Education*. Sherman Oaks, CA: Alfred Publishing Co., Inc., 1978. Readers interested in the problem of human autonomy and interdependence will find Chapter 2 of this book particularly helpful.

HARDIN, GARRETT. "The Tragedy of the Commons," *Science*, Vol. 162 (December 1968), pp. 1243–1248.

OLSON, MANCUR. *The Logic of Collective Action*. Cambridge: Harvard University Press, 1965.

SCHELLING, THOMAS. "On the Ecology of Micromotives," *The Public Interest* (Fall 1971), pp. 61–98.

Cooperation, perhaps more needed now than ever before, has to be learned and practiced. The following sources should help.

AXELROD, ROBERT. *The Evolution of Cooperation.* New York: Basic Books, 1984. A study of how cooperation can emerge and continue to flourish among self-seeking individuals when there is no outside authority to enforce it.

COLEMAN, ANDREW M. *Cooperation and Competition in Humans and Animals.* Berkshire, England: Van Nostrand Reinhold, 1982.

MAXWELL, GERALD, and DAVID R. SCHMITT. *Cooperation: An Experimental Analysis.* New York: Academic Press, 1975. This is a study of more than thirty interrelated experiments in search of the factors that inhibit, maintain, or promote cooperation.

MEAD, MARGARET. *Cooperation and Competition among Primitive Peoples.* Enlarged edition, with a new preface and appraisal. Boston: Beacon Press, 1961. Available in paperback.

Many philosophers and educators have grappled with the issue of educational aims. Among the most useful products of philosophical inquiry in this area are

DEWEY, JOHN. *Democracy and Education.* New York: The Free Press, 1966 [1916]. Available in paperback. Chapter 8 is titled "Aims in Education."

FRANKENA, WILLIAM F., ed. *Philosophy of Education.* New York: The Macmillan Co., 1965. Available in paperback. Part I compares four philosophers' views of the nature, aims, and principles of education.

WHITEHEAD, ALFRED NORTH. *The Aims of Education.* New York: The Free Press, 1967 [1929].

Summary of Section II

The school, especially the public school, is an agent of its culture. Its role is to bring the best of the culture to the young and to bring all the young into the culture. In the previous section, we learned that individuals and their cultures must be in supportive balance. This is especially true in democracies, where individual liberty is highly valued. One aim of education is to continually work out the balance between the individual and the culture. Other aims, such as self respect, cooperation, and critical intelligence, were discussed in the section.

Certain criteria exist for determining the warrant of educational aims. Such aims must be compatible with human nature; fit the conditions of society; be flexible, so they can be changed as conditions change; be clear enough to provide guidance in choosing subject matter and teaching methods; and be specific enough to allow teachers to determine whether they are making progress toward their chosen goals.

The aims we wish education to achieve reflect the core values of society. Here again, educators must pay close attention to balance. Core values in modern societies are always in flux and teachers must be conscious of value shifts. Schools will accommodate some value changes and may resist others. Educators also have to balance more values that appear to be contradictory.

Striving, success, activity, ambition, competition, individualism, conformity, obedience, and a belief in the abundance and controllability of nature are all core values of our society. Some of these values appear contradictory. For example, individualism seems to be in conflict with obedience and conformity, and schools are often caught in contests between these conflicting values.[1] Some values, such as a belief in the unlimited abundance and ultimate controllability of nature, are being challenged by ecological values and conservationism. Teachers must be aware of these value conflicts. At times, schools will avoid

---

[1] For example, should students be allowed to go to the senior prom unescorted or in casual dress, or is conformity to rules and dress codes a prerequisite for participation? Should students be forced to conform to school dress codes and hair-length regulations? Can students wear buttons in support of unpopular political causes? Court cases have been waged over these seemingly trivial matters.

value conflicts; at other times, they will mediate the conflict by trying to find a balance between contesting positions; and at still other times, schools may become instruments of value change.[2]

Parents are a child's first and most powerful teachers. When the home life of a child is educative, the power of the school is greatly enhanced; when the home life is miseducative, the work of the school is made more difficult. The American family is under extreme pressure today and so it is becoming increasingly difficult for parents to be effective teachers. Perhaps, the biggest problem is simply time. As mothers have entered the work force, they have less time to spend with the young. Work that would normally be done during the week now must be accomplished on the weekends. Television has become the great American baby-sitter and has cut into family communication. Other problems challenge traditional family practices. Families have become smaller; less stable; more private; less supported by the community and the megastructure; and more vulnerable to the mass media, advice from experts, and peer group pressures. At the same time, value shifts are occurring in the family. There is a new emotionalism, increased privatism, an equalization of sex roles, a new dependence on the family as a primary source of identity, and a new tolerance of divorce when identity needs are not met. Over 50 percent of today's first graders can expect to live for a time in a one-parent home before they graduate from college.

There is some debate over the health of the American family. Those who focus on surface strains tend to see families as damaged and in grave trouble. Others acknowledge that problems exist but insist that the family is a strong institution and that almost all parents are capable, caring, and knowledgeable. What families need from schools is not the assumption of family functions but simple assistance. Such assistance is most likely when schools function as mediating institutions.

The school's main function is education, especially literacy. But, in a democracy, the pursuit of literacy always entails a concern for civic education. Civic education is the process by which the young develop the sensibilities and skills needed to carry on the rights and obligations of citizenship. We find the influence of civic education expressed in politics and in popular culture, in textbooks, in the friction between religion and public schooling, and in the special concerns of moral education. Our review of these matters has taken us through much of the history of public schooling in America. Although civic education is a primary aim of schooling, it is trivialized when it is separated from other subjects and taught as a course in its own right. After much study and debate, it appears that the most efficacious way to impart civic education is through serious attention to the regular academic concerns of schooling: imparting culturally significant knowledge through teaching history, literature, art, and science and teaching the skills of critical thinking, debate, discussion, and persuasion.

Educational aims are ideals, ends in view for which we must strive even though they can never be perfectly achieved. Here again educators are confronted with questions of proportion and balance. If educational aims overemphasize conformity, schools will produce Philistines. If, on the other hand, the aims of

[2] The integration of the nation's schools is an example of a situation in which education became an instrument for actively supporting some American values and just as actively discouraging others.

education fall too heavily on the side of unrestricted choice, schools may encourage Bohemianism. We have argued that Philistine and Bohemian ideals have some appeal (each appearing most attractive after we have suffered the excesses of the other), but that ultimately these ideals are too rigid or unstable to maintain democracy. We have noted competing values in American society and have shown that values are made and revised continuously. Educational aims must allow for the rational evolution of values to meet the changing conditions of modern society. We believe that cooperation, caring, creative individualism and social intelligence best represent the core values of democratic culture and American education. Teachers who attend to these goals help maintain the delicate individual–culture balance. Because they value the culture and its past, they introduce its best ideas and greatest accomplishments to the young. Because they respect the individual, they nurture each child's development. And because they value the future, they nurture the critical intelligence of students so that their pupils will have the skills needed to shape the future.

Educational aims, once established, lead inevitably to the question of means. Do the training and socialization of teachers, the career patterns of the profession, the organization of schools, or the teaching methods typically employed in public school classrooms promote or discourage the democratic educational aims? The next two sections will deal with some of these matters.

The Teaching Profession: Ideals and Realities

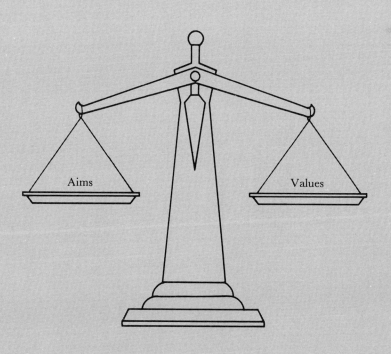

CHAPTER 9

Teacher Backgrounds: What Teachers Bring with Them to the School

Introduction

If schools are to be effective institutions, if they are to achieve the educational aims set for them, they must meet the needs of the people who work in them. Schools must satisfy the immediate and long-term goals of both students and teachers. This chapter will focus on teachers. Who are they? Where do they come from? Why are they teaching? What do they find rewarding about their work? What stands in the way of job satisfaction?

Social Class Origins of Teachers

A popular device for summing up the values and aspirations of teachers is to refer to them as being "solidly middle class." Although there is some truth in this description, it hides as much as it reveals. Teachers are a diverse lot and cannot be summed up so easily. For example, if we look at just one portion of the issue—the social class origins of teachers—we find that their backgrounds vary considerably depending on what group of teachers we are examining.

Until approximately 1920, urban teachers were drawn largely from the middle class, whereas rural teachers came primarily from farming and working-class backgrounds. As America became more industrialized and increasingly urban, the need for educated workers increased. Public education expanded, and students continued in school for longer periods of time. Compulsory attendance laws were passed in some states and newly enforced in others. These developments increased the demand for teachers and opened greater opportunities for upper lower-class and lower middle-class individuals.

As Americans migrated out of the country and into the city (off the farm and into the factory), a decreasing percentage of teachers came from agricultural backgrounds. Florence Greenhoe conducted a national study of 9000 public school teachers prior to World War II. She found that 38 percent of teachers came from farming backgounds.[1] By 1986 only 13 percent of teachers came from farming families and another 14 percent had fathers who were employed as unskilled workers, salesmen, or clerks. Recent studies by the National Education Association reveal that teachers now come from all classes of American society.[2] However, the largest portion of teachers have lower middle-class or upper lower-class origins. This fact is especially true of male teachers. These data indicate that the assumption that all teachers come from the middle class is unfounded. A large percentage of teachers is upwardly mobile. (See Table 9-1.)

Data gathered by the National Educational Association show a slight increase in the percentage of teachers coming from white-collar families. In 1986, 22 percent of all teachers came from families where the father did professional or semiprofessional work (see Table 9-1). However, 39 percent of new teachers (those under thirty) were raised in white-collar homes.[3] Anthony Dworkin's study of over 3000 teachers in a southwestern city reported similar findings.[4]

Teaching Salaries and Upward Mobility

Public school teaching will not make anyone rich, but traditionally it has provided an adequate income to support a small family. The humanitarian mission of teaching has given the profession greater prestige than its modest salary might suggest. As we shall see, however, these conditions are presently in flux. Inflation significantly diminished teachers' salaries in the last decade. In addition, the national concern over the quality of public education has harmed the public's opinion of the teaching profession and eroded the social status of teachers. These are important developments and we will return to them later in the chapter. Yet, as important as they are, they have not changed the fact that many of today's teachers have come from the working-class and lower middle-class backgrounds. Teaching has historically proven to be a well-traveled, easy-access route to the white-collar world of the middle class. Dan Lortie, who has written the best account of the teaching profession, explains, "Teaching is clearly white-collar, middle-class work and as such offers upward mobility for people who grew up in blue-collar or lower-class families."[5]

It may seem odd that some people are attracted to teaching for the salary and status it provides. It is generally conceded that teaching is a low-paying profession without much social clout, but this is a relative matter and begs the question, Compared to what? A secure salary and some social recognition can

---

[1] Florence Greenhoe, *Community Contacts and Participation of Teachers* (Washington, DC: American Council on Public Affairs, 1941).

[2] National Education Association, *Status of the American Public School Teacher: 1985–1986* (Washington, DC: NEA Research Division, 1987), p. 162.

[3] Ibid., p. 163.

[4] Anthony G. Dworkin, "The Changing Demography of Public School Teachers: Some Implications for Faculty Turnover in Urban Areas," *Sociology of Education*, Vol. 53 (April 1980), pp. 65–73.

[5] Dan C. Lortie, *School-Teacher: A Sociological Study* (Chicago: University of Chicago Press, 1975), p. 35.

TABLE 9-1. Teachers Report Their Fathers' Occupations

| | Total | | | | | Sex | | | | | | | | |
| | | | | | | Men | | | | | Women | | | | |
	1961	1971	1976	1981	1986	1961	1971	1976	1981	1986	1961	1971	1976	1981	1986
Farmer	26.5%	19.3%	15.2%	15.3%	13.1%	20.0%	16.3%	10.9%	13.0%	10.9%	29.5%	20.9%	17.1%	16.3%	14.0%
Unskilled Worker	6.5	8.4	9.9	9.3	8.7	8.7	9.6	11.8	11.1	9.4	5.4	7.8	9.0	8.5	8.4
Skilled or Semi-skilled Worker	23.4	25.7	28.6	29.3	29.9	30.3	34.3	38.4	33.6	37.1	20.2	21.2	23.8	27.4	26.7
Clerical Worker or Salesworker	7.1	5.5	5.7	5.7	5.0	7.3	6.1	4.7	5.8	4.8	7.1	5.2	6.3	5.5	5.1
Managerial or Self-employed Workers	22.0	21.1	20.5	22.2	21.5	21.9	16.7	19.2	19.0	17.5	22.1	24.9	21.1	23.9	23.2
Professional or Semi-professional Workers	14.5	18.9	20.1	18.2	21.9	11.8	17.0	15.0	17.6	20.3	15.7	19.8	22.6	18.4	22.6

SOURCE: Data from National Education Association, *Status of the American Public School Teacher: 1970–1971,* p. 61; *Status of the American Public School Teacher: 1975–1976,* p. 127; *Status of the American Public School Teacher: 1981–1982,* p. 184; *Status of the American Public School Teacher: 1985–1986* (Washington DC: NEA Research Division, 1987), p. 162.

Note: Columns may not add to 100 percent because of rounding.

be attractive incentives, especially for someone who grew up in the relative uncertainty of the working-class world. A great many teachers fall into this category. According to National Educational Association data, 57.4 percent of men teachers and 49.1 percent of women teachers had fathers who were farmers or unskilled, semiskilled, or skilled workers (see the 1986 data in Table 9-1). Another measure of the social class origins of teachers is found in the education levels achieved by their parents. The fathers of 38 percent of today's teachers did not graduate from high school.[6] Beyond social-mobility statistics, there is other evidence that suggests that teachers are attracted to their profession for monetary reasons. Dan Lortie asked nearly 6000 teachers in Dade County, Florida, what attracted them to teaching. The answers teachers gave are shown in Table 9-2.

Note that 11.9 percent of the teachers surveyed indicated that salary, respect, and influence were "most important" to them. It must be remembered, however, that teaching is a service-oriented profession, and many teachers pride themselves on their selfless devotion to students. That being the case, there is social pressure against teachers admitting (to themselves and to others) that they may be in teaching for the money and prestige the profession offers. Lortie therefore fashioned another kind of question that he posed to teachers in the Boston area. Instead of asking, What rewards do you get from teaching? he asked, What attracts and holds other teachers to the profession? This question allowed teachers to analyze the motives of others in the profession without revealing their own. Interestingly, 37 percent of respondents indicated that money attracted people to teaching, 34 percent said teaching offered security, and 12 percent said teaching offered prestige. Lortie concluded that income and prestige do make teaching an attractive profession, especially for individuals from working-class backgrounds.[7] Further evidence for this contention is found in a study supported by the National Center for Educational Statistics. A nationally representative sample of 3600 students in their final year of pres-

TABLE 9-2.   Reasons Teachers Give for Teaching

Question: Of the features grouped below, I think that the following (circle 1) is most important to me:	
The salary and respect received and the position of influence	11.9%
The opportunity to study, plan, and master classroom management, to "reach" students, and to associate with colleagues and children	76.5%
The economic security, time, freedom from competition, and appropriateness for persons like me	11.7%

Reprinted from, *School-Teacher: A Sociological Study* by Dan Lortie, by permission of the University of Chicago Press, 1975, pp. 105, 259, © 1975 by University of Chicago.

[6] National Education Association, *Status of the American Public School Teacher: 1985–1986*, pp. 162–163.
[7] Dan C. Lortie, *School-Teacher*, p. 31.

TABLE 9-3.   Average Salary of Instructional Staff in Public Elementary and Secondary Schools, and Average Annual Earnings of Full-time Employees in all Industries, United States, 1929–30 to 1985–86 in Adjusted Dollars, 1985–1986 Purchasing Power.

School Year	Average Salary of Instructional Staff	Earnings per Full-time Employee Working for Wages or Salary	School Year	Average Salary of Instructional Staff	Earnings per Full-time Employee Working for Wages or Salary
1929–30	$ 9,027	$ 8,811	1961–62	20,628	17,834
1931–32	10,696	9,043	1963–64	22,004	18,947
1933–34	10,081	8,791	1965–66	23,632	19,894
1935–36	10,165	9,191	1967–68	24,406	20,613
1937–38	10,448	9,308	1969–70	25,469	21,130
1939–40	11,220	9,982	1971–72	26,709	22,039
1941–42	10,527	11,009	1973–74	26,096	22,508
1943–44	10,801	12,689	1975–76	25,746	22,007
1945–46	11,909	13,562	1977–78	25,537	22,289
1947–48	12,320	12,567	1979–80	23,430	21,159
1949–50	13,831	13,463	1980–81	23,124	20,725
1951–52	14,279	13,750	1981–82	23,502	20,601
1953–54	15,471	14,674	1982–83	23,534	20,931
1955–56	16,822	15,883	1983–84	24,458	21,103
1957–58	17,901	16,279	1984–85	25,360	21,170
1959–60	19,162	17,155	1985–86	26,372	21,510

SOURCE: Data from Thomas D. Snyder, *Digest of Educational Statistics, 1987* (Washington, DC: Center for Education Statistics, 1987), Table 53, p. 63.

ervice teacher training were asked why they wanted to enter the teaching profession. Over 30 percent mentioned good income, and more than half mentioned job security as "very important" to them.[8]

The Financial Standing of Teachers

The salary of teachers, like the earnings of most American workers, has risen dramatically over the last fifty years. Using figures adjusted to account for inflation, we can determine the extent of the salary surge in education (see Table 9-3). In 1943–1944 the average annual salary for teachers was $10,801 (in 1986 dollars). By 1985–1986 that figure had jumped to $26,372. When we compare these earnings to the income of full-time employees in other industries, we see that teachers fared relatively well. The average earning for American employees in 1943–1944 was $12,689 (or 18 percent more than teachers). By 1985–1986 the average earning for American employees was $21,510, but the average salary of teachers was $26,372. Teachers are presently earning over $4000 (22 percent) more than the average American worker.

[8] Lewin and Associates, Inc., "The State of Teacher Education: 1977," Publication No. NCES 78–409 (Washington, DC: National Center for Educational Statistics, September 1978), p. 69.

Women and Teaching

More women than men from the middle class enter teaching. What draws middle-class women to this profession? In order to answer this question adequately, we must remember that until recently few occupations were open to women. Professional schools did not encourage women applicants and women were socialized to believe that they should not be interested in and were incapable of "man's work." Women desiring employment (or needing it) were guided into "female occupations" such as nursing, home economics, and, of course, teaching. It is little wonder, then, that two-thirds of American schoolteachers are women. They constitute 86 percent of all elementary schoolteachers, 56 percent of junior high teachers, and 47 percent of all high school teachers.[10]

A large number of middle-class women were attracted to teaching because it was one of the few professions open to women, and it paid better than other women-dominated occupations. It offered both respectability and security. This situation is still true today, although new options are opening up for women all the time. Nevertheless, teaching offers women many advantages not present in other professions. First, teaching does not conflict strenuously with the traditional demands family life puts on women. Second, it offers respectable employment during early adulthood, the time when women are likely to get married and begin family life. It brings in a second income, thus making it easier for the new family to get off to a secure financial start. Third, a married woman can leave teaching without penalty if the couple decides to have children. If she decides to return to the classroom, it is likely that she will find a job and that the school will not have changed much in her absence. Sixty-four percent of all women teachers surveyed by the National Education Association reported they had left teaching for a year or more in order to become homemakers and raise children.[11] Fourth, many women find it possible to carry on the traditional duties of motherhood while carrying out their teaching obligations. Their hours at school coincide conveniently with their children's school day, and during vacations they can be at home to care for the young. Lastly, for a woman a teaching certificate can serve as a long-term insurance policy. In the unhappy event of a husband's death or illness, or of divorce, she is prepared to support herself and her family.

Primary Motives for Teaching

Teachers enter the education profession for a wide variety of motives. Some are attracted by salary, status, and social mobility. Others plan to stay in teaching only until new career opportunities appear or until marriage or motherhood. But these are secondary motives for teaching and they are discovered by social scientists only after careful study. Primary motives for teaching are easier to study but are also important. When asked to explain why they entered the profession, teachers offer three primary motives more than any others:

---

[10] National Education Association, *Status of the American Public School Teacher: 1985–1986* (Washington, DC: NEA Research Divison, 1987), p. 119.

[11] Ibid., p. 114.

TABLE 9-4. Primary Motives for Choosing a Career in Teaching

	1971	1981	1986
Question: What are the three main reasons you originally decided to become a teacher?			
Desire to work with young people	71.8%	69.6%	65.6%
Interest in subject matter	34.5	44.1	37.1
Value or significance of education in society	37.1	40.2	37.2

SOURCE: National Education Association, *Status of the American Public School Teacher: 1985–1986* (Washington, DC: National Education Association, 1987), p. 56.

Note: Figures add to more than 100 percent because respondents were invited to give more than one answer.

1. The desire to work with young people.
2. An interest in a subject-matter field.
3. The value of education to society (see Table 9-4).

These primary motives are idealistic and activistic. Teachers share a faith that education and knowledge can make a difference in the lives of children and in the long-term well-being of society.

Secondary Motives for Teaching

When experienced teachers were asked why they remained in the profession they gave different responses. The primary motives for teaching—working with the young, working with subject matter, and contributing to society—remained strong. However, teachers admitted to secondary motives that were not clear to them at the start of their careers. For example, 36 percent of teachers listed long summer vacations as an important reason for their remaining in the field. Thirty-seven percent of men teachers (those most likely to come from the financially insecure world of the working class) said job security was one thing that kept them in teaching. Twenty-five percent of women teachers listed job security and 25 percent listed the need for a second family income as factors that kept them in teaching. Twenty-five percent of women teachers listed job

TABLE 9-5. Secondary Motives for Staying in Teaching

	1986	Men	Women
Question: What are the three main reasons you are still in teaching?			
Long summer vacations	36.1	31.9	38.0
Job security	28.9	37.3	25.1
Need for second income in family	17.1	0.5	24.6
Financial rewards	5.9	4.9	6.3

SOURCE: National Education Association, *Status of the American Public School Teacher, 1985–1986* (Washington, DC: National Education Association, 1987), pp. 57, 213.

Note: Figures add to more than 100 percent because respondents were invited to give more than one answer.

Teaching serves as a social elevator into the middle class. It offers a salary that compares well with the income of the average American, and to some degree it carries social recognition and prestige. Teaching offers women an opportunity to pursue a profession while carrying on the traditional roles of wife and mother. But are there other incentives to teaching? Dan Lortie suggests two which he labels *continuation* and *blocked aspirations*.

THE CONTINUATION MOTIVE.   Lortie found that some teachers so love their own schooling that they go into teaching to continue and share these positive educational experiences. One example of this phenomenon might be high school athletic heroes who enter coaching in order to remain on the scene of their past glories and to relive them vicariously through their students. If this phenomenon is true of some coaches, it is no less true of some teachers of English, math, history, home economics, and so on.

THE BLOCKED-ASPIRATIONS MOTIVE.   Some teachers come to the field because their first career choices did not pan out. Lortie calls this the "blocked-aspirations" motive for teaching. People who hope to become writers, actors, athletes, or artists but are unable to support themselves in these activities choose teaching because it supports them and keeps them active in their interest area. Thus some English teachers plan to stay in teaching only until they finish the great American novel, and some drama coaches direct high school plays as preparation for a career in acting.

Some other teachers are in the field because they are unable to meet the requirements of another profession. A student who fails a premed course may transfer to science education, and a student who cannot unravel the mysteries of binary topological algebra may feel comfortable teaching high school geometry. Some people move into teaching after becoming disillusioned with another line of work because of its lack of humanism, its boredom, its competitiveness, or its shady practices. For these people, teaching offers interesing and uplifting work that they find more compatible with their skills, values, and personalities.

Motives for Teaching and Conservative Bias

What are we to conclude from this discussion of why people come to teaching? For one thing, we see that teachers are not simply look alikes. They come to the field from different backgrounds and with different values and aspirations. There is no single "teacher personality"; there are instead many different kinds of people playing out the teacher role for very different reasons.[12]

However, some generalizations can be made about the teaching motives reviewed here. Those who choose teaching because it allows them to render service to the young and society are probably already convinced that schools function to achieve these ends. Teachers who see the school as giving them an opportunity to deal with interesting subject matter are likely to be satisfied with the schools as they are; schooling already offers them everything they ask of it.

[12] J. W. Getzels and P. Jackson, "The Teacher's Personality and Characteristics," in *The Handbook of Research on Teaching*, ed. N. L. Gage (Chicago: Rand McNally & Company, 1963), pp. 506–582.

Evidently, few teachers come to teaching bent on radical reform. They may wish to improve the system but do not see the need for sweeping change. Similarly, those teachers who see teaching as an easy access to the middle class may be reluctant to attack the system that elevated their social position. Teachers who are using teaching as a stopgap measure while they prepare themselves for another career are not likely to invest much time and energy in educational change; their interests lie elsewhere. The same might be said for those women teachers whose primary commitment is to the full-time role of the traditional wife and mother and who are only secondarily committed to the teaching profession. Their interests and the demands on their time make it unlikely that they will devote themselves to educational change.

In all likelihood, then, the motives that drive people into teaching also draw them away from considering large-scale changes in the operations of the school. Lortie makes this point, but he is quick to add that he is making generalizations about teachers and not setting down iron norms. Certainly there are teachers who desire to change schools, but their work is difficult because many, if not most, teachers come to teaching with motivations that support the status quo.

Social Class and Teacher Satisfaction

Until recently many teachers did not remain in teaching very long. One study determined that the average career expectancy for teachers was about two years.[13] This average has changed somewhat since the late 1970s, but the shift to longer careers has not been caused by changes in the teaching profession or in teachers but rather by economic changes in society. Leaving teaching has become an economic risk that few teachers are willing to run.

A number of factors appear to contribute to the decision to leave teaching. Dworkin asked teachers in his study if they had seriously considered leaving the field of education. Roughly a quarter of the teachers in his sample indicated that they had. When Dworkin analyzed the data he found the teachers who had considered leaving education were usually white, young, and of higher-status occupational origin. They were also likely to be working at schools where they would prefer not to teach.[14]

Dworkin's findings are confirmed by previous studies that have shown that minorities and people from low-income occupational origins are more likely to remain in teaching and to be satisfied with their work.[15] Many factors may explain this phenomenon. People from lower social class origins may find greater satisfaction in the modest financial rewards offered teachers. The fact that these groups often have to spend a greater percentage of their personal and family resources in education means that they have a greater initial investment in their teaching career. This may discourage them from branching out into other fields. It is also possible that these groups are less surprised by the conditions in poverty neighborhood schools and therefore less likely to quit out of frustration

---

[13] Herbert Walberg, "Professional Role Discontinuities in Educational Careers," *Review of Educational Research*, Vol. 40 (June 1970), pp. 409–420.

[14] Anthony G. Dworkin, "The Changing Demography of Public School Teachers: Some Implications for Faculty Turnover in Urban Areas."

[15] David Gottlieb, "Teaching and Students: Reviews of Negro and White Teachers," *Sociology of Education*, Vol. 37 (1964), pp. 345–353. See also Ronald Pavalco, "Recruitment to Teaching: Patterns of Selection and Retention," *Sociology of Education*, Vol. 43 (1970), pp. 340–353.

or disgust when assigned to these areas. They also have fewer contacts with affluent friends who can offer them inviting opportunities in other careers. National Education Association data allow us to explore the issue of dissatisfaction in more depth.

Teacher Dissatisfaction

There has been an alarming drop in teacher satisfaction over the last two decades, as can be seen from Figure 9-1. Of all teachers in 1966, 53 percent indicated that they would certainly choose to become teachers, if they had it to do again; by 1986, that figure had dropped to 23 percent. A more recent Harris poll found that 51 percent of a national sample of teachers had considered leaving teaching and that 27 percent of all teachers (and 36 percent of urban teachers) said they were likely to leave the profession in the next five years.[16] The poll also indicated that the best teachers (those who had won awards for their teaching) were the most likely to want to leave the classroom.

As we have seen, teachers from the working-class backgrounds generally take pride in their advancement into the white-collar middle class and take comfort in the security the teaching profession provides. They share an achievement orientation with colleagues from middle-class families but often expect more from the teaching profession than it presently delivers. An ethnographic study of middle and high school teachers revealed that their initial satisfactions with teaching were threatened when they discovered that

1. Their salaries were lower than most workers with comparable training and responsibility;
2. Their salary increases had fallen behind the rate of inflation;
3. Their profession provided limited opportunities for continued economic and status advancement;
4. Blue-collar wages in some areas met or significantly exceeded their own yearly earnings;
5. A stereotypical image of teachers' work and worth, promulgated by the press and widely held by the public, had lowered the status of the teaching profession; and
6. Teachers felt that their achievements went unrecognized by the public and school administrators.[17]

We will deal with these issues individually, though it is important to keep in mind that they are interrelated and together have a powerful effect on teacher satisfaction.

LOW SALARIES.   We saw earlier in the chapter that teachers' income had increased significantly over the years. These data do not tell the whole story, however. Teachers' salaries do not compare favorably with the earnings of individuals in other professionals. Data from a study by the National Center for Education Information indicates that the salaries of teachers rose to $24,559 in 1986. However, in the same year, the average salary of individuals with at least

---

[16] Quoted in *Teacher Education Reports*, Vol. 7 (September 26, 1985), p. 2.
[17] Patricia Ashton and Rodman Webb, *Making A Difference: Teachers' Sense of Efficacy and Student Achievement* (New York: Longman Publishing Company, 1985), pp. 29–54.

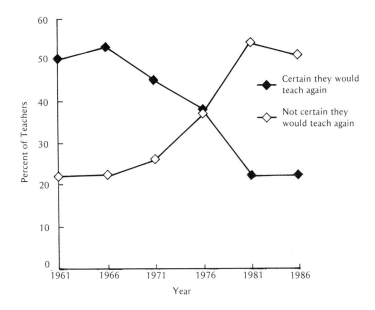

Figure 9-1   Percent of teachers who would certainly choose to teach again and percent who are not certain they would choose to teach again, 1961–1986. Those in the "not certain" category answered the question by saying they "certainly would not teach again," "probably would not teach again," or that "the chances were about even" that they would teach again. Those in the "certain" category said that they "certainly would choose to teach again." (*Source:* National Education Association, *Status of the American Public School Teacher: 1970–1971*, p. 61; *Status of the American Public School Teacher: 1975–1976*, p. 127; *Status of the American Public School Teacher: 1981–1982*, p. 184; *Status of the American Public School Teacher: 1985–1986* [Washington, DC: NEA Research Division], p. 58)

four years of college in the United States was $32,216. Teachers earn more than $7000 less than the average American worker with a college education.[18]

Salary differences begin to show themselves early in the careers of teachers. When we look at the entry-level salaries over time, we see that the salary gap between teaching and other professions is widening. In the decade between 1975 and 1985, the beginning salaries of teachers increased 187 percent. However, the increase for engineers was 225 percent; for chemists, 216 percent; for mathematicians, 217 percent; and for sales and marketing personnel, 204 percent (see Figure 9-2). Considering these findings, it is not surprising that for many middle-class men, and increasing numbers of middle-class women, teaching represents a step down the economic ladder.

THE RAVAGES OF INFLATION.   Salaries increased significantly for teachers between 1952 and 1972. After World War II, teachers were earning substantially less than the average American worker. In the late 1950s, in response to Sputnik and the growing arms race, more money was pumped into education and teachers' salaries rose significantly. By 1971–1972, the salary of the average teacher ($10,100) had not only caught up with, but significantly surpassed

---

[18] The disparity between these two figures is not great if we take into account that teachers are required to work 180 days a year, whereas most other full-time employees work a 250-day year. The average daily salary of teachers is $136, whereas the average daily salary of other employees is $129. Although the per-day pay of teachers is relatively high, the facts remain that their yearly salary is relatively low when compared with comparably educated employees, and their yearly salary determines their standard of living. C. Emily Feistritzer, *Profiles of Teachers in the U.S.* (Washington, DC: National Center for Education Information, 1986).

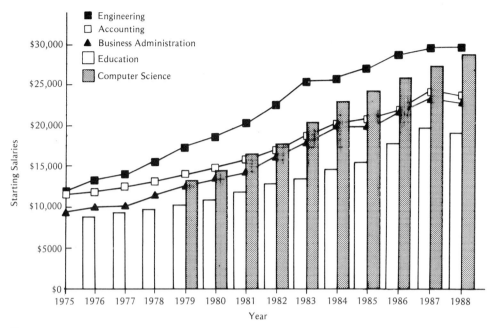

Figure 9-2   Starting salaries for college graduates entering various professions. (*Source:* U.S. Bureau of the Census, *Statistical Abstract of the United States: 1985* [Washington, DC: U.S. Government Printing Office, 1985], p. 141; Victor R. Lindquist and Frank S. Endicott, *Northwestern Endicott Report* [Evanston, IL: The Placement Center, Northwestern University, 1988], pp. 8–9; and the American Federation of Teachers, *Survey & Analysis of Salary Trends, 1987* [Washington, DC: American Federation of Teachers, 1987] p. 14.)

the earnings of the average American worker ($8334) (see Table 9-6). The 1970s, however, were a time of deep recession and high inflation. Governments at the local, state, and federal level were forced to cut expenditures. They accomplished this goal by holding pay raises of public employees below the national inflation rate, in effect cutting the employees' pay. Between 1971 and 1984, the average salary for teachers increased from $10,100 to $22,877, a seemingly significant gain. However, when inflation is taken into account, the buying power of teachers' paychecks actually dropped by $2251 during these years. The after-inflation income of the "average American" also fell, but only by $1027. By 1986, teachers had made up a lot of lost ground, but they were still earning less in constant dollars than they did in 1971.

In a national survey, 94 percent of teachers indicated that "providing a decent salary" would help keep good teachers in their chosen profession.[19] Among people who left teaching, 52 percent said that they might return to the classroom if salaries improved.[20] The declining buying power of teachers' paychecks is a matter of widespread concern in the profession. The financial trou-

---

[19] Quoted in *Teacher Education Reports,* Vol. 7 (September 26, 1985), p. 2.
[20] John C. Freed, "Teachers Who Quit Offer Their Reasons," *New York Times* (April 26, 1986), p. 15.

TABLE 9-6. Average Annual Salary of Instructional Staff[1] in Public Elementary and Secondary Schools and Average Annual Earnings of Full-time Employees in all Industries: United States, 1929–30 to 1985–86

| School Year[3] | Constant Dollars | | Constant 1985–1986 Dollars[2] | | |
	Average Salary of Instructional Staff	Earnings per Full-time Employee Working for Wages or Salary	Average Salary of Instructional Staff	Earnings per Full-time Employee Working for Wages or Salary	Ratio of Instructional Teachers to all Full-time Employees
1929–30	1,420	1,386	9,027	8,811	1.02
1931–32	1,417	1,198	10,696	9,043	1.18
1933–34	1,227	1,070	10,081	8,791	1.15
1935–36	1,283	1,160	10,165	9,191	1.11
1937–38	1,374	1,224	10,448	9,308	1.12
1939–40	1,441	1,282	11,220	9,982	1.12
1941–42	1,507	1,576	10,527	11,009	0.96
1943–44	1,728	2,030	10,801	12,689	0.85
1945–46	1,995	2,272	11,909	13,562	0.88
1947–48	2,639	2,692	12,320	12,567	0.98
1949–50	3,010	2,930	13,831	13,463	1.03
1951–52	3,450	3,322	14,279	13,750	1.04
1953–54	3,825	3,628	15,471	14,674	1.05
1955–56	4,156	3,924	16,822	15,883	1.06
1957–58	4,702	4,276	17,901	16,279	1.10
1959–60	5,174	4,632	19,162	17,155	1.12
1961–62	5,700	4,928	20,628	17,834	1.26
1963–64	6,240	5,373	22,004	18,947	1.16
1965–66	6,935	5,838	23,632	19,894	1.19
1967–68	7,630	6,444	24,406	20,613	1.18
1969–70	8,840	7,334	25,469	21,130	1.21
1971–72	10,100	8,334	26,709	22,039	1.21
1973–74	11,185	9,647	26,096	22,508	1.16
1975–76	13,124	11,218	25,746	22,007	1.17
1977–78	14,698	12,829	25,537	22,289	1.15
1979–80	16,715	15,095	23,430	21,159	1.11
1980–81	18,404	16,495	23,124	20,725	1.12
1981–82	20,327	17,818	23,502	20,601	1.14
1982–83	21,230	18,883	23,534	20,931	1.12
1983–84	22,877	19,740	24,458	21,103	1.16
1984–85	24,644	20,573	25,360	21,170	1.20
1985–86	26,372	21,510	26,372	21,150	1.22

[1] Includes supervisors, principals, classroom teachers, and other instructional staff.
[2] Based on the consumer price index, prepared by the Bureau of Labor Statistics, U.S. Department of Labor.
[3] Calendar-year data from the U.S. Department of Commerce have been converted to a school-year basis by averaging the two appropriate calendar years in each case.

SOURCE: U.S. Department of Education, National Center for Education Statistics, *Statistics of State School Systems;* and Center for Education Statistics, unpublished data; National Education Association, *Estimates of School Statistics,* 1985–1986 (copyright 1986 by the National Education Association. All rights reserved); and U.S. Department of Commerce, *Survey of Current Business,* July issues, Table 62B. (This table was prepared September 1986.)

bles of teachers are presently so great that 20 percent of teachers find it necessary to hold a second job.[21]

Teachers often discuss salary matters with great intensity. For example one teacher told Ashton and Webb:

> I'm looking more and more to getting out of teaching. It's not so much that I don't like teaching, it's because I'm not making any money. I think I do too many things too well to sit around here [making sixteen] thousand dollars a year when I can probably go and find some kind of business to get involved in and do much better than I'm doing. I think probably within the next three or four years I'll be out of teaching. It's the money. It's a real problem. . . . We're just not doing well at all.[22]

LIMITED OPPORTUNITY FOR ADVANCEMENT.   The career pattern that dominates the teaching profession is horizontal rather than vertical (see Figure 9-3). There are few ladders up the hierarchy unless one leaves the classroom for a job in the private sector or school administration. A person devoted to teaching can enter the profession after college and exit forty years later holding the same position in the same school, and perhaps even teaching in the same classroom. His or her salary typically will progress in fixed steps along a negotiated scale, with little or no financial recognition awarded for meritorious accom-

Figure 9-3   Typical career patterns in business and education.

---

[21] Ibid.
[22] Ashton and Webb, *Making a Difference*, p. 36.

plishment. Inadequate teachers advance along the salary schedule just as quickly as the excellent ones. A year or two before retirement, the veteran teacher will be earning less than twice the salary of new teachers in his or her school, a pay differential much lower than is typically found in private-sector professions. In other words, teachers start out financially behind most other college graduates and fall further and further behind as their careers progress.

Few school districts offer merit pay systems that reward good teaching. Gallup polls indicate that teachers oppose the idea of merit pay by a 2:1 ratio, 64 percent to 32 percent.[23] Teachers argue that until all in the profession are earning a decent salary, merit pay programs make little sense. The dollars given to a few will be subtracted from the already inadequate raises given to the rest. Teachers also worry that measuring merit is difficult and invites arbitrary or biased judgments. They contend that merit pay would create morale problems in schools and would set teachers in counterproductive competition with their colleagues. Teachers do not reject the merit pay idea out of hand, however. In another survey, 71 percent said that merit pay plans could work if the performance of teachers could be measured objectively. Thirty-nine percent thought an effective merit pay plan would attract and keep talented teachers in the profession.[24]

The absence of a career ladder distinguishes teaching from most other professions. Ernest Boyer has noted that

> two of the most troublesome aspects of the teaching profession are the lack of a career ladder and the leveling off of salaries. The irony is that to "get ahead" in teaching you must leave it. The notion seems to be that if you are good, you will move out of the classroom and become a school counselor or principal—or football coach. The lack of opportunity for advancement in teaching is in sharp contrast to other professions, where outstanding performance is rewarded.[25]

It would appear that teaching offers few formal rewards for excellence. This situation is made worse by the fact that only meager informal rewards are built into the profession. For example, an experienced doctor, lawyer, accountant, or auto mechanic is likely to be respected for what he or she has learned over the years. The opposite is true in education. Long-time teachers frequently are seen as "set in their ways" and are not venerated for their experience or knowledge.

BLUE-COLLAR ADVANCES.   The decade of real income decline for teachers was a period of advancement for some (though certainly not all) strongly unionized blue-collar workers. For example, between 1967 and 1978, the after-inflation income of coal miners advanced 31 percent; that of truck drivers, 23

---

[23] Alec Gallup, "The Gallup Poll of Teachers' Attitudes Toward the Public Schools," *Phi Delta Kappan*, Vol. 66 (October 1984), p. 103. In another study, 72 percent of teachers were familiar with the idea of merit pay and 71 percent opposed its use in education. Louis Harris, Michael Kagay, and Stuart Leichenko, *The Metropolitan Life Survey of the American Teacher, 1986: Restructuring the Profession* (New York: Metropolitan Life Insurance Company, 1986), p. 17.

[24] Louis Harris, Joshua D. Libresco, and Robert P. Parker, *The American Teacher* (New York: The Metropolitan Life Insurance Company, 1984), pp. 43–48. Fifty percent said that merit pay might provide valuable incentives for teachers to improve their performance. Harris, Kagay, and Leichenko, *The Metropolitan Life Survey*, p. 25.

[25] Ernest Boyer, *High School: A Report on Secondary Education in America* (New York: Harper & Row, 1983), p. 179.

percent; and the income of plumbers, over 11 percent.[26] Teachers who came from the middle class or advanced to that station from working-class origins were alarmed to see the incomes of many blue-collar workers equal or greatly exceed their own. For example, they were chagrined to find that in 1985 the entry-level pay of garbage collectors in Chicago was $26,000, over $10,000 higher than the average starting salary pay of teachers in that year.[27] Nationally, teachers are paid slightly less than unionized blue-collar workers though teachers have a longer workday.[28]

Teachers' sense of self-worth and social status is threatened by the real and comparative decline in their economic well-being. As Blumberg has shown, this problem is not unique to teachers; its effects are widespread within the middle class:

> Today, the middle-class struggle to maintain what have been for them appropriate income differentials is collapsing. Such salaried employees must inevitably develop the feeling that their income is no longer commensurate with their social worth.[29]

Teachers' doubts about their professional self-worth are experienced individually, but Ashton and Webb contend that they are now so widespread that they constitute a social issue and will require social solutions.[30] Today, unprecedented numbers of teachers believe that their work is important but underpaid, their accomplishments are impressive but unrewarded, and their dedication is deep but unappreciated.

BAD PRESS AND PUBLIC IMAGE.   Teachers complain that the public image of their profession has changed in recent years. Diane Ravitch, an educational historian, has pointed out that

> fifty years ago . . . there was almost an automatic respect for the teacher. The teacher was the most educated person in the community. That's no longer the case. Teachers find themselves perhaps the lowest ranking of all professions. [They] find themselves struggling for the respect of the communities, struggling for the respect of parents, and struggling for the respect of their students.[31]

Alec Gallup made a similar point, when reviewing the results of a national survey of teachers:

> Teachers rate their contribution to society the *highest* of twelve professions, including physicians, clergy, business executives, and lawyers. But they also feel that their status is the *lowest* of all these professions.[32]

A veteran high school teacher gives voice to the status concern Gallup describes:

> [The public is] demanding too much of teachers and not giving enough. . . . In the newspapers and all, we've lost a lot of respect. They blame the teachers be-

---

[26] Paul Blumberg, *Inequality in an Age of Decline* (New York: Oxford University Press, 1980), p. 78.

[27] Vol. 52 (Washington DC: International Management Association, 1985), p. 130.

[28] Marshall Frady, *To Save Our Schools, To Save Our Children* (Far Hills, NJ: New Horizons Press, 1985), p. 54.

[29] Blumberg, *Inequality in an Age of Decline*, p. 83.

[30] Ashton and Webb, *Making a Difference*, pp. 159–176.

[31] Quoted in Frady, *To Save Our Schools, To Save Our Children*, p. 59.

[32] Alec Gallup, "The Gallup Poll of Teachers' Attitudes," p. 323.

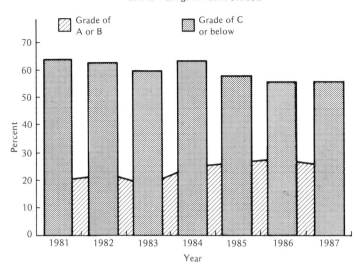

National Ratings of Public Schools

Figure 9-4   Percent of adults who give the nation's schools a grade of B or above, or C or below, 1981–1985. (*Source:* Alec M. Gallup and David L. Clark, "The 19th Annual Gallup Poll of the Public's Attitudes Toward the Public Schools," *Phi Delta Kappan,* Vol. 69 [September 1987], p. 2.)

cause students don't do well on tests. We're getting the blame when a lot of the blame should be placed on the home. There needs to be a lot more demanded of the home and less demanded of teachers. Give us [fewer] students and then see what we can do. . . . Pay us as professionals and let administrators treat us as professionals and then see what we can do.

Teachers are acutely aware that the public's confidence in public education has gone through a long period of decline. While polls indicate some improvement in recent years, public dissatisfaction is still widespread. In an annual Gallup poll on education, the public was asked to grade the *nation's* schools (not their local schools) in much the same way that a teacher might grade a student's homework. Only 26 percent of respondents gave the schools a grade of B or better. Most Americans (59 percent) assigned a grade of C or below (see Figure 9-4).[33]

One measure of the declining status of teachers is found in the fact that fewer parents are encouraging their children to enter teaching. Between 1969 and 1980, the number of parents who reported that they would like to see their children become teachers dropped from 75 to 48 percent.[34] More recent polls indicate a shift in these attitudes, an issue we will discuss shortly. The point to be made here is that the combination of poor pay and low status appears to have convinced many teachers that they are working in a precarious profession. Over half (53 percent) of the teachers report that they did not feel respected in today's society.[35] Of high school teachers, 71 percent say that the public's negative attitudes toward schools seriously eroded their job satisfac-

[33] Alec M. Gallup and David L. Clark, "The 19th Annual Gallup Poll of the Public's Attitudes Toward the Public Schools," *Phi Delta Kappan,* Vol. 69 (September 1987), p. 26.
[34] Alec Gallup, "The Gallup Poll of the Public's Attitudes Toward the Public Schools," *Phi Delta Kappan,* Vol. 62 (September 1980), p. 38. See also Boyer, *High School,* p. 154.
[35] Harris, Libresco, and Parker, *The American Teacher,* p. 22.

tion.[36] Half of all teachers say they are not sure they want their daughters to follow them into the teaching profession and 69 percent say the same thing about their sons.[37]

The teachers Ashton and Webb interviewed were troubled by their flagging image and low status. They claimed that the public generally did not understand the problems teachers face or appreciate their achievements. One teacher said that he did not

> think the average person knows what a teacher does. If I brought someone [into the classroom and he] knew the content [of the course], he would still have a tough time physically and mentally doing the job. . . . Teaching is a physical and mental strain. It's exhausting.

Another teacher pointed with pride to the fact that schools have been called upon to deal with many important national issues but that the public did not appreciate how well schools had responded to these challenges:

> In the last quarter century we have come a long way toward becoming a truly integrated society; not far enough, I'll grant that, but a long way, nevertheless. Schools helped to make that happen and I'm proud of the part I played in that process. We've accomplished a lot of things that quick-draw critics don't bother to mention. We helped reduce the drug abuse that was epidemic in schools a decade ago. The crisis isn't over, but, at this school at least, we have it under control. We reduced the dropout rate and got a lot of kids from poor homes through school. In the past they would never have been given a chance. We've helped heighten the professional aspirations of females. We didn't start the feminist movement, but we have helped it along. Now we are pulling test scores up. That will take time, but we're working on it. Teachers have done a lot for very little and I think it's time we got some recognition.

LACK OF RECOGNITION.   Teachers in many schools complain that they receive little support and recognition from administrators. Teachers say that their problems and achievements are often overlooked but that their mistakes and failures are widely advertised. An abundance of criticism and a paucity of praise make it difficult for teachers to maintain a positive sense of professional self-esteem. One seasoned teacher said that her husband had encouraged her to leave the profession:

> He sees how much teaching has devastated me over the years, and it has. A lot of these kids can break your heart. And he says I don't get much reward from teaching and I guess he's right; we certainly don't get much reward from the front office. We might get a pat on the back at a faculty meeting when the principal says, "You all have done a terrific job." But nobody comes in and says, "Thanks for stopping the riot at the basketball game"; that was something I did this year. . . . No one says, "We think you're doing a terrific job." I don't know of anybody in this school who has ever gotten that kind of recognition.[38]

Many teachers report that administrators are so wound up in front-office problems that they forget what it is like to be a teacher. A veteran teacher said, more in disappointment than in anger,

---

[36] Boyer, *High School,* p. 154.
[37] Gallup, "The Gallup Poll of Teachers' Attitudes," p. 323. In another survey, only 45 percent of teachers said they would advise a young person to pursue a career in teaching. See Harris, Libresco, and Parker, *The American Teacher,* p. 22.
[38] Ashton and Webb, *Making a Difference,* p. 40.

> My general complaint is how quickly administrators forget what it's actually like
> to be working in a classroom. They forget some of the problems and frustrating
> times that you go through. They forget that you need some support and under-
> standing. [But] it's very seldom . . . that you have someone [in the front office]
> who's genuinely interested and willing to lend an ear and listen to your prob-
> lems.[39]

Teachers worry that there is a one-way elasticity to the demands of their job:
their workload always expands, it almost never contracts; what is once accomplished is forever expected. If, for example, teachers put out a literary magazine, direct a class play, take children camping, or organize a mock United
Nations meeting, their efforts may be recognized and appreciated. However,
the novelty of each enterprise soon wears off. The extraordinary becomes ordinary and what was once appreciated is later simply assumed. Teachers who
wish further recognition must perpetually top their last accomplishment.

SURVEY DATA ON TEACHER DISSATISFACTION.   The problems reviewed here
are well documented in national surveys. One recent study asked dissatisfied
teachers why they considered leaving their chosen profession. Sixty-two percent mentioned low pay and 41 percent mentioned poor working conditions.
Others said that poor relations with students, parents, and administrators had
made teaching unpleasant. A quarter of the respondents said they were not
respected by society or their students (see Table 9-7). In another survey, 73
percent of teachers said they had to spend too much time on administrative
tasks.[40]

Despite these frustrations, teachers find areas of satisfaction in their work.
The greatest satisfaction comes not from pay but from teaching itself. *Ninety-
seven percent of all teachers in a national survey agreed with the statement, "I love to
teach."*[41] We turn now to the sources of teacher satisfaction.

The Rewards of Teaching

The difficulties teachers face have increased over the last decade and so has
teacher dissatisfaction. These trends are important and must be considered
carefully by anyone contemplating entering or advancing in the teaching
profession. Yet, despite these difficulties, many find teaching challenging, enjoyable, and personally satisfying. Most teachers hold proudly to the conviction
that they do vitally important work. As one middle-school teacher put it:

> I think that teaching is an inspired profession, I really do. For philosophical . . .
> reasons, I feel teaching [offers] a unique opportunity to help other individuals
> [and to make] a contribution . . . to . . . society. . . . We're spending . . . as
> [much time with students] as their parents do. . . . We're entrusted with [our
> students'] development. That's a great responsibility and . . . a great opportunity.
> I see it as both. I consider my position an exalted one . . . and I think that's one
> of the reasons I have stayed with [teaching. I] realize my rewards are . . . not
> . . . financial [but] I feel good about what I'm doing. I'm really contributing to

[39] Ibid.
[40] Harris, Libresco, and Parker, *The American Teacher*, p. 22.
[41] Ibid.

TABLE 9-7. Reasons Teachers Give for Seriously Considering Leaving Teaching

	Total	Men	Women
Question: What are the main things that made you consider *leaving teaching?*			
Inadequate, low salaries	62%	77%	53%
Working conditions (paperwork, nonteaching duties, school environment, class size, lack of autonomy, workload)	41	31	48
Student-related problems (lack of discipline and motivation, poor attitudes)	31	32	31
Administration-related problems (lack of support, incompetent administrators)	25	24	25
Lack of respect (society's attitudes, lack of respect from students and community, low status, lack respect)	25	22	27
Emotional issues (routine and boredom, stress, frustration, burnout)	22	20	23
Parent- and community-related problems (lack of support)	21	16	24

SOURCE: Louis Harris, Michael Kagay, and Stuart Leichenko, *The American Teacher, 1985: Strengthening the Profession* (New York: The Metropolitan Life Insurance Company, 1985), pp. 30–31.

Note: Figures add to more than 100 percent because respondents were invited to give more than one answer.

society and my fellow man. Maybe that's much more worthwhile than the dollar. So I guess that is a basic assumption; . . . that [teaching] is a calling.[42]

Ashton and Webb asked middle and high school teachers why they stayed in the profession. Teachers responded that students were their *primary* source of satisfaction. This is an interesting finding because it shows that teachers, though concerned about extrinsic rewards such as status and salary, are more interested in the intrinsic satisfactions (or what sociologists call *psychic rewards*) offered by the profession. Students make a teacher's work wearing or worthwhile. When relationships with students are troubled (when students are unappreciative, unproductive, or uncooperative), teachers find their work tedious and unrewarding. On the other hand, when classroom relationships are positive, teachers are likely to find joy in what they do.

Teachers were asked why they stayed in the classroom. These comments are typical of their responses:

• Well, it's all the kids. They make it worthwhile.
• I came into teaching because I like people; I'm a people person and I guess

---

[42] Ashton and Webb, *Making a Difference*, p. 105.

Teachers report that students are their primary source of satisfaction. (*Source:* National Education Association, Joe Di Dio.)

that's why I'm staying. I just like my students and as long as they continue to like me, I'll stick it out.
- I'd have to say it's the students. They frustrate you and they frustrate you some more and then, out of the blue, something goes right and you can see progress. That's what keeps me sane and keeps me coming back for more.
- Nothing is more satisfying than teaching someone to read. I don't think anything matches that. You see children's faces light up when they read for the first time and, well, it is wonderful. Wonderful! Where else could I get satisfaction like that?

When asked to elaborate on their answers, teachers referred to specific events they found satisfying. For example, they told of "getting through" to a reluctant student, receiving a letter of appreciation from a former pupil, helping a youngster through a difficult period, or helping a pupil get into college. Teachers described such accomplishments briefly and seldom elaborated on the circumstances of the events. Nevertheless, it was clear these achievements were important to teachers and a source of abiding satisfaction. Many keep artifacts of past successes (valentines, notes, letters of appreciation, pictures, news clippings, awards, and so on) to remind themselves of "what teaching was all about."

Teaching is, among other things, a performing art, and teachers understandably take pride when lessons "work out" and when "things just click" in the classroom. Experienced teachers report that during a "good class" they are in comfortable harmony with their students. Teachers described the characteristics of a "good class." Such classes came about when students were interested in the subject at hand, were motivated to learn what was being taught, respected the teacher's ability to make the material accessible, took some responsibility for the successes of the class, and took pride in their individual and collective accomplishments. In other words, there was an esprit de corps in the class because teachers and students worked together rather than at cross purposes.

The events teachers described were cherished, but they occurred unpredictably; teachers could not make them happen at will. Thus, even the most satisfied teachers are likely to suffer periods of doubt and worry. Nevertheless, most teachers find their profession personally satisfying. Forty-four percent of teachers report they are very satisfied with teaching as a career and another 35 percent report that they are somewhat satisfied.[43]

Another study compared the job satisfaction of teachers with that of other American workers. Respondents were asked to rank their job satisfaction along a scale where 1 indicated "extremely satisfied" and 10 "extremely dissatisfied." Ninety percent of public school teachers ranked themselves between 1 and 5. Two years earlier, the Gallup organization asked the same question to a national sample of adult workers. Then, 70 percent of all adults and 80 percent of college-educated adults ranked themselves somewhere between 1 and 5 on the ten-point scale.[44] Thus, while teachers face multiple problems—especially in terms of salary, working conditions, and professional status—they still find work intrinsically rewarding.

Understanding the Elements of Teacher Satisfaction

The issue of teacher satisfaction is complex and does not lend itself to easy summation. However, research in the area has uncovered some useful findings. In one survey, nearly two-thirds of public school teachers reported that the two most important aspects of their jobs were the chance to use their abilities and the opportunity to help students.[45] Not surprisingly, teachers are likely to resent anything that hinders their development in these areas. For example, they are frustrated by the myriad events that interrupt their teaching or that take time away from preparing for lesson plans and grading papers. Under present conditions, as much as 50 percent of a teacher's day is consumed by noninstructional tasks.

It is clear that working conditions in schools strongly influence faculty satisfaction.[46] Conditions that make teachers powerless, that hinder their ability to teach, or that disrupt their relationships with students diminish the joys of teaching. Conditions that empower teachers in these areas enhance job satisfaction. Teachers are most likely to be satisfied when

- The school has clear goals and standards;
- The administration is supportive and stays aware of what teachers are doing;
- The administration shares power and decision making with the faculty;
- Teachers are trusted and have autonomy in the classroom;
- Teachers collaborate to work out problems, policy issues, curriculum matters, and teaching strategies;

[43] Harris, Libresco, and Parker, *The American Teacher*, p. 51.
[44] C. Emily Feistritzer, *Profiles of Teachers in the U.S.* (Washington, DC: National Center for Education Information, 1986).
[45] Ibid.
[46] Harris, Libresco, and Parker, *The American Teacher*, p. 52.

- The school is safe and friendly;
- The rules of the school are clear, fair and enforced; and
- Teachers can get help when they need it.[47]

These conditions increase satisfaction because they give teachers *maximum access to the psychic rewards of teaching.*

It is worth noting that schools built on the model just described fit the democratic ideal discussed in Chapter 5. The aim of such schools, like the aim of democracy itself, is to improve institutional effectiveness by empowering those who work within them. Ideas are discussed; communal intelligence is brought to bear on problems of common concern; power is shared; and rationality, compromise, civility, and cooperation are valued. It is not surprising that the model of organization described here has been called workplace democracy. Proponents claim that workplace democracy increases worker participation, lessens dissatisfaction, increases productivity, and provides a community of purpose.[48]

The workplace democracy model holds promise as a way to improve school effectiveness, reduce faculty burnout, and raise teacher morale. These issues will be elaborated later in the text (see Chapters 10 and 23). Suffice it to say here that many of the stresses of teaching are better handled when teachers work together rather than alone.[49] Teachers are most likely to maintain their enthusiasm and effectiveness in the classroom when they have a network of collegial support within the school. As teachers, administrators, and policy makers become more aware of this fact, teaching is likely to become more satisfying and schools more effective.

Steps in a Positive Direction

Numerous commissions and blue ribbon panels studied our schools during the 1980s and reported their findings to the nation. (The reports are reviewed in detail in Chapter 23.) Though the reports work from different assumptions and offer different prescriptions, all share the goal of improving the quality of education offered in our public schools. Most call for increasing teacher pay, and some discuss the need for improving the working conditions for teachers. Although it is too early to predict whether the concern and interest generated by these reports will be translated into effective reform, it is clear that lasting reform is more likely today than it has been in many years. We now turn our attention to some of the areas where improvement appears likely.

[47] Ashton and Webb, *Making a Difference,* pp. 125–144, 159–176; Boyer, *High School;* John I. Goodlad, *A Place Called School: Prospects for the Future* (New York: McGraw-Hill Book Company, 1984), pp. 167–196, 254–270, available in paperback; Sara Lawrence Lightfoot, *The Good High School: Portraits of Character and Culture* (New York: Basic Books, 1983), available in paperback.

[48] See Arthur G. Wirth, *Productive Work in Schools and Industry: Becoming Persons Again* (Lanham, MD: University Press of America, 1983); available in paperback. See also Martin Carnoy and Derek Shearer, *Economic Democracy: The Challenge of the 1980s* (New York: M. E. Sharp, Inc., 1980); Mike Cooley, *Architect or Bee?* (Boston: South End Press, 1980); Daniel Zwerdling, *Democracy at Work* (Washington, DC: Association for Management, 1978).

[49] Goodlad, *A Place Called School,* p. 180; Barbara Benham Tye, *Multiple Realities: A Study of Thirteen American High Schools* (Lanham, MD: University Press of America, 1985), pp. 117–127, 327–333; Ashton and Webb, *Making a Difference,* pp. 125–144, 159–176.

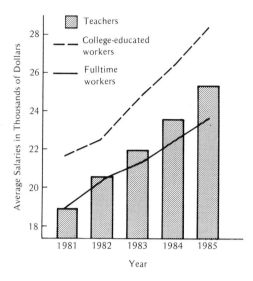

Figure 9-5   Average salaries of teachers, college-educated workers, and all workers in thousands of dollars, 1981–1985. Though still low, teacher pay is going up. Figures have not been adjusted for inflation.   (*Source:* The American Federation of Teachers, *Survey & Analysis of Salary Trends, 1987* [Washington, DC: Author, 1987].)

HIGHER PAY.   Most national reports and policy studies have called for substantially higher salaries for teachers, and it appears that these reports are having an impact on state legislatures. The after-inflation salaries of teachers are on the rise (see Figure 9-5). In thirty-five states, salary increases have been tied to pay-for-performance plans, usually called career ladders or master teacher plans. Teachers with seniority and proven records of accomplishment are given more money and added responsibilities, such as setting curriculum standards or supervising new teachers. In Tennessee, a "five rung" career ladder has been established. Thousands of teachers have applied for promotions that brought salary increases of up to $7000. The plan is controversial and has undergone major revisions. It is still unclear whether the state will fund the plan adequately and if it will encourage or dishearten teachers in the long run. Other states, Utah for example, developed programs that were funded at the state level but designed and implemented by local school districts.

The move to improve the income of teachers is well established and supported by such groups as the Carnegie Forum on Education and the Economy. In 1986, the Carnegie Forum issued a report suggesting that progressive levels of skill and responsibility be defined and that teachers be rewarded according to the ability they demonstrate and the responsibility they shoulder. The report suggests a salary norm of $35,000 rising to a top income of $72,000 for lead teachers.[50]

The leaders of the National Education Association and the American Federation of Teachers supported the salary provisions of the report. Myron Lieberman, a professor at Ohio University, is skeptical about the plan. He commented shortly after the report was issued that, "raising salaries by only 25 percent would [cost] billions of dollars. There's just no way that's going to hap-

---

[50] Carnegie Forum on Education and the Economy, *A Nation Prepared: Teachers for the 21st Century* (New York: Carnegie Forum on Education and the Economy, 1986).

pen."[51] Lieberman is probably right; salaries will not rise as far or as fast as the Carnegie Forum suggests. However, virtually every responsible call for school improvement has included a case for raising teachers' salaries and several states are beginning to act on these suggestions.

LEGISLATED REFORMS.   Salary increases in many states have been accompanied by reform legislation mandating more rigorous certification standards, teacher induction programs, teacher testing requirements, higher admission and graduation requirements for colleges of education, and merit pay plans. State legislators have been reluctant to increase the salaries of incompetent teachers. By 1986, thirty states required that all prospective teachers pass minimum competency tests before certification.[52] Ten states intended to require such tests by 1990, and four other states were considering pre-entry exams. The Carnegie Forum suggested a rigorous national proficiency exam for board-certified teachers, similar to the exams taken by lawyers and doctors. They have issued an $817,000 grant to Stanford University to develop such an exam.

Three states (Arkansas, Georgia, and Texas) have used tests to identify incompetent teachers already working in the classroom. Teachers failing state tests were allowed to take them again, but a passing score is a requirement for retaining certification. In Arkansas, 10 percent of the teachers failed the test the first time around. In Texas, the failure rate was 4 percent for both teachers and administrators. Eight thousand teachers took the first offering of a subject-matter test in Georgia and 12 percent did not pass. Critics of the tests argue that they do not accurately measure skills necessary for teaching. The test's defenders counter that the exams are designed to test basic skill knowledge and not teaching proficiency. They go on to say that teachers who cannot do sixth grade arithmetic problems cannot teach math effectively and probably could not do the arithmetic required in their everyday work.

Teacher organizations have been slow to endorse testing programs, especially those aimed at veteran teachers, fearing that the tests will be misused or will not actually measure a teacher's skill. However, as such programs have been implemented and where safeguards have been included to avoid the arbitrary systems of punishment and reward, teacher support has grown. For example, one survey asked teachers to judge the likely effect of a number of proposed reforms. As can be seen in Figure 9-6, a majority of teachers thought that career ladders and competency testing for teachers would help improve the quality of education in America's public schools.

IMPROVEMENT IN THE PUBLIC'S ATTITUDE TOWARD EDUCATION.   The flurry of educational reform that has been going on since 1980 is far from over, and the consequence of the school improvement effort will not be known for some time. Yet, one beneficial result is already becoming clear. Though the public still worries about the quality of public schools in general, attitudes toward *local*

---

[51] Jennet Conant, "Test Time for Teachers," *Newsweek* (May 26, 1986), p. 61.
[52] Valena White Plisko and Joyce D. Stern, *The Condition of Education, 1985* (Washington, DC: National Center for Education Statistics, 1985), p. 163.

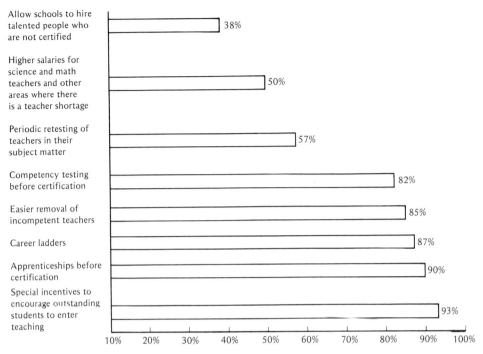

Percent of teachers contending that particular reforms will have a "Strongly Positive" or "Somewhat Positive" effect on the quality of teaching in America's public schools.

Figure 9-6   Whether suggested changes will have a positive effect on the quality of teaching.   (*Source:* Louis Harris, Joshua D. Libresco, and Robert P. Parker, *The American Teacher, 1985, Strengthening the Profession* [New York: The Metropolitan Life Insurance Company, 1984], p. 41. Figures add to more than 100 percent because respondents were invited to give more than one answer.)

schools (the schools people know best) have improved in recent years.[53] If the public's attitudes toward schools continues to improve, it is likely that the public's appreciation of teachers will improve also. There is already some evidence that this is happening. Recent polls show that the public's resistance to their own children entering teaching is beginning to diminish.[54]

Summary

Teachers are not all cut from the same cloth. They come to the profession from varied backgrounds and have myriad motives for choosing to become

[53] Today, the percentage of adults giving their *local* schools grades of A or B nearly equals the percent giving schools a grade of C or below. George H. Gallup, "The 17th Annual Gallup Poll of the Public's Attitudes Toward the Public Schools," *Phi Delta Kappan*, Vol. 77 (September 1985), p. 36. Figure 9-4 referred to schools in general, not to local schools.

[54] Gallup, "The Gallup Poll of Teachers' Attitudes," p. 324. Half of those surveyed said they would like to have a daughter of theirs enter teaching and 46 percent said that they would like to have a son of theirs enter the field.

teachers. If they share any single characteristic, it is that they want to work with the young and through that work contribute to society. Many are devoted to the subject matter they teach and work with the conviction that individuals and society are improved by the acquisition of knowledge and the ability to utilize knowledge critically. Inherent in these motives is the hope of bettering the human condition and a conviction that this can be accomplished through education. These are the *primary motives* for teaching and they constitute the single best hope for the improvement of the profession. The primary motives of teachers are idealistic, and, as we shall see in the next chapter, idealism plays an important role in education.

A number of *secondary motives* are also at work in the teaching profession. These motives are difficult to uncover and receive less attention than primary motives. Nevertheless, they have a significant impact on who enters teaching and who stays in the profession. Perhaps the most significant secondary motive is that teaching offers relatively easy mobility up into the middle class. Mobility out of the working class is accompanied by the promise, if not always the reality, of a comfortable income, job security, improved status, and increased respect.

Education has been a preferred occupation for women. One reason for this is that until recently other professions have been virtually off limits to women. The occupations open to women were often poorly paid and interfered with the traditional duties of homemaking and child rearing. Teaching, on the other hand, was (and still is today) the best-paid profession dominated by women. This may change in the future, as traditional prejudices decline and as women secure places in more lucrative professions. Another reason for the popularity of teaching among women is that the work and vacation schedule in teaching made it possible for women to work while their children were in school and to be home when the school day and term were over.

For some men and women, teaching is a convenient stopgap occupation, a means of earning a living while preparing for another line of work. For others, it is a second choice, which they fell into because they were unable to achieve some other (and in their view preferable) goal. And, for yet another group, teaching yields the opportunity to remember, and perhaps relive, happier days of personal success as an outstanding student or athlete. Dan Lortie suggests that the secondary motives for teaching constitute a conservative force in schools. They serve to lessen the activism and diminish the idealism of teachers. One of the great challenges facing the profession today is to discover ways to sustain the idealism of teachers and allow it to guide the practice of teaching.

A number of factors increase teachers' dissatisfaction. Teachers are poorly paid compared to other professions. Inflation has significantly diminished the salary gains teachers made during the 1970s. Limited career opportunities within teaching cause many talented teachers to leave the classroom for other professions or to accept nonteaching positions inside education. The public's declining confidence in the nation's schools has had a demoralizing effect on teachers in recent years. Upwardly mobile teachers are saddened to find that their profession has not provided the income or prestige they anticipated. In addition, the conditions of the work environment have made it difficult for teachers to reap the psychic rewards offered by the profession. Despite these problems, the intrinsic rewards of teaching remain abundant enough to sustain most individuals in teaching.

Teaching is a client-oriented occupation, thus, it is not surprising that students are a primary source of teacher satisfaction. As we shall see in the next chapter, students confirm or contradict a teacher's self-image of competence. When teachers "win over" their students, teaching is profoundly fulfilling. When teachers "blow it" or "lose the class," teaching can be arduous and demoralizing. Every teacher must build his or her own relationships with students. However, school policies and practices influence those relationships in profound ways.

Most teachers are frustrated by anything that interrupts their classes or hinders their ability to build friendly, productive relationships with students. Interruptions, such as needless announcements over the school PA system, give students the unsubtle message that teaching and learning are not particularly important. Good teachers resent that message. When schools lack an understandable and evenly enforceable code of conduct, students learn that civility is not valued in the school environment. Good teachers resent that lesson, too, because they understand that learning cannot take place in the midst of chaos.

The work of teachers is made easier and the morale of teachers is improved when schools are run democratically. Democratic schools are characterized by clear goals and standards, supportive leadership, shared decision making, teacher collaboration, clear and fairly enforced rules, and the possibility of professional development.

The future of the teaching profession looks brighter today than it has in many years. Every commission report has called for better pay and improved working conditions in education. The academic preparation of teachers is improving and numerous measures have been taken to assure that poorly prepared teachers will not enter or long remain in the profession. Career ladders and other pay-for-performance programs are being tested. Educational standards are improving and the test performance of students and their teachers is on the rise. The public's confidence in public education is moving up and there is some evidence that teachers' job satisfaction is increasing also.

No one can predict whether the improvements discussed in this chapter will be sustained over the next decade. However, it is clear that the nation's attention has been caught by the call for excellence in education. If the momentum of the past five years can be sustained, the chances are good that teaching will become the "exalted profession" it deserves to be.

Suggested Readings

Reading about the lives of teachers:

ASHTON, PATRICIA T., and RODMAN B. WEBB. *Making A Difference: Teachers' Sense of Efficacy and Student Achievement.* New York: Longman, 1986. This book grows out of research done for the National Institute of Education. It examines the degree to which teachers' attitudes regarding their ability to teach and their students' ability to learn may affect student achievement. In the course of the study, the investigators discovered that teachers' attitudes appeared to be affected by the conditions of their work. Chapter 2 investigates the social-psychological contexts of teaching, Chapter 4 investigates the effect of school organization on teacher attitudes, and Chapter 7 lays out a plan for educational reform.

BALL, STEPHEN J., and IVOR F. GOODSON, eds. *Teachers' Lives and Careers.* London: The Falmer Press, 1985. Growing out of a conference at St. Hilda's College, Oxford, in 1983, the book explores the contemporary situation of teachers' lives and careers in Britain and the United States. The editors supply an insightful introductory essay that sets the theoretical stage for the book.

BOYER, ERNEST L. *High School: A Report on Secondary Education in America.* New York: Harper & Row, 1983. In the tradition of James Conant's *The American High School,* Boyer examines the goals of American education and studies the high school as an institution. The chapter on teachers is short but insightful.

CARNEGIE FORUM ON EDUCATION AND THE ECONOMY. *A Nation Prepared: Teachers for the 21st Century.* New York: Carnegie Forum on Education and the Economy, 1986. This is a valuable source of data and policy proposals.

FEISTRITZER, C. EMILY. *Profiles of Teachers in the U.S.* Washington, DC: National Center for Education Information, 1986. This is an interesting, tough, controversial study.

FRADY, MARSHALL. *To Save Our Schools, To Save Our Children.* Far Hills, NJ: New Horizons Press, 1985. This book began as a three-hour special report broadcast over the ABC Television Network in September 1984. Over 8 million Americans watched reporters document what they called the shocking decline of the nation's schools. The section devoted to teachers and their careers is particularly relevant to the topic of this chapter.

GALLUP, ALEC. "The Gallup Poll of Teachers' Attitudes Toward the Public Schools," *Phi Delta Kappan,* Vol. 66 (October 1984). An excellent annual survey of teacher attitudes.

GOODLAD, JOHN I. *A Place Called School: Prospects for the Future.* New York: McGraw-Hill, 1984. Perhaps the most teacher-centered of all reports on American education, the book calls for schools to become more humane and rewarding environments for teachers and students alike.

HARRIS, LOUIS, JOSHUA D. LIBRESCO, and ROBERT P. PARKER. *The American Teacher, 1985, Strengthening the Profession.* New York: The Metropolitan Life Insurance Company, 1984. Here is another excellent source of data.

LIPSKY, MICHAEL. *Street-level Bureaucracy: Dilemma of the Individual in Public Service.* New York: Russell Sage Foundation, 1980. As the subtitle suggests, the focus of this book is not on the work experiences of teachers but on all who work for public agencies and who have wide discretion in the allocation of benefits and public sanctions. This highly original work goes a long way in explaining the day-to-day rewards and frustrations of client-centered work.

SIZER, THEODORE R. *Horace's Compromise: The Dilemma of the American High School.* Boston: Houghton-Mifflin Company, 1984. Cosponsored by the National Association of Secondary School Principals and the National Association of Independent Schools, this important book pays close attention to the work lives and desired commitments of teachers.

WIRTH, ARTHUR G. *Productive Work in Schools and Industry: Becoming Persons Again.* Lanham, MD: University Press of America, 1983. This award-winning book is a social-philosophical account of the democratic workplace movement. It documents research from around the world, places efforts to democratize the workplace in the theoretical context of American pragmatism, and shows the relevance of the movement for educational improvement in the United States.

The social class origins and present status of teachers have not received the attention they deserve. Nevertheless, some important studies are available.

BENNETT, WILLIAM S., and EDSEL L. ERICKSON. "Teacher Profile" in *The Encyclopedia of Education.* New York: Macmillan Publishing Co., Inc., 1971, pp. 43–49.

CARLSON, RICHARD O. "Variations in the Myth in the Social Status of Teachers," *Journal of Educational Sociology*, Vol. 35 (1951), pp. 104–118.

CHARTERS, W. W., JR. "The Social Background of Teaching" in *Handbook of Research on Teaching*, ed. N. L. Gage. Chicago: Rand McNally, 1963, pp. 718–722, 730–741.

DWORKIN, ANTHONY G. "The Changing Demography of Public School Teachers: Some Implications for Faculty Turnover in Urban Areas," *Sociology of Education*, Vol. 53 (April 1980), pp. 65–73.

GOTTLIEB, DAVID. "Teaching and Students: The View of Negro and White Teachers," *Sociology of Education*, Vol. 37 (1964), pp. 345–353.

HAVIGHURST, ROBERT J., and DANIEL U. LEVINE. *Society and Education*, 5th ed. Boston: Allyn & Bacon, Inc., 1979, pp. 513–530.

PAVALKO, RONALD. "Recruitment to Teaching: Patterns of Selection and Retention," *Sociology of Education*, Vol. 43 (1970), pp. 340–353.

SCHWARZWELLER, HARRY K., and THOMAS A. LYSON. "Some Plan to Become Teachers: Determinants of Career Specification Among Rural Youth in Norway, Germany, and the United States," *Sociology of Education*, Vol. 51 (1978), pp. 29–43.

Other studies that give information regarding the status of teachers in America today:

BROUDY, HARRIS S., ed. *The Real World of the Beginning Teacher*. Report of the National Commission on Teacher Education and Professional Standards Conference. Washington, DC: National Education Association, 1966. This series of essays examines the motivations of beginning teachers, variations in teacher preparation programs, the need for melding theory and practice in colleges of education, and the hopes and aspirations of beginning teachers.

DREEBEN, ROBERT. *The Nature of Teaching: Schools and the Work of Teachers*. Glenview, IL: Scott, Foresman and Company, 1970. This is a thorough analysis of who teachers are and what they do.

ELAM, STANLEY, ed. *The Gallup Polls of Attitudes Toward Education, 1969–1978*. Bloomington, IN: Phi Delta Kappa, 1978. This is a compilation of Phi Delta Kappa's yearly poll of public attitudes toward education. Many of the questions asked deal with the public's perceptions of teachers.

LORTIE, DAN C. *School Teacher: A Sociological Study*. Chicago: University of Chicago Press, 1975. This is the most complete and provocative account of the teaching profession.

NATIONAL EDUCATION ASSOCIATION. *Status of the American Public School Teacher, 1970–71* and *Status of the American Public School Teacher, 1975–76*. Washington, DC: National Education Association, 1971 and 1976. These are invaluable sources. Every five years, the National Education Association polls its membership. Questions of pay, workload, working conditions, attitudes toward teaching, social class backgrounds, and a host of other areas are asked of teachers.

ZEIGLER, HARMON. *The Political Life of American Teachers*. Englewood, Cliffs, NJ: Prentice-Hall, Inc., 1967. This book analyzes the factors that influence political behavior of high school teachers. Social class and gender turn out to be key variables. It brings up a number of issues that deserve further study.

CHAPTER 10

Teachers' Careers

RODMAN B. WEBB AND PATRICIA SIKES

Introduction

A career, as social scientists define it, is a pattern of organized professional activity for which individuals receive special training.[1] To train for and enter a career is not simply to "get a job" but to begin along a path of individual and social development. When Charles Eliot was twenty-one years old, fifteen years before he assumed the presidency of Harvard University in 1869, he wrote a friend asking, What shall I be? He went on to say,

> When a man answers that question he not only determines his sphere of useful-ness in this world, he also decides in what direction his own mind shall be devel-oped. The different professions are not different roads converging at the same end; they are different roads, which starting from the same point, diverge for-ever, for all we know.[2]

The young Eliot understood that the choice of a career was critical because it involves one's identity, future biography, material prospects, and relationship to society.

In everyday language the word *career* can refer to a line of work (a career in teaching) or to the course of an individual's professional life (*my* teaching ca-reer). These two meanings for the word reflect the fact that careers are con-structed both socially and individually. If we are to understand what a partic-ular career is like, we must study both the objective conditions of the work (job requirements, pay, advancement opportunities, social recognition, relationships with fellow employees, and so on) and people's own experience of employment (their motivations, dreams, surprises, troubles, and compromises). We must keep in mind that while careers are experienced subjectively by those who live them,

---

[1] Burton Bledstein, *The Culture of Professionalism* (New York: W. W. Norton, 1976), pp. 159–202.
[2] Letter from C. W. Eliot to Theodore Tebbets (January 29, 1854), Harvard University Archives, quoted in ibid., p. 159.

they also contain, as Stephen Ball and Ivor Goodson have put it, "their own organizing principles and distinct phases."[3]

Though every person's career is unique in some way, a study of a particular profession inevitably reveals similarities that tie the experiences of different individuals into recognizable patterns. These patterns are influenced by organizational structures (working in a hospital differs from working in a business office or a classroom), by historical events (teaching in the Depression was different from teaching in the boom era of the 1960s), and by the course of adult development (fifty-year-old teachers experience their work differently than novice twenty-two-year-olds). Career patterns in a profession are commonly divided into "stages" that are "linked to the process of aging."[4] Thus, it is possible to analyze the "life cycle" of a profession and spell out the career stages that people are likely to go through in the course of their professional lives.

The study of the life cycle of teachers is a relatively new line of research in the United States. Nevertheless, research into adult development indicates that career stages, identity, and aging are closely linked phenomena.[5] Drawing on two lines of research, studies of teachers' careers and research in adult development, allows us to identify and analyze the career stages that teachers are likely to pass through in the course of their professional lives. The stages discussed in this chapter are organized by the chronological age of the teachers. Of course, not all teachers travel through the stages of their profession in exactly the same way or at exactly the same pace. History, biography, social conditions, personality, and myriad other factors influence a teacher's career experience. The five stages discussed in the chapter simply indicate when certain patterns of experience, knowledge, and difficulty are likely to occur for most teachers.

There is an important limitation in studies of teachers' careers that deserves our attention at the outset. Much of the career development and life-stage research has focused exclusively on men. The careers of women have either been ignored[6] or, when considered at all, evaluated according to male norms.[7] Greater attention must be paid to the aspirations, achievements, and job experiences of women in general and of women teachers in particular. Only a few scholars have studied the careers of women teachers[8] and we will take account of their research in this chapter.

---

[3] Stephen Ball and Ivor Goodson, "Understanding Teachers: Concepts and Contexts," in *Teachers' Lives and Careers*, eds. Stephen Ball and Ivor Goodson (London: The Falmer Press, 1985), p. 11. Available in paperback.

[4] Ibid., p. 12.

[5] Daniel J. Levinson with Charlotte N. Darrow, Edward B. Klein, Maria H. Levinson, and Braxton McKee, *The Seasons of a Man's Life* (New York: Alfred A. Knopf, 1979), p. 49. Available in paperback.

[6] Judith Agassi, "The Quality of Women's Working Life," in *The Quality of Working Life*, eds. L. Davis and A. Cherns, Vol. 1 (New York: Free Press, 1975), pp. 280–298.

[7] Carol Gilligan, *In a Different Voice* (Cambridge: Harvard University Press, 1982). Available in paperback.

[8] Jennifer Nias, "A More Distant Drummer: Teacher Development as the Development of Self," in *Education and Social Change*, eds. Len Barton and Stephen Walker (London: Croom Helm, 1985); Sari Knopp Biklen, *Teaching as an Occupation for Women: A Case Study on an Elementary School* (Washington, DC: NIE, Final Report under grant No. NIE-G-81-007); Sari Knopp Biklen, "Can Elementary School Teaching Be a Career? A Search for New Ways of Understanding Women's Work," in *Issues in Education*, Vol. 3 (Winter 1985), pp. 215–231; Patricia J. Sikes, "The Life Cycle of the Teacher," in *Teachers' Lives and Careers*, eds. Ball and Goodson, pp. 27–60.

Stage 1. Early Adulthood: Initiation and Socilization (Ages Twenty-one through Twenty-eight)

Roughly between the ages of twenty-one and twenty-eight, individuals who have been trained for careers usually enter the job market. In the United States, indeed in all industrial nations, the initiation into a career is completed without much fanfare. Yet, those who graduate from college and land their first job understand that a significant change has occurred in their lives. Most college graduates separate from their immediate families and begin to establish an independent adult identity. A recent college graduate makes the point:

> I'll admit I'm excited. Until now, everything has been preparation. But now, at last, I'm doing things; not just *getting ready* to do things. I can't believe it; I'm a teacher and . . . I'm out on my own. I've got a job and my own apartment. (Laughing and raising her hands up over her head.) God, I think this means I'm grown up!

In a society where individualism is a core value, it should not surprise us that "being on your own" and "gainfully employed" are powerful indicators of adulthood. However, no one springs from late adolescence as a fully formed adult. There is a transition period between "growing up" and "settling down" that Levinson and other researchers call early adulthood. In this period, Levinson explains, individuals explore two, antithetical options: (1) "the possibilities of adult living," where individuals keep their options open, avoid strong commitments, and maximize their alternatives; and (2) "the possibility of creating a stable life structure," where individuals become more responsible, make commitments, "settle down" and begin to "make something of themselves." The challenge of young adulthood is to find a balance between the dual possibilities of exploration and commitment.[9]

There is always a danger that young adults will emphasize one of these options to the detriment or exclusion of the other. If individuals explore too long and fail to make commitments in work and in love, there is a danger that their lives will lose direction and meaning, a problem we call *under-commitment*. On the other hand, if individuals commit themselves too strongly or too early in their lives, they may eventually regret that they did not explore other options before settling down. We call this the problem of *early commitment*. Either of these problems, if left unresolved, may result in alienation later in life.

The Problem of Under-Commitment

As we saw in Chapter 9, some beginning teachers view teaching as a convenient stop-gap occupation that "provides a paycheck" and "long summer vacations" while they explore other career possibilities. It should not be assumed that individuals or the teaching profession are ill served when young adults teach for a few years and then move on to other things. Young adulthood, after all, is a time of experimentation. Thus, many intelligent, resourceful teachers enter the profession quite tentatively. Some contribute their talents for a short period

---

[9] Levinson et al., *The Seasons of a Man's Life*, pp. 58 and 79.

and then leave,[10] while others "get hooked" and decide to stay. Tentative teachers cause difficulty only when they lack commitment to their work, fail to do it well, or stay too long in a profession they find unsatisfying. One discontented sixth-grade teacher reported that she regretted becoming a teacher:

> I don't remember ever making a conscious decision to be a teacher. Never. I was a history major and . . . I was going to either go to law school or get a Ph. D. in history. I just picked up those education courses to have a teaching certificate. I never intended to end up here.

This particular teacher had a great deal to offer students, but she never incorporated teaching into the long-term plans she had for her life. She stayed in teaching longer than she wanted to but, in her thirties, decided to leave the classroom for law school. Certainly, education benefits from having talented people working in schools before moving on to other things. However, a profession cannot survive if too many of its members are transient and discontented.

The Problem of Early Commitment

Some teachers have "always wanted to teach" and thus never considered other career possibilities. After a few years in the classroom, however, a few begin to worry that they committed themselves too early to a life of chalk dust and red ink. They report feeling caught in a profession that turned out to be wrong for them. One such teacher explained,

> I don't feel I can get out of education because I've invested too much time in it. A lot of older teachers [like me] don't see any place else to go. Younger teachers . . . have more courage. They see the handwriting on the wall and get out. . . . But I've invested too much time to do that.

Another teacher said

> If I had it to do over again I might choose teaching; it's hard to say. But I certainly would think about it longer than I did. I would try to think of other options . . . I would do more serious thinking.

Career Dreams

The work of young adulthood is not merely to choose a career path (and probably a mate) but also to find satisfaction in the life choices that have been made and to plan a course for the future. Without commitment, young adults may feel that they lack direction and are unsure of who they are or where they are going. Like Biff, Willy Loman's hapless son in *Death of a Salesman*, they worry that they "can't take hold of some kind of a life."[11] However, once they have committed themselves, to a career and perhaps to another person, and have found some degree of direction and satisfaction through that commitment, they

---

[10] Lyndon Johnson, Golda Meir, John Dewey, Sam Levinson, Geraldine Ferraro, and Sylvia Ashton-Warner are but a few of the people who began their careers as teachers and went on to make a contribution in other fields. However, teaching left its mark on them all and they, in turn, continued to influence education.

[11] Arthur Miller, *Death of a Salesman* (New York: Viking Press, 1949), p. 54. Available in paperback.

must embark on the second major task of young adulthood, fashioning what Levinson calls a *dream.*

A dream is an idealized notion of what individuals hope to accomplish in their careers and private lives. Dreams usually begin as vague hopes and, in the case of teaching, with a self-confident idealism. Career dreams become better formed as individuals gather experience and begin to grasp their own potentials and limitations. We asked 127 college of education seniors, "How do you think you will do as a teacher?" Though the answers varied, all responses had two characteristics in common: They reflected a deeply felt idealism and they were expressions of career dreams in the early stages of formation. Here are five examples of the kinds of things students had to say:

> I'll be an excellent teacher. I enjoy the company of children and relate to them well. I understand them and am excited about being a part of their learning. I want to make a difference in their lives. I want them to trust me, confide in me, share their sorrows and joys with me, and I want to be more than just a teacher. I also want to be a friend. My classroom will be orderly but also fun.

> I will be a very effective and patient teacher; the kind of teacher who makes learning interesting. I will find new ways to help students learn and develop a love of learning. I will get along with my students and with "the system." I want to make learning enjoyable and to help them understand education is important.

> I will develop an atmosphere in my classes that will allow students to learn history honestly. I want students to understand past events and to explore the implications history has for the future. My students will be better citizens of the world because they will understand the course of human events and will have the skill of critical thinking.

> I want to teach my students the basics, but I also want to help them in other ways. I will help them develop strong self-concepts and creativity and I will encourage them to learn on their own and try new things. I will relate well to my students and transform their weaknesses and insecurities into strengths.

> I believe I will be a good teacher regardless of the obstacles that stand in my way. I'm in education to help others. I will always be there if students need help or guidance and I'll always be fair. I want my students to come back to me some day and say, "You made a difference in my life."

Carol Gilligan points out that the success-driven, competitive career dreams described in Levinson's research do not accurately depict the work experiences or career aspirations of women. Levinson's men dreamed of glorious achievements accompanied by social and economic advancement. Many women, according to Gilligan, speak "in a different voice," one that values relationships over power, care over conquest, and social responsibility over personal ambition.[12] If men tie their sense of identity to personal achievements in a competitive arena, women, according to Gilligan, are more likely to find identity in the links that connect caring, morality, responsibility, the mediation of conflict, and human relationships. Thus, the career dreams of women in general and of women teachers in particular should not be interpreted according to the standards laid down by the men in Levinson's study. The ambitions of the five students just quoted reveal an ethic of nurturance, responsibility, idealism, and

---

[12] Gilligan, *In a Different Voice,* pp. 151–174.

social morality. The achievements for which these teachers strive tend to be social rather than simply personal.

The five student quotes were typical of the comments collected from the 127 education majors. Of these students, 20 percent were men, and yet the career dreams of the men generally were indistinguishable from those of the women. This suggests that some male teachers share the social concerns of their female colleagues.

Reality Shocks

The career-choice problems of under- and over-commitment are not endemic to teaching but to young adulthood itself. The average American worker changes careers four times and most of these changes occur early in their working lives.[13] Therefore, it is not surprising that many young teachers leave the profession after just a few years in the classroom.[14] However, new teachers are particularly vulnerable to dissatisfaction because the first year of teaching is often so difficult. Many teachers experience "reality shock"[15] when they find that teaching is more difficult than they had expected. New teachers often are surprised by how little help they get during their first year and by how unprepared they feel. They are also surprised to find that they feel self-conscious in the teaching role, that they have problems disciplining their classes, that some students lack basic skills and are unmotivated, and that many more do not share the teachers' enthusiasm for the subject matter. Such shocks may jar the teachers' sense of competence and dampen their enthusiasm in the classroom. We will discuss each reality shock separately.

LACK OF HELP.   In most states and school districts, teachers are given very little help or attention during their first year on the job. Consider the reality shock of a high school science teacher during her first week at work:

> I was hired in late July. I can't remember the exact date, but I had less than a month to prepare for the classes I was told I would teach. The principal said I would be teaching two classes of general science, one class of computer science, two classes of biology. That gave me five classes and three preparations. I knew I could handle that, but I was also scared to death because I didn't know that much about computers. I had no idea what I was going to do in that class. On the first day of preplanning the principal showed me my classroom and the supply room, where there were no science supplies because last year's teacher had forgotten to order anything. He told me to "have a good year" and then just set me adrift. He didn't even tell me about the district curriculum materials or about the media lab. He didn't even introduce me to the head of the Science Department. Then, the day before school began, I was in my room decorating the walls, and the principal comes in and says ever-so-casually "I had to make some scheduling changes." He took away one of my biology classes and added an advanced computer class. That meant I had four preparations. I had to teach advanced computing the next day and I didn't even have a textbook. I was flabbergasted.

---

[13] *Teacher Education Reports*, Vol. 7 (September 26, 1985), p. 1.

[14] Herbert Walberg, "Professional Role Discontinuities in Educational Careers," *Review of Educational Research*, Vol. 40 (June 1970), pp. 409–420.

[15] Simon Veenman, "Perceived Problems of Beginning Teachers," *Review of Educational Research*, Vol. 54 (Summer 1984), pp. 143–148.

Not all new teachers are assigned new classes the day before school opens. Most principals would not set a new teacher "adrift" without discussing curriculum requirements and offering other assistance. However, when such things do occur they cause great stress in the lives of novice teachers.

Formal induction programs, when they exist at all, usually are structured to evaluate the adequacy of a new teacher's performance rather than provide support and assistance. A few states (most notably, to date, Arizona, Florida, Georgia, Kentucky, Michigan, Oklahoma, and Virginia) have initiated induction programs designed to be sources of help rather than stress. Little research has yet been done to evaluate the effectiveness of these new programs.[16] In the absence of strong induction programs, however, teachers are usually left on their own to find assistance. This is difficult because there are norms of noninterference at some schools that define offers of assistance as an implied criticism and requests for assistance as implied failure.[17] Thus, the successful first-year teachers are likely to be those who are insightful enough to see that they need assistance and resourceful enough to figure out how to get help in a social system that does not always offer it freely.[18]

Finding a mentor, according to Levinson, is an important part of young adulthood. Mentors serve as friends, confidants, guides, and quasi-parents. They ease an individual's transition into a career and, more crucially, facilitate the modification and eventual realization of the career dream. The comparative isolation in which teachers work and their limited opportunity for interaction with other teachers make it difficult for novice educators to establish mentor relationships within the school. When mentors cannot be found, new teachers must improvise. They may stay in touch with a helpful college professor or with college classmates who have just entered teaching. Many find support from other newly hired teachers in the school. While these relationships can be helpful, they seldom substitute adequately for a genuine mentor, who is "in the know" and can show the new teacher "the ropes."

COLLEGE PREPARATION.   Many teachers feel they were not adequately prepared in college for the "real world" of the classroom. When teachers in a national sample were asked to rate the quality of their own teacher preparation programs with a letter grade, 51 percent assigned a grade of C or below.[19] College of education graduates sometimes complain that their methods courses were not specific enough ("It taught me about teaching but it didn't teach me how to teach") or that they were not given enough opportunity to practice their skills in a clinical setting. Others say the methods presented in their classes were disconnected from reality. A second-year teacher commented,

[16] G. Griffin, "Teacher Induction· Research Issues," *Journal of Teacher Education*, Vol. 36 (1985), pp. 42–46.

[17] Gertrude McPherson, *Small Town Teacher* (Cambridge: Harvard University Press, 1972). See also J. M. Newberry, "The Barrier Between the Beginning and Experienced Teacher," *Journal of Educational Administration*, Vol. 16 (1978), pp. 46–56.

[18] J. H. Applegate, V. R. Flora, T. J. Lasley, G. M. Mager, K. K. Newman, and K. Ryan, "The First Year Teacher Study." Paper presented at the annual meeting of the American Educational Research Association, New York, April 1977 (ERIC Document Preparations Service, No. ED 135 766).

[19] Alec Gallup, "The Gallup Poll of Teachers' Attitudes Toward the Public Schools," *Phi Delta Kappan*, Vol. 66 (October 1984), p. 100.

> I was telling some friend from church the other day that there were many things that I wasn't prepared for [when I began teaching]. For example, no one told me what to do when half the class gets up and runs across the room screaming, "Johny farted." That happened last week. The students asked me to do something about it. I asked them, "What exactly do you expect me to do about that boy's gastro-intestinal troubles?" They don't tell you about those things; they don't even warn you about what it's really like.

When teachers speak positively about their college experience, they usually mention courses that presented relevant content and gave them an opportunity to think critically, practice their craft, and clarify their educational aims.

DIFFICULT STUDENTS AND CLASSES.   Many teachers find that they have been assigned difficult students or difficult classes in their first year. A second-grade teacher described such an experience:

> I had a bad time . . . at the beginning of the year. I had a real rough class but I thought it was me and that I was doing something wrong. The other classes were all well behaved but mine was a circus. Then I found that the previous spring the other second-grade teachers had chosen all the best-behaved kids for their own classes. I got the leftovers. You'd think they would have taken pity on me or on the kids. A bunch of troubled second graders don't need the new guy on the block; they need someone who knows what she's doing. I didn't have a clue what to do for them. But I stuck with it—what choice did I have?—and by the end of the year I had things going fairly well. I'm proud of that.

New teachers sometimes have more difficult schedules or more difficult students than other teachers in the school. They may have to work in "less desirable" schools in the district until they build up enough seniority to move to the "better schools" in the system.[20] Even when new teachers are not burdened with these extra problems, they can be exhausted by the everyday tasks of reading papers, planning lessons, writing unit plans, constructing activities and assignments, and developing an appropriate teaching style. A high school English teacher described the difficulties he faced in his first year:

> I've never worked so hard in my life. My tenth and eleventh grade classes each read a Shakespeare play and at least six novels. I had to read those books again just to figure out what to do in class. And there were the lessons in grammar and vocabulary I had to plan for. And we are required to have every student write at least once a week, so I have a mountain of papers to correct every night and on weekends. I'm always working, that's all I do. I'm always aware of how much I don't know and must learn if I really want to be an interesting teacher. My wife asked before Easter, "Hey, are we still married? I never see you these days." She's right. My head is always in a book or I'm correcting a pile of papers. I love it, but it better get easier next year . . . or I'll wear out.

DISCIPLINING AND MOTIVATING STUDENTS.   The most severe reality shock for new teachers, according to Peterson and Veenman, entails "coming to terms with problems of disciplining and motivating students."[21] One teacher de-

---

[20] Howard S. Becker, "Schools and Systems of Social Status" in *Sociological Work*, ed. Howard S. Becker (Chicago: Aldine Publishing Company, 1970), pp. 213–225.

[21] Warren A. Peterson, "Age, Teacher's Role, and the Institutional Setting," in *Contemporary Research in Teaching Effectiveness*, eds. B. J. Biddle and W. S. Elena (New York: Holt, Rinehart and Winston, 1964). See also Veenman, "Perceived Problems of Beginning Teachers," pp. 154–155.

scribed how surprised he was by the misbehavior of his students: "God, the abuse you have to put up with. . . . Discipline problems burn you out and make you feel useless." Another teacher said,

> My expectations were a lot different from what [teaching] turned out to be. It's a lot harder than I thought. It tries my patience much more than I thought it would. I have to find a way to control my classes without turning into a wild man.

During their first weeks on the job, many teachers are tested by their pupils. Students check to see how far the new teachers will let them go and if the teachers can successfully play the role they have claimed for themselves. Students usually remember testing incidents with humor and recount them fondly to college friends or at high school reunions. Teachers, however, find more stress than humor in these testing incidents. Compare the following stories told at separate times to a researcher by a seventh-grade student and his teacher:

STUDENT: Miss Zane is. . . , well, she is kinda nice. We like her and all. But she's so gullible. Like we told her on the first day that we had to sing a bunch of songs after the pledge [to the flag]. We started with *America* and before we were finished we were singing rock and roll. She was singing right along with us, and we told her all the classes did it and she believed us.

One time she was writing on the blackboard and backed up over one of those support things [that hold the blackboard up]. She goes "aaah" and then falls flat on her ass. She got real red, I mean real red, and we all began laughing like anything. It was so funny. Then we got the idea about putting the shot put in her purse, not the same day but on another day. . . . Eddy did that. It was my idea but Eddy did it. Miss Zane picked up the purse as she was kinda like running out the door. [The purse] swung off the desk and down she went again. You should have seen her face. We were like all really cracking up.

Now, she is a real drag. Well, not a drag exactly cause she's OK, but she gets on our case for every little thing.

TEACHER: I didn't understand what they were up to, though I guess I do now. At times, we would get along fine. We were having fun and getting work done, too. But things began to get out of hand and I could see I was losing them. They would pull some stunts that were just plain mean. They'd laugh like hyenas if you made the simplest mistake. They'd do it to me and they'd do it to each other. That made things real tense. I couldn't let my guard down.

I fell over the foot of a portable blackboard and they almost disintegrated; they thought it was so funny. I guess it was funny. But then they began to do hurtful things . . . just to make me look foolish. That's when I turned mean. I just clamped down hard and told them I wasn't going to tolerate their misbehavior. I started writing kids up, sending notes home, withholding privileges, and I did a fair amount of yelling, too. They don't pull that stuff any more because I've learned how to handle them. I don't think we are having as much fun in my class, but they behave. Maybe that's the price they have to pay for giving me a hard time. But, it's a price I have to pay, too, and it's a shame.

Teachers may resent being tested and complain that students do not care about their feelings or appreciate how hard they work. Eventually, of course, most teachers learn how to control their classes and find ways to invite and capture the interests of their students. They endure the reality shocks of the first year and find ways to adjust to the darker sides of classroom life. Teachers distill their recollection of these first-year adjustments into what sociologists call critical incidents,[22] and teachers are likely to call war stories. Critical incident stories are usually about situations in which students directly challenge a teacher's authority and professional identity. The teachers gain insight through the confrontation and that insight changes the course of future events. The teacher just quoted said that the "shot put incident was a turning point." As she explained,

> I decided then and there that this stuff was going to stop. I was losing control. But I wasn't going to be one of those teachers who is constantly harassed, I just wasn't. They were taking advantage of my efforts to be tolerant and nice. So I cracked down.

Not all teachers take the conflict between themselves and their students as seriously as this particular teacher, and, it will relieve new teachers to know, not all teachers are tested quite so imaginatively. The trick to handling such challenges is to recognize that they happen to most teachers, and that the challenge, by itself, does not say anything about a teacher's competence or the character of the students. Successful teachers usually "win" these confrontations if they stay calm, maintain some perspective, keep their humor, and resist taking either the incident or their "victory" too seriously.

SIZE AND MATURITY OF STUDENTS.   Some new high school teachers are surprised by the physical size and maturity of their students. Teachers often report that they need to "dress like teachers" to ensure that other members of the staff will not mistake them for students and that students will not mistake them for peers. Also, novice educators worry when they do not "feel like teachers" and say that they find it hard to "play the role" because they cannot believe it really fits them. As one rookie teacher put it, "I see kids getting in trouble and I know I'm supposed to side with the school. I do on the outside, but deep down I root for the kids." Part of the work of every new teacher is to learn how to play the teacher role unselfconsciously. This is part of the process of career socialization, a topic to be discussed in detail in Chapter 14.

STUDENT REACTION TO SUBJECT MATTER.   Next to discipline and learning to play the teacher role, the most significant reality shock for new teachers involves the students' reaction to the subject matter being taught. As we saw in Chapter 9, many junior and senior high school teachers come into teaching because they want to stay close to a subject they value and enjoy.[23] The subject is often a source of pride, identity, and security for these educators.[24] However, many teachers are disappointed to find that their students are unimpressed by

---

[22] Lynda Measor, "Critical Incidents in the Classroom: Identities, Choices and Careers," in *Teachers' Lives and Careers*, eds. Ball and Goodson, pp. 61–77. See also Anselm Strauss and Lee Rainewater, *The Professional Scientist* (Chicago: Aldine Publishing Co., 1962).

[23] Patricia J. Sikes, "The Life Cycle of the Teacher," in *Teachers' Lives and Careers*, eds. Ball and Goodson, p. 35.

[24] The significance of this variable appears to wane slightly over time. See National Education Association, *Status of the American Public School Teacher, 1980–1981* (Washington, DC: National Education Association, 1982), pp. 240–242.

the teacher's knowledge and unmoved by the subject matter the teacher finds so fascinating. These teachers complain that they must "water down" what they teach and hunt for ways to sell what they know to a reluctant clientele:

PSYCHOLOGY TEACHER: My biggest surprise had nothing to do with discipline. I expected some degree of rowdiness [because] I messed around a lot when I was in high school. But I was appalled by how ignorant my students were. I was trying to teach them something about psychology and I found that only about half of the kids were reading on grade level. Their writing skills were practically nonexistent. How can I help them understand psychology when they can't read well enough to understand the text?

SCIENCE TEACHER: I can't get any response from my students. I wish there was just some way, by trickery perhaps, that I could make them think that my course had some value. I have a lot to offer but they don't care. Last week I assigned an article and then showed a documentary on acid rain. It was a good film, but after ten minutes they were yawning and saying that the movie was "boorring." So I asked them what they thought the movie was trying to do. They said, "Put us to sleep." I asked why they didn't like it. At first, they just said it bored them, but when I pressed them they said that they "don't care about all that scientific stuff." My God, the trees of the eastern seaboard from Maine to Georgia and as far west as Kentucky are dying from pollution and there is good scientific evidence that explains the whole process. We know what's going on but these kids sit there and say they don't care. How can they not care about their own environment?

Another first-year teacher told a similar tale. She explained that when she was in college she

> assumed, and I guess the professors assumed, that students could read by the time they got to high school. All the courses I took in literature, creative writing, and grammar took it for granted that students knew how to read and write. I was learning how to teach students to read and write *better*.

She went on to say that she was unprepared when she confronted 120 students on her first day of teaching who "were reading way below grade level and could barely write at all." Here again, the examples we are using are extreme, but it is generally true that new teachers must adjust their expectations when they go into a classroom for the first time. There is always a danger that students' resistance to learning will become an excuse for not teaching them much of anything.

It is not unusual for teachers to face multiple reality shocks in their first year. Students may know less than the teacher expected, may not share the teacher's devotion to the subject matter or to schooling, and may continually challenge the teacher's authority and precarious professional identity. One such teacher began work in September and was considering quitting three months later:

> I came into this job with two master's degrees, one in chemistry and another in education. I have a lot of knowledge and experience to draw on. But I didn't get through to my classes at all. They were disrespectful and hard to control. They talked down to me. I don't think they care about school. They are all going to

work in agriculture when they graduate and they don't see any connection between their education and their future lives. I tried to show them the connections but they continually missed the point. They didn't give a hoot about biology even though I tried to make the material interesting and relevant. For example, I tried to show how the fishing industry in the state was being destroyed by pollution and greed. They said they didn't care because, get this, they don't like the taste of fish. That's what they said. What can you do with logic like that? I decorated the walls with posters from the Sierra Club that I bought with my own money and they drew all over them.

When teachers face multiple shocks their sense of professional identity is severely threatened and they are likely to concentrate more on survival than professional self-improvement.

Survival

Jennifer Nias, a British sociologist of education, studied ninety-nine teachers who had been working in elementary schools for up to nine years. The teachers reported that they worked long hours at school and at home, were continually tired, and were saddened that they did not have much of a social life outside of work. Many were exposed to childhood illnesses for which they had no immunity and spent much of their first year of teaching "lurching from one infection to another."[25] Nias tried to find out what sustained these teachers when their work was most difficult. She found that teachers "entered the profession with closely-defined values, beliefs and attitudes which . . . form[ed] . . . their personal identities."[26] Like the college of education seniors quoted earlier, Nias's teachers had idealistic visions of what they were going to accomplish in the classroom. They struggled to live up to those expectations and worked hard to become the kind of teachers they had always planned to be. Falling short was painful; it suggested that they had failed not simply as teachers but as people.[27] Teachers were not willing to give in to failure for reasons that were psychological ("I don't want to admit I failed.") and moral ("I can't let these students down.").[28] The idealism of teachers appears to be different from the individualistic ideals that dominate American culture. Teachers, as we have seen, often express their commitment to education in moral terms.[29] They mention their responsibility to students, to the subject matter, to the society, and to the profession. They do not enter teaching, as one might enter business, with the clear goal of individual advancement. Sari Biklen, in a small but interesting study of women teachers, found that

> The teachers focused on the content of their occupation, rather than on their work as a link to other occupational choices. Quality of performance overrode

---

[25] Nias, "A More Distant Drummer," p. 11.

[26] Ibid., p. 23.

[27] In our culture, as Michael Lewis discovered in a study of values, failure "threatens our self-esteem by causing us to doubt our character, our competence, or our quest for both. To the extent . . . that our aspirations go unrealized (whatever the reason) we are threatened or troubled by personal guilt." Michael Lewis, *The Culture of Inequality* (New York: The New American Library, 1979), p. 17.

[28] Jennifer Nias, "Commitment and Motivation in Primary School Teachers," *Educational Review*, Vol. 33 (1981), pp. 181–190.

[29] Nias, "A More Distant Drummer," p. 12.

career value. These teachers often thought of how they served the occupation rather than of how the occupation could serve them.[30]

The moral dimension of teachers' life worlds has not been given enough study. However, the research of Nias and Biklen suggests that the idealism of teachers is closely linked to their sense of social commitment and personal identity. Not living up to their ideals is a source of personal discomfort, but strong ideals are also a source of strength. The teachers in Nias's study were determined to fulfill their "obligation" to children, and this determination helped them survive the difficulties of the first year. As we shall see, idealism remains a factor throughout the careers of teachers.

Who Survives and Why

When all the different reality shocks and critical incidents that threaten beginning teachers are detailed, it invites the impertinent but essential question, Why does anyone stay in teaching? The shortest answer, though not the simplest, is that when things are going well in the classroom, teaching can be a wonderful experience. Consider the enthusiasm and sense of accomplishment reflected in the comments of this middle school language arts teacher:

> We had been working on poetry for a few weeks but nothing much was going on. We were just going through the motions and I knew it. I couldn't figure out why they were so resistant. It wasn't anything conscious on their part, they just weren't excited much by what we were doing. I was determined to make poetry live for those kids, so I kept trying new gimmicks. I read a poem to them every day. Sometimes we talked about the poem, sometimes we didn't. I got them to ask adults to identify their favorite poems and to bring the poems to class. We talked about why the adults might like those particular poems. We read and wrote haiku. All of that went all right, I guess, but there still wasn't any spark or enthusiasm. The classes were flat and the poems they wrote were dreary and predictable.
>
> One day, I gave the kids a list of phrases. I don't know where I got that idea, it just came to me. But I had a list of phrases like "My mind has wings," "In the purple image of fall," "Sad is not forever," and a lot more; it was a long list. A little schmaltzy—a lot schmaltzy—I'll admit, but I was desperate. I asked them to build poems around one of those phrases and, you know, it worked? The kids wrote *real* poetry for the first time. The best thing about it was that they knew they were doing good work; they could tell. It was only then that they began to take pride in their writing. They read the poems to each other, and we compared the poems in class. Then I gave them phrases from famous poems and they wrote around those phrases. That allowed us to compare their poems against the original works. And then, bless them, they asked if we could type the poems up so other classes could read them and so their parents could read them; so we started a literary magazine. Can you imagine a school like this having a literary magazine? And the kids did it all; the art work, the cover, the printing, collating, stapling, distributing, the whole thing. I can't tell you how great that experience was for me and it was for the kids, too.

As we can see from this sixth-grade teacher's experience, some critical incidents are positive. The successful poetry lesson convinced the teacher that teaching could be joyous, that his ideal was obtainable, that he had the potential to be a fine teacher, and that his students benefited from his efforts. Not all

[30] Biklen, "Can Elementary School Teaching Be a Career?" p. 224.

first-year teachers have such dramatic successes, but most catch glimpses of the possibilities that education holds for them and for their pupils. Even modest successes can be important for beginning teachers. For example, Betty's first months on the job were disappointing to her until she realized that she had a great deal to offer her students.

> The teacher I was replacing had the higher classes and I thought I would just take over her space. I was lured into the job because of that. When I got here I had the lower classes and I was really mad. But as I got to know the kids better and [learned] about their backgrounds, I started to like it better. I began to feel my job was more important because I realized that [these kids] really need a teacher, not [just] to teach them math, but also to give them guidance. I guess I had to realize that I was helping them.

First-year teachers learn numerous "tricks of the trade" that help them do a better job in the classroom. Teachers report that

- I've learned to budget my time better. I don't waste my time doing picky things that could be done by the kids or someone else or things that aren't necessary. I concentrate on the most important things and try to do them well.
- It has to do with balance, I think. I found out that it was vital to plan every part of the day; I mean right down to the minute. You have to know just what students were going to do and when. You'll have to change plans in mid-stream sometimes, but you better not be out there without a plan or you're sunk. You have to know where everything is and you have to have everything ready before the class begins. If you run out of things to do, or run out of materials—it's all over. If you don't keep the kids occupied, they'll keep themselves occupied, believe me. But you need to be flexible, too. If something isn't going well—you know, if it just isn't working—you have to make some fast changes. I'm getting better at thinking on my feet.
- I found out that twenty-four credits of literature courses didn't prepare me to teach. Maybe I could have taught advanced placement English, but I sure . . . wasn't ready for eighth-grade English. I had never read the stuff mid-dle-schoolers read today. The Kiddie Lit. [children's literature] course I took just gave an overview of the area. So I have read like crazy since I came here. I needed to know what to assign and what to recommend when someone likes a particular book and wants to me to suggest another to them. It's been a lot of work but I've had a great time. The more I learn, the more I have to share with students. We talk about the books we are reading and trade them back and forth. I find a good book and I can hardly wait to turn someone on to it.
- There is so much to know about this age group; their worries and moods and interests and humor and friendships and rivalries. I read about it in my child development courses but it didn't sink in because it wasn't real to me then. I guess I had to see it in action before I appreciated what it really meant. It fascinates me now. I think I could spend my life just studying how kids develop socially, morally, intellectually, and every other way. You know what I do in my free time? I read Piaget and Kohlberg.
- I've learned how important it is to have good feelings with the kids. I think of my relationships with kids as something I build, like a table or a book-case. It is a tangible thing that you can take pride in. If the relationship is bad, even good students will resist you. They won't put out the effort.

- It's all so much easier now because I'm more relaxed with children and I understand them better. I've learned how to trust them and am now able to catch their interest. I dare to laugh with them and not to confront them if I don't have to. You learn not to criticize or embarrass kids in front of their friends. That always backfires. I've gotten used to their language. I don't allow bad language in the class, but if I overhear something at a distance I don't go running over to chew someone out.

- It took me most of the year to understand how important it was for a teacher to be enthusiastic. I'm that way naturally, but I guess it took me a while to learn how to be natural in the classroom. I had to show the kids I really liked them and liked my subject before anything good happened in my classroom. Students need to know you care about the subject and that it's important to you.

- There is so much to teaching. I never dreamed it would be this complicated and demanding. I thought I would just ride on in there and wow them. There is so much to know. At first, I was overwhelmed by it all and worried that I would never be a good teacher. I was discouraged. But now I'm getting the feel of it. I don't know it all yet—I will never know it all—but I can see that I'm learning and that makes me feel good.

Teachers who survive the first year of teaching with some success find that their idealistic vision, while perhaps not wholly attainable, is viable and worth pursuing. Each success helps confirm not only the efficacy of schooling but the warrant of the teacher's ideals and the possibility of individual growth. The teacher begins to feel a part of something bigger than himself or herself. A new unity begins to connect the teacher's own idealism and professional identity with the work of the school and the aims of education.

Each success confirms the efficacy of schooling and warrants a teacher's ideals. (*Source:* National Education Association, Joe Di Dio.)

Trading on the Teaching Triangle

The teachers just quoted learned diverse lessons in their first year on the job, but all the lessons have one thing in common: They all dealt with some component in a complex triangle of classroom events (see Figure 10-1). The teachers reported the things they did that helped get students in harmonious and productive interaction with both the subject matter and the teacher. The art of teaching entails keeping these three elements in ongoing alliance.

Many factors influence this three-way relationship among students, their teachers, and the subject matter. When the relationship is positive, learning is enhanced; and when it is negative, learning is retarded. Successful teachers realize early in their careers that the teaching triangle is both important and complex. Students cannot be forced into a positive relationship with the teacher or the subject matter. Students, like all other human beings, have the power to say no to any other person's definition of reality. They sometimes can be forced to act (or to pretend to act), but they cannot be forced to believe in what they are doing. Successful teachers get their students to believe in the importance of what goes on in the classroom not by coercion but by agreement. Theodore Sizer, former dean at Harvard's Graduate School of Education, explains that getting such agreements is far from easy:

> If effective learning is to take place, students and teacher must agree on the objective [of the lesson] and the means to reach it. For the student this often requires trusting the teacher, as the objective and the ways to it are obscured by the student's inexperience. There is hurt in learning, and it is difficult to persuade someone to hurt himself. It is the castor oil problem: Take this and you'll feel better some time in the future. Expose your errors so that I, the teacher, can catalogue them for you, thus helping you make fewer in the future. Working hard with a teacher, or any mentor, is masochistic. Getting agreement . . . to pursue this often lacerating process of exposing that inexperience, and the errors it reaps, is a subtle, delicate business.[31]

Almost all the shocks and pains of first-year teaching derive from an inability to create harmony across the three elements of the teaching triangle. Conversely, most of teaching's joys spring from those moments when an agreement is reached, and the three elements are in productive coordination. As teachers attend to this coordination and nurture it, they experience their first classroom successes. Through these successes, they begin to see themselves, not as seasoned teachers, but as competent professionals who are beginning to master

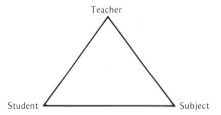

Figure 10-1   The teaching triangle.

---

[31] Theodore R. Sizer, *Horace's Compromise: The Dilemma of the American High School* (Boston: Houghton-Mifflin Company, 1984), p. 154.

their craft. In the process, they are also accomplishing the work of young adulthood. They are exploring the possibilities that exist in their chosen profession and within themselves and are beginning to establish a lasting commitment to their work. They are settling into their chosen profession, coming to recognize the skills and dispositions essential to teaching, and are developing these qualities within themselves.

Stage 2. The Age Thirty Transition: Reassessment and Connection (Ages Twenty-eight through Thirty-three)

The period of early adulthood is followed by what Levinson et al. call *the age thirty transition*. During this period individuals commonly reassess their life choices, evaluate accomplishments and shortcomings, readjust career dreams, and reset their career course. The period of exploration winds down in the late twenties and the need to reassess old choices and make new ones is felt with growing urgency as individuals move into their thirties.[32] Teachers who have known classroom success may congratulate themselves on their career choice and begin to plan their future with greater specificity. For some, this will mean staying in the classroom. Others set their sights on jobs such as guidance counselors, department chairpersons, curriculum specialists, or administrators. Still others will decide to leave teaching for other careers. Women who have not yet had children may begin to hear the tick of the biological clock and decide to start a family. During this period, teachers are likely to seek new challenges and responsibilities, greater recognition and fulfillment.

According to Levinson, the reevaluation that goes on in the transition period is possible because experience has made individuals more aware of their abilities and interests. The decisions people make in their early thirties are likely to determine the course of their future lives. Individuals lay a strong foundation for the future if their career and life-style decisions are compatible with their talents, needs, dreams, and personalities. If the decisions are inadequate or inappropriate, individuals are likely to pay a heavy price in later life; future career and personality development will be impeded and unhappiness is likely.[33]

Pat Sikes has emphasized that the transition from one stage of a career to another can be stressful. "For many people, life begins to get more serious now, commitments and responsibilities are increasing and it becomes more important to . . . work out and plan a life structure for the future."[34] For educators who decide that teaching is not for them, the prospect of starting a new career may appear frightening. Teachers who decide to move into administrative positions must give up their evenings and summer vacations or summer employment so that they can take graduate courses that will certify them for the positions they seek.

The decision to stay in the classroom can also be stressful. Contented class-

---

[32] Levinson et al., *The Seasons of a Man's Life*, pp. 84–89.
[33] Ibid.
[34] Sikes, "The Life Cycle of the Teacher," p. 44.

room teachers see that some of their colleagues are moving out of teaching or into administration. Friends in other lines of work may be moving into management positions that earn them greater prestige and financial reward. Some unionized, blue-collar workers may bring home pay checks that are substantially larger than those of teachers.[35] Educators in their thirties may begin to wonder whether they can raise a family and send their children through college on a teacher's salary. If, despite these problems, individuals choose to stay in the classroom, they must justify their decision first to themselves and then to others. It may seem surprising that anyone would be called upon (or feel obliged) to justify a decision to work with children; after all, the work that teachers do is vital to the well-being of society. However, it must be remembered that America runs on an ethic of self-improvement and upward mobility. When individuals decide to stay in the classroom, they are dropping out of the race for upward mobility. There is a great deal of pressure on men and a growing pressure on women to stay in that race and to prove their worth by ascending the status ladder. Thus when we asked a thirty-three-year-old middle-school teacher about his future plans, we were not surprised by the ambivalence his answer displayed:

> I want to keep doing what I'm doing now. That's what I'd like to do but I'm not sure if I should or if I will. I don't want to become a principal or anything like that because I like what I'm doing. I mean I didn't become a teacher so that I could shuffle papers in an office and take flak from everybody. I wouldn't be any good at that. [So you are not sure? Why is that?] Well, money is a big factor. It's the money and I guess I worry that I'm copping out. I ask myself if I'm just being lazy or just scared to give it [administration] a shot. But that kind of thinking makes me crazy.

Whatever choices teachers make, they are striving to create a stable basis for their future lives and to establish solid career identities. In Levinson's language, they are striving to become "their own person."[36] This involves testing career expectations against experience and deciding on a future course to which the individual can feel committed. Those who identified most strongly with the education profession in Nias's study, "expressed relatively high levels of job satisfaction, especially in terms of competency, and talked of feeling 'extended,' 'purposeful,' even 'fulfilled.' "[37]

Ironically, perhaps, the process of extending one's commitment to a career in education may entail a degree of separation from people and positions that gave support and guidance at the start of one's career.

Separating from Mentors

During young adulthood, teachers are junior members of their occupational world. They often have difficulty determining their own competence and must

---

[35] As we saw in Chapter 9, these conditions may cause "status panic." See Patricia T. Ashton and Rodman B. Webb, *Making a Difference: Teachers' Sense of Efficacy and Student Achievement* (New York: Longman, 1986), pp. 33–42. Available in paperback.

[36] Levinson et al., *The Seasons of a Man's Life*, pp. 60, 141, 144–149, 150–157.

[37] Nias, "A More Distant Drummer," p. 17.

rely on others to assess their progress and professional worth. Mentors are particularly helpful in this regard because they supply valuable information, friendship, support, and evaluative feedback to novice teachers. After a few years in the classroom, however, teachers begin to form their own standards of competence and feel capable of assessing their own achievements. They have less need of a mentor's advice and may look forward to filling the mentor role for someone else.

Separating from Students

When teachers first enter the profession, youth is the one advantage they have over their older colleagues. Reality shock may obscure this advantage, but once this has been overcome, new teachers are generally able to form friendly relationships with their students. They identify closely with their students' problems and experiences and may have a greater appreciation for, or tolerance of, the tastes and values of the young. As teachers grow into their thirties, most realize that the classroom is a strange and artificial world in which the young stay perpetually youthful but adults grow progressively older. As teachers gain experience and begin to fit more comfortably into their profession, they fit less comfortably into the culture of their students. A mathematics teacher described how her relationship with students changed as she moved into her thirties:

> It's not that I like my students any less, I think they're great, but one day I just realized that I . . . wasn't thinking of them in the same way and that they were treating me differently, too. They saw me much more as a teacher, maybe even as a parent, and I guess I saw them much more as students or as kids. I'm still close to them but not in the same way. I'm not as close in some ways. They don't tell me the same kind of things. It doesn't mean much of anything . . . except that I'm getting older and that I'm out of the club.

Some teachers are saddened to find that the young age-grade adults and that time is slowly but inexorably separating them from their pupils. Some teachers experience a sense of loss as they realize that they are "out of the club" and that they will never again recapture the intimate and friendly contact they once enjoyed with their pupils.[38] According to Sikes, a few teachers, "consciously hang on to an image of themselves as the 'young teacher' on the same side as the kids" even when students no longer see them as friendly allies.[39]

Not all teachers define being "out of the club" in negative terms. Some take pride in their own burgeoning abilities and define their new relationship with students in increasingly professional rather than personal terms. For example, a thirty-one-year-old teacher said:

> I think I can do more now for students; I know how to get things across better and I make things clearer. I don't know it all, but I know a lot more than I used to and my experience makes a big difference. There are fewer surprises for me now; I know what's coming and I know what to do when it comes.

---

[38] Peterson, "Age, Teachers' Role, and the Institutional Setting," pp. 272–277.
[39] Sikes, "The Life Cycle of the Teacher," p. 45.

However much teachers may be saddened by or relish their changing relationship with students, such changes are an inevitable part of growing older in the teaching profession.[40]

Separating from Imposed Structures

New teachers are likely to find security and guidance in curriculum guides, textbooks, and other prepackaged materials. With experience, however, teachers gain confidence and are likely to do more of their own planning. As a twenty-nine-year-old second-grade teacher said,

> Some of the things the school district suggests, or the things that you find in the teacher's guide [to the textbook] are just impossible. I can plan better lessons than that. [My lessons] might not work for another teacher, but they work for me.

A middle school teacher made a similar point:

> When I started [I] had every student in a textbook. [I would] just about sit down [during preplanning] and divide the chapters in the book into so many week's work. [Then I could figure out] that we were going to complete page so-and-so on Monday of the first week [and the next page] on Tuesday [and so on]. I didn't use any outside materials except [some things I put on] the overhead [projector]. Now I have students learning from a variety of materials. The kids use the library and the media lab. My strategies have changed, because I'm more experienced. I know what I'm doing.

Teachers with eight to ten years in the classroom are likely to have confidence in their abilities and take pride in what they have learned from experience. They are more willing, and usually more able, to try new teaching strategies, design new programs, and experiment. Their willingness to innovate is tied to their desire to find expression for and recognition of their newly established competence. Therefore, they may resist changes they think are being forced upon them or that will not allow them to use and expand their professional skills. On the other hand, they will embrace innovations that expand their abilities and improve their performance.

Separation from the First Jobs

When teachers become more self-confident and when their classroom successes confirm the warrant of their personal values and educational aims, they are likely to look for jobs that will allow the full expression of these beliefs and goals. As Nias explains, this often means "searching for a match between personal beliefs and attitudes and the values of the school."[41] Teachers may move three or four times in as many years until they find a teaching position that suits them. Some try jobs in other sectors of the educational system; for example, in private schools, residential treatment centers, church-related youth groups, children's hospitals, nursery schools, or schools for delinquents. Such moves, according to Nias, help young teachers' cement their commitment to teaching.[42]

[40] Nias, "A More Distant Drummer," p. 20.
[41] Ibid., p. 14.
[42] Ibid., pp. 12–14.

On the Way to Becoming One's Own Person

During the period of transition, individuals set the stage for becoming their own person, both professionally and in their private lives. They view themselves as full-fledged, capable adults and find it necessary to reassess their accomplishments and dreams. They are likely to either rededicate themselves to the career path they chose in their early twenties or to change direction. Sometimes, that change is large and leads them out of teaching, but frequently it entails only modest modification of their career plans. In any event, individuals seek to use the skills they have and to establish their own professional identity in a fulfilling career. They want to keep developing their expertise and have their accomplishments appreciated and rewarded. In the process of reassessing their professional direction, individuals may separate themselves somewhat from their past reliance on mentors, students, and imposed structures. They often look for teaching jobs that will allow them to "be themselves" and do what they "think is right." These separations may cause some initial stress, but they seldom cause psychological dislocation; in fact, the opposite is usually true. The separations help teachers consolidate their accomplishments and begin to view themselves as competent professionals. They begin to establish a more well-defined, autonomous sense of professional self-esteem.

The work that begins in the period of transition, roughly between the ages of twenty-eight and thirty-three, is continued well into the mid-forties.

Separation and Connection

Gilligan warns that Levinson's separation metaphor may not apply to the adult development of women and may even be misplaced when applied to men. In Levinson's depiction of adult development, men separate from anything that "threatens the great expectations of the dream."[43] The career dreams of men are described in terms of arduous competition for individual achievement. Social relationships play a subordinate role in the drama of male development. However, the career dreams of most women and many men teachers have a more social than individualistic orientation. Therefore, the separations just described should not be viewed as a rejection of former friends and aims. Instead, they suggest that teachers in their thirties feel competent and more able to have a positive impact on their students and their schools.

It's important to understand that the separations teachers go through in the age-thirty transition have more to do with connection than with disconnection. When individuals leave their first teaching jobs in order to find a position that better fits their educational goals, they are seeking a professional community of purpose and commitment. When youth no longer guarantees teachers the attention of their students, educators seek other ways to make contact with their classes. When teachers no longer need to rely on imposed structures and prepackaged lesson plans, they begin to play a greater and more creative role in their profession. Thus, these several separations merely set the stage for greater connection to and participation in the teaching profession. As we will see at the end of the chapter, the desire for connection is driven by teachers' idealism.

[43] Gilligan, *In a Different Voice*, p. 152.

Stage 3. Settling Down: Using Old Skills and Finding New Ones (Ages Thirty-three through Forty-four)

Trends begun during the transition period are continued in the settling-down stage of teachers' careers. According to Levinson et al., two tasks confront people entering this stage of adulthood:

1. to establish their niche in society, develop competence, and have that competence recognized by others, and
2. to finally become "one's own person"; that is, to establish a well-defined sense of professional self-esteem.[44]

Teachers in the settling-down stage of their careers often possess a high degree of energy and commitment. They have set their career goals and are anxious to exercise their hard-won professional competence. They feel less dependent and take pride in the fact that their abilities at last are recognized by principals, parents, pupils, and peers. Most have experienced success in the classroom and are now ready to take on new challenges. For some, this means expanding their repertoire of teaching skills. For others, it means extending their competencies beyond the classroom. Teachers may take on new professional responsibilities such as doing committee work, advising teacher interns, holding office in professional organizations, and leading extracurricular activities.[45]

For most teachers, this is a period of high activity and increased visibility. The occupational identification has been fully internalized and no small measure of pride and personal identity is derived from the successful performance of their teaching duties. The most satisfied teachers are likely to have worked in a number of schools and have found positions that are compatible with their philosophy of education and that allow them to teach the subjects and students they prefer.

During the settling-down stage of life, people in business and the professions typically strive for advancement up the organizational ladder. As was discussed in Chapter 9, however, teaching is a horizontal rather than vertical profession and offers few advancement opportunities for classroom teachers. If one wants to advance in the education profession, one must leave the classroom. In order to secure a post as a counselor, curriculum specialist, or administrator, a teacher must earn academic credentials. This often means considerable sacrifice in time, money, and effort.

Working for an advanced degree serves both manifest and latent functions. The most obvious reason for going back to school is to gain the "professional knowledge" deemed necessary for doing the work of administration and counseling, but latent functions are also being served. Those entering graduate school are publicly declaring their interest in advancement and demonstrating their

---

[44] Levinson et al., *The Seasons of a Man's Life*, p. 59, 141–165.
[45] Nias, "A More Distant Drummer," pp. 15–16.

seriousness through hard work and sacrifice. Pursuing an advanced degree serves another latent function; it tends to separate teachers from their teaching colleagues. Graduate study leaves little time to be with and share the concerns of fellow teachers. The very fact that a teacher declares an interest in leaving the classroom may cause some friction at the school where he or she works. Ambitious teachers are encouraged to identify with those filling the posts to which they themselves aspire. The net result of this "anticipatory socialization" process is that teachers on their way up to administration are likely to drift further and further away from the everyday concerns of classroom teachers, to define schooling in terms of the professional knowledge they are learning, and increasingly to see the school from the vantage point of the administrative culture.[46]

More men than women advance into administrative ranks in education, even though women outnumber men in the profession. In a national survey of teachers conducted by the National Education Association in 1986, 80 percent of all teachers worked for male principals.[47] Though it is generally recognized that women are offered fewer opportunities for advancement than are men, discussions of women's careers often mention reasons other than prejudice for the under-representation of women in leadership positions. For example, Dan Lortie contends that "most men reject teaching as an ultimate career goal; they see teaching as a means toward another end—an interim engagement." On the other hand, Lortie continues, "Women teachers do not hide their intention to put family matters first."[48] It is Lortie's belief that "men and women react differently" to the career lines open in education:

> The steps upward within teaching are too small to satisfy the ambitions of most male entrants; they want the greater rewards associated with administrative positions. But the gentle incline of teaching fits the aspirations most women bring with them; [to teach until they marry and have children, and then leave teaching, perhaps to return to the classroom at a later date].[49]

Sikes and Biklen contend that Lortie's explanation is incomplete. Sikes acknowledges that women may choose to make their school careers secondary to their home careers but points out that "this is what is expected of [women] and those who do not conform may well face social censure."[50] Biklen challenges the contention that women who have children are necessarily less committed to teaching. Her interviews with women teachers gave ample evidence that "they valued their work identities as teachers and did not want to choose between work and family."[51] They viewed themselves as teachers throughout their careers, even when they were full-time mothers.

Women teachers with children face several impediments to career advancement. They must find adequate child care so that they can go to work, must

---

[46] Howard S. Becker, "The Development of Identification with an Occupation," in *Sociological Work*, ed. Becker, pp. 189–201.

[47] *Status of the American Public School Teacher: 1985–1986* (Washington, DC: National Education Association, 1987), p. 148.

[48] Dan Lortie, *Schoolteacher: A Sociological Study* (Chicago: University of Chicago Press, 1975), p. 86.

[49] Ibid., p. 88.

[50] Sikes, "The Life Cycle of the Teacher," p. 48.

[51] Biklen, "Can Elementary School Teaching Be a Career?" p. 220.

wait until their children are old enough to fend for themselves before they take on the extra burden of graduate classes, and must eventually convince those above them that they "have what it takes" to be administrators. These decision makers are usually men and their conception of successful administration usually reflects the competitive individualism of the male culture.

The women Biklen interviewed were highly committed to teaching but maintained a social, rather than individualistic, orientation to their profession. As Biklen explained, they "focused their energies on the content of their work, not on its use to them for upward mobility."[52] While many were interested in taking on more responsibility in order to make greater contributions to students and the profession, they were seldom interested in advancement for its own sake. Some turned down promotions because they thought they were not yet qualified to fill them. Others were determined only to take positions that would allow them to be true to their values. Thus, Biklen concluded that the major frustrations of women teachers came "not when their hopes for advancement were crushed, but rather when they were forced to make compromises which they felt endangered their educational vision."[53]

Stage 4. The Midlife Transition: Coming to Terms (Ages Forty through Fifty to Fifty-five)

Of all the developmental stages, the midlife transition, often referred to as the midlife crisis, perhaps has received the most popular attention. During this period, individuals typically assess their accomplishments in relation to their earlier dreams and commitments. According to Levinson, individuals are likely to ask: "What have I done with my life? What do I really get from and give to my [spouse], children, friends, work, community—and self? What is it I truly want for myself and others?"[54] Such questions are sometimes answered easily, but frequently answers come only after a great deal of self-reflection and psychological turmoil.

Men Teachers in the Midlife Transition

Men who have not left the classroom for administrative posts become aware that their chances of promotion are growing increasingly remote. They must come to terms with the fact that they have been "passed over" for promotion and that younger teachers are likely to fill the jobs for which they once aspired. For some, this realization is difficult and they become embittered. Others, having read the handwriting on the wall, shift their career energies to a part-time occupation. For example, a forty-six-year-old, male high school teacher explained:

> I don't have much to do with the faculty here. I do my job and go home. I don't
> have the time or inclination to sit around bragging about my accomplishments or

---

[52] Ibid., p. 226.
[53] Ibid.
[54] Levinson et al., *The Seasons of a Man's Life*, p. 60.

complaining about the administration or the school board. I have a real estate office that takes a lot of my time.

Still other men teachers reassess their values and commitments and begin to place new emphasis on their homes and family and, perhaps, themselves.

Women Teachers in Midlife Transition

An interview and questionnaire study of over 400 elementary and secondary teachers by Miller and Taylor confirmed that men teachers begin to lose interest in promotion after the age of forty.[55] Limited opportunities for advancement force a reexamination of goals and priorities. The same was not true for women, however. Freed from home responsibilities as their children grow up and leave for college, women are often anxious to exercise their abilities in another arena. Thus, while men teachers in their forties are likely to reexamine their goals and focus increased attention on self and home, women teachers are moving in just the opposite direction. As a forty-two-year-old high school teacher explained:

> I came back [to teaching] six years ago when my youngest son and daughter entered middle school. We needed the money, but I was really ready to come back. I needed something to do and my kids didn't need me playing mom all the time. . . . I took a course [at the university] to renew my certification and I got hooked and went on to finish my master's. I'd like to go on and get a specialist degree but I'm not sure how to manage that because now I'm chairman of the math department and the job takes a lot of time.

That many women teachers in their forties are career oriented is consistent with the patterns revealed in other studies of adult development among women. Gail Sheehy's study of 115 men and women found that the midlife crisis occurs much earlier for women than for men, frequently around the age of thirty-five, and the reconciliation of that crisis often takes the form of greater assertiveness and career determination. Men enter the midlife transition later and sometimes emerge more passive and less career-oriented than they previously had been.[56]

Relationships with Students

Both men and women teachers in their forties begin to notice their relationship with students changing once again. In the beginning of their careers, most teachers enjoy a close, older-sibling type relationship with their pupils. As they move into their thirties most teachers feel a greater distance from students, who now view them as adult authority figures. Teachers in their forties notice that students see them more like parents and even grandparents and less like siblings or friends. Sikes quoted a forty-five-year-old teacher who discussed his changing relationships with students:

> I do seem ancient to some of these kids. I mean round here they get married early [so] I'm actually older than some of their grandparents. I mean, I go to

[55] J. Miller and G. Taylor, "The Teacher Force Is Aging," *The Canadian School Executive*, Vol. 2 (1983), pp. 12–14.

[56] See Gail Sheehy, *Passages: Predictable Crises of Adult Life* (New York: E. P. Dutton, 1976). Available in paperback.

concerts with my youngest daughter, I'm a real head banger, more with it than most of them. But they see an older man, like grandpa, and it affects their attitudes. It's bound to.[57]

The young are a constant reminder to teachers that they are getting older. As one physical education teacher put it, "the students keep me young in a lot of ways, I mean in my attitude and in my thinking, but being around youngsters all day long also makes me conscious of how old and flabby I'm getting. That can be depressing." A fifty-two-year-old elementary school teacher commented,

When I started teaching I was about the same age as the parents of my students. We had a lot in common and I made friends with a lot of them and some of them are still my friends even today. Now it's much different. The parents are younger—much younger—than I am and we don't have anything in common much at all. They ask advice and listen to what I say because they are uncertain. It rattles me to have them listen to me so attentively. That's not true of all of them but most of them. The same thing can be said for most of the young teachers around here.

Midlife Relationships with Fellow Teachers

As teachers grow older, they find themselves relating with fellow teachers in new ways. Some classroom teachers become authority figures in the school and find that colleagues come to them for guidance and advice. Many take on a mentor or quasi-parent role with younger faculty members.[58] Teachers who have been at a school for a long time may become sources of historical information or self-appointed guardians of school standards and tradition.[59] Teachers who have adjusted well to the turmoil of the midlife transition are likely to enjoy the new authority role.

Disgruntled individuals, who have not adjusted to their new circumstances, usually do not fare well as middle-aged teachers. They are likely, as one forty-six-year-old social studies teacher put it, to "just put in my hours and race the kids to the door at 3:00." Nias called such teachers "privatized workers" because they no longer get satisfaction from the job, students, or colleagues.[60]

Stage 5. Midlife: Taking Stock and Self-Acceptance (Ages Fifty to Fifty-five through Retirement)

Surprisingly little research has been done on the last season of career development, the period when workers are over fifty or fifty-five and before they reach the age of retirement. Levinson did not include many adults in this age

---

[57] Sikes, "The Life Cycle of the Teacher," p. 52.
[58] Peterson, "Age, Teachers' Role, and the Institutional Setting."
[59] Sikes, "The Life Cycle of the Teacher," p. 53. See also Colin Lacy, *Hightown Grammar* (Manchester, England: Manchester University Press, 1970). See also, Patricia Sikes, "Growing Old Gracefully? Age, Identity and Physical Education," in J. Evans, ed. *Teachers, Teaching and Control in the P. E. Curriculum* (New York: Falmer Press, 1988). Available in paperback.
[60] Nias, "A More Distant Drummer," pp. 21–22.

group in his sample and only briefly describes career patterns that occur in this period of life. Moving past the age of fifty, he suggests, prompts many men yet again to reexamine their goals and achievements. If the trauma of the midlife transition was not worked out adequately when individuals were in their forties, Levinson anticipates some degree of turmoil when they move into their fifties.

The period following the fifties transition (from roughly fifty-five until retirement) is relatively stable. Bernice Neugarten conducted extensive interviews with middle-aged and aging adults. She found that people in their fifties and sixties take increased interest in satisfying their personal needs and are characterized by what she called an increased "interiority of personality." In this period, according to Neugarten, "introspection seems to increase noticeably and contemplation and reflection and self-evaluation become characteristic forms of mental life."[61] Introspection in the middle years sometimes leads to self-criticism and change, but introspection in later years is characterized by an attitude of settled self-acceptance. As Roger Gould, a psychologist specializing in adult development, explains:

> We live with a sense of having completed something, a sense that we are whoever we are going to be—and we accept that, not with resignation . . . but with a more positive acceptance: "That's the way it is, world. Here I am! This is me!"[62]

Teachers may become more accepting of student foibles and less bothered by minor classroom disruptions. As one soon-to-retire teacher said:

> I'm quietly relaxed these days. That's because I've seen it all. I'm not bored, I don't mean to imply that, it's that I know what children are like. Little things just don't bother me like they used to. There was a time when I had quite a temper.

Teachers who have been at one school for a number of years are likely to have gained a reputation for themselves. When the reputation is positive, it can be a source of pride and pleasure for older teachers. One particularly candid sixty-one-year-old teacher explained why she no longer had discipline problems in her classes:

> I think I paid my dues a long time ago and students began to say, "Don't fool in Miss Tirrella's room, she'll pull you up short." They tell stories about me and, of course, I get credit for things I never did. The stories get exaggerated. So when students come into my class they are so filled with those stories that they don't dare misbehave. It's all rubbish, but I don't tell them that. They say, "Did you really do so and so to so and so?" and I say, "Yes, indeed."

Some particularly talented older teachers have enormous influence on students and the faculty. One such teacher had retired from the public school system to join the faculty of a private school where he taught three periods of English each day. He went home every afternoon for a nap and then, after dinner, read his students' compositions aloud to his wife. When a paper was particularly good or showed discernible progress or rank carelessness, the teacher phoned its author for a chat. The next day proud students would boast that

---

[61] Bernice Neugarten, "Adult Personality: Toward a Psychology of the Life Cycle," in *Middle Age and Aging*, ed. Bernice Neugarten (Chicago: University of Chicago Press, 1968), p. 140.

[62] Roger L. Gould, *Transformations: Growth and Change in Adult Life* (New York: Simon and Schuster, 1978), p. 331.

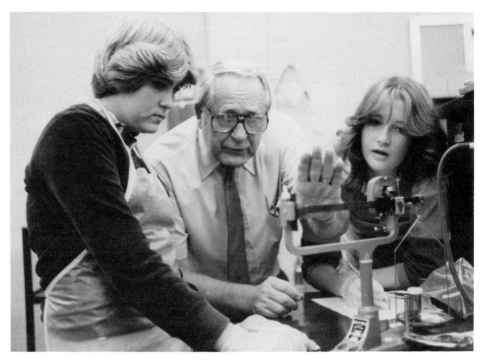

Having a reputation as a good teacher is a source of pride and pleasure.　(*Source:* National Education Association, Joe Di Dio.)

Mr. Henderson had called them at 11:15 just to compliment their work. Other students were less likely to admit that they too had been rousted from their beds to be told that they were still splitting infinitives and were not putting the proper effort into their writing.

Most older teachers do not enjoy the reputation of a Miss Tirella or Mr. Henderson. For them, the collective memory of their past history may provide more constraint than assistance. As one teacher in Sikes's study explained:

> They come into school with all sorts of ideas about you. In some ways it's nice but people change, courses change, and methods, and so on, and it's sometimes very difficult if people have these expectations about you.[63]

The greatest problem older teachers face, however, is not with the attention that comes from a well-earned reputation but with the invisibility created by inattention. As we saw in Chapter 9, there is a tendency in education not to honor past experience but to view older teachers as impediments to progress, "set in their ways," and "over the hill." When older teachers have power in the school, younger faculty may resent not being able to "put their own ideas into practice."[64] When older faculty members lack power, however, younger teachers often take no notice of them.

[63] Sikes, "The Life Cycle of the Teacher," p. 55.
[64] Ibid.

Older teachers may worry that they are losing touch with their community, faculty, subject matter, and students. They may lack interest in learning the vocabulary and methods of the latest innovations, in part because they lack the energy to change but also because they have watched "new ideas" come and go. A retired teacher laughed as she described her last ten years in the classroom.

> I just figured that I'd keep doing what I'd been doing all along. When you get to my age you can see that the whole thing runs in cycles—or in circles. (The teacher laughs.) They put the wine in new bottles, but it's the same old wine. I knew that if I waited long enough what I was doing would come back into style. So I decided not to go chasing after the fads but just to sit still and let [the fads] come to me.

As teachers approach retirement they are likely to spend time mentally reviewing their careers and the careers of past students. Meeting former pupils around town or hearing from students who have moved away is a source of great satisfaction:

> I meet students on the street and they say, "Remember me? You were my sixth grade teacher." Sometimes I don't remember them because they've changed so much but most of the time I do. And they tell me about their kids and their jobs. [What is it that makes these meetings so pleasant for you?] I like to see that everything has turned out all right. [Is that all?] Well, it's nice to be remembered and to know that they realized how much I cared about them. That is what teaching was all about for me.

Motives, Career Dreams, and the Power of Idealism

Teachers are an idealistic group and their idealism has been mentioned many times in this book. Teachers enter education because they want to help the young and contribute to the betterment of society. Most enjoy their work because it gives them an opportunity to use their minds, continue their own development, and help others. *Idealism* is an ambiguous word and for that reason often misunderstood. We will end this chapter by clarifying two different meanings of idealism and showing how one form of idealism can be detrimental to the aims of education while the other is essential to a career in teaching.

John Dewey made a useful distinction between what he called remote and genuine idealism.[65] When people refer to *remote idealism* they mean that an idea (or the person who presents it) is disconnected from reality and does not take into account the intricacies of the situation at hand. Used in this disparaging way (when, for example, we say that an idea is hopelessly idealistic), we mean that something is impossible, that it cannot be done. Of course, we may not be correct in that assessment. We can be sure, however, that remote idealists do exist and that they devote themselves to unattainable goals. We do not take such people seriously and with good reason; they are uninterested in reality and dangerously removed from everyday events. Their eyes are so fixed on lofty pursuits that they pay little attention to the actual problems around them

---

[65] John Dewey and James H. Tufts, *Ethics*, rev. ed. (New York: Henry Holt and Co., 1938 [1908]), p. 302. Available in paperback.

or the details of everyday life. Remote ideals are dangerous because, as Dewey explained, they tempt us to be "negligent."[66] The events of everyday life appear trivial in comparison to some far-off ideal of promised perfection.

Genuine idealism is of a different order. It has its roots in the felt problems and actual conditions of everyday life.[67] Genuine idealists want to make things better in the world around them and they apply creative intelligence to the problems they face. They recognize difficulties, envision a better situation, act on that vision, learn from their actions, and adjust their goals accordingly. For such people, ideals are not remote abstractions; they are genuine possibilities that are subject to ongoing refinement and change.

Some teachers pursue remote ideals. Such teachers, though few in number, are likely to be devoted to extreme ideologies or otherworldly religions. They see the classroom as a platform from which to preach their particular doctrine of political or religious salvation. Most teachers, however, are genuine idealists, though their idealism may not be fully formed. Such teachers do not take things simply as they are but devote themselves to making things better.

Genuine idealism is not something one is born with; like creative intelligence, it must be developed. Most teachers have idealistic intentions when they enter the profession and their idealism matures and deepens with experience. Idealistic hopes that are only vaguely articulated at the start of a career can develop into carefully considered educational aims.

The idealism of beginning teachers is often expressed in an extremely personal form. For example, one of the college seniors quoted at the start of the chapter said:

> *I will* be a very effective and patient teacher; the kind of teacher who makes learning interesting. *I will* find new ways to help students learn and develop a love of learning. *I will* get along with my students. (emphasis added)

These are not egotistical or remote aims, but they do reflect a certain self-centered naïveté. Beginning teachers often believe that they *single-handedly* can help students become critically intelligent, cooperative, self-assured citizens. First-year reality shock jars many teachers into recognizing that their aims can only be achieved with the cooperation of others.

Teachers begin to develop a mature sense of genuine idealism when they understand there must be a conscious connection between the small events of everyday teaching and the larger aims of education. Progress in education is the product of persistent effort and small achievements. Genuine idealism helps teachers see a simple but profound truth: *small actions and attitudes have large consequences, for ultimately the small acts accumulate and finally determine the character of individuals, institutions and societies.* In *Auguries of Innocence,* William Blake captured this point in just two lines:

> A dog starved at his Master's gate
> Predicts the ruin of the State.

Blake is saying that a society is in decay when its citizens no longer take notice of small cruelties. He is saying also that the moral integrity of a society is found not in its noblest claims but in what Blake called the "minute particulars" of

---

[66] Ibid.
[67] John Dewey, *A Common Faith* (New Haven: Yale University Press, 1960 [1934]), p. 48. Available in paperback.

everyday life. The point here is that the moral integrity of a teacher and of a school are expressed in the unity of everyday actions and in the degree to which those actions serve genuine ideals.

A respect for genuine ideals encourages teachers to pay close attention to everyday events and it infuses these events with enduring meaning. For example, teaching a group of children to recognize the letters of the alphabet and to associate specific letters with specific sounds is not, by itself, a particularly difficult or even interesting achievement. Yet, learning to read takes on limitless significance when considered in the context of a specified, genuine ideal, say, the ideal of democracy. In this context, we see that learning to read is not an isolated occurrence; it is an empowering activity that enables individuals to take greater control of their own development and gives them greater access to the goods and services of society. More important, it opens the way to fuller participation in the human community. Seen in this light, the small accomplishments of a phonics lesson are part of a much larger and significant undertaking. Genuine ideals remind teachers of the significance of their everyday activities. At the same time, genuine ideals guard teachers against seeing the learning of specific lessons and the mastery of specific skills as ends in themselves.

No genuine ideal is ever achieved completely because every advance exposes areas that need further improvement. No genuine ideal can be achieved by one person alone; every advance demands the cooperation of others. Thus, genuine ideals help individual teachers find unity in their own activities and see how their efforts are connected to the work of other teachers, with whom they share common goals. Genuine ideals, when they are fully developed, unite teachers in a professional community. They link the actions of teachers with the work of other educators who have taught their students in the past and who will teach them in the future. Genuine ideals do more. They connect teachers to the best traditions of their society. Teachers inherit ideals from the past. It is their responsibility to understand, conserve, rectify, enlarge, and transmit that heritage. When teachers do this work well, they shape the future.

Summary

The word *career* can refer to a line of work (a career in teaching) or to the course of an individual's professional life (my teaching career). Careers affect an individual's identity, biography, material prospects, and relationship with society and are characterized by patterned stages. Not all individuals pass through these stages at precisely the same age or experience them in exactly the same way.

Stage 1, early adulthood, is dedicated to the exploration of two antithetical options: the possibilities of adult living, where individuals maximize their alternatives; and the possibility of creating a stable life structure, where individuals make choices and settle down. Two problems for teachers in this stage involve early commitment to teaching (before fully exploring their potentials and interests) and under-commitment (considering teaching a stop-gap profession). Teachers who avoid these two problems begin to form career dreams that reflect their idealism and hopes for the future.

Entry into teaching is usually accompanied by reality shock. Teachers may find the work harder than anticipated and students difficult to discipline and motivate. They may find that they get little on-the-job assistance and that they are uncomfortable in their new role. Those who successfully weather first-year reality shock begin to experience and appreciate the joys of their work. They gain a greater sense of identity and purpose and a greater understanding of their own motives and idealism. Successful teachers find ways to forge a meaningful connection among students, themselves, and the subject matter under study.

Stage 2, the age-thirty transition, is a time of reassessment and new choices. Teachers may decide to leave the profession, recommit themselves to classroom teaching, or seek positions in administration or other education-related work. For those who stay in education, this stage entails a series of separations: from mentors, imposed structures, a reliance on youth, and their first teaching jobs. These separations set the stage for greater connections and commitment to their profession.

Stage 3, settling down, is characterized by the exercise of old skills and the development of new ones. Two tasks that confront people entering this stage of adulthood are (1) to establish a niche in society, to develop competence and have that competence recognized by others, and (2) to finally become their "own person," to establish a well-defined sense of professional self-esteem. Teachers are likely to look for new challenges and new areas within the profession where they can use their hard-won expertise. The ambitions of many men at this stage focus on career advancement. Many women, on the other hand, are more likely to focus on the content of their work. Gender roles are changing fast in the culture and these patterns may change with them. The idealism of teachers matures during this period and provides a greater support for a teachers' sense of professional self-esteem.

Stage 4, the midlife transition, is usually devoted to reassessments of career dreams and actual accomplishments. Men who have not become administrators are likely to give up on that pursuit. Some rededicate themselves to classroom teaching, others focus on other interests outside their work, and still others become bitter and isolated. Women, on the other hand, may find themselves with less burdensome family responsibilities. They often rededicate themselves to their careers and begin to consider administrative work. Teachers' relationships with students are likely to become more parentlike during the midlife stage of their careers. They may begin to fulfill mentor roles with younger colleagues and take a leadership role in important school matters.

Stage 5, midlife, is a period of taking stock. Teachers over fifty-five years old are likely to become increasingly introspective. At an earlier age, this kind of reassessment often led to change, but at this stage it frequently results in a new acceptance of one's self and one's life. The ideals that brought teachers into the profession, and that matured with them throughout their careers, now provide a sense of accomplishment, community, and perspective. The contentment of teachers in this stage is increased if their accomplishments are remembered and appreciated by colleagues and the community. Contentment is threatened when fellow teachers are unaware of what the teacher has done and no longer consider him or her a vital force in the school.

Genuine ideals are vitally important to the work of good teachers. Remote ideals are impractical and divert a teacher's attention away from the problems of everyday existence. Genuine ideals, on the other hand, grow from everyday existence and direct teachers' attention to the details of teaching. They make it possible for teachers to find meaning and unity in the work they do and to see how their efforts are a part of a larger undertaking. Genuine ideals link teachers to the achievements of the past and the promise of the future.

Suggested Readings

The literature on teachers' lives and careers is still sparse, but it is growing.

AGASSI, JUDITH. "The Quality of Women's Working Life," in *The Quality of Working Life*, eds. L. Davis and A. Cherns, Vol. 1. New York: The Free Press, 1975. This is a general paper but it has relevance to the study of teachers' careers.

BALL, STEPHEN, and IVOR GOODSON. "Understanding Teachers: Concepts and Contexts," in *Teachers' Lives and Careers*, eds. Stephen Ball and Ivor Goodson. London: The Falmer Press, 1985. This insightful essay sets current research in historical and theoretical context.

BIKLEN, SARI KNOPP. "Can Elementary School Teaching Be a Career? A Search for New Ways of Understanding Women's Work," in *Issues in Education*, Vol. 3 (Winter 1985), pp. 215–231. The author makes the case that we cannot judge the teaching careers of women with concepts uncovered in the study of men.

BLEDSTEIN, BURTON. *The Culture of Professionalism*. New York: W. W. Norton, 1976. This is an unsettling historical account of the role higher education has played and continues to play in the creation of "professionalism" in the United States.

GILLIGAN, CAROL. *In a Different Voice*. Cambridge: Harvard University Press, 1982. This ground-breaking book makes the case that psychology has persistently misunderstood the motives, moral commitments, and adult development of women.

LEVINSON, DANIEL J., with CHARLOTTE N. DARROW, EDWARD B. KLEIN, MARIA H. LEVINSON, and BRAXTON MCKEE. *The Seasons of a Man's Life*. New York: Alfred A. Knopf, 1979. This is a readable and interesting account of men's adult development.

LORTIE, DAN C. *Schoolteacher: A Sociological Study*. Chicago: University of Chicago Press, 1975. This is still the most complete and provocative account of the teaching profession.

MEASOR, LYNDA. "Critical Incidents of the Classroom: Identities, Choices and Careers" in *Teachers' Lives and Careers*, eds. Stephen Ball and Ivor Goodson. London: The Falmer Press, 1985, pp. 61–77. This paper draws data from an ongoing study of teachers' life histories directed by the British sociologist Peter Woods.

NATIONAL EDUCATION ASSOCIATION. *Status of the American Public School Teacher, 1980–1981*. Washington DC: National Education Association, 1982. A valuable source of primary data by the NEA, which conducts a national study of teachers every five years.

NIAS, JENNIFER. "A More Distant Drummer: Teacher Development as the Development of Self," in *Education and Social Change*, eds. Len Barton and Stephen Walker. London: Croom Helm, 1985. This is one of a series of fascinating articles on Nias's research into the careers of ninety-nine teachers.

PETERSON, WARREN A. "Age, Teacher's Role, and the Institutional Setting," in *Contemporary Research in Teaching Effectiveness*, eds. B. J. Biddle and W. S. Elena. New York: Holt, Rinehart and Winston, 1964. This book is an early and still useful examination of teacher development.

SIKES, PATRICIA A. "The Life Cycle of the Teacher" in *Teachers' Lives and Careers*, eds. Stephen Ball and Ivor Goodson. London: The Falmer Press, 1985. An application of Levinson's life stages to the career development of teachers, this interesting article is by a talented British sociologist of education.

VEENMAN, SIMON. "Perceived Problems of Beginning Teachers." *Review of Educational Research,* Vol. 54 (Summer 1984), pp. 143–148. This is a useful review of research on beginning teachers.

Students wanting to read further in the area of idealism are directed to the writings of John Dewey.

DEWEY, JOHN. *Democracy and Education.* New York: The Free Press, 1966.

DEWEY, JOHN. *A Common Faith.* New Haven: Yale University Press, 1960.

GOUINLOCK, JAMES. *John Dewey's Philosophy of Value.* New York: Humanities Press, 1972. Especially see the discussion of human ideals and nature in Chapter 6. This book, by one of America's foremost Dewey scholars, is exceedingly useful for both new and seasoned students of Dewey's work.

Summary of Section III

Teachers come to the profession from varied backgrounds and choose teaching for a variety of reasons. The most important thing they have in common is that most want to work with the young and, through that work, make a contribution to society. A large majority care about the subjects they teach and the students they serve. They believe that people are empowered by knowledge and by the skills and habits of critical intelligence. This is not to suggest that teaching is a selfless act. After all, teachers learn in the act of teaching and further their own development as they look after the development of others. Nevertheless, when teachers successfully spark the curiosity of their students, when they bring a subject to life and make it intelligible and relevant, when they help students develop and maintain the discipline necessary to grapple with important knowledge, when they help pupils attend to details and sharpen their skills of critical intelligence, when they prepare the young for a lifetime of learning, when they enhance pupils' self-respect by enhancing students' skills—when teachers do all this, they bring into being the best of all that is human. Put simply, good teaching touches humanity. These *primary motives* for teaching are genuinely idealistic and they constitute the foundation of the teaching profession.

A number of *secondary motives* coexist with the primary motives. Other secondary motives displace the primary motives for teaching and cause teachers to lose sight of the aims of education in a democratic society. In Section III, we discovered that some people are attracted to teaching because the profession offers easy mobility up into the middle class, a secure if modest income, improved status, and increased respect.

Teaching has long been a preferred occupation for many women. One reason for this is that teaching is still the best-paid profession dominated by women. This may change in the future as traditional prejudices decline and as women secure places in more lucrative professions. Another reason for the popularity of teaching among women is that its work and vacation schedule make it possible for women to work while their children are in school and to be home when the school day and term are over. Another reason may be that women have found the primary goals of teaching more compatible with their values than did men.

For men and women alike, teaching is sometimes a convenient stop-gap occupation, a way to earn a living while preparing for another line of work. Some people "fall into teaching" or "fall back on teaching" because other career plans did not pan out. Others are drawn to teaching because they wish to relive a high school experience as a leader, athletic hero, or good student. Such motives diminish activism and promote conservatism. One of the great challenges facing the profession today is to discover ways to sustain the idealism of teachers and allow it to guide the practice of teaching.

A number of factors increase teachers' dissatisfaction and loosen their commitment to the primary goals of teaching. Poor pay and limited career opportunities within teaching, declining confidence in the nation's schools, status panic, and difficult working conditions have forced many capable teachers out of the classroom. Despite these problems, the intrinsic rewards of teaching remain abundant enough to sustain most teachers.

Teachers tend to have greatest access to the intrinsic rewards of teaching when they work in a democratic environment. Democratic schools are characterized by clear goals and standards, supportive leadership, shared decision making, teacher collaboration, clear and fairly enforced rules, and the possibility of professional development.

Chapter 10 gave insight into the career patterns of teachers. Those patterns will not be reviewed here. Suffice it to say that career experiences can make teachers more reflective and able to effectively pursue the aims of education or they can detach teachers from their initial goals and motives. Teachers weather the reality shock experienced at the outset of their careers or they become disheartened and disillusioned. They experience some success and, through reflection, expand on that success, or they begin to worry that they do not have what it takes to teach or that their students don't have what it takes to learn. As they mature, successful teachers begin to recognize their own unique capabilities and how these abilities contribute to the school and its aims. Teachers who fail to see themselves as capable and "their own person" are likely to become stale. Their teaching becomes routine and they settle for the mere appearance of learning.

By midlife, teachers are forced to evaluate their career dreams against their actual accomplishments. Some teachers rededicate themselves to classroom teaching, others become embittered that they did not do as well in teaching as they might have liked, and still others prepare to move into administration or other lines of work. At the end of their careers, teachers are likely to take stock of what they have accomplished over the years. The ideals that brought them into the profession, and that matured with them over time, now provide a sense of accomplishment, community, and perspective.

Section III demonstrated why what Dewey called genuine ideals are vital to teaching. Remote ideals are impractical and divert a teacher's attention away from everyday problems. Genuine ideals, on the other hand, grow from everyday experience and direct teachers' attention to the details ("the minute particulars") of teaching. Ideals can motivate teachers, but they do much more. Genuine ideals reveal the meaning and unity in the work that teachers do. They make it possible for teachers to see how their efforts are a part of a larger undertaking and how that undertaking is linked to the deepest potentials in the human spirit.

No one can predict whether the reforms discussed in this section will be sustained over the next decade. It is clear that the nation's attention has been caught by the call for excellence in education. Excellence, however, is a mere slogan unless genuine ideals give substance and meaning to the idea and direction to the reform. Thus, ideals are not only important to daily work and career development of individual teachers; ideals also give direction to the entire enterprise of public education.

The School as a Social System: Institutionalizing Educational Aims

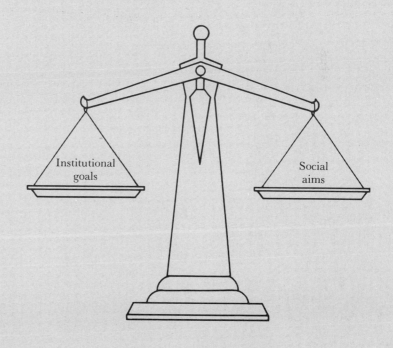

CHAPTER 11

Studying Institutions: Bureaucracy and Education

Introduction

This chapter presents a number of terms and concepts that you will need in order to understand the institution of the American school. Getting acquainted with definitions is seldom an exciting affair, but we have tried to limit the tedium by avoiding unnecessary technicalities and showing the relevance of each concept to the everyday workings of the school. The examples provided refer to educational settings and information that will be of importance to you as a teacher.

Institutions: What Are They?

Everyday life—for most of us most of the time—is an orderly affair. We move through a series of human interchanges that make sense. We know rather accurately how people will behave in each of these situations. We know the rules of the classroom, the church, the drive-in movie, the family, the bar, the bedroom, the supermarket, the corporation, the cocktail party, the Weight Watchers' meeting, the job interview, and so on. We know what to expect and are uncomfortable when we find ourselves in strange situations where we don't know the rules.[1] Our discomfort ends (we begin to feel more at home) when we discover the rules that regulate the new situation.

Everyday life brings us into many different situations, each with its own specific pattern of behavior. These regulatory patterns are called *institutions*. Notice

---

[1] For a sociological account of this discomfort, see two intriguing articles by Alfred Schutz, "The Stranger: An Essay in Social Psychology" and "Homecomer," in *Studies in Social Theory*, Vol. 2 of *Collected Papers*, ed. Arvid Brodersen (The Hague: Martinus Nijhoff, 1964), pp. 91–105 and 106–119.

that this technical definition of *institution* differs quite markedly from the everyday meanings attached to the term. For example, it is not uncommon for a football coach to be called *an institution* because he has been around for a long time. The term is occasionally used to refer to an organization that serves and somehow contains people of a certain kind, for example, an insane asylum, a prison, a hospital, a public school, and, yes, even a university. Sometimes we take a legalistic view and refer to such nontangible entities as "the state" or "the economy" as *institutions*. These common definitions are not wrong and we are not suggesting that they be drummed out of the language, but it is important to note that social scientists have a very specific meaning in mind when they use the term *institution*.

When we think of institutions as organized patterns of behavior, we stop thinking of schools (and other institutions) as fixed entities and begin seeing them as puzzles that can be pieced together and understood. For example, if we understand the subtle rules regulating a teacher's interaction with parents, we may work with parents more productively. In the next few chapters, we will examine the behavior patterns that characterize most American schools, but first we must clarify a few of the terms and concepts we will be using in our analysis.

Institutions organize human behavior.   (*Source:* National Education Association, Joe Di Dio.)

A Definition of *Status*

Institutions rarely require the same behavior of everyone. Instead, people holding different positions within an institution perform different functions and follow different sets of rules. A position within an institution is called a *status*. Within the typical school, we can find some people holding the status of teacher and others occupying the status of student, administrator, counselor, or custodian.

Individuals are likely to hold just one status within a particular institution, but because most people are involved in many institutions, it is possible to hold many statuses. For example, a person may be a teacher, a building representative for the union, vice-president of a local political organization, a member of the Friends of the Library, a parent, and a part-time graduate student. The total number of statuses an individual holds at any one time is called his or her *status set*. Having a wide variety of statuses is a characteristic of modern society and, as we saw in Chapter 1, can enrich an individual's life or contribute to alienation.

Status and Power

Attached to each status is a specific allocation of power. By *power* we mean simply the ability to get others to do things, whether they want to do them or not. Institutions rarely dole out power evenly. More typically, status is arranged hierarchically within the institution according to the power assigned to each position. Each status has some power over positions beneath it and decidedly less power over positions above it. The organizational chart of a typical large-city school is presented in Figure 11-1. The chart outlines the allocations of major responsibility and authority within a typical school system.

A Definition of *Role*

A person occupying a certain status (say, that of a teacher) does not necessarily treat all other status positions in the institution in just the same manner. Teachers are expected to do different things with different people. The work Mr. Smith does with his class demands one kind of behavior. His interactions with parents require other behaviors, and the work he does with fellow teachers, the principal, or the custodian requires still other behaviors. Yet, there are similarities in how he behaves when he works with different people occupying the same status. That is, he is likely to treat all his students in roughly the same way. If we were eavesdropping outside Mr. Smith's classroom door, we could probably tell whether he was talking to a student, a fellow teacher, a parent, or the school principal. The pattern of behavior that governs the interaction of one status-holder with another is called a *role*. A teacher plays one role with students and quite a different role with the school counselor. Thus, the status of teacher is made up of a large number of behavior patterns (roles) that regulate the teacher's interaction with other status positions. We can refer to all the different roles attached to a status as a *role set*.

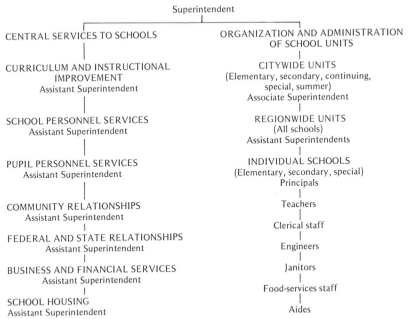

Figure 11-1   Allocations of major responsibilities and authority.   (*Source:*
Samuel Miller Brownell, "Superintendence of Large-City School Systems,"
in *Encyclopedia of Education,* Vol. 8 [New York: The Free Press, 1971],
p. 557. Copyright © 1971 Crowell Collier and Macmillan, Inc. Reprinted
by permission.)

A Brief Review

It may clarify things if we briefly review the definitions presented so far. *Insti-tutions* are social organizations that pattern human behavior in specific situa-tions. Thus, schools, families, bars, churches, and so on are all institutions be-cause they are social organizations that provide specific rules of conduct. Institutions often have different rules for people occupying different status positions. A *status* is a socially defined position in a social organization. Each status has attached to it a role set. A *role* is a behavior pattern regulating the interaction of one status with another. A teacher plays one role vis-à-vis other teachers and quite another role vis-à-vis students. We refer to all the different roles attached to a status as a *role set.* These definitions are represented graph-ically in Table 11-1. Notice that we have not listed all the statuses found within the institution of the school. In order to keep things simple, we have left out such status positions as crossing guards, school nurses, school board members, truant officers, school social workers, parents, and many more.

TABLE 11-1. Social Organization of the School

Status (position)	Roles (rules regulating status interaction)	
Principal	Principal–principal interaction Principal–counselor interaction Principal–teacher interaction Principal–custodian interaction Principal–student interaction	Role Set
Counselor	Counselor–principal interaction Counselor–counselor interaction Counselor–teacher interaction Counselor–custodian interaction Counselor–student interaction	Role Set
Teacher	Teacher–principal interaction Teacher–counselor interaction Teacher–teacher interaction Teacher–custodian interaction Teacher–student interaction	Role Set
Custodian	Custodian–principal interaction Custodian–counselor interaction Custodian–teacher interaction Custodian–custodian interaction Custodian–student interaction	Role Set
Student	Student–principal interaction Student–counselor interaction Student–teacher interaction Student–custodian interaction Student–student interaction	Role Set

Functions of Institutions, Statuses, and Roles

The most fundamental function of institutions is to keep our lives orderly and protect us from having to make too many choices. If at each moment we had to negotiate the rules of the games we play, we would be unable to play any games at all. Social order (and personal sanity) demands that we be able to take some things for granted. For example, you may have taken four or five courses in the last semester, each with a different subject matter, professor, syllabus, grading policy, and set of requirements. Despite these rather large differences, there was sufficient similarity in these experiences to allow you to know what was going on. You were able to play the role of student.

The term *playing a role* is derived from the theater and has some negative connotations in everyday language. It suggests insincerity (or incompetence) on the part of the role player. ("Don't pay any attention to Tom; he's just playing a role.") Although it is quite true that some people play their roles insincerely (remember our discussion of role distance in Chapter 2), this should not lead us to believe that role playing is always a game of hypocritical theatrics. The fact is that most of us believe our roles quite thoroughly.

Internalizing Roles: An Unconscious Process

Roles do not simply regulate our external behavior; they seep inside the self and significantly affect our attitudes and emotions. This is largely an unconscious process. As you begin to play a role, you grow into the kind of person you are "pretending" to be. Despite the discomfort you feel when you first become a teacher, you soon find yourself playing the role quite automatically. You begin to think as teachers think, feel as teachers feel, and, of course, do what teachers do. You begin to feel wiser when students ask you questions, more powerful as pupils succumb to your demands, more capable as you master the requirements of your job, and more professional when parents ask you to diagnose their child's learning problems. These internal changes happen without much thought. As they occur, they may (in fact, they often do) overpower your ideas about the kind of teacher you originally wanted to be.

A dramatic example of how quietly and unconsciously roles become internalized is provided in a study by Philip Zimbardo, a Stanford University psychologist. Students volunteered to take part in a mock prison experience. Those chosen by lot to become prisoners were dragged from their dorm rooms in the dead of night. They were dressed in prison uniforms, locked in cells, and watched over by fellow students playing the role of prison guards. In just a few days, Zimbardo observed that the students not only played their roles but also began to believe in them. The guards became authoritarian, even cruel, whereas the prisoners became apathetic, submissive, and conspiratorial. Zimbardo concluded that a social setting can be more powerful than an individual's personality or willpower in determining role behaviors.[2]

Studying Institutions

A social scientist who wants to study an institution does not just jump into the middle of it and begin to snoop around. Scientists have guidelines that tell them what to look for and methods that tell them how to do their looking. These guidelines come in the form of models (or theories) of what institutions are like. Obviously, the model that scientists have in mind will influence what they look for, what they see, and how they explain what goes on within the institution. This is not to say that social scientists first decide what they are going to find and then go out into the field to confirm their prejudices (although this accusation has been made more than once). It is to say, instead, that good social scientists have a theoretical base for their work. When they study human behavior, they test the adequacy of their theories. They ask, Does this theory help me understand what is going on? Does it account for what people do and why they do it? Does it help me predict future activities? In some cases, social scientists will conduct experiments in which they manipulate variables and thus better test the strength of their model.

[2] Philip Zimbardo, "Pathology of Imprisonment," *Society*, Vol. 9 (April 1972), pp. 4–8.

Two Models for Studying Institutions

Within the field of sociology there are dozens of models for studying institutions. We need not embroil ourselves in the family squabbles of the discipline. It will serve our purposes to discuss in general terms what the battle is about.[3] Sociologists disagree as to whether an institution is better understood from an objective or a subjective point of view. *Objectivists* see institutions as thinglike entities that can be analyzed in terms of status positions, role behaviors, social functions, and so on. In such an analysis, there is little need to discuss individual people, for their desires, personalities, and actions are seen as little more than reflections of institutional demands. *Subjectivists* take a different view of institutions. Although most would acknowledge the power institutions have over status holders, subjectivists pay careful attention to what status holders think, believe (consciously and unconsciously), and do. Whereas objectivists are primarily interested in institutions as things that are separate from human beings, subjectivists are interested in how individuals experience life within institutions.

It can be argued that these approaches, in the end, amount to the same thing. They both must account for institutional structures and how human beings behave within these structures—but the two models begin at different points and proceed in different directions (see Figure 11-2). Objectivists begin with an analysis of institutional order and proceed to show how this order is maintained through the assignment of status positions and role behaviors. With these findings established, the objectivist then may examine the actions and experiences of individual status holders. Subjectivists begin at the other end and investigate the experience of individuals playing their assigned roles (and perhaps engaging in nonconforming behavior). Whereas subjectivists begin with the individual and work up to the social system, objectivists begin with the social system and work down to the individual. Each accuses the other of not completing the trip. Subjectivists claim that objectivists do not fully appreciate human reality as it is experienced in the consciousness of individuals. Objectivists claim that subjectivists do not fully understand the workings of the social system. The accusations of both groups are probably correct—a point to which we will return later.

As we proceed with our analysis of the school as a social system, we will not

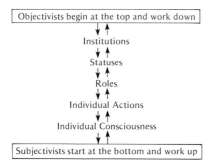

Figure 11-2   The subjectivist and objectivist study of institutions.

---

[3] For a fuller theoretical analysis, see George Ritzer, *Sociology: A Multiple Paradigm Science* (Boston: Allyn & Bacon, Inc., 1975).

limit ourselves to a solely objectivist or solely subjectivist approach. Instead, we will draw on sociologists from both persuasions so that we can get a full account of how schools work. Thus, not only will we focus on the behavior patterns attached to statuses and roles within the school, but we will also examine the experience of role players. What does the reality of the school mean to them? How do they experience the roles they play? In this way we can show that individuals do not always adapt to a ready-made environment; they help to construct the environment to which they adapt. Human beings are not simply role takers; they are sometimes role makers and role modifiers.[4]

What Are Schools Like?

There are many kinds of schools in America. Some are old, dilapidated, cramped, and ill equipped, whereas others are new, spacious, and equipped with everything from language laboratories and computer terminals to swimming pools and simulated spacecraft. Some schools serve impoverished populations, and others serve the affluent. Some have highly skilled, highly trained (the two need not go together), and highly motivated teachers; other schools have faculties with none of these qualities. Some schools are progressive and others conservative. Some are urban, others rural. Some serve homogeneous communities, whereas others draw from varied populations.

With all these differences (and many others that are not listed here) you might think that almost no generalizations could be made about American schools. Yet, despite this diversity, schools share patterns of behavior that make them instantly recognizable as schools. The status positions and roles assigned to individuals involved have impressive (not to say astonishing) similarities. School structures of governance and assignments of power are so familiar that these factors are taken for granted, not only by the staff and students but by the general public as well. The focus in the chapters that follow will be on the similarities among public schools. The examination will not apply to all schools equally but will have significant applicability even to the most unique public schools.

Bureaucratic Schools

Perhaps the most dramatic, certainly one of the most consistent, trend in American education has been growth in the size of schools and school districts. In 1941, there were 208,235 public schools in America spread across 115,493 school districts. By 1983, the number of schools had dropped to 84,740 and the number of school districts had shrunk to 15,880. As the number of school districts declined (by more than 86 percent), the number of students going to school skyrocketed from 25 to 43 million. The average school size quadrupled, moving from 120 to 480 students. As dramatic as this rise is, it is based on averages that mask the fact that most American children spend a considerable part of their childhood in schools that teach considerably more than 480 stu-

---

[4] For a fuller account of this point, see Ralph Turner, "Role-taking: Process vs. Conformity," in *Human Behavior and Social Processes: An Interactionist Approach,* ed. Arnold R. Rose (Boston: Houghton-Mifflin Company, 1962), pp. 20–40.

dents. This is especially true of high schools; the average high school enrollment now exceeds 900 students.[5]

As bureaucracies grow larger and larger, they require more and more administrators to manage them. Joel Spring, a historian who traced the growth of bureaucracy in education, has calculated that "in 1919–20 there was one supervisor or principal for every thirty-one teachers, librarians and other non-supervisory instructional staff." By 1929–1930, the ratio was one in twenty-two; by 1949–1950, it was one in nineteen; and by 1969–1970, it was one in sixteen.[6] The ratio did not change appreciably in the 1980s.[7] What has changed is the cost of administering these schools. Between 1970 and 1980, there was an after-inflation increase of 12.3 percent in expenditures for K–12 education in the United States. During the same period, however, the money spent on classroom instruction, including teachers' salaries, declined by 8 percent. The amount of money being spent to administer schools has increased while the amount devoted to teaching and learning has diminished.[8]

Characteristics of Bureaucracy

As schools grow in size, they become increasingly bureaucratic. The term *bureaucracy* is not easy to define, but we can list the characteristics of a bureaucracy.

SEPARATE ORGANIZATION.   Structurally, bureaucracies are separate organizations run by full-time staffs. In this respect, they are like other formal organizations. The staff's organizational life is distinctly separate from each member's personal life.

In order to illustrate this point, we can look back at the lives of teachers in colonial America. At that time, it was not unusual for a teacher to board with the families of his students, staying a few weeks at one home before moving on to another. Needless to say, colonial teachers were under constant scrutiny. Families came to know them and had a rather complete picture of their character. Similarly, teachers came to know their students well. The teachers' proximity to family life made it possible for them to bring education into the home and to bring family information into the world of the school. A teacher's private life was intimately connected with his or her public work. The two were inseparable entities. Contrast this arrangement with the educational system today. The school is a separate organization and has only formal contact with the home. (This point was discussed in Chapter 6.) Teachers may not even live in

---

[5] W. Vance Grant and Thomas D. Snyder, *Digest of Educational Statistics, 1985* (Washington DC: National Center for Educational Statistics, 1985). This figure is somewhat misleading. Most schools have fewer than 900 students, but some schools are very large indeed.

[6] Joel Spring, *Educating the Worker-Citizen* (New York: Longman, 1980), p. 90. Available in paperback.

[7] Grant and Snyder, *Digest of Educational Statistics*, p. 49.

[8] Lawrence W. Lezotte, "School Effectiveness: Reflections and Future Directions," paper presented at the Annual Meeting of the American Educational Research Association, San Francisco, April 1986, pp. 10–11.

the community where they teach, and their private lives are, for the most part, their own business.[9]

ORDERLY AND STABLE HIERARCHIES.   The fundamental characteristic of bureaucracies is their orderly hierarchical organization. In business bureaucracies, often national headquarters send directives to regional offices, which in turn oversee the work of local establishments. These likewise are divided into departments and individual jobs. Each segment of this supervision system has a carefully defined job and is governed by highly specific regulations.

Educational bureaucracies follow a similar pattern. The federal government increasingly plays a role in disbursing funds for education, implementing national educational legislation, and monitoring and enforcing court orders. State departments of education set licensing standards, conduct statewide tests, monitor the spending of state funds for education, and set out state curriculum requirements. Local school boards direct local policy, and school administrators have responsibility for all activities in their schools.

There is a clear chain of command in bureaucracies, and every bureaucrat's work is in some way monitored by another bureaucrat somewhere up the chain. Jobs have job descriptions that clarify the work to be done and classify the kinds of problems likely to be faced. For example, a teacher's handbook (or contract) may specify time schedules for arriving at and leaving work, teachers' "free periods" (if they have any), duty schedules for the playground and lunch room, due dates for grades, regulations for field trips, procedures for dealing with irate parents, general curriculum guidelines, disciplinary procedures, and much more. Once these expectations have been set out in writing and explained to the teacher, it is the bureaucratic assumption that job holders will be held accountable for their performance. If there are complaints (if someone feels that the regulations are inappropriate, that he or she has been unfairly judged, or that others are not doing their jobs), the bureaucracy provides an appeals procedure. The bureaucratic ideal is to define and classify all conceivable problems and set regulations regarding each eventuality. If the complaint reveals an unanticipated problem, the rules will be expanded to include the new issue. Thus, bureaucracies have an ever-expanding system of regulations based on a principle of inclusiveness.

FIXED JURISDICTIONS.   Bureaucracies have carefully defined kinds of work that they do according to carefully defined regulations. A police department, fire department, and school system may get their funding from the same tax source, but they have different jobs to do. A bureaucracy is expected to stay within its jurisdiction of expertise and to stay out of areas where it is incompetent. Teachers are not trained to put out fires, and firefighters are not skilled at catching criminals, but within its own jurisdiction each bureaucracy is held accountable (by the public, other bureaucracies, and the bureaucracy's own administration) for doing its job efficiently. For example, whatever else schools may try to accomplish, they are expected to help students acquire the basic skills of reading, writing, and arithmetic. If a child grows up to be an unhappy

---

[9] An extreme example is found in Judith Rossner's novel *Looking for Mr. Goodbar*, in which the heroine (if that is the right term) teaches school in the daytime and cruises bars to pick up stray men in the evening (New York: Simon & Schuster, Inc., 1975).

adult, the school is not held accountable. If the same adult ends a disastrous marriage in divorce, the school will not be blamed (even if the records show that he or she got an A in the school's "Marriage and the Family" course). But if students graduate from high school with passing grades yet cannot read or write, there is likely to be a public outcry. Some students have gone so far as to sue their own schools for incompetence because they graduated illiterate.

STATUS COMPETENCE.   If bureaucracies are held accountable for carrying out their functions, so are individual status holders within the organization. Officials presumably are selected on the basis of technical competence. Applicants may be tested, and their training, credentials, and past experience scrutinized. In the ideal bureaucracy, knowing someone, doing someone a favor, or having good looks will not get a person a job. Expertise is all-important. However, the ideal of expertise is not clear-cut. A bureaucrat doing the hiring (say, a school principal) is not only interested in whether the candidate can teach the third grade but also wants to know if he or she can get along in the school structure. Does she know how the game is played, and (as important) is she willing to play it? Will he be loyal to his organization and keep the "secrets of the office."[10]

To assure competence, many bureaucracies (or agencies that oversee bureaucracies) install testing procedures to measure the job-related knowledge of their applicants. Civil-service exams are a prime example of this method. The assumption behind such examinations is that a job in the bureaucracy can be described, and the skills needed for doing that job can be specified and measured. Bureaucrats, assuming that all job skills can be specified, are offended by the idea that good teaching cannot be defined. A growing number of states have attempted to list the competencies officially seen as essential to effective teaching and are testing teachers to see if they have mastered these competencies.

FORMAL COMMUNICATION.   The communication procedures on matters of "official business" are formal and impersonal within bureaucracies. There is a high dependence on written communication (memos, directives, reports, evaluations) and on formal conferences where "official minutes" are often taken. These communications become "matters of records" and are carefully filed so that they can be referred to in the future. Such records take on a power of their own. Children learn in the early grades that the statement "This will go on your record" can be a teacher's ultimate threat.

Teachers usually see their work in a personal and humanistic light and value their face-to-face interactions with students, yet schools have a high dependence on written communication. Government regulations, state curriculum mandates, teacher contracts, memos from the principal, student handbooks, report cards, homework assignments, counselor reports, and the rest are vital to the bureaucratic system of the school. The lifeblood of the bureaucracy is blue ink.

OBJECTIVITY AND RATIONALITY.   Bureaucracies are supposed to make sense. Procedures are spelled out, authority is clarified, and jurisdictions are outlined.

---

[10] This phrase is borrowed from the German sociologist Max Weber.

Ideally, bureaucracies are the epitome of rational social organization. Although we would have a hard time convincing some people of this rationality (say, a student facing the vagaries of registration at a large university), bureaucracies are much more rational and efficient than nonbureaucratic organizations.[11]

An essential element of rationality is objectivity. It is important to a bureaucracy that personal feeling not get in the way of assigned duties. People who accept bureaucratic logic define being "treated fairly" as being treated like everyone else. Teachers accused of biased grading, for example, can clear themselves of the charge by producing evidence that everyone's tests were graded in the same manner. True, bureaucracies are not free from bias, but they are probably far freer from such things than other forms of administration. Such objectivity leads to predictability for society. If we know the procedures that regulate a bureaucracy (admittedly no small task), it becomes possible to calculate how the bureaucracy will deal with us—and this is a point of great significance in a complex world. Such knowledge is clearly an essential element of life in a modern society.

Functions and Dysfunctions of Bureaucracies

The term *bureaucracy* was coined by Max Weber (1864–1920), one of the founding fathers of sociology. All of the characteristics of bureaucracy we have discussed can be traced to Weber's work.[12] He was impressed (perhaps overly so) by the positive functions of bureaucracy. Among these he included its reliability, functional rationality, coordination of complex activities, and minimization of personal (nonrational) considerations in decision making. These are positive functions essential to technological society, but bureaucracies also have negative consequences. A contemporary sociologist, Robert Merton, calls these the dysfunctions of bureaucracy.[13] Let us now examine some of the less attractive aspects of bureaucracy and see to what degree they are characteristic of educational institutions.

GOAL DISPLACEMENT.   One of the more troublesome characteristics of bureaucracy is the confusion of ends and means. A bureaucracy is established to achieve specific goals (the education of children, for example). But the bureaucratic emphasis on regulations encourages bureaucrats to forget their goals and to focus on rules for their own sake. For example, you may find a school board or a state board of education creating rules and demanding procedures, the sole purpose of which is to promote the smooth running of the bureaucratic

---

[11] Recently a university president attempted to quiet student objections to the chaos of registration by giving a purely bureaucratic response. He explained that the confusion was not caused by the university's procedures but rather by the university's willingness to allow students to choose their courses. If students would be willing to give up that freedom, if they would submit to the university's determining their class schedules, all chaos would be eliminated from the system. The students were not amused by the president's suggestion, but they might have been chagrined had they realized that he was not kidding. Bureaucrats, sad to say, are seldom humorists.

[12] Hans Gerth and C. Wright Mills, eds., *From Max Weber* (New York: Oxford University Press, Inc., 1958), pp. 196–244. Available in paperback.

[13] Robert Merton, *Social Theory and Social Structure* (New York: The Free Press, 1957), pp. 195–206.

machinery of the educational system. (Teachers sometimes feel these agencies do little else.) A careful study might show that some of these rules and regulations have little if anything to do with teaching or learning. The necessities of a bureaucracy can overpower the human necessities the organization was built to serve. As the regulations multiply, the levels of administration proliferate, paperwork increases, and it becomes ever more difficult to see the human beings who inhabit the bureaucratic structure. There are inner-city schools where sick and malnourished children have been denied health care for six months and more (even when health programs were funded and available) because school officials are unable to get the "proper signatures" on the needed forms to guide the paperwork through the "proper channels."

IMPERSONALITY.   The power of a status position resides in the position itself and not in the person who holds it. Thus the interaction of people in bureaucratic settings may not be a person-to-person exchange so much as it is a status-to-status confrontation. Each status occupant is aware of how the bureaucratic relationship impinges on the exchange. Each has different jobs and different amounts of power. Status occupants do not treat each other as unique individuals, for individual uniqueness is replaced by the standardization of status. What sociologists call the *primary relationships* of everyday life (where you are treated as a unique being) give way to the *secondary relationships* of formal organizations (where you are treated as a mere functionary). Secondary relationships are impersonal and increase the possibility of alienation (see Chapter 2). If bureaucratic interaction begins to dominate people's lives (if they cannot find primary relationships in the private sphere), they begin to feel the loss of meaningful connections with others. Alienation begins to take its toll.

To what degree is bureaucratic impersonality a characteristic of American schooling? This is a topic we will explore at some length in coming chapters. For now, suffice it to say that children's entry into school life is often their first experience at having a status assignment within a formal organization. In the school, children first experience written rules, formal procedures, inflexible scheduling, and, in extreme cases, treatment as a mere number. It has been claimed that schools are the nation's training ground for impersonality. Durkheim wrote directly to this point:

> Now, the class is a small society. It is therefore both natural and necessary that it have its own morality corresponding to its size, the character of its elements, and its function. . . . The individuals—teachers and students—who make it up are not brought together by personal feelings or preferences but for altogether general and abstract reasons, that is to say, because of the social function to be performed by the teacher, and the immature mental condition of the students. . . . The rule of the classroom cannot bend or give with the same flexibility as that of the family in all kinds and combinations of circumstances. It cannot accommodate itself to given temperaments. There is already something colder and more impersonal about the obligations imposed by the school. [Students] are now concerned with reason and less with feelings.[14]

Durkheim was not bothered by the cool impersonality of the school and would be less troubled than Rogers or Dewey about the formality it creates in the lives

---

[14] Emile Durkheim, *Moral Education*, trans. Everett K. Wilson (New York: The Free Press, 1973), pp. 148–149. Available in paperback.

of teachers and students. Today, many teachers and students find the impersonality of bureaucracy in conflict with their values and aims of education. We will return to this topic.

THE BUREAUCRATIC MENTALITY.   As we have learned, the roles people play affect both their external behavior and their internal beliefs and values. As David Riesman has pointed out, human beings tend to believe their own propaganda. It should not be surprising, then, that bureaucracies encourage the development of a personality peculiarly suited for work in bureaucratic settings. Perhaps the most fundamental attribute of the bureaucratic mentality is its acquiescence to authority. Successful bureaucrats are first and foremost interested in security—the security of the institution and their status within it. Bureaucrats enjoy the stability and rational predictability of the bureaucratic organization. They are not amused or excited by surprise and spontaneity. Bureaucrats are quite comfortable within the hierarchical chain of command of formal organizations. They do not usually challenge the authority of those above them and do not countenance those below them making waves. They accept supervision from above and expect their underlings to do the same.

An example of how this mentality pervades schools is found in a recent unpublished survey of Florida's sixth- through twelfth-grade teachers. Respondents were asked to record their degree of agreement or disagreement with each of these statements:

> Administrators are paid to make policy decisions. While teachers should be able to discuss these decisions, in the end they should abide by the administrator's directives.

> Teachers are paid to run classrooms. While students should be able to discuss issues with the teacher, in the end they should abide by the teacher's directives.

Seventy-eight percent of the teachers agreed with the first statement, and 84 percent agreed with the second. It would seem that teachers are quite comfortable with the hierarchical chain of command bureaucratic systems provide.

Hierarchical authority could make the position of bureaucrats insecure if the decision-making power of the higher-ups was unlimited. However, bureaucracies have carefully prescribed rules that define (and thus limit) the power of higher officials. For example, the tenure system frees teachers from concern over arbitrary firing. Contrary to public opinion, tenure is not a lifelong guarantee of employment, but it does guarantee that a teacher can only be fired for just cause (incompetence, dereliction of duty, unprofessional conduct, and so on).

The Positive Side of Bureaucracy

It is popular to criticize schools for their bureaucratic procedures. Telling commentaries by Jonathan Kozol *(Death at an Early Age)*, Paul Goodman *(Growing Up Absurd)*, Edgar Friedenberg *(Coming of Age in America)*, and Charles Silberman *(Crisis in the Classroom)* accuse schools of stifling creativity, destroying the spontaneous and critical capacities of the young, enforcing mindless conformity, attacking self-respect, perpetuating social inequality, and promoting other deadly sins. Are these accusations justified? The fact that they strike a responsive chord in a wide audience of readers, especially young readers who have recently undergone the school experience, suggests that there is some truth in what they are saying, but there are a few problems implicit in these accusations that should be noted.

First, the accusations are often descriptive rather than analytical. Critics tend to discuss what "evil" teachers do without first trying to understand the causes of their behavior. Readers come away with the impression that the essential problems in American education are to be found in the flawed personalities of specific teachers and administrators. This oversimplification is particularly treacherous for students training to be teachers. If they come to believe that all the problems in education are personality problems, and if they fail to see how the structural arrangements of the school help create these problems, then they are left with little understanding of how the system works and no tools for making it better.

Second, it is an oversimplification to suggest that bureaucracy has had only negative consequences in education. Ronald Corwin, a sociologist of education, has wisely pointed out that the massive growth of free public education in America would have been impossible without the organizational efficiency bureaucracy provides. Because the school system was separated from other government agencies, education was kept free from the patronage systems of corrupt government officials. The standardization of schools helped coordinate (if not homogenize) the diverse interests and values of a nation of immigrants. It also helped keep the cultural core open to renewal, yet protected it from disintegration during periods of unprecedented change.[15] Whatever criticism we might level at schooling, it has created a high rate of literacy and academic competence in America, and it has helped create a national expectation of increased competence. The bureaucratization of schooling played a part in these accomplishments.[16]

Third, while the standardized treatment of clients in bureaucratic organizations may cause impersonality, it also helps alleviate arbitrary or discriminatory prejudices from interfering with the education of poverty and minority students. The proliferation of record keeping may cause hardships for school officials (and may not always serve useful purposes), but it has on occasion helped government agencies to monitor funding policies, school population characteristics, and achievement data and to move against inequalities that might otherwise have gone unnoticed.

Fourth, although critics condemn the standardization of education, the general public seems concerned about too little regulation rather than too much. The Gallup poll on education continually shows that adults are concerned with a lack of discipline in schools more than almost any other problem in education.[17]

Fifth, there is diversity within any structure as large as the American school system. We have noted the vast similarities in American education, but we must not forget that not all teachers march to the bureaucratic drum. It is likely that

---

[15] Ronald Corwin, *Education in Crisis* (New York: John Wiley & Sons, Inc., 1974), pp. 1–13. Available in paperback.

[16] For a useful collection of materials dealing with the strengths of education in America, see Arthur Newman, *In Defense of the American Public School* (Cambridge: Schenkman Publishing Co., Inc., 1978). Available in paperback.

[17] Alec M. Gallup, "The 18th Annual Gallup Poll of the Public's Attitudes Toward the Public Schools," *Phi Delta Kappan*, Vol. 68 (September 1986), p. 44.

students will experience some diversity (though perhaps not a wide variety) of teaching styles and classroom arrangements before they leave public education.

Teacher Troubles and the Experience of Bureaucracy

Many of the problems of the teaching profession discussed in the last two chapters are traceable to the bureaucratization of American schools. As schools have grown larger, policy makers and administrators have become less accessible and teachers enjoy less control over the conditions of their work. Education policies are made in federal and state legislatures, in the courts, in state departments of education, and in downtown school board offices. The seats of power in education are far removed from classrooms where teachers do their work.[18] Top decision makers at every level of the system are protected by a small army of middle-management personnel, whose job it is to enforce rule compliance, protect the organization against internal and external criticism, and transmit the policies set by those above them to the employees who work below. This system often alienates teachers because it provides them with so little control over policies that affect the workplace.[19]

As bureaucracies grow, teachers have less voice in decisions, less contact with decision makers, more formal relationships with administrators, and less time with colleagues. In separate studies of American schools, Boyer, Goodlad, and Sizer found that teachers spend little time in the company of other adults and a lot of time on clerical and administrative chores seemingly unrelated to the education of their students.[20] Teachers increasingly feel that they are not serving students but the displaced goals of the bureaucracy: to keep the system orderly, to help it grow, and, above all else, to protect it from outside criticism. They find "the system" hard to comprehend and even harder to influence and reform. Many reify the bureaucracy and become convinced that they are individually and collectively powerless to instigate change. As one teacher explained,

> I think of myself as gutsy, as a scrapper. I'm willing to fight for what I believe in and I'm not scared of authority. But I don't know that my battles have done much good. It's like nailing Jell-O to the wall.

Alvin Gouldner, a sociologist who was particularly interested in how individuals cope in large institutions, said that bureaucracy is not designed to encourage participation or loyalty. Instead, bureaucracies are constructed to control the behavior of individuals who are assumed to be indifferent (and perhaps even resistant) to the goals of the institution.[21] Employee autonomy is limited because it is assumed that the freedom to work independently will result in

---

[18] Arthur Wise, *Legislated Learning: The Bureaucratization of the American Classroom* (Berkeley: University of California Press, 1979). Available in paperback.

[19] Rodman B. Webb and Patricia T. Ashton, "Teacher Motivation and the Conditions of Teaching: A Call for Ecological Reform," *Journal of Thought*, Vol. 21 (Summer 1986), pp. 43–60.

[20] Ernest L. Boyer, *High School: A Report on Secondary Education in America* (New York: Harper & Row, 1983), p. 158; available in paperback. John I. Goodlad, *A Place Called School: Prospects for the Future* (New York: McGraw-Hill Book Company, 1984), pp. 186–188; available in paperback. Theodore Sizer, *Horace's Compromise: The Dilemma of American High Schools* (Boston: Houghton-Mifflin Company, 1984), p. 92; available in paperback.

[21] Alvin Gouldner, *The Dialectics of Ideology and Technology: The Origins, Grammar, and Future of Ideology* (New York: The Seabury Press, 1976), p. 252.

employees working at cross purposes. Therefore, bureaucracies expend enormous resources in an effort to limit the parameters of choice available to their workers.

Limiting the choices of individuals, especially well-educated individuals, is difficult. First, there is the problem of figuring out exactly what behaviors should be mandated. Second, there is the problem of how to legitimate those behaviors and get employees to conform to the organization's rules and regulations. Both problems are solved by a growing reliance on technology. *Technology* was defined in Chapter 4 as the systematic application of scientific knowledge to practical tasks.

RELIANCE ON TECHNOLOGY.   To solve the first problem (figuring out what behaviors should be mandated), bureaucrats have increasingly relied on the advice of experts. For example, if a school system is under attack because students' reading scores are falling, policy makers may not involve teachers in the definition of the problem or the construction of its solution.[22] Instead, bureaucrats may consult experts who, in turn, will suggest a technological fix, say the adoption of a new reading series. What makes the new series attractive to the school system is not necessarily the content of its stories, but the tightly prescribed learning activities and teaching methods incorporated in the textbooks, workbooks, skillpacks, and teachers' guides. The series offers a technology of reading instruction, based, it is always claimed, on the very latest research.[23] The publisher's brochures promise that the technology is universally applicable (it will work for all students) and can be used effectively by every teacher in the system (it does not require special talents and is virtually foolproof).

The second problem (legitimacy and enforcement) also receives a technological fix. Rules governing employee behavior are justified by the claim that the new system is practical (it "works") and that it has been derived by "experts" from the latest scientific findings. Thus, the rules are depersonalized; they have not come from "know-nothing bureaucrats," but come from "all-knowing experts" who are thought to be more knowledgeable than either managers or employees. Everyone, therefore, is expected to recognize the legitimacy of the new policy and submit to it willingly. Just in case they do not, however, systems are constructed to check on employee compliance. Work schedules are prescribed, forms are to be filled out, employees are observed by supervisors, and the work of supervisors is double checked by district-level administrators and outside auditors.

In the case of our reading example, teachers may be trained to use the new technology by curriculum specialists in the school system and perhaps by representatives of the textbook publisher. In some cases, the teachers' manuals are so detailed that they make such training unnecessary. The manuals show teachers how to conduct a reading lesson, how to answer student questions, and how to administer tests and keep records. Administrators can monitor teacher compliance by reviewing the teachers' records to see that classes are proceeding at

---

[22] Sometimes teacher committees are set up to advise school officials on what course of action to take. Such committees may have real power or they may only rubber stamp the decisions made by the central administration.

[23] The research may be of value, but we are not dealing with that issue here. Instead, we are pointing out that those who sell technology give credibility to their product by claiming that it is based on "the latest" research.

the prescribed pace. One measure of our increasing reliance on technology in education is found in the growing complexity, not of textbooks themselves, but of the accompanying materials that spell out specific things to be done by both teachers and their supervisors. When technology dominates instruction, good teaching is defined as following prescribed procedures and keeping students busy, quiet, and compliant. Learning is measured by the scores students get on standardized tests.

DYSFUNCTIONAL TECHNOLOGY.   No one would argue against the efficacy of technology. Its appropriate application has improved the quality of human life enormously. However, the inappropriate or overzealous application of technology poses problems. Some difficulties are caused by the growing fusion of bureaucracy and technology in education.[24]

Technology is sometimes applied before there has been an adequate analysis of the problem to be solved. For example, let's assume that reading scores are declining in a school system and the administration, in consultation with experts, decides to adopt a new reading series to combat the problem. Within a year or two reading scores begin to climb in most schools. The technology appears to be "effective"[25] but, at one particularly troubled school, reading scores continue to go down. At this particular school, poor reading scores are merely a symptom of a much larger problem: The school itself is not a safe place for students or teachers, its educational aims are obscure, faculty and students are in perpetual conflict, discipline policies are unclear or unevenly administered, and pupils are bored and rebellious. The new reading program did nothing to restore the integrity of the institution. Indeed, because the new technology was administered with a heavy hand, it further alienated everyone in the school and diverted attention from pressing, systemic problems that plague the institution. Technology, no matter how attractive and powerful it may be, is ineffective when applied by the wrong people to the wrong problems. Such misapplications are likely when decision makers are far removed from the everyday workings of the institutions they run.

Another problem is that technological solutions are designed to cover typical problems. When atypical situations emerge, the technology may be ineffective or even counterproductive. For example, over the years, penicillin has cured gonorrhea. However, recent mutations of the disease actually produce an enzyme that attacks the drug and allows the disease to flourish.[26] The use of the typical remedy on the atypical case can have nasty results. Therefore, doctors must have the ability to diagnose these atypical cases and have leeway to adjust their treatment accordingly. Teachers confront similar problems.

Let us return to the example of the reading series. The new series may

---

[24] For a discussion of the fusion of technology and bureaucracy in education, see Charles A. Tesconi, Jr. and Van Cleve Morris, *The Anti-man Culture: Bureautechnocracy and the Schools* (Urbana: University of Illinois Press, 1972).

[25] Keep in mind that technologies carry their own definitions of effectiveness. An "effective" reading series is one that increases test scores, keeps students occupied and compliant, and that teachers find easy to use. There are other definitions of *effective*, however. For example, we might say that a reading program is effective only if students learn how to read and to love reading.

[26] Gerald I. Mandell, R. Gordon Douglas, and John E. Bennett, *Principles and Practice of Infectious Diseases*, 2d ed. (New York: John Wiley & Sons, 1985), p. 1198.

Reflective practitioners use experience to assess new problems, evaluate possible solutions, act, and evaluate the consequences of their actions.   (*Source:* National Education Association, Joe Di Dio.)

"work well" for average students in an average school, yet "work badly" for nonaverage pupils. Within any class there may be some advanced students who are bored by reading textbooks and anxious to tackle challenging novels. There may be a few others who are embarrassed to work in books their classmates have already read and now consider "easy." Both the high-achieving and low-achieving students may feel trapped in the narrow confines of the reading series. The teacher must recognize that the reading series is inappropriate for these few students and find other methods and materials for teaching them. Such teachers are what Donald Schön calls *reflective practitioners.*[27]

Reflective practitioners are professionals who use their expertise to carefully assess the problem at hand, evaluate possible solutions, act, and finally assess the consequences of their actions.[28] The process of reflection in action is complex because it entails an ongoing conversation with the problematic situation. For example, when some students do not respond to a reading program their teacher must recognize the situation. The teacher may not know exactly what

[27] Donald A. Schön, *The Reflective Practitioner: How Professionals Think in Action* (New York: Basic Books, 1983).

[28] Ibid., pp. 49–69, 128–162. The processes of what Schön calls *reflection in action* are very close to Dewey's views on reflective thinking. See John Dewey, *How We Think: A Restatement of the Relation of Reflective Thinking to the Educative Process* (Lexington, MA: D. C. Heath, 1933).

is going on but understands that things are "in a mess." Out of this messy situation, the teacher must define a problem, something that makes sense of the mess and suggests a solution. Drawing on all relevant knowledge and experience, the teacher formulates a plan (What if I tried this?) and acts on the plan. Unfortunately, the situation does not hold still while the teacher works. It stays in flux and it talks back. Reflection in action demands that the teacher respond to the back-talk. The situation speaks and the teacher listens, assesses, adjusts, and acts again. Reflection in action is a process of detecting and correcting errors in the teacher's own performance.

Technology can be of great use to reflective practitioners. When technology is used experimentally and its effects are assessed continually, reflective practitioners can improve their efficiency and sharpen their analytical skills. Trouble does not come from technology itself but from allowing technology to replace a teacher's creative intelligence.

TECHNOLOGY AS A SUBSTITUTE FOR INTELLIGENCE.   Too often, technology is used as a substitute for creative intelligence. In the nineteenth century, when craftsmen came out from behind their workbenches and took positions on factory assembly lines, they found that their unique skills were no longer needed. All the skills necessary to manufacture a given product were built right into the factory's machinery.[29] As Frederick Taylor, a pioneer in "scientific management," said to a factory worker, you are "not supposed to think; there are other people paid for thinking around here."[30] The skills of artisans were not needed and before long those skills were lost for lack of use. Technology had "deskilled" its work force. Some argue that a similar situation is occurring in education today.[31] Arthur Wirth, a social philosopher at Washington University, contends that the fusion of technology and bureaucracy in education is making teachers into mere technicians and robbing them of their skills as reflective practitioners.

> Skills that used to be considered essential to the craft of teaching—such as curriculum deliberation and planning; and the design of teaching strategies for specific children based on personal, intimate knowledge—are no longer necessary. With the influx of pre-packaged materials, planning is done by people external to the situation.[32]

Teachers who merely execute a technology designed by others are unlikely to notice when that technology is misapplied and ineffective. Such teachers are not in conversation with the teaching situation. Just such a case is documented by Elizabeth Bondy in a study of reading instruction in a first-grade classroom.[33] The teacher, a dedicated and intelligent woman, was working in a school

[29] Harry Braverman, *Labor and Monopoly Capitalism* (New York: Monthly Review Press, 1974). Available in paperback.

[30] Raymond E. Callahan, *Education and the Cult of Efficiency* (Chicago: University of Chicago Press, 1962), p. 28. See also Judith A. Merkel, *Management and Ideology* (Berkeley: University of California Press, 1980).

[31] Michael Apple, "Cultural Form and the Logic of Technical Control," in *Culture and Economic Reproduction in Education,* ed. Michael Apple (London: Routledge & Kegan Paul, 1982), pp. 250–257. Available in paperback.

[32] Arthur G. Wirth, *Productive Work—In Industry and Schools: Becoming Persons Again* (Lanham, MD: University Press of America, 1983), pp. 127–128.

[33] Elizabeth Bondy, "First Graders' Socially Constructed Definitions of Reading" (Ph.D. dissertation, University of Florida, 1984).

system that had been using a tightly structured reading series for some time. The teacher worked hard to master the system and was pleased when her students passed the mastery tests printed in the teacher's manual.[34]

Most students were reading on grade level, but a few, the poorest readers in the class, fell further and further behind their classmates. For these students, reading time was unproductive and painful. The teacher dutifully applied the technology but, for particular students, the required exercises were meaningless. For example, the lowest reading group had daily drills on letters, words, and sentences. These exercises had little or no meaning for students who did not yet understand what reading was or what it was for. They only vaguely knew that symbols stood for sounds and that together sounds stood for words. Some did not understand where words began and ended or that sentences are read from left to right. There was nothing in the reading exercises that helped students comprehend these essential details and the teacher did not supply them. What students learned was how to "psych out" the unit tests so they could get a passing grade. If one looked only at the tests results, it would appear that all students were progressing nicely. In fact, some pupils were getting more and more confused and unsure of their own abilities. Reading held no adventure, told no stories, and gave no knowledge. For these students, reading became a source of pain rather than pleasure.

The teacher recognized that something was amiss. She privately called her lowest group the *fragile readers* and was troubled when their performance in the reading group was so much worse than their performance on tests. The system was not working, yet the teacher could not identify the problem. Instead of modifying or abandoning the reading system, she applied it more vigorously. She concentrated on material that was on the unit tests so that students would be sure to pass. As the year progressed, the "low group" came to define reading simply as recognizing specific sounds and words.

The teacher did not analyze why some children were doing badly or attempt to modify the system for her low-achieving students. These options did not occur to her, not because she was uncaring or unintelligent (she was neither) but because she was no longer a reflective practitioner. The blind use of technology had ended her conversation with the situation and rendered such conversations irrelevant.

BECOMING TECHNICIANS.   Michael Apple suggests that the process of deskilling is accompanied by another process that he calls *reskilling*.[35] Teachers do not simply lose the talents they once had (or should have had); old talents are replaced with new skills and new assumptions. Bondy's reading teacher lost whatever capacity she had for reflection when she became a dutiful technician. She followed prescriptions exactly, attacked problems mechanically rather than analytically, and was totally dependent on the technology of teaching offered by the reading series.

When it was pointed out that the program was not working for low-achieving students, the teacher eagerly agreed to try something new. She asked for

---

[34] In fact, the series provided so much practice in testlike exercises that it was rare that students failed a mastery test. However, there was a question on just what was being mastered. Some students mastered test taking to the point that they could pass mastery tests even though they had not mastered the rudiments of reading.

[35] Apple, "Cultural Form and the Logic of Technical Control," pp. 250–257.

another program and when one was suggested, she embraced it enthusiastically but, once again, applied it mechanically. The teacher had learned to think of teaching as an application of prepackaged methods, not as a creative process that demanded judgment.

Bureaucracy, Technology, and Teacher Alienation

Deskilling teachers has had both social and psychological consequences. On the social level, schools populated by deskilled teachers tend to be intellectually and creatively flat. They are not "centers of inquiry,"[36] where reflective practitioners together hammer out aims, produce curricula, design teaching strategies, evaluate the effectiveness of their activities, and make improvements. Wirth points out that an overreliance on technology has had a negative impact on social relations within the schools:

> To the extent that pre-packaged systems become the basic curricular form, . . . interaction among teachers about ideas for teaching is no longer necessary. [Teachers] become detached from each other and from the stuff of their work. Whether or not one approves of the results of such efforts, . . . it is clear . . . that technology has effects on social relations. Those effects typically are not considered in the calculations of [the designers or consumers of prepackaged instructional materials].[37]

As we saw in the Chapters 4 and 10, there is a vital and fragile connection between individuals and the institutions in which they practice their skills and express their ideals and potentials. Healthy institutions foster human development and nurture the psychological well-being of their members. When schools isolate teachers, they destroy the community of purpose necessary to sustain genuine idealism. Teachers lose, as Sizer has noted, "a sense of ownership" in their work.[38] As they follow the prescriptions of experts and the directives of administrators, teachers begin to see themselves not as reflective practitioners but as interchangeable hired hands. They become alienated from the school, from students and colleagues, from the motives that drew them to teaching, and from their own creative potentials.

Technology has been applied to schools in order to make them more efficient, but it has not always had that result. Since the mid-1960s, a long series of technological innovations has been introduced into the nation's classrooms. Teachers have dutifully used prepackaged curricula, televised and computerized instruction, behavior modification, and competency testing. They have conformed to the requirements of modular scheduling, behavioral objectives, nongraded classrooms, the integrated core curriculum, and much more. During this period of unprecedented technological innovation in education, the academic competence of students and teachers fell dramatically. Of course, many factors have contributed to this decline and we cannot blame falling test scores simply on the application of educational technology. But it is fair to say that an overreliance on technology has alienated teachers and made it more difficult for them to become reflective practitioners.

---

[36] Robert Schaefer, *The School as a Center of Inquiry* (New York: Harper & Row, 1967).
[37] Wirth, *Productive Work—In Industry and Schools*, p. 128.
[38] Sizer, *Horace's Compromise*, p. 184.

Sizer poses a question that is relevant here:

> One wonders how good a law firm would be if it were given manuals on how to apply the law, were told precisely how much time to spend on each case, were directed how to govern its internal affairs, and had no say whatever in who its partners were.[39]

Under these conditions we can be sure that law firms would become inefficient. Lawyers would become alienated from their ideals and from each other. They would lose the most precious skill of their profession, informed discretion. They would no longer be reflective practitioners.

The future of education in the United States will be determined not merely by the quality of teachers who enter the profession or the quality of the training they receive, though these factors are vitally important. It will also be determined by the degree to which the schools can nurture the ideals and intelligence of teachers and help them become reflective practitioners. Technology can play a positive role, for technology itself does not damage reflection in action, but the mindless reliance on technology does. We will end this chapter by analyzing current reform suggestions to see if they are likely to enhance or retard the creative intelligence of teachers.

Reform and the Future of the Education Profession

Since 1981, a plethora of reports have reviewed and analyzed the condition of education in America and suggested reforms for the future.[40] In addition, state legislatures have enacted, or are considering, a wide range of reforms aimed at improving the quality of education. Some of these reforms were discussed at the end of Chapter 8. Our purpose here will not be to review material already covered but to discuss the reform movement in the context of what has been said about technology and teachers as reflective practitioners. It appears that some reforms rely heavily on technology while others are designed to improve the workplace and the professional competence of teachers.

Minimum Competency Testing

The most obvious application of technology in recent years has been the increased reliance on testing. By 1984, thirty states were administering minimum competency tests to students in one or more grades. Many other states left such testing to the discretion of local school districts. Twenty-one states required that students pass a minimum competency exam in order to graduate from high school. Six require that pupils pass state mandated tests before advancing to certain grades.[41] The Education Commission of the States reports that sev-

---

[39] Ibid.

[40] A detailed examination of the recent reports on public education can be found in Chapter 23.

[41] Valena White Plisko and Joyce D. Stern, *The Conditions of Education, 1985* (Washington, DC: National Center for Educational Statistics, 1985), p. 68.

enteen states have instituted or are contemplating the use of minimum competency testing at the college level.[42]

The very existence of standardized test data invites comparisons among students, classes, schools, school districts, states, and nations. Everyone wants to know how one or another unit is doing in comparison to the rest. When test scores are released they are often accompanied by calls for improved performance. For example, in 1984, the President challenged states to dramatically improve their students' academic performance. Goals were set for every state and each year the Secretary of Education issues a chart reporting how well states are proceeding toward their assigned goals. Scholastic Aptitude Tests (SAT) and the American College Testing Program (ACT) exams have been used as a primary measure of student achievement in these national comparisons.

Does an increasing reliance on the technology of testing help teachers do their work or does it hinder the development of reflective practitioners? No simple answer can be given to such a question. If national tests provide reasonably accurate measures of student performance, they could allow students, teachers, schools, school districts, and states to see how they measure up against national norms. If correctly interpreted, the information could identify areas of strength and weakness and help educators and students make important educational decisions. The problem comes when tests do not measure what they purport to measure, when they encourage spurious comparisons, and when test results provide the sole measure of student performance.

Some argue that the data we receive from the SAT and ACT are flawed because the tests are poor measures of student aptitude or achievement. Ralph Nader has criticized the SAT tests for being expensive, inaccurate, and run by an organization that has a virtual monopoly in the entrance examination business. Others suggest that class rank and high school grades are better predictors of college success than are the most widely used college entrance exams. Not surprisingly, test manufacturers dispute these claims.

Tests are not simply vessels that scoop up information about student achievement; they are (or can become) political instruments. Consider the issue of testing teachers to be sure that they possess necessary knowledge about the subjects they teach. When states mandate such tests, lawmakers must carefully gauge the consequences of their actions. The states must assure their citizens that they have rigorous academic "standards," so the cut-off scores must be set high enough to weed out incompetent teachers. At the same time, however, standards must be low enough to ensure that the vast majority of teachers will pass; lawmakers cannot afford to create a teacher shortage. Similarly, when states produce minimum competency tests for students, the determination of cut-off scores becomes a sensitive political issue. Again, the test must be difficult enough to give the appearance of rigor but easy enough to ensure that only the most academically troubled students fail.

The good that can result from state testing is obvious enough. When teachers and students are held to a higher standard, we have bench marks against which to measure improvement—and improvement is likely to be forthcoming. Teachers of low-achieving students report that minimum competency requirements for graduation have encouraged many pupils to take schoolwork seriously. Because the tests come from the state and not from the teacher, teachers

---

[42] Reported in *Higher Education Advocate*, Vol. 3, No. 2 (June 16, 1986), pp. 3–4.

can present themselves as helpers, there to assist students, rather than as villains, there to guard the gate to graduation.

Testing, like any technology, can serve productive or unproductive ends. Often tests have results that were quite unintended. For example, when the most difficult requirement for high school graduation becomes passing a simple exam, minimum competency requirements have a way of becoming maximum expectations, at least for some students. Standardized tests can also function as de facto determiners of what is taught in schools. Teachers have little incentive to teach and students little incentive to learn material that is not "on the test."

Mortimer Adler, who has been calling for reform in education for more than half a century, is dismayed by current efforts to improve schools through testing. Adler is interested in producing students who can think critically and continue their own education after graduation. His most recent call for school reform is set out in a widely read book, *The Paideia Proposal*.[43] In his opinion, tests are a sorry substitute for good teaching and real learning:

> The scores that we applaud are the worst possible measures of the ability to [think and] carry on [one's own education]. If the legislatures of the states mandate that certain score standards be established, if they mandate that certain content be covered, we can't get along. Those are the worst enemies of the Paideia reform. Covering the ground is the worst thing you can do.[44]

Adler believes that when students are asked to "cover the ground" simply for the purpose of passing an exam, pupils do not stay with ideas long enough to understand them, enjoy them, appreciate them, add to them, or be transformed by them. Standardized tests divert attention away from the true aim of education, the development of the mind, and focus attention instead on the lesser goal of acquiring facts.[45] As Norman Frederiksen of Princeton University and the Educational Testing Service has observed,

> It is clear that tests influence education, and—partly because of the influence of contemporary achievement tests—the educational emphasis today is on facts. Educational practices might change considerably if the testing program were expanded to include tests that require more complex cognitive activities.[46]

---

[43] Mortimer Adler, *The Paideia Proposal* (New York: Macmillan Publishing Co., 1982).

[44] Comments made during an interview with William F. Buckley, Jr., on the program *Firing Line* (January 27, 1986) on the Public Broadcasting Network, "How Does It Go with Revising Our Teaching?" Transcript #687 (Columbia, SC: Southern Educational Communication Association, 1986), p. 16.

[45] Adler's argument is that "the pursuit of [information] is a trivial pursuit. Information can be used and misused. Most of it is useless. The information we lose we can regain by going to the reference books. A great deal of the knowledge we have, the knowledge of fact, is unaccompanied by understanding [and thus is easily forgotten]. One never forgets what one understands. Understanding differs from knowledge. It occurred to me recently that one never says, 'I know the idea of liberty, I know the idea of justice, I know the idea of God.' One says, 'I understand [these things].' Ideas and even ideals are objects of understanding, not knowledge." In Adler's view, tests that encourage teachers and students to acquire facts without understanding are miseducative and should be abandoned. Comments made during an interview with William F. Buckely, Jr., on the program *Firing Line*, taped in New York City, January 27, 1986, and telecast on the Public Broadcasting Network. "Continuing to Learn," Transcript #683 (Columbia, SC: Southern Educational Communication Association, 1986), pp. 5–6.

[46] *E. T. S. Developments*, Vol. 32, No. 1 (Summer 1986), p. 9. See also Norman Frederiksen and Richard Wagner eds., *Practical Intelligence: Nature and Origins of Competence in the Everyday World* (New York: Cambridge University Press, 1986).

The power of tests to dictate the curriculum becomes more acute when the pay and status of teachers are linked to their classes' performance on standardized achievement tests. Under these conditions teachers are encouraged to "teach to the test." This does not mean that the teacher gives students test answers, though this has been known to happen, but that the teacher presents only test-related information and students practice only the skills required for the exam.

Critics contend that the political nature of test data opens the way for corruption. When government officials spearhead educational reforms, there is a temptation to make tests easier or otherwise manipulate results so that scores will suggest that the government's programs have been effective. For example, officials in New York City were accused of manipulating the test scores of summer-school students in a remedial program. The students had failed a minimal competency exam and were required to go to summer school before being advanced to the next grade. According to Kathryn Borman and Joel Spring, the school system benefited when they initiated the testing program and again when they subverted it. "The system showed it had standards by requiring tests for promotion, and . . . it looked good by providing a remedial program that seemed to work."[47]

Observation Instruments

Another element in recent reform efforts has been the development of instruments designed to measure the effectiveness of teachers' classroom performance. One such instrument is a part of the *Florida Performance Measurement System* (FPMS), which itself is a component in Florida's Beginning Teacher Program, a yearlong internship program for new teachers. The FPMS has four parts:

1. A handbook that presents research findings about effective teaching. The findings are organized into six domains of teaching: planning, management of student conduct, lesson organization and development, presentation of subject matter, verbal and nonverbal communication, and testing.
2. Instruments designed to measure teacher performance in four of these six domains.
3. An interview and portfolio process designed to further document teacher competency.
4. Learning materials that can be used by teachers who need to improve their performance in any particular domain.

When teachers begin their first job in Florida, each is assigned to an assistance and evaluation team, consisting of a peer teacher, a building-level administrator, and another educator (usually another teacher, a curriculum coordinator from the school district, or a professor from a nearby university). Teachers are told about the legal requirements of the Beginning Teacher Program, the minimum essential competency they must demonstrate before certification, and the FPMS instruments used to measure that competency.

Early in the year all new teachers are observed by a member of their team

---

[47] Kathryn M. Borman and Joel Spring, *Schools in Central City: Structure and Process* (New York: Longman, 1984), p. 95. See also Wayne Barret, "The Politics of Flunking," *The Village Voice*, Vol. 37, No. 22 (June 1, 1982), pp. 1, 24–26, 38.

and their behaviors recorded on the Summative Observation Instrument (Figure 11-3). The findings of the observation are shared with individual teachers and specific areas are targeted for improvement. The team and the teacher together tailor a professional development plan and the teacher's progress is monitored over the year. Formative Evaluation Instruments are used to evaluate how the teacher is doing. A minimum of nine observations are made between September and May.

The observation instruments are an important component of Florida's Beginning Teacher Program. Experts reviewed quantitative studies of teaching and identified specific teaching "behaviors that have been shown through research to be associated with . . . desired student learning and/or conduct." Their final product, the Florida Performance Measurement System (FPMS), was judged by an outside review panel to be a "comprehensive attempt . . . to translate the body of knowledge [on teaching] into instructional practice."[48] Care was taken to measure only behaviors that could be identified easily and that were "universally applicable." The review panel wrote in its report on the program, "The underlying premise [of the system] is that there is a single set of teaching behaviors that constitute effective teaching over all subject areas and grade levels."[49] Many states are devising evaluation systems similar to Florida's.

The FPMS technology includes an array of enforcement mechanisms. The state requires that every new teacher achieve at least minimum proficiency in each of the six domains deemed essential to good teaching. Four of the domains are measured by the Systematic Observation Instrument and the other two by interviews and an examination of the teacher's portfolio.[50] Teachers with deficiencies are given materials to help them improve and are observed and helped during the year. Failure to meet minimum proficiency levels results in the denial of certification. Studies are being conducted to see if school districts and school administrators follow the procedures mandated by the state.

Do technological innovations like the Florida Performance Measurement System help new teachers become reflective practitioners? Empirical evidence is not yet available on this point, but some common-sense observations can be made. Proponents claim that the program is a vast improvement over past evaluation systems that failed to identify, assist, or weed out incompetent teachers or strengthen the abilities of those who are competent.[51] They claim that the behaviors required by the FPMS are supported by research and that they "make sense."

[48] Patricia Kay, Carolyn Evertson, and Harold Mitzel, "Review of the Florida Performance Measurement System," in *Teacher Evaluation Project: Report for 1984–1985* (Tallahassee, FL: Department of Education, 1985), p. 208.

[49] Ibid.

[50] A folder containing the teacher's lesson plans, project ideas, evaluations, students' products, and other material pertaining to teaching.

[51] A review of a random sample of evaluative instruments used in Florida prior to adoption of the Beginning Teacher Program showed that 35 percent of all items had to do with teachers' ability to "get along with others" or with "appearance." Ten percent were related to teacher compliance. Twenty percent had to do with the self-concept of teachers, their communication skills, and the climate of their classrooms. Only 35 percent had anything to do with the activities of teaching, and these items often lacked specificity. John Hansen, "Teacher Evaluation," speech given to the annual meeting of the Alachua County Chapter of Phi Delta Kappa, Gainesville, FL, November 18, 1982.

DOMAIN		Freq	Freq	Freq	
3.0 Instructional Organization and Development	1. Begins instructions promptly				Delays
	2. Handles materials in an orderly manner				Does not organize or handle materials systematically
	3. Orients students to classwork/maintains academic focus				Allows talk/activity unrelated to subject
	4. Conducts beginning/ending review			▒	
	5. Questions: academic comprehension/lesson development — single factual (Dotn. 5.0)				Poses multiple questions asked as one, unison response
	5. Questions: requires analysis/reasons				Poses nonacademic questions/nonacademic procedural questions
	6. Recognizes response/amplifies/gives corrective feedback				Ignores student or response/expresses sarcasam, disgust, harshness
	7. Gives specific academic praise				Uses general, nonspecific praise
	8. Provides for practice				Extends discourse, changes topic with no practice
	9. Gives directions/assigns/checks comprehension of homework, seatwork assignment/gives feedback				Gives inadequate directions/no|homework/no feedback
	10. Circulates, assists students				Remains at desk, circulates inadequately
4.0 Presentation of Subject Matter	11. Treats concept—definition/attributes/examples/nonexamples				Gives definition or examples only
	12. Discusses cause-effect/uses linking words/applies law or principle				Discusses either cause or effect only/uses no linking word(s)
	13. States and applies academic rule				Does not state or does not apply academic rule
	14. Develops criteria and evidence for value judgement				States value judgement with no criteria or evidence
5.0 Communication: Verbal and Nonverbal	15. Emphasizes important points			▒	
	16. Expresses enthusiasm verbally/challenges students				
	17.		▒		Uses vague/scrambled discourse
	18.				Uses loud-grating, high pitched, monotonic, inaudible talk
	19. Uses body behavior that shows interest—smiles, gestures				Frowns, deadpan or lethargic
2.0 Mgt. of Std. Conduct	20. Stops misconduct				Delays desist/doesn't stop misconduct/desists punitively
	21. Maintains instructional momentum				Loses momentum—fragments nonacademic directions, overdwells

Figure 11-3   Summative Observation Instrument.   (*Source:* Florida Department of Education, Tallahassee, Fl.)

Critics contend that the research findings were drawn largely from studies of student achievement in the early elementary school grades and should not be generalized to all populations. Nevertheless, it is difficult to form a convincing argument against teachers beginning their classes on time, presenting material in a clear and orderly manner, providing appropriate praise, developing criteria and evidence for value judgments, demonstrating interest in the subject matter, or correcting students' misbehavior. Teachers who are not doing these things are not just told to do better; their exact deficiency is identified, a rationale for the "better behavior" is explained, and a program of improvement is set out in the professional development plan. Even teachers who are doing a good job are encouraged to improve their skills.

One of the most interesting parts of the Beginning Teacher Program is the occasion it provides for new teachers to discuss their teaching with other professionals, who are there to help. The program is designed to assure that new teachers are not "set adrift" in the first year but are observed, evaluated, and given guidance. Beginning teachers are invited into a conversation about their own teaching situation. Other educators take part in that conversation and give new teachers guided practice doing reflection in action.

Early compliance studies suggest that the program is not working as planned. Researchers have found that "the team concept . . . is . . . not being implemented in many cases."[52] They report that observation of new teachers is made almost exclusively by administrators and that peer teachers are playing only a token role in the program. New teachers either have no professional development plan or did not take an active part in the development of their plan.[53] Recommendations have been made to correct these problems, but as of now, the Florida Beginning Teacher Program appears to be driven by the Summative Observation Instrument and the power of the instrument is not being mediated effectively by team cooperation.

As with any technology, the FPMS contains within it some potential for abuse. It would be a travesty if anyone thought that good teaching required nothing more than conformity to the twenty-one behaviors listed on the Summative Observation Instrument. The system takes no notice of what is being taught and too little notice of the quality of thought demonstrated by teachers and their students. Lists of desirable teaching behaviors always run the risk of trivializing the art of teaching. They encourage teachers to "do it right" (that is, to be efficient and do all the things listed on the instrument). They do not always encourage teachers to "do what's right" (that is, to be effective and think continually about what they are doing and why).

As Schön points out, reflection in action is not a process of checklist conformity; instead, it entails looking at situations from many different angles. If the FPMS opens a wide-ranging analytical conversation about what a teacher is doing, it performs a great service. If, however, the conversation is only between the new teacher and the principal and if the topic of the conversation is limited to the twenty-one classroom behaviors on the observation instrument, then the system may do more to encourage compliance than competence.

It must also be noted that the behaviors identified as desirable on the instru-

---

[52] Florida Coalition for the Development of a Performance Measurement System, *Teacher Evaluation Project*, pp. 44–45.
[53] Ibid., pp. 36–45.

ment are most appropriate when teachers are engaged in didactic instruction, that is, when they are lecturing. Such behaviors appear less often when teachers are leading discussions or seminars. Teachers who want to do well on the instrument must devote more time to didactic instruction and less to seminar discussions.

Didactic instruction is further encouraged when merit pay raises or promotions are determined by the score a teacher receives on the Summative Observation Instrument. The instrument was used in Florida's Merit Teacher Program, in some school districts for annual review of personnel, and by one district in its own teacher incentive program.[54]

In conclusion, technology always holds a potential for good and harm. The minute particulars of its application will determine the net benefit. There are some encouraging signs that the technological innovations just discussed may become part of larger reforms designed specifically to empower teachers and help them to become reflective practitioners.

Teacher Empowerment

In Chapter 10, we discussed democratizing the workplace as a way to empower teachers and combat isolation and alienation. Here we discuss empowerment in the context of current reform proposals. Goodlad's *A Place Called School* is a widely read, highly praised recent report on education. The book reports findings from an investigation of thirty-eight schools, over 1000 classrooms, 1350 teachers, and 17,000 students. Goodlad contends that America will not significantly upgrade the quality of education until schools become more pleasant and cooperative places in which to work.

Schools differ but, according to Goodlad, only in small and subtle ways. Yet, when small differences are added together, they can have a powerful cumulative effect. Some schools Goodlad studied were not in charge of their own destinies. The instruction was uninteresting, the school's leadership confused or complacent, decision-making procedures did not involve the faculty members, and the schools lacked methods for identifying and combating problems. Teachers in these schools were engaged in few professional activities and were generally less satisfied with their work.

Other schools (Goodlad called them *renewing schools*) maintained "a state of readiness" to identify problems and consider solutions. Such schools were gratifying places to work because they were perceived by teachers as effective and able to take care of business. Renewing schools had a positive atmosphere. Teachers participated in schoolwide decisions and enjoyed a community of purpose with their colleagues. The administration was supportive and provided the resources and assistance teachers needed to do their jobs. Teachers were generally more satisfied in these schools and more likely to participate in professional activities, such as taking graduate courses and professional training programs, joining professional organizations, and reading professional journals. Teachers and students gave these schools high marks for academic rigor and the quality and relevance of the curriculum.[55]

[54] B. Othanel Smith and Donovan Peterson, *Teacher Evaluation Project: Abstract of Report for 1984–1985* (Tallahassee: Florida Coalition for the Development of a Performance Measurement System, 1985), unnumbered pages.

[55] Goodlad, *A Place Called School*, pp. 246–270.

The atmosphere in renewing schools was conducive to teacher empowerment and professional development. The process of reflection in action was visible within the workings of the institution itself. Goodlad claims that true reform of education will not come from piecemeal changes but, rather, by changing the structure of schools so that they become self-renewing institutions and by empowering teachers so that they can become reflective (self-renewing) practitioners.

Goodlad is not alone in these ideas. In 1986, the Carnegie Forum on Education and the Economy released the report of its Task Force on Teaching as a Profession. The report calls for "transforming the environment of teaching." Like Goodlad, the task force calls for "restructuring schools to provide a professional environment for teachers, freeing them to decide how best to meet state and local goals for children while holding them accountable for student progress."[56]

The task force recommends that states and school districts create schools that allow teachers the "discretion and professional autonomy that are the hallmarks of professional work." Under the Carnegie plan, the bureaucratic regulation of school practices would be "greatly reduced." Teachers would participate in the formation of educational aims and would be held accountable for their achievement. A variety of approaches to school leadership would be employed in order to foster collegial decision making. In addition, the plan calls for substantial increases in teacher pay, a career ladder system to reward achievement and professional development, a rigorous program of undergraduate and graduate education, and the hiring of support staff (secretaries, for example) to help teachers complete clerical and other nonprofessional work.

Legislators and the public are unlikely to act on reform suggestions without assurances that teachers are indeed capable of performing the new responsibilities being asked of them. The Carnegie proposal answers this concern with a call for the national licensing of teachers. The task force pointed out that every true profession has a codified body of knowledge and expertise that anyone practicing the profession must understand. Those practicing a profession with the sanction of its members are called on to demonstrate their command of that knowledge base and their ability to apply it, usually on a national, regional, or statewide exam.[57]

The Carnegie proposal makes a distinction between licensure and certification. Licenses, in the language of the report, are issued by the state but certificates are issued by the profession. The language here is a bit confusing because the licensing process that allow teachers to practice their profession in a particular state is usually called certification. In any case, the Carnegie Task Force proposed that states continue their present licensing practices, thus ensuring that teachers meet minimum standards. Over and above state requirements, the task force suggested the teaching profession establish its own national board for professional standards. The board would establish standards of excellence and issue certificates to those who meet those standards. Two levels of certification were suggested: a teacher's certificate and an advanced teacher's certificate. The first would be an entry-level certificate and "the second would be an advanced standard, signifying the highest levels of compe-

[56] Task Force on Teaching as a Profession, *A Nation Prepared: Teachers for the 21st Century* (New York: Carnegie Forum on Education and the Economy, 1986), p. 55. Available in paperback.
[57] Ibid., p. 65

tence as a teacher and possession of the qualities needed for leadership in the schools."[58] A majority of the board's membership would be elected by board-certified teachers. Other members would come from government officials, the public, and school administrators.

The Carnegie task force emphasized the need to set high standards and for standards of practice to be established by the profession itself. "The Board would judge the quality of candidates' general education, their mastery of the subjects they will teach, their knowledge of good teaching practices in general and their mastery of the techniques required to teach specific subjects."[59] The certification process would be voluntary but the report suggests that states should reward teachers who have been certified by the profession.

Here again we see a reliance on the technology of testing, yet this time with a difference. The Carnegie task force suggests testing not as a means of tightening bureaucratic controls over teachers, but as an instrument for loosening those controls. The debate over whether the Carnegie plan is feasible will continue for some time. The fact that board exams have worked well in law and medicine greatly enhances the Carnegie case.

Summary

This chapter provided a number of tools (terms and concepts) that will be of use in the upcoming analysis of the school as a social system. The terms *institution, status, status set, role,* and *role set* were defined with special reference to educational institutions. We not only discussed what these terms mean, but we investigated the function of each within the social system of the school.

Two approaches were presented for studying institutions, the subjectivist and the objectivist modes of analysis. Because each model has its strong points and limitations, both models will be used in upcoming chapters.

The rapid growth of the educational system and of school size has made the governace of education increasingly bureaucratic. Therefore, the characteristics of *bureaucracy* were reviewed and its functions and dysfunctions discussed. In the next chapter, we will look more specifically at bureaucracy in education in America.

There has been a dramatic increase in the size of schools and school districts since the turn of the century. As the size of schools has increased, more administrators have entered the system, and the administrator to teacher ratio is now smaller than the teacher to student ratio in the average class. The cost of administering the school bureaucracy has also grown. The growth of school bureaucracy has limited the autonomy and increased the distance between teachers and the makers of educational decisions. Teacher isolation and alienation have become major impediments to school improvement.

Gouldner pointed out that bureaucratic institutions typically limit the decision-making options of employees. Enormous resources in time and money are expended in an effort to scientifically determine the most efficient patterns of employee behavior, to train employees to conform to those patterns, and, when possible, to convince employees that the patterns make sense and are worth

[58] Ibid., p. 66.
[59] Ibid.

following. These tasks are accomplished through the wedding of bureaucracy and technology.

Technology is the systematic application of scientific knowledge to practical tasks. Technological solutions are usually claimed to be universally applicable. All contingencies are planned for and employees are expected to follow the prescriptions laid down by experts. Systems of enforcement are constructed to measure the level of employee compliance.

Technology is often enormously effective. Sometimes, however, it has caused more problems than it has solved. For example, technologies are sometimes applied to problems they were not designed to solve. Technologies never antic-ipate all possible contingencies. Thus, problems are likely to result when tech-nologies are applied rigidly to atypical situations.

Technologies are most effective when used to manufacture goods and some-what less effective when used by professionals who work with people. Schön's study shows that effective professionals do not simply follow a list of rules or apply preestablished procedures. Of course, competent professionals must be aware of these rules and accepted procedures and follow them closely when appropriate. However, professionals must remain in constant conversation with the situation before them. They must know when to apply typical procedures and when to deviate from those procedures. Schön calls this process of constant analysis *reflection in action*. Rigidly applied technologies disrupt reflection in ac-tion. They "deskill" professionals, make them less efficient, and make their professional lives less satisfying. Deskilled professionals do the work of techni-cians, and the institutions they inhabit resemble factories where isolated work-ers follow prescribed routines. They are not self-renewing centers of inquiry and they seldom nurture the potential of the people who work in them.

Current reform movements in education appear to be moving in two quite different directions. Legislated reforms are making increased use of the tech-nology of testing and systematic observation instruments. Reforms suggested by the Carnegie Forum on Education and the Economy and the research of John Goodlad support the empowerment of teachers through restructuring school governance. Other reports that deal with these issues will be discussed in Chapter 23.

National testing offers teachers data that can be useful for assessing achieve-ment and setting priorities. Critics point out that tests have the potential to become political instruments and may be misused. Others contend that the content of tests sometimes determines the curricula of schools and fosters teaching practices that encourage the accumulation of information rather than under-standing. Tests are likely to influence what and how teachers teach, when stu-dents' grades influence the reputation and pay of their teachers.

Observation instruments are a technological innovation made possible by a growing research literature that correlates specific teacher behaviors with stu-dent achievement. An example of this technology is Florida's Summative Ob-servation Instrument, which lists desirable and undesirable teaching behaviors that are said to apply in all teaching situations. Teachers must demonstrate that they understand and can apply these behaviors before they are certified to teach in the state.

The Florida Performance Measurement System fits all the requirements of technology. It is a practical application of research findings. It prescribes exact behaviors and includes mechanisms for their enforcement. It aims to change teachers' behavior and, not incidentally, influence the curriculum presented in colleges of education. Interesting elements have been built into the system to encourage teachers to discuss their teaching with other professionals and to discourage an overreliance on observation instruments. As yet, these safeguards do not appear to be working. Critics claim that a heavy reliance on the Summative Observation Instrument may encourage teachers to focus exclusively on didactic instruction and may discourage seminars designed to develop the critical thinking skills of students. Whether the Florida Beginning Teacher Program avoids the pitfalls of technology will depend on how alert administrators and teachers are to such problems and how willing they are to avert them.

Schools that are most likely to use technology well are those that are open to self-evaluation and renewal and have a faculty of reflective practitioners. Goodlad suggests that schools can be made more productive and satisfying if teachers are empowered to use their talents and creative potentials. A plan for implementing such changes is set forth by the Carnegie Forum on Education and the Economy. The Carnegie plan is to restructure schools by increasing teacher responsibility and autonomy. It proposes the creation of a national board for professional standards that would administer a certification program. The aim of the program is to ensure that teachers have a firm grasp of professional knowledge and the ability to apply that knowledge with informed discretion. Here again, we see a reliance on technology, but this time as a mechanism for loosening bureaucratic controls and for democratizing the workplace.

Suggested Readings

One of the most ubiquitous factors of modern life is the predominance of bureaucracy. The patterns that it imposes on thought and behavior seem obvious to us all. Yet, with careful study, we come to realize that there is more to bureaucracy than first meets the eye.

AIKEN, MICHAEL, and JERALD HAGE. *Social Change in Complex Organizations.* New York: Random House, Inc., 1970. The book deals with the question of institutional change and how bureaucratic decision-making processes can be utilized to introduce and carry out social innovation.

BENNIS, WARREN, ed. *American Bureaucracy.* New Brunswick, NJ: Transaction Books, 1970. This edited volume discusses the tendency of bureaucracies to become static and inflexible and the need for innovation.

GERTH, HANS, and C. WRIGHT MILLS, eds. *From Max Weber: Essays in Sociology.* New York: Oxford University Press, 1958. For good or ill, Weber's theory of bureaucracy still permeates the sociological study of formal organizations.

GOULDNER, ALVIN. *The Dialectics of Ideology and Technology: The Origins, Grammar, and Future of Ideology.* New York: The Seabury Press, 1976. This difficult book examines, among other things, the assumptions of bureaucratic consciousness.

The bureaucratization of education is discussed in the following works:

ANDERSON, JAMES G. *Bureaucracy in Education.* Baltimore: Johns Hopkins University Press, 1968. The author contends that bureaucratization is most structured and stringent in schools that serve students of low socioeconomic status and that are populated by teachers of lesser competence.

APPLE, MICHAEL, ed. *Cultural and Economic Reproduction in Education.* London: Routledge & Kegan Paul, 1982. This set of essays examines schooling from the perspective of critical theory.

BANKS, OLIVER. *The Sociology of Education*. New York: Schocken Books, 1976. This British-oriented text makes the case that schools are not as bureaucratized as is popularly thought.

BORMAN, KATHRYN M., and JOEL SPRING. *Schools in Central City: Structure and Process*. New York: Longman, 1984.

CALLAHAN, RAYMOND E. *Education and the Cult of Efficiency*. Chicago: University of Chicago Press, 1962. This is a classic study of how schools became susceptible to industry's efficiency experts at the turn of the twentieth century.

FEINBERG, WALTER, and HARRY ROSEMONT, eds. *Work, Technology and Education: Dissenting Essays in the Intellectual Foundations of American Education*. Urbana: University of Illinois Press, 1975. This collection of original essays is critical of the bureaucratization of education and much more.

KATZ, MICHAEL B. *Class, Bureaucracy and Schools*. New York: Praeger Publishers, 1975. One of the best revisionist historians analyzes the growth of bureaucracy in public education.

MACMILLAN, C. J. B., and SHIRLEY PENDLEBURY. "The Florida Performance Measurement System: A Consideration," *Teachers College Record*, Vol. 87 (Fall 1985), pp. 67–73. This article is an analysis of the presuppositions that undergird the FPMS and an excellent example of how philosophical analysis can inform policy decisions.

MOELLER, GERALD H. "Bureaucracy and Teachers' Sense of Power." *School Review*, Vol. 72 (Summer 1964), pp. 137–157. This is an early article arguing that bureaucracy provides teachers with an understandable and predictive ethos in which to pursue their profession. The predictability that bureaucracy provides, according to this author's research, heightens a teacher's sense of power and control.

RAVITCH, DIANE. *The Revisionists Revised: A Critique of the Radical Attack on the Schools*. New York: Basic Books, Inc., 1978. This is a convincing rebuttal to revisionist historians.

TESCONI, CHARLES A., and VAN CLEVE MORRIS. *The Anti-Man Culture: Bureautechnocracy and the Schools*. Urbana: University of Illinois Press, 1972. The book focuses on the public school system and its relationship to other segments of society. It seeks ways to counteract the dehumanizing effects of the bureaucratization of schooling and is an imaginative analysis, drawing on rich source material.

WISE, ARTHUR. *Legislated Learning: The Bureaucratization of the American Classroom*. Berkeley: University of California Press, 1979. This is an important study of how legislatures affect what goes on in the nation's classrooms.

Reform suggestions for lessening the negative effects of bureaucracy are discussed in the following reports:

GOODLAD, JOHN I. *A Place Called School: Prospects for the Future*. New York: McGraw-Hill Book Company, 1984. This is an examination of what public schools are in the United States and how they can be made better.

LIPSKY, MICHAEL. *Street-Level Bureaucracy: Dilemmas of the Individual in Public Service*. New York: Russell Sage Foundation, 1980. This award-winning book details the dilemmas facing individuals working in human service bureaucracies—schools, courts, welfare agencies—as they work with the public. This book is rich, provocative, well written, illuminating, and important.

SCHÖN, DONALD A. *The Reflective Practitioner: How Professionals Think in Action*. New York: Basic Books, Inc., 1983. This book does not address the work of teachers directly, but it has important things to say about how competent professionals go about their work.

SIZER, THEODORE. *Horace's Compromise: The Dilemma of American High Schools.* Boston: Houghton-Mifflin Company, 1984. This is a sympathetic look at how the school system encourages teachers to make compromises that diminish their effectiveness.

TASK FORCE ON TEACHING AS A PROFESSION. *A Nation Prepared: Teachers for the 21st Century.* New York: Carnegie Forum on Education and the Economy, 1986. This is an ambitious call for greater participation by teachers in the management of schools. It promises to create more change in schooling than any other single report issued in the 1980s.

WIRTH, ARTHUR G. *Productive Work—In Industry and Schools: Becoming Persons Again.* Lanham, MD: University Press of America, 1983. This is a particularly useful discussion of the nature and philosophical basis for democratic workplaces.

CHAPTER 12

Schools as Total Institutions

Introduction

The previous chapter reviewed the characteristics of institutions and a special kind of institution called *bureaucracy*. In this chapter we will go one step further and discuss a special kind of bureaucracy, what Erving Goffman has called the *total institution*.

Goffman arrived at his conception of the total institution when he was investigating, of all things, an insane asylum. He became convinced that what he discovered in the structure of the mental hospital had broad applicability to the study of other similarly organized bureaucracies. Indeed, Goffman was correct, for his discoveries are quite useful in helping us understand how schools operate.

In this chapter, the characteristics of total institutions will be examined. We will use an objectivist rather than a subjectivist perspective. Our focus for now will be on the structure of total institutions and not on how people respond to the structure. We will see to what degree schools fit Goffman's model of the total institution. Once the degree of fit has been established (and we must say in advance that it is by no means perfect), we can better understand the day-to-day things that go on in schools. Some taken-for-granted school activities will assume new significance. Once we form an understanding of what schools do, we will be in a better position to judge if the typical organization of schooling in America promotes or hinders the aims we set for education in Chapter 8.

Characteristics of Total Institutions

What are the characteristics of a total institution? Goffman discovered many, but here we will examine only six of his more important findings. As you read these characteristics, ask yourself to what extent they are typical of public schools in America.

1. *A Formally Administered Round of Life*. The total institution, according to Goffman, is a "place of residence and work where a large number of like-

situated individuals, cut off from the wider society for an appreciable period of time, together lead an enclosed, formally administered round of life."[1] Goffman goes on to say that all aspects of life in a total institution transpire in a single place and under the direction of a single authority. Activities are carried on in groups, and all individuals are treated alike and conform to the same scheduling. Prisons, asylums, and the military are quintessential examples of total institutions.

2. *Coercive Rule Structures.* The rules governing everyday life outside institutions are severely modified within the walls of the total institution, and rights that are taken for granted in the outside world often become privileges here. Prisoners who once decided for themselves when they would eat or go to the rest room find these activities restricted to specific times inside the jail. Deviation from the schedule, if allowed at all, requires the permission of the staff.

3. *Involuntary Membership.* Neither the client nor the staff has much choice as to who attends the total institution. Clients do not choose whether they will go to the institution, and the staff has no say in whether clients will be accepted. For example, the guards of the prison do not choose who will go to jail (that is the duty of the courts), and presumably the prisoners do not choose to spend time behind bars. (Prison escapes are a frequent phenomenon, but we have yet to hear of someone breaking into prison.)

In total institutions, clients have no choice but to attend, and staff have no say in whom they will serve. (*Source:* National Education Association, Joe Di Dio.)

[1] Erving Goffman, *Asylums* (New York: Doubleday & Co., Inc., 1961), p. xiii. Available in paperback.

4. *Externally Defined Roles.* The purpose of total institutions is defined by external agencies and is not determined solely by the institution's staff. Officially, state governments decide (or if you like, the public ultimately decides) whether prisons will have a punitive or a rehabilitative function. True, prison officials sometimes attempt to subvert the official definitions of their function, but when they do so, they are overstepping their authority.

5. *External Support.* Total institutions are not supported by client fees but rather by outside sources of revenue—usually taxes.

6. *Expert Servicing.* Total institutions are united in their effort to make some change in the character and behavior of their clients and are arranged to accomplish this end efficiently. It must be noted that the staff and public assume that behavior changes are in the best interests of society and the client. Insane asylums are supposed to make people sane, prisons are supposed to make them honest, and the army is supposed to build raw recruits into an efficient fighting force.

Schools as Total Institutions

To what extent do schools fit the ideal model of the total institution? Clearly the fit is not exact. The first characteristic discussed (a formally administered round of life) suggests that total institutions monitor a client's life around the clock. This is not the case in public schools, which demand attendance for only six hours a day, 5 days a week, and 180 days a year. Students spend most of their lives outside of school.

Another difference between the school and the total institution is even more significant. Schools typically serve the young, whereas inmates in total institutions are usually adults. What may be a humiliating experience for an adult (asking for permission to urinate, for example) may be a normal and untroublesome aspect of a child's life. For this reason, the characteristics of a total institution may have more significance at the high school level than at the elementary school level.

These differences between the total institution and the school, however, do not mean that we need to discard Goffman's model. In a number of areas, the correspondence between the characteristics of total institutions and schools is more exact. For example, within schools, students are typically managed in large groups. They are segregated by age and often by ability, attitude, behavior, and even by social class. The activities of students are enclosed within school walls and formally administered by institution officials. There is a tendency to treat all students alike, which, for school officials, is synonymous with saying that students are treated "fairly." Time is tightly scheduled and punctuated by official signals. ("Don't leave the room until you have been dismissed." "Stay at your desk until the bell rings.") And no matter how democratic the classroom, a part of a teacher's job is to guard the exits.[2]

Schools, like other total institutions, have their own set of rules that are different from the rules governing the outside world. For example, the rights of a student's home world may be the privileges of his or her school world. Students who are used to deciding for themselves when they will speak, go to the

---

[2] Philip W. Jackson, *Life in Classrooms* (New York: Holt, Rinehart and Winston, 1968), p. 31.

rest room, read a book, or walk around may have to ask permission to do these things when inside the school. (See the discussion of a total institution's coercive rule structures.)

There are other similarities between schools and total institutions. Students do not usually have a choice about attending school, may not be able to choose among schools, and very probably cannot choose among teachers within a school. Similarly, teachers do not have much say about who will be in their class. At most, a teacher can appeal to the school principal, "Look, I've had hell raisers for the last two years, and it's my turn to get some high achievers." In some school systems, especially large ones, teachers are subject to involuntary transfers from one school to another. (See the discussion of a total institution's involuntary membership.)

Functions of schooling are not decided solely by educators. If the public feels that schools have been concentrating too heavily on character building and too lightly on the three Rs, they may call for a move "back to basics." State agencies may establish standardized testing programs to monitor how well schools are accomplishing the back-to-basics objectives. (See the discussion of a total institution's externally defined roles.)

Schools receive external support. This gives outside agencies and the public greater power over what goes on in schools. If funds are provided for sex education, values clarification, peer-counseling programs, drug education, family-living classes, and the like, schools will expand their aims and add programs. If funds are not available for these purposes, schools will narrow their aims and cut their offerings. (See the discussion of a total institution's external support.)

Schools present themselves as rational organizations designed to effect desirable changes in the young. The organization of the school and the training of the staff are designed to maximize the likelihood of such change. Teachers are expected to facilitate learning in their students, to guide them toward good citizenship, and to prepare them for adult life. (See the discussion of a total institution's expert servicing.)

Client and Staff Behavior in Total Institutions

Goffman suggests that the organizational structure of total institutions (and the official ideology that undergirds this structure) significantly affects the behavior of the institution's inhabitants. In all institutions that share the characteristics we have discussed, we can expect to find certain predictable patterns of behavior. Goffman gives a thorough accounting of these behaviors, but space does not allow their full elaboration here. A few of the more interesting patterns will be discussed, however, so that you can determine if they coincide with what typically goes on in schools. As you study these patterns, check them against your knowledge of school life. Keep in mind that our effort is to understand how schools operate. At this point, we are not judging whether it is desirable for schools to be organized as they are or if the organization fosters learning. We will examine this question in Chapter 15.

Client–Staff Friction

Total institutions foster a split between the clients (usually a large group) and the staff (a relatively small group). There are many reasons for this friction. First, the staff is seen as expert, but the clients are defined as ignorant. According to the ideology of the total institution, the staff's expert status gives it the right (even the duty) to interpret the needs of clients. It is assumed that the staff can determine these needs more accurately than the clients themselves. Teachers frequently make such evaluations of students: "Tommy really isn't ready for the next book, although he certainly thinks he is." "Betty displays a disturbing lack of attention. Therefore, I have separated her from her friends and have her sitting where there are fewer distractions." "Larry acts tough, but this is all bluster. What he needs is someone to call his bluff."

A second reason for the client–staff split comes from their differing and often conflicting desires and goals. Teachers and students frequently define the school experience in different ways. What the teacher defines as educational, challenging, and useful, students may see as irrelevant and dull. What teachers define as constructive criticism students may see as ugly carping. A punishment the teacher believes to be fair and useful may be seen by students as unjust and spiteful. In all cases, however, the balance of institutional power resides with the teacher.

Stereotyping

The conflict between clients and staff encourages each group to think of the other in narrow, stereotypical terms. The staff is likely to define clients in groups, according to how difficult or easy the client makes the job of the staff member. The teacher may call a student a slow learner (meaning hard to teach), hyperactive (meaning hard to control), a good kid (meaning willing to follow the teacher's rules). Similarly, students stereotype teachers into groups according to how strict they are, how much work they assign, and how closely they adhere to the official role behavior of the teaching status.

Surveillance

Clients in total institutions are kept under the watchful eye of the staff at all times. There are many reasons for this surveillance. It ensures that the clients stay on task and can get staff help when they need it. It makes it less likely that clients will "get into trouble." These are the manifest functions of surveillance, but there are latent functions as well. Surveillance carries with it the message that clients are not to be trusted, that they are incapable of self-direction, and that if left to their own devices, they will raise havoc with the institution. When clients accept surveillance without resistance—when they come to take it for granted—they simultaneously accept these assumptions about their character and ability.

Surveillance is a dominant part of school life. Students must be accounted for at all times. Attendance is taken at the start of the day and repeatedly when students switch classes. There are few places in the school where students are not in the direct view of teachers. Some schools have no doors on rest room stalls. But not all schools are equally concerned about surveillance. Some high schools, for example, allow seniors to leave school grounds during their free periods.

Invasion of Selfhood: Violating the Informational Reserve

The avowed goal of total institutions is to serve the best interests of their clients. In order to do this efficiently, total institutions gather large quantities of information about their clients from a number of different sources. The staff has an appetite for information that is never fully satisfied. In schools, information is gathered from parents, counselors, test results, previous teachers, and from students themselves. Occasionally it is gathered from doctors, psychiatrists, the police, social workers, and other sources outside the school. Facts about a student's social status, past behavior (especially bad behavior), mental difficulties, family stresses, personality characteristics, and more are collected in records or filed in the memory of teachers. Information that might be private or privileged in other settings becomes open to the staff of total institutions. Significantly, clients do not have access to similar information about the staff.

Invasions of selfhood are not limited to bureaucratic fact gathering and record keeping. A student's privacy may be invaded in classroom settings. Let us look at one admittedly extreme, though unfortunately true, example. An elementary school teacher was told by the building custodian that a child had defecated in his pants and had left his underwear beside a toilet in the boys' room. By checking the restroom schedule, the custodian figured out what classroom the child was in but did not know which student had committed the "offense." The teacher asked the offending student to admit what he had done. Because no admission was forthcoming, the teacher marched all the boys into the rest room and asked them to lower their pants. The "guilty" child would be the boy without underwear. At this point, a student admitted to the incident and was sent to the office. Much might be said of this sad incident, but what is relevant here is that the teacher felt he had the right to invade the privacy of his students in order to "teach an important hygiene lesson" and to see "if the offending child had a health problem."

Obedience Systems

All institutions have rules, and total institutions are no exception, but the rules of the total institution enforce behavior that clients often resent. The staffs of total institutions have a two-pronged reaction to client resistance. On the one hand, they expect it and may even understand it. On the other hand, they are most satisfied when client resistance gives way to acceptance and enthusiasm. The goal of every teacher is to turn students around, guide them out of sullen defiance, and give them a love for school and learning. A total institution has done its work when clients stop viewing the system as a negative, coercive force and start seeing it as a "great opportunity."

There are many kinds of punishments total institutions can wield to discourage rule breaking and challenges to authority. Most punishments further restrict the rights ("privileges") of the client. The denial of rights is punishment in itself, but it is made more severe because it is public. For example, a student may be denied the right to sit with friends. When the teacher administers the punishment, the student must ceremonially move his desk. Its new position near the teacher makes him more vulnerable to the teacher's authority. Its placement also serves as a silent declaration of his previous misbehavior. Another student may be sent from the room and made to stand in the hall. Her punishment is observed by all who pass by and thus intensified.

All total institutions, including schools, severely restrict the activities of clients and fill their time with work that the staff defines as important. Punishment in total institutions further restricts the client's activities and increases the client's work. Thus, teachers may punish students by keeping them after school, keeping them in from recess, or giving them more homework. Some irony is revealed in all this. On the one hand, teachers claim that they want students to enjoy class, love learning, and look forward to school. On the other hand, they punish students by increasing schoolwork.

Privilege Systems

Every total institution has what Goffman calls a "privilege system." A few seemingly insignificant rewards are doled out to clients who in action and spirit fulfill the role expectations of their status. Such rewards might seem trivial to outsiders, but to insiders they take on great significance. Students may be allowed to deliver notes to the office, put up the flag, go to the library by themselves, or be the first in line for lunch. What makes these rewards attractive? They allow students to get away from adult surveillance and simultaneously slip the institutional assumption that they can't take care of themselves. Through these rewards, students regain a small measure of control over their own activities.

The Objectivist and Subjectivist Perspectives Revisited

In the preceding chapter, the characteristics of bureaucracy were discussed, and in this chapter, a special kind of bureaucracy, the total institution, was investigated. These analyses were made mainly from an objectivist perspective. The social organization of bureaucracies and total institutions was outlined, the status of staff and clients was reviewed, and interaction patterns between staff and clients were discussed. The school was examined to see if it fit the total institution model. The focus was on the system and not on the people who make it up.

One problem with the objectivist perspective is that it overlooks people and how they respond to their institutional roles. In doing so, it overlooks significant and often subtle aspects of the institution, which Goffman calls its *underlife*. For example, the objectivist point of view does not allow us to show how students slip out of sight of teachers and how they defuse teacher power. Another problem with the objectivist perspective is that it suggests that institutions are self-perpetuating and resistant to change. It is true that institutions resist change, but it is not true that they are unchangeable.

The next two chapters view the school from the total institution perspective, but this time with a subjectivist slant. Rather than looking at how the institution is organized, we will look at how people experience the institution. What is it like to be a student or a teacher?

Summary

Before we go off in this new direction, we should remind ourselves of where we have been. This chapter began with a discussion of the total institution. Several characteristics (involuntary membership, externally defined roles, external support, expert servicing, formally administered rounds of life, and coercive rule structures) were outlined. The school was evaluated with the help of the total institution model. A number of similarities between schools and total institutions were noted, but some dissimilarities were pointed out as well.

Determining that schools bore a partial resemblance to total institutions, we then looked to see if the patterns of behavior that characterize total institutions are found in schools as well. We found that within schools there are client–staff splits, stereotyped points of view, systems of surveillance, invasions of self-hood, obedience systems, and privilege systems.

We have examined the schools from a predominantly objectivist point of view. In the next two chapters, we will take a closer look at the thoughts and experiences of teachers and students, the actors who play the institution's roles.

Suggested Readings

The literature on total institutions is comparatively sparse as compared with, say, the literature on bureaucracies in general. However, the material that exists is of high quality.

EDDY, ELIZABETH M. *Walk the White Line: A Profile of Urban Education.* New York: Fredrick A. Praeger, 1967. This anthropological account of urban education makes good use of Goffman's model of the total institution.

GOFFMAN, ERVING. *Asylums: Essays on the Social Situation of Mental Patients and Other Inmates.* New York: Doubleday & Co., Inc., 1961. Students are advised to read this book with a pencil in hand, jotting notes in the margin when they come across information that applies to school.

JACKSON, PHILIP. *Life in Classrooms.* New York: Holt, Rinehart and Winston, 1968. This participant observation study of public schools exposes its hidden curriculum.

METZ, MARY. *Classrooms and Corridors.* Berkeley: University of California Press, 1978. This is a well-written investigation of students and teachers in desegregated secondary schools.

WOODS, PETER. *Inside Schools.* Boston: Routledge & Kagan Paul, 1986. This is a fine review of qualitative studies in school settings.

CHAPTER 13

The Student's View of the School

Introduction

The last chapter offered an objectivist look at the school as an institution. We turn now to a subjectivist examination of school life. Our focus will not be on the institution itself but rather on how individuals react to it. As W. I. Thomas suggested years ago, "A social institution can be fully understood only if we do not limit ourselves to the abstract study of its formal organization, but analyze the way in which it appears in the personal experience of various members of the group and follow the influence which it has upon their lives."[1]

In this chapter we attempt to put ourselves in the place of students as they make their way through the public school system. We attempt to catch a glimpse of the world as they see it, define it, and adjust to it. We want to uncover what happens to students as they become socialized into school life. Socialization is always a matter of learning to adjust to the environment. We learn to control our behavior so that we can get some desired response from the people around us. What is interesting about this procedure is that the controls over our behavior always remain within ourselves. Socialization is successful only if we choose to go along with it and if our environment provides us with the rewards we seek. Even in the Orwellian confines of the total institution, individuals retain their powers of choice.

What kinds of choices are open to students in schools? As we have seen, they are not free to leave their environment; the law insists that they go to school. They retain, however, three significant options: They can conform to the institution, rebel against it, or adopt a crafty middle position we shall call *making do*. Let us examine each of these options.

Conformity

Students who conform to the expectations of the school and internalize school values become what Goffman disparagingly calls the *programmed members* of the

---

[1] W. I. Thomas, *W. I Thomas on Social Organization and Social Personality*, ed. Morris Janowitz (Chicago: University of Chicago Press, 1966), p. 13.

organization. They accept their position within the school's hierarchical structure. They work hard, do what is expected, and see themselves as the institution defines them. They align themselves with the institution, may work to promote school spirit, and become active members of student government. They enjoy the roles they play, are good at playing them, and for doing so, receive rewards from teachers, parents, the community, and some fellow students.

What are the skills such individuals master on their way to becoming model students? Certainly there must be some mastery of the academic curriculum, but this is not nearly enough to win the model student label. Students must also learn obedience, self-control, punctuality, reliability, and respect for authority. They must learn patience, for much of school life consists of waiting. Students wait their turn to ask and answer questions, to use the rest room, to sharpen pencils, and to go to lunch. They must wait, for example, for report cards to be issued, papers to be corrected, and materials to be handed out. They must learn to subordinate personal desires to the demands of teachers, to accept public evaluation—praise and censure from teachers and occasionally from classmates—and to suppress anger and often the urge to laugh. They must compete willingly, win modestly, and lose gracefully. They must please teachers without alienating their peers. These nonacademic skills make up what Philip Jackson has called the *hidden curriculum* of the school. Mastering the hidden curriculum is the primary adjustment students must make to school life.[2]

For many students, conforming to the expectations of the schools is both edifying and rewarding. School success usually increases pupil interest and effort and these, in turn, encourage further academic improvement. Powell, Farrar, and Cohen concluded from their study of high schools that

> most . . . schools have at least one program that caters to the school's brightest and most ambitious students, the top-track shop, where the subject matter is demanding and the teachers are willing to work hard for their students. The students in the top-track programs have to be committed to the academic purposes of high school; in return they are recognized by being given a variety of services, resources, and privileges not available to others. Top-track students are a special group, and many teachers believe that it is this group that is best served by the school.[3]

The instruction given to high-achieving students is not uniformly good (indeed, too often it is inadequate), but the fact remains that top-track students almost always receive the best the school has to offer. The instruction and recognition encourage achievement and that, in turn, enhances self-esteem. Thus, there is little reason to worry when students conform to the academic and behavioral expectations of their teachers, so long as these expectations include demands for critical intelligence. There is reason to worry, however, when only a few students have a good deal expected of them or access to high-quality instruction.[4]

[2] Philip W. Jackson, *Life in Classrooms* (New York: Holt, Rinehart and Winston, 1968), p. 1–39.
[3] Arthur G. Powell, Eleanor Farrar, and David K. Cohen, *The Shopping Mall High School: Winners and Losers in the Educational Market Place* (Boston: Houghton-Mifflin Company, 1985), p. 119.
[4] Michael W. Sedlak, Christopher W. Wheeler, Diana C. Pullin, and Philip A. Cusick, *Selling Students Short: Classroom Bargains and Academic Reform in the American High School* (New York: Teachers College Press, 1986). Available in paperback.

Rebellion

Not all students become "programmed members" of the school. In most schools there are a number of individuals who actively resist the roles they are expected to play. Not all students rebel for the same reason. Some have carefully analyzed the assumptions that undergird the school and contend that such assumptions hinder learning and degrade individuality. Students who rebel on these grounds fall into this category. Rebellion can be a courageous act, but most school rebels lack the convictions of their courage.

Most frequently, rebels are students who never get the hang of school, are never able to "psych-out" what is expected of them, and, for that reason, never experience school success. An explanation for these frustrations might be found in the learning disabilities of the child or the teaching disabilities of the school. It could be that the values some children inherit from their families ill prepare them for the demands of the school. Rebellion can be expected whenever there is a mismatch between school demands and the student's desires. In some cases, students may accept the demands of the school, may want to conform to them, but are unable to do so. In these instances, there is a strain between the students' desires and their abilities. Rebellion is frequently born of this strain.[5]

Although it is tempting for teachers to put the blame for rebellion on students or their families, it is clear that schools are often implicated in student discontent. Students experience unrelenting public evaluation in classrooms. If they fail to do what is expected of them, they are given the unspoken label *failure*. The label comes early in the lives of some children, and it stays with them throughout their school experience.

Some social scientists contend that the presence of negative labels identifies people as being different, encourages others to see them as deviant, and eventually causes them to live up to their label. Once a student has been labeled *different,* he or she may find it rewarding to accept the label and to act accordingly. For example, consider children experiencing academic difficulty in school. Their failures are personally frustrating and publicly humiliating. In time, teachers label them *slow learners* and expect less of them academically. The label eases the pressure on them and, in that sense, is rewarding. Thus, some students work to keep the slow-learner label in place. A sixth-grader once took her teacher aside to say, "Look, when it comes to school, I'm really stupid. I have a low IQ or something." Because the teacher was new, the child was afraid he had not gotten the news of her "learning disability." The student advertised her school-assigned label. As if that were not sad enough, she herself had come to believe it. She was not trying to con her teacher; she thought of herself as dumb.

Although there are different causes of rebellion, the school experience for most rebels is the same. They experience failure early and often in their school career, making it difficult for them to feel comfortable in the student role or to identify positively with the institution. Feeling alienated, they seek out students who, like themselves, have been given negative labels. Together they fashion

---

[5] For a discussion of "the strain theory" of rebellion, see Albert Cohen, *Delinquent Boys: The Culture of the Gang* (New York: The Free Press, 1960). See also Arthur Stinchcombe, *Rebellion in a High School* (Chicago: Quadrangle Books, 1964).

an identity as "outsiders." This identity increases their alienation and reinforces their socialization to the role of rebel.

Many rebels drop out of school as soon as the law allows. Others are pushed out, suspended, sent to alternative schools, expelled, or are present but obviously disengaged.[6] Today, over 25 percent of students who enroll in the ninth grade drop out before they graduate.[7] Black and Hispanic students drop out at a substantially higher rate than their white classmates.[8] Tougher graduation requirements than are presently in place may discourage borderline students. For that reason, already-high drop-out rates may increase still further in years to come.[9] Most students who have quit high school say they did so because their grades were low and they had little interest in what schools offered. Others said they left school because of financial hardship.

Rebellion and dropping out are clearly related to academic performance and alienation from school life. In some schools, especially those in working-class neighborhoods, alienated youngsters form an antischool subculture. Such students entertain themselves and gain status among friends by opposing school norms, harassing teachers, and ridiculing students who conform to teacher demands. Antischool cultures support such values as informality, "having a good time," "partying," group loyalty, fighting, courage (not being "chicken"), being good with one's hands, confronting authority, possessing and spending cash, owning a car, being sexually active, controlling one's own time, and not squealing on friends. Academic knowledge and authority (especially the authority of teachers and the police) are not valued in the antischool subculture.[10] They challenge the legitimacy of schools and the authority of those who run them. At the same time, they provide members with a sense of belonging and self-esteem. They shield low-achieving students from the pain of school failure by ridiculing the academic enterprise and those who take it seriously.

Membership in the antischool culture severely limits the life chances of students. Paul Willis, a British sociologist, claims that belonging to the antischool culture virtually guarantees that working-class students will grow up to take working-class jobs, or, in a time of economic decline, to have no jobs at all. Schools do not provide such students with the knowledge, skills, values, or credentials needed for white-collar work, and students in the antischool culture have little desire to obtain them. Tragically, a youthful rebellion against authority and power assures that some students will remain forever powerless and in the grip of poverty.

Vocational programs exist in many high schools for students who are "turned off" by academic work and value working with their hands rather than with their minds. The argument for such programs is that they foster student inter-

---

[6] Sedlak, Wheeler, Pullin and Cusick, *Selling Students Short*, pp. 9, 19.

[7] Ernest L. Boyer, *High School: A Report on Secondary Education in America* (New York: Harper and Row, 1983), p. 240.

[8] Harold L. Hodgkinson, *All One System* (Washington, D.C.: Institute for Educational Leadership, Inc., 1985).

[9] Sedlak, Wheeler, Pullin, and Cusick, *Selling Students Short*, p. 30.

[10] Paul Willis, *Learning to Labor: How Working Class Kids Get Working Class Jobs* (New York: Columbia University Press, 1981). See also, P. Corrigan, *Schooling the Smash Street Kids* (London: Macmillan Press, Ltd., 1978); Ken Reid, ed., *Disaffection From School* (London: Methuen, 1986); Peter Fensham, *Alienation from School* (Routledge & Kegan Paul, 1986); Gene Muehbauer and Laura Dodder, *The Losers: Gang and Delinquency in an American Suburb* (New York: Praeger, 1983).

est and increase the opportunities open to nonacademic youngsters. Studies support the first contention but not the second. Students in vocational programs are generally convinced of their value and report that they find their content interesting and useful.[11] On the other hand, a recent comprehensive survey of the research concluded that students in vocational programs do not fare better in the job market than general education students who have not had the benefits of vocational training.[12] Critics contend that vocational students are being shortchanged. Their training does not adequately prepare them for skilled work and their lack of academic training leaves them unprepared for citizenship or self-improvement.[13] Thus, specialty programs designed to assist potentially rebellious students may do little more than reduce the dropout rate and keep the peace.

Making Do

Every institution has official role expectations that define how a person is expected to act. When we are conforming to these expectations, we are making what Goffman calls *primary adjustments* to the system. But within total institutions, Goffman found individuals who "decline in some way to accept the official view of what they should be putting into and getting out of the organization."[14] These individuals make *secondary adjustments* to the institution. They find subtle means of stepping out of their role to retrieve craftily what the institution has taken away. And so it is in schools. If the school will not allow students to sleep, some students devise cunning ways to hide their slumber behind a well-placed book. If they cannot copy other people's tests, some will invent other means for obtaining illegal answers. Their methods are sometimes ingenious. One student wrote chemistry formulas on a fully extended rubber band. When the rubber band was relaxed to normal size, the formulas disappeared into an inky line. During the test the student stretched the rubber band to retrieve formulas and relaxed it to hide the ruse. As we shall see, not all secondary adjustments are as drastic as cheating on tests or sleeping away school time. Students may make school more tolerable (and less profitable) by passing notes, getting the teacher off topic, negotiating down the level of required work, writing book reports from Cliff Notes, or becoming classroom monitors so that they are occasionally excused from class to run errands for the teacher.

The use of secondary adjustments places students in the wide territory that separates programmed members of the school from its rebels. If 10 to 20 percent of students attending an average school are generally conscientious programmed members and another 10 to 20 percent are in rather open rebellion,

---

[11] Powell, Farrar, and Cohen, *The Shopping Mall High School*, pp. 129–133. See also John I. Goodlad, *A Place Called School: Prospects for the Future* (New York: McGraw-Hill Book Company, 1984), pp. 55, 143–150, 343–344.

[12] Paul Osterman, *Getting Started: The Youth Labor Market* (Cambridge: MIT Press, 1980), p. 31. The one exception to this finding appears to be in the area of secretarial training. See Elinor M. Woods and Walt Haney, "Does Vocational Education Make a Difference: A Review of Previous Research and Reanalysis of National Longitudinal Data Sets," Final Report to the National Institute of Education (Cambridge: Horton Institute, September 1981), pp. 4–19.

[13] Ernest L. Boyer, *High School*, p. 123.

[14] Erving Goffman, *Asylums* (New York: Doubleday & Co., Inc., 1961), p. 304. Available in paperback.

Good teachers see the school through their students' eyes. (*Source:* National Education Association, Joe Di Dio.)

then the vast majority (60 to 80 percent) *make do* by passively disengaging themselves from some portions of school life.[15] Such students do not totally conform to the system but neither do they openly resist it. Instead, they maneuver their way around the institution's rules and occasionally stand somewhat apart from the institution's roles. Students may make secondary adjustments to some portions of school life but become programmed members in other portions. For example, a devoted English student may bluff his way through the mysteries of chemistry and totally devote himself to his drama class. A girl who hates all things academic may tolerate her classes in order to be with her friends and play on the basketball team. A student's experience of school may change over time. Someone who was totally alienated from school in his or her freshman year may get turned on to learning and be fully involved two or three years later.

Secondary adjustments are a way of making do in school without fully joining or totally rejecting what the institution offers. Let us now examine some areas of school life where secondary adjustments are commonly found. No useful distinctions can be made here between secondary and elementary school students except to say that it takes time to learn and perfect secondary adjustments. Though high school students may be more proficient at beating the system than elementary school students, a careful look will reveal an underlife even in a first-grade classroom.

<hr />

[15] Sedlak, Wheeler, Pullin, and Cusick, *Selling Students Short*, p. 9. Of course, these figures represent a mythical "average" school. At many schools the proportions are quite different. When rebels grow in number, many make-do students may be drawn to the rebel's ranks. When the percentage of devoted students grows, the likelihood is good that make-do students will take schoolwork more seriously and get more from it. If making-do becomes a respected art form among students, then schools slowly adjust their standards downward.

PRIVATE SPACE.   Secondary adjustments often entail the use of institutional facilities for illicit purposes. For example, students may use school materials (paper, tape, toilet paper tubes, and so on) to build elaborate marble shoots in their desks. Rubber bands and paper clips may be fashioned into sling shots. Rest rooms can be transformed into safe meeting places where students smoke, waste time, and swap information out of the view of their teachers.

SHORTCUTTING.   Students are expected to complete vast quantities of work, and they soon learn that the stream of assignments is unrelenting. The more they accomplish, the more they will be asked to do. In response, they devise ways to slow down the flow of work. They may complain about assignments, accuse teachers of being unreasonable, or seek shortcuts to completing the assignments. They may collaborate on homework, keep files of tests, plagiarize papers, and psych out what the instructor wants. All these devices cut down the work a student need do in order to get through school.[16]

A few years ago a sixth-grade teacher kept a notebook in which he recorded things he had learned about his students and himself. One student in particular taught the teacher a great deal about shortcutting. Betty had been kept after school to finish her arithmetic homework. The sixth-grade teacher was correcting papers in the back of the math teacher's classroom. These are some of the notes the sixth-grade teacher took as he observed the student and the math teacher.

> Mr. _____'s class, 3:15. I've been here 15 minutes, and Betty has gazed out the window the whole time.
>
> 3:20: Mr. _____ reminds Betty she can't leave until all her math is done. Betty says, "I know, but I can't remember how to do this first one here." Mr. _____ calls Betty to the desk and shows her how to start the problem. Betty says, "I get that, I know it; it's the next part I don't get." Mr. _____ works on guiding Betty through the second problem. He sends Betty back to her seat where she looks out the window again.
>
> 3:35: Mr. _____ asks Betty how she's doing. Betty says, "This one's different; I can't get it." Betty is called to the teacher's desk once more. Mr. _____ explains the problem, but Betty isn't listening; she's looking around the room. She sees me and smiles, as if to let me in on the secret. I think she's going to get Mr. _____ to do the whole assignment for her.

SECRET COMMUNICATION.   Schools severely limit legitimate communication among students. As Philip Jackson notes, classrooms are crowded places where spontaneous youngsters learn to act as if they were alone.[17] They are expected to concentrate on their work, keep their eyes on their own papers, stay in their own seats, and not distract their neighbors. Since these are difficult, if not impossible, things to do, students find ways around the regulations. Notes passed surreptitiously across the room, whispers concealed behind cupped hands, and elaborate, pantomimed messages are but a few of the more obvious devices students use to communicate with one another.

---

[16] Howard Becker, Blanche Geer, and Everett Hughes, *Making the Grade* (New York: John Wiley & Sons, Inc., 1968).

[17] Jackson, *Life in Classrooms*, p. 16.

AVOIDING CENSURE THROUGH IMPRESSION MANAGEMENT.   It is difficult for students (especially young ones) to keep themselves mentally and physically on task all the time, yet teachers are continually looking for signs of inattention. Students therefore learn to look attentive even when they are not. Jackson has reviewed some of the signs of pretended attention: eye contact with teachers; the appearance of concentration, interest, and activity; participation in class discussions; and completion of assignments. Students can avoid censure if they hide their mental leave-taking from official view. Daydreaming must take place behind a face that says, "I'm listening"; looks of interest must hide boredom; students can write letters in class if they look as if they are taking notes; and homework, even when carelessly done, must have the neat appearance of effort.

Students who adopt such techniques learn to monitor their activities and the impressions they are creating in others. They learn to give the impression of knowledge where none exists and the semblance of understanding where confusion reigns.

FALSE ADVERTISING.   Impression management extends to many areas of student life. The unrelenting questions teachers ask must be answered correctly if the student is to stay in the teacher's good graces. We all remember classroom situations where students frantically grabbed for answers—any answers—as long as they held the teacher at bay.

How do students appear knowledgeable when they are not? A favorite tactic is to give short, noncommittal answers:

TEACHER. What was the major cause of the Second World War?
STUDENT. Friction?
TEACHER. What kind of friction?
STUDENT. International, mostly!

Students learn early that most teachers cannot resist the urge to talk. If given the suggestion of an answer, teachers can be counted on to expand upon it and make it sensible.

Another tactic students use is to make sure they are asked questions they can answer. If, for example, certain students have only completed the first half of their arithmetic homework, they may work to be called upon early in the math class, or, if students don't know the answer to a question the teacher has just asked, they may try to avoid being called upon at all. They may look away from the teacher while giving the appearance of thinking about the question. If the teacher likes to call on students who appear confused or inattentive, the student may try a bolder technique. John Holt observed one such student, Emily, raising her hand and calling out, "I know, I know. Please call on me!" knowing the teacher would ignore her request. When the teacher, true to form, called on someone else, Emily nodded knowingly as the answer was given, as if to give her blessing.[18]

TEMPERING VULNERABILITY.   Teachers wield great power in schools, and keeping teachers happy is essential to student success. Students are vulnerable

[18] John Holt, *How Children Fail* (New York: Pitman Publishing Company, 1964), p. 33. Available in paperback.

to teachers' evaluations of their work and character. They are vulnerable to the rewards and punishments teachers dole out. The public nature of teacher sanctions makes rewards and punishments more powerful and increases student vulnerability. If a student respects teachers and values their judgment, critical comments from the front of the room can be devastating. Students can protect themselves from the pain teachers can inflict by devaluing teachers as people. By trivializing teachers, emptying them of personal significance, and conforming to their wishes only mechanically, students make themselves less vulnerable to the teacher's will. As Willard Waller observed many years ago, "By 'laughing off' the teacher, or hating him out of all existence as a person, by taking refuge in self-initiated activities that are always beyond the teacher's reach, students attempt to neutralize teacher control."[19]

Teachers often misunderstand why students are sometimes aloof and hard to reach. The reason may not be clear even to students themselves, but it is Waller's view that the social distance between teachers and students serves to protect students from undue pain. If they view teachers as mere role players (and significant ones at that), the teacher's evaluation of a student's work, worth, and behavior is not likely to matter. And if students cannot devalue the teacher by the sheer power of personal will, they can jointly force the teacher's character into the void of insignificance. Nicknames ("The Great Suspender," "Old Brass Ass," "Volcano Breath," and so on) are useful, if unkind, devices to make teachers seem less awesome. Few students worry that such maneuvers might hurt a teacher's feelings, because to devalue a person is to forget that he or she has feelings. It is important to remember that such techniques for handling teacher power reinforce the impersonality of the school and increase the social distance between teachers and students.

CURRYING FAVOR.   Another method for dealing with vulnerability is currying favor with teachers. As Philip Jackson put it, "One way of managing life in total institutions is by moving close to the source of power."[20] The apple-polishing technique has a long tradition that extends far beyond the academic years. The primary characteristic of apple polishers is their insincerity. A programmed member of the institution may identify with teachers and value them highly, but apple polishers feign sincerity in the hope of manipulating teacher behavior.

THE ENSIGN PULVER MANEUVER.   The play *Mister Roberts* is about life on a World War II supply ship. The crew of the ship struggles under the autocratic demands of an incompetent but ambitious captain. The central character, Mr. Roberts, protects the crew by drawing the captain's rage away from them and to himself. Another character, Ensign Pulver, adjusts to the total institution by hiding from the captain. In fact, he secrets himself so well that a full year passes before the captain ever sets eyes on him.

Some students use the Ensign Pulver maneuver effectively. Because they cannot hide below decks as Ensign Pulver did, they perfect the fine art of invisibility. They sit in the back of the room near the wall and strategically posi-

[19] Willard Waller, *The Sociology of Teaching* (New York: John Wiley & Sons, 1967 [1932]), p. 126. Available in paperback.
[20] Jackson, *Life in Classrooms*, p. 32.

tioned behind other students. They avoid eye contact with the teacher, never volunteer an answer, and when forced to speak, do so in the shortest possible sentences. They never do their assignments poorly enough to cause concern nor well enough to draw the teacher's attention. They disappear into the mass and wait out the school experience.

CUTTING CLASSES AND ABSENTEEISM.   One way students can ensure invisibility is simply not to go to class. The problems of tardiness, absenteeism, and class cutting grew in the 1960s and now have reached alarming proportions. Nonattendance is now a national concern.[21] Administrators in urban, suburban, and rural schools report that absenteeism is one of the most ubiquitous problems in their schools.[22] Students agree. In a recent study, 68 percent of high school seniors said cutting class was a significant problem at their school.[23] The Detroit school system recently reported that 20 percent of its total student body was absent from school on any given day. However, teachers' records revealed an absentee rate of over 30 percent, indicating that more students skip class than skip school. Imagine how difficult it would be for students to learn and teachers to teach if nearly a third of the class was not in class on any given day.[24]

No single factor fully explains the high nonattendance rates in schools today. Part of the problem probably can be traced to inadequate monitoring. Large schools have larger absentee rates than small schools, and children from single-parent homes are more likely to cut school than are children from two-parent homes.[25] It appears that large schools and single parents have the greatest difficulty keeping track of children's activities.

Probably another reason for nonattendance is that some teachers offer students uninteresting and unchallenging fare. In most of the 1000 classrooms studied by Goodlad, teachers dominated the talk, instruction, and decision making. Students were seldom involved in classroom discussions and took part in only a narrow range of activities: listening to their teachers, taking notes, answering questions, filling in blanks, and taking tests. Goodlad saw few activities that might encourage students to develop their powers of critical thinking. Instead students were rewarded for passivity and compliance.[26] In a recent survey of high school seniors, 33 percent agreed with the statement, "My school does not place enough emphasis on training students . . . to think" and 56 percent disagreed with the statement, "My school provides enough opportunities for student discussion of school problems."[27] Nonattendance, when it does not become chronic, is an easy (though costly) method for students to avoid tedium and hard work.

---

[21] Sedlak, Wheeler, Pullin, and Cusick, *Selling Students Short*, p. 84.

[22] Philip A. Cusick, *The Egalitarian Ideal and the American School* (New York: Longman, 1983), p. 27.

[23] United States Department of Education, National Center for Education Statistics, "High School and Beyond Study" (unpublished tabulations, October 1984). Reported in *Public Opinion*, Vol. 9 (Summer 1986), p. 38.

[24] Sedlak, Wheeler, Pullin, and Cusick, *Selling Students Short*, p. 84.

[25] Ibid., p. 86.

[26] Goodlad, *A Place Called School*, pp. 93–129, 233.

[27] David L. Clark, "High School Seniors React to Their Teachers and Their Schools," *Phi Delta Kappan*, Vol. 68 (March 1987), pp. 506–507.

STRIKING THE TACIT BARGAIN.   Arthur Powell and his colleagues studied American high schools and, like Goodlad, found that classrooms were generally orderly, quiet, and dull. Most teachers did not push their students or challenge them to put in their best effort. Many, if not most, students did a moderate amount of work but stopped far short of real effort or commitment. It appeared to Powell that a tacit agreement had been struck between teachers and their classes. Students agreed to do some work and avoid open rebellion. In exchange for classroom peace and cordial relations, teachers agreed not to demand much from their pupils and to tolerate slipshod work.[28]

Sometimes a teacher strikes a single agreement with an entire class. More often, different students negotiate their own bargains with the teacher. Pupils who want to excel put in extra effort and reap a greater share of classroom rewards. Others are content to make do with far less. As one student explained:

> If you want an education in this school, you can get it. You can learn a lot here if you want to. But you don't have to because nobody's going to make you do anything. Kids who don't want to do much aren't going to do much and everybody knows that. Like they refuse. The ones who want to go to college hit the books but the others just slide.

Classroom agreements work both ways. Teachers agree not to hassle their students and, in return, students agree not to give their teachers too hard a time. It is as if neither the teacher nor their students want to work very hard but neither is willing to admit—to themselves or others—that they were trying to avoid the discomfort of effort or conflict.[29] The bargaining process described by Powell is an adaptation to the school system, but long-term costs of that adaptation are high. Students and teachers become progressively disengaged from learning, and fewer and fewer pupils ever realize their potential or prepare themselves for gainful employment, thoughtful citizenship, or lifelong learning. Researchers agree that unprecedented numbers of students merely go through the motions of schooling[30] and never fully comprehend the aims of a liberal education.[31]

PRESERVING DIGNITY.   Although students work to limit their vulnerability, many get caught (at least occasionally) in situations that challenge their dignity and self-concept. Frederick Wiseman, in his documentary film *High School*, recorded the following exchange between a dean of discipline and a student of a big-city, middle-class high school:

DEAN: What do you mean, you can't take gym. Do you get dressed in the morning?

STUDENT: Yes.

---

[28] Powell, Farrar, and Cohen, *The Shopping Mall High School*, pp. 66–117.

[29] Ibid., p. 72.

[30] R. B. Everheart, *Reading Writing and Resistance—Adolescence and Labor in a Junior High School* (Boston: Routledge & Kegan Paul, 1983); Linda McNeil, *Lowering Expectations: The Impact of Student Employment in Classroom Knowledge* (Madison, WI: Center for Educational Research, February 1984); Powell, Farrar and Cohen, *The Shopping Mall High School*, pp. 66–117; Gary Sykes, "The Deal," *Wilson Quarterly*, Vol. 8 (1984), pp. 59–77;

[31] Sedlak, Wheeler, Pullin, and Cusick, *Selling Students Short*, p. 8.

DEAN: Do you get undressed?

STUDENT: Yes.

DEAN: Well, you can get into a gym outfit.

STUDENT: I can't take gym.

DEAN: Will you get into a gym outfit?

STUDENT: I can't take gym.

DEAN: We'll decide that.

STUDENT: But I have a doctor's appointment today.

DEAN: I'm sick and tired of you talking. You just . . .

STUDENT: My mom was in, though.

DEAN: I spoke to your mother.

STUDENT: I'm going to the doctor today.

DEAN: Now look, you better be in a gym outfit. We'll determine whether you take exercise or not.

STUDENT: I can't.

DEAN: We'll determine that.

STUDENT: I'm not even supposed to come to school.

At this point the dean, a muscular man with a barrel chest, rises from his desk and approaches the student. Shaking a pen in the student's direction, he says with quiet force, "Why don't you just stop. Now, look, I'm going to tell you something. You don't talk; you just listen. You'll come prepared in a gym outfit, and you'll go to gym. Is that clear?"[33]

The student realizes that the situation has escalated and that he is going to be defeated. His illness (real or professed) is not enough to keep him out of gym for the day. He will be forced to attend, dressed in a gym outfit. Others, more powerful than himself, will determine if he will "take exercise" or sit the period out. The student feels the press of institutional power as it questions his motives and ability to judge his own health. Further resistance appears fruitless. The dean ends his directions with the question, "Is that clear?" and the student answers, "Yes."

But the dean is not placated. "All right. Now don't tell us you're not going to do anything. We're going to put you in an uncompromising position. You'll come dressed in a gym outfit."

At this point, the situation changes slightly as the student attempts to end the discussion with his dignity still intact. What can he do? To challenge the dean further would invite trouble but to continue listening to the dean would prolong his humiliation. The student chooses another course. Cocking his head in a manner of mild defiance, but at the same time looking down in deference, he says softly but firmly, "I said I would."

The tactic here is subtle and easier to detect on film than in print. The student's words say he is giving in, but the way he says them suggests something else. He manages to imply that the dean has been unreasonable and that his victory is hollow because it rests on mere force. The dean can make the student dress for gym, but the student's mind is still his own. He does not acknowledge the dean's right to treat him in this way.

If such a tactic is to be successful, it must not be obvious. The object is to leave some doubt in the dean's mind about the meaning of what is being said.

---

[33] *High School* (1968), directed by Frederick Wiseman. Courtesy of Zipporah Films, Inc.

If the message is too clear, it will bring on more trouble. In this case trouble did follow. The student was suspended from school because the dean read the unspoken implication in his seemingly innocent sentence, "I said I would."

The purpose here is not to show that educators can be unreasonable (though in this case one certainly was) but rather to show how some students attempt to deal with situations they find humiliating. Rather than rebel totally or acquiesce completely, students subtly resist the teacher's power. They resist the definition the teacher places on the situation and advertise some portion of their defection while ritualistically fulfilling the role expected of them. Some fall into silence; others adopt a stance of cocky defiance; still others give in totally yet discredit their acquiescence with a hidden gesture of defiance when the teacher's back is turned.

VANDALISM. The last tactic, vandalism, is unlike other methods of making do. In some sense it would be better placed under the heading of open rebellion, but it is not just rebels who engage in vandalism. Many otherwise conforming students have been known to vandalize schools. In fact, schools may be the nation's most vandalized buildings. Working from government data, we calculate that school windows are broken in New York City at a rate of one every two minutes, around the clock, 365 days a year. How can we account for such widespread vandalism?

Certainly part of the explanation comes from the fact that schools house the young. School buildings are accessible, unguarded at night, and are usually surrounded by playgrounds that separate them from nearby buildings. These factors, however, really do not explain vandalism. Probably a better explanation is that a lot of kids just don't like school and strike out against it when they have the opportunity. An extensive study of the New York state school system sampled opinions of teachers and students in fifteen high schools throughout the state. They found that over 66 percent of the students surveyed claimed that they did not enjoy school. They reported that teachers did not help them, did not understand them, did not improve their academic skills, and did not care about their future. The report states,

> Students felt that administrators were not sufficiently accessible. They reported that the proliferation of school rules was oppressive, and, more importantly, that enforcement of discipline was unfair, arbitrary or discriminatory. . . .
>
> Teacher's perceptions of the school situation were substantially different from those of students. Teachers appeared largely unaware of the negative feelings of students. When asked to rate school morale as "positive," "average" or "negative," 52 percent of students picked "negative" while 64 percent of teachers picked "positive." Asked to assign the same ratings to the overall educational process, 52 percent of teachers chose "positive" compared with only 28 percent of students.[34] (See Table 13.1.)

Summary

This chapter has dealt with schools as they are experienced by students. We pointed out that socialization is a process of adjustment to the environment.

[34] *The Fleischmann Report: On the Quality, Cost, and Financing of Elementary and Secondary Education in New York State*, Vol. I (New York: The Viking Press, 1973), p.47.

TABLE 13-1.   Teacher-Student Attitudes

	Teachers		Students	
	Negative	Positive	Negative	Positive
How Teachers Treat Students				
Treat students as responsible	10.4%	52.4%	34.9%	37.0%
Listen to students' opinions	15.3	46.6	42.1	31.2
Understand student problems	21.8	41.7	52.7	21.0
Help students develop skills	12.9	49.6	43.0	29.2
Help students do best	8.9	55.1	40.1	29.9
Concerned about students' future	10.4	60.2	42.1	32.0
How Students Treat Teachers				
Students respect teachers	13.8%	52.8%	36.5%	29.2%
Students listen to teachers' opinions	18.3	39.6	35.3	28.9
Students help teacher do best	23.8	32.3	46.8	18.1
Students understand teachers' problems	63.3	9.3	61.7	14.9
Students can disagree with teachers	7.0	72.7	48.0	29.9

Not all students adjust to the school environment in the same way. Some join the system wholeheartedly and become model students. Others reject the institution and define themselves through rebellion. Another group, the large majority, learn to "make do" within the institution. They learn what the system expects of them and conform outwardly to its demands; but inwardly they distance themselves from their roles, make "secondary adjustments," and use the system for their own ends. We examined many of the tactics students use to work the system.

It is not likely that the activities described in this chapter square with your aims for education. The programmed members of the system look disturbingly like the people W. I. Thomas defined as Philistines. The rebels resemble Thomas's Bohemians. The crafty manipulators who make do in the institution seem too alienated and socially dishonest to fulfill the role of Thomas's creative individuals. We will have to reexamine our aims for education in the light of these findings. But before we tackle that issue in Chapter 16, we must look at the total institution once again—this time from the teacher's perspective.

Suggested Readings

There is no more important and perhaps no more difficult task facing the teacher than to stay aware of student perceptions and experience in schools. Many books are available to help teachers in this regard.

BECKER, HOWARD S., BLANCHE GEER, and Everett HUGHES. *Making the Grade: The Academic Side of College Life.* New York: John Wiley & Sons, Inc., 1968. This is a sociological exploration of undergraduate culture at the University of Kansas. It appears that college students, like their counterparts in elementary and secondary schools, are expert at working the system.

CLARK, DAVID L. "High School Seniors React to Their Teachers and Their Schools." *Phi Delta Kappan,* Vol. 68 (March 1987), pp. 506–507. This reports the results of an opinion poll of high school seniors about the schools they attend. The article argues that most students are contented with the quality of their education and the skills of their teachers.

EVERHEART, R. B. *Reading Writing and Resistance—Adolescence and Labor in a Junior High School.* Boston: Routledge & Kegan Paul, 1983. This is another useful study of how students come to resist schooling.

GOODLAD, JOHN I. *A Place Called School: Prospects for the Future.* New York: McGraw-Hill Book Company, 1984. This sensitive study of American schools pays a good deal of attention to the quality of students' lives in classrooms.

HOLT, JOHN. *How Children Fail.* New York: Pitman Publishing Co., Inc., 1964. A long-time teacher takes a child's-eye view of the classroom. A useful analysis of how students' fear of failure encourages them to "work the system."

LARKIN, RALPH W. *Suburban Youth in Cultural Crisis.* New York: Oxford University Press, 1979. The author finds suburban high schools populated with student types he labels *jocks, grinds, freaks, greasers,* and so on. The book emphasizes the relevance of the school experience for these students.

MUEHBAUER, GENE, and LAURA DODDER. *The Losers: Gang and Delinquency in an American Suburb.* New York: Praeger, 1983. This is a modest investigation of the dynamics of gang life in one American community.

POWELL, ARTHUR G., ELEANOR FARRAR, and DAVID K. COHEN. *The Shopping Mall High School: Winners and Losers in the Educational Market Place.* Boston: Houghton-Mifflin Company, 1985. This is a sensitive account of how teachers and students have learned to settle for less and less.

SCHRAG, PETER. *Voices in the Classroom.* Boston: Beacon Books, 1965. The book is a sensitive analysis by an adult who listens carefully to what children have to say.

SEDLAK, MICHAEL W., CHRISTOPHER W. WHEELER, DIANA C. PULLIN, and PHILIP A. CUSICK. *Selling Students Short: Classroom Bargains and Academic Reform in the American High School.* New York: Teachers College Press, 1986. This thoughtful book explores the ways in which students are systematically denied the education that democracy promises and requires.

STINCHCOMBE, ARTHUR. *Rebellion in a High School: High School Stinks.* Chicago: Quadrangle Books, 1964. This is an analysis of the relationship between school structure and student rebellion.

WALLER, WILLARD. *The Sociology of Teaching.* New York. John Wiley & Sons, Inc., 1967 [1932]. This is a classic study utlizing a conflict model of the school. Waller's descriptions of students remain remarkably fresh.

WILLIS, PAUL. *Learning to Labor: How Working Class Kids Get Working Class Jobs.* New York: Columbia University Press, 1981. This book shows with painful clarity how the rebellion of certain working-class students against school authority prepares them for working-class jobs. Students will find the first half of the book most accessible.

A number of ambitious studies, conducted for the government and private agencies, have analyzed the conditions of youth in modern America. All the studies agree that the young are playing a decreasing role in American society. They lament the growing alienation of the young from schools and make suggestions for future educational policy.

CARNEGIE COUNCIL ON CHILDREN, Kenneth Keniston, Chairman. *All Our Children: The American Family under Pressure.* New York: Harcourt Brace Jovanovich, 1977.

CARNEGIE COUNCIL ON POLICY STUDIES IN HIGHER EDUCATION. *Giving Youth a Better Chance: Options for Education, Work and Service.* San Francisco: Jossey-Bass, 1979.

LIPSITZ, JOAN. *Growing up Forgotten: A Review of Research and Programs Concerning Early Adolescence.* A Report to the Ford Foundation, Lexington, MA: Lexington Books, 1977.

REPORT OF THE PANEL ON YOUTH OF THE PRESIDENT'S SCIENCE ADVISORY COMMITTEE, James S. Coleman, Chairman. *Youth: Transition to Adulthood.* Chicago: University of Chicago Press, 1974.

WYNNE, EDWARD A., and MARY HESS. "Long-term Trends in Youth Conduct and the Revival of Traditional Value Patterns." *Educational Evaluation and Policy Analysis,* Vol. 8 (Fall 1986), pp. 294–308. The article reviews data regarding the growing antisocial behavior among American adolescents. It discusses suicide rates, homicide rates, sexual activity, rates of out-of-wedlock births, substance abuse, delinquency, psychiatric admission rates, declining academic achievement, and other disturbing trends.

A few books have appeared that investigate the school experience of females.

HARRISON, BARBARA GRIZZUTI. *Unlearning the Lie: Sexism in School.* New York: William Morrow & Company, Inc., 1974.

STACEY, JUDITH, SUSAN BÉREAUD, and JOAN DANIELS, eds. *And Jill Came Tumbling After: Sexism in American Education.* New York: Dell Publishing Co., Inc., 1974.

CHAPTER 14

The Teacher's View of the School

Introduction

Teaching is a difficult profession, much more difficult than most aspiring educators realize. Some of the difficulty resides in the mystery of teaching itself, some in the teacher–student relationship, and some in teachers' interaction with colleagues, parents, and the administration. The purpose of this chapter is to spell out the kinds of problems teachers face. Again, we will use a subjectivist mode of analysis so we can see the schools as teachers see them. We will not stop there, however, for we will also look at institutional arrangements and how they affect teacher behavior.

The Teacher–Student Relationship

The Desire for Primary Relationships

When teachers are asked why they chose teaching as a profession, the most common reply is, "Because I care about people." Surveys conducted by the National Education Association indicate that 62 percent of men and 67 percent of women enter teaching because they want to work with the young. Teaching is a helping profession that attracts individuals who feel an emotional and moral need to serve others.[1] There are other motives for teaching as we learned in Chapter 9, but service is the largest single reason teachers give for wanting to teach.

It may be that beginning teachers have a romanticized view of the relationships they will have with students. Most seek caring, mutually supportive relationships in which the student and teacher work in close alliance to achieve mutually important goals. As we have seen, the structure of the school is ill suited for primary relationships of this kind. Many teachers are disappointed to find that their initial interactions with students are cool, distant, and some-

---

[1] National Education Association, *Status of the American Public School Teacher. 1985–86* (Washington, DC: National Education Association, 1987), p. 211.

times manipulative. The disappointment drives some people out of teaching and serves to fix others in traditional teacher roles. Nevertheless, working with the young is still the single most important reason teachers give for staying in teaching.[2]

Getting Into the Role

As we saw in Chapter 10, most teachers graduate from college with an idealistic vision of their profession. They expect to be interesting, helpful teachers who are liked and appreciated by their students. They plan to address the "individual needs" of their pupils (a phrase they learned in college that meshed comfortably with their own desire to form *primary relationships* with the young). They expected to bring life to the subject matter and to trade profitably on the teaching triangle (Figure 10-1). Many are saddened to find that classroom realities fall somewhat short of their hopes. They are shocked to find that becoming a teacher is a difficult and sometimes lonely process. Being new in the school, they do not face a class of individuals they know well or can relate to personally. Despite their best efforts, they find themselves thinking of students as a group and treating them accordingly. Students, of course, do not know the new teacher either and cannot treat him or her as an individual. However, they know much about the role teachers play and fashion their behavior accordingly. Students may test the teachers to see if they can play the teacher role convincingly. When they do this, their behavior is leveled at the status of teacher and not necessarily at the person who fills it. However, teachers cannot help but take this test personally, as a challenge to their authority and as an affront of their self-respect. As one first-year teacher described her experience:

> I think sometimes I take things too personally with kids. But you can't be completely impersonal. Attacks are made on you all the time, personal attacks. Attacks that children make are extremely personal. They have no compunction about speaking about the way you look or talk. They really dehumanize you, and you have a terrible time reacting.[3]

Such a teacher may feel misunderstood and vulnerable. What she had intended as kind, students perceived as soft. What she had worked hard to make interesting, students perceived as boring. As students test the limits of the new classroom, the teacher begins to feel that students are taking advantage of her goodwill. She may decide to crack down before the situation gets out of hand, and as she does so, she progressively gives up the hope of developing warm, individualized relationships in her classroom. Another novice teacher describes his attitude transformation this way:

> The first year the most important thing to me was winning the kids' approval. Now I can look back and say, OK, I don't need it; I can be a good teacher without everyone liking me.[4]

The transformation described here can happen in any classroom, but it is most likely to occur when students dislike school and generally are distrustful of

---

[2] Ibid., pp. 240–241.

[3] Eli Bower, *Teachers Talk about Their Feelings,* DHEW Publication No. (HSM) 73–9032 (Washington, DC: National Institute of Mental Health, 1973), p. 6.

[4] Ibid., p. 2.

teachers. These attitudes are often found in homogeneously grouped classes of low-achieving students. In many schools, new teachers are placed in just such rooms.[5]

There is a tragic circularity to this teacher transformation process. Teachers with high hopes want to build primary relationships with students. Students misunderstand their intentions, view them as lax, and begin to test the limits of their new environments. Teachers do not understand this new behavior, take it personally, are threatened by it, and decide to clamp down. Their get-tough policy serves to reinforce the students' belief that teachers can always be trusted to act like teachers. As a result, the client–staff split of the total institution is maintained even though no one necessarily desires it. Of course, not all teachers march around this vicious circle. The point is that the classroom situation encourages—we might even say manufactures—the mentality and social distance that total institutions require.

Socialization by Default

The movement into the traditional role of teacher (businesslike, aloof, autocratic) may not happen quickly or consciously. Gertrude McPherson, a trained anthropologist, studied her own socialization into the teacher role and described her transformation this way:

> During my first few weeks of teaching, I was constantly aware that I was play acting, wearing the mask of a teacher rather than being a teacher. I emotionally identified with "disobedient" pupils rather than with the reprimanding teacher. The manner and actions of the other teachers seemed to me artificial, contrived, and even in some situations laughable . . . but I imitated [them] and watched myself imitating. I recall taking my class to a play during the second month of my first teaching year, sitting relaxed and watching the play, and then becoming aware that other teachers were glaring at me because some of my boys were misbehaving. I had to force myself to scold them as I had seen other teachers do, terribly afraid that my artificiality would show. . . . By the end of the year, I played policeman with the others without particularly noticing myself doing it. I began to forget I was wearing a mask, I found it harder to stand aside and watch myself being a teacher. The emotions I had simulated I began to feel. Johnny's misbehavior in the lunch line now annoyed me inside and not just because Mrs. Gregory [another teacher] would glare at me if Johnny acted up.[6]

Howard Becker describes such transformations as socialization "by default," because they are accomplished without conscious choice. Commitment grows through a series of seemingly innocent acts, each one of which brings individuals deeper into their official role. At first they awkwardly do the things expected of them and experience a considerable role distance in the process.[7] They are self-consciously aware that they do not believe their own acts and are not committed to them. Their behavior does not reflect their inner feelings.

---

[5] Elizabeth Eddy, *Becoming a Teacher* (New York: Teachers College Press, 1969), pp. 78–79. See also Howard Becker, "Social Class Variations in the Teacher–Pupil Relationship," *Journal of Educational Sociology*, Vol. 25 (April 1952), pp. 451–465.

[6] Gertrude McPherson, *Small Town Teacher* (Cambridge: Harvard University Press, 1972), pp. 70–71.

[7] See Chapter 2 for a discussion of role distance as a permanent rather than a transitory phenomenon.

But, as time goes on, these acts become less foreign. Individuals begin to have a bigger stake in carrying them off convincingly, until, without being aware of it, they begin to believe their own propaganda. They become committed to their roles not by choice but by default.[8]

Social Distance

The great enigma of teaching is that people enter the profession in order to work closely with the young and in the course of their work progressively distance themselves from their students. This is not a universal phenomenon, but it is common enough to deserve our attention.

Part of the reason for social distance is found in the client–staff split that characterizes total institutions. Students and teachers view education from different perspectives, and each group struggles to get its perspective to dominate the classroom. But there are other reasons for social distance. For example, social distance protects teachers from hurt, helps them keep control of their emotions, and guards them against the accusation of favoritism. Let's look at these issues in order.

PROTECTION FROM HURT.   Betsy West of Wichita State University has pointed out that some teachers use social distance as a shield against personal pain. As they embroil themselves in the lives of their students, they begin to realize, perhaps for the first time, the limits of their ability to help children. For example, if a child is suffering emotional distress because his mother is an alcoholic, he may find some comfort from his classroom teacher. However helpful that relationship might be, the teacher must send the child home to tragedy every day. This can be emotionally traumatic for the teacher, especially when it is repeated year after year with new students facing their own equally unsolvable problems. Some teachers rid themselves of this chronic trauma by distancing themselves from their students. As a veteran teacher expressed it to us,

> Students used to tell me a lot about their lives, about what they were up to, and most of all about their problems. I used to take it all in and do what I could to help. I mean I knew a lot of stuff about their family problems, drug use, personal stuff I had no business knowing. And I guess if I were truthful I would . . . say I felt good that they trusted me enough to confide in me. . . . But I realized one day that I was carrying around a lot of emotional luggage. I took it home, and I worried and worried about it. And then a student of mine got pregnant, and I had known what she had been up to because she had told me. That got me thinking about my responsibilities—shouldn't I have done something? Shouldn't I have told her parents? I guess I felt like an accomplice or something. So I said the hell with it, I'm not going to listen to that stuff any more. And I haven't.

Another source of teacher pain comes from the custom of passing a class to another teacher at the end of the school year. Just as teachers begin to understand and care for their students, to know what motivates the class, and to see signs of progress, they have to give up their pupils to someone else. Under

---

[8] Howard Becker, "Notes on the Concept of Commitment," in *Sociological Work* (Chicago: Aldine Publishing Company, 1970), pp. 261–273. See also John T. McArthur, "What Does Teaching Do to Teachers?" *Educational Administration Quarterly*, Vol. 14 (1978), pp. 89–103.

such conditions teachers can ill afford to establish deep and loving relationships with other pupils. Jules Henry explains what might happen if social distance were not institutionalized in the school: "Children would have to be dragged shrieking from grade to grade, and most teachers would flee teaching, for the mutual attachment would be so deep that its annual severing would be too much for either to bear."[9]

HOLDING NEGATIVE EMOTIONS IN CHECK. Teachers are expected to keep control of their classrooms without physically or verbally abusing students. The pressures of teaching—the need to be constantly alert, to make decisions quickly, to monitor student work, to reward positive behavior and redirect negative behavior—are so exhausting that they tax the reserves of even the most talented and vigorous teachers. Because teachers become physically and emotionally drained, because they work outside the view of other teachers, and because students are continually straining at the limits imposed by the institution, there is always the possibility that tempers will flare and teachers will lose control of themselves or their classrooms.[10] When this loss of control occurs, teachers can be flooded with guilt. Teachers control negative emotions by continually monitoring their behavior and allowing themselves very little emotional leeway. They try to channel their emotions within the narrow boundaries of the teacher role. Social distance is a device teachers use to keep their tempers within bounds.[11]

PROTECTION FROM THE ACCUSATION OF FAVORITISM. It has already been mentioned that teachers are expected to administer justice evenhandedly.[12] Social distance makes favoritism easier to resist. It also makes it less likely that others will misunderstand a teacher's intentions. The accusation of favoritism invites privileged students to take advantage and nonprivileged students to cry foul and perhaps to rebel.[13] Social distance is an easy way to uphold the appearance of impartiality.

Devices for Maintaining Social Distance

Teachers employ a number of devices for maintaining social distance from students. Perhaps the most obvious is teacher attire. Teachers typically dress more formally than their students, and their clothing becomes a visual symbol of social distance. In schools where teacher dress becomes indistinguishable from student dress, school officials often institute faculty dress codes.

Students are usually required to address teachers formally, whereas teachers address students on a first-name basis. Teachers who allow their students to call them by their first names are often challenged by other teachers, who see such informality as disrespect and a potential challenge to their own authority.

Another sign of social distance is found in the formalistic, businesslike manner that teachers employ when dealing with students. Inevitably, some student

---

[9] Jules Henry, "American Schoolrooms: Learning the Nightmare," *Columbia University Forum,* Vol. 6 (Spring 1963), pp. 24–30.

[10] Dan Lortie, "The Teacher's Shame: Anger and the Normative Commitment of Classroom Teachers," *School Review,* Vol. 75 (Summer 1967), pp. 155–171.

[11] Willard Waller, *The Sociology of Teaching* (New York: John Wiley & Sons, Inc., 1967), p. 223.

[12] See Chapter 11.

[13] Waller, *The Sociology of Teaching,* p. 223.

will attempt to crack the facade of formality and address the person behind the teacher mask. A student might ask intimate questions, such as "How come you never got married?" "Does it bother you that you're getting bald?" "Have you ever smoked grass?" "How old were you when you lost your virginity?" Teachers who are anxious to maintain social distance will quickly move the conversation back to more formal territory: "That is nothing we need to discuss. What does need to be talked about is the test you failed last week."[14] It's easier to maintain social distance if teachers never let students see them out of role. When teachers address each other in the presence of students, they are likely to speak formally: "Mr. Klinger, Mr. Proctor has called a committee meeting at 3:30 and would like you to attend."

Staying in role at all times is difficult to accomplish. Therefore, most schools provide a location where teachers can momentarily step out of role. The teachers' lounge, like the faculty rest room, is typically off limits to students. This segregation minimizes the possibility that students will catch a glimpse of the real person who plays the teacher role.

Goffman has found that total institutions provide formal occasions when the staff may step out of role—and so, in many schools, time is set aside for role-release activities. These may take the form of faculty skits, student–faculty volleyball games, or a nostalgia day when everyone (including teachers) comes to school dressed in the bobby sox garb of the 1950s. Officially sanctioned occasions for role-release can give the impression of intimacy when in fact none exists. Seeing teachers out of role no doubt makes them seem more human and fun-loving than they appear in everyday school life. Such activities, which release some of the tensions that build up as the result of social distance, promote school solidarity. At the same time, role-release activities are carefully monitored so that they stay within the confines of preplanned activities and time periods. Thus it becomes easy to slide back into role and reestablish social distance when the role-release activity is completed.

Social Distance and Teacher Authority

Social-distance devices are methods for maintaining teacher authority or, to put it more bluntly, teacher power. It may seem odd that teachers are concerned with maintaining power when, compared to students, they seem downright omnipotent. The power of teachers, however, is always limited. It is true that teachers control the privilege and punishment systems of the school, but these are potent forces only insofar as students care about grades, teacher opinions, or parent reaction to poor school performance. When students begin not to care about these things (as they appear to be doing in growing numbers), teachers become increasingly powerless. Every order a teacher issues runs the risk of being disobeyed. Although teachers have great power in confrontations with disobedient students, they also have a great deal to lose. Whereas teachers are expected to win every confrontation, students may gain a sense of victory and pride by simply standing up to teacher authority. It can be argued that teachers generally have more of themselves invested in the role of teacher than students have invested in the role of student. Teaching, after all, is a chosen career, but

---

[14] For a discussion of this phenomenon, see Willard Waller, *The Sociology of Teaching*, especially Chapter 17, "Social Distance: Buffer Phrases," pp. 279–291.

students are forced into the pupil role. Therefore, there is a tendency for teachers to take their status quite seriously, whereas students tend to devalue and distance themselves from the pupil status.

Teaching is an audacious act, for it assumes that teachers have something to offer students that is worth their time, obedience, and attention. It seems that teachers are the first people to be taken in by the audacity of their work. They value it and judge themselves according to how well they get the job done. However, for reasons explained in the last chapter, students do not usually attach much significance to their schoolwork and may derive little sense of self-hood from classroom assignments.

The Teacher–Student Relationship and the Classroom Audience

The teacher–student interaction goes on before an audience of other students, and this fact can significantly affect the content and tone of the exchange. However, there is power in privacy. Thus, veteran teachers and educational researchers advise novice teachers to discuss a student's misbehavior outside of class and away from other students. Freed from the pressure of onlookers, student–teacher skirmishes can usually be handled amiably. Compromise is possible, and each can afford to see the problem as the other sees it. When the confrontation is public, however, the antagonists often play to the perceptions of the onlooking group. The student who challenges a teacher's authority may be rewarded by peers for his or her courage. The challenge is the victory. Playing to peers, however, can blind such a student to the teacher's definition of the situation. Teachers know they must win such confrontations. To lose is to invite more disruption, increase their vulnerability, and challenge their feelings of professional adequacy. These pressures may blind the teacher to the student's definition of the situation.

The public nature of the student–teacher relationship makes personal communication difficult and increases social distance. We need not blame teachers or students for their narrow vision of the classroom world, but it is important to understand what part the institutional situation plays in creating hostilities and social distance. Teachers who do not understand the dynamics of the situation will not be able to change them. In fact, the situation may well change teachers in ways that leave them surprised, confused, and disappointed, as the following remarks by a first-year teacher exemplify all too vividly:

> I teach reading in the seventh grade, and I am faced with situations in which I feel myself being pushed so far by the kids that I am somebody so completely different I don't even recognize me as me. I'm really afraid I'm getting out of control, feeling myself faced with too many stresses.[15]

The Uses of Power and Authority

Discussions of power are often offensive to teachers because the term violates their belief in what teaching should be. They desire primary relationships with students who want to learn what they have to teach. Had they been interested in wielding power, monitoring behavior, and punishing disobedience, they might

---

[15] Bower, *Teachers Talk About Their Feelings*, pp. 8–9.

have chosen another occupation—police work, for example. The fact is, how-ever, that the need for authority is built into the teacher role, even in the best situations.

Let's take an example of a teenager who is highly motivated to learn to play the guitar and saves her money to pay for lessons. Despite her motivation, part of learning to play the instrument is difficult, unrewarding, and just plain dull. Rather than learn how to read music, she would prefer to go right to chord work. Rather than building finger dexterity and strength for bar chords, she would prefer to use simpler, more limiting techniques. Yet, because she is mo-tivated and because she trusts the advice of her teacher, she follows his instruc-tions. If we define power and authority as the ability to get people to do what they do not necessarily want to do, then this music teacher clearly has power over his student. Learning always begins with some degree (sometimes a great degree) of frustration. Teacher authority helps keep students on task and helps them resist the temptation to give up or to take some easy and unproductive way out of frustrating situations.

It is tempting to think that teachers have no need for power, but such a view misses the point that learning is inherently frustrating and that teachers can help students manage the discomforts that are quite naturally a part of learn-ing. The question is not Should teachers have authority? but What kind of authority should teachers possess?

Types of Authority: Personal Power and Positional Power

Max Weber made a useful and now classic distinction between positional and personal authority. These types of authority grow from different sources and are maintained by different methods. *Positional authority*[16] resides in the orga-nization and is assigned by the institution to a status. It is not earned by status occupants but comes with the office they hold. For example, the positional power of teachers demands that they be treated respectfully by students simply because they are teachers.

Personal authority is not bestowed by the institution; it grows from an individ-ual's personality. We do the person's bidding because we trust his or her judg-ment, experience, and expertise. For example, the music teacher just discussed had personal authority because the student trusted his judgment and valued his advice. She knew that she would not be asked to do difficult preliminary work if it would not help her later performance.

While positional authority demands social distance, personal power may re-quire the intimacy of primary relationships. We need information and contact with a teacher to know whether he or she qualifies for our respect and can be trusted. Positional power is built into the institution and is bestowed in equal measure upon all who occupy the status of teacher. Personal authority is the product of the primary relationships teachers forge with their pupils. Positional authority is immediately assigned by the school and requires social distance; personal authority grows over time and is given voluntarily to teachers by their pupils. Positional authority demands *obedience* from students; personal author-ity invites a negotiated *conformity* to shared goals.[17] Teachers who win personal

---

[16] Willard Waller uses the phrase *institutional authority* in *The Sociology of Teaching*, pp. 189–211.
[17] See Chapter 5 for a discussion of the distinction between obedience and conformity.

authority do not necessarily give up positional authority. The power of their status remains and can be used when the situation requires. Good teaching is difficult without establishing some degree of personal authority in the classroom.

There are no formulas for establishing personal authority any more than there are easy recipes for friendship. However, some general principles can give guidance to the novice practitioner. Effective teachers know their subject matter thoroughly, communicate its value to their pupils, make the material intelligible, stretch their pupils' abilities, and reward real accomplishment. The best teachers are those who love their subject and genuinely respect their pupils. They bring their subject alive in the classroom and, through the subject, give life to students' powers of understanding and creativity.

The Teacher and the Institution

So far the point of this chapter has been that the structure of schools significantly affects teacher behavior. This point of view, however, does not tell the whole story. Teachers come into the classroom with different beliefs, dispositions, and personalities, and these qualities interact with the institution in unique ways. An explanation of teacher behavior is not to be found totally within the institution or totally within the individual but rather in the interaction of the two.

It has been pointed out that the organizational arrangements of the school encourage teachers to rely on positional power, yet it is clear that some teachers resist these pressures and are able to establish personal authority with their students. How do they accomplish this feat? Part of the answer lies in the beliefs that teachers bring to the classroom, and part of it lies in how the teacher translates attitudes into action. Let's examine these issues one at a time.

Teacher Beliefs

Some teachers come to the profession with conservative values. They have faith that the universe is governed by fixed laws and that human behavior should be guided by fixed truths. They see education as a means for communicating unchanging wisdom. Though they have great respect for human accomplishments, they are keenly aware that the people are capable of ignoring truth and doing evil. They fault liberals for not taking such misconduct into account and look to institutions such as law, religion, the family, and the school to check humankind's most evil inclinations. Conservative teachers are not ideological undertakers intent on burying human imagination or hope. They see themselves as caretakers who are dedicated to preserving human wisdom and strengthening the institutions that productively channel human behavior. According to National Education Association data, about 20 percent of teachers consider themselves conservative and 45 percent say their beliefs tend to be conservative.[18]

On the opposite side of the ideological divide, we find liberal teachers. They do not have a faith in fixed truth but believe that human intelligence is capable of improving our understanding of how the world works. They see schools as

---

[18] National Education Association, *Status of the American Public School Teacher: 1985–86*, p. 89.

TABLE 14-1.   Teacher Beliefs Regarding Authority by Teacher Ideology

Authority Preference	Self-Assigned Ideological Labels			
	Conservative	Somewhat Conservative	Somewhat Liberal	Liberal
Personal Authority	46.9%	52.1%	64.3%	80.8%
Positional Authority	53.1%	47.9%	35.7%	19.2%
Total Percentage	100%	100%	100%	100%

SOURCE: An unpublished portion of a study of teacher attitudes: Rodman B. Webb and Sue Legg, "The Drug Education Controversy: Attitudes of Educators and Experts," *Research Bulletin,* Vol. 12, No. 2 (Fort Myers, FL: Florida Educational Research and Development Council, 1978).

places where children can develop their powers of reason. Liberal teachers generally trust human nature and see schools as an instrument for liberating the reasoning and cooperative capacities of students. According to National Education Association data, roughly 7 percent of teachers identify themselves as liberal, and 27 percent say their beliefs tend in the liberal direction.[19]

Both liberal and conservative teachers come into teaching with a strong desire to build a rapport with students, to win their allegiance, and to make a contribution to the lives of young people. The school experience, as we have seen, mitigates against personal relationships and pressures teachers to adopt positional power. Conservative teachers move more easily into positional power than do liberal teachers. It appears that conservative beliefs are more compatible with the bureaucratic ideology than are liberal beliefs. There is evidence to suggest that the beliefs of liberal teachers keep them conscious of the institutional pressures toward positional power and enable many to resist being socialized by default. Table 14-1 illustrates this point: A survey asked a sample of sixth- through twelfth-grade Florida teachers to choose which of the following statements more closely describes the ideal student–teacher relationship:

> Positional power: It is important that all teachers be treated with respect by students. Students must learn to respect authority because teachers are older, more experienced, and better informed than students.

> Personal power: Teachers should not be shown respect merely because of age and experience and because they are teachers. Students' respect must be earned.

Notice that a slight majority of conservative teachers indicated a preference for positional authority whereas a large majority of liberal teachers preferred personal authority. Although it is true that schools socialize teachers to be increasingly control oriented and decreasingly nurturing and caring, it is also true that teachers' ideological beliefs can advance or retard this socialization.

Creating Personal Authority

Every time teachers face new students, they are perceived by the class as wearing the garb of positional authority. Teachers need not apply for such authority; it comes with the job and, with the exception of the early elementary grades,

[19] Ibid.

Most teachers work hard to build primary relationships with their students. (*Source: National Education Association, Joe Di Dio.*)

it is built into the expectations of students. Few teachers can trade positional authority for personal authority at will. If teachers divest themselves of the authority that their roles provide, they often find themselves without any authority at all. As we have seen, this loss of authority invites disruption. Students, trained in the total institution setting of the school, rarely learn self-control or cooperative self-government. A relaxation of rules can degenerate into the pandemonium of a liberation celebration. It appears that teachers who successfully move from positional to personal authority make the transition gradually. They accept positional power as a fact of institutional life, yet understand that another kind of authority will eventually become available. They work patiently at developing positive relationships with students and educating them for democracy. By giving students a share in generating the rules that govern the classroom and a share in developing enforcement procedures, progressive teachers help students internalize the rules of cooperative interaction. As students become more proficient at self-control, as they get to know the teacher and get used to the idea of democratic classrooms, progressive teachers begin to divest themselves of positional power and utilize personal authority.

Teacher–Teacher Interaction

The Need for Allies

With all the pressures they face in the classroom, one might think that teachers would work to establish strong relationships with their fellow teachers. Such relationships could serve to alleviate self-doubt, reestablish self-worth, and rekindle teacher determination. They could help to establish and reinforce the educational aims of the school and facilitate the sharing of workable methods and worthwhile ideas. Yet, most studies of teacher–teacher interaction emphasize the insularity of teaching and the superficiality of teacher interaction.[20]

Teacher Insularity

The insularity of teachers is enforced by physical barriers and social norms within the school. Open-space schools and team teaching notwithstanding, the vast majority of teachers work behind closed doors, safely out of the eyesight and earshot of other teachers.[21] Opinions about what goes on in another teacher's classroom are based on sketchy knowledge. Teachers observe one another riding herd on students in public situations (lunchroom lines, gatherings in the auditorium, activities on the playground), but information about classroom activities is usually secondhand and based on a teacher's self-reports.[22]

A teacher's report of classroom success, even when couched in appropriately modest language, is often seen by colleagues as self-advertisement and may not be taken seriously. If such reports become too frequent and come to threaten the professional self-assurance of colleagues, the offending teacher may be pressured to change his or her behavior. Subtle pressure is especially likely if displays of classroom success become public and attract the attention of the administration, parents, and the community. For example, a teacher who publishes a class magazine, puts on a play for the school, or arranges a camping trip for the class may be told by colleagues, "It's wonderful that the children are having so much fun with you this year, but I just hope they don't forget how to study or they'll be in real trouble when they get to me." Or a high

---

20   McPherson, *Small Town Teacher;* Waller, *The Sociology of Teaching;* Howard Becker, "The Teacher in the Authority System of the Public School," in *Sociological Work* (Chicago: Aldine Publishing Company, 1970), pp. 151–164; Mary Bredemeier and Harry Bredemeier, *Social Forces in Education* (Sherman Oaks, CA: Alfred Publishing Co., Inc.), pp. 256–258; Robert Dreeben, *The Nature of Teaching* (Glenview, IL: Scott, Foresman & Company, 1970), pp. 41–81.

21   National Education Association, *The Status of the American Public School Teacher, 1975–76* (Washington, DC: National Education Association, Research Division, 1977), p. 22. NEA data reveal that only 16 percent of teachers are presently in team-teaching situations for all or part of the day.

22   For some useful discussions of teacher insularity, see Richard Warren, "Context and Isolation: The Teaching Experience in the Elementary School," *Human Organization*, Vol. 34 (Summer 1975), pp. 139–147; Alan Zucker, "Isolation at the Top, Degradation at the Bottom: A Reply to Philip Jackson," *School Review*, Vol. 86 (November 1977), pp. 104–108; Patrick Forsyth and Wayne Hoy, "Isolation and Alienation in Educational Organizations," *Educational Administration Quarterly*, Vol. 14 (Winter 1978), pp. 80–96.

school teacher whose students advertise that Miss Jones is a "great teacher" may find colleagues making the safely guarded point, "Anyone can entertain students; the real challenge is to teach them."

Because teachers do not see one another at work and because they often devalue the self-reports of colleagues, they are deprived of constructive evaluations of their own accomplishments and professional support for their methods. Teachers' professional self-confidence is largely self-constructed and is therefore quite vulnerable. A few bad experiences or a couple of mediocre days may throw them into self-doubt. Even when things seem to be going well, there is the lingering suspicion that they are fooling themselves, that they are really not as good as they pretend to be. This insecurity encourages isolation. Teachers who are uncertain about their ability do not enjoy situations where their competence can be evaluated by others. They fear they will be misjudged—or worse fairly judged—as incompetent. Teachers may be careful not to discuss their insecurities with colleagues for fear the comments of others might confirm their own worst suspicions.[23]

Because many teachers share these feelings of insecurity, norms of noninterference are easily established in schools. Teachers are expected to stay out of one another's classrooms. When some intrusion is necessary (when a teacher has to deliver a message, for example), the intruding teacher is expected to leave quickly and to punctuate the visit with profuse apologies. Goodlad reports that the teachers in his study seldom lent assistance to colleagues, observed one another teaching, shared ideas, dealt collaboratively on schoolwide problems, or hammered out the aims of education for their school.[24] In another study, a teacher told Ashton and Webb that she and her colleagues worked "in their own little world[s]. Everybody is doing their own thing and nobody is helping anybody else."[25] Isolated and uncertain about their accomplishments, many teachers perfect systems of impression management designed to convince colleagues of their capabilities and hide from their peers any hint of vulnerability. Another teacher explained that at her school you "never let another teacher find a weakness or an area you need help in." Such admissions increased teachers' sense of uncertainty and professional self-confidence. The teacher went on:

> You never go into the teachers' lounge and hear a teacher say, "Damn, I really failed . . . that kid today." You never hear that. You always hear how a teacher was on top of the situation. If there is any discussion of problems, teachers . . . make sure their admissions are always equal. Teachers aren't supposed to be vulnerable. In your classroom when you show vulnerability you lose control. You practice that behavior eight hours a day. So how can you help but having it affect your thinking outside the classroom?[26]

---

[23] Lipsky studied professionals who work in human service bureaucracies (teachers, social workers, public defenders, public health nurses, and so on) and found that they all worked in isolation and maintained norms of noninterference that inhibit them from seeking the guidance of colleagues because to ask for help is to "admit to a degree of incapacity." Michael Lipsky, *Street-Level Bureaucracy: Dilemmas of the Individual in Public Services* (New York: Russell Sage Foundation, 1980), p. 203. Available in paperback.

[24] John I. Goodlad, *A Place Called School: Prospects for the Future* (New York: McGraw-Hill Book Company, 1984), pp. 186–188.

[25] Patricia T. Ashton and Rodman B. Webb, *Making a Difference: Teachers' Sense of Efficacy and Student Achievement* (New York: Longman, 1986), p. 45.

[26] Ibid., p. 64.

The Functions of Isolation

Gertrude McPherson has called the norms that enforce teacher isolation "the ideology of noninterference" and contends that it is a major barrier to teacher cooperation.[27] She points out, however, that it serves some interesting social functions within the school. It enhances teacher solidarity by minimizing the opportunity for discord and competition. It prevents gaudy, self-serving displays of superiority that carry with them the unspoken but clear message that other teachers are inferior. As McPherson explains, "If one teacher did not interfere with another, she neither showed off her success nor threatened the shaky security of another."[28] Thus, the ideology of noninterference serves an important peace-keeping function within the school.

Teaching is a difficult occupation that invites insecurity. Teachers feel vulnerable to the misbehavior of students, the opinions of colleagues, the evaluations of administrators, the complaints of parents, and their own self-doubts. Understandably, they go to great lengths to maintain smooth relationships with their peers. Teacher discord could add intolerable pressure to an already pressure-filled profession.

Teachers are careful to avoid confrontations with one another and to keep school relationships calm and free of friction. They are slow to criticize each other (at least directly), and when compelled to do so, they usually keep their comments passionless and subtle. The closing of a classroom door may carry the message that the class next door is being too noisy. An angry look at a student may indicate that a fellow teacher is neglecting her duty. A general comment that children should never be humiliated may be a veiled criticism of a teacher's continued threat to dress misbehaving students in diapers.

The Dysfunction of Isolation

NO HELP.   Although the ideology of noninterference may keep the peace in schools, it has other less desirable consequences. It makes it difficult for teachers to get help from one another when they need it. McPherson found that teachers were reluctant to answer real requests for help, for fear that their suggestions or their intentions would be misconstrued as meddling. Thus, the teacher who asks in desperation, "What can I do with a class of behavior problems?" may get the flippant reply, "Have you tried dipping them in hot wax?" Similarly, when teachers disguise their criticism of colleagues behind subtle comments, the problem is only vaguely identified, and its solution remains a mystery. It is one thing to let a teacher know he should have better control of his class and quite another to give him the skills he needs to do it.

SUPERFICIAL TALK.   The desire to keep the peace not only affects what teachers say, but it also influences the language they use. Teachers may hold widely dissimilar aims for education. Some adhere to Durkheim's values, others to Rogers's ideals, and still others to Dewey's aims. We might expect that such divergent ideas would cause conflict, but this is usually not the case. The ideology of noninterference discourages teachers from discussing fundamental ideas

---

[27] McPherson, *Small Town Teacher*, p. 65.
[28] Ibid.

about education. When discussions turn in this direction, the conversation is often conducted in such general and essentially meaningless terms that basic disagreements stay safely hidden. The slogans of education (education should meet the needs of the child, promote moral development, help children reach their potential, encourage thought, and so on) are soft and inarticulate. They hide rather than clarify disagreements as to what children need, what constitutes moral development, what the definition of potential is, and what kind of thought best serves the interests of the child and the needs of society. Thus, professional discussions of educational aims, when they occur at all, often degenerate into a useless exchange of platitudes. As McPherson discovered:

> Talk among teachers tended to be light, superficial, and rarely serious. One teacher listened only sporadically and half-heartedly to another. . . . Many conversations hardly touched upon school matters: Those that did rarely focused on teaching methods, educational philosophy, or the content of class material.[29]

Such superficiality does little to promote sound educational policies, school programs, or professional development. It increases the insularity of teachers, protects their classroom autonomy, lessens conflict, and promotes teacher solidarity. In short, it helps teachers deal with their vulnerability to parents, students, the administration, and fellow teachers. By refusing to reveal their insecurities about education, they maintain a front of self-reliance. By refusing to discuss fundamental questions about education, they guard themselves against criticism from colleagues. McPherson found in her study that teachers tend to wear masks "of inscrutability and invulnerability. . . . If one teacher starts to drop the mask, the others at once help . . . replace it."[30] Yet all of this superficiality does not give teachers the feedback they need in order to know how they are doing. It hinders the development of worthwhile aims, substitutes apparent camaraderie for real community, and leaves teachers fundamentally alone, fatigued, and apprehensive.

Overcoming Teacher Isolation

A number of recent studies have identified teacher isolation as a serious problem that must be overcome if the quality of education in America is to be improved.[31] The reasons for teacher isolation are psychological as well as structural. Thus, teacher isolation will not be eliminated simply by telling teachers that they must share time and ideas. The physical barriers separating teachers can be diminished by redesigning schools so that there is greater potential for teacher interaction. There are many ways of accomplishing this end. For example, one school abandoned the traditional linear classroom design (see Figure 14-1) and adopted an hexagonal design (see Figure 14-2).

---

[29] Ibid., p. 73.
[30] Ibid., p. 75.
[31] Ashton and Webb, *Making a Difference*, pp. 19, 45–48, 59–66, 172; Ernest L. Boyer, *High School: A Report on Secondary Education in America* (New York: Harper & Row, 1983), pp. 157, 160, 171; Goodlad, *A Place Called School*, pp. 186–188; Lipsky, *Street-Level Bureaucracy*, pp. 203, 206, 208; Arthur G. Powell, Eleanor Farrar, and David Cohen, *The Shopping Mall High School: Winners and Losers in the Educational Marketplace* (Boston: Houghton-Mifflin Company, 1985), pp. 56–57, 167, 311, 319–320. Theodore R. Sizer, *Horace's Compromise: The Dilemmas of the American High School* (Boston: Houghton-Mifflin, 1984), p. 92.

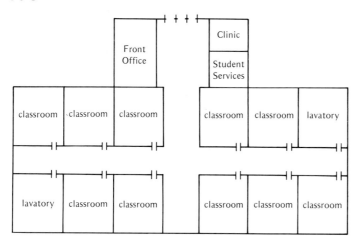

Figure 14-1 Traditional architectural arrangement of American schools. Classrooms are isolated and teachers cannot see one another at work.

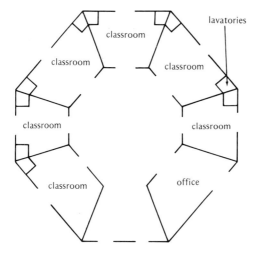

Figure 14-2 Innovative architectural arrangement. Classrooms open on to free space thus minimizing isolation and maximizing opportunities for observation, communication, collaboration, and assistance.

Abandoning the architecture of isolation promotes a visible community where people see one another at work, share activities, exchange ideas, lend assistance, and give support. However, an alteration of the physical arrangements of the school by itself cannot transform the social ecology of the institution. A belief system that legitimates cooperation and sharing must be developed.

An ideology of professional cooperation is established when the leadership of the school promotes faculty interaction and when teachers are given the time and opportunities to work together. Thus, school schedules must be adjusted to provide opportunities for teamwork. *Scheduled involvement* can be accomplished in several ways. Grade-level high school teachers might be given a common planning period for meetings and curriculum development. Middle school teachers might be divided into teams that stay with a class through its entire middle school career.[32] Such teaching teams have common planning times to

[32] Ashton and Webb, *Making a Difference*, pp. 91–124.

discuss student progress and develop an integrated curriculum that challenges the abilities and captures the interests of their pupils. On the elementary level, flexible scheduling would allow teachers to plan cooperative projects. Several national reports have concluded that teaches should be given more time for cooperative work and that their class loads need to be cut.[33]

Even if teachers work in settings designed to promote interaction, are encouraged to cooperate, and are given time to meet, the faculty still may retain their habits of isolation. Cooperation heightens the possibility of disagreement and puts uncertain teachers at risk. In order to make cooperation worth the risk and effort, administrators must be willing to give teachers a real say in decision making. Here again, we see the need for giving teachers greater control over the conditions of their work and greater say in decisions that affect their professional practice. As we learned in Chapter 9, the Carnegie Forum on Teaching and the Economy has called for greater collegial decision making in schools and significant reduction in the size and complexity of school bureaucracy.[34] The aim of such proposals is to help teachers to become reflective practitioners[35] and to unleash their collective intelligence on the problem of school improvement.[36]

Though no one of the proposed changes in the structure and organization of schools will necessarily eradicate isolation, together they can work in positive circularity to empower teachers and make the governance of schools more democratic (see Figure 14-3).

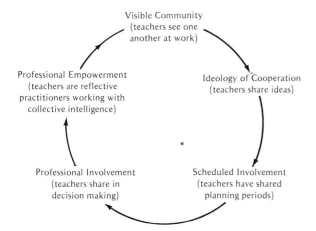

Figure 14-3   Empowering teachers and making the workplace more democratic by reducing isolation and the ideology of non-interference.

[33] Powell, Farrar, and Cohen, *The Shopping Mall High School*, pp. 319–320; Sizer, *Horace's Compromise*, p. 159.
[34] Task Force on Teaching as a Profession, *A Nation Prepared: Teachers for the 21st Century* (New York: Carnegie Forum on Teaching and the Economy, 1986). Available in paperback.
[35] Donald A. Schön, *The Reflective Practitioner: How Professionals Think in Action* (New York: Basic Books, 1983). Available in paperback.
[36] Bruce R. Joyce, Richard H. Hersh, and Michael McKibbin, *The Structure of School Improvement* (New York: Longman, 1983).

The Teacher–Parent Relationship

If teachers are isolated from colleagues, they are even more isolated from parents. We might have thought that the teacher–parent relationship would be close and lasting. After all, the two share a mutual interest in the child's welfare. As Waller has pointed out, however, the teacher–parent interaction is characterized more by distrust and enmity than by harmony and goodwill.[37] There are a number of reasons for this.

First, parents see their children differently from the ways in which teachers see them. The parent–child relationship is emotionally charged. Parents deal with the particular, unique characteristics of children. In the terminology of Talcott Parsons, the relationship is *particularistic*. The teacher–child relationship, on the other hand, is emotionally restrained and characterized by social distance. In Parsons's language, such a relationship is *universalistic*. Teachers must orient themselves toward one aspect of the child's school life—achievement—and must not let the child's emotional needs impinge too deeply on their relationship.[38] Teachers cannot play a parenting role but must treat children equally, according to "universal" criteria that are formal, abstract, and generalizable.

Conflicts can result from these different perspectives. As Sarah Lightfoot suggests, when parents ask that their children be given a fair chance, they are usually requesting that the special needs of the "particular" child be taken into consideration. From the teacher's point of view, however, giving children a fair chance means giving them the same opportunity open to other students, treating them equally, and judging them according to a universal standard.[39] Waller has contended that this fundamental difference in perspective makes teacher–parent conflicts natural and to some degree inevitable.[40]

Another source of parent–teacher conflict has been suggested by Harry and Mary Bredemeier. It revolves around the question of who gets credit when a student is doing well in school and who takes the blame when a child does poorly. From the teacher's vantage point, the child's success is the result of the teacher's patient labor. He aroused the child's interests, he disciplined her misbehavior, and he taught her the skills she now displays so proudly. But, from the parents' viewpoint, the child's abilities are family-based and the result of good parenting.[41]

If parents and teachers compete for credit when a child does well, they are equally anxious to rid themselves of blame when a child performs badly. A teacher's complaints about a child's disobedience seldom include the suggestion of personal failure on the part of the teacher. There is the unspoken message that the child's problem is home based. Parents read these subtle messages and may quickly respond, "We can't understand why Teddy would do such a thing. He never acts that way at home." The suggestion in this statement

---

[37] Waller, *The Sociology of Teaching*, pp. 68–79.
[38] Talcott Parsons, "The School Class as a Social System: Some of Its Functions in American Society," *Harvard Educational Review*, Vol. 29 (Fall 1959), pp. 297–318.
[39] Sarah Lawrence Lightfoot, *Worlds Apart* (New York: Basic Books, Inc., Publishers, 1978), p. 22.
[40] Waller, *The Sociology of Teaching*, pp. 66 ff.
[41] Mary Bredemeier and Harry Bredemeier, *Social Forces in Education*, pp. 274–279.

is that the problem resides not in the family or in the child but in the classroom and, more specifically, in the teacher. Much of this conflict rests on inadequate knowledge. Teachers cannot fully appreciate the position of parents because they do not see the parents in action in the home. The reverse is also true. Parents do not fully appreciate the accomplishments of teachers because they seldom see what teachers do in the classroom. Parent information about school activities is largely secondhand and usually comes from children.

Parents and teachers share control over the child, and there is sometimes a disagreement as to the location and the extent of this control. On the surface this seems a simple enough matter: The child is under teacher direction in the school and under parental control in the home. But these spheres of influence do not have clear boundaries. A parent may wish to take a child out of school for a family trip, or a teacher may want a child to stay after school for punishment or special help. At times, both teachers and parents attempt to extend their influence into the others' domain. A teacher may ask parents to monitor a child's homework or adopt a new discipline procedure in the home. A parent may send a sick child to school and ask that the teacher administer medicine or keep the child in during play time. As McPherson observes, such battles over turf and control are usually won by parents, unless the conflict severely challenges the authority of the school.

Parents as Potential "Troublemakers"

The informal intelligence network of any school carries the names of parents who are likely to give teachers "a bad time." Some parents are outspoken, are strong willed, have an eye for school problems, and are quick to bring these problems to light. Teachers often see such parents as "crackpots" or "troublemakers" and label them as such in the privacy of the teachers' lounge. But in public, teachers are usually more circumspect, knowing that even "crackpots" can cause teachers a good deal of grief. It is a careless teacher who speaks negatively about parents or students outside of school. Most educators take pains not to needlessly annoy or upset parents and will go out of their way to satisfy them. Parents with power in the community are seen as most potentially threatening. Not infrequently, children from influential families are given deferential treatment in classrooms in order to avoid problems with their parents.

Dealing with Parents

In any institution where there is a built-in strain between two groups, we find official and unofficial mechanisms for lessening conflict. One method for lessening conflict is the parent–teacher conference. Such meetings are officially scheduled once or twice during the school year. Other meetings can be called as needed. These meetings are formal, ritualistic, often perfunctory, and teachers tend to devalue them. "You only see the parents whose children are doing well; you don't see the ones whose kids are in trouble" is a typical teacher complaint. The meetings are often scheduled at fifteen- or thirty-minute intervals that allow little opportunity for a useful exchange of information, concerns, criticisms, or real negotiations once social pleasantries are exchanged.[42]

On special occasions, conferences may be requested by teachers or parents.

---

[42] Lightfoot, *Worlds Apart.*

Such meetings are usually called when specific students are experiencing difficulty rather than when teachers think things are going well. "Bad-news conferences" are occasions for anxiety on the part of teachers and parents alike and too rarely result in collaboration. Parents want their children to do well and are upset by news to the contrary. Teachers worry that parents may blame them for the child's poor performance. It is significant that the conferences take place in classrooms (the teacher's turf) with parents often perched on student-sized chairs. Well-prepared teachers bring to the meetings their grade book, the student's accumulative record, achievement test scores, and perhaps some examples of the student's work. This setting puts the parent at some disadvantage and helps establish the teacher's authority.

The demeanor of a seasoned teacher during these conferences is usually one of friendly, authoritative concern. Most avoid arguments, listen patiently to parental complaints, and try not to take accusations personally. The aim of experienced teachers is not so much to win a skirmish with parents as to contain it and avoid its escalating into a bigger battle that could be fought at higher levels.

The position of teachers is greatly enhanced if they have established themselves in the community and enjoy a reputation for fairness and excellence. Concerned parents may become less worried about what is going on in the classroom if their friends think well of the teacher.

As we indicated in Chapter 6 the parent–teacher relationship can be enhanced if schools function as mediating institutions. This would mean, among other things, that parents are kept abreast of school aims, curriculum design, classroom activities, and students' progress.[43] Newsletters; school newspapers; stories in the local press; television coverage of important educational events; school advisory committees; active Parent-Teacher Associations, where parents are given a real say rather than perfunctory power; homework hotlines; evening classes for parents on such subjects as child rearing, monitoring homework assignments, drug abuse, or the mystery of adolescents are all efforts to keep parents informed about and involved with the school. The mere willingness to listen to parents' suggestions sometimes significantly improves the parents' ability to work with the school. For example, parents at one school requested that teachers type out the week's assignments and send them home with students every Monday. Parents learned to expect the assignment sheets and to help their children organize their time accordingly. As a result, the homework completion rate rose and the quality of the work improved.

The Teacher–Principal Relationship

When all else fails, teachers expect the principal to protect them from marauding parents. According to one national survey, more than 75 percent of high schools have procedures for handling parent complaints.[44] Nearly 70 percent

---

[43] H. J. Becker and J. Epstein, "Parent Involvement: A Survey of Teacher Practices," *The Elementary School Journal*, Vol. 83, No. 2 (November 1982), pp. 85–102; Herbert J. Walberg, "Families as Partners in Educational Productivity," *Phi Delta Kappan*, Vol. 65, No. 16 (February 1984), pp. 397–400.

[44] Susan Abramowitz and Ellen Tenenbaum, *High School '77: A Survey of Public Secondary School Principals* (Washington, DC: National Institute of Education, 1978), pp. 34, 97.

of principals indicated that resolving or mediating conflicts is a very important part of their job.[45] These findings confirm work done by Howard Becker that indicated that for teachers the most important part of the principal's job is "backing the teacher up" in all cases of parental "interference."[46]

The job of the principal is difficult because it entails satisfying the conflicting interests of different groups. Principals must administer school-district policies, satisfy local parents, keep up teacher efficacy and morale, and deal with discipline problems that cannot be handled in the classroom. Despite these strains, principals are generally quite satisfied with their jobs. One national study indicated that 65 percent of high school principals were very satisfied and 29 percent were somewhat satisfied with their work.[47] Another survey of 1600 principals indicated that two-thirds found their jobs moderately prestigious and fulfilling.[48]

The principal–teacher relationship is an interesting one. On the one hand, principals need the cooperation of teachers in order to do their jobs effectively. Without the support of their faculty, principals are unable to administer district policies and are open to criticism from above. Principals, however, have little to offer teachers in exchange for their cooperation. Because salary raises are usually fixed by negotiated schedules, the loyalties of teachers cannot be bought, at least not financially. Principals must find other ways to reward faculty cooperation. Adam Scrupski found that teachers will accept a principal's authority if he or she will grant them autonomy over classroom practices. This agreement increases the isolation of teachers, but it also serves to minimize teacher–principal conflict.[49]

Principals have a few other perquisites that can be dispensed to cooperative teachers. For example, they can support teacher authority in disputes with students. As might be expected, given what we know about the student–teacher conflict, teachers feel administrative support is vital if they are to carry out their assigned duties. In a recent unpublished study, 95 percent of Florida middle school and high school teachers agreed with the statement, "Teachers must always be able to count on strong administrative support in cases involving student discipline."

Summary

This chapter has described the school experience of teachers. Teaching is a difficult occupation, beset with conflicts. Teachers have precarious relationships with students, fellow teachers, parents, and administrators. The structure of the school institutionalizes conflict but does not give the teacher ready allies. At times, the institution even sets the teacher against himself or herself, for it

---

[45] Ibid.

[46] Becker, "The Teacher in the Authority System of the Public School," in *Sociological Work*, pp. 151–163.

[47] Abramowitz and Tenenbaum, *High School '77*, p. 55.

[48] David Bryne, Susan Hines, and Lloyd McCleary, *The National Survey*, Vol. 1 of *The Senior High Principalship* (Reston, VA: National Association of Secondary School Principals, 1978).

[49] Adam Scrupski, "Administrative Support for Teachers and Teacher Legitimation of Administrative Authority: A Test of an Exchange Theory of the Social System of the School" (Ed.D. diss., Rutgers University, 1970). See also Robert Dreeben, *The Nature of Teaching*, pp. 57–75.

encourages teaching behaviors that may conflict with an individual's personal value structure.

By focusing on the problems of teachers and how they handle these problems, it is easier to understand some of the more mysterious aspects of schooling. For example, we can see that social distance from students serves to protect teachers from hurt, helps them to keep their emotions in check, guards them against accusations of favoritism, and helps maintain teacher authority.

It was suggested that authority is the vital part of the teacher role but that there are two kinds of teacher power: personal authority, which grows from the personality of the individual, and positional authority, which resides in a teacher's official status. We pointed out that personal authority is established only over time, whereas positional authority is immediately bestowed. A number of mechanisms move teachers toward institutionalized authority and discourage personal authority. However, some teachers are able to build personal power if they do not invite student disruption by giving up positional authority too quickly.

Teacher interaction is often limited by a school-based ideology of noninterference. This ideology guards teacher autonomy but it also limits cooperation and deprives teachers of a much-needed source of mutual support and professional improvement.

Teacher–parent conflicts grow from the differing relationships that teachers and parents have with children. Parent–child relationships are particularistic, whereas teacher–child relationships are generally universalistic. Furthermore, parents and teachers each tend to assign credit to themselves for a student's success and to blame the other for a student's failure. At times, they compete for control over the child's activity.

The principal–teacher relationship potentially invites conflict because principals usually evaluate teachers' work and implement school board policies that may run counter to teacher expectation. This conflict is reduced somewhat if principals help protect teachers' authority and autonomy and do not challenge their decision-making powers in the classroom.

Suggested Readings

Many teachers in recent years have taken time to report their classroom experiences. Though their accounts are often critical of the public school system, they provide detailed accounts of the pressures and joys that accompany teaching.

ASHTON-WARNER, SYLVIA. *Teacher.* New York: Simon & Schuster, 1963. This is a positive account of teaching.

HERNDON, JAMES. *Notes From a School Teacher.* New York: Simon Schuster, 1985. Herndon shows that the distance separating policy makers and classroom teachers is vast, and the communication between these two points in the educational system is nil.

HIGHET, GILBERT. *The Art of Teaching.* New York: Vintage Books, 1955. This is required reading for every aspiring or disheartened teacher and a useful antidote for the romanticism of Holt and Kozol.

JAMES, WILLIAM. *Talks to Teachers . . . and Students.* New York: Henry Holt, 1899. Still relevant today, the author predicted that psychological research in education would be of little use and risks replacing a focus on subject matter with a concern for teaching techniques.

More technical analyses of teachers and their work can be found in the following:

BALL, STEPHEN, and IVOR GOODSON, eds. *Teachers' Lives and Careers*. London: Falmer Press, 1985.

BECKER, HOWARD S. *Sociological Work*. Chicago: Aldine Publishing Company, 1970. The book contains, among other things, Becker's articles on educational organizations and experiences.

BOYER, ERNEST L. *High School: A Report on Secondary Education in America*. New York: Harper & Row, 1983. This is a comprehensive study of American high school education.

DREEBEN, ROBERT. *The Nature of Teaching: Schools and the Work of Teachers*. Glenview, IL: Scott, Foresman and Company, 1970.

EDDY, ELIZABETH M. *Becoming a Teacher: The Passage to Professional Status*. New York: Teachers College Press, 1969.

ELSBREE, W. S. *The American Teacher*. New York: American Book Company, 1939.

FEISTRITZER, EMILY E. *The Making of a Teacher: A Report on Teacher Education and Certification*. Washington DC: National Center for Education Information, 1984. This is an informative survey.

GOODLAD, JOHN I. *A Place Called School: Prospects for the Future*. New York: McGraw-Hill Book Company, 1983.

LIEBERMAN, MYRON. *Education as a Profession*. Englewood Cliffs, NJ: Prentice-Hall, Inc., 1956.

LORTIE, DAN C. *Schoolteacher: A Sociological Study*. Chicago: University of Chicago Press, 1975.

LORTIE, DAN C. "The Teacher's Shame: Anger and the Normative Commitments of Classroom Teachers," *School Review*, Vol. 75 (Summer 1967), pp. 155–171.

MARJORIBANKS, KEVIN. "Bureaucratic Orientation, Autonomy and the Professional Attitudes of Teachers," *Journal of Educational Administration*, Vol. 15 (1977), pp. 104–113.

METZ, MARY HAYWOOD. *Classrooms and Corridors: The Crisis of Authority in Desegregated Schools*. Berkeley: University of California Press, 1978. This useful ethnography contains a chapter entitled "Teachers' Definitions of Classroom Relationships."

POWELL, ARTHUR G., ELEANOR FARRAR, and DAVID COHEN. *The Shopping Mall High School*. Boston: Houghton-Mifflin, 1985. This well-financed study of American high schools brings a journalistic, historical perspective to understanding secondary education today.

SIZER, THEODORE R. *Horace's Compromise: The Dilemma of the American High School: Winners and Losers in the Educational Marketplace*. Boston: Houghton-Mifflin, 1984. Sizer details the compromises a dedicated teacher is forced to make as he faces large classes, an unyielding bureaucracy, disinterested students, and unhelpful administrators. The compromises made by Horace are a reflection of the pervasive compromises America has made.

CHAPTER 15

Bureaucratic Education: Its Supporters and Critics

Introduction

This chapter asks three questions:

1. What does being in a bureaucratic school system teach students?
2. Are the lessons of bureaucratic education worthwhile?
3. What is the future of bureaucratic education in America?

To answer the first question, we will not look at the formal elements of bureaucratic organizations (that topic has been covered in Chapter 11). Rather, we will focus on how students experience bureaucratic systems. We are interested in what their experience teaches them about the bureaucratic world. Therefore, we will examine the assumptions that students must take for granted if they are to cope successfully with American schooling.

The chapter's second question asks if the experience of bureaucratic schooling serves worthwhile educational aims. To answer this we will examine the contentions of supporters and critics of contemporary education.

The third question, regarding the future of bureaucratic education, is approached through an analysis of what bureaucracies do and how they grow. The chapter ends with some suggestions on how schooling might be simplified, made smaller, reorganized, and debureaucratized.

Lessons from the Bureaucracy

Schools are intricately connected to the societies in which they exist. Although they must reflect the outside culture, they need not replicate it exactly. Educators and the public must determine what portions of the culture should be emphasized in school and what aspects should be deemphasized or avoided.

Teachers within a particular school, let us say, may decide to emphasize critical intelligence, to discourage dishonesty and cruelty, and to avoid questions of religious preference. Such choices, of course, have educational consequences. Sometimes teachers evade these choices merely by accepting what has been handed down by tradition—curriculum guides, textbooks, administrative procedures, and so on. Even the failure to make a conscious decision, however, is a decision of sorts, and it too has educational consequences. The question, therefore, is not whether teachers will make choices regarding what they teach but whether these choices will be made consciously or thoughtlessly.

A basic tenet of this text has been that awareness is a prerequisite of rational choice and that rational choice is a necessary condition of freedom. Teachers must keep themselves conscious of all that is being taught in the school. They must be aware both of the lessons taught overtly through the formal curriculum and of those taught subtly through the hidden curriculum. They must remain sensitive to what is easily taken for granted. And, in the process, they must question what often goes unquestioned in the everyday operations of the school.

It is difficult to become aware of everything a school teaches because its students learn so much more than the content of their classwork. They learn from how the material is presented and from how they are expected to conduct themselves. These are the lessons carried in the *hidden curriculum* of the school. We have already examined many of these subtle lessons, but one issue remains unexplored—the question of *bureaucratic mentality*. This term refers to the assumptions that individuals must take for granted in order to deal successfully with bureaucratic organizations. The case will be made that schools quite successfully train students to understand and accept the bureaucratic structures of modern society; they help students adopt a bureaucratic mentality.

Ten Components of the Bureaucratic Mentality

In order to determine if schools train students to adopt a bureaucratic mind set, we must dissect the components of bureaucratic thinking. Some of this ground already has been covered and can be quickly reviewed here. As we venture into new territory, however, some elaboration will be necessary.

The first and most obvious component of bureaucratic consciousness has to do with impersonality. In order to make his or her way in modern society, one must learn to accept impersonal relationships and to tolerate being defined by one's status. As we have seen in earlier chapters, schools teach this lesson effectively.

Second, schools teach students about status and authority. Teachers hold their status by virtue of their credentials and specialized training. Their authority usually grows from their status, not from their personality.

Third, children learn that status-holders are essentially interchangeable. If only in theory, one teacher is just about as good as another. The school does not depend on the talent or personality of any single individual. If a teacher quits on Friday, a new teacher will be at work Monday morning. Students may be inconvenienced by this change, but the institution hums along.

Fourth, children learn that status-holders have limited domains of expertise and power. If they overstep their authority, teachers can be challenged. For instance, teachers are allowed to discipline a child's misbehavior, but in most states they cannot strike a student who gets out of line. A child who has been slapped by a teacher knows (or soon learns) that he or she can complain to a higher authority. Similarly, teachers are assigned to work within a specified subject area and can be reprimanded if they venture too far from their assigned turf. A sex-education teacher may talk about some issues in class that, presumably, a geometry teacher may not. With time, students learn that an individual's work and expertise have official boundaries; beyond these fixed limits individuals lose the official sanctions of their status.

Fifth, students come to expect that they should be treated impartially according to specified, universalistic standards. Educational rhetoric notwithstanding, students learn that they should be treated like everybody else. Furthermore, they learn that if an injustice has been done, they are to follow the official grievance procedures of the organization.

Sixth, schools teach children about the overriding orderliness of bureaucratic thinking. Schools are orderly institutions, or at least they try to be. Within them activities are tightly scheduled; power is hierarchically arranged; students are classified by grade, ability, and behavior; information is passed through official channels; lessons are presented in logical sequence; and, in all official activities, people and functions are assigned appropriate labels and time slots. In such a system, children are likely to learn that bureaucrats do not analyze and dissect phenomena so much as they classify them; they do not value understanding quite so dearly as they value order.

Seventh, schools teach children that the rich complexity of human knowledge can be cut into narrow subject areas and sorted by grade levels. Each area is assigned its specific period in the day and is overseen by a trained expert. Students can be scheduled to learn English from 9:03 to 9:53 A.M., history from 10:08 to 10:58 A.M., algebra from 1:18 to 2:03 P.M., and so on. This compartmentalization of time and knowledge is essential to bureaucracies. Schools train children to take this fragmentation of experience for granted. Students are led to believe that all course work, study assignments, and bits and pieces of subject matter that are accumulated during school will someday add up to something significant—something they are not yet prepared to understand. Thus, education not only dissects human experience; it also puts academic activity in service of invisible ends. Later, when students become adult workers, they will be prepared to carry out assigned duties without requiring a clear vision of the ends they serve. They will have learned to assume that someone in authority knows what is being done and why.

The point here may appear abstract. Let's bring it closer to home. In your study of education, when was the last time you asked for an explanation of your total curriculum? No doubt you have on occasion complained about courses you thought were trivial or irrelevant, but have you inquired into the logic of your course work, how your classes are connected, and what they all should add up to in the end? Have you checked to see if your professors talk with one another and if they understand how their own course material is supposed to relate to what is taught in other classes? If such questions never occurred to you, or if you believed you had no right to ask them, then we might conclude that your years of schooling masterfully prepared you for life in a bureaucratic society.

Eighth, schools categorize people just as effectively as they compartmentalize knowledge and time. Students are classified into ever-narrowing categories by age, IQ, social adjustment, attitudes toward school, learning styles, and so on. Once categorized, children are assigned to different classes or groups and given specific educational experiences. Each is assigned to a teacher who is specially trained to work with students of his or her "type." This categorization process will be repeated throughout their lives as they confront bureaucracies in the roles of customers, patients, employees, clients, victims, voters, members, and volunteers.

Ninth, children are told that schools classify them according to their personal achievements rather than their family's background or teachers' prejudices. In the private sphere of the family, children enjoy the ascribed status of son or daughter; in schools they occupy a status based (at least in theory) on achievement. One function of schooling is to introduce youngsters to the idea that they are responsible for their own achievements and ultimate placement in society. Students who do well can take credit for their accomplishments, but those who do poorly must accept blame for their failures. The selective process begins in schools and continues in later life, but it is in schools where children learn to take the selection process for granted and to perceive it as "just."

Schools teach students about life in the public sphere.   (*Source:* National Education Association, Joe Di Dio.)

Tenth, schools teach children that everyday life is segmented into public and private spheres. The organizational scheme and interactional patterns of public institutions are dramatically different from those of primary institutions such as the family. The two worlds are in an uneasy alliance, and individuals must divide their loyalties, their behavior, and their thinking between the two spheres. Relationships, information, and behavior appropriate in one sphere are not necessarily appropriate in the other. It takes children time to learn the distinctions between the school world (public sphere) and the home world (private sphere). A first-grader may innocently proclaim during share-and-tell time, "My Daddy pushed Mommy against the refrigerator last night and made a big dent in the door. Mommy said she was going to live with Grandma, and I'd like that. My Grandma makes good cookies." With experience, however, children begin to understand that the school world and the home world are quite different territories and that they must respect the information boundaries of the private sphere.

The Power of the Hidden Curriculum

Note that none of the ten items discussed is a part of the official curriculum of school. There is irony in the fact that some of the most enduring lessons of education come from the school experience rather than from the formal content of classroom instruction.

Edward Hall, an American anthropologist, has noted that "school life is an excellent preparation for understanding adult bureaucracies; it is designed less for learning than for teaching you who's boss and how bosses behave, and [for] keeping order."[1] Hall is no doubt correct. But it would be a mistake to believe that schools intentionally transmit the bureaucratic mentality. Educational institutions simply reflect, in their own way, the high value Americans place on efficiency, rational order, and productivity. In order to handle students in large numbers, to bring massive quantities of information to them, to train them in basic (and not so basic) skills, schools are organized bureaucratically. This organizational structure, in turn, passes on the values and preferences that motivate it.

Schools—by their organization and the values that underlie it—too often teach students to be passive receptacles of knowledge rather than active participants in learning, to tolerate impersonal treatment, to expect power to be arranged hierarchically, and to view authority as attached to a status rather than to a person. Students learn about status domains and that time, people, and knowledge can be compartmentalized. They learn to see the world as bifurcated into a public and a private sphere, and they learn that within the public sphere, their work is at the service of abstract ends and distant rewards. Rhea Buford conducted a study of Massachusetts high school students and found 91 percent

---

[1] Edward T. Hall, *Beyond Culture* (New York: Doubleday & Co., Inc., Anchor Books, 1977), p. 205. Available in paperback. See also Robert Dreeben, "The Contribution of Schooling to the Learning of Norms," *Harvard Educational Review*, Vol. 37 (Winter 1967), pp. 211–237, and Dreeben's *On What Is Learned in School* (Reading, MA: Addison-Wesley Publishing Co., Inc., 1968).

agreeing with the statement, "What we do in high school is essentially preparation for what will come later; the payoff will be in college or on the job."[2]

The hidden curriculum is as powerful as it is because human beings are capable of learning more than one thing at a time. They absorb both the content and the context of their lessons. Children learn the formal lesson of an arithmetic drill, but they also learn from the drill itself. They learn from how the class is arranged, how the students are treated, and how the teacher behaves. These are the *meta-lessons* of the school experience. In the view of many social scientists, they are the most potent lessons schools teach. Sadly, they are also the lessons to which educators pay the least conscious attention.

Parsons on the Hidden Curriculum

Are the lessons of the hidden curriculum compatible with the aims of education? Is it good that we train students for bureaucratic consciousness?

How we answer such questions, of course, depends on the aims we hold for education. Talcott Parsons, a sociologist and in many ways a theoretical defender of the status quo, saw the school as a model of functional efficiency. In Parsons's view, schools ease children away from the private sphere of the family, introduce them to the organizational assumptions of the public sphere, teach them the necessity of personal achievement, sort them according to how well they master the cognitive and behavioral curriculum, and point them toward adult careers based on their personal capacity and records of achievement. In short, Parsons believed schools effectively prepare students for adult life in modern society. Schools not only function rationally but also promote fairness and equal education opportunities. In so doing, Parsons contended, they serve the best interests both of society and of the children themselves. They give each individual the skills and values needed to maximize his or her abilities—and thus provide the human capital society needs in order to function efficiently.[3]

Parsons's critics do not agree with his analysis of schooling—nor with his sociological theory, for that matter. Irving Louis Horowitz claims that Parsons's work is little more than an "ideological celebration of the corporate personality."[4] Another critic, Alvin Gouldner, contends that "Parsons is a rare creature: the contented moralist," whose analysis of the social system induces "a smug satisfaction with things as they are."[5] According to Gouldner, Parsonians invite us to be content with the status quo:

> Instead of telling . . . how bureaucracy might be mitigated, they insist that it is inevitable. Instead of explaining how democratic patterns may, to some extent, be fortified and extended, they warn us that democracy cannot be perfect. Instead of controlling the disease, they suggest that we are deluded, or more politely, incurably romantic for hoping to control it. Instead of assuming responsibilities as

---

[2] Rhea Buford, "Institutional Paternalism in the High School," *Urban Review*, Vol. 2 (1968), pp. 13–15, 34. See also John I. Goodlad, *A Place Called School: Prospects for the Future* (New York: McGraw-Hill Book Company, 1983).

[3] Talcott Parsons, "The School Class as a Social System: Some of Its Functions in American Society," *Harvard Educational Review*, Vol. 29 (Fall 1959), pp. 297–318.

[4] Irving Louis Horowitz, *Professing Sociology* (Chicago: Aldine Publishing Co., 1968), p. 11.

[5] Alvin Gouldner, *The Coming Crisis of Western Sociology* (New York: Basic Books, Inc., Publishers, 1970), p. 290.

realistic clinicians, striving to further democratic potentialities wherever they can, many social scientists have become morticians, all too eager to bury men's hopes.[6]

One way to determine the extent to which Parsons's claims are warranted is to measure them against some criticism of bureaucratic education.

The Critics' Contentions

Many educators have come to the conclusion that bureaucratization of schooling hinders learning. Rhea Buford sums up these arguments:

> In virtually every important respect the behaviors and attitudes appropriate to all bureaucracies are quite opposite of those appropriate to education. Educational relationships are diffuse, the student is treated as a "whole" person, but the hallmark of the bureaucratic institution is its specificity; education best proceeds in personal settings, through "primary" contacts, but bureaucracies are formal and impersonal . . . education is responsive to the needs of the student, instruction is "individualized," but bureaucracies are first and always agencies of control.[7]

Many critics, perhaps most notably John Goodlad, Paul Goodman, and Ivan Illich, give analytical support to Buford's assertions. Goodman contended that, "In advanced countries, a chief cause—perhaps the chief cause—of the alienation of the young has been the school systems themselves." The failure of education, in Goodman's view, is that it does not effectively help students to "have a world," that is, to be an active part of the community. Schools separate students from adults, from real participation in their own education, and ultimately from genuine curiosity and learning. They are deprived of situations where they can "pursue their own interests, use their powers, exercise initiative." They have little opportunity to "act and realize themselves."[8]

Goodman accused schools of being run by a logic of social engineering rather than by humane education. Social engineering, he insisted, is inherently miseducative, because it "rules out too many human powers to learn." It attempts to restrict tightly the behavior and thinking of people and, in so doing, inhibits their ability to create, innovate, and meaningfully connect with what there is to know. For Goodman,

> the academic problem at present is to unblock the intellect in the young, to prove that it is possible for persons to display intellectual virtues . . . and to use them in the community and the world without futility.[9]

Goodman was not against institutions or socialization; he recognized the vital nature of both. But, he insisted, institutions become less useful to individuals as they become more impersonal, remote, and abstract. This development creates alienation and subverts worthwhile socialization. "If the institutions of so-

---

[6] Alvin Gouldner, "Metaphysical Pathos and the Theory of Bureaucracy," *American Political Science Review,* Vol. 49 (1955), pp. 506–507.

[7] Buford, "Institutional Paternalism in the High School," *Urban Review,* pp. 13–15, 34.

[8] Paul Goodman, *New Reformation* (New York: Random House, Inc., 1970), pp. 67, 49. See also Ivan Illich, *Deschooling Society* (New York: Harper & Row, Publishers, Inc., 1970). Both available in paperback.

[9] Goodman, *New Reformation,* p. 76, and Paul Goodman, *Compulsory Miseducation and the Community of Scholars* (New York: Random House, Inc., Vintage Books, 1964), p. 309. Available in paperback.

ciety were made vital and functional," said Goodman, if the young could "identify with them, be free in them, participate in their management," then children would be socialized into what is best and most humane in our society.[10] Goodman believed that open-ended organizations allow primary relationships and enrich human potential. In such settings, individuals learn effectively, work cooperatively, and become more fully human. "It is not that good institutions make possible good educational systems," explained Goodman, "they are the good educational system."[11] Schools must not aim for indoctrination, regimentation, or prestructured efficiency. They should instead furnish a congenial environment for the development of community, learning, and human values.

More recently a new set of educational critics has emerged. Though less radical than their predecessors, Boyer,[12] Goodlad,[13] Wirth,[14] and Sizer all question the efficacy of bureaucratized schools. As Sizer explained, the bureaucratic structure is getting in the way of learning because it loses track of its primary objectives, mandates sameness, disempowers teachers, renders students docile, and alienates parents from the education of their children.[15] Recent critics do not call for a dismantling of the school system, but, as we shall see, they do call for a radical restructuring of the educational bureaucracy.

Who Defends Bureaucratic Education?

While the bureaucratic education system has defenders such as Talcott Parsons, it can be argued that it really does not need theoretical support. Bureaucracy never emerges for its own sake but always in service of something else, namely, "progress" and "efficiency." Therefore, no one needs to proclaim the benefits of bureaucracy or to challenge the contention of critics such as Goodman or Illich. To assure its own growth, the system needs only to wait for problems to emerge that call for greater control of human events and educational outcomes. Almost inevitably, the official response to all problems (from school violence, decline in test scores, and increased drug use to inequality, immorality, and inflation) will lead to the increased bureaucratization of education. We saw evidence of this trend in Chapter 11 when we discussed how technology has been used to limit teachers' options and tighten administrative control over the classroom.

Efficiency and the History of Education

We can get a clearer view of this phenomenon (the self-perpetuation of bureaucracy) if we look at some history. Early in the century, two great problems faced American education. The first of these was a massive extension of secondary schooling. By 1920, 50 percent of youths aged fourteen to seventeen

---

[10] Ibid., pp. 109–110.
[11] Ibid., p. 110.
[12] Ernest L. Boyer, *High School: A Report on Secondary Education in America* (New York: Harper & Row, 1983), p. 159
[13] John I. Goodlad, *A Place Called School*, pp. 189–90, 224–225.
[14] Arthur Wirth, *Productive Work—In Industry and Schools: Becoming Persons Again* (Lanham, NY: University Press of America, 1983), pp. 16–17, 19, 120, 214–216. Available in paperback.
[15] Theodore R. Sizer, *Horace's Compromise: The Dilemma of the American High School* (Boston: Houghton-Mifflin, 1984), pp. 205–213.

were in school. Within a generation, attendance figures jumped to 90 percent. At the same time, the school system was coping with a flood of immigrants. Twenty-seven million arrived in the United States between 1876 and 1926, and well over 9 million landed between 1906 and 1915.

The school system was called upon to assimilate the newcomers into the American mainstream. Ellwood Cubberley, a prominent educator of the day, defined the task of the public school system in stark, ethnocentric terms. He called on schools to alter drastically the habits and beliefs of these foreign, and in his view "inferior," people.

> These southern and western Europeans are of a very different type from the northern Europeans who preceded them. Illiterate, docile, lacking in self-resilience and initiative, and not possessing the Anglo-Teutonic conceptions of law, order, and government, their coming has served to dilute tremendously our native stock, and to corrupt our civic life. . . . Our task is to break up these groups or settlements, to assimilate and amalgamate these people as a part of our American race, and to implant in their children, so far as can be done, the Anglo-Saxon conception of righteousness, law, and order, and popular government.[16]

The dual challenges of expansion and immigration were quickly defined as problems of production and efficiency. The schools, Cubberley proclaimed, were "factories in which the raw materials [children] are to be shaped and fashioned into products to meet the various demands of life."[17] With this metaphor, the process of education was defined in bureaucratic-technological terms. The "best" (most efficient) way to ensure high-quality education was to treat students as material to be shaped, rather than as human beings to be nurtured.

Human beings, of course, differ from raw materials in that they have opinions, values, and desires of their own and can resist manipulation. However, this did not discourage educators from adopting a factory model for schooling. In schools, as in industry, efficiency experts were called upon to minimize human resistance through the use of "scientific management techniques." In 1912, James Phinney Munroe began his book *New Demands in Education* with the statement, "The fundamental demand in education, as in everything else, is for efficiency—physical efficiency, mental efficiency, moral efficiency." Schools, he claimed, were needlessly wasting human resources. To alleviate this waste,

> We need "educational engineers" to study this huge business of preparing youth for life. . . . Such engineers would make a thorough study of (1) the pupils who constitute the raw material of the business of education; (2) the buildings and other facilities for teaching, which make up the plant; (3) the school boards and the teaching staff, who correspond to the directorate and the working force; (4) the means and methods of instruction and development; (5) the demands of society in general and of industry in particular upon boys and girls—this corresponding to the problem of markets; and (6) the question of the cost, which is almost purely a business problem.[18]

---

[16] Ellwood P. Cubberley, *Changing Conceptions of Education* (Boston: Houghton-Mifflin Company, 1909), pp. 15–16.

[17] Ellwood P. Cubberley, *Public School Administration* (Boston: Houghton-Mifflin Company, 1916), p. 338.

[18] James Phinney Munroe, *New Demands in Education*, quoted in Raymond E. Callahan, *Education and the Cult of Efficiency* (Chicago: University of Chicago Press, 1962), p. 62. Available in paperback.

Recent Examples of School Bureaucratization

Once the connection between efficiency and tight organizational structures was established in the public mind early in the century, virtually every educational problem served to expand the bureaucratic presence in the school system. Similar conclusions might be drawn from more recent occurrences in education.

The pressure to cut school costs led to massive school consolidation in the 1950s and 1960s because, it was claimed, the unit cost of schools decreased as school size increased. The cry for better discipline has been answered by an increased use of behavior-modification techniques. The demands for better teaching have brought the technology of television, teaching machines, computers, language labs, and a vast array of classroom gadgetry into the schools.

Even the press for more personalized attention in schools has given rise to the development of IQ, aptitude, and personality instruments designed to "fairly" assess and categorize individuals for efficient processing by the school. The growing worry over the quality of education has led to the competency testing and performance evaluation of teachers and students alike.

The most significant development in educational software has been psychological testing. We have tests for almost everything: tests of intelligence, achievement, vocational interests, personality traits, hyperactivity, learning disabilities, minimal brain dysfunctions, predelinquency characteristics, maladaptive tendencies, and so on. The list is long and still growing.

All these developments have resulted, not from any direct call for bureaucratic expansion, but rather as answers to specific, pressing educational problems. Even calls for reform, aimed at personalizing education, have instigated changes (such as psychological testing) that have served to increase the bureaucratization of schools.

The Further Bureaucratization of Education

Is it possible that schools will become even more bureaucratized than they are today? There is some indication that school officials and the general public are beginning to look more carefully at the problems caused by bureaucratization of education. As a case in point, a number of recent studies challenge the assumption that consolidation in schools is economically efficient.

Proponents of consolidation have focused on the reduced unit costs incurred when schools grow larger. They argue that it is cost effective to build, say, one gymnasium for a school of 1800 students, rather than three gymnasiums to serve three schools of 600 students each. But critics point out that such assumptions often ignore the added costs of consolidation. Jonathan Sher and Rachel Tompkins have pointed out:

> The bulk of relevant research ignores the additional capital expenditures, salaries and operating costs, associated with the greatly increased transportation required by consolidation. Children who formerly walked to school now must be bussed. Children who used to ride for four or five miles per day now must frequently ride twenty or more miles to reach the "centrally located" school. All of this means

more buses, more drivers, higher fuel costs, and faster depreciation than was the case prior to consolidation.[19]

The point here is not that school consolidation always inflates costs but that an assumption that consolidation saves money is not always warranted. Nor can we assume that larger, better equipped schools inevitably increase student learning.

The "more-is-better" approach to education was argued forcibly by James Bryant Conant in his study of American high schools. "The number of small high schools must be drastically reduced through district reorganization," said Conant. "Aside from this important change, I believe no radical alteration in the basic pattern of American education is necessary in order to improve our public high schools."[20] By simply making schools larger, Conant claimed, America could solve its educational problems.

Later research by James Coleman assaults Conant's conclusion. Coleman states that school size is "a variable not significantly correlated with achievement." In fact, Coleman suggested that the "size of the twelfth grade is negatively correlated with verbal achievement . . . each additional 200 students is associated with the decline of one-fifth grade level in achievement."[21] Similarly, work by A. Summers and B. Wolfe indicates that "higher achievement results correlated with smaller schools at both the elementary and senior high school levels."[22]

Research findings such as these have led educators to look beyond the accounting ledger to determine cost efficiency. Roger Barker and Paul Gump, in an extensive review of the literature on school size effectiveness, point out that large schools can inhibit rather than enlarge the educative experiences of the young. Students can get lost in the machinery of large school systems, and this submersion can limit both the extent and the quality of their participation in academically enriching activities. The researchers came to this conclusion:

> The proportion of participants was three to twenty times as great in the small schools as in the largest school. The number of extracurricular activities and kinds of activities engaged in during their four-year high school careers was twice as great in the small schools as in the large schools.[23]

These findings are important, especially in the light of Coleman's finding that students' feeling of control over their own destiny "appears to have a stronger relationship to achievement than all 'school' factors together."[24] As Coleman notes, fate-control attitudes are likely to be influenced by the quality of students' experience of school, the extent of their school involvement, and their perceptions of competence. Barker and Gump conclude that small schools

[19] Jonathan P. Sher and Rachel B. Tompkins, "Economy, Efficiency, and Equality: The Myths of Rural School and District Consolidation," in *Education in Rural America: A Reassessment of Conventional Wisdom*, ed. Jonathan P. Sher (Boulder, CO: Westview Press, Inc., 1977), pp. 46–47. Available in paperback.

[20] James Bryant Conant, *The American High School Today*, Carnegie Series in American Education (New York: McGraw-Hill Book Company, 1959), p. 40.

[21] James S. Coleman et al., *Equality of Educational Opportunity* (Washington, DC: Department of Health, Education and Welfare, U.S. Office of Education OE38001, 1966).

[22] A. Summers and B. Wolfe, "Which School Resources Help Learning?" *Business Review* (February 1975).

[23] Roger G. Barker and Paul V. Gump, *Big School, Small School* (Stanford, CA: Stanford University Press, 1964), p. 196.

[24] Quoted in ibid.

produce "more satisfactions relating to the development of competence, to being challenged, to engaging in important actions, to being involved in group activities, to achieving moral and cultural values."[25]

More recently Goodlad found that small schools offered students a greater opportunity for involvement.[26] Perhaps because students are more involved in school activities, the drop-out rate is lower in small schools.[27] Goodlad also discovered that teachers in small schools had greater knowledge about and communications with their colleagues and were more involved in solving schoolwide problems.[28]

Such conclusions show that there is now a formidable body of evidence that questions the wisdom of the growth-for-growth's-sake mentality in education. It is not yet clear that this evidence will appreciably slow the bureaucratization of education. Bureaucracy, as we have seen, is propelled by the power of its own assumptions. The tendency to translate human problems into technological terms and to define efficiency in bureaucratic terms makes increased bureaucratization almost irresistible in industrialized societies.

The Larger Picture

Few questions in education can be understood in isolation from the larger society. When we question the desirability of bureaucracy in education, we inevitably become entangled in larger questions such as the general desirability of bureaucracy in society. It is necessary, therefore, to clarify the boundaries of our discussion and to specify when we are talking exclusively about education and when we are merely using education as an example of a larger, society-wide issue.

The push to simplify the organizational structure of schools is, for some people, a part of a larger movement to demodernize society. Certainly, the criticisms that Goodman and Illich level against education are in keeping with their more general criticisms of technological life. They see the debureaucratization of education as but one step toward the simplification of modern society. This fact may explain why their criticisms have had so little impact on educational practice. To accept their arguments in education is to question the pervasive logic of modern life.

Americans (educators included) are generally unwilling to consider seriously the dismantling of modern technology. There is good reason to assume that Americans have become nostalgic for the supposed unity, identity, and general wholeness of a past age. They are made uncomfortable (some are driven insane) by a lost sense of community and the division of modern life into public and private spheres. Many feel helpless as they are processed by society's megastructures. In response, some join the newest pop psychology craze, reinvestigate religion, undergo counseling, get divorced, get remarried, have children by natural childbirth, take up organic gardening, study meditation, and so on—all in an effort to combat the alienation of modern life. Yet this is not

---

[25] Ibid., p. 197.
[26] Goodlad, *A Place Called School*, p. 188.
[27] Harold L. Hodgkinson, *All One System: Demographics of Education—Kindergarten Through Graduate School* (Washington, DC: Institute for Educational Leadership, Inc., 1985), p. 12.
[28] Goodlad, *A Place Called School*, p. 225.

to say that the majority of Americans would embrace an all-out effort to demodernize society. Thus, the reading of Goodman's and Illich's works, like the reading of *The Whole Earth Catalog,* amounts to little more than an entertaining diversion. It is not taken seriously and certainly is not acted upon by most Americans.

Why won't Americans seriously consider demodernization? One reason is simple enough. We like most of what modernization delivers. We may be troubled by some consequences of bureaucracy and technology (alienation and depersonalization, for example), but we also enjoy the freedom modernization provides, at least within the private sphere. Modernization, for all its faults, has freed Americans from the stifling confines of small-town life, tradition, and restrictive collective codes. The price of this liberation has been a heightened alienation, and, it appears, most Americans are willing to pay the fare.

A second reason for the American reluctance to demodernize is that we so thoroughly enjoy abundance and efficiency. We like being able to call in an expert when our microwave oven, color TV, gall bladder, marriage, or mind goes on the fritz. Certainly, we complain about depersonalization, but we complain even louder and longer about inefficiency.

The weakening bonds of community have left us utterly dependent upon rationality, predictability, and efficiency. For all its impersonality, bureaucracy is the institutional embodiment of these three pillars of modernity. When they fail to support us—when bureaucracy appears irrational, unpredictable, and inefficient—we become enraged. Yet, our anger is not an attack on the basic functions of bureaucracy but rather on its failure to do its job well. Thus, many complaints that appear to be indictments of bureaucracy are more accurately a call for better service and efficiency—demands that are answered by a further expansion of the bureaucratic order.

Although critics like Goodman and Illich argue insightfully against bureaucracy, their cries are drowned out by the national demand for expanded services. If we judge people's desires by their actions, it would appear that few of us truly want to end our dependence on technology. Only a small percentage of the population would be willing to become sandalmakers in Vermont or to live in communes on the Arizona desert. *The Whole Earth Catalog* makes entertaining reading, but few of us take seriously its suggestion that we give birth to our children on the kitchen floor and pass the placenta around to onlookers as a celebration of community. Even alienation is more inviting than that.

For good or ill, and barring catastrophe, we will be living in a technological, bureaucratized world for some time to come. Even critics of modernization are wedded to the benefits of technological life, often in ways they themselves barely recognize. Peter Berger tells an amusing story that makes just this point:

> A few months ago my friend Richard Neuhaus was in an airplane, thirty thousand feet over the Middle West somewhere. He wanted to sleep. Next to him was a young man in full counter-culture regalia who wanted to talk. Neuhaus (otherwise a very passive type) became hostile. "You know," he said to the young man, "this is really a swinging airline. I was talking to the pilot before we took off, in the bar. He told me really mind-blowing things about this airline. They really hang loose, you know. Like none of this bit about not drinking when they're flying. In fact, they smoke pot right on the plane, most of the time. They even screw the stewardesses right there in the cockpit." And so on. Please remember that this conversation took place at about thirty thousand feet over, like, Indiana. Not sur-

prisingly, the young man became very nervous indeed. As a matter of fact, to coin a phrase, he became positively uptight.

Does the moral of this story have to be spelled out? Perhaps not, but let me, anyway. Whatever his private "life style," there was no doubt that the young man wanted the pilots (and, by extension, everyone connected with the technology of getting the plane safely to its destination) to be as "square" as they come—at least while they were handling the plane in which he was flying. He wanted them . . . to be strictly and stringently "abstract" (all those gadgets!), functionally specific ("schizophrenic," "repressed"—never mind!), performance-oriented, affectively neutral, "alienated" as they come. Why? Simple: Because he had excellent reason to think that, otherwise, the plane would crash. You cannot fly an airplane by the values of the counter-culture.[29]

Berger is no doubt correct. We cannot run technological-bureaucratic organizations by any laid-back system of values, whether they are generated by a present-day youth movement or by the small-town simplicity of a long-gone agrarian America. We share the ambivalence of the young man on the plane; we yearn for wholeness, community, identity, and a saner pace through life. Yet, we want to be able to fly safe airlines, enjoy efficient telephone service, have our diseases diagnosed and cured through medical technology, have our energy needs met, and plan our getaway weekends around reliable weather forecasts. We want to have our bureaucracy and escape it, too. If faced with a choice between the wholeness of a simpler time and the abundance of the complex present, however, Americans (like the citizens of other modern nations) would choose abundance. It may well be a bad choice, but it is the choice being made.

The Future of Bureaucracy in Education

Bureaucracy is likely to remain a significant part of American life, but this likelihood does not imply that it need remain a dominant force in education. The cost of bureaucratic education is too high and its benefits too few. Allowing schools to function as total institutions sets teachers and students at cross-purposes, depersonalizes human relationships, alienates youngsters from the learning process and the student role, and encourages them to use impression management to work the system.

There is no single formula for the debureaucratization of schools, but central to any effort in this direction would be a renewed concentration on the school experience of individual students. Attention would be focused on the quality of a student's interaction with peers, teachers, and, of course, subject matter. These things would be most effectively accomplished if class size and school size were drastically reduced and if closer connections existed between the home and the school. To remake a point developed at the end of Chapter 6, schools would have to become mediating organizations and resist their internal compulsion to become megastructures. The projected decline of school enrollments through this decade offers unprecedented opportunity to accomplish these ends.

Most of the aims we have proposed for education are difficult or impossible

[29] Peter Berger, "The Liberal as Fall Guy," *The Center Magazine*, Vol. 5 (July/August 1972), p. 43. See also Peter Berger, Brigitte Berger, and Hansfried Kellner, *The Homeless Mind: Modernization and Consciousness* (New York: Random House, Inc., Vintage Books, 1973), pp. 182–230.

to achieve in bureaucratic settings. The development of self-esteem, creative intelligence, and cooperative individualism demands a more open and personal climate than bureaucracies can provide. It makes sense, then, to delay bureaucratic socialization at least until youngsters have had the chance to develop self-respect and social skills. They need to learn something about themselves—who they are and what they can accomplish (individually and in cooperation with others)—before they can function creatively and responsibly in a bureaucratic environment.

If students do not experience bureaucracy in schools, will they be prepared to face society's megastructures as adults? There is reason to believe they will. It is unlikely that schools will totally eliminate their bureaucratic orientation. Students will doubtless still be exposed to bureaucratic consciousness as they proceed through the school system. Ideally, however, exposure to such thinking will come later in their educational careers than is presently the case. Moreover, schools are not the sole source of bureaucratic experience for children. They learn small bureaucratic lessons from a number of other sources: hospitals, organized athletics, their parents' work experience, and so on. Bureaucratic consciousness is not particularly complicated. It can be learned relatively quickly. Students do not need twelve years of education to teach them bureaucratic thinking.

If students are graduated from our nation's schools knowing who they are and what they can accomplish, if they understand initiative and cooperation, if they have developed problem-solving skills and have experienced academic success, then they will be prepared to deal with the bureaucratic realities of modern life. Contrary to popular thought, bureaucracy is not an environment wholly inhospitable to intelligence and creativity. Research by Melvin Kohn has shown that many bureaucrats are notably resourceful, responsible, and creative.[30] But bureaucracy is not an environment conducive to the development of these skills and attitudes. If bureaucrats do not approach their work with such skills already intact, it is unlikely they will develop them on the job.

The explanation for this phenomenon is found in Charles Cooley's insight that social ideals (intelligence, love, freedom, justice, cooperation, empathy, tolerance, creativity, and so on) are not born in large institutions or from abstract thought, but rather in face-to-face, primary-group interactions. The moral unity of Edmund Burke's "little platoon" is the mother of social ideals and individual development.[31] The same point was made by Emile Durkheim. He warned that the growth of large institutions endangered the "little aggregations" in which individuals have found community, identity, and moral purpose throughout history. He pointed out that people who "never acquired the habit of forming associations" early in their lives were unlikely to do so in later times of crisis or confusion.[32]

[30] Melvin Kohn, "Benefits of Bureaucracy," *Human Nature*, Vol. 1 (August 1978), pp. 60–66.

[31] Edmund Burke, the father of modern conservatism, wrote: "To be attached to the subdivision, to love the little platoon we belong to in society, is the first principle (the germ, as it were) of public affections." Quoted in Peter L. Berger and Richard John Neuhaus, *To Empower People: The Role of Mediating Structures in Public Policy* (Washington, DC: American Enterprise Institute for Public Policy Research, 1977), p. 4.

[32] Quoted in ibid., p. 4. Durkheim, referring to mediating institutions, wrote: "A nation can be maintained only if, between the state and the individual, there is intercalated a whole series of secondary groups near enough to the individual to attract them strongly in their sphere of action and drag them, in this way, into the general torrent of social life." Emile Durkheim, *The Division of Labor in Society*, trans. George Simpson (New York: The Free Press, 1964), p. 28.

The problems we have discussed in earlier chapters—the "tragedy of the commons," the impersonality of megastructures, the alienating forces of modernization, the fragile and underinstitutionalized nature of the private sphere—will only be overcome if we find ways to build and maintain corporate values. Traditionally, this work has been accomplished by the mediating structures of American society. The vitality of the democratic system, as Alexis de Tocqueville discovered in the last century, grows from the creative powers of voluntary associations.

Today, our mediating structures are in danger. The family is being buffeted by changing patterns of work, increasing rates of divorce, growing importance of adolescent peer groups, and the intrusion of television into the living room. Neighborhood communities are being weakened by government planning, the mobility of the American work force, and the mass exodus from urban centers to the latch-key living of suburbia. Religious institutions are undergoing change and challenge and appear less able than they once were to provide spiritual sustenance to their congregations. Local governments are becoming increasingly aloof: They respond more readily to the desires of agencies at the state and federal levels than they do to the needs of their local constituency. And, as this chapter has attempted to illustrate, schools have become more bureaucratic and less accessible to the public they were created to serve.

The dangers of this state of affairs work in two directions. On one side, the weakening of mediating structures threatens the stability of the private sphere. It loosens the ties of community, deprives individuals of a shared morality, and sets them adrift to do their own thing. On the other side, the weakening of mediating institutions deprives megastructures of their only source of morality and social purpose. Mediating institutions are essential to the megastructure, because, as Berger has put it,

> No society, modern or otherwise, can survive without . . . moral values that have general authority. The megastructures, because of their remoteness and sheer vastness, are unsuitable for the generation and maintenance of such a general morality.

Megastructures cannot create moral aims or social values. They must depend on institutions and social formations far below for their "moral sustenance."[33]

It behooves us to establish educational strategies that foster the primary ideals of creative intelligence, self-esteem, civility, and cooperative individualism. Youngsters who grow up possessing these attributes will not only be prepared to perpetuate modern society but also to improve it. They will not only be able to survive in bureaucratic institutions but also to infuse these institutions with humanity and ethical purpose.

Mediating institutions prepare people to work in the public sphere by providing them with the habits of civility, morality, empathy, sharing, community, and informed discretion. They also protect individuals from the sometimes unreasonable and destructive demands of the megastructure. Parker Palmer warns that in a mass society the individual too often stands alone "without a network of associations to protect personal meaning, to enlarge personal power, or [through which] to learn the habits of democracy.[34] Etzioni enlarges on the

---

[33] Peter Berger, "In Praise of Particularity: The Concept of Mediating Structures," in *Facing up to Modernity, Excursions in Society, Politics, and Religion* (New York: Basic Books, Inc., Publishers, 1977), p. 134.

[34] Parker J. Palmer, "A Place Called Community," *Christian Century* (March 16, 1977), p. 253.

point. He contends that mediating institutions do vital work in mass society because they can "make the individual much less dependent on—and hence less vulnerable to—the [pervasive power of the megastructure].[35] Palmer agrees: "Families, neighborhoods, work teams, church or other voluntary associations mediate between the lone individual and the power of the state. They amplify the individual's small voice so that it can be heard.[36]

Mediating institutions are empowering because they are fundamentally participatory and thus vitally connected to the processes of democracy. Democracy limits governmental power through popular participation. At the same time, the practical foundation for democratic participation (and not incidentally for individual dignity and self-respect) is lodged in voluntary associations within local communities.[37]

Mediating institutions provide individuals with opportunities to discuss important issues and deeply felt problems with people they value and who, in return, value them. Such discussions help citizens plan problem-solving strategies and strengthen the bonds of democracy at the community level. Democracy can work in a mass society only if it is practiced locally, where people live, work, raise their families, and educate their children. As Peter Berger has observed,

> Popular participation in social life, and specifically in the decision-making processes of society, is not confined to the political area proper. Thus there is a great variety of . . . subpolitical institutions through which people participate in the life of the larger society. . . .[38]

Mediating institutions have been called "schools for democracy."[39] While acknowledging that such institutions prepare individuals for the formal processes of democratic politics, we contend that they do much more. When mediating institutions function well, when they empower individuals, they are institutional expressions of democracy in action. They anchor democracy in the face-to-face interactions of community life.[40]

We argue that mediating institutions serve multiple purposes. They promote fundamental "human goods" that cannot be fostered in a bureaucratic society. Included on our list of human goods are the habits of tolerance, cooperation, morality, intelligence, empathy, dignity, self-respect, love, and belonging. At the same time, mediating institutions protect individuals against the most dehumanizing elements of mass society. Voluntary associations "amplify the voices" of dissenters and help them to be heard by fellow citizens and those in power. They prepare individuals for the processes of democratic politics by building democratic practices into the face-to-face interactions of community life. In short, mediating institutions promote the human development within the individual, community, large organization, and mass society.

[35] Amitai Etzioni, *An Immodest Agenda: Rebuilding America for the 21st Century* (New York: McGraw-Hill Book Company, 1983), pp. 99.

[36] Palmer, "A Placed Called Community," p. 253.

[37] Robert N. Bellah, Richard Madsen, William M. Sullivan, Ann Swidler, and Steven M. Tipton, *Habits of the Heart: Individualism and Commitment in American Life* (Berkeley: University of California Press, 1985), pp. 38–39, 191–192, 196–199.

[38] Peter L. Berger, *The Capitalist Revolution: Fifty Propositions about Prosperity, Equality, and Liberty,* (New York: Basic Books, 1986), p. 84.

[39] Ibid., p. 85.

[40] Bellah, Madsen, Sullivan, Swidler, and Tipton, *Habits of the Heart*, p. 39.

It would be naive to suggest that schools will solve all the problems of modern life by becoming mediating institutions. But if schools can become more personalistic, they will contribute less to the problems of modern existence and more to their solution. As Berger and Neuhaus have pointed out, "Mediating structures are the value-generating and value-maintaining agencies in society."[41] Such institutions give a measure of stability to our private lives; they help us transfer meaning and moral direction to our public lives in the megastructures of modern society.

Summary

This chapter began with a discussion of the elements of bureaucratic consciousness. We pointed out that all the elements of bureaucratic thinking are carried in the hidden curriculum of most schools. If teachers are to achieve the aims they set for education, they must remain aware of what is being taught in both the formal and hidden curricula of the schools.

Talcott Parsons defended the teaching of bureaucratic consciousness, because, he claimed, it prepares students for adult life and encourages societal harmony. Parsons's critics disagree. Rhea Buford claims that bureaucratic arrangements disrupt the process of education. Paul Goodman and Ivan Illich extend this indictment of schooling, arguing that bureaucratic schools alienate students from institutions, learning, and ultimately from themselves.

Given the strength of such criticisms, we might wonder why educators and the public tolerate bureaucratic educational systems. But, as the chapter pointed out, bureaucracy needs no proponents; it is propelled by the force of its taken-for-granted assumptions. As long as we assume that more is better, that size equals quality, and that efficiency can be guaranteed through human engineering, the bureaucratization of schooling will continue. Expansion will be checked only if educators and the public directly confront these assumptions to determine if they are warranted.

Although there is reason to believe that bureaucratic settings are ill suited for education, we need not assume that society must abandon bureaucracy in all its forms. Americans are unlikely to take such suggestions seriously. It is possible to reduce bureaucracy's hold on education without jettisoning all bureaucracy from the American scene. This modest proposal has some chance of succeeding; certainly it could serve to lessen some of the problems bureaucracy engenders in the public sphere. If schools were to become personalistic, mediating structures, they could more effectively foster creative intelligence, self-respect, and cooperation. In so doing, they would help instill primary values in our public institutions. This change would be a revolution of no small dimension.

Up to this point in the text, we have made only a moral case for the aims of self-respect, creative intelligence, and cooperation. We have addressed the logical desirability of these aims, but now we must approach the issue from another direction and ask if they can indeed be accomplished. Are they achievable? This is an empirical question that can be answered only if we examine relevant educational research. That is the task of the next chapter.

[41] Berger and Neuhaus, *To Empower People*, p. 6.

Suggested Readings

The study of bureaucracy is usually associated with sociology. Yet, sociologists who neglect history do so at great peril. We are likely to gain a deeper understanding of the role bureaucracy plays in education if we examine historical developments.

CALLAHAN, RAYMOND E. *Education and the Cult of Efficiency.* Chicago: University of Chicago Press, 1962. This is a fascinating, readable, and scholarly account of the administrative mentality in education during the early part of this century.

KATZ, MICHAEL B. *Class, Bureaucracy, and Schools: The Illusion of Educational Change in America.* Expanded edition. New York: Praeger Publishers, 1975. This book traces the emergence of educational bureaucracy in the context of educational reform. "From Voluntarism to Bureaucracy in American Education," in *Power and Ideology in Education,* edited by Jerome Karabel and A. H. Halsey. New York: Oxford University Press, 1977, pp. 386–397, presents variations on the same theme.

SPRING, JOEL. *Educating the Worker-Citizen: The Social, Economic, and Political Foundations of Education.* New York: Longman, Inc., 1980. A revisionist historian investigates the increasing political power of professional experts in American society.

A number of studies have investigated the multiple effects bureaucratization of the schools has had on student life, curriculum, student achievement, teacher–student relationships, and the thought processes of students and teachers alike.

APPLE, MICHAEL. *Ideology and Curriculum.* London: Routledge & Kegan Paul, 1979. This is an imaginative examination of school curriculum.

BOYER, ERNEST L. *High School: A Report on Secondary Education in America.* New York: Harper & Row, 1983. This book is a comprehensive study of American high school education.

EGGLESTON, JOHN. *The Sociology of the School Curriculum.* London: Routledge & Kegan Paul, Ltd., 1977. An English sociologist examines the nature of the curriculum experience from the point of view of teachers and pupils. He makes the case for breaking the curriculum out of its present bureaucratic encasements.

GOODLAD, JOHN I. *A Place Called School: Prospects for the Future.* New York: McGraw-Hill Company, 1983. In an ambitious study of the American education system, the author calls for the empowerment of teachers and the debureaucratization of schools.

POWELL, ARTHUR G., ELEANOR FARRAR, and DAVID COHEN. *The Shopping Mall High School: Winners and Losers in the Educational Marketplace.* Boston: Houghton-Mifflin Company, 1985. Though not explicitly about bureaucracy, this study of schooling concludes that schools and classes must get smaller if they are to get better.

SIZER, THEODORE R. *Horace's Compromise: The Dilemma of the American High School.* Boston: Houghton-Mifflin, 1984. This entertaining yet disquieting account of the compromises teachers make in the course of their careers examines the ways in which bureaucratic organizations promote settling for less.

WIRTH, ARTHUR. *Productive Work—In Industry and Schools: Becoming Persons Again.* Lanham, NY: University Press of America, 1983. This award-winning book offers a thorough review of the literature on democratic workplaces.

A number of books address the broader issue of effects of bureaucratization on society in general. Among the best of these are

BELL, DANIEL. *The Coming of Post-Industrial Society.* New York: Basic Books, Inc., Publishers, 1973. The author elaborates on the enduring changes that industrialization has brought to our economy, class structure, and political institutions. It is a debatable though upbeat venture in social forecasting.

BERGER, PETER L. *The Capitalist Revolution: Fifty Propositions about Prosperity, Equality, and Liberty.* New York: Basic Books, 1986. This book is primarily an attempt to understand the specific social consequences of socialism and capitalism in the modern world. In so doing, it examines from a conservative perspective the needed balance between the individual and society.

BERGER, PETER, BRIGITTE BERGER, and HANSFRIED KELLNER. *The Homeless Mind: Modernization and Consciousness.* New York: Vintage Books, 1973. This book traces the effects of technological production and bureaucracy on the consciousness of individuals, presenting a provocative expansion of the sociology of knowledge.

ELLUL, JACQUES. *The Technological Society,* translated by John Wilkinson. New York: Vintage Books, 1964. This French sociologist shows how technological society has brought one human activity after another within its bureaucratic grasp. It is difficult reading but worth the effort.

GOODMAN, PAUL. *New Reformation.* New York: Random House, Inc., 1970. In this, as in many of his earlier works, Goodman shows the profound and sometimes debilitating effects social structure has on the development of individual autonomy and communal creativity. His call for the reconstruction of community in America has been misread by some critics as romantic nostalgia. It is much more than that.

Students wishing to learn more about the concept of mediating institutions are invited to look at the following:

BELLAH, ROBERT N., RICHARD MADSEN, WILLIAM M. SULLIVAN, ANN SWIDLER, and STEVEN M. TIPTON. *Habits of the Heart: Individualism and Commitment in American Life.* Berkeley: University of California Press, 1985. This book is a fundamentally liberal examination of individualism and the possibility of community in America.

BERGER, PETER. "In Praise of Particularity: The Concept of Mediating Structures," in *Facing up to Modernity: Excursions in Society, Politics, and Religion,* edited by Peter L. Berger. New York: Basic Books, Inc., Publishers, 1977.

BERGER, PETER L., and RICHARD JOHN NEUHAUS. *To Empower People: The Role of Mediating Structures in Public Policy.* Washington, DC: American Enterprise Institute for Public Policy Research, 1977.

ETZIONI, AMITAI. *An Immodest Agenda: Rebuilding America for the 21st Century.* New York: McGraw-Hill Book Company, 1983. This is a middle-of-the-road attempt to balance individual freedom and community reconstruction in an age of extreme individualism.

JANOWITZ, MORRIS, ed. *W. I. Thomas on Social Organization and Social Personality.* Chicago: Phoenix Books, The University of Chicago Press, 1966.

NOVAK, MICHAEL, ed. Democracy and Mediating Structures: A Theological Inquiry. Washington, DC: American Enterprise Institute for Policy Research, 1980.

Further readings on bureaucracy are found in the bibliography following Chapter 11, "Studying Institutions."

CHAPTER 16

Educational Aims Revisited

Introduction: Three Necessities for Education

The aims of education suggested in Chapter 8 have three major components. The first deals with rationality and creativity. We contended that the personal troubles individuals suffer and the social problems they share together can be solved only by creative thought and cannot be handled by blind conformity or impassioned rebellion. The second aim emphasizes that the problems of modern life are essentially human problems that call for cooperative solutions. The third educational aim is related to the first two. If individuals are to develop their capacity for independent thought and a propensity for cooperative effort, they must have a secure sense of selfhood and an enduring sense of community. This chapter is devoted to a reexamination of these issues. Now that we know something of how schools work, we can better determine if schools promote or retard these aims for education. Where schools succeed, we will examine how they might capitalize on their success. Where they fail, we will look for ways they might improve.

This chapter asks three questions:

1. Is it possible to increase the creative intelligence of students in schools?
2. Do cooperative classrooms advance or hinder learning?
3. Is it possible to develop student self-respect?

Creative Intelligence

What Is Intelligence?

Discussions of intelligence in education are often dominated by considerations of IQ scores and the technology of testing. For our purposes, however, the use of the term *intelligence* will refer to something broader and more encompassing than a score on a test or a mass of memorized knowledge. When W. I. Thomas spoke of creative individuality, he was referring to the dispositions, interests, and problem-solving skills needed for life in a fast-changing world. Thomas's ideas on intelligence were similar to Dewey's. As we saw in Chapter 2, Dewey put the question of intelligence at the center of his philosophy. In his view, the capacity for creative intelligence frees individuals from reliance on routine, authority, superstition, and prejudice. A developed intelligence guides us through the myriad choices life lays before us.

Intelligence is called for when we find ourselves in problematic situations—when we are caught between conflicting desires and alternative possibilities. How can such problems be resolved? We can ignore them and hope they will go away or will somehow resolve themselves; we can ask someone, perhaps an expert, to tell us what to do; we can read our horoscope, a Ouija board, or the entrails of a chicken for signs and omens; we can flip a coin. All of these alternatives leave us at the mercy of authority or luck.

Intelligent action, on the other hand, entails ordered and thoughtful inquiry. We examine the makeup of a problem: analyze its diverse factors in an attempt to clarify what is obscure and thus easily missed; define the problem in the light of this knowledge; consider various ways of handling the problem; trace the consequences of each possible solution in our imagination to judge how well it might work; decide upon the alternatives that seem most promising; and finally, we act and check the results to see if the anticipated consequences of our actions square with what actually transpired. This is called a *problem-solving procedure*, and whether it is used to get a date for Saturday night or solve a riddle in atomic physics, it constitutes intelligence as Dewey defined it.[1]

By this definition, intelligence is not something that belongs solely to the highly educated or gifted; it is a possible component in all human beings and human activity. An important aim for education, therefore, is to develop our individual and collective ability for intelligent behavior.

The Critics' Contentions

Do schools encourage intelligence as Dewey hoped they would? It's not possible to give a yes or no answer to this question. Different students draw different things from the school experience. Some are excited by school and the activity it offers, others are bored but muddle through, and still others may suffer harm. Critics of education often speak as if schools are everywhere the same, and as if all students experience them in identical ways. Such generalizations oversimplify complex issues, but the critics point out that their criticisms of education, though not universally applicable, are nevertheless generally valid.

Many critics contend that schools promote narrow conformity to externally imposed and often meaningless rules. The institutional pressure of most schools encourages obedience and routine rather than creative exploration and intelligent action. Creativity, when it is found at all, exists in the underlife of the school or is carefully compartmentalized so as not to challenge the smooth

---

[1] John Dewey, *Reconstruction in Philosophy* (New York: The New American Library, Inc., 1950), esp. p. 133. Available in paperback. For a more detailed analysis, see Dewey's *How We Think: A Restatement of the Relation of Thinking to the Educative Process* (Lexington, MA: D. C. Heath, 1933). Available in paperback.

working of the system. Students may be encouraged to do creative writing but are not allowed uncensored expression in the school newspaper or student assemblies. They may be afforded instruction in creative movement but may not be allowed to move freely around the school classroom. They are told about the ideals of democratic government but are seldom given an effective voice in the governance of the school. Critics contend that the domains of creativity are so limited (at least in traditional schools) that what is called creativity looks suspiciously like conformity and acquiescence.

The critics go further. They contend that schools are run by teachers and administrators whose positions and experience inhibit their own creative juices. If students are not allowed to challenge the system, neither are teachers. As evidence for this contention, critics give examples of teachers who have lost their jobs when they dared to oppose the authority of the system. In one such case, Jonathan Kozol was fired when he introduced fourth-grade ghetto students to an angry poem by Langston Hughes, "The Ballad of the Landlord." According to official records, the reason for his dismissal was that the poem "could be interpreted as advocating defiance of authority." Kozol was informed that the school system had to protect children "from ideologies and concepts not acceptable to our way of life." Although Kozol was told he possessed "an enthusiastic spirit, a high degree of initiative, and other fine qualities found in the best teachers," he was fired because he was not adequately committed to "the rules and regulations" of the school.[2]

John Holt, after many years of teaching, came to the conclusion that the prisonlike atmosphere of some classrooms inhibits the development of creative intelligence.

> To a very great degree, school is a place where children learn to be stupid. A dismal thought, but hard to escape. Children come to school curious; within a few years most of that curiosity is dead, or at least silent.
>
> * * *
>
> A child is most intelligent when the reality before him arouses in him a high degree of attention, interest, concentration, involvement—in short, when he cares most about what he is doing. This is why we make schoolrooms and schoolwork as interesting and exciting as possible, not just so that school will be a pleasant place, but so that children in the school will act intelligently and get into the habit of acting intelligently. The case against boredom in school is the same as the case against fear; it makes children behave stupidly.[3]

Holt's contention that schools make children stupid is not easily proven. Its power is more rhetorical than scientific, but his analysis of schooling, especially in his book *How Children Fail,* indicates that schools do not do enough to promote creativity intelligence. Some research into children's thinking skills also suggests that schools are neglecting this vital area.

Research on Thinking

Recent assessments of educational progress show that over 80 percent of students in grades four, eight, and eleven can perform informative writing tasks

[2] Jonathan Kozol, *Death at an Early Age* (Boston: Houghton-Mifflin Company, 1967), pp. 225–227. Available in paperback.

[3] John Holt, *How Children Fail* (New York: Pitman Publishing Company, 1964), pp. 196, 198–199. Available in paperback.

at a minimal level or better. However, only 20 to 25 percent are able to add an analytic element to their informative writing. Analytic writing demands that students explain their assertions, provide supporting evidence, and compare and contrast their views with those held by others. Two out of three eleventh graders can perform at least minimally on tasks that require persuasive writing, but only one in three perform adequately or better. Only 18 percent of American eleventh graders can write an adequate piece of imaginative writing.[4] These results indicate that most students have minimal mastery of the mechanics of writing. However, many experience difficulty when asked to do writing that requires them to find knowledge, pursue understanding, present ideas in an orderly fashion, and make coherent and warranted judgments out of that understanding and knowledge. In short, the majority of American students can not do the kind of writing that requires thought, or what we are calling creative intelligence.

The same point can be made in regard to reading. A recent study of educational progress concluded:

> The thoughts of teenagers may be long, . . . but as far as literature is concerned, their thoughts [lack] depth and sophistication. For many American seventeen-year-olds, thinking about what they have read and expressing their thoughts coherently appear to be a difficult and unfamiliar task.[5]

During the 1970s and early 1980s, teenagers' ability to understand and analyze literature declined and so did their knowledge of literature. Investigators noted that "students seem satisfied with their initial interpretations [of what they have read] and seem genuinely puzzled at requests to defend or explain their points of view."[6] When pressed, students defended their opinions but in most cases their explanations were superficial and made few references to what they had read or to related material. Students performed best on multiple choice and short answer questions that focused on facts but did poorly when asked to write analytically or to discuss a passage's mood, theme, or characters.

No single factor explains the decline in students' thinking skills over the past two decades. However, most recent studies of schooling suggest that students are no longer expected to stretch their talents or test their abilities. All too often schools sell students short.[7] John I. Goodlad and others who have studied classrooms over the past decade contend that many of the instructional strategies popular today fail to actively engage students in classroom learning.[8] Others suggest that much of the teaching in elementary school—with its em-

---

[4] National Assessment of Educational Progress, *NAEPGRAM 8* (Princeton, NJ: National Assessment of Educational Progress, 1986), pp. 1–2.

[5] National Assessment of Educational Progress, *NAEP Newsletter*, Vol. 14 (Fall 1981), p. 1. See also, National Assessment of Educational Progress, *Reading, Thinking and Writing* (Denver: National Assessment of Educational Progress, 1981); Jonathan Kozol, *Illiterate America* (Garden City, NY: Anchor Press, 1985).

[6] Ibid.

[7] Michael W. Sedlak, Christopher W. Wheeler, Diana C. Pullin, and Philip A. Cusick, *Selling Students Short: Classroom Bargains and Academic Reform in the American High School* (New York: Teachers College Press, 1986). Available in paperback.

[8] John I. Goodlad, *A Place Called School: Prospects for the Future* (New York: McGraw-Hill Book Company, 1984); available in paperback. Larry Cuban, *How Teachers Taught: Consistency and Change in American Classrooms, 1890–1980* (New York: Longman, 1984). Jeannie Oakes, *Keeping Track: How Schools Structure Inequality* (New Haven: Yale University Press, 1985). Norris B. Johnson, *West Haven: Classroom Culture and Society in a Rural Elementary School* (Chapel Hill, NC: University of North Carolina Press, 1985).

phasis on independent seatwork, correct answers rather than understanding, and drill over discussion—does not prepare students for the demanding dialogues that many recent reports suggest are at the heart of the education process.[9] Gary Sykes, formerly of the National Institute of Education, concluded that

> at the middle and secondary level, . . . when students are expected to develop complex skills and to deepen mastery of subject matter, serious achievement problems clearly emerge. Yet the problem is in part rooted in elementary-level teaching. Prolonged, intense emphasis on drill-skill approaches to reading in the elementary grades drives out attention to comprehension, to the critical process of making meaning from written work.[10]

Other factors also account for the decline in students' thinking skills. Students, especially those in the middle and lower tracks, are being asked to do less homework, and the work they do often requires little higher-order thinking. The proliferation of elective courses and the move away from core courses have fragmented the curriculum in many high schools.[11] Course content and degrees of difficulty are often determined by individual teachers, who are expected but not required to follow curriculum guidelines, and by students, who are free to resist what the teacher offers.[12] Schools lack clear academic goals and instructional priorities are often unclear.[13]

Schools and the Status Quo

A few critics, most notably Jules Henry, contend that schools almost inevitably promote conformity over creativity. Throughout history, Henry says, we find cultures promoting acquiescence rather than originality in children. The implicit aim of education historically is to maintain the culture, to get people to accept social standards as the one best measure of individual worth, and to

[9] Mortimer J. Adler, *The Paideia Proposal* (New York: Macmillan, 1982); available in paperback. Mortimer J. Adler, *Paideia Problems and Possibilities: A Consideration of Questions Raised by the Paideia Proposal* (New York: Macmillan, 1983); available in paperback. Mortimer J. Adler, *The Paideia Program: An Educational Syllabus* (New York: Macmillan, 1984); available in paperback. Theodore R. Sizer, *Horace's Compromise: The Dilemma of the American High School* (Boston: Houghton-Mifflin, 1984); available in paperback.

[10] Gary Sykes, "Public Policy and the Problem of Teacher Quality: The Need for Screens and Magnets," in *Handbook of Teaching and Policy*, eds. Lee Schulman and Gary Sykes (New York: Longman, 1983), p. 100.

[11] Mortimer J. Adler, *The Paideia Proposal,* 1982; available in paperback. Ernest L. Boyer, *High School: A Report on Secondary Education in America* (New York: Harper and Row, 1983); available in paperback. Education Commission of the States, *Action for Excellence: Task Force on Education for Economic Growth* (Denver: Education Commission of the States, 1983); available in paperback. Goodlad, *A Place Called School,* 1984; available in paperback. Theodore R. Sizer, *Horace's Compromise: The Dilemma of the American High School* (Boston: Houghton-Mifflin, 1984). Available in paperback.

[12] Philip A. Cusick, *The Egalitarian Ideal and the American High School* (New York: Longman: 1983); available in paperback. Arthur G. Powell, Eleanor Farrar, and David Cohen, *The Shopping Mall High School: Winners and Losers in the Educational Marketplace* (Boston: Houghton-Mifflin Company, 1985); available in paperback. Sedlak, Wheeler, Pullin, and Cusick, *Selling Students Short.*

[13] Boyer, *High School;* Goodlad, *A Place Called School.*

guard the status quo against the dangers of divergent thinking. Therefore, it does not surprise Henry that American schools serve to narrow the perceptions of children and to limit their options. Schools traditionally work in service of the status quo.[14]

Aiming for Intelligence

Given Henry's insight into the historical purpose of education, must we abandon the hope that education can serve to encourage rationality, originality, and curiosity? Not at all. His comments serve to remind us of the exciting duality of human nature. Although human beings need order, they are also capable of creativity; although they are autonomous decision makers, they are inextricably interdependent; although they are products of their culture, they are also its producers. The problem that Henry identifies is that schools have too narrowly served one portion of our being (our need for order and our urge to conform) and have woefully neglected other aspects of our nature (our capacity to understand, cooperate, and create). As Edward Hall put it,

> Our schools are a vignette of how man, in the development of civilization and its core institutions, has managed to ignore or disregard some of the most compelling aspects of his own nature.[15]

Real learning helps individuals to grasp the order of things, to understand what is going on, and to increase control over human events. To promote creative intelligence and learning is to take part in humankind's most essential evolutionary task. Learning entails a great deal more than acquiring standard recipes for solving standard problems. Intelligence is needed when we face tough problems for which standard recipes do not exist or are no longer useful. Promotion of intelligence does not mean that schools must give up order or forget what has been learned from past experience. As Jules Henry has pointed out, creative intelligence is the product of discipline and involvement. Creativity and democracy are poisoned by laxity and chaos. Neither Henry nor Dewey suggests that intelligence will emerge spontaneously out of disarray. Instead, they claim that if intelligence is a warranted aim for education, teachers must dedicate themselves to its development. Rather than promote mindless conformity to the status quo, schools must become steadfastly loyal to the pursuit of knowledge, the skills of inquiry, and the expansion and continual reinterpretation of truth.[16]

At this point, Henry's argument breaks away from Dewey's. Henry's view of creativity is less optimistic than Dewey's and more elitist. Says Henry,

> As for the creative individual, the history of great civilizations seems to reveal little about creativity except that it has an obstinate way of emerging only in gifted individuals, and that it has never appeared in the mass of people.[17]

---

[14] Jules Henry, *Culture Against Man* (New York: Random House, Inc., Vintage Books, 1963), pp. 319–320.

[15] Edward T. Hall, *Beyond Culture* (New York: Doubleday & Co., Inc., Anchor Books, 1977), p. 205.

[16] Henry, *Culture Against Man*, pp. 283–321.

[17] Ibid., pp. 319–320.

Training for Creative Intelligence

Psychologists have developed tests that attempt to measure and quantify human creativity. Such tests give the subject a number of opportunities for original thinking. For example, a test may present three seemingly unrelated words (blue, cake, cottage) and ask for a word that is related to all three.[18] More typically a test will ask for unusual uses of a common object (a sugar cube, for example) or will ask for coordinated uses for two objects (how many uses can you think of for a book and a ruler?). These test instruments are imperfect, but they give us a way to investigate the complicated issue of creativity. For example, they help us evaluate Jules Henry's suggestion that creativity is a natural gift, inevitably limited to a fortunate few. Is it true that creativity is something that we are born with, something we either have at birth or do not have at all? Scientific evidence is not abundant, but what exists suggests that creativity is only partially inherited. Although people may be born with a genetic potential for creativity, the more significant research finding is that creativity is a modifiable trait.[19]

I. M. Maltzman designed a study in which he trained students in word-association techniques. He found that students who received the training were more able than a nontrained control group to produce abundant and original word associations.[20] Similarly, N. R. F. Maier found that giving students formal instruction in the techniques of problem solving significantly increased their ability to tackle difficult problems successfully. Maier's training was not elaborate. Students were informed that problem solving entailed breaking out of habitual ways of thinking. The mind must be kept open for new meanings and new ways of viewing the situation. Because such thinking cannot be forced, students who were having difficulty with a problem were encouraged to stop thinking about it, to work on something else and to return to it later with a fresh outlook and from another direction.[21] Studies by R. S. Crutchfield and others have shown that problem-solving skills can be improved through carefully designed instruction on how to generate hypotheses and recognize incongruities in situations.[22]

Other studies show that students' problem-solving abilities are enhanced when teachers explicitly model their own problem-solving procedures. Such modeling entails verbalizing what is going on in their heads when attacking a problem. Teachers describe how they decided on their problem-solving approach, why they eliminated other approaches, how they determined what options to consider at various points in the problem-solving process, and how they recognized

---

[18] A possible answer here is the word *cheese*.

[19] E. Paul Torrance, "Creativity Research in Education: Still Alive," in *Perspectives on Creativity*, eds. Irving Taylor and J. W. Getzels (Chicago: Aldine Publishing Co., 1975), pp. 278–296.

[20] I. M. Maltzman, "On the Training of Originality," *Psychological Review*, Vol. 67 (1960), pp. 229–242.

[21] N. R. F. Maier, "An Aspect of Human Reasoning," *British Journal of Psychology*, Vol. 24 (1933), pp. 144–155.

[22] V. Covington and R. S. Crutchfield, "Experiments in the Use of Programmed Instruction for the Facilitation of Creative Problem Solving," *Programmed Instruction*, Vol. 4 (1965), pp. 3–4, 10. See also Robert Olton and Richard S. Crutchfield, "Developing the Skills of Productive Thinking," in *Trends and Issues in Developmental Psychology*, eds. Paul H. Mussen, Jonas Langer, and Martin Covington (New York: Holt, Rinehart and Winston, 1969), pp. 68–87.

errors and recovered from false starts. Such modeling helps students see that the teachers do not just "know the answer" to a given problem; they think their way to the answer. When teachers verbalize their thinking processes they see how the problem-solving process developed.[23]

Thinking and Subject Matter

Traditionally, teachers have assumed that thinking skills were acquired in the course of studying academic subjects. However, as early as 1924, Thorndike, a pioneering psychologist, showed that the problem-solving skills learned in one subject do not necessarily transfer over to other disciplines or to everyday life.[24] More recent approaches have tried to teach problem-solving strategies directly.[25] For example, the CoRT Thinking Program was developed by Edward de Bono of Cambridge University in England. CoRT, an acronym standing for the Cognitive Research Trust, is a course in critical thinking that consists of six units of ten lessons each. The goal of the course is to teach students to scan problematic situations, organize their thinking into discrete steps or operations, analyze different sides of a debate or disagreement, apply creative thinking, weigh the implications of ideas by comparing those that are more desirable against those that are less desirable, apply values and emotions reflectively, direct the thinking toward decisions and action, defend the decisions with evidence, and evaluate the consequences of the decisions.[26]

There is great benefit to be gained from making students aware of their own thinking processes and letting them in on the thinking processes of others. Too often, teachers teach facts and solve problems without sharing how the facts were established or how the problem-solving process was developed. Students need to see good minds at work so that they can become more aware of their own thinking habits. However, there is a danger in making "thinking" a course in its own right, as if thinking was somehow separate from subject matter. After all, human beings do not simply think; they think *about* something. The subjects taught in school are important because they represent the most significant products of human inquiry. The idea that we can teach creative intelligence without exposing students to content is misguided. Thinking with informed discretion is not an ancillary portion of education or a skill one develops in order to gain access to education; *it is education.* For that reason, thinking skills must be dealt with explicitly and consistently in the context of every course.

---

[23] Thomas L. Good and Jere E. Brophy, *Looking in Classrooms,* 4th ed. (New York: Harper & Row, 1987), pp. 181–188, 335–336; available in paperback. Dale H. Schunk and Antoinette R. Hanson, "Peer Models: Influence on Children's Self-Efficacy and Achievement," *Journal of Educational Psychology,* Vol. 77 (1985), pp. 313–322.

[24] E. Thorndike, "Mental Discipline in High School Studies," *Journal of Educational Psychology,* Vol. 15 (1924), pp. 1–15, 83–98.

[25] Robert J. Marzano and C. L. Hutchins, *Thinking Skills: A Conceptual Framework* (Aurora, CO: Mid-Continent Regional Educational Laboratory, 1987).

[26] Edward de Bono, "The CoRT Thinking Program," in *Thinking and Learning Skills. Vol. 1: Relating Instruction to Research,* eds. J. Segal, S. Chipman, and R. Glaser (Hillsdale, NJ: Erlbaum, 1985). Edward de Bono, "The Direct Teaching of Thinking as a Skill," *Phi Delta Kappan,* Vol. 64 (1983), pp. 703–708. Another problem-solving method is called IDEAL, an acronym standing for a five-step program of problem-solving strategies: 1. Identify the problem; 2. Define the problem; 3. Explore the problem; 4. Act on these strategies; 5. Look at the effects of your actions. J. Bradford and B. Stein, *The IDEAL Problem Solver* (San Francisco: Freeman, 1985).

Good teachers provide opportunities for students to solve problems and to explain their problem-solving procedures to others. (*Source:* National Education Association, Joe Di Dio.)

Feuerstein and his colleagues developed the Instrumental Enrichment Program to help culturally disadvantaged students in Israel. Their goal was ambitious. They set out to change the cognitive structures of disadvantaged youngsters and improve their higher-order thinking skills. They wanted to help students become autonomous, inventive thinkers capable of initiating and elaborating original ideas. To accomplish that goal, Feuerstein developed a set of instructional strategies, collateral exercises, and paper and pencil tests.[27] Students were given exercises to help them become aware of their own cognitive processes and increase what is called their metacognitive activity. *Metacognition* is the ability to stay aware of one's own thought processes and problem-solving strategies.

Research into Feuerstein's techniques has been done in Israel, Venezuela, Canada, and the United States, and the results have been generally positive. Taken together, these studies suggest that the program produces lasting improvements in the intellectual ability of disadvantaged students. Results have been strongest on standard, nonverbal intelligence measures. Treatment effects are most powerful (1) when students get a good deal of instruction in Feuer-

---

[27] R. Feuerstein, Yaacov Rand, Mildred B. Hoffman, Roland Miller, *Instrumental Enrichment: An Intervention Program for Cognitive Modifiability* (Baltimore: University Park Press, 1980). Units included such topics as organization of dots, orientation in space, comparisons, categorizations, analytic perception, family relations, temporal relations, numerical progressions, instructions, illustrations, representational stencil design, transitive relations, and syllogisms.

stein's program (over eighty hours in a given year) and (2) when the program is taught by a teacher who also teaches academic courses and applies Feuerstein's methods to regular course work.[28]

The research into Feuerstein's program gives empirical support to the contention that the teaching of thinking should be integrated into the teaching of good ideas and significant subject matter.[29] What is said for the teaching of thinking must also be said for the teaching of reading and writing. These are not basic skills developed on the way to something else; reading and writing are the heart and spine of education. They must be a part of *every* course because *reading and writing are instruments of thought.* Literacy means reading and writing with what Jefferson called *informed discretion* or what we call *creative intelligence.* Reading analytically brings us into direct contact with someone else's thinking.[30] Writing is vital to the education process because it demands thought and because writing exposes our thoughts and thought processes to public scrutiny. Thus, any serious attempt at writing is a metacognitive enterprise.[31]

Democracy of the Intellect

One last point needs to be made before we move on to other matters. The levels of creativity investigated in the studies cited earlier were modest when compared to the world-changing originality of a Galileo, Newton, Shakespeare, Beethoven, or Einstein. However, such research reminds us that although not everyone can be a creative genius, individuals can expand their creative problem-solving abilities. If given the opportunity, people can become more skilled at making choices and solving problems.

Jules Henry is, no doubt, correct that high-caliber genius is a rarity, but he might agree that a general upgrading of our creative intelligence is not only desirable but essential to human survival. The problems of modern life are essentially moral problems that must be solved collectively if we are to avoid the tragedy of the commons. We cannot rely on the brilliance of a few to chart our course through future events. The future will be determined not by momentous decisions of the few but by myriad choices made by millions of autonomous individuals. The insights of an intellectual elite will not be enough to see us through. What is needed, J. P. Bronowski tells us, is a "democracy of the intellect."[32] Human beings must share a dedication to intelligence, freedom,

---

[28] Jeffrey Messerer, Edmond Hunt, Gertrude Meyers, and Janet Lerner, "Feuerstein's Instrumental Enrichment: A New Approach for Activating Potential in Learning Disabled Youth," *Journal of Learning Disabilities,* Vol. 17 (1984), pp. 322–325. Joel M. Savell, Paul T. Twohig, and Douglas L. Rachford, "Empirical Status of Feuerstein's 'Instrumental Enrichment' " (FIE) Technique as a Method for Teaching Thinking Skills," *Review of Educational Research,* Vol. 56 (Winter 1986), pp. 381–409.

[29] See also Selma Wassermann, "Teaching for Thinking: Louis E. Raths Revisited," *Phi Delta Kappan,* Vol. 68 (February 1987), pp. 460–465.

[30] Mortimer Adler and Charles Van Doren, *How to Read a Book* (New York: Simon and Schuster, 1972).

[31] See E. D. Hirsch, Jr., "Cultural Literacy," *The American Scholar,* Vol. 52 (Spring 1983), pp. 159–169. See also E. D. Hirsch, Jr., "English and Formalism," *The American Scholar,* Vol. 53 (Summer 1984), pp. 369–380.

[32] J. P. Bronowski, *The Ascent of Man* (Boston: Little, Brown & Company, 1973), p. 435. Available in paperback.

and the possibility of moral choice. Knowledge, like intelligence, said Bronowski,

> is not a loose-leaf notebook of facts. Above all, it is a responsibility for the integrity of what we are [intelligent, choice-making beings], primarily of what we are as ethical creatures [capable of moral choice]. You cannot possibly maintain that informed integrity if you let other people run the world for you while you . . . continue to live out of a ragbag of morals that come from past beliefs.[33]

When Bronowski calls for a "democracy of intellect," he is not suggesting that great minds are of no use to us. He means only that an aristocracy of intellect will not see us through the pressing problems of our time. We need a *generalized intelligence*. Perhaps only a gifted few can investigate the mysteries of atomic physics, but the uses of atomic power are of such cosmic importance that we dare not leave decisions concerning them to mere specialists alone. Seen in this light, intelligence is not just a possibility; it is a human necessity. If we fail to aim for creative intelligence in education, our future as a nation and as a species is bleak indeed.

For the purposes of this section, we defined intelligence as ordered, thoughtful inquiry. Critics contend that schools do not foster intelligent action because they do not adequately focus on problem-solving processes. Too much emphasis is placed on memorization, obedience, and passivity and not enough on creative problem solving. Yet, there is evidence that creative intelligence can be fostered in school settings. If schools made the development of problem-solving skills an explicit aim, and if they ordered student activities with this objective in mind, we might realize Bronowski's hope for the democratization of intellect in America.

Cooperation

Schooling and Competition

Competition, as we saw in Chapter 5 ("Some American Values"), is a core value in America, and therefore it is not surprising that schools teach children the "importance" of out-competing others. As Talcott Parsons put it, schools give children the experience of "achieved status." Children are told throughout the school experience that they are responsible for their own work, that they are to do assigned tasks, and to accept gracefully teachers' evaluations of their performance. Each student is expected to maximize personal gain. As we learned in Chapter 8 ("Educational Aims for American Society"), however, the problems we face today demand increased levels of cooperation. The struggle to maximize individual gain can lead to communal catastrophe (the tragedy of the commons).

It is often assumed that competition is a natural state, that it is part of human nature, and that it cannot be altered. Such an assumption is a prime example of lazy-fallacy thinking.[34] Competition, like cooperation, is a value we learn from the culture. Both competition and cooperation are found in abun-

---

[33] Ibid., p. 436.
[34] See Chapter 3, "The Question of Human Nature," for a discussion of lazy-fallacy thinking.

dance in American society. Thus, what is being called for here is not an eradication of all competitive behavior (competition serves many useful purposes) but rather an extension of our cooperative capacities and an understanding that cooperation plays a vital role in our present society.

Alternative Reward Structures

Cooperation is behavior directed toward the benefit of a group rather than an individual. Teachers using *competitive reward structures* might grade on a curve (only 15 percent of the class gets As, 30 percent Bs, and so on). Under such a structure, one student's success necessitates a fellow student's failure. Another teacher may give group assignments. In this *cooperative reward structure*, the project is evaluated and all members of the group receive the same grade. In such situations, individual success depends upon the success of the group.

The cooperative and competitive reward structures do not exhaust the reward options open to teachers. An *individualistic goal structure* differs from the others in that it sets a student in competition with his or her own past performance. For example, individualized instruction may allow students to proceed at their own pace through alternative materials. They are allowed to stay with a skill until it has been mastered. Under such conditions, an individual's success is not connected to the success or failure of other pupils.

The Consequences of Competitive Classrooms

Traditionally, schools have used competitive reward structures to the near exclusion of other options. Children are taught the value of performing well or better than their fellows. To get higher grades or display more knowledge than others is taken as a sign of superiority, and "being number one" becomes a primary value. Goodlad and others have commented on the noncooperative character of most American classrooms. It is tempting, he says, to compare teachers to coaches, directors, or conductors. He goes on to warn that the analogy has limited usefulness because it suggests that the class is a team, cast, or orchestra, when, in most cases, it is not. There is only a "loosely knit group" in which every student plays the same position, acts out the same role, performs on the same instrument, and plays the same tune. He concludes,

> There is little or nothing about classroom life as it is conducted . . . that suggests the existence of or need for norms of group cohesion and cooperation for achievement of a shared purpose.[35]

Cultural values and classroom practices that emphasize competition to the seeming exclusion of cooperation help explain why American children are usually more competitive than children from other nations and why they become increasingly competitive the older they grow and the longer they remain in school.[36] There is also evidence to suggest that middle-class children have internalized competitive norms so thoroughly that they compete even when it is

---

[35] Goodlad, *A Place Called School*, p. 108.

[36] M. C. Madsen, "Developmental and Cross-Cultural Differences in the Cooperative and Competitive Behavior of Young Children," *Journal of Cross-Cultural Psychology*, Vol. 2 (December 1971), pp. 365–371; and A. Shapiro and M. C. Madsen, "Cooperative and Competitive Behavior of Kibbutz and Urban Children in Israel," *Child Development*, Vol. 40 (1969), pp. 609–617.

Figure 16-1   Cooperation.

self-defeating to do so. Madsen, a social psychologist, devised a game where children are asked to sit at the four corners of a large square piece of plywood. In each corner there is a painted circle. Each child holds a string that is attached to a single marking pen at the center of the board. By pulling the string, a child can move the pen in his direction, and by relaxing his hold, he allows other children to move the pen toward their circles. (See Figure 16-1.) As Madsen arranged the game, children were first placed in a cooperative reward structure (children were rewarded if they moved the marker through all four circles in sequence) and later were put in a competitive reward structure (children were rewarded each time the marker traveled to their own circle). Madsen found that many middle-class American children were so highly competitive that competition dominated the game even when a cooperative reward structure was in place.

Research by L. Nelson and S. Kagan found that American students seldom cooperate spontaneously in experimental situations. In fact, American youngsters are more willing than children from other parts of the world to reduce their own rewards in order to reduce the rewards of their peers. The researchers found that

> Anglo-American children are not only irrationally competitive, they are almost sadistically rivalrous. Given a choice, Anglo-American children took toys away from their peers on 78 percent of the trials even when they could not keep the toys for themselves. Observing the success of their actions, some children gloated "Ha! Ha! Now you won't get a toy." Rural Mexican children in the same situation were rivalrous only half as often as the Anglo-American child.[37]

Cooperative vs. Competitive Classrooms

American educators use competitive reward structures because they assume that competition increases student interest, productivity, and competence. There is evidence to disprove these assumptions. Research indicates that competitive situations can impede adaptive problem solving.[38] The threat of failure is particularly damaging to students who believe they cannot win. Such students may

---

[37] L. Nelson and S. Kagan, "Competition: The Star-Spangled Scramble," *Psychology Today,* Vol. 6 (September 1972), pp. 53–56, 90–91.
[38] Ibid.

withdraw or simply go through the motions of participation.[39] Although these students may appear to enjoy competitive situations, a careful analysis has shown that what they most deeply enjoy is winning or at least chasing the carrot of victory. When it is clear to them that they cannot win the game, the situation becomes less appealing.

Contrary to the popular notion that students enjoy competition, a number of studies indicate that they prefer to cooperate.[40] Studies also indicate that, although elementary school students are aware of the competitive nature of their classrooms, most would prefer more cooperative arrangements.[41]

The assumption that competition will increase student performance is seldom supported by empirical evidence.[42] A review of the research by David Johnson and Roger Johnson indicates that competition increases performance only when the work to be done is simple, repetitive, mechanical, and requires little imagination and no assistance from others. However, when problem solving is involved, cooperative situations are most effective. Students in cooperative classrooms solve problems more accurately, retain more information, and perform as well or better than other students on individually completed achievement tests. In one study, researchers divided fifth-grade, inner-city students into four groups with fifteen students in each group. Each group was put into a different reward structure.

- Reward structure I: Each student was given a play-money reward (refundable for goods) for each individually solved problem that was completed correctly.
- Reward structure II: All students in the group were given the same reward depending upon the average scores of the four lowest performances in the group.
- Reward structures III and IV: Two other reinforcement conditions gave children different proportions of rewards for both individual achievement and the average of the four lowest achievement scores in the group.

The results of this experiment showed that individual problem-solving ability and accuracy were improved for all students in cooperative settings; the greater

[39] R. E. Dunn and M. Goldman, "Competition and Noncompetition in Relation to Satisfaction and Feelings Toward Group and Nongroup Members," *Journal of Social Psychology*, Vol. 68 (1966), pp. 299–311.

[40] D. L. DeVries and K. J. Edwards, *Learning Games and Student Teams, Center Report No. 142* (Baltimore: Johns Hopkins University, Center for Social Organization of Schools, 1972). See also Alfie Kohn, *No Contest: The Case Against Competition* (Boston: Houghton-Mifflin, 1986), especially Chapter 4, "Is Competition More Enjoyable?" pp. 79–95.

[41] R. Johnson, D. E. Johnson, and B. Bryant, "Cooperation and Competition in Classrooms: Perceptions and Preferences as Related to Students' Feelings of Personal Control," *Elementary School Journal*, Vol. 74 (December 1973), pp. 172–181. See also David Johnson and Roger Johnson, "Instructional Goal Structures: Cooperative, Competitive, or Individualistic," *Review of Educational Research*, Vol. 44 (Spring 1976), pp. 213–240.

[42] David W. Johnson and Robert T. Johnson, "The Internal Dynamics of Cooperative Learning Groups," in *Learning to Cooperate, Cooperating to Learn*, eds. Robert Slavin, Shlomo Sharan, Spencer Kagan, Rachel Hertz Lazaeowitz, Clark Webb, and Richard Schmuck (New York: Plenum Press, 1985), pp. 112–113. David W. Johnson, Robert T. Johnson, and Geoffrey Maruyama, "Interdependence and Interpersonal Attraction Among Heterogeneous and Homogeneous Individuals: A Theoretical Formulation and a Meta-analysis of the Research," *Review of Educational Research*, Vol. 53 (1983), pp. 5–54.

the degree of cooperation, the greater the degree of improvement. The highest rate of improvement was observed among low-achieving students, but the performance of high-achieving students was also improved by cooperative experiences.[43]

Cooperation is a process that appears to promote a large number of effects that are desirable for the individual and for society. For example,

- Empathy and sensitivity: Children in cooperative settings are more likely to take the interests and needs of others into account.[44]
- Encouraging others: Children who work cooperatively are more likely than those working in individualistic or competitive settings to encourage and support the self-enhancement of others.[45]
- Communication: Cooperation has been found to be an effective method for improving the quality and quantity of communication among students. In early experiments, Deustch compared undergraduates working under cooperative and competitive conditions. He found that students who worked cooperatively verbalized more ideas and group members "were more attentive to one another. . . . They had fewer difficulties in communicating with or understanding others." In competitive groups, on the other hand, communication tended to be "unreliable and impoverished."[46]
- Interest: Students who work cooperatively not only enjoy the group activities but show greater interest in the subject matter they are studying.[47]
- Friendship: Students who work cooperatively, rather than competitively, tend to like one another more. Students who work competitively are more likely to distrust one another and display hostility.[48]
- Trust: Research shows that trust is likely to grow in cooperative settings and that it is virtually absent in competitive settings.[49]
- Integration: Cooperative settings have been shown to promote greater in-

[43] John S. Wodarski, Robert L. Hamblin, David R. Buckholdt, and Daniel E. Ferritor, "Individual Consequences Versus Different Shared Consequences Contingent on the Performance of Low-Achieving Group Members," *Journal of Applied Social Psychology*, Vol. 3 (1973), pp. 276–290.

[44] Emmy A. Pepitone, *Children in Cooperation and Competition: Toward a Developmental Social Psychology* (Lexington, MA: Lexington Books, 1980), p. 209. Gillian A. King and Richard M. Sorrentino, "Psychological Dimensions of Goal Oriented Interpersonal Situations," *Journal of Personality and Social Psychology*, Vol. 44 (1983), pp. 140–162.

[45] Brenda K. Bryant, "The Effects of the Interpersonal Context of Evaluation on Self- and Other-Enhancement Behavior," *Child Development*, Vol. 48 (1977), pp. 885–892. David W. Johnson and Robert T. Johnson, "Motivational Processes in Cooperation, Competitive, and Individualistic Learning Situations," in *Research on Motivation in Education*, Vol. 2, eds. Carole Ames and Russell Ames (Orlando, FL: Academic Press, 1985), pp. 10.

[46] Morton Deustch, *The Resolution of Conflict: Constructive and Destructive Processes* (New Haven: Yale University Press, 1973), pp. 26, 353. Similar findings have been reported in eight other studies. See Johnson, Johnson, and Maruyama, "Interdependence and Interpersonal Attraction Among Heterogeneous and Homogeneous Individuals," p. 5–54.

[47] David Johnson and Roger Johnson, "Instructional Goal Structures." See also David Johnson and Roger Johnson, "Cooperative, Competitive, and Individualistic Learning," pp. 3–15.

[48] Johnson, Johnson and Maruyama, "Interdependence and Interpersonal Attraction Among Heterogeneous and Homogeneous Individuals," p. 22.

[49] Dean Tjosvold, David W. Johnson, and Robert T. Johnson, "Influence Strategy, Perspective-Taking and Relationships Between High- and Low-Power Individuals in Cooperative and Competitive Contexts," *Journal of Psychology* Vol. 116 (1984), p. 199. See also Deustch, *The Resolution of Conflict*, p. 24.

teraction and understanding among children from different backgrounds. Researchers reviewing the literature on this issue concluded

> intergroup cooperation promoted more positive cross-ethnic and cross-sex inter-action than did intergroup competition. These results disconfirm the position that competition among groups leads to attraction among collaborators . . . and they provide some support for the position that the more pervasive the cooperation, the greater the interpersonal attraction.[50]

The skills and dispositions just listed are essential for the moral and social development of individuals. They are also vital to the workings of democracy. Reviewing scores of studies, Johnson and Johnson conclude that competition engenders distrust and hostility, interrupts group cohesiveness, and lowers productivity. Cooperation heightens trust, increases both the quantity and quality of communication, engenders group cohesiveness, stimulates student interest, increases creative problem-solving abilities, and improves achievement.[51] The weight of the evidence clearly indicates that cooperative skills can be enhanced in classroom settings that encourage and reward cooperative interaction among students. Indeed, cooperative classrooms are ideal environments for promoting creative intelligence.

Is Cooperative Education the Answer?

The research on cooperation is so encouraging that teachers should seriously consider the option of cooperative techniques in their classrooms. Johnson and Johnson go so far as to suggest that cooperative goal structures should predominate in American schools. However, supplemental use of individualistic reward structures also can serve some useful purposes. For example, learning simple tasks may be hampered by group procedures. Johnson and Johnson suggest that competition can be exciting and productive when the victory is not particularly important, when students are evenly matched and have an equal chance of winning, when rules are clear and correct answers unambiguous (ambiguity ruins competition), and when the standing of all competitors is shown on a running scoreboard throughout the game.

It should be emphasized that the cooperative reward structure does not mean that schools need to abandon evaluating individual student achievement, interests, and skill levels. Testing (as a diagnostic procedure) is not only possible in cooperative settings, but it is also essential to the advancement of learning there. Student achievement and teacher effectiveness are enhanced by frequent monitoring of student progress. Diagnosis allows students and teachers to know how things are going, where problems exist, and when change is called for.[52]

At some point, of course, student achievement will have competitive implications, for example, when a student applies to medical school or to a college

---

[50] Douglas Warring, David W. Johnson, Geoffrey Maruyama, and Robert T. Johnson, "Impact of Different Types of Cooperative Learning on Cross-Ethnic and Cross-Sex Relationships," *Journal of Educational Psychology,* Vol. 77 (1985), p. 58.

[51] David Johnson and Roger Johnson, "Instructional Goal Structures." See also David Johnson and Roger Johnson, "Cooperative, Competitive and Individualistic Learning," pp. 3–15.

[52] Harry Bredemeier, "Schools and Student Growth," *The Urban Review,* Vol. 2 (April 1968), esp. p. 21.

of education. Under these conditions, students and society are well served by procedures that help ensure that professional schools accept the students most suited to each profession. Competitive testing has a place in education, but its place is limited. Furthermore, noncompetitive testing can serve useful functions in cooperative classrooms.

Individualistic reward structures (setting a student in competition with his or her own past performance) can limit the debilitating effects of competition, but when they are used, it is important that assigned tasks be valued by the student. As Johnson and Johnson have pointed out, effort in individualistic reward structures is essentially self-motivated. Students must have adequate space, privacy, and materials to complete their assigned tasks. It is also important that the student understand what is to be done; directions must be clear. The drawbacks of individualistic instruction are obvious enough: They do not foster social skills, give little or no opportunity for publicly explaining ideas, and can engender loneliness. However, in moderate doses and for appropriate tasks, individualistic methods provide a useful diversion from cooperative routines.

The major points made in this section can be summed up as follows. The problems facing Americans are predominately human problems (moral problems) that demand cooperative effort. The competitive structure of schools clearly retards children's ability to cooperate and hinders learning. Cooperative classrooms not only enhance the learning process, but they also increase group cohesiveness, student empathy, and moral development. It is clear that cooperation can be taught in schools and is a warranted aim for education. However, there is also room for competitive and individualistic reward structures under specific conditions.

Privatism and Self-Respect

As we learned in Chapter 8 ("Educational Aims for American Society") and Chapter 2 ("Identity and the Social Order"), Americans are growing increasingly anxious and alienated from their social roles. In order to deal with the situation, growing numbers of people are pulling into themselves in the belief that independence is the best way to preserve identity and self-respect. Are such ideas justified? To get at this question, we must first define our terms.

John Rawls, Harvard's noted social philosopher, has defined self-respect as an individual's sense of personal value. According to Rawls, self-respect rests on two factors. First, self-respect is possible only when we are doing things worth doing. Second, something is worth doing when it excites our interest, is within our range of ability (we are confident we can do it well), challenges and increases our competence (we do not find it easy), and is recognized and valued by others (significant others confirm the worth of our activity, recognize our competence, and take pleasure in our accomplishments).

Notice that by Rawls's formula, self-respect is located both within oneself and within the community. It demands that we be engaged in activities that we ourselves think are important but that are also recognized as important by others. Self-respect demands that we extend our competence, our intelligence, and our unity with others. As Rawls put it, "The more someone experiences his own way of life as . . . fulfilling, the more likely he is to welcome [someone else's] attainments."[53] That is to say, the more secure our feelings of self-re-spect, the more able we are to contribute to the self-respect of others. Con-versely, as the self-respect of others is put in jeopardy, so are our personal feelings of competence. Self-respect is hindered whenever intelligence is stifled, individual interests are ignored, or community cohesion is loosened. When these things happen together, alienation grows and privatism flourishes.

Rawls's insights bring us once again to the vital connection between individ-uals and the community. To paraphrase another philosopher, George Herbert Mead, society does not simply stamp its pattern on individuals. It helps individ-uals develop minds that enable them to improve society and, in so doing, to improve themselves. We are autonomous creatures, capable of making our own decisions, but we are also interdependent creatures, because our actions always affect others.[54] The great challenge of modern life is to keep the dual forces of the individual and society in productive harmony. Many social institutions are involved in this work but none more vitally than the school.

Schools and Self-Respect

Justice Felix Frankfurter insisted that the central function of education is to teach children the "habits of community"—the ability to act and interact pro-ductively.[55] Rawls expands this idea by claiming that the role of education is to enable "a person to enjoy the culture of his society and to take part in its affairs, and in this way to provide each individual a secure sense of his own worth."[56]

Do schools help or hinder self-respect? Here again, no easy answers are pos-sible. John Holt, in his aptly titled book *The Underachieving School*, asserts that education dismantles student identity and competence. In another book, *What Do I Do Monday?* he goes further:

> I now feel the damage goes still deeper, and that the schooling of most children destroys a large part, not just of their intelligence, character and identity, but their health of mind and spirit, their very sanity.[57]

Such accusations are more startling than convincing. What they lack in scien-tific evidence they attempt to make up for in uncompromising generalizations. More realistically, we might contend that schooling is a happy and challenging experience for some children, one that advances their abilities and self-respect. But for others—those who fail in school or who make do by working the sys-tem—schooling can be an inhibiting experience that damages (or at least does not enhance) their abilities and self-esteem. Unfortunately, there is little empir-ical evidence that speaks directly to these issues. We must extrapolate from related studies and fashion logical, rather than statistical, arguments to make this case.

---

[53] John Rawls, *A Theory of Justice* (Cambridge: Belknap Press, Harvard University Press, 1971), p. 441. Available in paperback.

[54] George Herbert Mead, *Mind, Self and Society,* ed. Charles Morris (Chicago: University of Chi-cago Press, 1934), p. 263. Available in paperback.

[55] Quoted in R. Freeman Butts, "The Public School: Assaults on a Great Idea," *The Nation* (30 April 1973), pp. 553–560.

[56] Rawls, *Theory of Justice*, p. 101.

[57] John Holt, *What Do I Do Monday?* (New York: E. P. Dutton, 1970), p. 54.

Working the System

We learned in previous chapters that many students bluff their way through school and distance themselves from the student role. They do not deny their roles or rebel against them; instead, they play them without inner conviction and with only an appearance of commitment.[58] Such activities, as we already have seen, are common in modern society.[59] The German sociologist Georg Simmel has contended that, except at the highest levels of bureaucratic organizations, "the individual life and the tone of the total personality is removed from social action. Individuals are merely engaged in exchange of performance and counter-performance that takes place according to objective norms."[60] Role distance and impression management can easily lead to alienation and estrangement from ourselves and our social roles.

To the degree that schools promote role distance, they endanger the self-respect of students. Remember that self-respect is only possible if our activities are important to us, challenge our abilities, and are valued by others. Students who merely go through the motions of learning—who fake interest, attention, and understanding—enjoy none of these conditions for self-respect. They are engaged in a form of personal and social dishonesty, which, Philip Jackson has noted, is sometimes "accompanied by feelings of cynicism and self-hatred."[61] At just the period of life when students would benefit most from commitments that challenge their intelligence and encourage moral development, they find themselves in a setting that tolerates (and perhaps even encourages) pretense.[62]

Role distance holds two dangers for students. First, it can alienate them from a significant social institution (the school) and from an important segment of the school community (the teachers). Second, it can alienate them from themselves (a form of alienation we called *self-estrangement* in Chapter 2). Students who memorize a few key phrases in order to appear knowledgeable on an essay test or who remain silent in class for fear of publicizing their ignorance can, over time, lose faith in their own powers of intelligence. Their desire to create the right impression can overpower their ability to think for themselves, to commit themselves to their own ideas, and to gain intrinsic satisfaction through committed involvement with people and learning. If schools are to promote creativity and cooperation among students, they must bring the young into clearer connection with their own abilities, their institutions, and with one another. Instead, it would seem, schools encourage estrangement, role distance, and impression management.

Research on Impression Management in Schools

Some evidence of how deeply students are committed to impression management was uncovered through an extensive study of student attitudes by Edgar

---

[58] Erving Goffman, "Role Distance," in *Encounters: Two Studies in the Sociology of Interaction* (Indianapolis: Bobbs-Merrill Co., Inc., 1961), pp. 85–152. Available in paperback.

[59] See Chapter 2, "Identity and the Social Order," for a discussion of the problems of role distance.

[60] Georg Simmel, "How Is Society Possible?" in *Essays on Sociology, Philosophy and Aesthetics*, ed. K. H. Wolff (New York: Harper & Row, Publishers, Inc. Torchbooks, 1965), p. 347.

[61] Philip W. Jackson, *Life in Classrooms* (New York: Holt, Rinehart and Winston, 1968), p. 32.

[62] For a discussion of impression management in schools, see Chapter 13, "The Student's View of the School."

Friedenberg and others. One portion of the study asked pupils to choose from a list of names and descriptions the students they would most like to have represent their school during a visit with a foreign dignitary. The instructions indicated that the dignitary ("a king from a country like Denmark") wanted to meet interesting, representative students. It was pointed out that the king had a "notable interest in spirited young people."[63] After interviewing eleventh- and twelfth-grade students in nine schools across the country, Friedenberg interpreted his findings. He was interested that respondents took few risks. They believed, rather uniformly, that the king's visit was a public-relations problem, and they therefore chose students who they thought would create a "good impression." The king's request that he meet "spirited young people" was ignored. Respondents did not choose students who displayed self-assurance or unique skills but rather those who were more affable than interesting, whose records revealed they were masters of impression management, and who could be trusted not to rock the boat or challenge authority.

Friedenberg and his colleagues concluded that schools were a grim training ground for the nagging alienation of adult life. We must be careful, however, not to go beyond the evidence. The point is not that schools are major (or even minor) causes of modern alienation. Such an assertion is speculative. It can be more safely contended that schools do not do enough to fortify young people against the strains of modern life. They do not do enough to build the self-esteem necessary to endure the impersonality of the public sphere. The bureaucratization of education hinders the formation of identity, personal integrity, and moral purpose that are essential to creative intelligence and democracy.

More recent research has emphasized the degree to which students have become docile and thoughtless in school.[64] Sizer has pointed out that docility not only debilitates students' capacity to learn, it also lowers their self-esteem. Sizer found that two incentives dominate in schools today, pupils' desire to graduate and their need "to respect themselves and be respected."[65] Respect is difficult to come by when students are patronized and the tasks they are required to do fail to challenge their ability or excite their interests. "The best respect is high expectations for [pupils] and a level of accountability more adult in its demand than childlike,"[66] according to Sizer.

Teaching Self-Respect

Teachers have long been aware that education can affect the self-respect of students. Indeed, many educators believe that students who are hindered by a low self-concept will have a difficult time learning. Research has uncovered a clear and significant relationship between self-concept and academic achievement. What is not clear is the causal direction of the relationship: Does high self-concept increase academic performance or does the successful performance increase self-concept?

[63] Edgar Friedenberg, *Coming of Age in America* (New York: Random House, Inc., Vintage Books, 1963), p. 53. Available in paperback.
[64] Goodlad, *A Place Called School*, pp. 91–129. Powell, Farrar, and Cohen, *The Shopping Mall High School*, pp. 81–100.
[65] Sizer, *Horace's Compromise*, p. 59.
[66] Ibid., p. 34.

Logically, we might assume that self-concepts grow from experience. Therefore, the experience of academic success would enhance an individual's self-respect, and the experience of long-term failure would encourage perception of personal helplessness and incompetence. There is growing evidence that these dynamics are the case.[67] The relationship between self-concept and achievement, however, is complex and cannot usefully be reduced to a one-way, this-causes-that formula. Self-concept and achievement are reciprocally related, and (as in the case of the proverbial chicken and egg) it does little good to haggle over which came first.

What does this analysis imply for teachers? We can conclude from the research that teachers must pay close attention to their students' experiences of success and failure. C. S. Dweck has found that the damage done by repeated failure is not erased even when it is followed by repeated success.[68] Children's skills and self-confidence are enhanced when they are given experiences that extend but do not exceed their abilities. Students' self-concept is most likely to grow when there is a genuine and objective basis for heightened self-esteem.[69] It is important that students experience frequent, consistent, and long-term success. In studies of first-, second-, and third-grade impoverished children, whose initial self-confidence was low and whose achievement was significantly below average, it has consistently been found that student achievement is facilitated by asking questions that students can answer correctly 80 percent or more of the time.[70]

If a teacher continually exposes pupils to material they cannot master, students may come to believe that success is beyond their control. An interesting study by R. M. Arkin and G. M. Maruyama showed how college students interpreted their academic performance according to the grades they received on a test. The students were asked to attribute their test performance to either ability, preparation, test difficulty, or luck. Students who scored well on the test attributed their success to internal attributes, ability, and preparation. Students who performed poorly, however, attributed their failure to test difficulty and luck. These results suggest that, as students experience continual failure, they begin to see academic performance as controlled by external forces that are

[67] E. Kifer, "Relationships Between Academic Achievement and Personality Characteristics: A Quasi-Longitudinal Study," *American Educational Research Journal,* Vol. 12 (1975), pp. 191–210; R. J. Calsyn and D. A. Kenny, "Self-Concept of Ability and Perceived Evaluation of Others: Cause or Effect of Academic Achievement?" *Journal of Educational Psychology,* Vol. 69 (1977), pp. 136–145; B. Bridgeman and V. C. Shipman, "Preschool Measures of Self-Esteem and Achievement Motivation as Predictors of Third-Grade Achievement," *Journal of Educational Psychology,* Vol. 70 (February 1978), pp. 17–28.

[68] C. S. Dweck and E. Elliott, "Achievement Motivation," in *Handbook of Child Psychology, Vol. IV: Socialization, Personality, and Social Development,* ed. P. Mussen, 4th ed. (New York: Wiley, 1983). See also, C. S. Dweck, "Children's Interpretation and Evaluation of Feedback: The Effects of Social Cues on Learned Helplessness," *Merrill Palmer Quarterly,* Vol. 22 (1976), pp. 105–110; and C. S. Dweck, "The Role of Expectations and Attributions in the Alleviation of Learned Helplessness," *Journal of Personality and Social Psychology,* Vol. 31 (1975), pp. 674–685.

[69] A. Bandura, *Principles of Behavior Modification* (New York: Holt, Rinehart and Winston, 1969), p. 91; and A. Bandura, "The Self System in Reciprocal Determinism," *American Psychologist,* Vol. 33 (1978), p. 344–358.

[70] Donald M. Medley, *Teacher Competence and Teacher Effectiveness: A Review of Process–Product Research* (Washington, DC: American Association of Colleges of Teacher Education, 1977).

beyond their control.[71] This view of the world posits an "external locus of control."

Changing Self-Concepts

The damage done by prolonged school failure is not easily overcome. Failure produces attitudes of self-doubt and a perception that poor performance is a result of external causes. These attitudes in turn disturb student concentration and effort, and lead to further academic failure. This spiral of defeat becomes self-perpetuating and cannot be stopped until changes are made both inside the child and in the external environment.[72]

External changes might include examining the child's level of competence and assigning tasks that are well within his or her range of ability. Self-concept change is most likely to occur when a student's performance provides a genuine, objective basis for feeling competent.[73] Short-term changes are not usually sufficient for basic alterations in self-concept. Students must experience consistent and prolonged success.

Students also benefit from training that helps alter their thoughts about failure. Dweck found that it was possible to help students to take responsibility for their failures (to adopt an internal locus of control) and thereby to improve their performance.[74] Helping students to extinguish negative thoughts about themselves and their work serves two useful functions. It allows children to concentrate more fully on their work, and it improves their performance. This latter change in turn reinforces their growing sense of competence and self-confidence.[75] Encouraging students to verbalize their thoughts when working on problems helps them avoid internal dialogues of defeat ("I don't get this: I'll never get this stuff. I wish it were recess time; when will this class end?"). It is important to change the self-defeating attitudes of students, but it is naive to think that these attitudes can be altered by simple devices (by a teacher saying something nice to every child every day, for example). Negative self-concepts grow from long-term, concrete experiences, and their alteration calls for an equal, if not stronger, dose of positive experiences. There is, therefore, not much chance of improving a student's academic self-concept without improving performance.

Rawls suggests that self-esteem is only possible when significant others recognize and value an individual's achievements. Research bears out his philo-

---

[71] R. M. Arkin and G. M. Maruyama, "Attribution, Affect and College Exam Performance," *Journal of Educational Psychology*, Vol. 71 (1979), pp. 85–93. See also, Jacqueline Eccles and Allan Wigfield, "Teacher Expectations and Teacher Motivation," in *Teacher Expectancies*, ed. Jerome B. Dusek (Hillsdale, NJ: Erlbaum, 1985).

[72] J. B. Rotter, "Generalized Expectancies from Internal vs. External Control of Reinforcement," *Psychological Monographs*, Vol. 80 (1966), pp. 1–28.

[73] A. Bandura, *Principles of Behavior Modification*, p. 91.

[74] C. S. Dweck, "Children's Interpretation and Evaluation of Feedback: The Effect of Social Cues on Learned Helplessness," pp. 105–110. See also Carol S. Dweck and E. Elliott, "Achievement Motivation," in *Handbook of Child Psychology, Vol. IV: Socialization, Personality, and Social Development*. Related findings show that students are helped by verbalizing their thought processes. See Bonnie W. Camp and Marry Ann S. Bash, *Think Aloud: Increasing Social and Cognitive Skills: A Problem-Solving Program for Children, Primary Level* (Champaign, IL: Research Press, 1981).

[75] D. Meichenbaum, "Enhancing Creativity by Modifying What Subjects Say to Themselves," *American Educational Research Journal*, Vol. 12 (Spring 1975), pp. 129–145.

sophical assertions. A study by Wilbur Brookover and others showed that self-concept change was facilitated when students were working with teachers they respected and with whom they enjoyed a positive rapport.[76] Self-concept change is unlikely when the teacher–student relationship is strained, when teachers are perceived as critical and judgmental, when classrooms are disruptive, or when teachers do not enjoy student respect and personal authority.

Summary

A central theme of this book has been that education should work to enhance creative intelligence, cooperation, and self-respect. In previous chapters, we investigated why these are warranted aims for education in a democratic society. We also learned how the organizational structure and dominant values of the American school system can inhibit the achievement of these aims. In this chapter, we looked at a more fundamental issue—if it is possible for schools to enhance creativity, cooperation, and self-respect. The research evidence suggests that these are achievable goals.

It is important to note, before leaving this topic, that the aims of education proposed here are not achieved easily. They certainly will not be accomplished by the mechanical administration of a few innovative teaching techniques or by simply adopting some gimmicky policy such as the elimination of grading. Educational aims must guide a teacher's policy decisions at every level of the educational enterprise. Teachers who are guided by these goals should keep them in mind as they develop curricula, make lesson plans, decide on disciplinary techniques, decide on the structural arrangements of the classroom, develop the classroom reward structure, evaluate friendship patterns, plan free-time games, and so on.

The point is that those elements of schooling that inhibit intelligence, discourage cooperation, and damage self-respect are pervasive. If, as teachers, we plan to change this situation, it is necessary for us to design the educational environment in ways that will continually support the achievement of our goals. Clearly, therefore, it is not enough that individual teachers pursue these goals on their own; they must work to establish a communal dedication to them. The staff of a school, with the cooperation of parents, must design educational policies that support these goals.

As we have already seen, the culture of the teaching profession and the structure of the school encourage teachers to work in isolation, apart from their colleagues, without the guidance of clearly developed educational aims. Because of this situation, a teacher who sees wisdom in adopting the aims we have discussed here might understandably become discouraged by the suggestion that teachers should adopt these goals collectively. Don't be disheartened too quickly; there is reason to believe that these goals are in keeping with the personalistic objectives that motivate most teachers. In fact, many of the situations that teachers find most distressing (their social distance from students, their separation from peers, their inability to assess whether they are making a

[76] Wilbur Brookover et al., *Self-Concept, Ability and School Achievement*, Cooperative Research Project No. 1636 (East Lansing: Bureau of Educational Research, Michigan State University, 1965).

difference) could be affected positively if they collectively adopted creative intelligence, cooperation, and self-respect as warranted educational aims. Teachers would have some criteria by which to judge their effectiveness. They would enjoy the camaraderie and pride that come from working successfully toward a communal goal. They would have a basis for carrying on professional discussions and for determining the merit of various school policies. In short, the adoption of clear educational aims can go far toward enhancing the self-esteem of teachers. Rawls's formula for self-respect is as appropriate for the teaching profession as it is for students. If teachers are to find self-respect in what they do, they must know that what they are doing is worthwhile. They must have some criteria (some educational aims) by which they can judge the worth of their work. Everything we know about teachers suggests that the enhancement of student creativity, cooperation, and self-respect are goals that would excite their interest. Educational research suggests that these goals are achievable, yet challenging. No matter how successful we become, there is important work still to be done. If teachers hold these goals in common, they will be able to take pride in their accomplishments, to recognize the accomplishments of others, and to take pride in the accomplishments of the school.

The point of the argument presented here is that democratic aims are not easily accomplished; they demand a communal effort. Although some teachers may be discouraged by the enormity of the task, it is important to keep in mind that democratic aims of education are within reach, that they are compatible with the personalistic objectives of many teachers, and that their adoption would go far toward solving many of the problems that face the teaching profession today.

Suggested Readings

The literature on creativity, cooperation, and self-esteem is growing at a furious pace. The references in the footnotes for this chapter, as well as this bibliography, will be helpful. Recent issues of the journals mentioned here will also contain new articles on these themes.

Creativity, Intelligence, and Metacognitive Awareness

CAMP, B., and M. BASH. *Think Aloud: Increasing Social and Cognitive Skills: A Problem-Solving Program for Children, Primary Level.* Champaign, Il: Research Press, 1981.

DE BONO, EDWARD. "The CoRT Thinking Program." In *Thinking and Learning Skills. Vol. 1: Relating Instruction to Research,* edited by J. Segal, S. Chipman, and R. Glaser. Hillsdale, NJ: Erlbaum, 1985.

DE BONO, EDWARD. "The Direct Teaching of Thinking as a Skill," *Phi Delta Kappan,* Vol. 64 (1983), pp. 703–708.

DWECK, CAROL S., and E. ELLIOTT. "Achievement Motivation." In *Handbook of Child Psychology, Vol. IV: Socialization, Personality, and Social Development,* 4th ed., edited by Paul H. Mussen. New York: Wiley, 1983.

FEUERSTEIN, R., Y. RAND, M. B. HOFFMAN, and R. MILLER. *Instructional Enrichment: An Intervention Program for Cognitive Modifiability.* Baltimore: University Park Press, 1980.

GOOD, THOMAS, and JERE BROPHY. *Educational Psychology: A Realistic Approach,* 3d ed. New York: Longman, 1986.

GOULD, STEPHEN JAY. *The Mismeasure of Man.* New York: W. W. Norton, 1981.

MARZANO, ROBERT J., and C. L. HUTCHINS. *Thinking Skills: A Conceptual Framework,* Aurora, CO: Mid-Continent Regional Educational Laboratory, 1987.

MCKEAN, KEVIN. "The Assault on I. Q.," *Discover,* Vol 6 (1985), pp. 25–44.

SAVELL, JOEL M., PAUL T. TWOHIG, and DOUGLAS L. RACHFORD "Empirical Status of Feuerstein's 'Instrumental Enrichment' (FIE) Technique as a Method for Teaching Thinking Skills," *Review of Educational Research,* Vol. 56 (Winter 1986), pp. 381–409.

SCHUNK, D. H. "Self-Efficacy and Classroom Learning," *Psychology in the Schools,* Vol. 22, (1985), pp. 208–223.

SCHUNK, D. H., and A. R. HANSON. "Peer Models: Influence on Children's Self-efficacy and Achievement," *Journal of Educational Psychology,* Vol. 77 (1985), pp. 313–322.

WEINSTEIN, C., and R. MAYER. "The Teaching of Learning Strategies." In *Handbook of Research on Teaching,* edited by M. Wittrock. New York: Macmillan, 1986.

ZIMMERMAN, B. J., and R. BLOTNER. "Effects of Model Persistence and Success on Children's Problem Solving," *Journal of Educational Psychology.* Vol. 71 (1979), pp. 508–513.

Cooperation

JOHNSON, DAVID W., and ROBERT T. JOHNSON. "The Internal Dynamics of Cooperative Learning Groups." In *Learning to Cooperate, Cooperating to Learn,* edited by Robert Slavin, Shlomo Sharan, Spencer Kagan, Rachel Hertz Lazaeowitz, Clark Webb, and Richard Schmuck, pp. 112–113. New York: Plenum Press, 1985.

JOHNSON, DAVID W. and ROBERT T. JOHNSON. "Motivational Processes in Cooperation, Competitive, and Individualistic Learning Situations." In *Research on Motivation in Education,* Vol. 2, edited by Carole Ames and Russell Ames. Orlando, FL: Academic Press: 1985.

JOHNSON, DAVID W., ROBERT T. JOHNSON, and GEOFFREY MARUYAMA. "Interdependence and Interpersonal Attraction Among Heterogeneous and Homogeneous Individuals: A Theoretical Formulation and a Metaanalysis," *Review of Educational Research,* Vol. 53 (1983), pp. 5–54.

KOHN, ALFIE. *No Contest: The Case Against Competition.* Boston: Houghton-Mifflin Co., 1986.

KING, GILLIAN A., and RICHARD M. SORRENTINO. "Psychological Dimensions of Goal Oriented Interpersonal Situations," *Journal of Personality and Social Psychology,* Vol. 44 (1983), pp. 140–162.

PEPITONE, EMMY A. *Children in Cooperation and Competition: Toward a Developmental Social Psychology* (Lexington, MA: Lexington Books, 1980).

TJOSVOLD, D., DAVID W. JOHNSON, and ROBERT T. JOHNSON. "Influence Strategy, Perspective-Taking and Relationships Between High- and Low-Power Individuals in Cooperative and Competitive Contexts," *Journal of Psychology,* Vol. 116 (1984).

WARRING, D., DAVID W. JOHNSON, GEOFFREY MARUYAMA, and ROBERT T. JOHNSON. "Impact of Different Types of Cooperative Learning on Cross-Ethnic and Cross-Sex Relationships," *Journal of Educational Psychology,* Vol. 77 (1985).

Self-Esteem

ALLEN-MEARES, PAULA. "The Effects of Remedial Reading Services on Self-esteem and Self-concept of Ability," *Educational and Psychological Research,* Vol. 1 (1981), pp. 103–117.

BURKE, JOY P., ROBERT M. MIDKIFF, and R. VANCE WILLIAMS. "The Role of Self-esteem in Affective Reactions to Achievement-related Situations," *Educational and Psychological Research,* Vol. 5 (1985), pp. 191–203.

BYRNE, BARBARA M. "The General/Academic Self-concept Nomological Net-work: A

Review of Construct Validation Research," *Review of Educational Research*, Vol. 54 (1984), pp. 427–456.

COLEMAN, J. M., and B. A. FULTS. "Self-concept and the Gifted Classroom: The Role of Social Comparisons," *Gifted Child Quarterly*, Vol. 26 (1982), pp. 116–120.

FLEMMING, J. S., and W. A. WATTS. "The Dimensionality of Self-esteem: Some Results for a College Sample," *Journal of Personality and Social Psychology*, Vol. 39 (1980), pp. 3–17.

HANSFORD, B. C., and J. A. HATTIE. "The Relationship between Self and Achievement/Performance Measures" *Review of Educational Research*, Vol. 52 (1982), pp. 123–142.

MARSH, H. W., J. W. PARKER, and I. D. SMITH. "Preadolescent Self-concept: Its Relation to Self-concept as Inferred by Teachers and to Academic Ability," *British Journal of Educational Psychology*, Vol. 53 (1983), pp. 60–78.

MARSH, H. W., and J. W. PARKER. "Determinants of Student Self-concept: Is It Better to Be a Relatively Large Fish in a Small Pond Even If You Don't Learn How to Swim as Well?" *Journal of Personality and Social Psychology*, Vol. 47 (1984), pp. 213–231.

ROSS, ALLAN, and MAROLYN PARKER, "Academic and Social Self-concepts of the Academically Gifted," *Exceptional Children*, Vol. 47 (1980), pp. 6–10.

SHAVELSON, RICHARD J., and ROGER BOLUS. "Self-concept: The Interplay of Theory and Methods," *Journal of Educational Psychology*, Vol. 74 (1982), pp. 3–17.

THOMAS, JOHN W. "Agency and Achievement: Self-management and Self-regard," *Review of Educational Research*, Vol. 50 (1980), pp. 213–240.

WEST, C. K., FISH, J. A., and R. J. STEVENS. "General Self-concept, Self-concept of Academic Ability, and School Achievement: Implications for 'Causes' of Self-concept," *Australian Journal of Education*, Vol. 24 (1980), pp. 194–213.

WINNIE, PHILLIP H., and JOHN WALSH. "Self-concept and Participation in School Activities Reanalyzed" *Journal of Educational Psychology*, Vol. 72 (1980), pp. 161–166.

WINNIE, PHILLIP H., M. J. WOODLANDS, and B. Y. WONG. "Comparability of Self-concept among Learning Disabled, Normal, and Gifted Students," *Journal of Learning Disabilities*, Vol. 15 (1982), pp. 470–475.

Summary of Section IV

Section IV dissects the organization of schools to see how it influences the people who work in them. We wanted to know whether schools maintain or retard the genuine ideals of teachers and whether they serve the aims we have suggested for education. In order to answer these questions, we had to learn something about how institutions are studied, the benefits and problems connected with bureaucracies, the characteristics of total institutions, how students and teachers experience schools, and what educational research tells about the efficacy of the aims we propose for education. It should be reiterated here that students are under no obligation to accept the aims we propose. Our effort is not to impose our aims but rather to open the conversation about aims and to provide an example of the kinds of things that must be considered when educators and the public grapple with the goals of education.

The rapid growth of the educational system and the size of schools has made the governance of schools increasingly bureaucratic. It was pointed out that, in bureaucratic school systems, policy decisions are almost always made by administrators who are far removed from the everyday life of the school. Administrators often define the goals of the system and increasingly select technological methods for reaching those goals. Technology, especially when it is strictly enforced, can deskill teachers; make them less responsible, creative, and reflective; and, in extreme cases, alienate teachers from their work.

Some recent educational reforms (for example, competency testing for teachers and students, classroom observation instruments, and pay-for-performance merit increases for teachers) have relied heavily on technology. Other reforms (for example, the Carnegie Forum's plan for reforming the teaching profession and the Florida Beginning Teacher Program) have employed technology but have also worked to loosen bureaucratic control and make the workplace more democratic.

In Chapter 12, we learned about a special kind of bureaucracy, the total institution. Schools do not share all the characteristics of total institutions, but such elements as client–staff friction, group stereotyping, client surveillance, invasions of selfhood, obedience, and privilege systems are prevalent. These consequences of total-institution arrangements are not always negative, but they sometimes hinder learning and dishearten students. Educators must continually analyze the effects institutional arrangements have on students and make necessary adjustments.

Chapters 13 and 14 examined how students and teachers typically experience schools. We learned that some students conform easily to the school's expectations, that others rebel, and that most make do. Making do allows students to avoid some portions of the school experience while embracing others. In recent years, however, disturbing numbers of students have avoided the intellectual aspects of their education. Teachers and students, though they benefit from primary relationships with one another, sometimes find safety in social distance. Students protect themselves from the high expectations and criticism of someone they care about. Teachers maintain positional authority, keep their emotions in check, and protect themselves from hurt and accusations of favoritism.

As teachers become socialized into the profession they begin to learn that norms of noninterference limit the help and cooperation they can receive from colleagues and administrators. They learn that schools often discourage parent participation and make it difficult for teachers and parents to work in close cooperation. To change institutional norms that encourage isolation and discourage cooperation, schools need clear goals, democratic leadership, a reflective teaching staff, and determination.

Chapter 15 places the discussion of school bureaucracy in a national context. The movement toward debureaucratization in education is a part of a larger movement combating the depersonalization of modern life. We can all understand why people are put off by the cold efficiency (and sometimes maddening inefficiency) of bureaucracies. Nevertheless, few of us are willing to give up the benefits of bureaucracy. The question then becomes Do schools have to be run bureaucratically? We suggest that they do not. All the best potentials of the human spirit (the ability to learn, love, reason, communicate, cooperate, empathize, and act morally) come to life and are given shape in close primary (not remote secondary) relationships. Bureaucracies are not inhospitable environments for people who have already developed these potentials—bureaucracies can be run by loving, reasonable, empathic, moral people—but bureaucracies are not good environments in which to develop these potentials.

Schools are no substitute for families, and they cannot be run on a family model. However, they can become mediating institutions that stand between megastructures and the private sphere. As such, schools would work to promote a closer, more meaningful connection between students, teachers, and the subject matter. They would pursue clear aims and would work in closer cooperation with parents. They would enhance the competence and self-esteem of students and their teachers.

It makes little sense to ask schools to promote critical intelligence, cooperation, and self-respect, if these goals are beyond the influence of teachers. Educational research suggests that these are ambitious but achievable goals for all students. That is not to say that all children, no matter what their family background or native propensities, will benefit to the same degree or in the same way if schools are guided by these aims. It is to say that all but the most injured child can learn and cooperate and that every child desires self-respect and deserves the chance to achieve it. *These common capacities are what make us human.* Though individual differences exist—and we celebrate them—such differences are only differences in degree never in kind. It is the purpose of education to maximize these essential human capacities in every child.

The aims discussed in this section have social as well as individual utility. Democracy is hobbled when its citizens cannot respect themselves or one another, when they lack informed discretion, and when they cannot work together productively and with social intelligence.

No school can be better than its teachers and students, but schools can be, and too often are, much worse. Institutions fulfill their social and moral function when they empower those within them to realize their potential and extend their talents. Thus, the work of educators is to build the interpersonal relationships, classroom arrangements, and institutional environments needed to maximize learning and social responsibility. To accomplish these vital goals, teachers must learn to work together and to spark the social intelligence of the school.

Social Class and Education: Balancing Equity and Equality

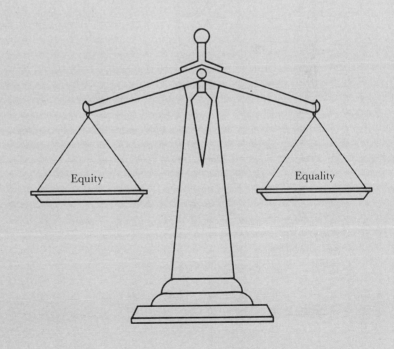

CHAPTER 17

Social Class in American Society

Introduction

When asked about their social class membership, most Americans will describe themselves as middle class. We might conclude from this self-identification that the United States is a nearly classless society, where economic differences are of little significance. But this, as we shall see, is not the case. There are vast financial disparities, and these inequalities affect the lives of individuals in significant ways.

This chapter defines social class membership and identifies the broad characteristics of five classes. It will discuss the effects of social class and spell out the consequences of being rich and poor in modern society.

Defining Social Class

The study of social class is a difficult undertaking. The workings of the stratification system are often obscure, and uncovering them requires sophisticated techniques. Our common-sense knowledge about stratification is deeply believed but often in error.

Not surprisingly, sociologists differ in their interpretations of social stratification. Stratification theories focus on varying aspects of the social-class phenomenon. Marxists are most concerned about who owns the nation's wealth and, more important, who controls the means of production. They see the social classes as engaged in a struggle for power over production—a conflict that, when resolved, Marxists claim, will lead to a new and more harmonious social order.

Max Weber constructed a theory of stratification in opposition to the Marxist view. Weber contended that Marx misunderstood social stratification because he focused too narrowly on its economic aspects. There is more to stratification, he contended, than dollars and cents. Weber offered a threefold analysis of stratification: (1) class—the economic aspect of stratification that largely determines the path your life will follow (what Weber called your *life-chances*), (2) power—the ability to get your way in situations of conflict, and (3) status—social esteem, or what we generally mean when we use the word *prestige*.

These aspects of stratification are not mutually exclusive. Some individuals and groups enjoy the benefits of class, power, and status all at the same time, but the categories are not always conjoined. Some people have a lot of money (class), a good deal of influence (power), but little or no status. Examples might be the successful cocaine salesman or the central character in F. Scott Fitzgerald's novel *The Great Gatsby*. Similarly, someone may have status and power but no fortune in the bank. Some presidents, Harry Truman being one instance, fall into this category. Teachers appear to have more status than they have class or power, though their status has waned in recent years.

Weber's differences with Marx notwithstanding, he agreed with the intellectual revolutionary that economic factors are important in society. He contended, however, that there is more to stratification than control of capital and production. By separating class, power, and status, Weber provided a theoretical framework with which we can study virtually any aspect of stratification.

Criteria for Ranking

The issue of stratification prompts the question, Who is doing the ranking? Is social class a label we place on ourselves? Is it hung on us by others in the community? Or, is it attached to us by some unseen sociologist who suffers the bureaucrat's need to sort and classify people into homogenous categories?

Each approach has something to be said for it, although obviously each leads in a different direction. You might place yourself at one spot in the pecking order, those around you might place you in another, and the snoopy sociologist just mentioned might peg you in yet a third position. Which of these would best represent reality?

When W. Lloyd Warner faced this problem in the early 1930s, he dealt with it in an innovative way. Using techniques developed in anthropology, Warner undertook an exhaustive study of social-class ranking in Newburyport, Massachusetts. The system he used involved questioning people about the community's ranking system. Informants were asked what kinds of strata existed in the community and who belonged to each ranking. Of course, people did not agree on the number of classes involved or who made them up. However, by comparing large numbers of responses, Warner was able to piece together a rather precise ranking system for the community. It soon became clear that there were distinct strata, each with its own membership characteristics and its own level of prestige.

Warner then examined the characteristics of each classification. He looked at such things as the occupations of the people belonging to a class, their sources of income, the types of houses in which they lived, and the locations of their homes in the community.[1] He found that an individual's prestige was highly correlated with his or her occupation and economic standing. This finding was confirmed in a number of other community studies. Such a conclusion may seem obvious today, but in its time, it was an important finding. It meant that social scientists could safely study stratification using just a few key variables as reliable indicators of class rank. It relieved investigators of having to repeat

---

[1] W. Lloyd Warner, Marchia Meeker, and Kenneth Eells, *Social Class in America: The Evaluation of Status* (New York: Harper & Row, Publishers, Inc., Torchbooks, 1960). Available in paperback.

Warner's arduous and costly method every time they wished to study some aspect of stratification.

Warner's work has had a significant impact on American sociology, although in recent years it has been criticized. Some sociologists contend that class is not simply a subjective phenomenon and disagree with Warner's assumption that "class is pretty much what people say it is." Critics are distressed by Warner's reliance on measures of prestige and complain that his techniques ignore the often hidden, but nevertheless powerful, economic aspects of social class.

America's Five Classes

Any brief description of America's social classes is, by necessity, highly abstract. Although our discussion of criteria will accurately reflect the characteristics of one strata or another, these criteria are not equally applicable to all individuals who inhabit a class. What is presented is a broadly descriptive account of the social, cultural, and personality outcomes of class. It is based upon the accumulated research findings of many interpretative and empirical studies, but it must not be read as a set of iron rules that encase all members of a single class.

Just how many social classes exist in America is a topic hotly debated in sociology today. The issue is complicated by the fact that different communities have slightly different class structures. Furthermore a person who holds a lofty position in a small town may not have the same high status if he or she moves to a wealthy suburb of a large city.

A social class is made up of families and unrelated individuals who share roughly equivalent benefits, such as financial assets, prestige, and power. In Max Weber's terms, they share similar life-chances. Thus, as a family changes its social class, family members will experience new social benefits or deficits, depending on the direction of their mobility.

Class I (The Upper Class)

Upper-class families make up the social elite of American society. They number less than 1 percent of the total population.[2] This group is wealthy, wields great power, and has more influence than any other single group in America. But money, by itself, does not secure placement in elite society.

Those in the upper class have, for the most part, inherited social privilege from others. The further back the family's prosperity extends (the older the money), the more secure their placement among the social elite. E. Digby Baltzell, a sociologist and himself a descendent of wealth, explains that upper-class families descend from individuals who generations earlier amassed great fortunes. These families

> are descendents of successful individuals (elite members) of one, two, three or more generations ago. These families are at the top of the social class hierarchy; they are brought up together, are friends, and are intermarried one with another;

[2] Ibid., p. 14. G. William Domhoff, *Who Rules America?* (Englewood Cliffs, NJ: Prentice-Hall, Inc., 1967), p. 7.

. . . they maintain a distinct style of life and a kind of primary group solidarity which sets them apart from the rest of the population.[3]

The offspring of Class I families tend to marry the children of other families in their class, thereby consolidating their fortunes and lineage. There are exceptions to this, of course, and such events are unusual enough to provide grist for the mill of any self-respecting gossip columnist. Family stability is comparatively high among members of this strata. The class is characterized by high life expectancy, good mental health, great material comfort, high psychic satisfaction from primary and secondary associations, and easy access to the levers of power.

As will be learned in Chapter 19 ("Social Class and Child Rearing: What Children Bring with Them to School"), wealthy families socialize their children to uphold the family name. In this way, each generation is prepared to guard the family's fortune, reputation, and position of privilege.

G. William Domhoff, a psychologist who has studied Class I extensively, has listed a few handy, though not perfect, indices of Class I membership. Among these he includes (1) attendance at elite private preparatory schools, usually located in the Northeast, (2) listing in the social register of specified cities, (3) membership in selective gentlemen's clubs, (4) being the offspring of a millionaire or an executive earning $300,000 a year, and (4) marriage to a Class I member.[4]

Few would deny that the upper class marshals great wealth and influence, but there is disagreement as to how far its real power extends. One group contends that Class I individuals hold inordinate power, which they protect through an informal, elitist network of class and family affiliations. The most articulate (and controversial) proponent of this view, C. Wright Mills, contended that

> The men of the higher circles are not representative men; their high position is not a result of moral virtue; their fabulous success is not firmly connected with meritorious ability. Those who sit in the seat of the high and mighty are selected and formed by the means of power, the success of wealth, the mechanics of celebrity, which prevail in their society. They are not men selected and formed by a civil service that is linked with the world of knowledge and sensibility. They are not men shaped by nationally responsible parties that debate openly and clearly the issues this nation now so unintelligently confronts. They are not men held in responsible check by a plurality of voluntary associations which connect debating publics with the pinnacles of decision. Commanders of power unequaled in human history, they have succeeded within the American system of organized irresponsibility.[5]

Those opposing the power elite hypothesis contend that the explosive growth of managerial positions in industry has drawn to its rank middle-class individuals, who, by virtue of special training and technological competence, are well

---

[3] E. Digby Baltzell, *Philadelphia Gentlemen: The Making of a National Upper Class* (New York: The Free Press, 1958), p. 7.

[4] G. William Domhoff, *The Higher Circles: The Governing Class of America* (New York: Random House, Inc., 1970), figures have been adjusted for inflation.

[5] C. Wright Mills, *The Power Elite* (New York: Oxford University Press, Inc., 1956), p. 361. Available in paperback.

prepared for such work.[6] By this analysis, there has been a democratization of managerial rule in the country. Upwardly mobile managers hold no class loyalty to the uppermost strata but are overwhelmingly loyal to the profit motive and to whatever organizations pay their salary. David Reisman expresses this view when he writes:

> There has been in the last fifty years a change in the configuration of power in America, in which a single hierarchy with a ruling class at its head has been replaced by a number of "veto groups" among which power is disbursed.[7]

In other words, highly competent managers, working in competition rather than in cahoots, guard the nation against a class-based monopoly of power.

Who is correct: those supporting the power-elite hypothesis or those endorsing the managerial-democracy position? The answer is not clear (debates seldom rage over clear-cut issues), but a look at the available research is instructive.

In an earlier era of American history, Class I males were often men of leisure who did not need to work. Currently, however, upper-class individuals usually hold jobs and are heavily involved in banking, corporate law, industry, and government. Domhoff examined the background of corporate directors of the top insurance companies, banks, and industrial corporations and found that 53 percent were from Class I families.[8] Other, more detailed, studies suggest that upper-class families appear to predominate (that is, they contribute 40 to 70 percent of the leadership hierarchy) in high-level banking, law, and business.[9] In government, individuals of Class I origins are disproportionately represented in diplomacy, on the Supreme Court, and in the Cabinet.[10] These are the areas where significant decisions are made and policies are established. This evidence lends credibility to C. Wright Mills's contention that America is ruled by a power elite, but it falls far short of rendering this claim indisputable. Numerical evidence does not prove that Class I individuals act in unison to protect their class interests.

Another upper-class group—we will call them the lower uppers for purposes of distinction—share all the material benefits of those above them except for lineage (that is, a family history of wealth and power). Those who have earned their own fortunes (rock stars, for example) are not likely to achieve membership in the upper-upper class. Inheritance (or what those in other classes often call *old money*) is an indispensable requirement for upper-upper class membership. This requirement can be frustrating to people who have ascended through two or three classes only to find their final ascent to the pinnacle of society blocked by requirements they cannot possibly meet. That, of course, is exactly

[6] S. Keller, *Beyond the Ruling Class: Strategic Elites in Modern Society* (New York: Random House, Inc., 1963), p. 261.

[7] David Riesman, Nathan Glazer, and Reuel Denney, *The Lonely Crowd* (New York: Doubleday & Co., Inc., Anchor Books, 1953), p. 239.

[8] Domhoff, *Who Rules America?* p. 51. Other research puts the figure somewhat lower. See Thomas R. Dye, *Who's Running America?* (Englewood Cliffs, NJ: Prentice-Hall, 1976), p. 152; available in paperback.

[9] Domhoff, *Who Rules America?* pp. 53–55; and P. M. Blumberg and P. W. Paul, "Continuities and Discontinuities in Upper-Class Marriages," *Journal of Marriage and the Family*, Vol. 37 (1975), pp. 63–77.

[10] Keller, *Beyond the Ruling Class*, pp. 297–303; and Domhoff, *Who Rules America?* pp. 97–103.

why the old-line requirement was established; it protected the upper-upper class against status assaults from below.

There are distinguishing characteristics that separate the upper uppers from the lower uppers. Those in the higher reaches of the upper class do not need to work, though many busy themselves at tasks that are important to themselves and/or society. For example, they may sit on the boards of well-established foundations, prestigious universities, powerful banks, influential think tanks, or take an active role in such organizations as the Council on Foreign Relations or the Foreign Policy Association.

People in the upper-upper class often live in fashionable, nongarish houses nestled comfortably on family estates. Most upper-upper homes cannot be seen from the road and are protected by high fences and elaborate gates. The rooms of the house are filled with heirloom furnishings that sit on hardwood floors covered by old, frequently threadbare, Oriental rugs. Walls, often paneled in dark wood, are covered with valuable oil paintings and portraits in ornate, gilded frames. Upper-upper families are likely to have new, but probably not ostentatious cars in the garage, but may prefer to drive an old and dirty Jeep, Chevy, or Plymouth around town.

Those in the lower-upper class tend to display their wealth more conspicuously and to lead lives more public than those higher up the class ladder. Their houses are usually large and showy. (Think, for example, of William Randolph Hearst's San Simeon, Hugh Heffner's Playboy Mansion in Chicago, those monuments to conspicuous consumption that inhabit the shoreline of Newport, Rhode Island, or for that matter, think of the White House.) Sometimes, we can see lower-upper homes as they stand proudly on some high piece of ground, but if not, no matter—many in lower-upper class families are willing (perhaps, anxious) to open their doors to photographers from *Architectural Digest, Better Homes and Gardens,* or regional journals such as *Southern Living.*

The lower-upper class world is depicted through countless plays and novels in the tragic tradition of *The Great Gatsby* and slapstick antics of "Beverly Hillbillys." Lower-uppers also are more prone than members of other classes to write (or commission the writing of) books that celebrate their own success. There is a ready market for such material because Americans have a nearly insatiable appetite for information about "the life-styles of the rich and famous." We revere success and, at the same time, take perverse pleasures in the graceless efforts of the lower-uppers to gain entry into the highest reaches of the upper class. Of course, not all of the newly rich are shunned by the older inhabitants of Class I. Some in the lower-upper class simply have too much talent and/or power to bear for long the brunt of upper-class snobbery.

Class II (The Upper-Middle Class)

The upper-middle class consists of professionals, managers, leading scientists, high corporate executives, and their families. Membership in this class does not depend solely on family background, but it usually requires extensive education (preferably at "good schools") as well as socially acceptable manners, tastes, and patterns of consumption.

Class II families are well off financially. They usually own their own homes and have two or more cars and many other conspicuous possessions (swimming pools, country club membership) that enhance their comfort and advertise their status. Because of soaring inflation rates, the salary range of this and other classes is difficult to set. The matter is further complicated because the salary perimeters of Class II differ when considered on a national level and within the confines of a particular community. Thinking in terms of 1988 dollars and considering the issue nationally, we calculate that the salary range of Class II would begin at $87,000 or higher.

Many members of Class II are new arrivals who successfully rode the wave of industrial expansion into affluence. Understandably, most are proud of their accomplishments and view upward mobility as the product of hard-won skill. They are often politically conservative and would prefer that government stay out of their business or professional practices. Because they have been upwardly mobile, they believe others with talent and determination can do the same. Therefore, they support only minimal welfare aid.[11] This group does tend to support civil liberties issues, however, and will often take liberal positions on foreign policy matters.[12]

The upper-middle class is politically active. They are likely to belong to political organizations (usually Republican), contribute to candidates, work for their election, and perhaps run for office themselves. Members of Congress, as well as officials at state, local, and federal levels, often come from this strata of society. They are frequently the major beneficiaries of national and local legislation.[13]

A smaller percentage of the upper-middle class—what Herbert Gans has called the "liberal professional" groups to distinguish them from the larger, more conservative managerial segment of this class—are likely to take a liberal stance on political issues. It was the children of the "liberal professional" group who spearheaded the civil rights movement and initiated the antiwar movement on the campuses of prestigious colleges in the 1960s and 1970s. Far from representing an intense rebellion from their parents (as is often contended), many radical campus leaders were merely extending and putting into practice views they had learned at home.[14]

At work, the upper-middle class are not usually policy makers but are rather those charged with devising ways to implement policy and achieve the goals of the institution. Whereas Class II individuals wield considerable power and enjoy high income and status, they are largely dominated by the still greater power of those above them in Class I. This fact does not appear to bother upper-

[11] R. Hamilton, *Class and Politics in the United States* (New York: Wiley, 1972), p. 198; and R. Bendix and Seymour M. Lipset, "Political Sociology: An Essay and Bibliography," *Current Sociology*, Vol. 6 (1957), pp. 79–169.

[12] Samuel Stouffer, *Communism, Conformity and Civil Liberties* (New York: Doubleday & Co., Inc., 1955). Clyde Z. Nunn, Harry J. Crockett, Jr., and J. Allen Williams, Jr., *Tolerance for Nonconformity* (San Francisco: Jossey-Bass, Inc., Publishers, 1978).

[13] Donald R. Mathews, *The Social Background of Political Decision-Makers* (New York: Random House, Inc., 1954). See also Donald Mathews, *U.S. Senators and Their World* (Chapel Hill: The University of North Carolina Press, 1960).

[14] Seymour M. Lipset and Gerald M. Schaflander, *Passion and Politics* (Boston: Little, Brown & Company, 1971); Richard Flacks, "The Liberated Generation: An Exploration of the Roots of Student Protest," *Journal of Social Issues*, Vol. 23 (July 1967), pp. 52–75; Irwin Unger, *The Movement: A History of the American New Left, 1959–72* (New York: Dodd, Mead & Company, 1974).

middle class workers. Most studies show them to be highly satisfied with their work and in generally good mental health.[15]

Class II jobs require considerable training, high motivation, mental flexibility, graceful managerial skills, a willingness to adjust to changing techniques and new work situations, and often a willingness to put work at the center of one's life. The chances of acquiring the values and habits requisite for Class II work are greatly enhanced if an individual has been raised in a middle- or upper-middle class home.

Class II men tend to marry college-educated, stylish women who share a commitment to their husbands' careers. The fast-changing role of women in American society makes generalizations in this area dangerous, but traditionally Class II women have not worked outside the home.[16] Their work is more usually to support the husband's career plans by running an orderly, noncontroversial home and playing the role of companion (with whom the husband can unwind), organizer (who orchestrates family functions), teacher (who oversees the children's school activities), counselor (who revives her husband's spirits during moments of depression or insecurity), and gracious hostess (who gives good parties and can impress influential people).[17] Research indicates that not all women approach Class II marriage with the expectation of playing the role of corporate wife, but most find themselves filling that niche as their husbands' careers develop.[18]

Child-rearing patterns among Class II families, it will come as no surprise, emphasize achievement, motivation, independence, and excellence. The young are encouraged to do well academically and to take part in extracurricular activities. Although not as affluent as the upper class, the offspring of the upper-middle class seldom lack material comfort. Some studies indicate, however, that a minority of Class II children suffer from boredom, a sense of superfluousness, and unmet needs for meaningful activity in the home and community. Ralph W. Larkin concluded a study of youth in an upper-middle class community with this trenchant assessment:

> The problem of [upper] middle-class youth is that the family is isolated and the bread winner is involved in an intense struggle for status. The family, as the repository of status, assumes the external manifestations of the status of the bread winner. However, the more the bread winner(s) involves him or herself in the struggle for status, which occurs in the world of work, the more the family becomes merely a material adjunct of the status struggle. The internal workings become harnessed to the strivings of the adults and the emotional tenor of the family relationships are attenuated and subsumed by the necessity to maintain or increase status. Children become fetters on the status strivings, since they require time out from labor in the world of work.[19]

[15] C. M. Bonjean, "Mass, Class, and the Industrial Community: A Comparative Analysis of Managers, Businessmen, and Workers," *American Journal of Sociology*, Vol. 72 (1966), pp. 149–162.
[16] W. H. Whyte, Jr., "The Wives of Management," *Fortune*, Vol. 44 (1951), pp. 86 ff.
[17] R. M. Kanter, *Men and Women of the Corporation* (New York: Basic Books, Inc., Publishers, 1977).
[18] M. Komarovsky, "Cultural Contradictions and Sex Roles: The Masculine Case," *American Journal of Sociology*, Vol. 78 (1973), pp. 873–884.
[19] Ralph W. Larkin, *Suburban Youth in Cultural Crisis* (New York: Oxford University Press, Inc., 1979), pp. 198–199. Available in paperback.

Larkin's conclusions are drawn from one study and cannot be applied to all Class II families. However, his findings are confirmed in enough other research to suggest that the problems he identifies are widespread.[20]

The homes of the upper-middle class usually have more rooms than are needed in everyday life and can easily accommodate overnight guests and holiday gatherings. Living and dining rooms in Class II homes often are reserved for formal entertaining and, thus, seldom get daily use. The family congregates in the "family room," where magazines such as *The New Yorker, Smithsonian, Forbes, Business Week,* and the *New York Review of Books* may be piled neatly waiting to be read. On the bookshelf, there may be a collection of mysteries (usually read) and headier fare such as Churchill's *History of the Second World War* (often unread). Meals are usually served in a "dining area" off the kitchen. Pets (pedigreed dogs are preferred) may be given names that advertise the family's sophistication and/or humor. A particularly randy canine, for example, might be called Caligula. Leisure time is spent playing golf or tennis at the country club rather than on public links or city courts. Those who populate Class II are likely to drive expensive foreign cars (BMWs, Mercedes, and Volvos) though they may temper this ostentation by claiming they are being "practical," "we got an unbelievable deal," or "the repair bills on my old car were so large that it was actually cheaper to buy a dependable new car."

Class III (The Lower-Middle Class)

The lower-middle class is largely although not totally, a white-collar class. Its members are middle-income business people, small business proprietors, independent professionals, and sometimes farmers. It also includes semiprofessionals (teachers, clergy, social workers, nurses, police officers, and fire fighters), sales and clerical workers, draftsmen, bank tellers, bookkeepers, and middle-management personnel in business and government. Such jobs require a high school education and, increasingly, at least some college training. Generally, work-related decision making in this group is allowed only within a narrow and clearly specified range of activities.

Some white-collar, Class III jobs, such as teaching, demand attention to detail and a high degree of mental activity. Other work, such as keypunching or clerical work, can be routine and factorylike. Therefore, a wide spectrum of activities, talents, values, and dispositions are represented in Class III. Clerical work can be dull and uninvolving and may demand little skill or commitment, whereas running a small business, social work, or teaching requires a high degree of commitment, involvement, knowledge, skill, and, we presume, intelligence.

Family patterns in Class III tend to be stable, though such generalizations are dangerous in an age of increasing matrimonial disarray. Husbands and

---

[20] Kenneth Keniston, *The Uncommitted: Alienated Youth in American Society* (New York: Dell Publishing Co., Inc., 1960); available in paperback. Kenneth Keniston, *Young Radicals* (New York: Harcourt Brace Jovanovich, Inc., 1968); available in paperback. James S. Coleman et al., *Youth: Transition to Adulthood* (Chicago: University of Chicago Press, 1974); available in paperback. Kenneth Keniston and the Carnegie Commission on Children, *All Our Children* (New York: Harcourt Brace Jovanovich, Inc., 1977); available in paperback.

wives generally share interests, participate in one another's worlds, and jointly care for the children. Parental roles are less sex-segregated than in most other classes.

Child-rearing patterns of the middle class are clearly related to the type of work done by the primary breadwinner. Those holding jobs characterized by relative autonomy and freedom from supervision stress the importance of achievement, internal motivation, high aspirations, self-control, rationality, postponement of gratification, respect for authority, and the significance of an internal locus of control. In short, parents prepare children for the types of work they themselves do.[21] Those holding jobs in which autonomy is limited and supervision is tight are likely to train their children in obedience, acceptance of authority, docility, respectability, and generally lower status and economic aspirations.[22] No matter what the parents' occupation, Class III children are usually taught that education is a prerequisite for social mobility.

The salary range for this class is quite wide, stretching well above the $80,000 mark on the upper end of the scale and down to about $23,000 at the bottom (1987 dollars). Class III individuals usually live in apartments or in modest homes, which increasingly must be rented due to the recent skyrocketing prices of building or buying a house. Many individuals of the lower-middle class can trace their ancestry back to the heavy immigration of the mid- or late 1800s. Membership in fraternal organizations such as the Elks, Moose, and Masons is high in this stratum, as is church membership.

The political orientation of the lower-middle class is somewhat uncertain. A number of conservative presidential hopefuls have run campaigns designed to appeal to the "forgotten American."[23] This individual is depicted in political speeches as a hard-working, law-abiding, taxpaying, long-suffering, patient, middle-class American who has become fed up with liberal taxation and government meddling in business, education, and the private sphere of American life. The "forgotten American," right-wing politicians contend, is fundamentally conservative. Available evidence, however, does not indicate that the lower-middle class moves consistently to the conservative ideology. This group, at least in urban America, tends to vote the Democratic ticket and to support such liberal proposals as national health insurance.

Class III individuals tend to be discontented with their lot. After reviewing job satisfaction literature, Beth Vanfossen contends that Class III individuals frequently "feel caught in the prestige squeeze between the salaried administrators on the upper side and the increasingly affluent skilled worker on the

---

[21] Melvin Kohn, *Class and Conformity: A Study in Values*, 2d ed. (Chicago: University of Chicago Press, (1977); available in paperback. J. A. Kahl, *The American Class Structure* (New York: Holt, Rinehart and Winston, 1957). Jonathan H. Turner, "Entrepreneurial Environments and the Emergence of Achievement Motivation in Adolescent Males," *Sociometry*, Vol. 33 (June 1970), pp. 147–166.

[22] Ibid. G. H. Elder, "Family Structure and Educational Attainment," *American Sociological Review*, Vol. 39 (February 1965), pp. 81–96. G. Mackenzie, *The Aristocracy of Labor: The Positions of Skilled Craftsmen in the American Class Structure* (London: Cambridge University Press, 1973). Herbert Gans, *The Levittowners: Ways of Life and Politics in a New Suburban Community* (New York: Random House, Inc. 1967); available in paperback.

[23] These views date far back in American history and were given their clearest, if inaccurate, elaboration by William Graham Sumner. "The Forgotten Man" and other essays appear in *Social Darwinism: Selected Essays of William Graham Sumner* (Englewood Cliffs, NJ: Prentice-Hall, Spectrum Books, 1963).

lower side."[24] This dissatisfaction is most prevalent when their jobs are unchallenging, economically unrewarding, deficient in autonomy, and lacking in responsibility commensurate with their training. Dissatisfaction is heightened when those in the lower reaches of Class III begin to suspect their children will not be able to advance beyond the economic status of their parents.

The lower-middle class is characterized, in literature and in fact, by the desire to belong and be respectable. Middle-class families usually lead conventional, noncontroversial lives in neat homes set on roadside lots with well-kept lawns. Friendliness and openness are valued and attention is paid to "keeping up appearances." At the upper end of the class, positions that may lead to management and executive responsibilities are highly praised. (A typical boast on a holiday greeting card might be: "Tommy graduated last spring from State University where he majored in business administration. He's now an executive trainee with the local gas company and has already been given his first promotion.") At the lower ends of the class, where jobs offer less opportunity for advancement, workers derive pride and reflected status by working in the proximity of power. For example, a secretary to the vice president of a company claims greater status than someone who works for middle management.

Lower-middle class families own smaller homes on smaller pieces of land than their upper-class counterparts. In the typical Class III living room stands a television set, perhaps nestled into a prefabricated "wall unit" of shelves and cupboards. On the top of the television (or nearby) may be displayed an array of family photographs depicting marriages, sporting events, military service, and other significant occasions or accomplishments. On a nearby shelf, there may be some neatly arranged "collectibles" and perhaps a few mail-order books published by Time-Life or Reader's Digest. On the coffee table are usually such magazines as *National Geographic, T.V. Guide, Reader's Digest,* or *Family Circle.* Copies of the same publications, together with collections of catalogues, perhaps, may be found in a rack in the bathroom.

Class III bathrooms often are monuments to cleanliness. Toilet brushes and plumbers helpers (perhaps cleverly decorated), air fresheners and scouring powders, water picks and electric tooth brushes, hair dryers and hair curlers stand beside scented soaps, unguents, pastes, shampoos, and gels as testimony to the family's concern for "proper grooming." Class III bathrooms are not much different from those in Class II homes, except the former are more likely to be decorated with cute artifacts (turtle-shaped soap dishes, for example) and the latter may have space enough for side-by-side sinks, a sunken bathtub, and, perhaps, a jacuzzi.

Class IV (The Working Class)

Class IV is composed largely, though again not exclusively, of workers in blue-collar, skilled, semiskilled, and unskilled occupations. There is a great diversity

---

[24] Beth Vanfossen, *The Structure of Social Inequality* (Boston: Little, Brown & Company, 1979), p. 324. See also E. N. Glenn and R. L Feldberg, "Degraded and Deskilled: The Proletarianization of Clerical Work," *Social Problems,* Vol. 25 (1977), pp. 52–64. See also C. Wright Mills, *White Collar: The American Middle Classes* (New York: Oxford University Press, 1951); available in paperback.

White-collar workers now outnumber blue-collar workers in the
work force. (*Source:* National Education Association, Joe Di Dio.)

among blue-collar jobs and the boundary separating Class III from Class IV is
blurred. Some white-collar employees, by virtue of their low pay and the routine nature of their work, find themselves embedded in Class IV. Some skilled
blue-collar workers, by virtue of their higher pay and technical expertise, might
be considered in Class III.

Class IV occupations can be divided into skilled workers (consisting of 20 to
25 percent of the blue-collar work force), semiskilled workers (30 to 35 percent), unskilled workers (about 10 percent), service workers (about 25 percent),
and some farmers and farm laborers (roughly 6 percent). Table 17-1 indicates
the wide range of occupations collected under the blue-collar heading.

America is fast becoming a service-oriented, rather than industrial economy.
White-collar workers now outnumber blue-collar workers in the labor force.
The percentage of the population in blue-collar jobs has declined from 55 per-

TABLE 17-1.   Types of Work in Blue-Collar Occupations

Skilled Workers (craft workers)	Semiskilled Workers (operators)	Unskilled Workers (laborers)	Service Workers
bakers	assemblers	car washers	beauticians
carpenters	dressmakers	construction laborers	bartenders
cobblers	gas pump operators	farm workers	dental assistants
electricians	machine operators	ditch diggers	garbage collectors
heavy equipment operators	meat cutters	gardeners	janitors
mechanics	public transportation operators	longshoremen	nurses' aides
opticians	sailors		ushers
printers	telephone operators		
tailors			

cent of all workers in 1915 to 33 percent in 1986.[25] That decline was gradual from 1940 to 1970, but in the last two decades it has accelerated considerably. Many contend that declining numbers of blue-collar jobs and expanding numbers of white-collar jobs signals an upgrading of the occupational structure.[26] This is only partly true. Certainly, some new jobs pay well and require great skill. Others, probably a majority of newly created white-collar jobs, are low-skill, low-opportunity positions that carry no authority and require little training or native ability. Some of the fastest growing job opportunities today are for fast food employees, word processors, and sales clerks. At the same time, increased reliance on automation and robotics is gradually diminishing the need for a large, highly skilled, blue-collar work force. Modernization in America appears to be doing two things simultaneously: It is increasing the skills and education needed at the top end of the workforce and decreasing the skills and training required at the low end.

A belief that has grown popular in recent years is that blue-collar workers earn higher pay and enjoy better benefits than their white-collar counterparts. Who has not heard a white-collar worker complain that his or her salary no longer compares well to that of big-city sanitation workers or bus drivers? Today, the average salary for automobile workers is 50 percent higher than that of librarians and 42 percent higher than that of teachers.[27] Although these data may well be accurate, it would be dangerous to draw from them the conclusion that blue-collar pay generally exceeds white-collar salaries. It is important to remember that not all blue-collar workers earn the wages prevailing in the effectively unionized auto industry. A majority of Class IV families earn salaries below what the U.S. Department of Labor estimates to be a "moderate standard of living."[28]

The economic life of most blue-collar workers is characterized by poor job security. Bureau of Labor statistics show that 81 percent of unemployed men are blue-collar workers.[29] Once unemployed, Class IV individuals are likely to remain out of work for longer periods than white-collar employees. Leonard Beeghley notes that when plumbers, electricians, and other construction workers are well paid, it is often because their wages are a hedge against periodic unemployment.[30]

Blue-collar workers tend to have fewer fringe benefits, longer work hours, and shorter vacations than their white-collar counterparts. They often do more dangerous work, are injured more frequently, stay disabled for longer periods, and are exposed to more numerous and serious occupational diseases than other workers. Also, their work offers fewer opportunities for advancement than are found in other occupations. They are more likely to have to do shift

[25] Spencer Rich, "Study Shows Dramatic Changes in Americans Over 70 Years," *Gainesville Sun* (November 7, 1986), p. 5A.

[26] Peter L. Berger, *The Capitalist Revolution* (New York: Basic Books, 1986), pp. 57–58.

[27] Ibid., p. 63. See also Paul Blumberg, "White-Collar Status Panic," *The New Republic* (1 December 1979), pp. 21–23.

[28] U.S. Bureau of the Census, "Money Income in 1974 of Families and Persons in the United States," *Current Population Reports*, Ser. P-60, No. 101 (Washington, DC: Government Printing Office, 1976), Tables 45 and 69.

[29] Bureau of Labor Statistics, *Handbook of Labor Statistics, 1976* (Washington, DC: U.S. Government Printing Office), Table 60.

[30] Leonard Beeghley, *Social Stratification in America: A Critical Analysis of Theory and Research* (Santa Monica, CA: Goodyear Publishing Co., Inc., 1978), p. 160.

work and often find it necessary to hold down a second job in order to make ends meet.[31]

There is also evidence that blue-collar workers are more alienated from their work than other groups. One study asked workers in Chicago a number of questions regarding their work satisfaction. In all areas, white-collar workers felt greater satisfaction than blue-collar workers. One can conclude from these findings that blue-collar employees gain little intrinsic satisfaction from their work and find it endurable only by virtue of the salary it provides. (See Table 17-2.)

The family structure of blue-collar homes is generally less stable than that of the upper classes. Divorce, desertion, and alcoholism, although not the rule, are not uncommon. Blue-collar young people tend to marry young, partly by tradition, sometimes to escape an unhappy home life, and, in some cases, as a rite of passage to adulthood. Studies indicate that husband and wife roles are still narrowly defined in many Class IV homes. Marriage tends to be a stabilizing force for blue-collar men, providing sexual security, emotional support, and material help (through the salary of a working wife and the services of housewifery). Despite all this, some studies of blue-collar attitudes suggest that men of this class hold women in low esteem. Lillian Rubin asked blue-collar men why they got married. They usually answered stereotypically, saying, "She finally caught me." When interviewing her subjects, she found little discussion of love, companionship, or even respect.[32] Women, for their part, report that, although marriage has affectionate beginnings, life after marriage often grows hard and love sometimes sours. Studies indicate that these feelings of discontent are most likely in the middle and lower reaches of Class IV.[33]

Social scientists have frequently accused blue-collar workers of having authoritarian personalities: of being prejudiced, rigid, ethnocentric and prone to support military solutions to foreign policy problems. Archie Bunker stands as the prototypical working-class authoritarian. A number of studies challenge the accuracy of this image. For example, Clyde Nunn and his associates did an extensive study of tolerance in the United States and found no significant difference between the attitudes of white-collar and blue-collar workers if educational level was held constant.[34] Similarly, studies of attitudes toward the Viet-

---

[31] F. Wallick, *The American Worker: An Endangered Species* (New York: Random House, Inc., Ballantine Books, Inc., 1972). Available in paperback. See also Metropolitan Life Insurance Company, "Work Disability by Occupation," *Statistical Bulletin*, Vol. 56 (November 1975), pp. 9–11.

[32] Lillian Breslow Rubin, *Worlds of Pain: Life in the Working Class Family* (New York: Basic Books, Inc., Publishers, 1976). See also E. LeMasters, *Blue Collar Aristocrats* (Madison: University of Wisconsin Press, 1975), available in paperback; and Joseph T. Howell, *Hard Living on Clay Street* (New York: Doubleday & Co., Inc., Anchor Books, 1973), available in paperback.

[33] Rubin, *World of Pain*, pp. 69–113.

[34] Nunn, Crochett, and Williams, *Tolerance for Noncomformity*, p. 62. Other research has found "that political tolerance is a norm or cluster of norms, very strongly related to cultural sophistication, or 'cosmopolitanism,' and thus to the level of education achieved—and *very little else*" (author's emphasis): M. Trow, "Small Businessmen, Political Tolerance and Support for McCarthy," *American Journal of Sociology*, Vol. 54 (1958), p. 273. See also Louis Harris and Associates, *The Playboy Report on American Men: A Study of Values, Attitudes and Goals of U.S. Males, 18 to 49 Years Old* (Chicago: Playboy Publishing, 1977). For the other side of the debate, see Seymour Martin Lipset's "Working-Class Authoritarianism," in *Political Man* (New York: Doubleday & Co., Inc., Anchor Books, 1963), pp. 87–126.

TABLE 17-2. Percentage of 1257 Chicagoans Who Agree with Various Statements about Work, by Occupation, 1972

Statements	Agree, Percent						
	Higher Executives and Major Professionals (N=62)	Managers and Lesser Professionals (N=157)	Small Businessmen and Semi-professionals (N=138)	Clerical and Sales (N=367)	Skilled Laborers (N=199)	Semiskilled Laborers (N=198)	Unskilled Laborers (N=93)
I don't really expect to get much pleasure out of work.	0%	6%	14%	22%	23%	42%	57%
My job does not bring out the best in me.	11	22	24	31	37	41	61
The most important thing about my job is that it provides me the things I need in life.	46	56	67	71	80	87	88
I have to accept my job as it is, because there's nothing I can do to change it.	15	21	25	41	44	59	72
I can put up with a lot on my job as long as the pay is good.	47	49	61	62	70	75	79
As soon as I leave work, I put it out of my mind.	29	36	43	63	64	79	78

SOURCE: From *The Structure of Social Inequality*, by Beth E. Vanfossen. Copyright © 1979 by Beth Vanfossen. Reprinted by permission of Little, Brown & Company in association with The Atlantic Monthly Press. Original data adapted from material provided by Leonard Pearlin, National Institute of Mental Health.

nam War showed blue-collar workers more likely than white-collar employees to support a cease-fire or withdrawal of U.S. troops.[35]

The political orientation of blue-collar workers is much discussed but often misunderstood. When they vote, they usually vote for Democratic candidates. (About one-third of the blue-collar class never vote or vote only irregularly.) Their attitudes tend to be liberal on economic issues (national health insurance, minimum wage and labor legislation, and so on) but conservative on civil rights, racial integration,[36] and foreign policy.

Blue-collar homes of well-paid workers resemble those at the lower end of the white-collar stratum; most are neat and comfortable. Three pieces of furniture typically are found in the living room: a television set, a sofa, and a comfortable chair (perhaps a recliner). Few books adorn the shelves of a typical Class IV home. *Reader's Digest, T. V. Guide, Popular Mechanics*, and paperback romances are often favored reading material. The family car (or cars) is usually American made, often second-hand, and may have ornaments (stuffed dice, a garter, or baby shoes) hanging from the rearview mirror. Pickup trucks are also popular in rural areas and may have gun racks across the rear window.

Class V (The Lower Class)

Being poor means, above all else, lacking money. This statement would be too obvious to mention were it not for the fact that most Americans see poverty in other terms. Middle-class conversations about the poor often depict them as lazy, promiscuous, and criminal. Misconceptions about the poor are so widespread that it is difficult to appreciate fully what life is like at the lowest stratum of society.

THE EXTENT OF POVERTY.   There is disagreement as to how poverty should be measured, and therefore statistics on the extent of poverty vary considerably. Most experts studying poverty agree that between 10 and 20 percent of the American population lives in need. According to Census Bureau figures, about 34 million people (or 14.4 percent of the population) are presently poor.[37] In 1984, a family of four was classified as poor if it had a cash income of less than $10,609.

The population living in poverty is largely unseen in America. The poor often live in out-of-the-way neighborhoods ("on the other side of the tracks"), conveniently out of view of the affluent. Many poor people are tethered to their communities by a lack of convenient and/or affordable public transportation. Others are old and/or sick and cannot venture far from home. Growing numbers of homeless live in shelters or on the streets of our towns and cities. Because most poor people live out of the sight of the affluent, middle-class Americans often underestimate the full extent of poverty in the United States.

[35] J. D. Wright, "The Working Class, Authoritarianism and the War in Vietnam," *Social Problems*, Vol. 20 (Fall 1972), pp. 133–150.

[36] H. Edward Ransford, *Race and Class in American Society* (Cambridge, MA: Schenkman Publishing Co., Inc., 1977), pp. 179–193.

[37] Gordon Green, "Note to Correspondents," United States Department of Commerce News, September 1985, Table A.

Americans have more than tripled their standard of living since the turn of the century. Although less than half of married couples owned their own home in 1915, today more than three-quarters of such families are home owners. Worker productivity has more than doubled in the last decade. Workers enjoy longer retirements than ever before. They retire earlier, are generally healthier, and live longer.

Progress has been made in the amelioration of poverty, as can be seen from Table 17-3. The poverty rate today is eight percentage points lower than it was in 1959. However, these figures tell only a part of the story. Poverty rates have been rising steadily since 1979. Some groups have been hit worse than others, and the fastest growing group appears to be children.[38] Nearly two-thirds of all people living in poverty today are under eighteen years old. The percentage of blacks falling into poverty since 1980 has been twice that of whites. Almost half of all black children (46.7 percent) are now living in poverty and the percentage is highest (49.5) among black children under six.[39] Children in poverty often live in one-parent households. Almost half of the female-headed families with children under eighteen presently are poor, and such families constitute about a third of the total living in poverty.[40] Women (especially black women and single mothers) and children (especially black and Spanish-speaking children) are the groups most likely to fall into poverty and to stay there for long periods.[41]

Other Americans have fared much better. The largest reductions in poverty have taken place among the elderly. Between the mid-1960s and the early 1980s, the rate of poverty for people over 65 dropped by nearly 90 percent.[42] High

TABLE 17-3. Percent of Persons below Poverty Level by Race and Sex, 1959–1984

	1959	*1966*	*1969*	*1975**	*1979**	*1984**
All Persons	22.4	14.7	12.1	12.3	11.7	14.4
White	18.1	11.3	9.5	9.7	9.0	11.5
Black	55.1	41.8	32.2	31.3	31.0	33.8
Spanish-speaking	N.A.	N.A.	N.A.	26.9	21.6	28.4
Male Head of Household	18.7	10.8	8.0	7.8	10.2	13.1
Female Head of Household	50.2	41.0	38.4	34.6	30.4	34.5

SOURCE: U.S. Department of Commerce, Bureau of the Census, *Current Population Reports,* Series P-60, No. 149, Table B and No. 127.

*Beginning in 1975, not strictly comparable with prior years due to revised procedures.

[38] Congressional Budget Office, *Reducing Poverty among Children* (Washington, DC: Congressional Budget Office, May 1985), p. xi.

[39] Center on Budget and Policy Priorities, *Falling Behind: A Report on How Blacks Fared under the Reagan Policies,* (Washington, DC: Center on Budget and Policy Priorities, 1984), pp. 4–5.

[40] Institute for Research on Poverty, "Transfers, Market Income, and the Trend in Poverty," *Focus,* Vol. 8 (Summer 1985), p. 8.

[41] Institute for Research on Poverty, "Family Background, Family Structure, and Poverty," *Focus,* Vol. 8 (Summer 1985), p. 9.

[42] Calculations were made on income figures that were adjusted to include in-kind transfer payments such as the market cost of health care. Institute for Research on Poverty, "Transfers, Market Income, and the Trend in Poverty," *Focus,* Vol. 8 (Summer 1985), p. 2.

poverty rates among the young and lower poverty rates among adults have led Senator Daniel P. Moynihan to suggest that we "may be the first society in history in which children are distinctly worse off than adults."[43]

Some demographic and political facts of life help explain why children are falling into poverty at just the time that the elderly are being lifted out of it. As the baby boom abated in the late 1960s and early 1970s, the number of children under fifteen fell by 7 percent. During the same period, the death rate for people over 65 declined by 54 percent.[44] Their growing ranks have given retirement-aged adults considerable political clout. Understandably, senior citizens have organized to protect their benefits in economically troubled times and they have been successful. Social security benefits have been protected while funds for food stamps, education and training programs, legal aid, tuition assistance, aid to dependent children, and other social programs have been cut back severely. Politicians who neglect the health and welfare of the elderly do so at some political risk. However, children don't vote and adults who live in poverty have little political savvy and even less political power.

CORRELATES OF POVERTY.   Impoverished families tend to live in substandard housing in crowded areas of the inner city. The sheer density of slum life has debilitating effects. Studies show that high-density housing is associated with stress, mental anxiety, increased mental illness, and a lessening of social communication.[45] The lack of privacy that results when large families are crowded in small apartments makes it difficult to escape from family turmoil. Small arguments, aggravated by cramped living conditions, can flare into major confrontations simply because a child or spouse cannot withdraw to the privacy of a room of his or her own. The only avenue of escape is the street, which is crowded and provides its own source of stress.

Contrary to the popular myth that people in poverty lead slow, peaceful lives, untroubled by the hassles of middle-class striving, life among the poor is fraught with tension. Alexander Mood describes conditions all too prevalent in impoverished families:

> Poor families . . . are endlessly forced to trade time for money—to search for work, to moonlight, to find cheap food, to seek out an acceptable inexpensive place to live, to try to find cheap second hand spare parts for a disabled car or appliance, to try to find out how to replace the parts themselves or to try and find a knowledgeable neighbor who can spare a little time to help them out, to search for a person who would loan a little money in an emergency at less than a confiscatory rate of interest, to struggle with the vast complication of bureaucracies . . . to stave off frightening installment collectors in order to catch up with payments to even more frightening ones, to plead with merchants who have overcharged

[43] Senator Daniel Patrick Moynihan, "Family and Nation," The Godkin Lectures, Harvard University, April 8–9, 1985, p. 1.

[44] Samuel H. Preston, "Children and the Elderly in the U.S.," *Scientific American*, Vol. 251 (December 1984), p. 44.

[45] James S. Plant, "Family Living Space and Personality Development," in *A Modern Introduction to the Family*, eds. Norman W. Bell and Ezra F. Vogel (New York: The Free Press, 1960); Carl J. George and Daniel McKinley, *Urban Ecology: In Search of an Asphalt Rose* (New York: McGraw-Hill Book Company, 1974); William Griffith and Russell Veitch, "Hot and Crowded: Influences of Population Density and Temperature on Interpersonal Affective Behavior," in *Issues in Social Ecology*, eds. Rudolph H. Moos and Paul M. Insel (New York: National Press Books, 1974).

them to be merciful, to lose one's way in the maze of public transportation trying to get a day's work in a strange neighborhood, to walk and walk and walk when one does not have bus fare, to entreat the landlord to honor his commitment, to trudge all day through the mystifying maze of the county hospital with a crying sick child in search of a little reassurance, to endure sneering petty persons who dispense free public service to the poor. The debilitating struggle to keep alive without money in a complex, highly organized, society is so frightening, so humiliating, so emotionally exhausting, that one's patience and strength are totally spent when one finally gets home to one's children.[46]

It is little wonder that the homes of the poor are plagued with instability.[47] The energy expended keeping body and soul intact leaves little time for middle-class togetherness. Sex roles in such homes are often segregated and provide less opportunity for husband–wife communication.[48]

Divorce and separation, common now at all levels of society, are found most frequently among the poor. The reasons for this incidence are directly connected to poverty. National studies have revealed that when a low-income husband experiences serious unemployment, the chances of marriage disruption rise from 7.6 to 24 percent in white families and from 12 to 30 percent in black families.[49] Other studies have shown that the lower the husband's wages the more likely the chances of marital separation.[50]

These data show how public-policy decisions (such as the choice by government and industry to curb inflation through increased unemployment) are intimately connected with the private troubles of low-income citizens. A rise in unemployment will be followed by an increased incidence of divorce and, it now appears, suicide.[51]

The problem of divorce in low-income families is not simply one of money; it involves stigma and pride as well. Studies have shown that while government assistance helps the unemployed financially, it does not add to marital stability. The stigma of unemployment and welfare aid—and all that this implies in our society—damages pride and causes friction in the home. A newly divorced young man explained to a reporter from *The New York Times* that his wife left him because "She lost respect for me as a man because I could not support us."[52]

Poor families tend to be larger than those in other classes, enforcing the stereotype that poor people are sexually active and irresponsible. This fact also feeds the belief that impoverished families have children for the express purpose of increasing their Aid to Families with Dependent Children payments

[46] Alexander M. Mood, "Foreword," in *A Study of Our Nation's Schools*, eds. G. W. Mayske et al., DHEW Publication No. (OE) (Washington, DC: U.S. Department of Health, Education and Welfare, 1972).

[47] P. Cutright, "Income and Family Events: Marital Stability," *Journal of Marriage and the Family*, Vol. 33 (May 1971), pp. 291–306.

[48] Lee Rainwater, *What Money Buys: Inequality and the Social Meanings of Income* (New York: Basic Books, Inc., Publishers, 1974).

[49] John Bishop, *Jobs, Cash Transfers, and Marital Instability: A Review of the Evidence*, Special Report Series SR-19 (Madison: Institute for Research on Poverty, 1977), pp. 3–4.

[50] Daniel Rossides, *The American Class System* (Boston: Houghton-Mifflin Company, 1976), pp. 185–187.

[51] Warren Breed, "Occupational Mobility and Suicide among White Males," *American Sociological Review*, Vol. 28 (April 1963), pp. 179–188. See also Ronald W. Maris, *Social Forces in Urban Suicide* (Homewood, IL: Dorsey Press, 1969).

[52] *The New York Times* (September 9, 1977).

(AFDC). Evidence does not support these stereotypes. Sixty-eight percent of all AFDC families have two children or less.[53]

Contrary to popular belief, poor men and women are somewhat more inhibited in sexual matters than their middle-class counterparts.[54] Discussions of birth-control methods—the nature of their use and acquisition—are viewed as an indelicate, if not a shocking, topic of conversation by many in the ranks of poverty.[55] Reluctance to talk about such matters leaves it unclear which partner will take responsibility for contraception and further ignorance regarding family planning.[56]

There is a stereotype that the poor have children to prove the virility of the man and the femininity of the woman. Whether these feelings are any more prevalent among the poor than among the nonpoor is a highly debatable question. One thing is clear, however: The poor do not desire large families.[57] If the poor were provided adequate birth-control information and access to affordable abortions when necessary, the official rate of poverty would be reduced by half.[58]

MYTHS ABOUT THE POOR.   Americans have become concerned about the rising costs of welfare and social insurance programs.[59] They are aware that almost half of the federal budget each year goes to support these programs.[60] They are also convinced that some able-bodied people are abusing the system and that the easy availability of welfare makes families permanently dependent on social assistance. The poor are thus seen as different from other Americans. They are accused of lacking gumption and the will to break out of poverty. These assumptions are dangerously exaggerated.

Over 70 percent of the poor are people we do not normally expect to work: children and young people under sixteen, the old or disabled, students, and mothers with children under six.[61] Increasingly, poor Americans look very much like their more affluent counterparts. As Robert Reich has noted:

> Between 1975 and 1985 one out of every three Americans fell below the poverty line at least once. Half of all who did remained there only one or two years. The

---

[53] U.S. Department of Health, Education and Welfare, *A Chartbook: Aid to Families with Dependent Children*, HEW Publication No. OSSA, 79-11721 (Washington, DC: U.S. Government Printing Office, 1979).

[54] The famed Kinsey Reports showed that the higher the social-class level, the more variegated and imaginative marital sex life tends to be. Of course, great changes have occurred in American sexual practices since Kinsey's studies, but the general trend he discovered remains intact today. Alfred Kinsey, Wardell Pomeroy, and Clyde Martin, *Sexual Behavior in the Human Male* (Philadelphia: W. B. Saunders Company, 1948). See also Louis Harris and Associates, *The Playboy Report on American Men*.

[55] Lee Rainwater and K. K. Weinstein, *And the Poor Get Children* (Chicago: Quadrangle Books, 1960).

[56] N. B. Ryder and C. F. Westoff, *Reproduction in the United States, 1965* (Princeton: Princeton University Press, 1971).

[57] H. B. Presser and L. S. Salsberg, "Public Assistance and Early Family Formation: Is There a Pronatalist Effect?" *Social Problems*, Vol. 23 (December 1975), pp. 226–241.

[58] P. Cutright, "Income and Family Events: Family Income, Family Size, and Consumption," *Journal of Marriage and the Family*, Vol. 33 (February 1971), pp. 161–173.

[59] "Poverty in America," *Public Opinion*, Vol. 8 (June–July 1985), pp. 25–31.

[60] Robert B. Reich, *Tales of a New America* (New York: Times Books, 1987), p. 157.

[61] Ibid., p. 181. See also U.S. Bureau of the Census, *Current Population Reports*, Series P-60, No. 144 (1983).

poor did not shun work to live off welfare: Two-thirds of the nonelderly poor lived in households where someone worked, and most of these families received no welfare payments at all.[62]

The cost of social programs is massive and the possibility for abuse is real. However, cash assistance to the nonelderly poor amounts to less than 1 percent of the federal budget. As a proportion of that budget, the costs of programs aimed to help the poor have not mushroomed; in fact, they have not increased since 1972. America has spent billions on public assistance programs, but most of that money has gone to support very popular programs, such as Social Security and Medicare. These programs are popular for two reasons. First, the programs have been promoted, not as welfare for the poor, but as insurance for everybody. They are not seen as a mechanism for redistributing wealth, though, of course, they do exactly that. Second, the benefits of these programs are open to us all. No means tests are applied to see if we actually need the assistance we receive at age sixty-five. Thus, Social Security and Medicare have not come under popular or political attack even though they are massively expensive. At the same time, welfare programs are not popular, especially in economically troubled times, and have been vulnerable to the budget-cutting axe.

The Distribution of Income and Wealth in America

Social class is a powerful force in America that significantly influences human relationships within and among classes. The most significant determinant of class in America is economic (see Table 17-4). Thus, an understanding of class necessitates an understanding of the distribution of income and wealth in the nation.

There is a popular notion that economic inequality has diminished in America since World War II. These claims are exaggerated. Table 17-5 displays the income distribution in the United States since 1960. The percentage of all personal income received by each fifth of the population is listed. As you can see, the poorest fifth of the nation received 4.8 percent of all personal income in 1960 and 4.6 percent in 1986. The percentage received by the richest fifth rose from 42.7 to 43.7 percent over the same period. These figures show that enormous disparities of income exist in the United States, but the actual differences are far greater than these figures convey. The data on which Table 17-5 is based include only "money income" (salaries, transfer payments, property-rental income, interest, dividends, and the like). They do not include realized capital gains or nonmonetary income, such as expense accounts, company cars, company-paid club memberships, and stock options, all of which mask real income data, especially for those at the top of the economic scale.[63] When these factors are taken into account, the top fifth of the population received over 48 percent of the nation's personal income, while the share received by the poorest fifth shrank to about 4 percent.[64]

[62] Ibid., pp. 174–175.
[63] E. Smolensky, "The Past and Present Poor," in *A Reinterpretation of American Economic History*, ed. S. Engerman (New York: Harper & Row, Publishers, Inc., 1971), pp. 84–96.
[64] Bob Howard and John Logue, *American Class Society in Numbers* (Kent, Ohio: Kent Popular Press, 1981), p. 17.

TABLE 17-4. The American Class System

Class (and approximate percentage of population)	Income	Occupation (responsibilities)	Wealth	Status	Family Life	Personal Satisfaction, Mental Health, Life Expectancy	Education	Political Persuasion and Participation
I Upper class (1 to 3%)	Very high income	Executives of big business, large-scale banking (makers of large-scale, long-term policies; goal setters)	Great inherited wealth increased via investments and added earnings	High inherited status	Stable	Good mental and physical health, high life expectancy, reported satisfaction with work and life	College education, liberal arts major, elite schools	High participation, Republican, seldom run for office
				High earned status				
II Upper-middle class (10 to 15%)	High income	Professionals, high-ranking business executives, military officers, civil servants (second-level decision makers, determiners of means not ends)	Some inherited wealth (usually after death of parents), but largely accumulated wealth via savings and investments		Stable; some sex-role differentiation	Autonomous, good mental and physical health, long life expectancy, reported satisfaction with work and life	Graduate training, often at elite schools	High participation, conservative Republican (some "professional liberals"), may run for office
	Comfortable income			Middle status				
III Lower-middle class, white-collar workers (30 to 35%)	Comfortable income	Owners of small businesses, low-level professionals and semi-professionals, sales workers (few decisions; narrow range of responsibilities), clerical workers	Little, if any, inherited wealth		Higher incidence of women working; generally stable, but higher incidence of divorce; sharing of family duties	Higher stress, higher incidence of illness and job-related hazards, lower life expectancy, less reported satisfaction with life and work	College; Some college	Votes less frequently; Democrat, sometimes votes Republican

	Income	Savings	Occupation	Status	Family	Health/Life	Education	Politics
IV Working class blue-collar workers (40 to 45%)	Moderate income / Low income	Some savings	Skilled workers, semiskilled and service workers, unskilled workers	Low status	Unstable family life	Higher stress, higher incidence of illness and job-related hazards, lower life expectancy, less reported satisfaction with life and work	Junior college training, post-secondary vocational training, high school, some high school, grade school	Doesn't run for office, Democrat, conservative on some issues
V Lower class (10 to 20%)	Poverty income	No savings	High unemployment	Stigma of poverty status	Highest incidence of divorce, separation, and desertion	Poorer physical and mental health, lowest life expectancy, lowest reported satisfaction with life and work	Some high school, grade school, highest incidence of functional illiteracy	Seldom participates; Democrat

419

TABLE 17-5.   Money Income of Families—Percentage of Aggregate Income and Income at Selected Positions Received by Each Fifth and Highest 5 Percent: 1960 to 1986

Income Rank	1960	1965	1970	1975*	1981*	1986
Percentage of Aggregate Income						
All families	100.00	100.00	100.00	100.00	100.00	100.00
Lowest fifth	4.8	5.2	5.4	5.4	5.0	4.6
Second fifth	12.2	12.2	12.2	11.8	11.3	10.5
Middle fifth	17.8	17.8	17.6	17.6	17.4	16.8
Fourth fifth	24.0	23.9	23.8	24.1	24.4	24.0
Highest fifth	41.3	40.9	40.9	41.1	41.9	43.7
Highest 5 percent	15.9	15.5	15.6	15.5	15.4	17.0

SOURCE: U.S. Department of Commerce, Bureau of the Census, *Statistical Abstract of the United States*, 1988, Table No. 70, p. 428.

*Beginning 1975, not strictly comparable with earlier years due to revised procedures.

Income inequality appears to be growing, not diminishing. At present, the poorest 40 percent of families control a smaller share of the nation's income (15.4 percent) than at any time since 1947. On the other hand, the wealthiest 40 percent receive a 67.7 percent of the national income, the highest percentage since 1947. The unequal distribution of wealth affects blacks more acutely than whites. Almost half of all black families are found in the poorest fifth of the population but only 7 percent enjoy a place among the richest fifth.[65]

Yearly income figures are misleading for they do not take into account disparities in *accumulated wealth*. Looking at figures for 1983 (the latest figures available), we find that the richest 0.5 percent of all U.S. households controlled 35.1 percent of the national wealth. The extent of wealth accumulation among the richest Americans is put into perspective when it is realized that all together the bottom 90 percent of the nation's households control only 28 percent of U.S. wealth. Compare these figures with 1962 data. In that year, a study found that the richest 0.5 percent of U.S. households controlled only 25.4 percent of the national wealth and the bottom 90 percent controlled 34.9 percent. When we look at accumulated wealth (as we have done here) rather than just yearly income (as we did in the past paragraph), it becomes clear that the distribution of resources is shifting in favor of the richest segment of the population. If wealth is power, then the rich are more powerful today than at any time since the great depression.[66]

Trouble in the American Dream

In 1969, the United States Department of Health, Education and Welfare announced with pride that "The most obvious fact about American income is that it is the highest in the world and rising rapidly. In terms of gross national product per capita—or any other measure of the average availability of goods

[65] Center on Budget and Policy Priorities, *Falling Behind*, p. 3.
[66] Report of the Joint Economic Committee, July 25, 1986, quoted in Los Angeles Times News Service, "Top 0.5% in U.S. Have 35% of Wealth," *Gainesville Sun* (July 26, 1986), p. 9A.

and services—the United States outranks its nearest competitors."[67] Americans cannot make the same claim today. The performance of the economy has deteriorated to such a degree that a half dozen northern European countries now have larger per capita gross national products than does the United States.[68] Though family incomes look as if they have risen dramatically in recent years, in fact they have declined when the figures are adjusted for inflation. For example, in 1971, the average income in the United States was $22,039 (when figured in 1986 dollars). By 1986, the median income had dropped to $21,510.[69] The income decline of the late 1970s stalled in the mid-1980s and there have been some signs of modest recovery since then.[70] However, one conclusion is unavoidable: Over the past decade, most Americans have not improved their income or standard of living.

A basic component of the American Dream is that hard work will bring advancement and an improved standard of living. Such expectations can no longer be taken for granted by the average citizen. Inflation and a faltering economy have significantly lessened the number of people who successfully will live out the dream. The decline in family income in America is distressing, but think how much more severe it would have been had married women not entered the work force in unprecedented numbers (see Chapter 6). The income of women has kept many middle-class families in the middle class and many working-class families out of poverty.[71]

Even as the average income in America has dropped, the cost of self-improvement and participating in society has been rising steadily. This is especially true in such vital areas as health care, transportation, home ownership, and the cost of raising children.[72] As a college education has become more accessible to the general population, a college diploma has become almost mandatory for access into the middle class. Entry-level jobs that once went to high school graduates now go only to those with college diplomas. It is clear that the economic forces that have brought many wives and mothers into the paid work force will not soon relent. It is also clear that most Americans in the forseeable future will have to work harder and harder, not to get ahead, but to just stay even.

The Consequences of Class

When Max Weber coined the term *life-chances*, he was suggesting that class membership determined, in large measure, the course of one's life. He had many things in mind: occupational status, educational attainment, income lev-

[67] Quoted in Oxford Analytica, *America in Perspective*, p. 57.
[68] Switzerland, Denmark, West Germany, Belgium, Norway, and Sweden.
[69] Thomas D. Snyder, *Digest of Educational Statistics* (Washington, DC: Center for Education Information, 1987), Table 53.
[70] Institute for Research on Poverty, "Are We Losing Ground?" *Focus*, Vol. 8 (Winter, 1985), Figure 2.1, p. 58.
[71] Ibid., p. 91. Sixty-one percent of married women with husbands present in the home and with children under eighteen years of age are in the work force. They are there for complex social, psychological, philosophical, and legislative reasons. But, above all, they are there out of economic necessity.
[72] Ibid., p. 93.

els, choice of marriage partners, chances of marital happiness, preferred values, life-styles, and tastes—in fact, almost every social characteristic by which individuals vary. From the viewpoint of equal opportunity, Weber's conception of class-related life-chances is shocking. It suggests that the rhetoric of the American promise may not square with the realities of our practices. It further suggests that the best things in life (by which we presumably mean happiness, health, self-esteem, and love) are not free at all.

Life Expectancy and Class

At the most elemental level, life-chances must refer to life expectancy. Everyone must die, but it appears that the poor die sooner than the rest of us. Infant mortality rates are higher among the poor,[73] and total life expectancy is lower among low-income groups.[74] The lower strata of society experience a higher incidence of chronic diseases, tooth decay, obesity, and a number of other health-related problems.[75] They have poorer diets[76] and have less access to medical facilities than other classes.[77] The poor are also the most likely to die in war[78] and to be sentenced to death for criminal offenses.[79]

Happiness and Class

The pursuit of happiness is a part of the American ideology, and we would like to think it is a human commodity equally accessible to all. Sadly, the evidence suggests otherwise.

Large-scale studies of happiness, self-esteem, and life satisfaction show a clear and consistent relationship between these factors and socioeconomic status (SES). To cite just one example, Leonard Pearlin, in a study for the National Institute of Mental Health, found that the self-esteem of 2300 Chicago

[73] National Center for Health Statistics, *Infant Mortality Rates: Socio-economic Factors*, United States Vital and Health Statistics, Series 22, No. 14, DHEW Publication No. (HSM) 72-1045 (Washington, DC: U.S. Government Printing Office, 1977).

[74] Aaron Antonovsky, "Social Class, Life Expectancy and Overall Mortality," in *The Impact of Social Class*, ed. Paul Blumberg (New York: Lippincott & Crowell, Publishers, 1972), pp. 467–491; and Evelyn M. Kitagawa and Phillip Hauser, "Education Differentials in Mortality by Cause of Death: United States, 1960," *Demography*, Vol. 5 (1968), pp. 318–353.

[75] John Kosa, Aaron Antonovsky, and Irving Zola, eds., *Poverty and Health: A Sociological Analysis* (Cambridge: Harvard University Press, 1969).

[76] U.S. Senate Select Committee on Nutrition and Human Needs, *The National Nutrition Survey Hearings*, Part III (Washington, DC: U.S. Government Printing Office, 1969).

[77] P. Bierman, "Meeting the Health Needs of Low-Income Families," *Annals of the American Academy of Political and Social Science*, Vol. 337 (1961), pp. 103–113.

[78] M. Zeitlin, K. A. Lutterman, and J. W. Russell, "Death in Vietnam: Class, Poverty, and the Risks of War," *Politics and Society*, Vol. 3 (Spring 1973), pp. 313–328. See also Albert J. Mayer and Thomas Ford Hoult, "Social Stratification and Combat Survival," *Social Forces*, Vol. 34 (December 1955), pp. 155–159.

[79] Elmer H. Johnson, "Selective Factors in Capital Punishment," *Social Forces*, Vol. 36 (December 1957), pp. 165–169; and Marvin E. Wolfgang, Arlene Kelly, and Hans C. Nolde, "Comparison of the Executed and the Committed Among Admissions to Death Row," *Journal of Criminal Law, Criminology and Police Science*, Vol. 53 (September 1962), pp. 301–311.

TABLE 17-6.   Family Income and Self-esteem

| | Family Income* | | | |
Self-esteem	Less than $8,000	$8,000 to $16,000	$16,001 to $24,000	More than $24,000
High	24%	38%	44%	58%
Moderate	21	23	29	18
Low	55	39	27	24
Total	100%	100%	100%	100%
Number	(571)	(947)	(325)	(149)

*1972–73 income.

SOURCE: *The Structure of Social Inequality* by Beth E. Vanfossen. Copyright © 1979 by Beth Vanfossen. Reprinted by permission of Little, Brown & Company in association with The Atlantic Monthly Press. Original data adapted from material provided by Leonard Pearlin, National Institute of Mental Health.

residents was closely related to family income (see Table 17-6). Money, it appears, has much to do with psychological satisfaction in America.[80]

Measures of friendship and love are also related to social class. Divorce rates among lower-income groups are four times greater than are found in higher-income groups. If marriage stability is at all related to romance and affection, then we might have to rethink the popular idea that "money can't buy you love." Other studies have shown that friendship patterns are similarly related to economic status. One study found that 30 percent of unskilled workers (as compared to 10 percent of upper-income white-collar workers) reported that they had no close friends.[81]

A substantial body of evidence indicates that low-paying jobs satisfy few mental needs, provide little intrinsic reward, and leave workers depressed and dissatisfied.[82]

Mental Health and Social Class

There are clear and direct relationships between economic class and rates of mental illness, types of mental illness, and the effectiveness of treatment that

[80] Leonard I. Pearlin, "Social Origins of Stress," (Washington DC: National Institute of Mental Health, 1975). In another study, people were asked to rate themselves on a scale of happiness and unhappiness. Thirty-eight percent of individuals with incomes over $10,000 reported being "very happy," whereas only 14 percent of those with incomes under $3,000 made the same claim. Norman Bradburn and David Caplowitz, *Reports on Happiness* (Chicago: Aldine, 1965).

[81] Joseph Kahl, *The American Class Structure* (New York: Holt, Rinehart and Winston, 1957).

[82] A. Levison, *The Working Class Majority* (New York: Penguin Books, 1974); available in paperback. Leonard I. Pearlin, "Social Origins of Stress" (Washington, DC: National Institute of Mental Health, 1975); E. E. LeMasters, *Blue Collar Aristocrats: Life Styles at a Working-Class Tavern* (Madison: University of Wisconsin Press, 1975).

mental patients receive.[83] Although poor people are more likely to suffer mental disorders, they appear less likely to seek and receive treatment for these conditions. When they do get help, they are likely to be treated by interns and residents rather than by psychiatrists. They are also more likely to receive shock treatment, to be lobotomized (an infrequent occurrence since the advent of psychokinetic drugs), and to be given drugs more frequently than affluent individuals.[84]

Justice

Evidence abounds that the legal system of the United States does not administer justice evenhandedly. It is well known that individuals in the lower classes are arrested more frequently than individuals in the upper strata, but they are not necessarily arrested because they commit more crimes than affluent Americans. To illustrate this point, we can look at some of the evidence on juvenile delinquency. Because reform schools tend to house lower-class youth, it is widely assumed that poor children are more prone to delinquency than other youngsters. The President's Committee on Law Enforcement expressed the view this way: "There is still no reason to doubt that delinquency and especially the most serious delinquency is committed disproportionately by slum and lower-class youth."[85]

Studies of undetected delinquency—most usually questionnaire studies that ask respondents to report their crimes anonymously—give us reason to question the Law Enforcement Commission's assumptions.[86] It appears that middle- and upper-class youth are just about as prone to break the law as are the poor. The President's Commission reached its conclusion because it looked exclusively at official records of delinquency rather than at the law-violating behavior that the self-report studies measure.

If affluent youth are breaking the law as frequently as the poor, why are juvenile prisons filled with impoverished youth? The reasons are numerous. First, middle-class children caught in a criminal act may be reported to their parents rather than to law-enforcement authorities. Police officers may take such children home rather than press charges. When middle-class children are reported to the police, their parents sometimes are able to get them off the

[83] August B. Hollingshead and Frederick C. Redlich, *Social Class and Mental Illness: A Community Study* (New York: Wiley, 1958); Jerome K. Myers and Bertram H. Roberts, *Family and Class Dynamics in Mental Health* (New York: Wiley, 1959); Jerome K. Myers and Lee L. Bean, *A Decade Later: A Follow-up of Social Class and Mental Illness* (New York: Wiley, 1968); Leo Strole et al., *Mental Health in the Metropolis: The Midtown Manhattan Study* (New York: McGraw-Hill Book Company, 1962).

[84] Ibid.

[85] President's Commission on Law Enforcement and Administration of Justice, *The Challenge of Crime in a Free Society* (Washington, DC: U.S. Government Printing Office, 1967), p. 75.

[86] Ronald L. Akers, "Socio-economic Status and Delinquent Behavior: A Retest," *Journal of Research in Crime and Delinquency,* Vol. 1 (January 1964), pp. 38–46; Robert A. Dentler and Lawrence Monroe, "Social Correlates of Early Adolescent Theft," *American Sociological Review,* Vol. 26 (October 1961), pp. 733–743; LaMar T. Empey and Maynard Erickson, "Hidden Delinquency and Social Status," *Social Forces,* Vol. 44 (June 1966), pp. 546–554; J. R. Williams and Martin Gold, "From Delinquent Behavior to Official Delinquency," *Social Problems,* Vol. 20 (Fall 1972), pp. 209–229; Harwin Voss, "Socio-economic Status and Reported Delinquent Behavior," *Social Problems,* Vol. 13 (Winter 1966), pp. 314–324.

hook by talking to friends in power or hiring expensive, effective lawyers. In court (and at every stage of the legal process preceding the court appearance), middle-class offenders are likely to conform to the American image of ideal youngsters. They are likely to have caring parents, to speak well, to dress neatly, to present a properly contrite image, and to impress officials that, with just a bit of guidance, they could avoid further trouble.

Summing up a large quantity of research on juvenile crime, the following conclusions appear warranted:

1. Juvenile crime is extensive. Between 1932 and 1983, the arrest rate for people under eighteen increased almost eightyfold. The size of the youth population has been shrinking in the 1980s and as a result the rate of crime among youth has declined somewhat. These declines, though welcome, are not dramatic. Violent crimes by persons under eighteen are still up over 250 percent since 1960. Persons under twenty-five account for one in every two violent crimes, and three out of four crimes against property each year.[87]

2. More young people commit crimes than are ever caught.

3. Our traditional assumption that the poor are more prone to crime is probably exaggerated. However, poor youngsters are more likely to be arrested and sentenced to reformatories than are their more affluent peers.

4. Most young people violate the law at one time or another, although only a minority do so frequently or commit serious crimes.

Summary

Human beings differ not merely as individuals but as social types. Society is divided into blondes, brunettes, and redheads; doctors, dilettantes, and ditch-diggers; Catholics, Protestants, Jews, and the religiously undecided; the young and the old; and thousands of other differentiations. Some of these (hair color, for example) are of little consequence. Other factors that are tied to the social stratification system have an enormous impact.

Social stratification, the system by which society ranks and differentially rewards its members, is not unique to the United States, to capitalist countries, or even to the modern era. As far as social science can determine, all societies are stratified. However, they use vastly dissimilar criteria for stratification. Some societies take age as a sign of wisdom and give status and respect to the elderly. Other cultures reward scholarship, physical strength, hunting skills, or the ability to speak to the gods. In the United States, the criteria for ranking include

1. Family background, which involves economic status factors as well as race and ethnic origins.
2. Current income, wealth, and occupation.
3. Personal achievements, including education and job performance.
4. Status and power.

---

[87] Edward A. Wynne and Mary Hess, "Long-term Trends in Youth Conduct and the Revival of Traditional Value Patterns," *Educational Evaluation and Policy Analysis*, Vol. 8. (Fall 1986), pp. 300–301.

One of the conceptual problems in the study of stratification is to distinguish which factors cause an individual's status and which are a consequence of economics, power, and rank. For example, is educational achievement the cause or consequence of economic standing? We will address this and related questions in later chapters.

The American class system includes roughly five classes, each displaying its own pattern of values, behaviors, and life-chances. These classes reflect a top-heavy distribution of income and wealth—a pattern that has remained reasonably stable over time.

Income disparities between the rich and the poor have consequences in almost every area of human life. As two sociologists, Hans Gerth and C. Wright Mills, explain, class standing crucially influences "everything from the chance to stay alive during the first year after birth to the chance to view fine art, the chance to remain healthy and grow tall, and if sick to get well again quickly, the chance to avoid becoming a juvenile delinquent—and very crucially the chance to complete an intermediary or higher educational grade."[88]

The social lives and emotional identities of Americans are closely identified with their class affiliations. The socioeconomic distinctions that give rise to social classes also constrain patterns of association and friendship. Friendships tend to cluster within class groups and do not usually cross class lines. People may not approve of the values and behaviors expressed in classes below them, but they also feel greater estrangement from classes above them.[89]

The story of socioeconomic status (SES) is a tale of inequality. Teachers must understand this inequality if they are to fulfill their professional obligation to provide equal opportunity through high-quality education. But, in order to comprehend fully the class system and how it works in families, schools, and society, we must peer around the corner of our taken-for-granted assumptions. The next chapter, which looks at child rearing and social class, is designed to aid in that important endeavor.

Suggested Readings

A trip to the catalog of any major library will reveal a vast literature on stratification. No effort will here be made to exhaust that literature. What follows, instead, is a listing and brief description of books that interested education students may find helpful.

GENERAL REFERENCE BOOKS

A number of texts have appeared in recent years, any one of which would provide a useful and important overview of social class in America.

BERGER, PETER L. *The Capitalist Revolution: Fifty Propositions About Prosperity, Equality, and Liberty.* New York: Basic Books, 1986. This is a broad-ranging attempt to isolate the essential features and consequences of capitalism. It is witty, fair-minded, and conservative.

CENTER ON BUDGET AND POLICY PRIORITIES. *Falling Behind: A Report on How Blacks*

---

[88] Hans Gerth and C. Wright Mills, *Character and Social Structure: The Psychology of Social Institutions* (New York: Harcourt Brace Jovanovich, Inc., 1964), p. 313. Available in paperback.

[89] Mary R. Jackman and Robert R. Jackman, *Class Awareness in the United States* (Berkeley: University of California Press, 1983). Available in paperback.

Have Fared under Reagan Policies. Washington, DC: Center on Budget and Policy Priorities, 1984. The book presents an analysis of poverty trends in recent years.

MURRAY, CHARLES. *Losing Ground: American Social Policy, 1950–1980.* New York: Basic Books, 1984. Murray gathers data to support the popular notion that the programs of the Great Society did not work and, in fact, worsened the circumstances of the very groups they were designed to help. He contends that welfare and other social policies encourage the poor to act in ways that are beneficial in the short run but destructive over the long term.

MCLANAHAN, SARA, GLEN CAIN, MICHAEL OLNECK, IRVING PILIAVIN, SHELDON DANZIGER, and PETER GOTTSCHALK. *Losing Ground: A Critique.* Iroquois' Special Report No. 38. Madison WI: Institute for Research on Poverty, 1985. The authors analyzed Murray's data on unemployment, the family, education, and crime and challenge his conclusions. While agreeing that changes must be made in the present welfare system, McLanahan et al. reject Murray's broad condemnation of the Great Society effort to improve the conditions of the poor.

FUSSELL, PAUL. *Class.* New York: Ballantine Books, 1983. This is a shrewd and entertaining, semiserious look at the American class system.

GOODWIN, LEONARD. *Causes and Cures of Welfare: New Evidence on the Social Psychology of the Poor.* Lexington, MA: Lexington Books, 1985. The book reports on findings of research into the values and behavior of the poor.

GREEN, PHILIP. *The Pursuit of Inequality.* New York: Pantheon Books, 1981. This is an egalitarian attack on the logic of inequality and the system that supports it.

JACKMAN, MARY R., and ROBERT R. JACKMAN. *Class Awareness in the United States.* Berkeley: University of California Press, 1983. This is probably the best study of class awareness since Centers wrote *Psychology of Social Class* in 1949.

PALMER, JOHN L., and ISABEL V. SAWHILL, eds. *The Reagan Record: An Assessment of America's Domestic Priorities.* Washington, DC: The Urban Institute, 1984. This is a mid-term assessment of how a conservative administration changed the direction of various domestic programs.

THE HIGHS AND THE LOWS

DOMHOFF, G. WILLIAM. *The Higher Circles: The Governing Class of America.* New York: Random House, Inc., 1970. This is one of the finer explorations of upper-class power in America.

DYE, THOMAS R. *Who's Running America? Institutional Leadership in the United States.* Englewood Cliffs, NJ: Prentice-Hall, Inc., 1976. This readable book effectively answers the question it poses in its title.

HOWE, IRVING, ed. *The World of the Blue Collar Worker.* New York: Quadrangle Books, 1972. This is a literate collection of relevant articles discussing various aspects of blue-collar life.

HOWELL, JOSEPH T. *Hard Living on Clay Street.* New York: Doubleday & Co., Inc., Anchor Books, 1973. This is a young man's sensitive and penetrating report of a blue-collar neighborhood in Washington, D.C.

RUBIN, LILLIAN BRESLOW. *Worlds of Pain: Life in the Working Class Family.* New York: Basic Books, Inc., Publishers, 1976. Rubin describes the sad childhood memories of men and women of the poor and near-poor and the frightening ambiguities of their lives. The great strength of the book is that she allows her respondents to describe for themselves the troubles of their marriages, the mind-numbing sameness of their work, their uncommunicative sex lives, and their frenzied effort to find "good times."

Another useful source of information is the Institute for Research on Poverty at the University of Wisconsin. This group publishes a quarterly newsletter, *Focus.* Free subscriptions may be obtained from the Institute for Research on Poverty, 3412 Social Science Building, University of Wisconsin, Madison, Wisconsin 53706.

CHAPTER 18

Equal Educational Opportunity and the Ideology of Stratification

Introduction

America is generally believed to be the "land of opportunity," and its people are defined as "created equal." Yet we are a class-ridden society, where vast disparities exist between the life-chances of our rich and our poor. Whether or not we find a contradiction between America's professed equality and manifest inequality depends largely upon our definition of terms.

Some use the term *equality* to refer to equal *conditions:* people having the same income, health care, and general life-chances. Others view equality in terms of *opportunity:* people having an equal chance to develop their native skills and to pursue their chosen dreams.

The first section of this chapter views the question of equality historically. It presents the argument that, from the beginning, Americans have opted to define equality in terms of opportunity. In fact, one might view the course of American history as an attempt to make good on the original promise to equalize opportunity for all citizens. Education, as we shall see, has played an important part in this effort.

The second section updates the equality debate by looking at public opinion regarding stratification and opportunities. The public school system has become the primary agency for equalizing opportunity in America. Although teachers generally believe in the ideal of equality, they are often ill prepared in training and disposition to turn the ideal into reality.

The Founding Fathers' View of Equality

America has never been a nation of extreme ideological antagonisms. Unlike other nations, where widely divergent political ideas have gained a substantial foothold, the United States has been characterized by the relative narrowness of its ideological debate. Most of our national discussions have been dominated by the generally moderate ideas of liberals and conservatives rather than the more radical views of Fascists, Communists, and anarchists.

This moderation in America's political debate has given its participants an easy access to compromise. The narrowness of the political spectrum, however, sometimes obscures significant differences between the opposing sides. This section will highlight some of the different ways early American conservatives and liberals looked at important issues: the nature of human nature, the role of government, the meaning of equality, and the aim of education (Table 18-1).

The Conservative View of Human Nature

Central to the thinking of most conservatives during the colonial period was the Calvinist doctrine that "human nature is not fit to be trusted."[1] One of the founding fathers, Alexander Hamilton, spoke repeatedly of "the folly and wickedness of mankind" and "the ordinary depravity of human nature."[2] Although this seems a dark and even cynical view of humankind, Hamilton and his friends claimed that they were describing people realistically. Any government, they thought, that failed to take human depravity into account would be consumed by the inherent evils it failed to recognize.

TABLE 18-1. Contrasting Views of Human Nature, the Role of Government, and Progress, Inequality, and Education as Defined by Conservatives and Liberals in Early American History

	Conservatives	*Liberals*
Human Nature	Distrust of people: People are basically driven by self-interest.	Trust in people: People are basically moral.
Role of Government	Should control the evil nature of people, channel self-interest and discord into productive enterprise, and protect the status quo.	Should nurture the moral sense of individuals, which is the basis for happiness and community, and improve the human condition.
Progress	A slow-moving, evolutionary process that should not be accelerated by the misguided hope of liberal reform. Failure to respect the past leads to failure in the duty to protect the accumulated wisdom of humankind.	A human process that can be accelerated by a deliberate effort to improve society. Failure to work for improvement in society leads to failure in the duty to leave the world better than we found it.

[1] Quoted in Vernon Parrington, *The Colonial Mind*, Vol. 1 of *Main Currents in American Thought* (New York: Harcourt Brace Jovanovich, Inc., 1930), p. 312.
[2] Quoted in Clinton Rossiter, *Conservatism in America* (New York: Random House, Inc., Vintage Books, 1962), p. 105. Available in paperback.

TABLE 18-1. *(Continued)*

	Conservatives	Liberals
Inequality	People are created unequal by nature. No social policy can alter this fact.	People are created equally capable of morality, social intercourse, benevolence, and ultimately happiness.
	Those who hold power in a free-enterprise republic are usually deserving of their advantaged position. Their leadership should not be endangered by the votes of an unruly majority. The vote should be restricted.	Those who hold power in a democracy should be the most talented. Their leadership must be underwritten by popular vote. Voting rights should be extended.
	Attempts to narrow economic and political inequalities tamper with the natural order and invite disaster.	Economic and social inequalities must never be so great as to create jealousy and suspicion, disrupt the democratic process, cut useful communication, and petrify the social order.
Equal Opportunity	Support for the idea of equal opportunity.	Support for the idea of equal opportunity.
Poverty	Poverty is an incentive that spurs people to work harder.	Poverty is debilitating. It destroys the moral sense necessary to community, happiness, and the development of creative intelligence.
Education	Education is important, but it is more of a privilege than a right.	Education is vital to democracy, and equal educational opportunity is a right the government must guarantee to all citizens.
Major Accusations Leveled at the Opposition	Liberals are too trusting of human nature and too willing to give power and privilege to the poor.	The conservative distrust of the poor is used as an excuse for maintaining the power of the rich. Conservatives are more interested in maintaining the status quo than they are in equalizing opportunity.
	Liberals aren't really interested in equalizing opportunity: They want to restrict the rights of the affluent.	Conservatives aren't really interested in equalizing opportunity: They use this rhetoric to restrict the rights of the poor and to protect their privileged position.

The Conservative View of Government

According to Hamilton, the first principle of good government is to acknowledge that "the vast majority of mankind is eternally biased by motives of self-interest"[3] and to fashion policies that provide for this reality. Thus, the purpose of government is not to eradicate avarice (such an effort, said Hamilton, would be folly) but to channel it into productive activity. This result would be best achieved by instituting a system of laws supported by a strong central government.

Conservatives worried, however, that the government itself could become the instrument of evil if it were to fall into untrustworthy hands. From the conservative perspective, no group was more untrustworthy than the majority—that vast, unruly mob that liberals called *the people*. "The proposition that the people are the best keepers of their own liberty is not true," exclaimed John Adams long before he took office as the second President of the United States.[4] "The passions and desires of the majority are insatiable and unlimited."

In Adams's view, the people are not to be trusted. In a letter to a wealthy friend, he spelled out his objection to majority rule: "If you give [the people] command . . . they will vote all property out of the hands of you aristocrats."[5] When given control, they would be "as unjust, tyrannical, brutal, barbarous and cruel as any king."[6] Thus, Adams opposed spreading too widely the right to vote. He agreed with Chancellor Kent of New York that "universal suffrage jeopardizes property and puts it into the power of the poor and profligate to control the affluent."[7]

Hamilton and Adams both argued vigorously for a government that would protect the interest of the affluent against the ignorance and avarice of the poor. Hamilton favored limited suffrage and a strong executive with absolute veto power, office for life, and power to appoint state governors; in effect, a king. Adams's less extreme proposals found their way into the Constitution. He supported a strong senate, which, he supposed, would be controlled by the rich. The power of the senate would be checked by a house of representatives, which would represent the poor. "The rich," said Adams, "ought to have an effectual barrier in the Constitution against being robbed, plundered and murdered"[8] by the greedy public—that group that Chancellor Kent referred to as "the motley crowd of paupers, immigrants, journeymen, manufacturers and those undefined classes of inhabitants which a state and city like ours is calculated to invite."[9] But the poor deserved similar protection against the excesses of the rich; and this protection, Adams said, "can never be [effected] without a House of Representatives of the people."[10] The historian Vernon Parrington, however, correctly observed that "Adams invalidated his entire sys-

---

[3] Quoted in Vernon Parrington, *The Colonial Mind*, p. 298.
[4] Ibid., p. 316.
[5] Ibid., pp. 315–316.
[6] Quoted in Clinton Rossiter, *Conservatism in America*, p. 112.
[7] Quoted in Sidney Lens, *Radicalism in America* (New York: Thomas Y. Crowell Co., 1966), p. 48.
[8] Vernon Parrington, *The Colonial Mind*, p. 317.
[9] Sidney Lens, *Radicalism in America*, p. 48.
[10] Quoted in Vernon Parrington, *Main Currents in American Thought*, p. 318.

tem [of checks and balances] by refusing to provide the necessary machinery by which the House could represent the small man."[11] By limiting the vote to men with property and education, Adams effectively disfranchised the poor, renters, and other people of modest means. The House, like the Senate, was to be controlled by the interests of property and wealth.[12]

Conservatism and Equality

Colonial conservatives regarded inequality as a necessary and inevitable fact of social life. Physical and intellectual inequality, said Adams, "is established unchangeably by the Author of nature . . . and society has the right to establish other inequalities it may judge necessary for its good."[13] Intellectual and physical inequalities are quickly transformed into economic differences. "All communities divide themselves into the few and the many," wrote Hamilton. "The first are the rich and well born and the other, the mass of the people."[14]

The logic of the conservative argument is straightforward enough. Nature provides for an unequal distribution of talent, which, when augmented by hard work, allows some individuals to accomplish more than others. As a result, the productive few become a wealthy elite, and the less productive earn more modest stations in life. Thus, when Adams and Hamilton worked to protect the interests of the wealthy and well born, they were protecting what they took to be a natural aristocracy, ordained by nature to lead those less talented than themselves. Hamilton summed up this view succinctly when he stated that the "power which holds the purse-strings absolutely must rule."[15]

Both Adams and Hamilton opposed schemes to narrow the economic and social distance between the poor and the wealthy. Inequality was a plan ordained by nature, and to tamper with it was as unjust as it was impossible. "There are inequalities . . . which no human legislator ever can eradicate," warned Adams.[16] "No two men are perfectly equal in person, property, understanding, activity, and virtue, or ever can be made so by any power less than that which created them."[17] According to colonial conservatives, human beings are equal only before God and the law.

The entire apparatus of colonial conservative thought rested on an assumption of human inequality and equal opportunity. If an unworthy aristocracy became entrenched by heredity, wealth, or raw power, it could block the ad-

---

[11] Ibid., p. 319.

[12] The liberals of the day understood that the poor had not been given representation in the Constitution, and many opposed its adoption for just that reason. Amos Singletary, a Massachusetts politician, spoke for his rural constituency when he said, "These lawyers, and men of learning, and moneyed men, that talk so finely, to make us poor illiterates swallow down the pill, expect to get all the power and money into their hands and then they will swallow up all of us little folk." But most liberals supported the document, though sometimes grudgingly, because they saw in it the promise of progress toward a more perfect democracy. It was their hope that a new government would, in time, provide the poor with a more equal opportunity in life. Quoted in Sidney Lens, *Radicalism in America*, p. 48.

[13] Quoted in Russell Kirk, *The Conservative Mind* (New York: Avon Books, 1968), p. 100. Available in paperback.

[14] Quoted in Vernon Parrington, *The Colonial Mind*, p. 302.

[15] Ibid., p. 299.

[16] Quoted in Peter Viereck, *Conservatism* (Princeton, NJ: D. Van Nostrand Company, 1956), p. 20. Available in paperback.

[17] Quoted in Russell Kirk, *The Conservative Mind*, p. 103.

vance of the "natural aristocracy" that nature had designed. Thus, to be consistent and to rid themselves of the charge that they were interested in protecting the established interests of property and wealth, conservatives had to work to guarantee equal opportunity.

It is here, liberal critics of that time contended, that conservatives failed their philosophical assumptions and revealed their true interests: Conservatives were unwilling to take the bold action needed to provide a genuine equality of opportunity for the poor.

The Liberal View of Human Nature

At the opposite end of the political spectrum from conservatives stood liberals, whose political philosophy sprang from a radically different conception of human nature. Whereas Adams "could never understand the doctrine of the perfectability of the human mind,"[18] Jefferson was committed to its infinite "improveability."[19]

In old age, Jefferson and Adams—having been at loggerheads for decades—entered into a lengthy correspondence, in which they explained to each other their differences and renewed a friendship badly bruised by long political battles. Whereas Adams saw progress curtailed by the evil inclinations of human nature, Jefferson envisioned limitless progress. Those who advocated social reform, Jefferson wrote his old foe, "maintained that no definite limits could be assigned to . . . progress. The enemies of reform [Jefferson had Adams in mind] denied improvement, and advocated steady adherence to the principles, practices and institutions of our fathers . . . beyond which the human mind could never advance."[20] This statement nicely sums up the differing dispositions of the liberal and conservative minds in early America. Conservatism was cautious, respectful of accumulated wisdom, generally protective of the status quo, and mindful of human folly and the need for authority. Liberalism was bold, eager to assault new frontiers, willing to change a corrupt present for something better, and trusting of human nature and its unbounded powers of benevolence and intelligence.

No one better personified the liberal spirit than Thomas Jefferson. Whereas Hamilton and Adams saw the inflexible need of self-interest as the driving force behind society, Jefferson dwelt upon sweeter possibilities. If rightly organized, he was convinced, human beings were capable of civic brotherhood, intelligence, justice, and kindly discourse.

The Liberal View of Government

Jefferson was offended by the conservative assumption that selfishness was the prime motivator of human action. To him, such thoughts degraded the human spirit and rendered social harmony impossible. He reasoned that one could not erect social unity out of individual discord. He preferred to base his theory of government on more harmonious grounds. The natural world for human beings

[18] Quoted in Peter Viereck, *Conservatism*, p. 117.
[19] Quoted in Garry Wills, *Inventing America* (New York: Random House, Inc., Vintage Books, 1979), p. xxiii. Available in paperback.
[20] Ibid.

was, in his eyes, one of sharing and harmony, not of selfishness and battle. This fundamental faith in human goodness and improvability permeates Jefferson's work and is the key to understanding his philosophy.

Jefferson did not believe that human beings always did what was just and good. The evidence was ample that this was not the case. He was convinced, however, that human beings are endowed with a powerful instinct to do what is right. Being social animals, he argued, we are propelled into associations with others, associations that we desire to be virtuous and mutually satisfying. "The essence of virtue," Jefferson believed, "is doing good to others."[21] He agreed with Scottish philosophers that human beings are endowed with a moral sense that guides them into virtuous associations with one another.[22]

Although far-reaching, Jefferson's faith in human nature was not unlimited. He understood that the moral sense of human beings could be stunted by deprivation and disuse. Just as a human limb will atrophy if not exercised, so will moral capacity be crippled if not put into action. If a people are poorly governed; if they are denied a voice in their own rule; if they are deprived of the information and education needed for warranted judgments; if they are pushed around by tyrants, distrusted by those in power, or kept vulnerable by poverty, their moral sense will diminish. The social bonds of community will decay.

For Jefferson, the purpose of government was to promote human happiness, which he associated with social harmony and virtuous living. Government, in Jefferson's view, would liberate human goodness rather than control human evil. When he took over the presidency from John Adams, he spelled out his hopes for government in his first inaugural address: "Let us restore to social intercourse that harmony and affection without which liberty and even life are dreary things."[23] Years earlier, Jefferson had forcefully expressed the same idea to the American people and the world. "Governments are instituted," he wrote in the Declaration of Independence, to secure the rights of "life, liberty and the pursuit of happiness." Happiness for Jefferson, as we have seen, was more than a state of narcissistic joy; it was a social condition brought about through benevolence, a recognition of our interdependence, and an understanding of our mutual obligations. "When government becomes destructive of these ends," he stated unequivocally, "it is the right of the people to alter and abolish it."[24]

What a contrast this provides to conservative thought. Whereas Adams emphasized human depravity and the need for order, Jefferson emphasized human morality, the pursuit of happiness, and, when necessary, revolution.[25] During his exchange of letters with Adams, he focused on this important difference in their thinking. "We both love the people," he wrote, "but you love them as infants whom you are afraid to trust without nurses, and I as adults whom I freely leave to self-government."[26]

---

[21] Ibid., p. 213.

[22] This aspect of Jefferson's philosophy has recently been explored and persuasively explicated by Garry Wills in *Inventing America.*

[23] Quoted in Wilson McWilliams, *The Idea of Fraternity in America* (Berkeley: University of California Press, 1973), p. 219. Available in paperback.

[24] From the Declaration of Independence.

[25] In Jefferson's view, revolution provides a general cleansing of the body politic. "God forbid that we should ever have twenty years without . . . a rebellion," he wrote. Quoted in John Randall, Jr., *The Making of the Modern Mind*, rev. ed. (Boston: Houghton-Mifflin Company, 1954), p. 356.

[26] Ibid., p. 357.

Liberalism and Equality

Jefferson wrote a famous phrase into the Declaration of Independence: "We hold these truths to be self-evident, *That all men are created equal.*" Adams took such a statement to mean that we are equal before the law, but the author of these words had more in mind. He believed human morality to be "the brightest gem with which the human character is studded."[27] The capacity to do good, he claimed, is found equally in us all. If we give a moral problem to a professor and a plowman, the plowman would be at no disadvantage, for the principles of good and evil are equally legible to everyone. Equality, for Jefferson, meant equality in the moral sense. He saw little wisdom in the conservative argument that the wealthy are more virtuous than the poor. "I have never observed men's honesty to increase with their riches,"[28] he observed.

The equality of the moral sense was vitally important to Jefferson's philosophy, for he saw it as a source of human benevolence, civic brotherhood, and ultimately human happiness. He would freely admit that inequalities existed among men in size, strength, intelligence, education, wisdom, and talent; but these were pale differences when compared to the moral sameness of human nature.

Jefferson opposed all social conditions that might disrupt the natural exercise of the moral sense. His major concern was that the rich would gain control of the government, be corrupted by their own power, and distort democracy. He knew that, without some degree of economic security, individual citizens would be distrustful of one another and that vast economic differences would engender jealousy and disrupt kindly interaction. Large cities and social institutions, he feared, would fail to bring forth the feelings of involvement and affection necessary to democratic government. He dreaded any system that would solidify the social classes and inhibit the ability of those at the bottom to rise by their talent to the top.

The economy of colonial America was simple and agrarian. Its population was made up of self-sufficient country folk living on farms and in villages, managing their affairs in an uncomplicated manner. The distance between the top and bottom rungs of the social ladder was not great, and economic mobility was possible. But Jefferson warned that America would lose its moral sense if people "get piled upon one another in large cities"[29] and social mobility became impossible. He worried that a day might arrive when economic inequalities would become so wide and obvious that they would disrupt the social order.

It was perhaps in anticipation of this condition that Jefferson copied into his notebook a plan for a periodic census that would examine the extent of economic inequality in the country. If the disparity between the rich and the poor proved too great, the plan suggested a redistribution system to reduce gross disparities.[30]

It would be wrong to say that Jefferson was a champion of the *equality of condition* as an ideal; his focus was on *equality of opportunity.* He did, however,

---

[27] Wills, *Inventing America*, p. 211.
[28] Quoted in Vernon Parrington, *Main Currents of American Thought*, p. 354.
[29] John Randall, Jr., *The Making of the Modern Mind*, p. 356.
[30] Wills, *Inventing America*, p. 208.

support aggressive action to bring about this latter equality. He might also have fought to reduce economic inequalities if these could have been shown to be petrifying and thus endangering the moral sense of the nation's citizens.

Conservative and Liberal Views on Education

The differences between the liberal and conservative traditions of equality are subtle but important. Both groups recognized inequality as a fact of life and were willing to capitalize on human differences in order to bring the most talented people to the top of the social ladder. Both groups supported equal opportunity. Both opposed an aristocracy based on the arbitrary advantages of wealth, birth, and power. At these points, however, the similarities ended and significant differences began to emerge.

Conservatives feared human nature and were especially worried about the ignorance and avarice of the lower classes. Thus, although they supported the ideal of a natural aristocracy, they were not convinced that much talent was to be found in the lower reaches of society. They did not often advocate programs that would seek out talent among the poor, and they were virtually oblivious to the argument that poverty not only camouflaged talent but also prevented its development. Thus, they had little interest in government efforts to improve the lives of the poor so that their natural talents might emerge.

Liberals were optimistic about human nature and the possibility of social improvement. They distrusted concentrated power and therefore felt power should be distributed widely among the people. They advocated systems of free public education wherein the children of the rich and the poor would study together and advance by merit. Education, in the liberal tradition, had many aims. It would inform the general population, enlighten its moral sense, and promote an unswerving devotion to democratic government. It would lessen the arbitrary disadvantages that accompany poverty and thereby help equalize opportunity among the American people. Last, but not least, it would provide a means for the early identification and nurture of a natural aristocracy of talent. "Democracy," Jefferson wrote in 1782, could not survive without

> those talents which nature has sown as liberally among the poor as the rich, but which perish without use, if not sought for and cultivated. . . . Every government degenerates when trusted to the rulers of people alone. The people themselves therefore are its only safe depositories. *And to render even them safe, their minds must be improved to a certain degree.* This indeed is not all that is necessary, though it be essentially necessary.[31]

Conservatives were rarely champions of public education and equal opportunity.[32] Jefferson's idea for common schools, in which the rich and the poor

---

[31] Quoted in Henry S. Kariel, *The Decline of American Pluralism* (Stanford, CA: Stanford University Press, 1961), pp. 245–246. Available in paperback.

[32] Although conservatives did not support public education with Jefferson's hopeful enthusiasm, they were not always hostile to the idea of public schooling. In 1780, Adams helped formulate the Constitution for the Massachusetts Commonwealth, which vigorously supported equal educational opportunity. The pertinent portion of that Constitution reads as follows: "Wisdom and knowledge, as well as virtue, diffused generally among the body of the people, being necessary for the preservation of their rights and liberties; and as these depend on spreading the opportunities and advantages of education in the various parts of the country, and among the

would sit side by side, offended the class prejudices of many conservatives. Some opposed common schools, fearing that the close proximity of poor children would hinder their own children's educational progress. Others fought free schooling, arguing that children who received something for nothing early in their lives would grow up to be idle and lazy adults.[33] Alarmists saw free education as the driving wedge of socialism and social leveling.[34] Still others, thinking public schools were too expensive, were willing to underwrite education only for children of the poorest families. As the result of this opposition, by 1840, only one-half of New England children, one-seventh of those in the middle states, and one-sixth of those in the western territories were receiving free public education.[35]

When conservatives did support free schools, their objective was seldom to equalize opportunity. Instead, they thought schools would preserve the class structure of society by producing disciplined workers and patriotic citizens hostile to the dangerous disruptions of foreign ideologies, unionization, and revolution. Thus, in education as in government, the conservative propensity was to protect the people from ignorance and gullibility. Liberals, on the other hand, saw education and government as liberating forces promoting individualism and equal opportunity. Though conservatives and liberals disagreed on many important issues, they were united in their opposition to the European feudal system they had left behind. Under that system, power, privilege, and prestige were determined by birth and fixed by law. Titled aristocrats owned the land, influenced the government, enjoyed the fruits of working-class labor, and believed that their privileged position was ordained by God. Under the feudal system, upward mobility was impossible.

Slowly, there grew up in European towns and cities a stratum of craftsmen and tradesmen that became increasingly independent of the feudal system. Improvements in transportation and communication made it possible for large numbers of people to improve their economic position and the life-chances of their children through hard work. This new class, called the *bourgeoisie*, became increasingly powerful in Europe and especially in the new world. Their first and most persistent political demand was for legal equality. This meant that economic privilege would no longer be determined by birth but by what a person contributed to the processes of production.

The American Revolution was a powerful expression of the bourgeois desire for legal equality. Liberals, as we have seen, wanted legal equality to be far-reaching. They worried that the aristocrats of the old feudal system might be replaced by an equally repressive bourgeois aristocracy. Bourgeois conserva-

---

different orders of the people, it shall be the duty of legislators and magistrates, in all future periods of this commonwealth, to cherish the interests of literature and the sciences, and all seminaries of them; especially the university at Cambridge, public schools and grammar schools in the towns . . . to countenance and inculcate the principles of humanity and general benevolence, public and private charity, industry and frugality, honesty and punctuality in their dealings; sincerity, good humor, and all social affections and generous sentiments, among the people." Quoted in R. Freeman Butts, *Public Education in the United States* (New York: Holt, Rinehart and Winston, 1978), p. 14.

[33] Merle Curti, *The Social Ideas of American Educators* (Totowa, NJ: Littlefield, Adams & Company, 1966 [1935]), p. 87.

[34] Ibid., p. 88.

[35] Ibid., p. 78.

tives worried that their hard-won economic gains might be lost if the under classes were guaranteed too much legal power. The liberal desire to extend opportunity to all and the conservative desire to protect the interests of the already successful live on today.

The American political tradition has endured tensions between liberals and conservatives largely because of the accommodation worked out between these two groups in the early days of the republic. Because they shared important core values, they could disagree without extending their differences beyond the limits of compromise. They were united in their dedication to representative government and to the settling of disputes by democratic rather than by violent means. They agreed that, if democracy were to survive, it must possess and actively pursue a vision of a just society where all citizens have an equal opportunity to achieve success and happiness.

With the passage of time, liberals and conservatives have divided the theoretical and political work of the nation between them. Liberals have generally championed the extension of democracy, the expansion of human rights, and the equalization of opportunity. Conservatives have guarded the accomplishments of the past against the onslaughts of rapid social change and the unbridled optimism of the liberal vision—paradoxically working to preserve the existing order, which has become profoundly liberal institutionally and ideologically.

Drawing Your Own Conclusions

The liberal–conservative debate in early America has modern significance because the themes of that argument persist today. An understanding of these themes can help you untangle the complexities of the current debate over social stratification.

An excursion into history may also help you clarify your own thinking on the equality issue. Adams and Jefferson were extraordinarily orderly thinkers. They expressed their views of human nature, government, equality, and education with a clarity and controlled intensity all too rare today. Their ideas should help one to appreciate the importance of these issues and to discover and clarify one's own views of them.

Updating the Stratification Debate

This section deals with public opinion on the issues of poverty, education, and equal opportunity, or what we will broadly call the *ideology of stratification*. We will use the headings *conservative* and *liberal* just as we did in the last section, but a few warnings are in order. First, headings will be used here as labels for a narrow range of opinions, those dealing with stratification, and not as broad political classifications. Second, liberal and conservative views of stratification will be presented as though they represented mutually exclusive visions of the world. Few Americans, however, express attitudes that totally conform to one or the other of these ideal types. Instead, most of us borrow opinions from both ideologies and stake out a territory somewhere between these extremes. Often our cross-hatched ideas of stratification are not extensively thought out and may even be self-contradictory. Third, one should keep in mind that much has happened since 1776; present-day liberal and conservative opinions do not exactly replicate the views that dominated an earlier time. Conservatives have come to welcome free public education and to accept past advances toward equal opportunity. Liberals of the 1980s have become less and less sure that opportunity can be equalized without attacking poverty directly as well as through education.

The Conservative Ideology of Stratification

Most people in most nations hold conservative views of the world. They do not hold these views because they find conservative arguments persuasive; in fact, they pay little attention to political theory. They are conservative in the sense that they take for granted the structures of society and attempt to lead their lives in harmony with the order these structures provide. As long as the social system seems to be working and places no undue hardship upon them as individuals, they are not disposed to change it. Theirs is an unreflective, untroubled conservatism, spawned less by theory than by common-sense knowledge of the world.

Common-sense knowledge (the views persons hold in common with others) is limited because it grows from personal experience and from the experience of others one knows well.[36] It carries an assumption that most people experience the world pretty much as we do. Thus, if hard work has paid off for us, we assume it will pay off for others. If we manage to get by when the economy turns down, we assume others can do the same. If we encounter people on the street corner or in the news who seem not to be making it in society, we tend to interpret their situation in terms of our own experience. We remind ourselves of what hard work has done for us and assume it will do the same for them. The usual conclusion we draw is that they had their chance but failed to put it to good use.

Ideas such as these are quite common, and they feed the assumption that we have pretty much achieved equal opportunity in America. One public opinion poll found that 80 percent of whites and 60 percent of blacks surveyed agreed with the statement, "There's plenty of opportunity [in America today], and anyone who works hard can go as far as he wants."[37] Such a view carries a good deal of freight. It assumes that people generally earn their position on the social-class ladder; that getting ahead is a warranted reward for drive and talent; and that staying behind is largely a consequence of laziness and inability.

A number of surveys confirm that these ideas are widely dispersed throughout American society. Michael Lewis asked people in a midwestern city to re-

---

[36] The definition of common-sense knowledge used here and the idea that it is a valid topic for sociological study are borrowed from Alfred Schutz. See his article, "Equality and the Meaning Structure of the Social World," in *Studies in Social Theory*, Vol. II of *Collected Papers of Alfred Schutz*, ed. Arvid Brodersen (The Hague: Martinus Nijhoff, 1964), pp. 226–273.

[37] Joan Huber Rytina, William H. Form, and John Pease, "Income and Stratification Ideology: Beliefs About the American Opportunity Structure," *American Journal of Sociology*, Vol. 80 (January 1975), p. 707. A survey of high school students' attitudes showed very similar results. Seventy-nine percent of white high school students and 78 percent of black high school students answered this question affirmatively: "America has often been called the 'land of opportunity.' Do you think almost everyone in America today can get ahead if he or she wants to?" See Nancy Dearman and Valena Plisko, *The Condition of Education, 1979* (Washington, DC: National Center for Education Statistics, 1979), p. 222.

flect on the cause of poverty. Respondents reported that the poor do not want to succeed and will not apply themselves as others have done.[38] This view undergirds the conservative ideology of stratification and *individualizes* the problem of poverty. It identifies poverty's causes as endemic to the character of the poor themselves.

One of the most extensive studies of public attitudes toward poverty was conducted by Joe Feagin, a social scientist at the University of Texas. He asked a cross-section of Americans to identify the major causes of poverty. The most common reasons given in reply were

1. Lack of thrift and proper money management by poor people.
2. Lack of effort by the poor themselves.
3. Lack of ability and talent among poor people.
4. Loose morals and drunkenness.[39]

The conservative ideology of stratification individualizes the cures as well as the causes of poverty. The pain of poverty and the contrasting comfort of affluence are seen as the driving motivations for hard work and self-improvement. Thus, Americans generally are skeptical of programs that significantly reduce the discomfort of poverty. A survey by the Opinion Research Corporation found that 72 percent of Americans supported guaranteed-job proposals, so long as they would not raise taxes, but that only 38 percent supported guaranteed-income plans.[40] When Lee Rainwater asked Boston residents why they opposed guaranteed-income schemes, most people responded that such programs would reward those "who do not want to work and . . . do not really deserve a decent living."[41]

The Liberal Ideology of Stratification

The liberal diagnosis of inequality is usually more theoretically based than popular conservative opinion. It demands that individuals step out of the taken-for-granted structures of common-sense knowledge and consult a theoretical (or sometimes merely ideological) body of thought.[42] Liberal thought provides *structural* rather than *individualistic* explanations of poverty. Instead of focusing on what is "wrong" with people who are poor, liberals tend to see what's "wrong" with society that makes people poor.

Liberals accuse conservatives of blaming poverty on its victims and ignoring the social conditions that are its root cause. Conservative ideology, liberals claim, defines the poor as flawed and the social system as flawless.[43] In this way, say liberals, conservatives can preserve the status quo while evading their obligation

---

[38] Michael Lewis, *The Culture of Inequality* (Amherst: University of Massachusetts, 1978).

[39] Joe R. Feagin, *Subordinating the Poor: Welfare and American Beliefs* (Englewood Cliffs, NJ: Prentice-Hall, Inc., 1975), p. 97.

[40] Ibid., p. 136.

[41] Lee Rainwater, *What Money Buys: Inequality and the Social Meanings of Income* (New York: Basic Books, Inc., Publishers, 1974), p. 181.

[42] This view is true for most liberals except those living in poverty. Their common-sense knowledge may include explanations for their plight.

[43] For discussion of this issue, see C. Wright Mills, "The Professional Ideology of Social Pathologists," *American Journal of Sociology*, Vol. 49 (September 1943), pp. 165–180.

to equalize opportunity.[44] By failing to equalize opportunity, liberals conclude, "the privileged . . . systematically prevent the talent of the less privileged from being recognized or developed."[45]

By liberal definition, poverty is a social rather than an individual problem. It represents entrapment in the seamier aspects of an unjust social system rather than deviance from a flawless norm. Liberals, therefore, focus their attention on those portions of the socioeconomic system that they say take advantage of the poor. To illustrate, Joan Huber has observed that a

> sizeable proportion of American jobs pay such low wages that a grown man or woman supporting two or three children can only live at the poverty level. . . . The sociological question is why, in the richest nation of the world, do such jobs exist?[46]

Another sociologist, Herbert Gans, answers this question by suggesting that the existence of poverty serves the interest of the affluent. In *More Equality*, Gans almost satirically outlines the ways in which the existence of poverty benefits those who are not poor.

1. There are many undesirable jobs to be done in America, which no one would do unless forced to by the circumstance of poverty. The poor represent a low-wage labor pool readily on call for dangerous, dirty, temporary, menial, dead-end work. "Indeed, this function is so important that in some Southern states welfare payments have been cut off during the summer months when the poor are needed to work in the fields."

2. "The poor subsidize, directly and indirectly, many activities that benefit affluent people and institutions." Money not spent on decent wages is available as profit or for reinvestment into the economy.

3. Poverty creates jobs that are filled by individuals in the middle class. Without the poor, we would have fewer jobs for social workers, mental-health professionals, police personnel, public-health nurses, poverty warriors, urban-renewal experts, slum lords, drug dealers, racketeers, faith healers, and, yes, even college professors who write and teach about poverty and education.

4. The poor will buy goods that the affluent do not want. These include everything from the intestines of pigs to dilapidated automobiles; from second-hand clothes to poorly made, pseudo-signs of affluence such as elaborate-looking but inefficient hi-fi equipment. The poor also "provide income for doctors, lawyers, teachers, and others who are too old, poorly trained, or incompetent to attract more affluent clients."

5. The "deserving poor," those whose economic condition is a result of illness or disaster rather than of laziness or incompetence, are a source of emotional satisfaction to the affluent. "They evoke compassion, pity, and charity,

[44] For a thorough explication of this view, see William Ryan, *Blaming the Victim*, rev. ed. (New York: Random House, Inc., Vintage Books, 1976). Available in paperback.

[45] William J. Goode, "The Protection of the Inept," *American Sociological Review*, Vol. 32 (February 1967), p. 5.

[46] Joan Huber, "Mechanisms of Income Distribution," in *The Sociology of American Poverty*, eds. J. Huber and H. Chalfant (Cambridge, MA: Schenkman Publishing Co., Inc., 1974), p. 103. Available in paperback.

thus allowing those who help them to feel that they are altruistic, moral, and practicing the Judeo-Christian ethic."

6. The poor help the affluent see themselves as hard-working, worthy people. The under classes provide a sense of accomplishment and security to those above them on the economic ladder. "The poor function as a reliable and relatively permanent measuring rod for status comparison, particularly for the working class, which must find and maintain status distinctions between itself and the poor, much as the aristocracy must find ways of distinguishing itself from the nouveaux riches."

7. The poor assist the social mobility of those who are not poor. Because the poor exist, working-class individuals can begin upward mobility as store owners or politicians, as policemen, teachers, or social workers working in slum areas. "In fact, members of almost every immigrant group have financed their upward mobility by providing retail goods and services, housing, entertainment, gambling, and narcotics to later arrivals in America (or in the city), most recently blacks, Mexicans, and Puerto Ricans."

8. The poor have borne the brunt of economic growth in America by absorbing its costs and inconveniences and by providing cheap labor. Urban factories, universities, and hospitals expand easily into ghetto areas; highway extensions can be cut through poor neighborhoods where powerless residents can offer little resistance. The poor have provided the labor for the beginning of industrialization by working in sweatshops, digging canals, laying railroads, and so on. In recent times, they have provided the bulk of our front-line troops during wartime.[47]

By the liberal analysis, poverty is not simply caused by the flawed character of the poor but rather by a social system that tolerates and in some ways profits from the existence of poverty. Michael Harrington expresses the liberal explanation for poverty in *The Other America:*

> The real explanation of why the poor are where they are is that they made the mistake of being born to the wrong parents, in the wrong section of the country, in the wrong industry, or in the wrong racial or ethnic group.[48]

Self-Interest and Inequality

These liberal and conservative views of inequality are ideal types. Although some Americans replicate one or the other of these positions almost exactly, a large majority do not. Instead, most Americans piece together some combination of these views and hold both individuals and society responsible for poverty. Indeed, opinion polls show Americans to be compassionate and more than a little confused about poverty. On the one hand, over 85 percent favor government action on behalf of the poor, 75 percent say the poor only barely get by on public assistance, and almost 60 percent say the government should spend more to help those in economic trouble. A slight majority believe that most

[47] Quotations from Herbert Gans, "The Positive Function of Poverty and Inequality," in *More Equality* (New York: Pantheon Books, Inc., 1973), pp. 102–123.

[48] Michael Harrington, *The Other America: Poverty in the United States* (New York: Penguin Books, 1963), p. 21. Available in paperback.

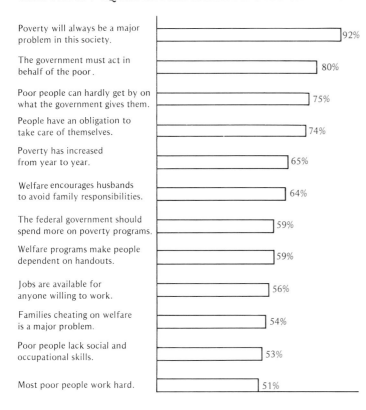

Figure 18-1 Attitudes toward poverty among American adults: A story of ambivalence. (*Source:* Los Angeles Times Survey, April 20–25, 1985. Quoted in "Poverty in America," *Public Opinion,* Vol. 8 [June/July 1985], pp. 25–31.) Reprinted with permission of American Enterprise Institute for Public Policy Research.

poor people are hard working. On the other hand, 92 percent contend that poverty will always be a problem in this country, 74 percent say people are responsible for their own well-being, 59 percent believe that welfare makes people dependent, 56 percent believe that jobs are available for anyone willing to work, and 54 percent believe many people get too much welfare rather than too little[49] (see Figure 18-1).

Although Americans claim that ample opportunity exists in this country, they also admit that the children of the rich have better opportunities than the children of the poor.[50] Although they claim that inefficiency, laziness, and lack of ability are major causes of poverty, they do not fail to recognize that poor schooling, low wages, and discrimination keep some people poor.

The question then becomes, Which of these explanations is more likely to come into play when the more affluent think about poverty? Researchers have found that although individuals may hold conflicting opinions, they usually resort to one or another ideology of stratification when urged to make a deci-

[49] Los Angeles Times Survey, April, 20–25, 1985. Quoted in "Poverty in America," *Public Opinion,* Vol. 8 (June/July 1985), pp. 25–31. See also Jennifer Hochschild, *What's Fair?* (Cambridge: Harvard University Press, 1981), especially Chapters 8 and 9; and Joe Feagin, *Subordinating the Poor,* p. 97.

[50] For an interesting exploration of this phenomenon, see Rytina, Form, and Pease, "Income and Stratification Ideology," pp. 703–716. See also Joe Feagin, *Subordinating the Poor,* p. 97.

sion. Often the direction they choose is determined by self-interest.[51] For example, in economically affluent periods, the cost of liberal programs can be absorbed by the expanding economy. The liberal definition of poverty and the programs that spring from that definition can be accepted easily by middle-of-the-road families because such programs inflict little economic hardship on them. However, in economically precarious times, liberal policies tax already scarce resources and eventually threaten the standard of living enjoyed by the middle class. Under these conditions, middle-of-the-roaders typically side with conservatives, as they did in the 1980s. When an economic downturn is severe enough to put a middle-of-the-road breadwinner out of work, downwardly mobile families may again support liberal policies.

The connection between perceived self-interest and ideological preference has led Gans to conclude that poverty will not be reduced significantly in the United States because its elimination will always cost comfortable citizens more than they are willing to pay. Poverty will only be addressed when the price for not helping the poor becomes greater than the price for helping them. If, for example, the cost of crime, the prosecution of criminals, law enforcement, prisons, and the parole system becomes too high; if poverty populations grow in urban centers to the point where cities become unpleasant or unsafe for the middle and upper classes; if public schools become hubs of cultural conflict rather than centers of learning; if parks, streets, and train stations are overrun by the homeless and dispossessed; then, and only then, according to Gans, will America make an all-out commitment to the elimination of poverty.[52]

Teachers and Inequality

Few researchers have systematically studied the attitudes of teachers regarding the poor, although a number of them have inferred teacher beliefs from teacher behavior. It is an educational cliché, though one which holds a good deal of truth, that teachers generally favor middle-class children who adapt most readily to the behavioral standards of the school.[53] In what has become a famous study, Howard Becker found teachers describing poor children in generally negative terms:

> They don't have the right kind of study habits. They can't seem to apply themselves as well. Of course, it's not their fault; they aren't brought up right. After all, the parents in a neighborhood like that really aren't interested. . . . But, as I say, those children don't learn very quickly. A great number of them don't seem to be really interested in getting an education. . . . They simply don't respond.[54]

[51] Beth E. Vanfossen, *The Structure of Inequality* (Boston: Little, Brown & Company, 1979), pp. 18–20.

[52] Herbert Gans, *More Equality*, p. 120.

[53] Some early studies of education and stratification make this point: W. Lloyd Warner, Robert J. Havighurst, and Martin B. Loeb, *Who Shall Be Educated?* (New York: Harper & Row, Publishers, 1944); August B. Hollingshead, *Elmtown's Youth: The Impact of Social Class on Adolescents* (New York: Wiley, 1949), available in paperback; Allison Davis, *Social-Class Influences upon Learning* (Cambridge: Harvard University Press, 1948), available in paperback.

[54] Howard Becker, "Social-Class Variations in the Teacher–Pupil Relationship," in *Sociological Work: Essays by Howard Becker* (Chicago: Aldine, 1970), p. 140. See also Jere Brophy and Thomas Good, *Teacher–Student Relationships* (New York: Holt, Rinehart and Winston, 1974), pp. 161–165. Available in paperback.

Impoverished students offended the "moral sensibilities" of teachers. In teachers' eyes, such students were unhealthy, immoral, unwilling, and unable to learn. Here are a few of the teachers' comments:

It's just horribly depressing, you know. I mean, it just gets you down. I'll give you an example. A kid complained of a toothache one day. Well, I thought I could take a look and see if I could help him or something so I told him to open his mouth. I almost wigged when I saw his mouth. His teeth were all rotten, every one of them. Just filthy and rotten. Man, I mean, I was really shocked, you know. I said, "Don't you have a toothbrush?"

I decided to read them a story one day. I started reading them "Puss in Boots" and they just burst out laughing. I couldn't understand what I had said that made them burst out like that. I went back over the story and tried to find out what it might be. I couldn't see anything that would make them laugh. Later one of the other teachers asked me what had happened. . . . I told her I didn't know; that I was just reading them a story and they thought it was extremely funny. She asked me what story I read them and I told her "Puss in Boots." She said, "Oh, I should have warned you not to read that one." It seems that Puss means something else to them. It means something awful—I wouldn't even tell you what. It doesn't mean a thing to us.

We had one of the [teachers] who just came to school last year and she used to come and talk to me quite a bit. I know that it was just terrible for her. . . . She came to me one day almost in tears and said, "They don't want to learn, they don't even want to learn. Why is that?" Well, she had me there.[55]

The moral alarm teachers expressed to Becker indicated that they had taken a predominantly individualist view of poverty. A team of researchers at the University of Florida found similar results in a recent study of elementary school teachers working in impoverished areas. The study was conducted in three communities across the country: a large city, a small city, and a middle-size university town in the Midwest. The report concluded:

Educators believe America to be an open society where the children of the poor have a good chance at upward mobility. They believe education is important to mobility and that, generally speaking, schools serve the poor well. They acknowledge the existence of poverty but feel that most poor people could extract themselves from the lower classes if they had the will to do so. They deny that poverty is a result of bad luck (with the possible exception of illness) and contend that the poor have what it takes in terms of native ability and talent to enter the world of the middle class. They are confident that as educators they are good judges of student ability. We found no overwhelming support for the idea that schools can change mental ability, but neither is there strong support for the contention that the poor are lacking in this area. The majority believe that our economic system will reward those who work hard and, therefore, the majority of educators explain poverty in terms of a lack of will or drive rather than of mental deficiencies, victimization by the economic system, or a fatalistic turn of bad luck.[56]

The individualistic explanations that most teachers used to explain poverty were in keeping with the attitudes of Americans in general. Although these

---

[55] Ibid., pp. 146–148.

[56] Rodman Webb, Sandra Damico, and Afesa Bell-Nathaniel, *Teacher and Para-professional Perceptions and Attitudes toward Poverty and Racism*, Parent Education Follow-through Program, 1977–78 Annual Report, Vol. III (Chapel Hill: University of North Carolina School of Education, 1978), p. 62.

teachers recognized that some schools fail to provide equal opportunity and relevant education to poor children, they did not believe this was true of their teaching or of their schools or of schools in general. In most cases, they did not blame students directly for the problems they encountered in school. The teachers' dedication to young people and their knowledge that the home environment has significant effects on children's learning caused the teachers to lay the blame for student failure at the doorstep of the family. As one teacher explained it,

> I get mad—well, frustrated you might say—because of the way these kids act up. . . . But it is not their fault, not really. They've got parents who can't read or hold a job . . . who let them stay up all hours watching late night crap on TV . . . [who] dress them in any old clothes. You'd think the parents would make things better for their children, but they don't seem to care. They don't even come to school for conferences when I send notes home. No, I don't blame the kids, but I sure get aggravated at their parents. If they're not at fault, who is?

As this particular teacher saw it, a child who has experienced ten years of poverty has little ability to conform to school norms, but parents who have experienced many more years of poverty are blameworthy. She believed they would be able to help themselves and their children if only they wanted to. Although many teachers in this study acknowledged that schools could do a better job of educating poor children, that industry could pay higher wages, that the rich sometimes take advantage of the poor, and that discrimination hinders equal opportunity, a majority nevertheless agreed with the statement: "Most adults on welfare could overcome their difficulties if they wanted to."[57]

Many teachers find it difficult to adapt to the realities of classrooms of impoverished students. They are offended by the behavior of poor students and their parents and are unconvinced that such children can make significant academic progress. Some teachers express frustration that they are unable to exercise their talents as educators and are deprived of a sense of accomplishment at the end of the year. This frustration explains why many teachers assigned to lower-class schools request transfers to middle-class neighborhoods.[58] The exodus of experienced teachers in turn guarantees that low SES schools will have a disproportionate percentage of inexperienced teachers, who are either incompetent and unable to get jobs elsewhere or are biding their time until spots open elsewhere in the system. As a teacher in Becker's study reported:

> When you first get assigned you almost naturally get assigned to one of those poorer schools, because those naturally are among the first to have openings because people are always transferring out of them to other schools. Then you go and request to be transferred to other schools near your home or in some nicer neighborhood. Naturally the vacancies don't come as quickly in those schools because people want to stay there once they get there. I think that every teacher strives to get into a nicer neighborhood.[59]

---

[57] Ibid., p. 40.

[58] Howard Becker, "The Career of the Chicago Public School Teacher," in *Sociological Work: Essays by Howard Becker*, pp. 165–175. See also Ronald Corwin, *Education in Crisis* (New York: Wiley, 1974), p. 141.

[59] Ibid., p. 169.

The high turnover rate in schools in poor areas and the values and attitudes of teachers that motivate their exodus help put poor students at a disadvantage. The problems that poverty brings to a child's life are compounded when teachers view them as morally offensive, educationally incompetent, and bewilderingly "different."

Summary

The American view of equality dates back to a time when, in Europe at least, those in power held their position by reason of birth rather than of talent. American patriots felt that this distribution of power and prestige was inequitable because it was not related to individual merit. They proposed a system of government that would reduce the arbitrary advantage of birth and would allow people to compete for status, privilege, and power. In effect, the idea was to equalize the opportunity of individuals to become unequal. Jefferson, Adams, and Hamilton were in basic agreement on this point. However, Jefferson was more fervently committed to the ideal of equality and more willing than his adversaries to make equality of opportunity the central focus of social policy.

The contemporary debate over stratification and inequality concerns itself with the same differences that separated liberals from conservatives during the colonial period. Today, conservatives still tend to view inequality as a natural phenomenon and to assume generally that those at the top and those at the bottom of the economic ladder have earned their positions.

Today's liberal position goes far beyond Jefferson's programs for equalizing opportunity. However, the view that equality of opportunity cannot be attained without social policies to support it is in keeping with Jeffersonian belief. Contemporary liberal opinion reflects Jefferson's contention that conservatives are primarily concerned with protecting their own self-interests—and are not adequately committed to equalizing opportunity.

The research suggests that teachers support a conservative ideology of stratification. They tend to hold negative views of the poor, and poor students in general offend their "moral sensibilities." Although teachers may not blame impoverished students for the trouble they meet in school, it is not unusual for teachers to attribute student failure to the home environment.

Sociologists have been caught up in the stratification debate, and we will examine their ideological loyalties in Chapter 21. Before moving in that direction, however, we will look in Chapter 19 at the research on family life and social class in America. In Chapter 20, we will turn to the research on social class and teaching. Our objective in that chapter will be to determine how social-class factors impinge upon the classroom practices of teachers.

Suggested Readings

Students wishing to explore the content and development of the ideological spectrum of American thought will find rich source material in the footnotes of this chapter.

APPLE, MICHAEL, and LOIS WEIS. *Ideology and Practice in Schooling*. Philadelphia: Temple University Press, 1983. This book points out that schools are designed to reproduce the culture's dominant ideological structures in the minds and lives of students. Students sometimes reject what the school offers, making the school something like an ideological battleground.

BEST, JOHN HARDIN, and ROBERT T. SIDWELL. *The American Legacy of Learning: Readings in the History of Education.* Philadelphia: J. B. Lippincott Company, 1967. This is a useful collection of primary sources.

BUTTS, R. FREEMAN. *Public Education in the United States: From Revolution to Reform.* New York: Holt, Rinehart and Winston, 1978. This readable and convincing text focuses on, among other things, the relationship between schooling and the constitutional ideals of liberty, equality, justice, and obligation for the public good.

BUTTS, R. FREEMAN, and LAWRENCE A. CREMIN. *A History of Education in American Culture.* New York: Holt, Rinehart and Winston, 1962. This is still one of the best history of education texts.

CHURCH, ROBERT L., and MICHAEL W. SEDLAK. *Education in the United States.* New York: The Free Press, 1976. This is a chronological social history of American educational ideals and institutions from the Revolutionary War to the present.

CREMIN, LAWRENCE A. *The Transformation of the School.* New York: Vintage Books, 1961. This is the first and still finest history of the Progressive Education movement.

CREMIN, LAWRENCE A. *American Education: The Colonial Experience: 1607–1783.* New York: Harper Torch Books, 1970. The book is a splendid history of the roots of American education.

CURTI, MERLE. *The Social Ideas of American Educators.* Totowa, NJ: Littlefield, Adams & Co., 1966. First published in 1935, Curti's book still stands as the single best examination of the social aims of America's leading educators.

ITZKOFF, SEYMOUR W. *A New Public Education.* New York: David McKay Company, Inc., 1976. This is a historical interpretation of the interaction between schools and our nation's evolving sense of community life and social structure.

KATZNELSON, IRA, and MARGARET WEIR. *Schooling For All: Class, Race and the Decline of the Democratic Ideal.* New York: Basic Books, 1985. This book departs from the standard "progressive," "revisionist," and "functionalist" schools of educational history. It argues that public education has shaped and been shaped by the working class.

PERKINSON, HARRY G. *Two Hundred Years of American Educational Thought.* New York: David McKay Company, Inc., 1976. This is an exploration of educational theories as they were developed by some of America's foremost intellects.

PERKINSON, HARRY G. *The Imperfect Panacea: American Faith in Education, 1865–1965.* New York: Random House, Inc., 1968. The book details America's high hopes for education and the difficulties of trying to obtain those goals.

SHERMAN, ROBERT R., ed. *Understanding History of Education,* rev. ed. Cambridge, MA: Schenkman Publishing Company, Inc., 1984. This invaluable collection of essays and introductory material is designed to help students better study and understand the history of education.

TYACK, DAVID B., ed. *Turning Points in American Educational History.* Lexington, MA. Xerox College Publishing, 1967. This unique book combines primary source material and interpretative essays in order to illuminate eleven major turning points in the history of American education.

CHAPTER 19

Social Class and Child Rearing: What Children Bring with Them to School

Introduction

Before children have ever been in school, they have learned a great deal about the world. Their knowledge comes largely from parents, siblings, friends, and their community. The experience of the home and neighborhood provides a sense of self (what educators call a *self-concept*) and a sense of how the world works (what philosophers call a *world view*). Thus, what goes on in the micro-world of the family profoundly affects how children perceive and experience the macroworld beyond the home.

They learn that people can be trusted, or they cannot; that the world is orderly and predictable, or it is not; and that they have the power to make things happen, or they don't. These generalized feelings about themselves and the world are drawn from thousands of major and minor events that punctuate their early years. Born helpless and without knowledge, children soon learn that food is plentiful, tasty, and supplied whenever hunger threatens, or that it is scarce, unappealing, and provided only sporadically. They learn that adults are nurturing, loving, and on call when needed, or that they are unpredictable and indifferent. Robert Coles, a psychiatrist who has spent much of his career working with the young, explains that children learn many other things as well:

> They learn that their parents work, or that they can't find work. They learn that their mother feels reasonably happy and contented, or that she is really up against it, and afraid from day to day of one or another danger. They learn that their fathers bring home no money, or barely enough money, or so much money that they do not know what to do with it all. They learn that their fathers feel like failures or, to some extent, feel successful. They learn that they don't have a father, or they do have one but he dare not come home if the "welfare lady" is

Economic class affects the life chances of all Americans.   (*Source:* Alan Wieder.)

around. They learn, in short, just about everything economists or political scientists talk about.[1]

These are profound and lasting lessons that are largely (though not totally) the legacy of economic class. Economic pressures influence family life and thus can (and usually do) affect the parent–child relationship. A child born to poverty experiences a different world from that of a child born to affluence. Financial position often means that an individual's life will follow a predictable pattern. It determines, in larger measure than most Americans like to admit, how people view the world and their place in it. It helps formulate a family's values, fears, and aspirations, all of which in turn influence a child's sense of self.

This chapter examines family life and social class in the United States. Rather than examine all five classes, we will limit our discussion to three broad groups: the poor (Class V and some members of Class IV), the middle class (Classes II, III, and the upper end of Class IV), and the rich (Class I). We will not examine stratification statistics or theories used to explain why classes exist. Instead, we will try to capture something of the experience of poverty and affluence. The goal of this experiential analysis is to provide a better understanding of the consequences of social class in America.

There are certainly dangers in classifying the American population in just three categories. Although class lines suggest patterns of behavior, they do not guarantee them. If we assume that all people who are poor have been raised in a certain way, we stereotype individuals and run the risk of ignoring real

[1] Robert Coles, *The South Goes North*, Vol. III of *Children of Crisis* (Boston: Little, Brown & Company, 1967), pp. 580–581.

and important differences among them. However, if we ignore the reality of class in America, we run an equally dangerous risk of ignoring the real (though certainly not universal) effects that poverty life can have on individuals. Readers are encouraged to keep these dangers in mind. The effort here is to familiarize the reader with some of the common experiences that exist within three broad social class categories.

Growing Up Poor

Who are the poor? It is possible to give complex answers to this question. For our purposes, however, we can keep the issue simple. The poor are those who do not have enough money to buy the goods and services accepted as essential for human welfare. This definition is tight enough to help us identify those about whom we are talking, yet loose enough to accommodate the escalating standard of living in modern society. What are now thought of as essentials (flush toilets, for example) were seen as high luxury in the not-so-distant past.

Among the poor, we find people in a wide variety of circumstances. Some belong to the working class. They hold skilled, unskilled, or semiskilled jobs for which they receive an hourly wage. Some of the poor work only sporadically. Many others have no employment whatever and maintain themselves on public assistance. Clearly, life for the hard-core unemployed is more difficult than life for those who are poor but working regularly. Yet, despite the differences that exist among these groups, they share a vulnerability that affects their lives. Those with steady employment may own a modest home, be settled in a community, enjoy occasional weekend vacations, and hope that their children will grow up to join the middle class. Despite this relative comfort, they may suffer financial setbacks, may occasionally overextend their credit, and may sometimes fall victim to the high interest rates of finance companies. But generally, they manage to keep their heads above water. In this sense, they have little in common with the down-and-out poor, who work only sporadically and face hardships on a daily basis. These two groups (and all the families that fall between these extremes) are discussed together under the umbrella category of "poverty" because they share one important characteristic—vulnerability.

Working-class adults often hold jobs that could end with little warning. Local events such as the completion of a construction project or general events such as a downturn in the national economy can abruptly cut off all family income. If the worker is without a job for a month or two, the family stands to lose its car, home, and other belongings. Of course, such adversities can also befall members of the middle class, but with the middle class they are not a way of life. Among the poor, even at this group's upper reaches, families live with a daily knowledge that their hard-earned comforts are always precarious, always in danger, and cannot be taken for granted. When a family loses this sense of vulnerability, they have probably moved across the invisible line that separates the upper-lower class from the lower-middle class.

Out of Sight and Out of Mind

Most Americans live a world apart from the truly poor. They know little about what long-term poverty is or what it does to people. Their daily routines do not bring them into contact with the reality of poverty. They do not have opportunity to talk to poor people, to work with them, or to win their friendship, but this lack of experience does not prevent Americans from forming strong opinions about what "the poor" are like, how they act, and how they should set about improving their lot. Since popular opinion is often formed in ignorance of the facts of a life in poverty, it is difficult to investigate poverty objectively. Let us attempt to hold preformed opinions in check so that we can concentrate on what poverty is actually like for those who live with it on a daily basis.

The Experience of Poverty

Children learn the lessons of their physical and social environment; they learn the world they grow up in. What is that world like for a child born to poverty?

Above all else it is a precarious world that can be changed overnight by far-off events and invisible decision makers. Policies emanating from Washington regarding welfare eligibility can affect the amount of food a family has on the table and the kind of home or apartment available to it. Uncontrollable events can determine if Daddy must leave home or can stay put. Decisions made in corporate board rooms can provide work or deprive the family's breadwinner of a job. Edicts emanating from school board offices (and sometimes from judges' chambers) can determine where the kids will go to school and how they are to get there. The evaluations of principals, teachers, and staff psychologists will determine if a child will take the normal route through school or will be relegated to special classrooms for disruptive kids or slow learners. And so it goes. Life-changing decisions circumscribing the poor are seldom made by the poor themselves but rather by people who live far from poverty, who know little and may care less about the human consequences of their actions. Poverty not only deprives people of needed goods and services but also puts them at the mercy of outside forces.

Children brought up in such an environment (especially children of very poor families) soon get the message that they have little if any control over their personal fates. An impoverished mother reflects upon the course of her family's life:

> You can't change things, no you can't and all you can do is to say to yourself that it is true, that we've got a long hard row to hoe, and the Lord sometimes seems to have other more important things to do than to look after us.[2]

The grinding experience of poverty can and often does wear children down. Parents in extreme poverty may feel helpless to reverse the process. Some try to instill in their children a capacity for denial. As a thirty-four-year-old truck driver put it:

> I tell my kids all the time—it's better to forget about things that bother you; just put them out of your mind, otherwise you will just be sitting around feeling sorry for yourself all the time. Just put those things out of your mind is what I tell them, just like I did; then they will not get at you.[3]

[2] Robert Coles, *Uprooted Children* (Pittsburgh: University of Pittsburgh Press, 1970). Quoted in *Life at the Bottom,* ed. Gregory Armstrong (New York: Bantam Books, Inc., 1971), p. xix.
[3] Lillian Breslow Rubin, *Worlds of Pain* (New York: Basic Books, Inc., Publishers, 1976), p. 29.

Resignation and denial are attitudes that bind people to the present and make it impossible to plan the future. You cannot plan events over which you have no control. A thirty-six-year-old refinery worker recounts the view of the world he learned in childhood:

> I did not think much about it. I just kind of took things as they came. . . . There was not much point in dreaming. I guess you could say in my family we did not— maybe I should say we could not—plan our lives; things just happened.[4]

A migrant laborer explains what she tells her children to prepare them for life:

> My husband told me, don't try to convince them that everything is going to be good later on. Don't tell them lies. Do not tell them that we are going to change the world, and they are going to have a new life. Let the priest talk about "a new life"; we're not going to have any life but this one, and that goes for our kids and their kids—not while we're here on this earth. That is what kids have to know, and that's what I tell them.[5]

Fatalism is a shield that at least partially blocks out the stark facts of poverty. By ignoring the future, some individuals avoid the most painful fact of all— that events are beyond their control. Such avoidance is, alas, always temporary. Eventually, powerlessness is bound to become too obvious to ignore. At such times, fatalism gives way to fear and hopelessness. A thirty-year-old mother of six recalls how the fear of unemployment crippled her father:

> My father couldn't find a job either, not a steady one, anyway. I remember my mother telling us how he walked and walked, practically begging for work. She said he would almost offer to work for nothing rather than sit around home doing nothing. The day he applied for relief was the saddest day of his life. It broke him. He hated himself ever after. He was always against taking charity, and to have to ask for it was too much for him. When the war came he got steady work again, but my mother said he was never the same. He was always nervous, worried about losing his job, like in the thirties. . . . He was plain scared for the rest of his life. To be truthful, I think he died happy. It was like a relief for him. . . . He used to say to [my mother] that whether it was Heaven or Hell the good Lord chose for him, it would be better than the worry and the trying to make ends meet of this world.[6]

Poverty can frighten people, wear them down, and eventually wear them out. The process need not take long. It can happen to children. Teachers in poor neighborhoods have commented that large numbers of their students do not grow up so much as they grow old. Open, happy, capable, curious children can turn sour on life. They grow suspicious, sullen, sad, and sometimes violent. What happens? A mother describes the process:

> They are alive, and you bet they are, and then they go off and quit. I can tell it by their walk and how they look. They slow down and get so tired in their face, real tired. They get all full of hate, and they look cross at you, as if I cheated them when I brought them into the world. I have seven, and two of them have gone that way, and to be honest, I expect my every child to have it happen—like

---

[4] Ibid., p. 39.

[5] Robert Coles, *Privileged Ones*, Vol. V of *Children of Crisis* (Boston: Little, Brown & Company, 1977), p. 521.

[6] Coles, *The South Goes North*, pp. 268–269.

it did to me. I just gave up when I was about fourteen or so. And what brings us back to life is having the kids and keeping them with us for awhile, away from the outside and everything bad. But there comes a day when they ask you why it's like it is for us, and all you can do is shrug your shoulders, or sometimes you scream. But they know already, they're just asking for the record. And it doesn't take but a few months to see that they are no longer kids, and they've lost all the hope and the life you have tried to give them.[7]

The process may not always happen so quickly. Some children swing between joy and sorrow, hope and despair. They do not give up easily. When Rod Webb taught elementary school in an impoverished neighborhood, he was often struck by the sudden mood swings that would overtake his students. Happy, giving children would turn sullen and suspicious without warning, only to return to happiness again a moment later. It was as if happiness, trust, friendship (all those elements that make human interaction joyous) were precarious entities that these children fought to believe in but worried would soon disappear. To lose oneself in a group activity, to enter into a friendship, to allow oneself to trust an adult, was to find happiness but also to risk (even to invite) disappointment. This disappointment was made more intolerable because such children yearned for a predictable world where the pursuit of happiness was not a game of chance with its odds stacked against success.

The Special Strengths of Poor Children

A life forged by stress and hardship can, of course, create special strengths. Some children endure the experience of poverty with amazing grace and emerge into adulthood with a profound insight into themselves and the human condition. Yet, poverty does devastating damage to most children, damage that makes it easy to overlook the resilience and vitality alive in many of poverty's young. If large numbers of slum children are forced by life to give up hope, they do not do so without a struggle. We make a mistake if we look only at the negative aspects of their lives. Robert Coles found that, after many years of working among the poor, he had only cataloged the harm done by poverty. He had failed to record the good that many poor children had created and maintained for themselves despite their circumstances:

> For a long time I . . . looked only for the harm inflicted on the boys and girls who grow up on the wrong side of the tracks. . . . Determined to record every bit of pathology I could find, I failed to ask myself what makes for survival in the poor; indeed, sometimes for more than that—for a resourcefulness and vitality that some of us in the therapy-prone suburbs might at least want to ponder, if not envy.[8]

Aided by an insight into our single-mindedness, we may find it easier to see, as Coles did, that poor children cannot be summed up by a mere list of problems and pathologies. What accounts for survival in the poor? I have been impressed by the humor that many poor people use to keep themselves open to the world. The blues lyric, "When you see me laughing, baby, it is to keep from crying," is no doubt drawn from a common life experience in the world of poverty. Coles mentions

[7] Ibid., p. 590.
[8] Ibid., p. 587.

[the] considerable energy and "life" [of slum children]. Many ghetto children I know have a flesh and blood loyalty to one another, a disarming code of honor, a sharp, critical eye for the fake and pretentious, a delightful capacity to laugh, yell, shout, sing, congratulate themselves, and tickle others. Their laugh is often strong and expressive, their drawings full of action, feeling, and even searing social criticism.[9]

Some fellow social scientists join Coles in his praise of lower-class culture. Frank Riessman lists the positive attributes he found in impoverished families:

The cooperativeness and mutual aid . . . the avoidance of the strain accompanying competitiveness and individualism, the equalitarianism, informality and warm humor; the freedom from self-blame and parental over-protection; the children's enjoyment of each other's company and lessened sibling rivalry.[10]

Not all social scientists view the attributes of poverty so positively. Robert Havighurst states:

There is substantial doubt that the socially disadvantaged children in our big cities have any positive qualities of potential value in urban society in which they are systematically better than the children of families who participate fully in the mass culture. The writer does not know of any comparative study which shows American lower-class children to be superior in any positive respect to American upper working-class or middle-class children.[11]

Whatever virtues disadvantaged children may possess, we can be sure they can be maintained only if they are understood, nurtured, and appreciated by teachers, parents, and others who work with the young. Otherwise, they will be bullied out of existence by the relentless pressures of poverty.

To sum up what has been said so far, the experience of powerlessness makes it difficult for poor children to build self-confidence—difficult for them to view themselves as capable of changing the conditions of their lives or as responsible for what happens to them. Some critics of the poor say that these self-depreciatory attitudes are the real cause of poverty. Others claim that such attitudes are just an accurate assessment of their life conditions. According to this latter view, the only way to raise the self-confidence and responsibility of the poor is to eradicate conditions that render the poor powerless, that is to say, we must eradicate poverty itself.

Child Rearing among the Poor

If you were poor and lived in the inner city, if you loved your children and desired for them a better life than you yourself enjoyed, if you knew from bitter experience that outside your apartment door lay an invitation to drug use, crime, and despair—what would your child-rearing strategies be?

INSULATION.   It is possible that your major concern would be to protect your children, to insulate them as best you could from the corrupting forces that

---

[9] Ibid., pp. 589–590.

[10] Frank Riessman, "Lower Income Culture: The Strengths of the Poor," *Journal of Marriage and the Family* (November 1964), p. 419.

[11] Robert J. Havighurst, "Who Are the Socially Disadvantaged?" in *Education and the Social Crisis,* eds. Everett T. Keach, Jr., et al. (New York: Wiley, 1967), pp. 23–30.

surround them. And so it is with the poor. A twenty-eight-year-old plumber's assistant describes his effort to keep his children cocooned from the hostile world outside the home:

> You've got to watch out over the kids all the time if you expect them to grow up decent. I know from when I was a kid how easy it is to get into trouble, and I don't want my kids into none of that kind of stuff. That is why [my wife] makes sure she knows where they are and who they're playing with all the time.
>
> All you need is one rotten apple, one bad kid on the block, and there's no telling what a kid will do, especially a boy when he gets to be a teenager. You got to start off teaching them right from wrong when they are just little kids.[12]

OBEDIENCE.   Another strategy that you might employ would be to teach children to adhere to a strict set of rules. When your children leave the apartment, when they wander unsupervised in the streets, there is nothing to protect them from trouble except what you have taught them about the world and obedience to rules.

When we see that poor parents (especially those among the working class) are trying to protect their children by enforcing rules, their tactics seem less severe and authoritarian. But, this heavy emphasis on authority has consequences. Studies show that impoverished parents may lay out rules without consulting their children or explaining the reasons for the rules. This custom has led social scientists to label the parent–child relationship in poverty homes as *parent-centered* rather than *child-centered*. Low-income parents tend to focus on the consequences of their children's behavior and are not much interested in the child's intentions. Transgressions of rules are punished, often physically, but not necessarily unkindly. Children learn that they are expected to conform to authority. This push for conformity combines with the condition of their economic lives to heighten their sense of powerlessness. In some children, it brings home the lesson that one legitimate way to solve problems is to resort to physical force.

If these child-rearing practices seem a far cry from what you experienced as a child, or from the "more desirable" practices you have learned in your child psychology classes, keep in mind what poor parents are trying to accomplish. Strictness and obedience are seen by them as the only available means for keeping children out of trouble.[13] And remember, too, that obedience to externally imposed rules is central to the life experience of a lower-class, law-abiding adult. As one moves down the employment ladder, the jobs encountered become increasingly routine and narrow. Lower-working class adults have little opportunity for autonomous decision making. Their work is often repetitious and offers little intrinsic satisfaction. As a consequence, such workers must fashion an aptitude for passive obedience. They, like all parents, tend to pass on to their children the values they find functional in their own lives.[14]

---

[12] Rubin, *Worlds of Pain*, p. 86
[13] Ibid.
[14] Albert K. Cohen and Harold M. Hodges, Jr., "Characteristics of the Lower Blue Collar Class," *Social Problems*, Vol. 10, No. 4 (Spring 1963), pp. 303–334. See also Melvin L. Kohn, *Class and Conformity*, 2d ed. (Chicago: University of Chicago Press, 1977); available in paperback.

The Poor Child Goes to School

Many middle-class teachers are shocked when poor parents pull them aside and say something like this: "My kid is a real hellion. He needs a good whack now and then to keep him in line. So if he acts up, just give him a few good licks. It is okay with me. I know he needs it and I will give the same when he gets home."

It is easy for a teacher to assume that such parents are unloving and even cruel. Yet, as we have seen, this assumption is not necessarily true. Teachers misunderstand the intentions of poor parents, and the reverse is also true. Note, for example, the comments of a young mother as she explains why she decided not to send her two children to nursery school:

> I think little kids belong home with their mothers, not in some nursery school that is run by a bunch of people who think they're experts and know all about what's good for kids and how they are supposed to act. I saw some of those kids in a nursery school once. They act like a bunch of wild Indians.[15]

Sending children off to school is not always a happy experience for the poor. It often marks the beginning of the breakdown of parental control.[16] Not only do peer groups grow in influence, but the school itself also is regarded as a potentially disruptive force. Child-centered teachers do not maintain the rigid discipline many poor parents see as essential for their children's survival in a hostile world. One study found that mothers from working-class communities were considerably more likely than their middle-class counterparts to prefer teachers who emphasized discipline and mastery of subject matter rather than individual creativity and initiative.[17]

Working-class parents are also concerned about what is taught in schools. They are distressed when the study of values clarification, situational ethics, or evolution violates the strict doctrines of their personal beliefs. The textbook controversy of recent years is a classic example of social-class conflict over the aims of education. Working-class parents look to schools to enforce conformity, set out unambiguous rules, and demand obedience.[18] They do not expect schools to change their children or to alienate them from the beliefs of the family. Schools by and large have a more middle-class orientation: They attempt to foster internal rather than external control and inquiry rather than docility. In so doing, they unknowingly challenge the values of the impoverished home.

Working-class children are caught in the middle of this conflict. Their experience of the world leads them to believe that they have little or no ability to influence what happens to them. Their parents' insistence on obedience leaves many children overly dependent on, first, their elders and, second, their peers. They seldom become sure of their own abilities. These insecurities are height-

---

[15] Rubin, *Worlds of Pain*, p. 87.

[16] Lee Rainwater, *What Money Buys: Inequality and the Social Meaning of Class* (New York: Basic Books, Inc., Publishers, 1974), pp. 13–14.

[17] Sam D. Dieber and David E. Wilder, "Teaching Styles: Parental Preferences and Professional Role Definitions," *Sociology of Education*, Vol. 40 (Fall 1967), pp. 302–315. See also Sarah Lawrence Lightfoot, *Worlds Apart* (New York: Basic Books, Inc., Publishers, 1978), pp. 164–167.

[18] Herbert J. Gans, *The Levittowners* (New York: Random House, Inc., Vintage Books, 1967), p. 26.

ened when they enter school and begin what for many is a decade's experience of daily academic failure. Failure serves to confirm their growing sense of worthlessness and powerlessness. With the onset of pubescent pessimism, many poor children give up all hope of a rewarding future. They derive what rewards they can from the relative security of the peer group. All too often, this recourse leads them into a deepening spiral of trouble. By then the worst fears of their parents have come true. Lee Rainwater, a sociologist who has specialized in the study of poverty, explains the tragedy:

> When [the] strategy for protecting children from the morally and socially threatening world around them breaks down, parents often salvage what self-respect they can by disavowing responsibility for the child's behavior. They say that it is impossible to control him. Given their poverty and the little protection they can offer their children from the insults and deprivation of their world, they are often right. In their relation with their parents and from the negative identities their parents in anger often offer to them, children come to look upon themselves as persons of whom not much good can be expected. Their experiences at school can drive this lesson home day in and day out.[19]

The Aspirations of Poor Families

It is often assumed that lower-class parents do not have high aspirations for their children and do not expect much from them in school. A number of studies support this contention.[20] But more recent studies have begun to question the strength of the relationship between social status and educational aspirations.[21] For example, The Coleman Report collected data on over 645,000 pupils from all sectors of American society. Coleman's findings show that black students (who are overly represented in populations living in poverty) have exceptionally high educational aspirations.[22] Coleman and others contend that these aspirations are unrealistic because poor children have little chance of achieving their goals. Furthermore, it is contended that lower-class parents do not reinforce these high aspirations by overseeing their children's study, rewarding good grades, monitoring academic progress, and conferring with teachers. Irwin Katz has suggested that poor children (especially blacks) internalize the educational goals their parents hold for them but are unable to master the behaviors needed to meet these goals. This failure results in much anxiety for lower-class children.[23] A study by Arthur Stinchcombe concludes that it is precisely this combination of high aspirations and poor academic performance that leads to rebellious behavior in high school students.[24]

---

[19] Lee Rainwater, *What Money Buys,* p. 14.
[20] See William Sewell and Vimal Shah, "Social Class Parental Encouragement and Educational Aspirations," *American Journal of Sociology,* Vol. 73 (1968), pp. 559–572.
[21] Ralph Turner, *The Social Context of Ambition* (San Francisco: Chandler, 1964).
[22] A number of studies have confirmed this finding. See, for example, Christopher Jencks et al., *Inequality: A Reassessment of the Effect of Family and Schooling in America* (New York: Basic Books, Inc., Publishers, 1972); and Morris Rosenberg and Roberta Simmons, *Black and White Self-Esteem: The Urban School Child,* Arnold M. and Carolyn Rose Monograph Series (Washington, DC: American Sociological Association, 1971), p. 145
[23] Irwin Katz, "Academic Motivation and Equal Educational Opportunity," *Harvard Educational Review,* Vol. 38 (Winter 1968), pp. 57–65.
[24] Arthur Stinchcombe, *Rebellion in a High School: High School Stinks* (Chicago: Quadrangle, 1964).

Why don't low-income parents help their children to become academically successful? The easy answer (one which teachers often give) is that these parents do not care about their children's academic work. No doubt this is true for some parents, yet ample evidence demonstrates that most low-income parents care deeply about their children's school achievement. Then, why don't they help? Of course, some do, but, for many, a confrontation with their children's schoolwork is a painful reminder of their own school failures. Feelings of academic inadequacy make them uncertain of what they can do to help their children. As one parent told me, "When I work with my kid, it is a case of the blind leading the blind. I swear it is." Understandably, many poor parents regard education as a function of the school. They view teachers as better prepared to help their children with schoolwork than they are.

It seems unfortunate, to say the least, that low-income parents are either blamed for having low educational aspirations for their children or conversely for having unrealistically high aspirations. We must find ways to help parents and children turn their reasonable aspirations into reality. The picture drawn here is not complete nor is it pretty, but it is accurate in broad detail and provides some of the information teachers must understand if they are to teach impoverished children successfully. Later in the text, we examine teaching strategies that have proven successful in classrooms with disadvantaged students. We hope that, in this section, we have provided some understanding of what it is like to grow up poor.

Growing Up in the Middle Class

In all likelihood, most students reading this book are familiar with family patterns in the middle class.[25] Therefore, the purpose of this section will not be to give you new information so much as to help you organize and analyze what you already know.

In the preceding section, we suggested that most parents (no matter what their economic class) attempt to reproduce in their children the skills they have found necessary in their own lives. Low-income families emphasize authority, conformity, and docility because these behaviors are appropriate to the kind of jobs they hold. Middle-income occupations demand a different orientation. Better paying jobs require skills in manipulating ideas (rather than objects) and in dealing tactfully with other people. Middle-class occupations are not closely supervised. They demand self-direction and call for a tightly scheduled sense of time.[26] They require that a person analyze complex situations, choose a course of action, and see it through to the finish. Thus, middle-class parents encour-

---

[25] A 1977 report indicates that increasing numbers of education students are coming from middle-class backgrounds. See *The State of Teacher Education, 1977* (Washington, DC: National Center for Education Statistics, 1978).

[26] Melvin Kohn, *Class and Conformity* (Homewood, IL: Dorsey Press, 1969), pp. 34–35. Middle-class children learn to live under tight time schedules in school, but the importance of time is reinforced in the home. A look at the intricate planning needed to figure out how Tommy will get home from Little League, how Sally will get to and from the Brownie meeting, when Dad will pick up the lawn mower at Sears, and how Mom will find time to type up the minutes of the last League of Women Voters' meeting should explain where middle-class children learn to plan ahead and meet deadlines.

age their offspring to be expressive, self-directed, self-controlled, self-reliant, responsible, and ambitious. Curiosity and consideration of others are empha-sized.

The most extensive study of how parents pass on job-related values to their children was conducted by Melvin Kohn and others and reported in *Class and Conformity*. Kohn found that

> middle-class parents . . . are more likely to emphasize children's *self-direction*, and working-class parents to emphasize their *conformity to external authority*. . . . The essential difference between the terms, as we use them, is that self-direction fo-cuses on *internal* standards for behavior; conformity focuses on *externally* imposed rules.[27]

An example may help sharpen this distinction. Kohn found that working-class mothers are likely to punish children for both wild play and fighting. They do not distinguish between the two activities because both are seen as overstepping social rules. Working-class mothers are generally interested in the absolute nature of behavior and are less interested in a child's intentions. Mid-dle-class mothers, on the other hand, do make a distinction between wild play and fighting. Fighting is seen as a loss of self-control and is punished. But wild play, however boisterous, need not represent a loss of self-control and may be ignored. The internality of the middle-class mother's orientation causes her to focus on the psychological aspects of her children's behavior. She believes it vital that her children develop an internal standard of behavior (as exemplified by group play), but she becomes concerned when these standards break down (as evidenced in fighting). Thus, wild play is acceptable in the middle class whereas fighting generally is not.

It is interesting to note that Kohn found middle-class parents as likely as working-class parents to punish their children for certain behaviors (fighting, for example). As we have seen, the reason for punishment was different in the two groups. Kohn also found that working-class mothers are more likely to retract the punishment if the children resist. The reason for this is not clear. It may be that mothers in the middle class are more aware of the importance of consistency. It may be, too, that the daily difficulties facing a working-class mother so exhaust her that she cannot easily manage to follow up on her stated intentions. Consistency may be another one of the many benefits of affluence.

Middle-Class Aspirations

Most middle-class parents value education. Because they were at least moder-ately successful in school themselves, they see education as vital to success in life. Thus, they are likely to take an active interest in their children's academic progress. Many schedule and monitor a special time for their children to do homework. They attend parent–teacher conferences, question their children about how the school day went, display their children's work around the home, brag to neighbors about their children's test scores (when these are impressively high), and plan ahead for their children's college education.

Middle-class parents are likely to be alert to any interests their children may develop. A few questions the kindergartner asks about dinosaurs will send con-

---

[27] Ibid., pp. 34–35.

scientious parents scurrying to encyclopedias, libraries, bookstores, and museum gift shops for information on the subject. Pictures, models, puzzles, and games with a prehistoric theme may turn up at the child's next birthday or under the Christmas tree. Middle-class parents are more apt to take their children on educational excursions to zoos, museums, plays, and historical sites and to monitor their children's television viewing.

Reason is a virtue highly valued in middle-class homes. Children are not only told rules; they are told the reasons behind them. "I do not want you to run in the living room because there are a lot of things you might bang into, and you could hurt yourself. There are a lot of breakable things in here that Mommy and Daddy love. So if you are going to run, run outside where it is safer."

Middle-class parents may resort to physical punishment, at least for offenses that violate the norm of self-control. They are far more likely than lower-class parents, however, to use the withdrawal of approval and affection as a discipline technique. When pushed to extremes, such tactics can be as debilitating as corporal punishment.

The middle-class family is more child-centered than lower-class families. Parents play with their children more, reason with them, look after their interests, and maintain control for a longer period of time. Some parents do these things more successfully than others. Not all middle-class parents produce children who are self-reliant, reasoning, and academically successful, but the background and economic situation of the middle class make these outcomes more likely than they are in poor homes.

Middle-Class Family Values

The history of the United States since the eighteenth century—indeed, the history of the industrialized West—has been the story of triumph for middle-class values and culture.[28] Perhaps one of the strongest institutional products of that culture has been the child-centered, middle-class family. Within its confines, individuals have found a haven from the onslaughts of modern life and a locus of morality and personal identity.[29] The middle-class family also has motivated and socialized its members to participate and often prosper in the public sphere.[30]

Raising and educating children is the "great mission" of the modern middle-class family and a host of "bourgeois virtues" support that enterprise. Among these virtues are hard work, discipline, diligence, attention to detail, delayed gratification, the cultivation of will power, achievement motivation, decency, dependability, civility, politeness, respect, responsibility, individualism, and fairness.[31] Such values may be ridiculed because they can, and sometimes do, turn ugly when driven to extremes. In distorted form, bourgeois virtues may turn to avarice, greed, narcissism, philistinism, prejudice, conformity, timidity,

[28] Philippe Aries, *Centuries of Childhood: A Social History of Family Life* (New York: Knopf, 1962). See also Peter Laslett, *The World We Have Lost* (New York: Charles Scribner's Sons, 1965).
[29] Robert N. Bellah, Richard Madsen, William M. Sullivan, Ann Swindler, and Stephen M. Tipton, *Habits of the Heart: Individualism and Commitment in American Life* (Berkeley: University of California Press, 1985), p. 88.
[30] Ibid., pp. 85–88, 107–112.
[31] Brigitte Berger, "The Fourth R: The Repatriation of the School," in *Annual Editions in Education: 1987–1988*, ed. Fred Schultz. (Sluice Dock, CT: Annual Editions, 1987), p. 19.

Raising and educating children is the "great mission" of the modern middle-class family. (*Source:* National Education Association, Carolyn Salisbury.)

pettiness, smug self-satisfaction, and other antisocial values. Some contend that these distortions are more common today than in the past.[32] Others argue that over the last 200 years, the middle-class family has been able to maintain some degree of balance between individualism and social responsibility, autonomy and community, acquisitiveness and altruism, and civility and conformity.[33]

Modernization has not been kind to the modern family. As the public sphere has grown in significance, the family receded in importance. No longer are the family and local community the uncontested socializing agents for society. The mass media (especially television,[34] but also radios, music, magazines, and movies), peer groups, youth recreation industries, the medical establishment, guidance counselors, and child-care facilities now compete for the attention and loyalties of the young. As growing numbers of children give themselves up to

[32] Some social scientists contend that the middle-class values have been thrown badly out of balance and that the modern family is no longer serving the social and individual aims it served in the past. See, for example, Bellah, Madsen, Sullivan, Swindler, and Tipton, *Habits of the Heart*, pp. 275–296.

[33] Some social scientists contend that the modern, middle-class family is still strong and well worth preserving. See, for example, Brigitte Berger and Peter L. Berger, *The War over the Family: Capturing the Middle Ground* (Garden City, NY: Doubleday, 1983).

[34] Joshua Meyrowitz, *No Sense of Place: The Impact of Electronic Media on Social Behavior* (New York: Oxford University Press, 1985), pp. 237–265.

drugs, delinquency, careless sexuality, peer-group conformity, and suicide, middle-class parents have become less and less sure of their parenting skills. Anxious parents, wanting to help and be helped, have turned to experts for advice and guidance. Many have become willing clients of what Brigitte Berger has called the *educational-therapeutic complex*.[35] It is hardly surprising that parents should become fearful as they feel less capable. Nor is it surprising that "helping professionals" should offer assistance. However, Berger and others worry that the educational-therapeutic complex is promoting values that undermine the traditional values of the middle-class family. Thus, Berger calls for a new breed of educator who will

> rediscover what an earlier generation of educators took for granted: a positive home environment that emphasized parental understanding, parental control, and involvement is still the best precondition for a child's successful performance in school and life.[36]

It should be pointed out that middle-class values are not the sole property of the middle class. Many working-class families have adopted and maintained bourgeois values, because they believe adherence to such values will improve the opportunities open to them and their children. It is not always easy to maintain such values when local communities and schools operate according to different value structures. However, when these values are maintained at home, rewarded at school, and internalized by the children, those children are likely to out-perform their classmates and greatly improve their life chances.[37]

Children of Privilege

Affluence expands the realm of choice for children and adults. From an early age, children of privilege are exposed to (if not overwhelmed by) a staggering variety of things they can have, see, and do. Toys are abundant and within easy reach in rooms set aside for play. Homes, often accessible by private roads and set on well-manicured lawns, offer numerous rooms, wings, and secondary buildings where children can play and explore. More elaborate fun is available from easily accessible facilities for ice skating, skiing, sailing, horseback riding, tennis, and so on. The family may shuttle between a city apartment and a country estate with an additional cottage by the sea or in the mountains.

If choosing among the advantages of affluence is a problem, then the life of wealthy children is beset with problems. Selecting among alternative sources of pleasure, however, is not the central focus of growing up wealthy. The real problem is grappling with the reality that one is set apart by virtue of one's family's social position and life-style. In a narrow sense, wealthy children share with poor children a feeling of being different from the rest of society. Of course, affluent children are envied and sought after, whereas poor children

---

[35] Brigitte Berger, "The Fourth R," p. 21.

[36] Ibid., p. 23.

[37] Reginald M. Clark, *Family Life and School Achievement: Why Poor Black Children Succeed or Fail* (Chicago: University of Chicago Press, 1983). See also Karl R. White, "The Relation Between Socioeconomic Status and Academic Achievement," *Psychological Bulletin*, Vol. 91, No. 3 (May 1982), pp. 461–481. This article is important because it shows that it is not socioeconomic status that determines student achievement but the values and the quality of a child's homelife.

are rejected or pitied by the world around them. The experience of being set apart has many roots. In the experience of the affluent, it begins with the family's pride in the family name. Children soon see that they are not only individuals, valued in their own right, but also links in a generational chain of family tradition. They are warned that misbehavior is not only bad in itself but also a reflection upon the family.

This sense of family significance is underscored for children as they observe how the world treats their parents. Family servants bend every effort to keep in the good graces of the family. Successful and important people come to talk business with Father and wait anxiously for his arrival. When such a meeting begins, participants choose their words carefully and listen intently to whatever Father has to say. This deference is repeated in all social situations outside the family's sphere of close friends. It becomes magnified in the minds of wealthy children as they realize that newspapers, magazines, radio, and television do more than report the impersonal news of the world: The news is often about their family and close acquaintances. It begins to dawn on children that they live in a stratified world in which they occupy a privileged position.

Child Rearing and Wealth

Wealth frees people from the daily routines that fill the lives of individuals in other economic classes. Wealthy mothers need not scurry to finish the shopping before school ends so that they can be free to transport their children to Little League games and dancing lessons. Chauffeurs pick up and deliver the children; governesses dress, bathe, look out for, and pick up after them; hired servants shop, cook, and clean. If the children encounter trouble in arithmetic, parents need not personally ponder the mysteries of the new math. They can hire a tutor or send their children to schools where special tutoring comes with the high cost of tuition.

All this delegation of responsibility means that children of privilege are not of necessity thrown together with their parents in the rounds of everyday life. As a result, they are less closely tied to their parents and are likely to form attachments to their nannies or to other servants charged with their care. Yet, if the parent–child relationship is not emotionally charged, it is usually friendly. Parents can pay others to set and reinforce rules for their children, thus freeing the parent–child relationship from many sources of conflict. When trouble does arise, children can be shunted off to servants for an afternoon's supervision. If the trouble proves persistent, the child can be sent to summer camp, to Europe for a trip, or to a private boarding school until the problem passes.

The combination of family wealth, social position, and political leverage nurtures self-confidence and self-worth (often, even a smug sense of superiority) in rich children. On the other hand, their insulation from pain and stress may make it difficult for them to endure troubles when these do arise. Realizing this possibility, concerned parents may encourage their children to test themselves through simulated difficulties such as wilderness training and other character-building activities. Ironically, they attempt to buy the traumas that ordinary life provides at other levels of society.

Life among the "upper crust" is not always joyful for children. Wealthy families are generally aware of the problems that money and power can inject into the lives of the young. Most take care that their children learn to avoid the appearance of condescension. Children are taught to wield their inherited power unobtrusively. They are instructed in how to carry power and position with grace. Aware that money guarantees a comfortable life, parents worry that their children will grow soft and self-indulgent. They know that there is but a thin line separating self-assurance from narcissism. They are not merely worried that their children will fulfill the caricature of the spoiled rich kid but are concerned that the experience of wealth will make it difficult for their children to care about others. They seek to avoid what F. Scott Fitzgerald called the carelessness of the rich.

It is probably this concern, together with the tradition of family pride, that causes the wealthy to stress to their children the importance of high ideals and lofty standards. One child, not yet out of grade school, explained his father's expectations: "He wants me to have *principles;* that is the word he always uses. He says you should know where you would draw the line, and not budge an inch."[38] Having principles and standards engenders a high sense of responsibility in some wealthy children. Note the world view expressed by one eleven-year-old boy. He felt responsible for everything, including his personal health:

> When I get a bad cold, I feel disappointed in myself. I don't think it's right to be easy on yourself. If you are, then you slip back, and you don't get a lot of the rewards in life. If you really work for the rewards, you'll get them.[39]

Compare this conception with the world view of the typical poor child. Whereas poor children see themselves as powerless, this child of wealth sees himself as omnipotent, responsible for all things, even the common cold. Another eleven-year-old, this one a child of a bank president, related what he had learned about hard work and high standards:

> My Dad says if you want to get some place, you should make up your mind, and never be satisfied until you've won. My mother says that she'd be happy, no matter what work I did, so long as I was good at it.[40]

Coping with Wealth

Parents of wealthy children encourage idealism, although it is an idealism with clear boundaries and intricate subtleties. Wealthy children are likely (if only by accident) to discover that while they enjoy the comforts of wealth, others suffer the indignities of poverty. It is a complex puzzle for inquisitive, fair-minded children and one that parents (who perhaps have not yet sorted out their own thinking on this issue) find difficult to explain. A preadolescent girl—whose home is in Westport, Connecticut, but who vacations in Nantucket, the Rocky Mountains, and Captiva Island, Florida—recalled when she first learned about the poor:

> I asked my mother once why we have all the food in the freezer and in the refrigerator and in the cabinets, and there are those people dying. You see them on television. They are a majority, the man said—most of the people on this planet. He said we throw away more than most people eat in a day. That sounded bad. I

---

[38] Coles, *Privileged Ones*, p. 477.
[39] Ibid., p. 405.
[40] Ibid., p. 485.

asked my mother why it's like that. She was mad with our governess, because we were not supposed to be watching that program or any programs like it.[41]

The child's parents dealt with the situation through denial. They instructed the children to watch less television, for as they put it, watching shows like that would make them "morbid." They instructed the governess to monitor more carefully the children's television viewing. Should they see any more shows on this topic, she would be fired. But children are not easily denied access to disturbing questions. Eventually parents must provide a belief system that legitimates the family's comfort even while explaining (and justifying) other families' pain.

> My mother says that the trouble with this country is that people are becoming soft; they want a lot of things, but they're not going to work as hard as they should to get them. They want jobs. But do they really try hard on the job? They want things for nothing. But do they know that you can't get something for nothing? There has to be *someone* who pays for everything. It is getting so that the people who work hardest and make the most money end up paying for everything, and the people who want to loaf all day end up expecting to get anything they want just by snapping their fingers.[42]

Not all parents present the ideology of entitlement in such harsh terms. Instead, many explain that they do not have enough money to help everybody. They emphasize that charity is important and point out that they give large sums to "worthy causes." But the stronger message is that without an abundance of hard work on the part of the poor, all the charity in the world would "not make one whit of difference." This is, of course, a debatable assertion and one with which we need not deal here. The important point is that the ideology of entitlement is believed by many wealthy parents and that they pass it on to their children.

Such a tightly knit ideology could unravel were children to learn that indolence is not a major cause of poverty. Many poor families work hard yet cannot make ends meet. But there is little likelihood that young wealthy children, given the insular character of their lives, will discover this. The ideology of entitlement impresses upon the young the importance of living up to rigorous standards, doing things excellently, and working hard. The more children come to see wealth as a just consequence of merit, the more likely it is that they will come to see poverty as the equally just consequence of failure. Such beliefs legitimate the family wealth while providing an explanation for poverty. It is important to note that the belief system of the eleven-year-old quoted here is not unique to her class. Such ideas are popular in the less affluent middle class as well, but the fact that it has been mastered by someone so young is evidence of its importance in the world of the wealthy.

The Aspirations of the Wealthy

In a world where almost all desires are met, dreams and aspirations take on a sense of impending reality. Children considering the future are not so much concerned with preparing themselves for careers as they are with choosing which

[41] Ibid., p. 490.
[42] Ibid., p. 491.

career they want. Preparations are a secondary matter. These can be arranged once the child has demonstrated a compelling interest.

Some affluent families stress education highly and insist that only a thoroughly educated child makes intelligent choices and develops meaningful interests. For such families, the privileges of money are compounded since children are provided the finest education that money can buy. The young attend the best nursery schools, move on to private country-day schools, graduate to exclusive boarding schools, and wind up at colleges often in the Ivy League.

But for other families, formal education is not so important. They see no need to add the credentials of a liberal arts education to the more formidable credentials of family background and wealth. Formal schooling for children in these families might be interrupted or even ended if a child develops a deep interest in, say, photography, skin diving, anthropology, hunting, or some other pursuit. For such families, general-education requirements serve no purpose in themselves. They are seen as getting in the way of the child's more compelling personal interests.[43]

Summary

This chapter has examined child-rearing practices within three very broad categories: the poor, the middle class, and the affluent. (See Table 19-1.) The approach has been experiential rather than theoretical. The aim was to give you a feel for what it is like to grow up in circumstances different from your own. Within categories as broad as these, generalizations must be made with caution. Economic class significantly alters the lives of Americans, yet it is not the sole determinant of how parents interact with their children. Other conditions play their part and may even override the experience of economic class. Some families are influenced by religion, others by an ethnic or cultural heritage. Community support systems, close friends, artistic or academic skills, and sensitivities and individual eccentricities all exert their own pressures on family life. Certainly the incidence of alcoholism and illness (physical and/or mental) can cripple parent–child relationships in any class.

Even after making these generalizations and qualifications, it is possible to sort out the common experiences of families within a given class and to conclude that such experiences will have lasting effects on most members of that particular class. In this chapter, you have studied some of these common experiences.

The most common experience among the poor is the pain caused by inadequate income. Life for the poor is precarious. The children of the poor have little to convince them that what they do will make a difference in how they live. This deprivation promotes a fatalistic view of the world that can easily turn to despair. Concerned parents strictly supervise their children in an effort to protect them from hostile environments and keep them out of trouble. Rigid standards are set down, and children are expected to obey them. Schools are expected to reinforce family standards, to promote learning, and to support parental authority. Children respond to such restrictions by seeking to break free of parental control and by finding refuge in peer groups. This response

[43] Ibid., pp. 452–456.

TABLE 19-1.   Child-rearing Attitudes and Behavior among Three Social Classes

The Poor	*The Middle Class*	*The Wealthy*
Differences in Child-rearing Methods		
Parent-centered	Child-centered	Parent- and child-centered
Commanding	Reasoning and discussing	Reasoning and discussing
Sporadic warmth and affection	Continuous warmth and affection	Warmth and affection but less parent–child contact
Interest in consequences of behavior	Interest in motivation of behavior	Interest in consequences and motivation
Physical punishment	Some physical punishment; also guilt-provoking withholding of love	Guilt-provoking withholding of love
Differences in Values		
External locus of control (your actions make no difference)	Internal locus of control (you can make a difference)	Internal locus of control (you can do anything)
Externality (you are judged by others)	Internality (you are judged by self)	Internality-externality (you are judged by self but live up to family name)
Focus on the present and forget the painful past	Plan for the future	Respect the past, enjoy the present, and prepare for the future
The world is harsh, cruel	The world is good and getting better	The world is your oyster
People should develop physical toughness conformity acceptance docility	People should develop competitive skills reasoning skills interactive skills self-control intellect initiative curiosity	People should develop high standards lofty principles deep interests determination good manners intellect taste reasoning skills social graces

SOURCE: Adapted with major changes from Lucile Duberman, *Social Inequality* (Philadelphia: J. B. Lippincott Company, 1976), p. 120.

causes conflicts in many homes, but generally lower-class children break free from parental control earlier than the children of the middle class. Many poor children, especially poor blacks, have high educational aspirations. Although poor families may not know how to fulfill these aspirations, schools also have neither successfully capitalized on these dreams nor found ways to turn them into reality.

Middle-class families live in a far more comfortable world, where it is easy to believe that hard work, rational thought, and a good education will lead to future success. Not surprisingly, middle-class parents endeavor (with varying degrees of proficiency) to instill self-direction, self-control, interpersonal skills, responsibility, and ambition into their children. Curiosity and thoughtful concern for others are highly valued. Education is promoted not as an end in itself but as a means to a more valued end—a well-paying job. Parents take an interest in their children's academic work and plan for their future education.

Wealthy children live in a world of heightened choice. An emphasis is placed on the family name, and, unless wealth is a recent occurrence, careful attention is given to lineage. Children learn early that wealth sets them apart from the rest of society. They learn they are different by observing how the world deals with their parents and themselves. People are invariably polite, attentive, and sometimes sycophantic. The abundance of personal attention, physical comfort, and material goods engenders in many wealthy children a healthy self-confidence. Nevertheless, there are risks. Children can become overwhelmed by possessions and retreat from a concern for individuals into a concern for things and self-comfort. Self-confidence can slip into self-importance, and self-importance gradually into narcissism. Concerned parents may attempt to counter such forces by insisting that their children adhere to high standards and maintain lofty ideals. But even here children are vulnerable, especially when they begin to question, as one child put it, "why God is not as kind to everyone as he has been to us." In order to explain such mysteries, parents are apt to provide their children with an ideology that justifies their wealth and explains why others are less fortunate.

One of the advantages of wealth is easy access to an excellent education. Children may attend well-funded public schools or enroll in excellent and costly private academies. Most wealthy children go to college, and many go on to do graduate work. But for the wealthy, education is not the necessity that it is for the middle class. Education can be valued for itself and not merely as an avenue to employment. This outlook may be altered if a child chooses a career in law or medicine. The idea that education can be valued for its own sake is even more clearly accentuated when a youngster develops an interest in some specialized pursuit. In such a case, education may be focused solely on that narrow interest, and a diploma may lose its significance, unless it is needed as a credential.

Suggested Readings

The aim of this chapter has been to point out differential patterns of child rearing in three separate social classes. The following books might be used to follow up this point:

BERGER, BRIGITTE. "The Fourth R: The Repatriation of the School," *Annual Editions in Education: 1987–1988*, edited by Fred Schultz. Sluice Dock, CT: Annual Editions, 1987, pp. 17–24. This conservative sociologist calls for a fuller appreciation of middle-class values.

CLARK, REGINALD M. *Family Life and School Achievement: Why Poor Black Children Succeed or Fail.* Chicago: University of Chicago Press, 1983.

COLES, ROBERT. *Privileged Ones*, Vol. V of *Children of Crisis.* Boston: Little, Brown & Company, 1977. This is a sensitive account of the problems and benefits of being reared in a wealthy family.

COLES, ROBERT. *The South Goes North*, Vol. III of *Children of Crisis.* Boston: Little, Brown & Company, 1967. This is a sensitive account of poor white southerners transplanted to northern urban settings.

GANS, HERBERT. *The Urban Villagers*. New York: The Free Press, 1962. This book depicts life in a working-class family.

HARRINGTON, MICHAEL. *The New American Poverty*. New York: Holt, Rinehart and Winston, 1984. This is a socialist account of poverty in America.

KOHN, MELVIN. *Class and Conformity*, 2d ed. Chicago: University of Chicago Press, 1977. This explains the value differences often found between middle-class and working-class Americans and shows the connection between the values and work.

LEWIS, OSCAR. *The Children of Sanchez*. New York: Random House, Inc., 1961. The book describes family life in the "culture of poverty."

MURRAY, CHARLES. *Loosing Ground: American Social Policy, 1950–1980*. New York: Basic Books, 1984. This is a conservative analysis of government efforts to help the poor.

RUBIN, LILLIAN BRESLOW. *Worlds of Pain*. New York: Basic Books, Inc., Publishers, 1976. This is a moving account of life and love at the bottom of the social class heap.

SEELEY, J. R., R. A. SIM, and E. W. LOOSLEY. *Crestwood Heights*. New York: Basic Books, Inc., Publishers, 1956. This book describes family life in a North American suburb.

CHAPTER 20

Schooling and the Stigma of Poverty

Equality of opportunity is a core value in American democracy and a compelling aim of education. As a broad ideal, it is accepted by both the liberal and conservative traditions in the United States. Yet, it has become increasingly clear that the equalization of opportunity is exceedingly difficult to achieve—more difficult than the Founding Fathers ever imagined. In their view, opportunity was equalized if people were left alone; if the frontier were open for fresh starts and development; and if opportunities for farming, trade, and small business were abundant.

Since the time of Jefferson and Adams, conditions have changed. The frontier has vanished. The mechanisms of production have moved from rural to urban settings, from agriculture to industry, and from small groups of workers to large ones. The growth of vast corporations has made it difficult for small business ventures to survive. With the passing of generations, the nation has become more clearly stratified. Poverty has become an obvious and vexatious problem.

These changes have alerted us to many hitherto unexplored facts. Social scientists are coming to understand that a class system that dispenses unequal rewards allocates unequal life-chances as well. They are beginning to comprehend the inadequacy of the standard liberal and conservative ideologies of stratification. The systems that keep people disadvantaged do not exist solely in the character of individuals, as many conservatives would have us believe; nor is poverty simply the result of a usurious social system, as many liberals contend.

We learned early in the text that humans are interactive beings. As W. I. Thomas wrote:

> In the continual interaction between the individual and his environment, we can say neither that the individual is the product of his milieu nor that he produces his milieu; or rather, we can say both. For the individual can indeed develop only

under the influence of his environment, but on the other hand during his development he modified this environment.[1]

If we are to understand human behavior, we must pay close attention to how the world treats individuals and how they, in turn, define and act upon their world. This is a complicated matter, for we must investigate both human events and the meaning of those events for the actors involved.

Any adequate explanation of poverty demands an interactive perspective that is sensitive to these issues. Chaim Waxman of Rutgers University provides such a perspective in *The Stigma of Poverty*. He points out that poverty is neither "solely internally generated nor . . . solely externally generated."[2] We will misinterpret the motivation and meaning of poor people's behavior if we look only at the poor themselves and ignore the social structure in which they live. Much is to be gained, Waxman contends, from an examination of the interactions of the poor with others in society. Specifically, he would have us examine "the perceptions and definitions which the non-poor have of the poor in American society."[3] As we already have seen, a majority of Americans entertain negative opinions of the poor. Those existing in poverty, especially those receiving public assistance, are *stigmatized* as being deviant and undesirable.

The Meaning of Stigma

The concept of stigma is important, for it helps us clarify both the internal and external causes of poverty. It provides a means for understanding what transpires when stigmatized individuals share social situations with nonstigmatized individuals. We'll call the latter group *normals*.

Erving Goffman has observed that stigmatized individuals are defined by "normals" as "not quite human."[4] When we stigmatize people as deviant, we subtly free ourselves of the obligation to treat them politely or with trust. Because of pity, disgust, or fear, the "normal" individual feels little obligation to be attentive to the stigmatized individual's definition of the situation. Goffman contends further that when we stigmatize an individual, we

> exercise varieties of discrimination, through which we effectively, if often unthinkingly, reduce his life-chances. We construct a stigma-theory, an ideology to explain his inferiority and to account for the danger he represents.[5]

Stigma and Schooling

Schools are a good place to study the stigma of poverty. It is here that lower-class children first experience long-term contact with middle-class adults. The

---

[1] W. I. Thomas, *W. I. Thomas on Social Organization and Social Personality,* ed. Morris Janowitz (Chicago: University of Chicago Press, 1966), p. 32. Available in paperback.
[2] Chaim Waxman, *The Stigma of Poverty: A Critique of Poverty Theories and Policies* (Elmsford, NY: Pergamon Press, Inc., 1977), p. 66. Available in paperback.
[3] Ibid., p. 68.
[4] Erving Goffman, *Stigma* (Englewood Cliffs, NJ: Prentice-Hall, Inc., 1963), p. 5. Available in paperback.
[5] Ibid.

tender age and comparative powerlessness of the students make them particularly vulnerable to the stigmatizing assumptions of teachers. Remembering Goffman's contention that stigmatized individuals are viewed as "not quite human," consider Herbert Kohl's observations of his fellow teachers in a ghetto school:

> After a while the word "animal" came to epitomize for me most teachers' ambiguous relations to ghetto children—the scorn and the fear, the condescension yet the acknowledgement of some imagined power and unpredictability. I recognized some of that in myself, but never reached the sad point of denying my fear and uncertainty by projecting fearsome and unpredictable characteristics on the children and using them in class as some last primitive weapon. . . . I remember a teacher from another school I taught in, a white Southerner with good intentions and subtle and unacknowledged prejudices. He fought for the good part of the semester to gain the children's attention and affection. He wanted the children to listen to him, to respond to him, to learn from him; yet never thought to listen, respond, or learn from the children, who remained unresponsive, even sullen. They refused to learn, laughed at his professed good intentions, and tested him beyond his endurance. One day in a rage and vexation, it all came out.
>
> "Animals, that's what you are, animals, wild animals, that's all you are or can be."
>
> His pupils were relieved to hear it at last, their suspicions confirmed. They rose in calm unison and slowly circled the raging trapped teacher, chanting, "We are animals, we are animals . . ." until the bell rang and mercifully broke the spell. The children ran off, leaving the broken, confused man wondering what he'd done, convinced he had always been of good will but that "they" just couldn't be reached.[6]

Of course, not all teachers consciously stigmatize poor youngsters. Most would agree that children should be seen as being of equal worth. Despite differences in ability and family background, children should be equally deserving of respect, equally worthy of membership in the school community, and equally entitled to develop their unique potentials.

These ideals are widely held and, at least on abstract levels, vigorously defended. But they exist in many teachers' minds side by side with negative attitudes about poor adults. When a teacher has difficulty teaching impoverished children, it becomes an easy matter to define them as unreachable and to blame their home lives. As an illustration, consider James Herndon's description of his first day teaching at a junior high school in a low-income area in California. On his way to his first class, a veteran teacher offered him this advice:

> "Jim, you ever worked with these kids before?"
>
> "No," I admitted.
>
> "I thought so. Well, now, the first thing is, you don't ever push 'em, and you don't expect too much. If you do, they'll blow sky-high and you'll have one hell of a time getting them down again. May never do it. Now, it's not their fault, we all know that. But you have to take them as they are, not as you and me would like them to be."[7]

---

[6] Herbert Kohn, *36 Children* (New York: The New American Library, Inc., 1967), pp. 187–188. Available in paperback.

[7] James Herndon, *The Way It Spozed to Be* (New York: Bantam Books, 1969), p. 14.

Stigma and Self-Esteem

One of the most debilitating effects of prejudice is that the stigmatized individuals often come to believe the definitions "normals" assign them. As Goffman put it:

> The standards he has incorporated from the wider society equip [the stigmatized individual] to be intimately alive to what others see as his failing, inevitably causing him, if only for moments, to agree that he does indeed fall short of what he ought to be. Shame becomes a central possibility, rising from the individual's reception of . . . his own attributes as being a defiling thing to possess.[8]

Once individuals have internalized the stigma they have been assigned, they can erase it only with great difficulty. While working with sixth-grade youngsters in a slum neighborhood, Elise and Rodman Webb were continually confronted by students who would deny the worth of their work. Even when their poems, paintings, or math assignments were done well, they would publicly declare, "This is junk," or "I screwed this up." It was as if they wanted to define themselves as incompetent before anyone else had a chance to do it. This behavior was clearly a coping strategy, designed to protect themselves against the pain of negative evaluation. They had learned the stigma of failure and were now applying it rigorously to themselves.

Such behavior is common among poverty children who have experienced failure in school. Teachers frequently refer to such children as having low self-concepts. The term dangerously individualizes the phenomenon. It suggests that the "trouble" resides only within the child. Although this is partially true, it ignores the significant part the school has played in this self-deprecation process. As discussed in Chapter 16, combatting low self-esteem is not easily accomplished. It demands a long-term effort to establish new, more productive relationships between the child, his or her work, the teacher, and the class.

Stigma and the Self-Fulfilling Prophecy

Impoverished students usually begin school at an academic disadvantage. At the start of the first grade, they may lack familiarity with the alphabet, not recognize colors and shapes, and lag behind their classmates in reading-readiness skills. They may not be familiar with the meaning of phrases common in workbook instructions, namely, "Circle the biggest . . . ," "Draw a line between . . . ," "Who has the fewest . . . ?" There is also evidence that their verbal skills are generally not as well developed as those of middle-class children.[9]

Poor children, especially those from the very poorest families, are easily identified in the classroom. They may not dress like their classmates, may not behave in conformity with teacher expectations, may not perform well academically, and may not speak in standard English.

As we saw in the preceding chapter, impoverished parents are less likely

---

[8] Erving Goffman, *Stigma*, p. 7.

[9] Basil Bernstein, "Social Class and Linguistic Development: A Theory of Social Learning," in *Education, Economy and Society,* ed. A. H. Halsey, J. Floud, and C. A. Anderson (New York: The Free Press, 1961), pp. 288–314. See also Basil Bernstein, *Class, Codes and Control,* Vol. 3, *Towards a Theory of Educational Transmissions* (London: Routledge and Kegan Paul, 1975).

than middle-class parents to stress the behaviors that teachers tend to reward: self-control, responsibility, consideration of others, and curiosity as to how things work and why they happen. Teachers are aware that the single most powerful predictor of academic performance is a student's socioeconomic background. Thus, the signs of poverty are easily read by them as indicators of coming failure.

The assumption that poor children will not do well in school is not concocted out of thin air by teachers with prejudices against the poor. It is clear that growing up in severe poverty ill prepares children for what they face in school. However, too ready an assumption that such children will perform inadequately inevitably adds to their school difficulties. The actual extent to which teacher expectations account for school performance is not clearly known, but numerous studies reveal that teachers generally favor students whom they perceive as high achievers and give short shrift to those they believe to be slow learners. Research shows that teachers call on the "low expectation group" less frequently to recite;[10] are more publicly critical of such pupils;[11] have fewer positive interactions and shorter exchanges with them;[12] pay less attention to their comments;[13] reinforce their behavior inappropriately; and wait less time for answers to teacher questions.[14]

Findings such as these raise the possibility that at least some of the problems low-SES students have in schools are caused by teachers and not solely by the home. Robert Merton's conception of the self-fulfilling prophecy is relevant here. As Merton describes it:

> The self-fulfilling prophecy is, in the beginning, a *false* definition of the situation evoking a new behavior which makes the original false conception come *true*. The specious validity of the self-fulfilling prophecy perpetuates a reign of error. For the prophet will cite the actual course of events as proof that he was right from the very beginning. (emphasis Merton's)[15]

Applying Merton's concept to the classroom, it is possible that a teacher's expectation that low-SES students will fail will increase the likelihood of their poor academic performance. A study by Robert Rosenthal and Lenore Jacob-

[10] Thomas Good, "Which Pupils Do Teachers Call On?" *Elementary School Journal,* Vol. 70 (January 1970), pp. 190–198.

[11] W. Dalton, *The Relations between Classroom Interaction and Teacher Ratings of Pupils,* Peabody Papers in Human Development, Vol. 7, No. 6 (1969). See also Pamela Robovits and Martin Maehr, "Teacher Expectations: A Special Problem for Black Children and White Teachers," in *Culture, Child and School,* eds. Martin Maehr and William Stallings (Monterey, CA: Brooks/Cole Publishing Company, 1975), pp. 249–259.

[12] A. Tyo and P. Krans, "A Study of the Verbal Behavior Patterns of Teachers in Interaction with Migrant and Non-migrant Pupils" (Unpublished manuscript, Millersville State College, 1973).

[13] Mary Budd Rowe, "Science, Silence, and Sanctions," *Science and Children,* No. 6 (1969), pp. 11–13. See also Mary Budd Rowe, "Wait-Time and Rewards as Interactional Variables: Their Influence on Language, Logic, and Fate Control." Paper presented at the annual meeting of the National Association for Research and Science Teaching, 1972.

[14] Irwin Katz, "Factors Influencing Negro Performance in the Desegregated School," in *Social Class, Race and Psychological Development,* eds. M. Deutsch et al. (New York: Holt, Rinehart and Winston, 1968). See also F. Williams, *Language, Attitude, and Social Change* (Reading, MA: Addison-Wesley Publishing Co., Inc., 1969).

[15] Robert Merton, *Social Theory and Social Structure,* enl. ed. (New York: The Free Press, 1968), p. 47.

son, reported in *Pygmalion in the Classroom,* focused public attention on this possibility.[16] These two social scientists administered standard intelligence tests to students at a San Francisco elementary school. However, teachers of the classes involved were told that these were a special variety of tests that could identify students who were ready to make significant academic gains. Approximately 20 percent of the tested children were randomly selected by the researchers. Their names were given to teachers at the beginning of the school year with the message that these students were going to "bloom." Of course, the test the students took offered no such prediction of academic success. The important variable in the study was that teachers *believed* it did.

When the students were tested several months later, then at the end of the school year, and again in the following year, results showed that the randomly selected group of "bloomers" did indeed show significant gains compared to their classmates. It is probably fair to assume that these gains were somehow caused by the special attention they received from teachers who perceived them as potential achievers.

There were a number of weaknesses in the study. Classroom teachers, who were told who was supposed to bloom and who was not, administered the follow-up tests. This raised the possibility of contaminated results. The teachers might in some way have helped the target children to do well on the test. Furthermore, only children in the first and second grades made significant gains. The study was also criticized because IQ scores among the students tested were so low that the reliability of the instrument was questioned. The most serious criticism, however, is that numerous efforts to replicate this research have produced only modest support for the self-fulfilling prophecy hypothesis.[17]

Despite these difficulties, evidence does appear to support the contention that high expectations and the behaviors it engenders in teachers can indeed affect student performance.[18] It does not appear easy to change teacher attitudes, but when high expectations occur naturally (when they are part of the teacher's personality and teaching style), they can positively influence student performance.[19]

The Phenomenon of Learned Helplessness

In the mid-1960s, three psychologists, Stephen F. Maier, J. Bruce Overmier, and M. Michael Seligman, were doing experiments in fear conditioning when they discovered an unexpected phenomenon. Using methods most of us would

---

[16] Robert Rosenthal and Lenore Jacobson, *Pygmalion in the Classroom: Teacher Expectation and Pupils' Intellectual Development* (New York: Holt, Rinehart and Winston, 1968). For a short description of their work, see Robert Rosenthal and Lenore Jacobson, "Teacher Expectation for the Disadvantaged," *Scientific American,* Vol. 218 (1968), pp. 19–23.

[17] Paul Braun, "Teacher Expectation: Sociopsychological Dynamics," *Review of Educational Research,* Vol. 46 (Spring 1976), pp. 185–213.

[18] J. Philip Barker and Janet L. Crist, "Teacher Expectancies: A Review of the Literature," in *Pygmalion Reconsidered,* eds. Janet Elashoff and Richard Snow (Worthington, Ohio: Charles A. Jones Publishing, 1971), pp. 48–64.

[19] Jere E. Brophy and Thomas L. Good, *Teacher–Student Relationships* (New York: Holt, Rinehart and Winston, 1974); available in paperback. See also J. Duske, "Do Teachers Bias Children's Learning?" *Review of Educational Research,* Vol. 45 (1975), pp. 661–684; and Harris Cooper, "Pygmalion Grows Up: A Model for Teacher Expectation, Communication and Performance Influence," *Review of Educational Research,* Vol. 49 (Summer 1979), pp. 389–410.

think cruel, the psychologists attempted to teach dogs to associate the sound of a buzzer with pain. During the training phase of the study, an experimental group of dogs was restrained and given a series of shocks. After each shock, a buzzer sounded. Another group of dogs, the control group for the study, was given no such training.

Following the conditioning phase of the experiment, all the dogs were placed in a shuttle box, one at a time. The box was arranged with a low barrier in the middle and an electrical device designed to shock the captive animal. However, the dog could turn off the shocks by jumping over the barrier in the middle of the box. When the current was turned on, most dogs would jump frantically. When they jumped the barrier, the current was cut off. Before long, the dogs learned to associate jumping the barrier with avoiding the pain of an electric shock.

The scientists discovered that the experimental group (the dogs that had been restrained and given unavoidable shocks during the training phase of the experiment) behaved differently from control group dogs. When shocked, dogs from the experimental group would react only for a short time before lying down and whining. Seligman identified this phenomenon as "learned helplessness." Those dogs who had learned during the training phase that shocks were unavoidable lost motivation to escape. Further experiments showed that learned helplessness was easily produced in other laboratory animals.[20]

Scientists must be cautious about generalizing from the behavior of one species to the behavior of another. We cannot assume, without evidence, that human beings learn helplessness as readily as dogs. However, Donald Hiroto conducted studies with college students that nearly replicated Seligman's earlier work.[21] Hiroto found that students who had been put in situations in which they could not escape loud noises were less able than other students to figure out how to turn off the noise when that possibility was available to them. Furthermore, Hiroto discovered that all human beings do not learn helplessness at the same rate of speed.

The students in Hiroto's study were administered a personality inventory prior to the noise experiment to determine their "locus of control of reinforcement." Individuals with an external locus of control believe that reinforcement in life occurs by chance or luck and that their fate is out of their control. People with an internal locus of control, on the other hand, believe that they have some control over the reinforcement they receive from their environment.

Hiroto found that "high external" subjects learned helplessness more readily than "high internals." Other experimenters have found that the helplessness learned in one situation can affect the behavior of individuals in another, seemingly unrelated, situation.

Learned Helplessness in School

An experiment by R. A. O'Brien tells us something about how induced helplessness affects learning in children. Kindergartners were shown two "junk ob-

[20] Martin E. P. Seligman, *Helplessness: On Depression, Development, and Death* (San Francisco: W. H. Freeman and Company, 1975).

[21] Don S. Hiroto, "Locus of Control and Learned Helplessness," *Journal of Experimental Psychology*, Vol. 102 (1974), pp. 187–193.

jects," say, a block and a spoon. Subjects were asked to choose one of the objects. Each time a subject chose a spoon, he or she was rewarded with an M & M candy, but when the subject chose the block, no reward was given. Before long, children learned a *cognitive strategy*—-always choose the spoon.

O'Brien divided students into three groups. The first group was given a standard block/spoon problem and was rewarded appropriately. The second group was put into a helpless situation where no cognitive strategy was appropriate to solving the problems; rewards were presented indiscriminately. A third group (the control group) received no problem at all. Finally, students in all three groups were given a series of easy problems to solve. The helpless group had by far the greatest difficulty in solving the problems; the control group solved the problems efficiently; and the cognitive-strategy group had the fastest problem solvers.[22]

Results of this experiment suggest that students who experience continual failure in school may be learning a helplessness mind set that makes further academic progress difficult.

The School Career of Poor Students

Drawing the points of this section's argument together, we can begin to appreciate how the stigma of failure can be assigned to a child early in his or her school career. Teachers who expect poor children to fail are likely to treat them in ways that ensure that this prophecy will come true.

The school experience of some impoverished youngsters is so fraught with failure that it can induce a mind set of helplessness. To appreciate how this mind set can develop, we must look into the daily activities of a classroom of disadvantaged youngsters. As we do, however, it must be kept in mind that research on helplessness in school is not extensive. We have no reliable estimates as to how many youngsters—poor or affluent—learn helplessness in classrooms. The case made here is, therefore, logical rather than statistical. It attempts to describe the processes by which helplessness can be learned in classrooms, but it does not document the extent to which this process occurs.

Harold Cadmus conducted a year-long study of a first-grade classroom that is useful for our present purposes. The school in which the study was conducted was located in a large metropolitan area on the eastern seaboard. About 45 percent of the school population was black and poor; the larger white population came from affluent homes. The first-grade teacher was white, had twenty-five years of classroom experience, and was considered by parents and administrators to be one of the best teachers in the district. At the beginning of the school year, the class had sixteen students (seven black and nine white). All white students in the class, but none of the blacks, had attended kindergarten. All of the whites scored at the sixth stanine or higher in the Metropolitan Reading Test, but only one black student scored as high as the fourth stanine, and all others scored at the second stanine.

During the first thirteen days of class, Cadmus recorded all communications from the teacher to her students regarding their academic and behavioral per-

---

[22] Quoted in Seligman, *Helplessness*, pp. 155–156.

TABLE 20-1.   First-Grade Teacher's Communications Record During the First Thirteen Days of School

Race of Student	Number of Students	Social Skills		Academic Skills	
		Positive Message	Negative Message	Positive Message	Negative Message
Poverty Black	7	4	145	52	109
Affluent White	9	10	56	166	29

SOURCE: Harold Cadmus, "The Behavioral and Instructional Dynamics of Social Stratification as Manifested in a Racially Integrated First Grade Classroom" (Ph.D. diss., College of Education, University of Florida, 1974), p. 69. Reprinted by permission of Harold Cadmus.

formance. These messages were coded as positive or negative and were recorded by the race of the student. Table 20-1 summarizes the researcher's findings and draws a numerical picture of the teacher's behavioral patterns at the start of the school year. The pattern established during the first three weeks of class did not change appreciably throughout the year. Poor black children received about 75 percent of all negative messages, and affluent white students about 75 percent of all positive teacher comments.

Cadmus kept a record of the positive and negative comments directed at each child by subtracting the total number of negative comments from all positive comments. Cadmus was able to assign each child a number that crudely indicated the kind of attention he or she was receiving from the teacher. The scores ran from a high of plus 35 to a low of minus 65.[23] All white youngsters received positive scores; that is, the number of positive comments exceeded the number of negative comments directed at them. All but one black student received scores in the negative range.

At the end of the third week, the researcher took the children aside one at a time to play a game. Cadmus played the role of a school principal, and each student pretended to be a teacher. Pictures of the class were spread before the student. "The priniipal" asked "the teacher" to send him the "best student in the class." The youngster playing the role of "the teacher" would select one of the pictures and hand it to "the principal." Cadmus would then ask for the next best student and the next best and so on until all the pictures had been selected. By averaging the ranking the students provided, Cadmus was able to arrive at an overall ranking of the students in the class. When he compared the overall student ranking with the ranking constructed from teacher messages, he found close agreement: a correlation of .90.[24] In other words, by the third week of class the students had become part of the process that stigmatized impoverished youngsters. They figured out the teacher's pecking order and used it to discriminate "good students" from "bad students."

---

[23] Harold Cadmus, "The Behavioral and Instructional Dynamics of Social Stratification as Manifested in a Racially Integrated First Grade Classroom" (Ph.D. diss., College of Education, University of Florida, 1974), p. 94.

[24] Ibid., p. 106. Further rankings throughout the year showed even higher correlations.

The Stigmatizing Process

Students learn a teacher's pecking order effectively through mundane teacher-centered activities that are probably familiar to us all. Cadmus describes the process:

> When [questioned] by the teacher, a child would provide his response after which the class would wait for the teacher's evaluation. Her response to those whose efforts revealed a higher level of academic development was always lavish and animated. For those whose efforts fell short of these standards the inevitable result was an invitation to the class members to correct or to enlighten the one whose response was unacceptable. While a correct response would inevitably elicit a response of "good," "correct," "very nice" or "excellent," an unacceptable answer was usually met with the teacher directing her attention immediately away from the responding child and addressing the class as follows:
>
> Day 2: "Who can tell us what letter this is?"
> Day 3: "Tod, can you tell him?"
> Day 4: "Who knows the correct answer?"
> Day 5: "How many think they know the right answer?"
> Day 8: "Does this show that this person loves this room?"
> Day 9: "Maybe someone else was paying more attention."
>
> For the students providing correct answers an additional complimentary remark was frequently added. . . .
>
> Day 2: "Judy is a smart girl; isn't she, class?" (choral response)
> Day 4: "Very nice, Natalie. I want you to come up here and show the class your writing."
> Day 9: "Come up here and show the class your picture. I want everyone to see what beautiful work you do."
> Day 12: "I'm so proud of that girl. She knew how many oranges were in a dozen."[25]

Students were drawn into the stigmatizing process in other, more subtle ways. For example, the teacher rarely referred to herself in the first person singular while chastising or complimenting students. By employing pronouns such as *we* or *us* (rather than *I* or *me*), she would lend the weight of the class to her sanctions. Cadmus recorded the following illustration:

> Day 3: "Where is your paper? We're having to wait for this, child."
> Day 5: "We don't like people who leave their desks in a mess."
> Day 12: "You can't sit with us because you didn't come when you were called."[26]

Similarly, the teacher would invite the class to laugh at student mistakes. "Does horse begin with an M? Has anyone ever seen a morse?"[27] When the class exploded in laughter, the teacher would suggest, "It's not nice to make fun of your classmates." But this message was hollow, for she had initiated the humiliation process.

As the year progressed, Cadmus noted an increase in verbal aggression among the students. Children worked to elevate their position in the pecking order in two ways. First, they attempted to present themselves and their work in the

---

[25] Ibid., pp. 85–86.
[26] Ibid., p. 87.
[27] Ibid., p. 86.

best possible light; wherever possible, they would hide their mistakes and ex-
aggerate their accomplishments. Second, they would work to expose the flaws
of fellow students. Cadmus's field notes provide examples of the latter behavior:

> Day 17: [The teacher dots words which have been poorly written.] Those who
> have . . . their words dotted are ridiculed by others. Tod stated, "I used to have
> my words dotted but now I can write good." Said to Tabby.
>
> Day 23: Students' public comments on workbook lessons—Natalie to Tabby,
> "Don't you know what letter this is?" Betty to David, "He doesn't know his letters."
> Terry to Jessie, "She won't know that."
>
> Day 30: David stated, "That book is easy," referring to a book given to Terry.
>
> Day 32: [The class was taking part in a newspaper drive and the student who
> brought in the most newspaper was made "captain."] Natalie stated, "Judy! Betty
> brought in two hundred pounds of paper. You won't be paper captain now."
>
> Day 32: Carol stated, "Natalie! What are you doing reading that book? I fin-
> ished that long ago. It's easy." Natalie responded, "Shut up, stupid."
>
> Day 44: David, Terry, Sally, and Mary are in a special reading book—teacher
> told them they could take it home and read it—so excited and proud. Ted, Natalie
> and Carol looked on—Terry came up to them and explained with pride their
> achievement. Natalie stated, "We finished that long ago." Carol stated, "That's
> simple." Ted replied, "Those were easy." Terry stated, "So what?"
>
> Day 55: Teacher asked Terry to listen to Harold read. She was a tyrant—not
> at all helpful—screamed at him, "Put on your brains, stupid."
>
> Day 61: Blaine reads to me—Charles sitting next to Blaine, puts out a steady
> flow of depreciating remarks such as, "That's easy," "That's simple."
>
> Day 80: Carol [playing the ranking game with Cadmus] looking at the last four
> pictures stated, "These are the dumbest persons in the whole class." Looking at
> the last ten pictures, she said. "This is a bad group here. They are all hippie
> people."[28]

The sense of isolation felt by the poor students in the class was immense.
The academic work they were given provided little opportunity for success.
Continual failure instilled little motivation to improve. The locus of control for
positive and negative reinforcement from their environment was slipping from
their hands.

Adding to academic isolation was social isolation as well. By the forty-fifth
day of class, the day of the Halloween party, the extent of this isolation was all
too apparent. Cadmus describes the experience of three black children:

> As the children entered the classroom, they began showing each other the cos-
> tumes they would wear to the class party later that day. It soon became apparent
> that Louis, Tabby, and Mary did not have costumes. Tabby cried all morning and
> finally called her mother who brought her costume to school just prior to the
> party. Mrs. Jones' [the teacher] efforts to stop Tabby's crying were totally ineffec-
> tual as she sobbed and wailed for most of the day. Mary sat with tears in her eyes,
> unable to do any school work, deeply depressed and despondent. She continually
> approached the observer throughout the day pleading that she wanted to go home,
> that she was sick and wanted to go to the health room. Louis also manifested
> extreme discomfort and continually asked the teacher to call his grandmother and
> tell her to bring a costume. The full tragedy of the experience can only be com-
> municated by one's actual participation in the events of this day. The observer's
> notebook included the following comments:

[28] Ibid., pp. 140–141.

Day 45: Mary, Tabby, and Louis didn't have costumes or masks—their reactions were extremely tragic—one can't imagine the deep humiliation and feeling of isolation they manifest—are deeply embarrassed—would apparently do almost anything to avoid this situation. As the time came for the party, Mary took a Halloween face mask they had made in art class last week from the bulletin board and held it to her face—it had no eyes in it yet she kept it in place most of the time. Louis couldn't be found—we finally located him in the teacher's closet—he climbed in there, closed the door, and hid under one of the shelves.[29]

The Vicious Circle

The Cadmus study provides a school-based example of Waxman's theoretical analysis of poverty. You will remember Waxman's insistence that poverty is not born of purely internal or solely external causes. The persistence of poverty and the behavior of the poor, Waxman claims, "have both internal and external sources which are reciprocally related."[30] The behavior patterns and attitudes of those in poverty are not simply evidence of deviance. Rather, they are predictable (and in some senses, rational) adjustments to the stigma of poverty. The logic of Waxman's analysis of poverty is increased when we realize how early the stigmatization process begins in the life of the child and how unrelenting that stigma can be.

Of course, we cannot generalize the findings of the Cadmus study to cover all public schools. The conclusions Cadmus draws are confirmed, however, in a wide variety of research. We can safely conclude that he describes a widespread, though thankfully, not universal phenomenon.[31] There is a sad circularity to the school experiences of many poor children. Negative school behavior and low initial achievement arouse negative teacher behavior, which in turn arouses more negative behavior on the part of the student. This is answered by still more negative sanctions from the teacher.[32]

It is important to emphasize—as some educational researchers do not—that the initiating behavior of the student may be disruptive and educationally defeating. The academic deficiencies of poor students are often quite real, not

---

[29] Ibid., p. 83.

[30] Chaim Waxman, *The Stigma of Poverty*, p. 98.

[31] J. A. Dunn, "The Approach-Avoidance Paradigm as a Model for the Analysis of School Anxiety," *Journal of Educational Psychology*, Vol. 59 (1968), pp. 388–394; M. Deutsch, "Minority Group and Class Status as Related to Social and Personality Factors in Scholastic Achievement," *Monograph of the Society of Applied Anthropology*, Vol. 2 (1960), pp. 1–32; Daniel Bar-Tal, "Attributional Analysis of Achievement-Related Behavior," *Review of Educational Research*, Vol. 48 (Spring 1978), pp. 259–271; Harris Cooper, "Pygmalion Grows Up," pp. 389–410; C. S. Dweck, "The Role of Expectation and Attribution in the Alleviation of Learned Helplessness," *Journal of Personality and Social Psychology*, Vol. 31 (1975), pp. 674–68; T. Hawkes and R. Koff, "Social Class Differences in Anxiety of Elementary School Children" (Paper presented at the annual meeting of the American Educational Research Association, Los Angeles, February 1969); T. F. Pettigrew, *A Profile of the Negro American* (Princeton, NJ: D. Van Nostrand Company, 1964); B. Phillips, *Schools Stress and Anxiety* (New York: Human Sciences Press, Inc., 1978); R. C. Rist, "Student Social Class and Teacher Expectation: Self-fulfilling Prophecy in Ghetto Education," *Harvard Educational Review*, Vol. 40 (1970), pp. 411–450; R. C. Rist, "Social Distance and Social Inequality in a Kindergarten Classroom: An Examination of the 'Culture Gap' Hypothesis," *Urban Education*, Vol. 7 (1972), pp. 241–260; R. C. Rist, *The Urban School: A Factory for Failure* (Cambridge, MA: MIT Press, 1973).

[32] Louis M. Smith and William Geoffrey, *The Complexities of the Urban Classroom* (New York: Holt, Rinehart and Winston, 1968), pp. 65, 81, 268.

simply figments of a prejudiced teacher's imagination.[33] Sadly, however, teacher reactions to these children can aggravate rather than ameliorate those same difficulties.

Robert and Ruth Soar conclude from their systematic observation research that low-SES students learn less in classrooms where large numbers of negative messages emanate from teachers and fellow students. A negative emotional climate in the classroom severely retards the possibility of learning. As the Soars point out,

> this finding suggests a problem for education. If, as seems reasonable, pupils of low socioeconomic status come to school with patterns of behavior that the teacher dislikes and responds to with negative affect, a vicious circle is created that makes it difficult for such pupils to learn.[34]

The school experience of too many poor children deprives them of significant opportunities to confirm their worth and encourage their progress. When values and skills foreign to a child dominate in school, failure is almost guaranteed. Deprecatory messages about his or her character and capabilities will ensue. Belief in what others are saying is easily acquired. As Hans Gerth and C. Wright Mills have pointed out, when the environment carries the message that

> those at the bottom are there because they are lazy, unintelligent, and in general inferior, then these appraisals may be taken over by the poor and used in the building of an image of themselves.[35]

As poor youngsters come to view themselves as helpless in academic settings, as they begin to see achievement to be a result of luck rather than of ability and effort, they are made unknowing conspirators in their own bondage. Insofar as schooling increases the disadvantages faced by impoverished children, it fails in its task to equalize educational opportunity.[36]

Teachers who read the research explaining how schools act to limit the educational opportunities of low-income children often find the studies unconvincing because they do not square with the teachers' classroom experience. They know that they personally have worked hard to help such children learn in school. They complain that the research does not adequately describe either their effort on behalf of students or how vehemently some students resisted those efforts. For example, a teacher who had been assigned a class of low-

---

[33] This point is well made by Jerome Karabel and A. H. Halsey, eds., *Power and Ideology in Education* (New York: Oxford University Press, Inc., 1977), p. 56.

[34] Robert S. Soar and Ruth M. Soar, "Emotional Climate and Management," in *Research on Teaching: Concepts, Findings and Implications*, eds. Penelope L. Peterson and Herbert J. Walberg (Berkeley, CA: McCutchan Publishing Corporation, 1979), p. 105.

[35] Hans Gerth and C. Wright Mills, *Character and Social Structure* (New York: Harcourt Brace Jovanovich Inc., 1953), pp. 88–89. As other sociologists have put it, "The person who has been typed, in turn, becomes aware of the new definition that has been placed upon him by members of his group. He, too, takes this new understanding of himself into account when dealing with them. . . . When this happens, a social type has been ratified, and a person has been socially reconstructed." E. Rubington and M. Wienberg, *Deviance: The Interactionist Perspective* (New York: Macmillan Publishing Co., Inc., 1973), p. 7.

[36] Adele Thomas, "Learned Helplessness and Expectancy Factors: Implications for Research in Learning Disabilities," *Review of Educational Research*, Vol. 49 (Spring 1979), pp. 208–221. See also Daniel Bar-Tal, "Attributional Analysis of Achievement-Related Behavior," *Review of Educational Research*, Vol. 48 (Spring 1978), pp. 259–271.

When stigmatized youngsters view themselves as helpless in academic settings, and when they see achievement to be the result of luck rather than effort, they become conspirators in their own bondage.   (*Source*)*:* National Education Association, Joe Di Dio.)

achieving students from impoverished backgrounds described her experience this way:

> I thought [the] student would be willing to work, [but they were not]. I had a number of very, very extreme behavior problems in the class. [I had] forget-abouts who would only talk about food, or boys, or what to wear. Some kids were . . . out of it. What could I do? They were constantly being suspended . . . or truant, or in fights, or in the courts. I don't think teachers are prepared to teach children like this.

Some researchers, especially in Britain and Australia, have shown that student resistance to school is not only traceable to the negative behaviors and attitudes of their teachers but also can be traced to the values and attitudes of some students. For example, Willis studied a group of low-achieving, working-class boys in an English comprehensive school. He found that a group of boys (who called themselves *the lads*) banned together to actively resist the education offered by the school. In their view, manual labor was preferable to mental labor. Part-time work, when it could be had, gave the lads independence, self-esteem, and access to clothes, entertainment, alcohol, and girls. School offered no such rewards. Teachers promised that hard work in school would give students knowledge and that knowledge would eventually bring financial security, but the lads did not believe it. They understood that the economy in their city was in trouble and saw that working-class graduates were faring no better than nongraduates. Education offered no future, or so it seemed to the lads. Instead, schools offered only drudgery and humiliation. The lads preferred to rebel, or, as they put it, to "have a laugh." They humiliated teachers, got into fights, came to school drunk, and generally raised hell.[37]

Other studies have shown similar results. Michelle Fine studied drop outs from alternative high schools in the South Bronx of New York City. She discovered that the drop outs were not those who had "learned helplessness," but rather those who were at greatest odds with school values and practices. As Fine put it,

> Much to our collective surprise (and dismay) the drop outs were those students who were most likely to identify injustice in their social lives and at school, and most likely to correct injustice by criticizing or challenging a teacher. The drop outs were least depressed and had attained academic levels equivalent to students who remained in school.[38]

Resistance, whether it comes from British lads or American drop outs, diminishes teachers' ability to teach and can eventually diminish their determination to overcome students' resistance. Whatever the causes of that resistance (thoughtlessness, cultural values, peer pressure, insight into economic conditions, sensitivity to injustice, or anger at dull, prejudiced, or careless teaching), antischool students are deprived of the knowledge, skills, and credentials they need to extricate themselves from poverty. They never discover that critical thinking is a powerful tool of social and personal transformation.[39]

Reversing the Vicious Cycle

Efforts to narrow the achievement gap that separates the poor from the affluent have been discouraging, but there is evidence that particular schools and individual teachers can make a difference in the academic achievement of their pupils. Teachers who concentrate on student achievement are generally more effective than those that devalue students' work.[40] Direct instruction is most effective when low-achieving students are being taught low cognitive-level material. Teachers employing direct instruction techniques teach small pieces of information at a time, ask questions regularly to check student understanding, give opportunities for practice in what has just been learned, check practice

[37] Paul Willis, *Learning to Labor* (New York: Columbia University Press, 1981); available in paperback. See also R. W. Connell, D. J. Ashenden, S. Kessler, and G. W. Dowsett, *Making the Difference: School, Families and Social Division* (Sydney, Australia: George Allen & Unwin, 1982); available in paperback.

[38] Michelle Fine, "Examining Inequity: View From Urban Schools" (Unpublished manuscript, University of Pennsylvania, 1982).

[39] The connection between intelligence and change is elaborated in John Dewey, *Democracy and Education* (New York: Free Press, 1966); available in paperback. For another interpretation of the same point, see Stanley Aronowitz and Henry Giroux, *Education under Siege: The Conservative, Liberal and Radical Debate Over Schooling* (South Hadley, MA: Bergin & Gravey Publishers, 1985).

[40] Patricia T. Ashton and Rodman B. Webb, *Making a Difference: Teachers' Sense of Efficacy and Student Achievement* (New York: Longman, 1986).

work to ensure it has been done accurately, assign daily homework so students practice at night what they learned during the day, review homework to ensure that students have mastered the material, correct errors and reteach that which has not been mastered, hold students accountable and keep them on task, run orderly classrooms, and maintain friendly relationships with students.[41] Teachers with a high sense of efficacy (those who believe they can teach and that their students can learn) generally have higher achievement gains in their classes than teachers with a low sense of efficacy.[42] Schools that maintain a positive, academic environment increase student achievement significantly more than schools where the ethos is negative and nonacademic.[43]

We have made the point in this chapter that negative student behavior and negative teacher behavior reinforce one another with devastating consequences. It does not matter much where the cycle starts; its effect is to lessen the likelihood that teachers will teach or that students will learn. This sad cycle can be reversed. Teachers who capture student interest, win family support, enforce standards, maintain discipline, remain friendly, and insist on achievement have a positive effect on students. Such teachers are most likely to be found in schools where there are clear social and academic aims. As students give more time to their work and experience some academic success, they become more willing and able to take advantage of the educational opportunities schools offer. Teachers, too, are encouraged by student success and are likely to increase their efforts when they can see positive results. When the values of the school are reinforced in the home, the likelihood of academic success is greatly enhanced. Thus, it is important that schools become mediating institutions (see Chapters 8 and 16) and keep in close and productive contact with parents. When children do not receive academic help and encouragement at home, parent education programs are often helpful.

The measurable effects of remedial programs are not great. Achievement levels have been raised as a consequence of good teaching and effective discipline but, even after remedial help, the test scores of low-SES students tend to remain far below those of their high-SES classmates. Yet, it is essential that teachers understand that what they teach and how they teach does have an effect. The difference made by teachers is not as great as social scientists predicted it would be when War on Poverty funds were being funneled into education in the 1960s. Nevertheless, good teaching enhances learning, increases the chances of graduation from high school, and ultimately increases the life-chances of students. Thus, teachers who help students learn to learn are giving a precious and world-changing gift.

---

[41] Rodman B. Webb, Patricia T. Ashton, and Samuel T. Andrews, "The Basic Skills Instructional System: A Manual for Improving the Reading and Language Arts Skills of Low-Achieving Students," *Research Bulletin* (Florida Educational Research and Development Council), Vol. 17 (Fall 1983), pp. 1–36.

[42] Ashton and Webb, *Making a Difference.* See also S. Gibson and Myron Dembo, "Teacher Efficacy: A Construct Validation," *Journal of Educational Psychology,* Vol. 76, No. 4 (1984), pp. 569–582.

[43] Wilbur Brookover et al., *School Social Systems and Student Achievement: Schools Can Make a Difference* (New York: Praeger, 1979). Also see Wilbur Brookover et al., *Creating Effective Schools* (Holmes Beach, FL: Learning Publications, 1982).

Summary

The stigma of poverty is a powerful force in American classrooms. It manipulates teacher behavior in ways that educators themselves seldom realize. It can lower a teacher's expectations for a child, can change the teacher's behavior toward the child, and can initiate a self-fulfilling prophecy of failure.

Studies from social psychology show that human initiative can be immobilized if people are put in painful situations over which they have no control. In-depth studies of life in elementary classrooms have suggested all too persuasively that poor students actually can be taught academic helplessness. Similar studies indicate that such students often receive a disproportionate number of negative messages regarding their ability and character. These messages begin in the early grades and may persist through a child's entire school career. Under such conditions, it is likely that children will internalize the definitions others give of them. When this process occurs, school failure is virtually guaranteed and the already limiting life-chances of disadvantaged children become still further restricted.

Research on poverty and education is sufficiently extensive to draw a rather detailed picture of what school is like for low-SES children and to assure us that the picture drawn in this chapter is accurate in broad detail. But, as yet, we lack sufficient information to know what percentage of children must endure the negative experiences sketched here. It is probably safe to say that such experiences are widespread, but it would be unwise to conclude that they are universal.

For anyone who takes seriously the ideal of equal opportunity, the findings discussed in this chapter are disheartening. We all would wish that schools could do a better job of preparing disadvantaged children for ascent into the middle class. There is a sad significance to the research findings, but it is important to keep in mind that this research also provides a base for improving teacher performance. Knowing what can go wrong in a classroom is, after all, the first step toward making things go right.

As we shall see in the next section, much can be done to improve education in America. Research is available that informs us what needs to be done in order to make schools more effective. However, two important topics remain to be considered before we can get to this question. First, we must look more broadly at the issue of equality and see if the United States is indeed an open society deserving of the title, The Land of Opportunity. Second, we must look at the issue of race in America to determine if education is promoting the opportunity of blacks and other minority groups. These are the topics of the next two chapters.

Suggested Readings

This chapter has emphasized the school experiences of low-achieving impoverished students. It is an easy matter for even well-intentioned teachers to neglect the child's view of classroom activities. Such neglect has sad consequences.

CONNELL, R. W., D. J. ASHENDEN, S. KESSLER, and G. W. DOWSETT. *Making the Difference: School, Families and Social Division.* Sydney, Australia: George Allen & Unwin, 1982.

FUCHS, ESTELLE. *Teachers Talk.* Garden City, NY Doubleday & Company, Inc., 1969. Teachers talk and Fuchs analyzes their comments.

HENTOFF, NAT. *Our Children Are Dying.* New York: The Viking Press, 1966.

HERNDON, JAMES. *The Way It Spozed to Be.* New York: Bantam Books, 1968.

HERNDON, JAMES. *How to Survive in Your Native Land.* New York: Simon & Schuster, 1971.

KOHL, HERBERT R. *36 Children.* New York: The New American Library, 1967. This is a heartrending account of life in an urban classroom.

KOHL, HERBERT R. *Teaching the "Unteachable."* New York: The New York Review, 1967.

KOZOL, JONATHAN. *Death at an Early Age.* Boston: Houghton-Mifflin, 1967.

KOZOL, JONATHAN. *The Night Is Dark and I Am Far from Home.* Boston: Houghton-Mifflin Company, 1975. The author accuses public education of destroying the hearts and minds of poor children.

RIST, RAY C. *The Urban School: A Factory for Failure.* Cambridge: M.I.T. Press, 1973.

RIST, RAY C. *Invisible Children.* Cambridge: Harvard University Press, 1978.

WILLIS, PAUL. *Learning to Labor.* New York: Columbia University Press, 1981.

Instructional strategies that have been proven effective for low-SES students are outlined in the following sources.

BLOOM, BENJAMIN S. *Human Characteristics and School Learning.* New York: McGraw-Hill Book Company, 1976.

BROOKOVER, WILBUR, et al. *School Social Systems and Student Achievement: Schools Can Make a Difference.* New York: Praeger, 1979.

BROOKOVER, WILBUR, et al. *Creating Effective Schools.* Holmes Beach, FL: Learning Publications, 1982.

GIBSON, S., and MYRON DEMBO. "Teacher Efficacy: A Construct Validation," *Journal of Educational Psychology,* Vol. 76, No. 4 (1984), pp. 569–582.

HENTOFF, NAT. *Does Anybody Give a Damn?* New York: Alfred A. Knopf, Inc., 1977.

LEMLECH, JOHANNA K. *Handbook for Successful Urban Teaching.* New York: Harper & Row, Publishers, 1977.

MEDLEY, DONALD M. *Teacher Competence and Teacher Effectiveness: A Review of Process-Product Research.* Washington, DC: American Association of Colleges for Teacher Education, 1977.

PETERSON, PENELOPE L., and HERBERT J. WALBERG, eds. *Research on Teaching: Concepts, Findings and Implications.* Berkeley, CA: McCutchan Publishing Corporation, 1979.

RUTTER, MICHAEL, et al. *Fifteen Thousand Hours: Secondary Schools and Their Effects on Children.* Cambridge: Harvard University Press, 1979.

WALBERG, HERBERT J., ed. *Educational Environments and Effects: Evaluation, Policy, and Productivity.* Berkeley, CA: McCutchan Publishing Corporation, 1979.

WEBB, RODMAN B., PATRICIA T. ASHTON, and SAMUEL T. ANDREWS. "The Basic Skills Instructional System. A Manual for Improving the Reading and Language Arts Skills of Low-Achieving Students," *Research Bulletin* (Florida Educational Research and Development Council), Vol. 17 (Fall 1983), pp. 1–36.

Students wishing to learn more about the genesis and consequences of teachers' expectations will find the following literature useful:

ASHTON, PATRICIA T., and RODMAN B. WEBB. *Making a Difference: Teachers' Sense of Efficacy and Student Achievement.* New York: Longman, 1986.

BAR-TAL, DANIEL. "Attributional Analysis of Achievement-Related Behavior," *Review of Educational Research,* Vol. 48 (1978), pp. 259–271.

COOPER, HARRIS M., and THOMAS L. GOOD. *Pygmalion Grows Up: Studies in the Expectation Communication Process.* New York: Longman, 1983.

DUSEK, J. "Do Teachers Bias Children's Learning?" *Review of Educational Research,* Vol. 45 (1975), pp. 661–684.

DWECK, CAROL. "The Role of Expectation and Attribution in the Alleviation of Learned Helplessness," *Journal of Personality and Social Psychology,* Vol. 31 (1975), pp. 674–685.

GOOD, THOMAS L., and JERE E. BROPHY. *Looking in Classrooms,* 4th ed. New York: Harper & Row, 1987.

PHILLIPS, B. *School Stress and Society.* New York: Human Science Press, 1978.

ROSENTHAL, ROBERT, and LENORE JACOBSON. *Pygmalion in the Classroom: Teacher Expectation and Pupils' Intellectual Development.* New York: Holt, Rinehart and Winston, 1968.

THOMAS, ADELE. "Learned Helplessness and Expectancy Factors: Implications for Research in Learning Disabilities," *Review of Educational Research,* Vol. 49 (1979), pp. 208–221.

WEBSTER, M., and J. E. DRISKELL. "Status Generalization: A Review and Some New Data," *American Sociological Review,* Vol. 43 (1978), pp. 220–236.

CHAPTER 21

Education and the American Meritocracy

Introduction

The possibility of social mobility is a fundamental component of the American Dream. It is widely believed that the United States is an open society where individuals can rise as far as their ability and gumption can take them. It is further assumed that the United States offers greater opportunities for upward mobility than any other nation in the world. Americans take it as their birthright to better their stations in life and to make it possible for their children to surpass their accomplishments. It is also assumed that the best and most direct avenue to upward mobility is through free, public education. Whether or not these assumptions are correct is the subject of this chapter.

Examining the Meritocracy Hypothesis

Elements of a Meritocratic Society

The ideal of equal opportunity implies an open rather than closed society. In a closed society, privilege (access to goods and services), power (the ability to get one's way despite resistance), and prestige (status and respect) are determined by birth and reinforced by custom and law. There is little mobility (movement up or down the stratification ladder), because social position is determined at birth. In a perfectly open society, access to material goods and services, which means access to money, would be determined solely by individual achievement. That is to say, in a perfectly open society all privilege is purchasable and access to money is determined solely by merit. Such a society is called meritocratic because privilege, prestige, and power are products of individual merit (ability and effort) rather than inherited privilege.

Education plays an essential role in meritocratic societies. It serves as a sorting agency, where the most talented individuals, no matter what their social

Schools in meritocratic society serve as sorting agencies. (*Source:* National Education Association, Joe Di Dio.)

class origins, are identified and groomed for further schooling. The most capable, high-achieving students go through college (and often on to graduate school) and then take high-paying jobs. Other students go as far as their talents will take them in school and then take more modest employment. Figure 21-1 depicts the role schools play in perfectly open, meritocratic societies.

Of course, no society is perfectly open. Family origins will help or hinder a child's access to good schools and ultimately his or her participation in the economy. Gender and race may also influence an individual's access to privilege. Thus, we must always think of "openness" in relative than absolute terms.

Few would argue that the United States is a totally open society, although it is generally believed that we are more open than any other nation and getting more open all the time. As evidence of our openness, Americans point to rags-to-riches stories of success, to the vast expansion of the educational system, to second-chance programs such as adult education and high school equivalency examinations, and to the increased use of standardized tests, which, it is claimed, greatly reduce teacher bias and more accurately depict native ability.

Testing the Hypothesis of Meritocracy

Sociological knowledge in the area of social mobility is far from perfect. However, recent research allows us to examine the meritocracy hypothesis more carefully than ever before.

Despite disagreements among the social sciences about social class, there is consensus on one fact: Since the industrial revolution, there has been a major shift in the occupational structure of the western world. A new stratum, the industrial working class, has come into being. The middle class has grown in numbers and in comfort, and the old upper-class aristocracy has been displaced by a stratum of successful capitalists. It is clear that industrialization has increased the life-chances of the population as a whole and increased opportunities for upward mobility. However, other questions still remain: Are opportunities for mobility increasing? Do people from all classes have an equal chance

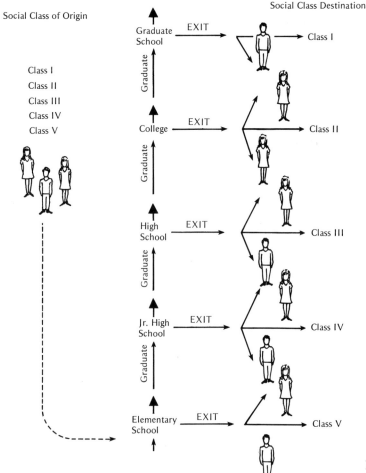

Figure 21-1   The meritocratic ideal: schools as sorting agencies.

to improve their economic position? And, does America provide greater mobility than other nations?

Recent research indicates that there is considerable social mobility in the United States today. A study of mobility rates among American men led Featherman and Hauser to draw the following conclusions:

- Overall, 68 percent of American men have experienced upward or downward mobility. Only 32 percent of American men have stayed in the same social class throughout their lives.
- The instances of upward mobility outnumber the instances of downward mobility 3 to 1.
- Mobility rates in the United States have not changed much over the past few decades and perhaps since the turn of the century.

- Mobility rates are no higher in the United States than they are in most other western industrial nations.[1]

We can conclude that though social mobility is possible in the United States, it is no easier or fairer today than it was three or four generations ago. Further, it appears that social mobility is not explained by the meritocracy hypothesis (talented, low-SES individuals out-competing less talented high SES individuals in the job market). Rather, American mobility rates in the twentieth century have been powered by an expanding economy. Blue-collar young people were pulled into white-collar occupations because economic growth created more white-collar jobs than middle-class youth could possibly fill.[2] Had the economy not grown so fast in the twentieth century, it is probable that many young people from working-class families would not have had the opportunity to compete for white-collar jobs. This point has two important implications for the future:

- If the growth of the economy slows down, we can expect a decline in upward mobility rates.
- If the economy stalls, we can expect an increase in downward mobility rates.[3]

Other Evidence of an Expanding Meritocracy

Mobility data are not abundant enough to tell us conclusively whether America is becoming more or less meritocratic. Therefore, researchers have found it necessary to look for less perfect (but more accessible) data that might shed light on the issue.

Because educational attainment is so closely associated with occupational placement, some researchers have focused on the question of equal opportunity within schools. They reason that, if it can be shown that schools increasingly reward achievement and ability rather than circumstances of birth, then we might conclude that America is becoming a more open society. To get at these issues, researchers have focused their work on a number of areas: increased retention rates (students completing more years of schooling), equal

---

[1] David L. Featherman and Robert M. Hauser, *Opportunity and Change* (New York: Academic Press, 1978). See also Oxford Analytica, *America in Perspective: Major Trends in the United States Through the 1990s* (Boston: Houghton-Mifflin, 1986), pp. 64–72; Peter Blau and Otis Dudley Duncan, *The American Occupational Structure* (New York: Wiley, 1967).

[2] As Hauser and his associates expressed this point: "There is minimal evidence of change in the process of occupational mobility beyond that induced by the changing occupational structure." Robert M. Hauser, John N. Koffel, Harry P. Travis, and Peter J. Dickinson, "Temporal Change in Occupational Mobility: Evidence for Men in the United States," *American Sociological Review*, Vol. 40 (1975), p. 280; Robert Hauser and David Featherman, "Trends in the Occupational Mobility of U.S. Men, 1962–1970," *American Sociological Review*, Vol. 38 (1973), pp. 302–310; Robert M. Hauser, Peter J. Dickinson, Harry P. Travis, and John N. Koffel, "Structural Changes in Occupational Mobility among Men in the United States," *American Sociological Review*, Vol. 40 (1975), pp. 585–598; Raymond Boudon, "Education and Social Mobility," in *Power and Ideology in Education*, eds. Jerome Karabel and A .H. Halsey (New York: Oxford University Press, Inc., 1977), pp. 186–196.

[3] Oxford Analytica, *America in Perspective*, pp. 67–68.

opportunity in public education, and meritocratic practices in higher education. We will look at these issues one at a time.

INCREASED RETENTION RATES.   The Bureau of the Census keeps close track of the educational attainments of Americans. By March 1987, well over 100 million Americans had completed high school; of those, one in five had completed college. The typical adult over twenty-five years of age had completed 12.6 years of schooling, up from 9.0 years of schooling in 1947. Figure 21-2 shows the growth in educational achievement in the United States between 1947 and 1985. The percentage of adults who completed college has nearly quadrupled over the past forty years; the percentage with less than 5 years of schooling has been dropped to under 3 percent.

These figures are encouraging because they suggest that growing numbers of people are being prepared for upward mobility. However, the fact that Americans are getting more schooling today than ever before is not, by itself, proof of increased opportunity. We cannot tell from these figures if talented graduates from low-SES homes are being treated fairly in the job market. Nor can we be sure, by looking at the numbers, that the schools themselves are meritocratic. It is necessary, therefore to take a look at what goes on inside schools.

EDUCATIONAL OPPORTUNITY AT THE ELEMENTARY AND SECONDARY LEVEL. The question of equal opportunity within the educational structure has received considerable attention in recent years. As we learned in the last chapter,

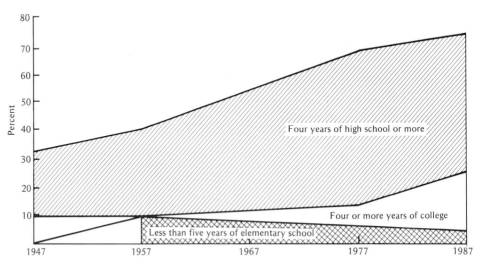

Figure 21-2   Level of school completed by persons twenty-five years old and over: United States, 1947–1987. *Note:* Data are based on sample surveys that include the civilian noninstitutional population and members of the Armed Forces living off post or with their families on post.   (*Source:* U.S. Department of Commerce, Bureau of the Census, *Current Population Reports;* Series P–20, Nos. 15, 77, 169, and 314, and Thomas D. Snyder, *Digest of Education Statistics* [Washington, DC: Center for Education Statistics, 1987], p. 13.)

some teachers identify impoverished youngsters early in the school year and systematically (though perhaps not intentionally) discourage their academic development.

Ray Rist, while investigating elementary schools in St. Louis, observed that after only eight days a kindergarten teacher had organized her classroom into ability groups, even though no formal evaluation of ability or achievement had taken place. The arrangement did not, in fact, reflect proven ability but rather the social-class origins of students. As Rist described it: "The poor children from welfare families all sat at one table, the working-class sat at another, and the middle-class at a third."[4] The groups were granted different degrees of autonomy, control, praise, discipline, and academic interaction by the teacher. By the second grade, the groups were still intact (no one had been moved from one group to another) and had picked up names along the way. The high-SES group was called the Tigers, the middle group the Blue Birds, and the lowest group the Clowns. Rist was able to show that what began as a subjective evaluation by the kindergarten teacher took on objective power as children moved through the school.[5]

The practice of grouping students by ability (or, more accurately, by achievement) has been studied extensively. Early studies tended to show that students in ability-grouped classes (called *homogeneous classrooms*) out-performed students in mixed-ability classes (called *heterogeneous classrooms*).[6] More recent research suggests that ability grouping produces no reliable effects on student achievement.[7] Some researchers suggest that the achievement of heterogeneous classes would improve if teachers adopted teaching methods appropriate to the subject matter being taught and to the level of students in the class.[8] Others worry that students, once labeled low achievers, will slide through school without being stretched or excited by challenging teachers and significant subject matter.[9]

Aaron Cicourel and John Kitsuse conducted research in an upper-income suburban school adjoining a large metropolitan area.[10] They found that in cases

---

[4] Ray Rist, "On Understanding the Process of Schooling: The Contribution of Labeling Theory," in *Power and Ideology in Education*, eds. Jerome Krabel and A. H. Halsey (New York: Oxford University Press, Inc., 1977), p. 298. For a more detailed and sophisticated examination of teacher expectations and student achievement, see Harris M. Cooper and Thomas L. Good, *Pygmalion Grows Up* (New York: Longman, 1983).

[5] Rist, ibid.

[6] R. O. Billett, *The Administration and Supervision of Homogeneous Grouping* (Columbus: Ohio State University Press, 1932); and R. B. Ekstron, *Experimental Studies of Homogeneous Grouping* (Princeton, NJ: Educational Testing Service, 1959).

[7] R. Slavin, "Ability Grouping and Student Achievement in Elementary Schools: A Best-evidence Analysis" (Unpublished manuscript, Center for Effective Elementary and Middle Schools, Johns Hopkins University, 1986).

[8] Thomas L. Good and Jere E. Brophy, *Looking in Classrooms*, 4th ed. (New York: Harper & Row, 1987), p. 406.

[9] Philip A. Cusick, *The Egalitarian Ideal and the American High School* (New York: Longman, 1983); John L. Goodlad, *A Place Called School: Prospects for the Future* (New York: McGraw-Hill Book Company, 1983), pp. 150–165; Richard H. deLone, *Small Futures: Children, Inequality and the Limits of Liberal Reform* (New York: Harcourt Brace Jovanovich, 1977); Michael W. Sedlak, Christopher W. Wheeler, Diana C. Pullin, and Philip A. Cusick, *Selling Students Short: Classroom Bargains and Academic Reform in the American High School* (New York: Teachers College Press, 1986).

[10] Aaron Cicourel and John I. Kitsuse, *The Educational Decision-Makers* (Indianapolis: The Bobbs-Merrill Co., Inc., 1963).

where a discrepancy existed between the test ability and the school achievement of students, counselors were unsure whether to place the students in the college-qualified or noncollege-qualified track. Counselors consistently resolved these dilemmas by placing low-SES students in noncollege tracks and high-SES students in college preparatory programs, despite the desires of the individual students.

The academic ineffectiveness of tracking and the stigma that accompanies low-ability placement have convinced many educators and social scientists that tracking limits the educational opportunities of the poor. As two severe critics of the tracking system put it:

> The track system provides a formal basis for translating . . . class-based factors into academic criteria for separating students into different groups: those who will drop out; those whose diplomas will not admit them to college; those who will be able to enter only two-year or junior colleges; and the lucky few in the honors classes who will go on to elite institutions and to graduate or professional schools. Thus while tracking may assure the "failure" of lower-class students, as a system it allows the schools to "succeed" in serving middle class interests by preparing their children to fill the technical and professional needs of corporate society.[11]

Not all educators would agree with the unhappy conclusions reported in this section. Utilizing sophisticated techniques of statistical analysis, however, some researchers have uncovered substantial evidence of equal opportunity in high schools. For example, Robert Hauser conducted a study of the socioeconomic background and educational performance of Nashville youth and found little evidence of ascriptive treatment. Instead, he found a relatively loose stratification system in schools where achievement rather than background was the primary mode of placement.[12] In a study of 2788 New York state students, Richard Rehberg and Evelyn Rosenthal concluded that academic achievement

> reflected much more of the student's scholastic ability and educational ambition than it did social class origin. No evidence . . . was found that would indicate that in the distribution of classroom grades, teachers overtly discriminate in favor of students from the middle class.[13]

---

[11] Paul Lauter and Florence Howe, "How the School System Is Rigged for Failure," in *Class and Conflict in American Society*, ed. Robert Lejeune (Skokie, IL: Rand McNally & Company, 1972), p. 207.

[12] Robert Hauser, *Socioeconomic Background and Educational Performance* (Washington, DC: Rose Monograph Series, American Sociological Association, 1971), p. 155. "Our results present a picture of the relationship between family origin and educational performance quite different from that which sociologists sometimes draw. The contrast is one between a relatively loose process of stratification in which achievement is the primary mode of ascent or descent, and a rather tight process in which ascriptive treatment . . . perpetuates past inequalities. The present results appear to substantiate the view of the process of stratification as rather loose."

[13] Richard Rehberg and Evelyn Rosenthal, *Class and Merit in the American High School: An Assessment of the Revisionist and Meritocratic Arguments* (New York: Longman, 1978), p. 252. These findings are different from those reviewed earlier in the section. In considering these differences, it is useful to keep in mind the nature of the research reported here. The Rehberg and Rosenthal study examined questionnaire and achievement data. It did not investigate the educational processes or classroom interaction patterns that make up the everyday life of the school. Their conclusions quite appropriately refer to the lack of overt class bias (systematically giving poor grades to academically able children from low SES backgrounds, for example). They do not touch the issue of subtle bias others, such as Rist, explored. These subtler forms of bias, if they existed in the classrooms Rehberg and Rosenthal studied, might have had effects on student achievement that would have escaped the vision of the researchers and the statistical techniques they employed.

Still, we cannot conclude, on the basis of available evidence, that high schools today are truly merit-based and even-handedly competitive. Rehberg and Rosenthal make the informed guess that "the role of social class *at the secondary level* has been declining since . . . the end of World War II."[14] This assessment is probably correct, yet it does not mean that the battle to equalize educational opportunity has been won. As high school graduation becomes a nearly universal phenomenon, more and more emphasis has been placed on college graduation. Christopher Jencks and his associates make this point clear in *Who Gets Ahead*, their massive reanalysis of available research.[15] Progress toward equalizing opportunity at the secondary level is of little benefit unless it is matched with equal accomplishments in higher education.

HIGHER EDUCATION.   Research into equality of opportunity in higher education is not voluminous, but it is growing rapidly. Some of the most ambitious research has been done by William Sewell and his associates at the University of Wisconsin. Much of their work is based on a longitudinal study of about 9000 randomly selected students whose careers have been followed since their senior year in high school. (See Table 21-1.)

The researchers found "enormous differences in educational opportunities among students of different socioeconomic backgrounds."[16] By Sewell's estimates,

> a high SES student has almost 2.5 times as much chance as a low SES student of continuing in some kind of post-high school education. [Such a student] has an almost 4 to 1 advantage in access to college, a 6 to 1 advantage in college graduation, and a 9 to 1 advantage in graduate or professional education.[17]

Such advantages appeared for both sexes but were greater for men than for women. Low-income women are handicapped not only by economic discrimination but also by gender discrimination.

TABLE 21-1.   Percentage of 9007 Wisconsin High School Students Who Attended College, by Measured Intelligence and Social Origin

Social Origin	Intelligence			
	High	Middle	Low	Total
High	91.1	78.9	58.0	84.2
Middle	64.9	43.3	24.0	46.8
Low	40.1	22.9	9.3	20.8

SOURCE: From William H. Sewell and Vimal P. Shah, "Parents' Education and Children's Educational Aspirations and Achievements," *American Sociological Review*, Vol. 33 (1968), Table 3, p. 199. Reprinted by permission of the American Sociological Association. Social origin is measured by education of father and mother; intelligence is measured by the Henmon-Nelson Test of Mental Ability.

[14] Ibid., p. 254.
[15] Christopher Jencks, et al., *Who Gets Ahead?* (New York: Basic Books, Inc., Publishers, 1979).
[16] William Sewell, "Inequality of Opportunity for Higher Education," *American Sociological Review*, Vol. 36 (October 1971), p. 794.
[17] Ibid., p. 795.

The socioeconomic differentials in education found by Sewell remained even when academic ability was taken into account. High-ability, low-SES students were about half as likely to attend college as high-SES students of equal talent.

> A similar pattern holds for the chances of graduating from college, where corresponding ratios range from 9 to 1 among low-ability students to 2 to 1 among high-ability students. At the level of graduate or professional school entry, where we would expect ability considerations to be determinative, the odds are 3.5 to 1 in favor of high SES over low SES students, even in the high-ability category.[18]

Sewell's findings severely challenged the notion that higher education provides equal opportunity for poor but talented young people. A number of other studies report similar results.[19] The disadvantages that low-SES students face in education do not disappear when they enter college. Such students are often less well prepared for college work, must hold a job or borrow money in order to attend college, and must defer badly needed income while getting an education. They are further hampered because they may not receive encouragement at home, from college faculty, or from their peers.[20]

When considering the disadvantages faced by low-income youth, we must keep in mind that higher education in America is itself stratified. High-prestige institutions (selective private colleges and universities) provide their graduates easier access to prestige graduate schools and to higher paying jobs. However, such institutions are infrequently open to low-SES students.[21] Such students, when they attend college at all, usually go to junior colleges or state-run schools that offer only limited access to high-paying jobs.

As you can see from Table 21-2, most low-SES, college-bound students end up in two-year institutions. Here they are guided into a two-pronged tracking system: one track leads students with ambition and scholastic talent toward four-year colleges, and the other leads students without interest or academic talent to terminal degrees and early entry into the job market.

This two-pronged tracking system gives junior college students a choice of study and may serve their career intentions. However, some researchers conclude that the two-tiered tracks sort students into noncompeting clusters by social class. Whereas low-SES students become candidates for a terminal degree, students from more affluent backgrounds are encouraged to prepare for further education. Critics contend that low-SES students who aspire to further

18 Ibid., pp. 295–296.

19 Natalie Rogoff, "Local Social Structure and Educational Selection," in *Education, Economy and Society*, eds. A. H. Halsey et al. (New York: The Free Press, 1961), p. 246. See also John C. Flannagan and William Cooley, *Project Talent: One-Year Follow-up Studies* (Pittsburgh: University of Pittsburgh School of Education, 1966); William H. Sewell and Vimal P. Shah, "Socioeconomic Status, Intelligence, and Attainment of Higher Education," *Sociology of Education*, Vol. 40 (Winter 1967), pp. 1–23; and Samuel Bowles and Herbert Gintis, "I.Q. in the U.S. Class Structure," *Social Policy*, Vol. 3 (November/December 1972, January/February 1973), p. 65–96.

20 Christopher Jencks, Marshall Smith, Henry Acland, Mary Jo Bane, David Cohen, Herbert Gintis, Barbara Heyns, and Stephen Nichelson, *Inequality: A Reassessment of the Effect of Family and Schooling in America* (New York: Harper & Row, Publishers, Inc., 1972), pp. 138–141.

21 J. K. Folger, H. S. Astin, and A. E. Bayer, *Human Resources and Higher Education* (New York: Russell Sage Foundation, 1970), p. 312; J. L. Speath and A. M. Greeley, *Recent Alumni and Higher Education: A Survey of College Graduates* (New York: McGraw-Hill Book Company, 1970), p. 154; L. L. Medsker and J. W. Trent, *The Influence of Different Types of Public Higher Institutions on College Attendance for Varying Socioeconomic and Ability Levels*, Monograph (Berkeley, CA: Center for Research and Development in Higher Education, 1965).

TABLE 21-2. Father's Occupational Classification by Type of College or University Student Entered

| Type of College or University | Father's Occupational Classification | | | |
	Skilled, Semi-Skilled, Unskilled	Semi-Professional, Small Business, Sales and Clerical	Professional and Managerial	Total
Public two-year college	55%	29%	16%	100%
Public four-year college	49	32	19	100
Private four-year college	38	30	32	100
Public university	32	33	35	100
Private university	20	31	49	100

SOURCE: L. L. Medsker and J. W. Trent, *The Influence of Different Types of Public Higher Institutions on College Attendance for Varying Socioeconomic and Ability Levels,* Monograph (Berkeley, CA: Center for the Study of Higher Education, 1965). Reprinted by permission.

education are gently weeded out by the system and convinced "that a transfer program is inappropriate for [them] without seeming to deny . . . the equal educational opportunities that Americans value so highly."[22]

This weeding-out process may be based on ability or on social-class bias (the evidence is not clear), but it convinces lower-track students that they have gone as far as their abilities will take them. Thus, their failure to achieve upward mobility is internalized ("I guess it's my fault") and is not blamed on the system. This process of easing students out of the educational process and convincing them that they themselves are responsible for ending their education has been labeled *cooling out.*[23]

The weight of evidence indicates that American higher education does not equalize opportunity for its students. Wealthy students carry their advantages on to the college campus just as poor students bring with them the disadvantages of their background. In the competition for grades and high-status jobs, poor students are at a distinct and enduring disadvantage.

HIGHER EDUCATION, SOCIAL CLASS, and ABILITY. Michael Olneck and James Crouse, after a careful study of academic ability and adult success, concluded,

> Socioeconomic background adds significantly to explaining inequalities in educational attainment and early occupational status. The vast preponderance of inequality in schooling, occupational status, and earnings has no relationship to differences in measured cognitive ability. Even when men[24] have the same [mental ability], differences in educational attainment have significant effects on economic

[22] J. Karabel, "Community Colleges and Social Stratification," *Harvard Educational Review,* Vol. 142 (November 1972), pp. 521–562.

[23] Ibid.

[24] Data available to Olneck and Crouse included only men.

success, but when men have the same amount of education, differences in measured ability have little effect on occupational status."[25]

Higher education, like schooling at other levels, is more beneficial to the middle and upper classes than it is to the poor. It comes closer to fulfilling the prejudices of Alexander Hamilton than the promises of Thomas Jefferson.

Available evidence does not support a contention that higher education is becoming increasingly meritocratic. Access to college (especially to prestige colleges), grades during college, and graduation from college are as dependent on one's economic background as they have been in the past.[26] This fact remains true even though high school graduation may have become increasingly egalitarian over the same period. If opportunity programs in colleges and business actually have increased in recent years, changes in opportunity have not yet shown up in research data.

Inequality in schooling, of course, bears consequences beyond the school yard and the college campus. Jencks and his associates calculated that an extra year of elementary or secondary schooling raises an individual's later earnings by "four or five percent, while an extra year of college raises earnings by seven to nine percent."[27] Although the financial return from higher education may have fallen somewhat in recent times, it remains clear that the failure to make education meritocratic serves to perpetuate inequalities of income that are unrelated to differences in ability, incentive or productivity. Although some progress has been made in equalizing opportunity through education in this century, we still have a long way to go. Public schools are not the great social equalizers Americans often suppose them to be.

Summing up the Hypothesis of Meritocracy

The evidence presented so far enables us to conclude that social mobility, although substantial, does not appear to be markedly increasing in America. Such mobility as does exist will not usually advance individuals far above their social-

---

[25] Michael Olneck and James Crouse, "The I.Q. Meritocracy Reconsidered: Cognitive Skill and Adult Success in the United States," *The American Journal of Education* (formerly *School Review*), Vol. 88 (November 1979), p. 24. See also Michael Olneck and James Crouse, *Myths of the Meritocracy: Cognitive Skill and Adult Success in the United States,* Institute for Research on Poverty, University of Wisconsin, Madison, Wisconsin, Discussion Paper No. 485–78, 1978. This paper, an earlier version of the "Meritocracy Reconsidered" paper, reported the following results:
1. The influence of family background on educational attainment, occupational status, and earnings has not fallen over time nor has the effect of measured cognitive ability risen.
2. The principal impact of so-called meritocratic criteria (that is, tested ability) is to connect men to their backgrounds rather than to free them. The effects of background are, however, mediated principally by factors other than ability.
3. Measured ability does affect adult standing, but socioeconomic success is determined principally by factors unrelated to cognitive ability.
4. Superior ability does not function as a necessary prerequisite for desirable jobs.
5. The effects of education on occupational status and earnings cannot readily be explained by the relationship between education and measured ability.
6. Men with high test scores do not benefit from additional education more than men with low test scores, suggesting that the exclusion of low-ability individuals from higher education cannot be justified on grounds of economic efficiency.
[26] William G. Spady, "Educational Mobility and Access: Growth and Paradoxes," *American Journal of Sociology,* Vol. 73 (November 1967), pp. 273–286.
[27] Christopher Jencks et al., *Who Gets Ahead?* p. 228.

class beginnings and is best explained by the pull of an expanding economy rather than by increasing meritocracy. Educational requirements have escalated with the economy so that high school diplomas have become a virtual prerequisite for even low-level work. High school graduation has become more common, and secondary schools do appear to run more meritocratically than in the past. However, progress in this area is apparently offset by continued class-related advantages in higher education.

Confronted with findings such as these, educators and social scientists have reexamined the traditional view that education is the great equalizer of opportunity in America. The thrust of this reanalysis has been to expand the inequality debate beyond the narrow perimeters of the Hamilton-Jefferson dialogue. We turn now to an examination of the current debate over equality in schooling.

Equality in Schooling: The Current Debate

Inequality in Society

As researchers come to realize that American schools do not provide the full opportunity we like to think they do, new attention is being given to the question of inequality in society itself. This development has had the effect of extending the social science debate over inequality. Many people, representing different disciplines and points of view, have entered into this discussion. Their ideas can be grouped, without intolerable distortion, under three headings: hereditarians, classical liberals, and the new egalitarians. We will discuss the views of each group separately.

The Hereditarian Position

The hereditarian position contends that economic inequalities in society and academic inequalities in schools are caused by differences in the genetic endowments and psychological dispositions of the wealthy and the poor. Such differences, it is argued, are biologically inevitable, socially productive, and morally just. Social mobility, as we have seen, has become rather fixed, and educational achievement continues to be heavily related to socioeconomic factors. This state of affairs exists, the hereditarians claim, because the stratification system has successfully sorted people according to their ability and initiative. The hereditarians point to the correlations that exist between high IQ scores and social-class placement and claim these as evidence that we are fast approaching a meritocratic society.[28]

Arthur Jensen, a professor of educational psychology at the University of California, uses the hereditarian analysis to explain differences between IQ scores of blacks and whites, income, and educational achievement. According to his much criticized view, the fifteen-point disparity between average IQ scores

---

[28] N. Stewart, "Army General Classification Test Scores of Army Personnel Groups by Occupation," *Occupations*, Vol. 26 (1947), pp. 5–41.

of blacks and whites is best explained by heredity rather than by environment (by nature rather than by nurture).[29]

Richard Herrnstein, a Harvard psychologist, is less concerned with race differences than with IQ differentials between occupations and social classes. The growing correlation between IQ scores and occupational standing is seen by Herrnstein as happy evidence of an advancing meritocracy.

> Intelligence tests, and the related aptitude tests, have more and more become society's instrument for the selection of human resources. Not only for the military, but for schools from secondary to professional, for industry, and for Civil Service, objective tests have eroded the traditional grounds for selection—family, social class, and, more important, money. The traditional grounds are, of course, not entirely gone, and some social critics wonder if they do not lurk surreptitiously behind the scenes in our definition of mental ability. . . . But at least on the face of it, there is a powerful trend toward meritocracy—the advancement of people on the basis of ability, either potential or fulfilled, measured objectively.[30]

The tighter the link between ability and monetary reward, Herrnstein argues, the better off society will be.

> The ties among I.Q., occupation and social standing make practical sense. The intellectual demands of engineering, for example, exceed those of ditch digging. Hence, engineers are brighter, on the average. If virtually anyone is smart enough to be a ditch digger, and only half the people are smart enough to be engineers, then society is, in effect, husbanding its intellectual resources by holding engineers in greater esteem, and, on the average, paying them more. . . . By directing its approval, admiration, and money towards certain occupations, society promotes their desirability, and hence, competition for them. To the extent that high intelligence confers a competitive advantage, society thereby expresses its recognition, however imprecise, of the importance and scarcity of intellectual ability.[31]

The analyses of Jensen and Herrnstein set liberal-environmentalist orthodoxy on its head. The ravages of poverty do not cause stupidity, as environ-

---

[29] Arthur Jensen, "How Much Can We Boost I.Q. and Scholastic Achievement?" *Harvard Educational Review*, Vol. 39 (1969), pp. 1–123. According to Jensen's analysis, "We are left with various lines of evidence, no one of which is definitive alone, but which, viewed altogether, make a not unreasonable hypothesis that genetic factors are strongly implicated in the average Negro–white intelligence difference. The preponderance of the evidence is, in my opinion, less consistent with the strictly environmental hypothesis than with a genetic hypothesis, which, of course, does not exclude the influence of environment or its interaction with genetic factors." See also William Shockley, "Models, Mathematics and the Moral Obligation to Diagnose the Origin of Negro I.Q. Deficits," *Review of Educational Research*, Vol. 40 (October 1970), pp. 369–377; William Shockley, "Dysgenics, Geneticity, Raceology: A Challenge to the Intellectual Responsibility of Educators," *Phi Delta Kappan* (January 1972), pp. 297–307; Michael Townsend and Brian Keeling, *Genetics and Education* (New York: Harper & Row, Publishers, Inc., 1972); Arthur Jensen, "The Differences Are Real," *Psychology Today*, Vol. 7 (December 1973), pp. 83–87; Arthur Jensen, "Relationship of Level I and Level II Cognitive Processes to Test of Associative Responding," *Journal of Educational Research*, Vol. 70 (January 1977), pp. 127–130; Hans J. Eysenck, *The I.Q. Argument: Race, Intelligence and Education* (La Salle, IL: Open Court Publishing Company, Library Press, 1971).

[30] Richard Herrnstein, *I.Q. in the Meritocracy* (Boston: Little, Brown & Company, 1973), pp. 60–61.

[31] Ibid., p. 124.

mentalists had long contended, rather, stupidity causes poverty. Educational programs designed to help the poor are bound to fail because the poor are, according to the hereditarians, ill equipped to benefit from them. In their view, government programs, designed to redistribute wealth or to provide job training, are doomed to fail for the same reason.[32]

The policy implications of this line of thought incorporate benign neglect, intensified tracking (designed to give poor children low-level job training commensurate with what hereditarians take to be their low-level potential), and maintenance of the status quo. If Adams's hope for a natural aristocracy has not yet been reached, the hereditarians insist that it is at least within our grasp. What is needed now, they tell us, is a more rigorous application of ability testing and an acceptance of the inevitability of inequality.

Classical Liberalism

Classical liberals inhabit the wide middle position in the meritocracy debate. In the last chapter, we distinguished between liberals and conservatives. Here we combine the two groups because, despite important differences, today they share some basic beliefs. Classical liberals, like hereditarians, support social stratification and the resultant inequalities associated with meritocratic competition. They are convinced that competition is a social mechanism for individual and social improvement. However, classical liberals see merit as springing from individual achievement rather than from family genetics and believe that talent is distributed widely (if not evenly) across the social strata. Classical liberals are sensitive to the possibility that the poor are not getting an equal opportunity to improve their position through fair competition. Of course, some classical liberals are more sensitive to this issue than others, but, as a matter of principle, classical liberals support the equal opportunity ideal.

Because classical liberals support the equal opportunity ideal, such thinkers are vehemently opposed to racism and prejudice in all their ugly guises. Daniel Bell, one of the most articulate and prolific of the classical liberal group, has written, "We must insist on a basic social equality, in that each person is to be

---

[32] Edward C. Banfield comes to a similar conclusion, although his arguments are not tied tightly to genetics: "So long as the city contains a sizable lower class, nothing can be done about its most serious problems. Good jobs may be offered to all, but some will remain chronically unemployed. Slums may be demolished, but if the housing that replaces them is occupied by the lower class it will shortly be turned into new slums. Welfare payments may be doubled or tripled and a negative income tax instituted, but some persons will continue to live in squalor and misery. New schools may be built, new curricula devised, and teacher–pupil ratio cut in half, but if children who attend these schools come from lower-class homes, the schools will be turned into blackboard jungles, and those who graduate or drop out from them will, in most cases, be functionally illiterate. The streets may be filled with armies of policemen, but violent crime and disorder will decrease very little. If, however, the lower class were to disappear—if, say, its members were overnight to acquire attitudes, motivations, and habits of the working class—the most serious and intractable problems of the city would all disappear with it. The lower-class forms of all problems are at bottom a single problem: the existence of an outlook and style of life which is radically present-oriented and which therefore attaches no values to work, sacrifice, self-improvement, or service to family, friends, or community." Edward C. Banfield, *The Unheavenly City Revisited* (Boston: Little, Brown & Company, 1974), pp. 234–235.

given respect and not humiliated on the basis of color, or sexual proclivities, or other personal attributes."[33]

Similarly, classical liberals are troubled by exploitive systems that place some workers at higher financial risk than others. Bell contends, "We should reduce invidious distinctions in work, whereby some persons are paid by the piece or the hour and others receive a salary by month or year, or a system whereby some persons receive a fluctuating wage on the basis of hours or weeks worked and others have a steady, calculable income."[34] Classical liberals are also disturbed by systems that allow the poor to suffer humiliation, hunger, and health problems while others enjoy prosperity. In Bell's view,

> We should assert that each person is entitled to a basic set of services and income which provides him with adequate medical care, housing, and the like. These are matters of security and dignity which must necessarily be the prior concerns of a civilized society.[35]

These conditions represent how far classic liberals are willing to go in the pursuit of equal opportunity. If these conditions are met (the elimination of racism, the eradication of invidious distinctions in work, the establishment of an economic floor below which no individual would be allowed to sink), most classical liberals would contend that we are well on the way to achieving a just society.

More ambitious efforts at equalizing opportunity are generally opposed by this group because, it is claimed, such efforts assault basic presuppositions of class. They disrupt social order and efficiency, disturb traditional definitions of fairness, and create a harmful backlash of resentment. Classic liberals admit (as hereditarians do not) "that the United States today is not a meritocracy," but they insist that this fact "does not discredit the principle."[36] Progress toward realizing the meritocratic ideal is likely to be made by an expansion of technology and increased economic growth (which pulls many blue-collar workers up to white-collar jobs) and by keeping the individual (rather than class, race, or gender) the primary unit of society.

Affirmative Action programs, bussing policies, and quotalike regulations emanating from Washington offices are usually opposed by classic liberals. They believe such policies put the group rather than the individual at the center of social policy. Peter and Brigitte Berger give clear expression to this concern:

> It is one thing for the Supreme Court to say in 1954 that to bar a child from a particular school solely because of his race was a violation of the child's rights: it is quite another thing for the Federal Courts and for agencies of the Federal Government to impose specific patterns of racial "balance" on school systems. It was one thing when both federal and state Fair Housing laws prohibited discrimination against individuals on the basis of race in the renting or selling of housing;

---

[33] Daniel Bell, *The Coming of Post-Industrial Society* (New York: Basic Books, Inc., Publishers, 1973), p. 452; available in paperback. Peter Berger, another of the classical liberal group, although he prefers the label *conservative*, has written, "Of all evils in American society, racial oppression is the most intolerable. Of all priorities for American society, the attainment of racial justice is the most urgent." Peter Berger and Brigitte Berger, "The Assault on Class," in Peter Berger, *Facing up to Modernity: Excursions in Society, Politics, and Religion* (New York: Basic Books, Inc., Publishers, 1977), p. 43.

[34] Bell, ibid., p. 452.

[35] Ibid.

[36] Ibid., p. 450.

it is quite another thing if political and legal power should now be used to design a demographic composition of a community or an entire region. Similarly, it was one thing for the Civil Rights Act of 1964 to prohibit racial discrimination in employment; the establishment of a system of racial and other group quotas by government fiat bears little resemblance to that original intention. One further commonality should be noted in each of these three cases. The original prospective actions were designed to test the rights of the individuals; the prescriptive policies now coming to the fore no longer focus on individuals but on collectivities. Indeed, it is becoming popular to cite the social desirability of furthering the collectivities in question (be they racial, ethnic, or other groups) in cases where the rights of an individual seem to be infringed upon. In other words, injury to the individual, regrettable though it may be, is legitimated in terms of this or that collective destiny. This constitutes not only a fundamental change of policies but an ideological reversal. Concern for the rights and welfare of the individual, regardless of his or her group membership, has been one of the great moral themes of modern liberalism. It is deeply ironic that a moral impetus rooted in this same liberalism should now be in process of giving birth to an ethic of collectivities that is profoundly illiberal in its implications.[37]

The classical liberal position accepts the existence of class and the desirability of achieved rather than ascribed status. Classical liberals support an equal opportunity society that is open at the top, provides economic protection at the bottom, and allows individuals to reap the rewards of their own efforts. They look at America's high mobility rates (albeit these rates are caused by the changing nature of occupations rather than by a lessening of status inheritance) and conclude that meritocracy is near at hand. Because social actions to increase the life-chances of the poor would entail a concentration on group privileges rather than on individual rights, they conclude that such changes are not wise.

The New Egalitarians

America has always had an active minority of egalitarians anxious to narrow the gap between the haves and the have-nots. Determined to provide all citizens with the means of participating fully in society, egalitarians have worked to secure voting rights and employment opportunities for minorities and women, to extend government services to the poor, and to narrow the extreme income differences between the top and the bottom of the economic ladder. With a few radical exceptions, early egalitarians looked very much like classic liberals. They share that group's loyalty to the equalization of opportunity.

Since the 1960s, however, egalitarians have moved further and further away from the classical liberal position. This change came as a result of the perceived failures of government efforts to change the social order through an equalization of educational opportunity.

The Kennedy and Johnson administrations made equal opportunity the centerpiece of social policy. Education was seen as the gateway to the middle class. The nation embarked on an unprecedented effort to expand the life-chances of the poor through better schooling. This effort was not a matter of equalizing educational equipment or diverting high-quality teachers to schools in poor neighborhoods; it was instead a massive attempt to give impoverished children the educational extras they needed to break the gravitational pull of poverty.

[37] Peter Berger and Brigitte Berger, "The Assault on Class," p. 49.

Head Start programs offered preschoolers the educational stimulation they were not getting at home; Follow Through programs were designed to help these same children progress through the early grades of the public school; Title I funding provided millions of dollars to improve the achievement of low-status schools at the elementary and secondary level.

The results of these programs will be discussed in the last section. Suffice it to say here that egalitarians were distressed by the apparent lack of success of these compensatory education programs. Such programs, they concluded, were not going to end the cycle of poverty or narrow the chasm that separated the rich from the poor in America.

This conclusion spurred many egalitarians to a new analysis of the American economic system. What was it, they asked, that really caused economic inequality? The question was, of course, not new, but new sociological and statistical research methods were available to dig out an answer.

Christopher Jencks and a team of seven colleagues at Harvard undertook a five-year reanalysis of an enormous body of prior research in an effort to discover the roots of inequality. The general conclusion was startling: Neither family background, cognitive skill, nor educational or occupational attainment fully explained inequality.

> We cannot blame economic inequality primarily on genetic differences in men's capacity for abstract reasoning, since there is nearly as much economic inequality among men with equal test scores as among men in general. We cannot blame economic inequality primarily on the fact that parents pass along their disadvantages to their children, since there is nearly as much inequality among men whose parents had the same economic status as among men in general. We cannot blame economic inequality on differences between schools, since differences between schools seem to have very little effect on any measurable attributes of those who attend them.[38]

Jencks amassed substantial evidence that the hereditarian analysis of society was wrong: Neither cognitive ability nor education was the key determinant to success. He had evidence that the classic liberals were mistaken as well: The determinants of family background and schooling were not major contributors to success. In other words, variations in income were not strongly related to any of the factors normally associated with inequality. "Economic success," Jencks concluded, "seems to depend on varieties of luck and on-the-job competence that are only moderately related to family background, schooling, or scores on standardized tests."[39]

The conclusion that luck and peculiar competencies (the ability to sing, pitch a baseball, win votes, or make quick boardroom decisions) were the major determinants of success contradicted the meritocracy analysis of classic liberals and the policies that emanated from that analysis. Because luck and individual competence were not directly changeable through government action, the way to reduce inequality was not by equalizing opportunity (how could one equalize luck?) but by redistributing wealth. As Jencks put it,

> Instead of trying to make everyone equally lucky or equally good at his job, we would have to devise "insurance" systems which neutralize the effects of luck, and

[38] Christopher Jencks et al., *Inequality*, p. 8.
[39] Ibid.

income-sharing systems which break the link between vocational success and living standards.[40]

Jencks's suggestions for education were no less radical than his income-distribution recommendations.

> Given: a) that differences in schooling have only minor effects on cognitive achievement, and b) that equalizing opportunity is almost impossible without reducing the absolute inequalities that lead to unequal opportunities, we must abandon the notion of education as a means to some non-educational end. Rather, we should view education in the context of the internal life of schools and try to equalize distribution of those resources that affect the immediate experience of schooling, forgetting entirely the idea of long-term benefits.[41]

In a second, even more ambitious project, Jencks and eleven colleagues looked again at the causes of success and reported their findings in *Who Gets Ahead?*[42] Working with vastly improved data, the team produced an elaborate portrait of American society. It was a picture of a class-ridden system where family factors (income and education of parents, number of siblings, race, and ethnicity) have a dominant impact on a child's future occupational status. It was a portrait of a rigid system where early test scores divide students into two groups: those with promise and those without. This grouping shapes the academic expectations of children themselves and of others toward them. It was a portrait of a superficial system that rewards such surface characteristics as college credentials, skin color, and symbols of class more thoroughly than knowledge, ability, ambition, and moral character.[43] The combined influences of family background, test scores, education, and adolescent personality development account for between 70 and 75 percent of a person's future occupational status and 35 to 50 percent of future earnings. (See Figure 21-3.)

Unlike *Inequality,* the Harvard team's earlier work, *Who Gets Ahead?* puts much less emphasis on luck. Jencks, however, stood by his conclusion that the only effective way to reduce inequality is instituting programs for direct economic redistribution. The conclusion to be drawn from *Who Gets Ahead?* is that there is no single determinant of success in America (neither family, schooling, IQ, nor personality) but that the combination of these factors gives some people great advantage over others. People with one or two things going for them (say, intelligence and perseverance) have only an average chance of success. Others with a series of advantages (say, high-status parents, high-status college education, average intelligence, and the ability to create a good impression) have a good chance at success. Programs that attempt to minimize the arbitrary advantages of birth and maximize the effects of hard work and ability are a long way from succeeding. Equality of opportunity cannot be achieved by the educational system alone. As Samuel Bowles, another egalitarian, expresses it,

---

[40] Ibid., p. 9.

[41] Donald Levine and Mary Jo Bane, *The "Inequality" Controversy: Schooling and Distributive Justice* (New York: Basic Books, Inc., Publishers, 1975), p. 5.

[42] Jencks et al., *Who Gets Ahead?*

[43] For a short interpretation of Jencks's work, see Daniel Yankelovitch, "Who Gets Ahead in America?" *Psychology Today,* Vol. 13 (July 1979), pp. 28–34, 40–43.

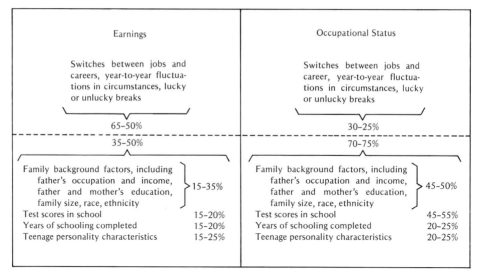

Figure 21-3   Influences on success: Factors affecting differences in earnings and occupational status (men, 25 to 65 years old, as of the early 1970s).   (*Source: Psychology Today*. July 1979, p. 33. Copyright © 1979. American Psychological Association. Reprinted by permission.)

> The achievement of some degree of equality of opportunity depends in part on what we do in the educational system but also, to a very large degree, in what we do elsewhere in the economy, in the polity, and in the society as a whole.[44]

Egalitarians urge classic liberals to acknowledge this fact and to join them in calling for a direct assault on the vast disparity between the rich and the poor in America. "We are . . . disturbed by the fact that the best-paid fifth of all white workers earn 600 percent more than the worst-paid fifth."[45] Egalitarians are also disturbed that families pass social-class advantages and disadvantages on to their children. Richard deLone uses mobility and opportunity data to show the power of class in American society. He asks us to imagine two second-grade boys, one named Bobby and the other Jimmy. They are both attentive students, reading above grade level and both have slightly better than average IQ scores. The only significant difference between the two boys is that Jimmy's father is a successful lawyer, whose salary puts him in the highest 10 percent of American workers, and Bobby's father is a custodian, whose salary puts him in the lowest 10 percent of American workers. What does life hold for these two children? Of course, we cannot tell in any exact sense, but statistical data make it possible to calculate their relative life-chances. Jimmy is four times more likely than Bobby to go to college and at least twelve times more likely to graduate. By the time he is 40, Jimmy is twenty-seven times more likely than Bobby to earn a salary equivalent to that of Jimmy's affluent father.[46] These

---

[44] Samuel Bowles, "Toward Equality of Educational Opportunity," in *Equal Educational Opportunity*, expansion of the Winter 1968, special issue, *Harvard Educational Review* (Cambridge: Harvard University Press, 1969), p. 121.
[45] Christopher Jencks et al., *Inequality*, p. 14.
[46] Richard H. deLone, *Small Futures*, pp. 3–4.

are disturbing findings for anyone who believes in the meritocratic ideal. Yet, deLone's calculations were made from data collected in less economically troubled times. Today, Bobby's life-chances are not as good. And if Bobby is black or female or both, his or her life-chances are even worse.

The new egalitarians contend that until the economic disparity between the rich and the poor is diminished, it is folly to think these groups can compete on anything approaching equal terms. For that reason, new egalitarians call for a radical redistribution of American wealth. They also call on schools to teach an emancipatory curriculum. By this they mean that schools should help working-class students analyze their position in society and actively encourage them to become politically active in support of democratic socialism.[47]

The analysis and suggestions of the new egalitarians are not new; in the 1930s George Counts was encouraging educators to help build a new social order.[48] However, like Counts, the new egalitarians are finding it difficult to convince teachers to abandon their historical effort to perfect the meritocratic ideal.

Summary

This chapter began with the question. Is America an open society that allows social mobility? The answer you give to this question depends on whether you are inclined to see the glass as half full or half empty.

Those who tend to see the glass as half full would be impressed by the Blau and Duncan data that indicate that over half (56.4 percent) of American men are upwardly mobile. They would be gratified by other data that indicate that mobility in America is as high or higher than in other industrialized nations.[49] They would be heartened by the findings of Hauser and his associates that mobility rates have increased slightly in recent years, and they would be further encouraged by data that indicate that there has been a general upgrading of salaries in the country. Although this upgrading does not alter the relative distribution of wealth in America, it does improve the living conditions of most people in the society.[50]

Those who see the glass as half empty would focus on a different set of findings and come to less optimistic conclusions. Although they would acknowledge the benefits of economic mobility, they would stress that mobility is associated with an expanding economy more than with an expanding meritocracy. In their view, this is important to consider, especially in a time of declining economic growth. If the economy ceases to expand at an accelerated rate, we can expect a new hardening of class lines in America. These would encourage us to consider the possible social consequences of educating American young people for new white-collar positions that may not materialize in a restricted economy.

Social scientists are more widely divided on the equality of opportunity issue

---

[47] Stanley Aronowitz and Henry A. Giroux, *Education Under Siege: The Conservative, Liberal and Radical Debate Over Schooling* (South Hadley, MA: Bergin & Garvey Publishers, 1985).

[48] George S. Counts, *Dare the Schools Build a New Social Order?* (Carbandale, IL: Southern Illinois University Press, 1978 [1932]). Available in paperback.

[49] Gerald Lenski, *Power and Privilege* (New York: McGraw-Hill Book Company, 1966), p. 411.

[50] Seymour Martin Lipset, "Social Mobility and Equal Opportunity," *Public Interest*, Vol. 29 (Fall 1972), pp. 90–98.

than are Americans in general. Their myriad opinions can be collectively discussed under three headings: the hereditarian position, the classic liberal position, and the new egalitarian position.

Hereditarians interpret social science evidence to mean that, largely, merit is genetically determined. They conclude that the inequalities in America today are the result of "natural" rather than "artificial" differences among people.

Social scientists taking the classic liberal position support the traditional notion of a "natural aristocracy," which, if given the chance, will rise by merit to positions of power and prestige. They support the ideal of equal opportunity and generally contend that opportunities have increased in the last century. They are not convinced, however, that we have yet reached a truly meritocratic society. Most would be willing to establish an economic floor to ensure that everyone enjoys the basic necessities of life. They are distrustful, however, of programs designed to help groups rather than to protect individual rights.

The third group, the new egalitarians, question both the efficacy and the morality of the social-class system. Their analysis of today's social stratification shows that the American economic system protects the class position of the wealthy and systematically limits the opportunities of the poor. They see America as too class bound to allow significant mobility by merit.

Some egalitarians move their argument far away from traditional quarrels over social class. Why, they ask, in a society that claims a distaste for such arbitrary advantages as aristocracy and wealth, should we not be equally repelled by other chance advantages like athletic ability, good looks, high IQ scores, or a facility for leadership? John Rawls states the case:

> There is no more reason to permit the distribution of income and wealth to be settled by the distribution of natural assets than by historical and social fortune. Furthermore, the principle of fair opportunity can be only imperfectly carried out, at least as long as the institution of the family exists. The extent to which natural capacities develop and reach fruition is affected by all kinds of social conditions and class attitudes. Even the willingness to make an effort, to try, and so to be deserving in the ordinary sense is itself dependent upon happy family and social circumstances. It is impossible in practice to secure equal chances of achievement and culture for those similarly endowed, and therefore we may want to adopt a principle which recognizes this fact and also mitigates the arbitrary effects of the natural lottery itself.[51]

If we cannot secure equality of opportunity, so the egalitarians claim, we should attempt to secure an equality of results. Suggestions on how far we should go toward equalizing income differ, depending on which egalitarian one reads, but all are united in the belief that the gap that separates the rich from the poor must be significantly reduced before we can claim to be a just society.

Suggested Readings

Books and articles that investigate the degree to which the American educational system supports the meritocratic hypothesis:

Collins, Randall. *The Credential Society: An Historical Sociology of Education and Stratification.* New York: Academic Press, Inc., 1979.

---

[51] John Rawls, *A Theory of Justice* (Cambridge: Harvard University Press, 1971), p. 74. Available in paperback.

CURTIS, R. F., and E. F. JACKSON. *Inequality in American Communities.* New York: Academic Press, Inc., 1977.

GIARELLI, JAMES M., and RODMAN B. WEBB. "Higher Education, Meritocracy and Distributive Justice," *Educational Studies,* Vol. 2 (Fall, 1980), pp. 221–238.

HURN, CHRISTOPHER J. *The Limits and Possibilities of Schooling.* Boston: Allyn & Bacon, Inc., 1978.

REHBERG, RICHARD, and EVELYN ROSENTHAL. *Class and Merit in the American High School: An Assessment of the Revisionist and Meritocratic Argument.* New York: Longman Group Limited, 1978.

TESCONI, CHARLES A., JR., and EMANUEL HURWITZ, JR. *Education for Whom? The Question of Equal Educational Opportunities.* New York: Dodd, Mead & Company, 1974.

THE HEREDITARIAN POSITION

BLOCK, N. J., and GERALD DWORKIN, eds. *The I.Q. Controversy.* New York: Pantheon Books, 1976. This useful collection of essays helps sort out the IQ controversy.

EYSENCK, HANS J. *The I.Q. Argument: Race, Intelligence and Education.* La Salle, IL: Open Court Publishing Company, 1971.

HERRNSTEIN, RICHARD. *I.Q. in the Meritocracy.* Boston: Little, Brown, & Company, 1973.

JENSEN, ARTHUR. "How Much Can We Boost I.Q. and Scholastic Achievement?" *Harvard Educational Review,* Vol. 39 (1969), pp. 1–123.

JENSEN, ARTHUR. *Genetics and Education.* New York: Harper & Row, Publishers, 1972.

JENSEN, ARTHUR. *Bias in Mental Testing.* New York: The Free Press, 1980.

KAMIN, LEON J. *The Science and Politics of I.Q.* New York: Wiley, 1974. This is a critical discussion of the hereditarian position and the use of IQ tests to determine merit.

THE CLASSIC LIBERAL POSITION

BELL, DANIEL. *The Coming of Post-Industrial Society: A Venture into Social Forecasting.* New York: Basic Books, Inc., Publishers, 1973.

BERGER, PETER, and BRIGITTE BERGER. "The Assault on Class," in *Facing up to Modernity,* edited by Peter Berger. New York: Basic Books, Inc., Publishers, 1977, pp. 43–55.

LIPSET, SEYMOUR MARTIN. "Social Mobility and Equal Opportunity," *Public Interest,* Vol. 29 (1972), pp. 90–98.

MOSTELLER, FREDERICK, and DANIEL P. MOYNIHAN, eds. *On Equality of Educational Opportunity.* New York: Random House, Inc., 1972. See especially Chapter 1.

MOYNIHAN, DANIEL. "Sources of Resistance to the Coleman Report," *Harvard Educational Review,* Vol. 38 (1969), pp. 25–38.

THE NEW EGALITARIAN POSITION

APPLE, MICHAEL W., and LOIS WEIS, eds. *Ideology and Practice in Schooling.* Philadelphia: Temple University Press, 1983.

ARONOWITZ, STANLEY, and HENRY A. GIROUX. *Education Under Siege: The Conservative Liberal and Radical Debate over Schooling.* South Hadley, MA: Bergin & Garvey Publishers, 1985.

BOWLES, SAMUEL, and HERBERT GINTIS. *Schooling in Capitalist America: Educational Reform and the Contradictions of Economic Life.* New York: Basic Books, Inc., Publishers, 1976.

CONNELL, R. W., D. J. Ashenden, S. Kessler, and G. W. DOWSETT. *Making the Difference: Schools, Families and Social Division.* Sydney, Australia: George Allen & Unwin, 1982.

GIROUX, HENRY A. *Theory and Resistance in Education.* South Hadley, MA: Bergin & Garvey Publishers, 1983.

WILLIS, PAUL. *Learning to Labor.* New York: Teachers College Press, 1981.

CHAPTER 22

Race, Poverty, Democracy, and the Common School

The Politics of Inclusion

Public education in the United States has been dominated by an ideology of inclusion. The civic aims of education, as we learned in Chapter 7, rest on the assumption that schools are instruments of socialization and that important benefits accrue when the children of all economic classes are educated in the same schools and the same classrooms. Thus, from the early days of the republic, Americans have shared a commitment to free schools where all the children of a community are educated together. We call such institutions *common schools* because they are open to all and promote values that community members hold in common. Inherent in the common-school ideology is the belief that all children must come to understand and appreciate civic virtues and democratic values. It is part of our common faith that schools contribute to social harmony, strengthen democracy, and help mold a population of disparate cultures into a single nation. At the same time, we hope that common schools will promote self-respect and creative intelligence, and will enhance the life-chances of disadvantaged children.

Of course, common schools and the ideology of inclusion have been contested throughout our history. There have always been those who wished to separate the children of various classes into different schools. These individuals and groups generally have been overpowered by the nation's commitment to common school education.

Though the politics of inclusion usually have triumphed in political debates involving social class, the same cannot be said about race. Here, the resistance to inclusion has been fierce and the forces supporting racial segregation in public schools have been powerful. The United States has a long history of racial prejudice and, because of that prejudice, the nation has tolerated overt and covert efforts to exclude minorities from free, equal, and integrated public education. Americans also have tolerated a contradiction between the American creed (which extols the virtues of freedom, equality, opportunity, and lib-

The civic aims of education rest on the assumption that there are benefits when the children of all economic classes are educated together. (*Source:* National Education Association, Joe Di Dio.)

erty) and the systematic practice of racial discrimination.[1] Racial minorities have had to struggle against great odds to gain the rights denied them by the majority and a great part of that struggle has centered on the right to be educated. Minorities have persisted, however, because they have viewed education as a vehicle to freedom and full citizenship.

In this chapter, we will discuss the role education has played in the struggle for racial equality. We will examine racism—why it exists and how it is maintained—and review what social science tells us about eliminating racial prejudice. We will sketch some of the battles blacks have fought to gain access to public education and will point out what those battles have accomplished. We end the chapter with a discussion of where the equality struggle stands today and what challenges lie ahead.

Prejudice, Discrimination, and Racism

The terms *prejudice, discrimination,* and *racism* are often used interchangeably, but they have different meanings. *Prejudice* refers to a negative attitude toward a group. Because prejudice refers to an attitude, it is not an observable entity.

---

[1] Gunnar Myrdal, *An American Dilemma: The Negro Problem and Modern Democracy* (New York: Harper & Brothers, 1944).

Prejudice is a mental construct that is both evaluative and enduring. *Discrimination*, on the other hand, refers to observable behavior. People act on their prejudices and give preferential treatment to members of their own group and less favorable treatment to other groups. The United States Commission on Civil Rights defines *racism* as, "any attitude, action, or institutional structure which subordinates a person because of his or her color."[2] By this definition, racism involves both prejudicial attitudes and discriminatory practices.

Theories of Prejudice

Researchers have been studying the causes and dynamics of prejudice since almost the beginning of social science and have produced a number of theories to help us understand why prejudice exists, how it is maintained, and what can be done to eliminate it. The theories of prejudice can be classified under four broad headings: group conflict theory, social learning theory, cognitive process theory, and psychodynamic theory. We will examine these theories separately but will show later that they are not necessarily inconsistent and, in fact, complement one another.

Group Conflict Theories

Group conflict theory focuses on the social causes and social dynamics of racial prejudices. Proponents of the theory contend that prejudice develops when two or more groups find themselves in competition for scarce resources. It does not matter what those resources might be—jobs, money, territory, status, awards, recognition, mating opportunities—the greater the competition for scarce resources, the greater the chances that prejudicial attitudes will begin to form.

The focus of conflict theory is on the group rather than the individual. Conflict theorists ask why groups hold prejudicial attitudes rather than why a single individual is prejudiced. According to this theory, groups hold the deepest feelings of prejudice when they feel threatened by some other identifiable group.[3] Thus, when minority workers begin to compete for jobs traditionally held by whites, it becomes more likely that threatened whites will form negative attitudes toward minority workers. Examples of this phenomenon occurred recently in fishing communities in Texas, Florida, and California.

Vietnamese immigrants entered the fishing industry in these areas and, because they were talented and hard-working, soon became more economically successful than the local fishermen. Hard work and improved methods are usually respected in a free market economy, but the local fishermen were angered by the quick success of this new group of immigrants. In Texas, Vietnamese fishing boats were burned, homes were fire bombed, and a packing plant that employed Vietnamese refugees was destroyed. Hooded Ku Klux Klansmen rode out on fishing boats to harass Vietnamese fishermen. In Cali-

[2] The United States Commission on Civil Rights, *Racism in America and How to Combat It* (Washington, DC: U.S. Government Printing Office, 1969), p. 1.

[3] Myron Rothbart, "Achieving Racial Equality: An Analysis of Resistance to Social Reform," in *Toward the Elimination of Racism*, ed. Phyllis A. Katz (New York: Pergamon Press, 1976). Available in paperback.

fornia, some buyers, under pressure from white fishermen, refused to deal with the Vietnamese. Local fishing groups in Florida convinced the state to outlaw the use of the large nets used on Vietnamese fishing vessels.[4] According to conflict theory, the kind of prejudicial attitudes and discriminatory behavior displayed by white and Hispanic fishermen toward the Vietnamese is explained by the threat to other fishermen posed by the success of the Vietnamese.

Whether a group's interests are threatened by another group is, in part at least, a subjective matter. People may perceive a threat that is not there or think that a tangible threat is larger than it really is. To account for the subjective factor, researchers have introduced the notion of *relative deprivation*. This term refers to people's perception that they (individually or as a group) are deprived relative to some other "less deserving" group.[5] Thus, whites may begin to feel antagonistic when they believe that blacks are making more economic progress than they are. Men may feel hostile when they perceive that women are being given preferential treatment on the job.[6] Middle-class parents may become antagonistic if they think that the bulk of college scholarship money goes to the children of the poor. Apparently, the threat does not have to be experienced directly by all members of the group for prejudical attitudes to take hold. Group members appear to be quite sensitive to symbolic signs of their group's well-being.

Conflict theory holds that prejudice is the result of frustration and the *perception* that one group is blocking the deserved aspirations of another. As frustration mounts, so does prejudice. When a group loses hope that they will better their situation, it becomes more likely that they will resort to violence. The racial violence directed at the Vietnamese fishermen is an example of what can happen when the frustration over relative deprivation rises to the boiling point.

Social Learning Theory

Supporters of social learning theory contend that prejudicial attitudes must be "carefully taught." The most obvious source of such information is the family where parents pass on the social norms (including prejudices) of their reference group to their own children. Sometimes these lessons are passed on overtly, through direct statements, and sometimes subtly, through behavior and body language. Children acquire prejudiced attitudes in the normal course of socialization and when they grow up, pass on those same prejudices to their children.[7]

Studies suggest that racial awareness is acquired early in a child's life, beginning before the age of three and becoming well established before the child enters the first grade.[8] Of course, racial awareness is not always attached to

[4] Karl Zinsmeister, "Asians: Prejudice Top and Bottom," *Public Opinion*, Vol. 10, No. 2 (July–August 1987), pp. 8–10, 59.

[5] M. Bernstein and F. Crosby, "An Empirical Examination of Relative Deprivation Theory," *Journal of Experimental Social Psychology*, Vol. 16, (1980), pp. 442–456.

[6] Teacher status panic, a phenomenon we examined in Chapter 10, provides another example of how a group can feel deprived relative to other segments of society.

[7] R. D. Ashmore and F. K. Del Boca, "Conceptual Approaches to Stereotypes and Stereotyping," in *Cognitive Processes in Stereotyping and Intergroup Behavior*, ed. D. L. Hamilton (Hillsdale NJ: Erlbaum, 1981).

[8] Phyllis A. Katz, "The Acquisition of Racial Attitudes in Children: Can the Twig Be Straightened?" in *Toward the Elimination of Racism*, ed. Phyllis A. Katz, pp. 125–150.

prejudice, but if parents are prejudiced, children are likely to pick up those attitudes at an early age. School experiences may reinforce the lessons learned at home or contradict those lessons. If a child's school experience reinforces home-learned prejudices, those attitudes will be very difficult to change in later years.[9]

The homes and schools teach vital lessons about tolerance and intolerance and so do the media. Those lessons sometimes carry negative stereotypes that reinforce prejudicial attitudes learned elsewhere. For example, in a content analysis of prime-time television series between 1955 and 1986, researchers found that blacks and Hispanics have been underrepresented, though progress has been made in some areas in recent years.[10] Blacks made up less than 1 percent of the characters on TV in the 1960s. Today, 10 percent of TV characters are black and of that percentage, 15 percent have starring roles. More frequently than ever before, blacks are being portrayed positively and are sometimes seen working in harmony with whites. Some differences still remain, however. Blacks are twice as likely as whites to play lower-middle class characters who have not graduated from high school. The researchers point out that "during the past three decades, whites have portrayed 94 percent of the educated professionals and business executives [and] blacks have portrayed 5 percent."[11] Other studies show that appearances on TV by blacks tend to be brief and, in most cases, show little interaction between blacks and whites. Cross-racial interactions tended to be formal, even ritualistic, especially when they involved men and women.[12]

The picture is less positive for Hispanics. This group represents only 2 percent of today's TV characters, a figure that has not changed in three decades. When Hispanics were shown on prime-time TV, they played negative characters 41 percent of the time. These characters were twice as likely as whites to commit crimes and the crimes they committed were more likely to be violent.[13]

A child who takes in the accumulative lessons taught by TV might believe that whites seldom interact with minorities, that their interactions are more formal than personal, and that most blacks and Hispanics hold poorly paid, nonprofessional jobs. Perhaps this is an improvement over what TV offered in the past, but such messages do little to counteract racial stereotypes. On the other hand, it is fair to say that TV programs do occasionally condemn racism and seldom support obvious prejudices.

Social learning theory maintains that prejudicial attitudes are learned at home, from parents and siblings, from the media, from the peer group, and from larger reference groups. The lessons are sometimes overt and sometimes subtle, but once prejudicial attitudes are in place, they are difficult to dislodge. After all, such attitudes are not independent thoughts; they are tied to an individual's view of the world and supported by people the individual loves and admires. Giving up prejudices learned at home and reinforced in the local

---

[9] Ibid., pp. 213–235.

[10] S. Robert Lichter, Linda S. Litchter, Stanley Rothman, and Daniel Amundson, "Prime-time Prejudice: TVs Image of Blacks and Hispanics," *Public Opinion*, Vol. 10, No. 2 (July–August 1987), pp. 13–16.

[11] Ibid., p. 16.

[12] R. H. Weigel, J. W. Loomis, and M. J. Soja, "Race Relations on Prime Time Television," *Journal of Personality and Social Psychology*, Vol. 39 (1980), pp. 884–893.

[13] Lichter, Litchter, Rothman, and Amundson, "Prime-time Prejudice," p. 16.

community means that an individual must adjust his or her thinking in many sensitive areas.

Cognitive Process Theories

Group conflict theory and social learning theory examine how prejudices are manufactured and maintained by groups within the culture or by the culture as a whole. *Cognitive process* theorists move the analysis to the level of the individual. These theorists are interested in how individuals perceive the world and the mental processes that influence individual perception. Human beings do not perceive everything that the world puts before them. We see some things and we do not see others; some things are relevant to the problem at hand and grab our attention (a car is honking behind us) and some things are unimportant and so we ignore them (we don't notice the color of the driver's necktie, unless, of course, we manufacture ties). The processes of selecting some things for attention and ignoring others is seldom voluntary. The selection process goes on below the level of conscious reflection or, to borrow a term from philosophy, *prereflectively*.

The processes of perception and prereflection are made possible by the ability of people to classify objects, individuals, groups, and ideas by type. Some things are seen as dangerous and others safe; some can be eaten while others should be avoided; some are heavy and others light. The process of classifying things into categories was called *typification* in Chapter 4. There, we suggested that children learn at an early age that people can be classified by type. Some individuals are male, others female; some short, others tall; some fat, others thin; some pleasant, others difficult; some are white and others are shades of black, brown, red, or yellow.

Typifications are organized in the mind and form schema. *Schema* are organized cognitive structures that include information, typifications, emotions, and values. For example, the schema we may have of a computer hacker[14] might be of someone, usually a male, who owns a computer; has great knowledge of and interest in programming but is primarily interested in the machine itself; possesses great powers of concentration; demands perfection; is compelled by things that can be brought under his control; works late into the night; feels a bit different from his peers, and therefore has a restricted social life; feels uncomfortable conforming to school regulations and certain cultural norms; watches *Star Trek* reruns; and reads books like Pirsig's *Zen and the Art of Motorcycle Maintenance* and Florman's *The Existential Pleasures of Engineering*.[15]

Schema are important because they help us efficiently process enormous quantities of information.[16] Of course, schema may not be accurate and some are more open to modification than others. In any case, schema help us know what to expect in various situations. Violations of what is expected help us learn new things and thus modify the schema, making it more accurate and

---

[14] See Sherry Turkle, *The Second Self: Computers and the Human Spirit* (New York: Simon and Schuster, 1984), especially Chapter 6. Available in paperback.

[15] Robert Pirsig, *Zen and the Art of Motorcycle Maintenance* (New York: Bantam Books, 1979); and Robert Florman, *The Existential Pleasures of Engineering* (New York: St. Martin's Press, 1976). Both available in paperback.

[16] S. T. Fiske and S. Taylor, *Social Cognition* (Reading, MA: Addison-Wesley, 1984).

more useful. When schema refer to groups of people and are not open to easy modification, they are called *stereotypes*. Stereotypes are more directive than most schema. They tend to censor information that is not in tune with an individual's prejudices. For example, in one classic study, subjects briefly were shown a picture of black and white people riding together on the subway. One person was holding a knife. When the picture was removed and subjects were asked to describe what they had seen, prejudiced subjects said that the knife was being held by a black man. In fact, however, the knife was held by a white. The respondents were not lying to the researchers; the stereotypes were so powerful that they actually changed what the subjects perceived.

Psychodynamic Theories

The last category includes *psychodynamic* theories of prejudice. These theories focus not on the cognitive processes of individuals in general, but in the personalities of specific individuals. The best known of the psychodynamic theories grows out of the work of Adorno and others on the authoritarian personality.[17] This work grew out of a post-World War II interest in what made people susceptible to Nazism and anti-Semitism. Adorno and his colleagues found that prejudiced individuals

- are conforming and tend to adhere rigidly to middle-class, conventional values;
- are uncritically submissive to authority;
- value punishment;
- distrust feelings, imagination, and tendermindedness;
- are superstitious and employ "magical thinking";
- see people in terms of rigid stereotypes;
- respect power and toughness;
- display a generalized hostility and distrust of others;
- view the world in conspiratorial terms; and
- have an exaggerated interest in sexual matters.

An archetypal authoritarian personality is embodied in Archie Bunker, the almost lovable bigot in the popular TV series, *All in the Family*. The series was well named because Adorno and his colleagues believed that the personality characteristics just listed are developed in childhood and may be reinforced by historical events. Authoritarian parents raise authoritarian children. Such parents brook no disobedience from their offspring and rigidly enforce conventional values. When children disobey they are likely to be punished physically and with ridicule. Gloria, Archie's daughter, escaped her father's authoritarianism because her upbringing was mediated by her sensitive and accepting mother.

Historical events can reinforce authoritarian values. In a series of interesting studies, Sales found that comic strip characters are more likely to display power and toughness in periods of economic instability and that books on the occult and astrology sell best in periods of social disruption.[18]

---

[17] T. W. Adorno, Else Frankel-Brunswik, Daniel J. Levinson, and R. Nevitt Sanford, *The Authoritarian Personality* (New York: Harper, 1950).

[18] S. M. Sales, "Threats as a Factor in Authoritarianism: An Analysis of Archival Data," *Journal of Personality and Social Psychology*, Vol. 28, pp. 44–57.

A problem with Adorno's work was that it focused exclusively on right-wing authoritarianism and did not explain the prejudices of the left. For example, Adorno's research gives us no insight into the equally rigid thinking of Mike, Archie Bunker's politically liberal son-in-law. In order to remedy the limitations of Adorno's work, Rokeach and others investigated *dogmatism,* which they defined as the tendency to be closed-minded and authoritarian, independent of any particular political ideology. Not surprisingly, Rokeach found that dogmatism and a propensity toward prejudice exist on both ends of the political spectrum.[19]

A Comparison of the Four Theories of Prejudice

The four categories of prejudice theories are not necessarily inconsistent with each other. Each theory addresses the problem of prejudice at a different level. Social learning theory and group conflict theory analyze prejudice at the level of small or large groups. Cognitive process theory and psychodynamic theory move the analysis down to the individual level. Thus, all the theories may assist us in understanding how prejudice actually works, and no single theory offers a complete explanation.

It appears that prejudice and discrimination are caused by a complex interaction of events. For example, prejudice and discrimination do not always appear when groups compete over scarce resources. However, if group members have been raised to think of the competing group in stereotypical terms, prejudice might develop. Cognitive theory tells us how stereotypes influence perceptions. Once a group begins to think in stereotypical terms, its perceptions will reinforce its prejudices and a vicious feedback loop is created: Prejudice distorts perception and perception reinforces prejudice, which, in turn, increases the distortion. You have experienced such things yourself. When a person does something that angers you in one area, you may begin to find fault with the person in other areas as well. The tension mounts until something is done to interrupt the cycle. Psychodynamic theory tells us that all people can harbor prejudicial attitudes, but some people are particularly prone to think in rigid terms.

Reducing Prejudice

Deeply held, culturally reinforced prejudices are extremely difficult to dislodge. The reason that prejudice is so tenacious is found in the theories just examined. Many children are socialized to take certain prejudices for granted. They learn at home and in their neighborhood to trust some people but to be suspicious of others. Prejudicial attitudes often serve the interests of one group and help group members believe they are entitled to certain advantages over others in the competition for resources. Once again, prejudices distort perceptions and distorted perceptions reinforce prejudices. All these pieces fit tightly together and provide groups with a degree of comfort and solidarity. No wonder, then, that prejudiced individuals feel threatened when their attitudes are challenged. The theories also suggest ways in which prejudice might be reduced. Most, as we shall see, involve bringing knowledge to individuals, be-

[19] Milton Rokeach, *The Open and Closed Mind* (New York: Basic Books, 1960).

cause prejudice feeds on ignorance. This is one reason that schools in a democracy must work to promote creative intelligence and to retard prejudice, discrimination, and racism. Prejudice is an example of what happens when people begin to think narrowly and act unreasonably.

Role Playing

Jane Eliot, a third-grade teacher, wanted to do something to combat prejudice in her school. She knew that her eight-year-olds would not grasp a sophisticated concept like prejudice unless she brought it close to their own experience. Ms. Elliot informed the class that it was a well-established fact that blue-eyed children were better looking, better behaved, smarter, and cleaner than brown-eyed children. As you might imagine, this came as a surprise to her pupils. However, the biggest surprise was yet to come. She told the class that she was going to withhold privileges from the brown-eyed children because they were less deserving and was going to give extra privileges to their blue-eyed classmates because they were superior. She went out of her way to criticize brown-eyed kids and to praise those with blue eyes.

The brown-eyed children were distressed to hear of their second-class citizenship, and their blue-eyed classmates celebrated their new status. Friendships that had existed throughout the year ended abruptly as in-group children refused to play with their out-group classmates. Names were called, arguments broke out, and tears were shed.

The next day the tables were turned. The teacher told the class that she had made a mistake and that it was the blue-eyed children who were inferior. Roles were immediately switched as brown-eyed kids took revenge on their newly humbled classmates. At the end of the day, the teacher admitted that she had not told them the truth and asked her surprised and relieved pupils to share their thoughts and feelings.[20] In the course of the conversation, much of what social scientists know about prejudice was revealed.

There is evidence that such experiments do diminish prejudice in children and adults and that the changes appear to last for some time.[21] It seems that playing the role of someone who is oppressed brings first-hand experience and a good deal of knowledge. That knowledge increases a person's ability to empathize with others who suffer the consequences of arbitrary oppression. However, teachers must think carefully before rushing into exercises in classroom prejudice. Such experiments demand great attention to every child's well-being and careful monitoring to be sure that the situation does not get out of control. Only teachers who have received training should attempt such an experiment and then only with the cooperation of the administration and parents.

Group Contact

Another source of information is group contact. After all, stereotypes are easy to maintain when we have little contact with the group we are prejudging. But,

[20] M. J. Weiner and F. E. Wright, "The Effects of Undergoing Arbitrary Discrimination upon Subsequent Attitudes toward a Minority Group," *Journal of Applied Social Psychology*, Vol. 3 (Summer 1973), pp. 94–102. See also William Peters, *A Class Divided* (New Haven: Yale University Press, 1987).

[21] Ibid.

when we are put in direct contact with the people we stereotype, we have the opportunity to learn that our stereotypes are flawed.

Research suggests, however, that it is not usually enough for people merely to meet and interact. Prejudicial attitudes may distort perceptions and encourage discriminatory behavior. People tend to see what they expect to see in others. The conditions of the interaction are important. In general, the following conditions are conducive to attitude change:

- the social norms in the integrated group favor acceptance and discourage hostility
- there is ample opportunity to know the other person as an individual
- the contact is pleasant and mutually rewarding
- resources are equal for all
- the members of the groups share a common goal
- the status of individuals is equal
- the reward structure of the tasks individuals do together is cooperative rather than competitive[22]

We will discuss the research on school desegregation momentarily, but an important point can be made here. It is clear that when we integrate schools but do nothing else to promote interracial contact and understanding, it is not likely that we will reduce prejudice in the student body.

Passing Laws

We have all heard it said that "you can't legislate morality," that "you can change people's behavior but you can't change their attitudes." There is some limit to what can be done through the passage of laws, but legislation has certainly changed things dramatically in recent history. Schools that were once segregated by law are now integrated; black elected officials now govern in areas where, twenty-five years ago, they could not even vote; and blacks now live in areas from which they were once banned. Attitudes have changed as well. In 1948, 63 percent of Americans reported they would prefer not to have blacks move into their neighborhood; in 1987, only 13 percent registered this concern. In 1963, 61 percent of Americans thought there should be a law against interracial marriage; by 1985, the number had dropped to 28 percent.[23] In the early 1960s, Governor George Wallace stood in the doorway of the University of Alabama and proclaimed, "segregation now, segregation forever." Ten years later, he was back at the university to crown the first black homecoming queen.

People did not change their minds about race simply because a law was passed. But laws ending segregation made it more difficult to keep the races apart and that meant that people of different races began to work together and know one another. Over time, prejudicial attitudes began to erode. Antidiscrimina-

---

[22] Jane R. Mercer, Peter Iadicola, and Helen Moore, "Building Effective Multiethnic Schools," in *School Desegregation: Past, Present, and Future,* eds. Walter G. Stephan and Joe R. Feagin (New York: Plenum Press, 1980), pp. 281–304. See also T. A. Weissbach, "Laboratory Controlled Studies of Change of Racial Attitudes," *Toward the Elimination of Racism,* ed. Phyllis A. Katz p. 163.

[23] "The State of Intolerance in America," *Public Opinion,* Vol. 10, No. 2, (July–August 1987), pp. 21–40. See also Howard Schuman, Charlotte Steeh, and Lawrence Bobo, *Racial Attitudes in America: Trends and Interpretations* (Cambridge: Harvard University Press, 1985).

tion laws did something else as well: They reminded people of the American creed and that racism stands in stark violation of our most cherished principles. Before looking at what schools can do to promote integration and reduce prejudice, we must examine some of the history of racism. Our purpose in the next section is to put the present into the context of the struggle for racial equality in America.

Black Education: The Struggle for Access to the Common School

From Slavery to Emancipation

Blacks first came to America in 1619, landing in Jamestown, Virginia, not as slaves but as indentured servants. They proved to be good workers; so good, in fact, that many Virginians refused to release them from their indentured status after they had met their contractual obligation. In 1661, the Virginia legislature legalized this practice by bonding all indentured blacks to their masters for life. Two years later, Maryland passed a similar law.

The reasons for slavery were purely economic; the colonies were labor poor and slavery provided a low-cost work force. Blacks made good slaves because if they escaped, they could not just disappear into the general population. Of course, no one admitted that greed was the prime motivator behind slavery. People seldom admit their own barbarity, even to themselves. Instead, slave owners erected an elaborate scaffolding of beliefs to make their practices appear rational and even humane. Slavery was defended on the grounds that blacks were being converted to Christianity and thereby saved from "damnation." It was asserted, also, that blacks were inferior to whites and were intended by God to serve as slaves.

Most Americans were indifferent to the practice of slavery and took "white supremacy" for granted. For example, Thomas Jefferson wrote that blacks were "ugly," "dull," and possessed "a very strong and disagreeable odor." He advanced a theory that "blacks . . . are inferior to whites in the endowment of both the body and mind."[24] Some groups, most notably the Quakers, recognized slavery for what it was and worked for its abolition.[25] From the beginning, those opposing slavery made education a key weapon of their work to free the slaves. For example, Quakers set up schools for freed slaves and helped smuggle books to slaves who wanted to learn to read.

By the time of the Revolution, the population of the nation was growing and the economic benefits of slavery were in slow decline. Some southerners, including Thomas Jefferson, were talking openly about freeing their slaves. However, when steam power was harnessed to spinning and weaving machinery, a prosperous new industry was born. The introduction of the cotton gin created a huge demand for cotton, a crop that grew well in the American South.

[24] Quoted in Thomas F. Gossett, *Race: The History of an Idea in America* (Dallas: Southern Methodist University Press, 1963), p. 42.
[25] The first recorded protest against slavery was organized by Quakers in Germantown, Pennsylvania, in 1688.

Because cotton is a labor-intensive crop, growers found a convenient source of cheap labor in slavery. Within a few years, slavery had become a part of the economic fabric of the nation.

As the practice of slavery grew, the number of people opposing the practice grew as well. In 1829, David Walker, a freed slave, wrote a pamphlet calling for insurrection. Three years later, Nat Turner, an itinerant preacher, led a rebellion that killed about sixty Virginians. In the 1830s and 1840s, the abolitionist cause gathered strength and abolitionist newspapers, such as the *Liberator* and *National Era*, grew in circulation.

In the South, white slave owners feared the growing abolitionist sentiment in New England. The abolitionist cause threatened the South's new-found prosperity, and calls for open slave rebellion made slave owners fear for their lives. To keep blacks ignorant and disorganized, "compulsory ignorance" laws were passed, making it a crime for anyone to teach slaves to read. An 1823 Mississippi law forbade the gathering of six or more blacks for the purposes of education. In Louisiana, a person who taught a slave to read or write was subject to a year in jail. In North Carolina, it was against the law for freed slaves to learn to read. However, slaves and abolitionists saw education as a necessary condition for freedom and set up clandestine schools to teach literacy. A child of a slave, Susie King, described her experience going to a clandestine school in Savannah, Georgia, this way:

> We went every day about nine o'clock, with our books wrapped in paper to prevent the police or white persons from seeing them. We went one at a time, through the gate, into the yard to the . . . kitchen, which was the schoolroom. . . . The neighbors would see us going in sometimes, but they supposed we were learning trades. . . . After school we left the same way we entered, one by one, then we would go to a square, about a block from the school, and wait for each other.[26]

Clandestine schools were widespread in the South. Freed slaves held classes in their homes at night and preachers secretly taught reading and writing during Sunday school. Slaves risked a great deal to become educated and, though clandestine schools did not eradicate illiteracy, they did represent the ongoing faith among blacks that education was an instrument of freedom.

Blacks living in the North enjoyed greater freedom, but life was not easy and access to education was still difficult. For example, even in Pennsylvania where Quakers were most prevalent, black children were excluded from public schools. Freed slaves established a number of organizations to promote education among blacks. A black leader wrote that in Pennsylvania in 1838 there were "26 day schools, 20 Sabbath schools, 125 Sabbath school teachers, 4 literary societies, 2 public libraries, 2 tract societies, 2 Bible societies, and 7 temperance societies" devoted to the education of the black population.[27]

In all states, even those where segregation was expressly prohibited by law, blacks had to fight to gain access to public education. When those efforts failed, blacks—often with the help of abolitionists—established their own private schools. Such schools were set up in Portland, Boston, New Haven, and Philadelphia. In some areas—Canterbury, Connecticut, and Zanesville, Ohio, to name just

---

[26] Quoted in Meyer Weinberg, *A Chance to Learn: A History of Race and Education in the United States* (New York: Cambridge University Press, 1977), pp. 13–14.

[27] Robert Purvis, *Liberator* (April 13, 1838). Quoted in ibid., p. 21.

two—whites burned down black schools as fast as they were built. Black parents persisted, however, and eventually established a number of private schools for their children.

Black leaders understood that private schooling was never going to be sufficient to educate the entire black population. Therefore, they used the experience they gained in the fight to establish private schools to launch a battle for free, public education. The new battle was difficult and sometimes violent, but slowly the doors of public schools began to swing open for black citizens. At first, public schools in the North were segregated but blacks flocked to them because education was valued so highly. For example, Ohio established segregated schools and, between 1853 and 1863, the number of black children receiving a public school education rose tenfold, from 702 to 7229 students. In 1860, about 90 percent of blacks attending schools in the North were being educated in segregated settings.[28]

Wherever the right to segregated education was won, the battle for access to integrated education soon followed. In some areas, blacks refused to pay taxes to support schools their children could not attend. In Boston, Nantucket, Rochester, Buffalo, and Lockport, black parents boycotted segregated schools. Political organizing helped elect abolitionists to school boards and state legislatures. Sometimes, battles were won at the local level and school boards abandoned segregationist policies; sometimes, they were won at the state level (the Massachusetts legislature outlawed segregated schools in 1855); and sometimes, they were won in state courts. When the time came to fight in a civil war that promised to end slavery, ex-slaves fought proudly and well. If there was a foreboding message in the fact that the Union Army paid white soldiers more than black soldiers to carry on this battle, the message was not lost on blacks. The struggle for freedom had always been costly and the policies and practices of white institutions had seldom been fair.

From Civil War to Civil Rights

The Civil War ended slavery, but it did not bring equal citizenship to blacks. After Reconstruction, a period when the North visited reprisals on the South, southern states instituted a number of laws and practices to keep blacks as second-class citizens. For example, Mississippi disfranchised citizens who could not read and write and did little to help black citizens gain these skills. As a result of such actions, by the turn of the century, no blacks were eligible to vote in southern elections.[29]

Southern states resisted providing public schools for black children. In some areas, no schools were provided for blacks though black taxes helped support schools for whites. In other areas black schools were built only after blacks paid a second tax to finance "their schools." Thus, in Florida, Texas, and Kentucky, blacks were often doubly taxed. Where schools were not provided, blacks established schools of their own. Ex-slaves, who had learned to read and write in clandestine schools or by working as house servants for whites, now became teachers in private schools. The most successful students were soon pressed into service as teachers.

---

[28] Ibid., p. 23.
[29] United States Commission on Civil Rights, *Twenty Years after Brown: Shadows of the Past* (Washington, DC: U.S. Commission on Civil Rights, 1974), p. 49.

In 1865, Congress passed a law creating a Freemen's Bureau to assist freed slaves to find food and shelter. A year later, the law was amended so that the bureau could assist in the creation of black schools. With financial assistance from the Freemen's Bureau and contributions from black citizens, newly freed slaves were able to obtain land, build schools, and pay a modest wage to teachers. By 1870, almost 10 percent of southern blacks were attending some kind of school.[30]

Whites were angered and fearful of the determination of blacks to obtain an education and retaliated with violence. Whites burned black schools and attacked teachers. In one year, all the black schools in eight Mississippi counties were destroyed. Similar campaigns were carried on throughout the South.

The passage of the Fourteenth Amendment to the U.S. Constitution brought major changes in the South. The amendment made the safeguarding of civil rights primarily a federal function. At last, blacks began to gain access to public education, and they flocked to school. Even when children were needed at home to work the farm, black parents found a way to get them to school. For example, a black educated during this period in Alabama described how he and his brother shared their work and education:

> I took turns with my brother at the plow and in school; one day I plowed and he went to school, the next day he plowed and I went to school; what was learned on his school day he taught me at night and I did the same for him.[31]

Efforts through the courts failed to gain the rights of full citizenship for blacks. In *Plessy* vs. *Ferguson*, a case argued before the Supreme Court in 1896, the court ruled that the separation of races in public accommodations did not violate the civil rights of blacks or suggest a status of inferiority. Though the South had been forced by the Fourteenth Amendment to provide schools for blacks, southerners worked hard to ensure that black schools would remain badly underfunded. Within a decade, funding for black education had been reduced to a trickle. In Owensboro, Kentucky, for example, $770 was set aside for a school that served 500 black students. The school for whites, that served just 200 more students, was given $9,400. The school for blacks was open for just three months during the year, but the school for whites ran for nine months. Court cases challenged such practices, and, indeed, the courts ruled that states could not employ such discriminatory practices. However, nothing the court said disallowed discrimination at the local level.[32] Thus, state funds that were distributed equitably at the state level were distributed inequitably at the local level. In 1895, for example, the per pupil expenditure for white children in South Carolina was three times the expenditures for black students.

The push for black rights was further hindered by the "separate but equal" doctrine laid down by the Supreme Court in *Plessy* vs. *Ferguson* in 1896. That decision, which argued that segregation was not prohibited by the Constitution, was used to justify the existence of two societies in America, one black and one white. Separate, though seldom equal, schools, churches, hospitals, restaurants, hotels, clubs, labor unions, and cemeteries were established for blacks and whites. Even the pets of black families were buried separately from those of white

---

[30] Weinberg, *A Chance to Learn*, p. 43.
[31] Quoted in ibid., p. 46.
[32] *Claybrook* vs. *Owensboro*, 16 Fed R 302 (1883). See also *Puitt* vs. *Commissioners*, 94 NC 519 (1886).

families. Employment was also segregated. Blacks were given menial work and were paid outrageously low wages.

According to Horace Mann Bond, a black historian and educator, the condition of black education did not improve much between 1875 and 1900, and from 1900 to 1930 conditions deteriorated badly.[33] Black students used books and equipment already worn out at white schools. Classes were overcrowded, teachers were underpaid, and per capita funding for black students was sometimes only a tenth of that for white students. Money was allocated for the transportation of white students to school but seldom for black pupils. Blacks fought back in every way they could: They launched petition drives, filed law suits, and tried to defeat bond issues for funds that would support white-only schools. Such efforts were seldom successful. When the efforts of blacks looked as if they were going to be successful, the Ku Klux Klan and other racist organizations would terrorize blacks in the community. Between 1889 and 1922, 3436 people were lynched; most of the victims were black and most lived in the South.

Discouraged by white opposition and by the lack of opportunity in the South, blacks began migrating to northern cities for the promise of factory work and union wages. The North proved to be no promised land, but new migrants from the South joined with the local black population to continue the battle for equal education. Summing up the period from the Civil War through the first half of the twentieth century, W. E. B. Du Bois wrote, "probably never in the world have so many oppressed people tried in every possible way to educate themselves."[34]

The Brown Decision

When Linda Brown was seven years old, her father, the Reverend Oliver Brown, watched his daughter depart every morning for a school in Topeka, Kansas. His daughter walked six blocks between train tracks to a bus stop where she would wait for a bus that would take her two miles to school for black children. On some mornings, in cold weather, Linda returned home in tears. One day, after his daughter had run home to escape the cold, her father took Linda's hand and walked her to the school for white children just four blocks away. To the principal's surprise, the Reverend Brown asked that his daughter be admitted. Linda described the day:

> Mother said that she had never seen him so angry. He was so fed up with the cruelty and injustice of it all that he decided then and there that this was going to . . . stop. Daddy told me, "I know they aren't going to accept you, but I'm going to try." I don't know what they said, but they spoke very sharply.[35]

The principal turned Linda and her father away. As they walked home, the Reverend Brown decided that he would call a friend, an attorney for the National Association for the Advancement of Colored People (NAACP), John Scott.

---

[33] Horace Mann Bond, *Education of the Negro in the American Social Order* (New York: Octagon, 1966 [1934]), p. 115.

[34] W. E. B. Du Bois, "The United States and the Negro," quoted in Weinberg, *A Chance to Learn*, p. 80.

[35] United States Commission on Civil Rights, *Twenty Years after Brown* (Washington, DC: U.S. Commission on Civil Rights, 1974), p. 9.

tation, twelve other parents joined Oliver Brown in what would be a historic case that, three years later, would be argued before the U.S. Supreme Court.

Plaintiffs in the Brown case did not argue that the black school Linda had been attending was separate but unequal; such cases had been argued and won in the past. Instead, the plaintiffs attacked the very idea of segregation. Thurgood Marshall (today a Justice of the U.S. Supreme Court but then a NAACP lawyer) assembled a group of prominent social scientists to argue against segregation. They put forth two arguments. The first was that the idea of race was meaningless because no pertinent differences existed between races. The second argued that racial separation did irreparable harm to black children.[36] On May 17, 1954, the court ruled unanimously in favor of Brown and his fellow plaintiffs. The change in American life would be lasting and dramatic. As Diane Ravitch put it:

> Never before had the Supreme Court reached so deeply into the lives, laws, and mores of so many people; nearly half the states of the nation were living according to laws the Court had [now] ruled unconstitutional. Approximately 40 percent of the public school pupils in the nation were enrolled in segregated systems.[37]

Chief Justice Warren wrote the majority opinion for the court. In it, he argued that

> education is perhaps the most important function of state and local governments, [so important that] it is doubtful if any child may reasonably be expected to succeed in life if he is denied the opportunity of an education.

He went on,

> We come then to the question presented [in the case]: Does segregation of children in public schools, solely on the basis of race, even though the physical facilities and other "tangible" factors may be equal, deprive the children of the minority group of equal educational opportunities? We believe it does. [Separating black] children from others of similar age and qualifications solely because of their race generates a feeling of inferiority as to their status in the community that may affect their hearts and minds in a way unlikely ever to be undone. We conclude that in the field of public education the doctrine of "separate but equal" has no place. Separate educational facilities are inherently unequal.

A year later, in what came to be known as the Brown II decision, the court ruled that because local conditions varied so much, the implementation of desegregation would have to be carried out by local authorities under the supervision of federal courts. School boards were required to act "with all deliberate speed" toward integration. The debate that accompanied the Brown II decision lingers on today. Some argued that Brown II played into the hands of segregationists because it gave flexibility to local communities—where blacks were least powerful—and denied blacks immediate relief from the unconstitutional practice of segregation. This group, that we can call *interventionists*, wanted a single standard of integration designed by the court and implemented with the

---

[36] Diane Ravitch, a historian of education, argues that the two arguments are contradictory, that one argues that school policies should be color blind (that is, not take race into account) and the other argues that school policies should be color conscious (that schools should purposefully mix races). Diane Ravitch, *The Troubled Crusade: American Education, 1945–1980* (New York: Basic Books, 1983), p. 128.

[37] Ibid.

full strength of the federal government. Justice, they claimed, was best served by uniformity.

A second group, we will call them *localists*, wanted to keep the courts out of educational issues. They preferred that all educational decisions be made at the local level. The localists claimed that justice was best served by allowing for maximum diversity.

Brown II adopted a "centrist" approach. The court established in Brown I that segregation was intolerable in public education and established integration as an ideal toward which the nation should strive. Minimal standards and general principles were established. At the same time, the court gave localities the leeway to determine for themselves how best to apply those principles and meet those standards. This opened the possibility of local debate, compromise, local involvement, and voluntary compliance. When the process failed, cases could be brought before district courts, where decisions could be made on a case-by-case basis. Thus, the ideology of inclusion was affirmed, the acceptability of segregation was denied, the possibility of political compromise was maximized, and the all-or-nothing extremes advocated by the localists and the interventionists were avoided.[38]

Some areas of the country moved quickly to comply with the Brown decisions. Effective desegregation plans came about when local leaders expressed a willingness to comply with the decision, when they worked with community groups to formulate effective desegregation plans, when many groups were involved and had an opportunity to be heard, when community leaders supported the planning effort, and when time was taken to draft plans that had a chance to work.

In the deep South, opposition to integration was fierce and the flexibility of the Brown II decision made it easier for segregationists to delay and obstruct the integration process. In defiance of Brown, states passed laws designed to resist the integration of public schools. School closures were permitted, compulsory attendance laws were repealed, private schools were established and sometimes funded, sex-segregated schools were set up, teacher tenure was revoked, and aid was withheld from desegregated schools.[39] In Alabama, a bill was passed outlawing the NAACP.

Legislative resistance to integration in the deep South was effective. A decade after Brown I, little progress had been made toward integration. When obstructionist laws failed, violence by whites was unleashed on blacks who tried to enroll in schools for whites. For example, when nine black students enrolled at all-white Central High School in Little Rock, they were met by the bayonets of the Arkansas National Guard. The governor had called out the Guard and ordered them to prevent the integration of Central High. A mob of whites jeered as the children were turned away from the school. One of the students described the experience:

> They glared at me . . . and I was frightened and I didn't know what to do. I turned around and the crowd came toward me. Somebody started yelling, "Lynch her! Lynch her!" I tried to find a friendly face . . . someone who maybe would help. I looked at the face of an old woman and it seemed a nice kind face, but when I looked at her again she spat on me. [I ran to the bus stop and sat down

---

[38] For an elegant and empirical exploration of this argument, see David L. Kirp, *Just Schools: The Ideal of Racial Equality in American Education* (Berkeley: University of California Press, 1982).

[39] Reed Sarrat, *The Ordeal of Desegregation: The First Decade* (New York: Harper & Row, 1966).

exhausted.] I don't think I could have taken another step. The mob crowded up and began shouting. . . . Someone hollered, "Drag her over to this tree! Let's take care of the nigger!" Just then a white man sat down beside me, put his arm around me and patted my shoulder. He raised my chin and said, "Don't let them see you cry." Then a white lady came over. . . . She put me on the bus and sat beside me.

The National Guard was withdrawn in response to a court order, but mobs remained around the school. Finally, Central High was integrated when President Eisenhower ordered national paratroops to restore order and enforce the law.

These spectacles of resistance gave white citizens an insight into the extent and consequence of prejudice. At the same time, it energized and expanded the goals of the civil rights movement. Blacks were not simply fighting for access to the common school in America; they were fighting for full participation in the political process and in the American dream.

The Quest of Civil Rights

On the evening of December 1, 1955, Rosa Parks climbed wearily onto a city bus and made her way to the section in the back reserved for blacks. The ritual was nothing new to her; she had spent a lifetime in the South and, for some years, had taken the bus to and from her work as a seamstress. On this day, however, in her own quiet way, she was going to make history. Martin Luther King, Jr., described what happened:

> Tired from long hours on her feet [Mrs. Parks] sat down in the first seat behind the section reserved for whites. Not long after she took her seat, the bus operator ordered her, along with three other Negro passengers, to move back in order to accommodate boarding white passengers. If Mrs. Parks had followed the driver's command she would have to stand while a white male passenger, who had just boarded the bus, would sit. The three other Negro passengers immediately complied with the driver's request. But Mrs. Parks quietly refused. The result was her arrest.[40]

Small acts of courage sometimes change history. Though Mrs. Parks had no way of knowing at the time, her refusal to succumb to injustice convinced hundreds and then thousands of others that segregation had gone on too long and now had to be ended. Blacks in the city boycotted the bus company, saying that, if they could ride only as second-class citizens, they would not ride at all. The boycott demonstrated the injustice of segregation and brought the nation's attention to Montgomery. It also put financial pressure on the city's transit system. When blacks could not get a ride from the car pools that were organized during the bus boycott, they walked. Each day the streets of Montgomery were filled with blacks walking to and from work. When an elderly lady was asked by a reporter if so much walking had made her tired, she responded, "My soul has been tired for a long time: now my feet are tired, and my soul is resting."[41]

[40] Martin Luther King, Jr., *Stride Toward Freedom: Montgomery Story* (New York: Harper, 1958), p. 43.
[41] Quoted in United States Commission on Civil Rights, *Twenty Years after Brown: Shadows of the Past* (Washington, DC: U.S. Commission on Civil Rights, 1974), p. 64.

The Montgomery boycott showed the power of nonviolent protest, and the tactic spread. In 1960, students from North Carolina Agricultural and Technical College for Negroes went shopping at a local five-and-dime store. Having made their purchase, they sat down at the for-whites-only lunch counter and waited to be served. Again a small act was the catalyst for something larger. Within days sit-ins were carried out at lunch counters across the South.

College students were at the forefront of the sit-in movement. Whenever blacks protested in their own communities, whites would exert financial pressure to bring the protest to an end. Sit-ins were done in violation of local laws, and protesters were often jailed. Students were not as vulnerable to financial pressures of the white community and were able to withstand the hardships of going to jail.

Voter registration drives increased the political participation of blacks. As a result of growing political pressure from blacks and growing support from whites, Congress passed the Civil Rights Bill of 1964. The law contained incentives for those districts working to integrate their schools. The legislation also gave the federal government a way to punish school districts that remained segregated. The Civil Rights Bill provided financial and technical assistance to school districts that were implementing desegregation plans. It also gave the Attorney General the power to bring individual or class-action suits on behalf of persons denied access to public school solely because of race. Further, it denied federal funds to programs that discriminated on the basis of race, color, religion, or national origin. The latter provision was powerful. It meant that school districts that resisted integration stood to lose millions of federal dollars. New federal pressure augmented a growing number of demonstrations—from Atlantic City, New Jersey, to Woodville, Mississippi—in support of integration. The rate of integration increased significantly, especially in the South.

"By 1972," wrote one historian, "the kind of segregation that had existed before the Brown decision had nearly been eliminated." Two years before Brown, southern schools were universally segregated. Twenty years later, "91.3 percent of all southern black students attended schools with whites."[42] In the North and West the statistics were less impressive. Here segregation did not exist as a result of law (de jure segregation) but did exist in fact (de facto segregation) because of housing patterns, discriminatory zoning, gerrymandering, and subtle practices designed to keep blacks congregated in minority-dominated schools. Perhaps, the distinction between the two forms of segregation was only academic, because subsequent court rulings indicated almost every case of de facto segregation could be shown to be an unconstitutional case of de jure segregation. The fact remained that, in 1972, half of all black students in the South (46 percent) attended schools with a majority of white students, but in the North and West only 28 percent of black students went to schools where whites were in the majority. By these measures, segregation had become a bigger problem in the North and West than it was in the South.

The Brown decision required integration but said nothing about racial balance. However, the existence of de facto segregation and growing evidence that the academic achievement of black students was low in minority-dominated schools got the attention of civil rights leaders, education policy makers, the

---

[42] Ravitch, *The Troubled Crusade,* p. 176.

Justice Department, and the courts. In *Swan* vs. *Charlotte–Mecklenburg*, the U.S. Supreme Court ruled that the local desegregation plan had not integrated the schools. The school district was instructed to "make every effort to achieve the greatest possible degree of actual desegregation."[43] In order to achieve "the greatest possible degree of integration," local authorities could not be color blind; they had to be color conscious and they had to use race as a criterion for school assignment. If, in Brown, schools were told to ignore race, in Swan, they were told to take race into account as they worked to achieve racial balance.

Achieving desegregation has been more difficult in the North and West than it was in the South. As we shall see later in the chapter, a migration of blacks from the land and into urban areas has been going on since the 1930s. More recently, whites have been moving to the suburban rim of metropolitan areas. In some cities, blacks now make up a majority of the urban population and over three-quarters of the public school population. In the remainder of the chapter, we will examine the effects of integration on the education of blacks and whites. We will also consider what present demographic trends suggest for the future of the common school in America.

The Effects of Integration

The Initial Debate

When the battle over integration was being waged in the 1950s and 1960s, proponents sometimes promised that an end to segregation would bring about an educational transformation. Academic achievement among black students would increase greatly, the self-concept of black students would improve, more blacks would enter higher education and win well-paying jobs, white student achievement would not be harmed, prejudicial attitudes among all children would be diminished, and within a generation or two, race would no longer be a significant determinant of an individual's academic or economic life-chances. Opponents of integration predicted just the opposite. They predicted that blacks would not be able to compete with their white classmates, academic achievement would decline among both groups, self-concept among black students would decline, racial tensions would increase, and the social fabric of the nation would begin to unravel.

Can we tell now, more than three decades after the Brown decision, which side best predicted the future? A quick answer would be that both sides were wrong. Proponents of integration were overly optimistic and opponents were far too pessimistic. We will review the desegregation research; however, it is worth emphasizing that the research on integration was not conducted to see whether the integrationists or the segregationists correctly predicted the future. The integration debate that dominated the educational scene thirty years ago is no longer relevant. The law of the land makes clear that segregation in public education is an unacceptable practice. It is significant that a growing majority of Americans agree that it is wrong to segregate our public schools.

---

[43] *Swan* vs. *Charlotte–Mecklenburg*, 402 US 1 (1971).

Characteristics of Good Research

If we really want to know the effects of desegregation, we would have to design a study that randomly selected similar children from similar homes in the same community. One group would be assigned to a segregated school and the other to an integrated school. The schools to which the children were assigned would have to be equivalent in every way except, of course, for racial composition. That is to say that the curriculum, the quality of instruction, the characteristics of teachers, the size of classes, and other factors would have to be the same, or we could not tell whether later differences between the two groups were caused by desegregation or some other factor.

The two groups would be tested before the experiment started. We might measure their academic achievement in basic subjects, their self-concepts, their racial attitudes, their aspirations for the future, and other relevant variables. Then at specified intervals (perhaps, every year), the groups would be tested again. By comparing the results, we could determine the results of the experiment. To eliminate the chance of spurious findings, we would have to repeat the experiment in a number of settings.

The research design just described follows a classic four-cell model. An experimental group (those attending an integrated school) and a control group (those who attend a segregated school) are tested at one point in time (time one) and then again at a second time (time two). An effort is made to assure that the groups are the same in every way, so the effect of one difference (attending a segregated or integrated school) can be accurately measured. (See Figure 22-1.)

Few situations permit the kind of experimentation depicted in Figure 22-1. Education policies are seldom enacted for the convenience of researchers. It is difficult to find comparable groups of children and assign them to comparable schools simply to satisfy the requirements of scientific research. Other interests (those of public policy, the law, parents, and students) must take precedence. Thus, we find that some studies (longitudinal studies) investigate just one group before and after segregation. These two-cell studies lack a comparable control group. Other studies (quasi-experiments) have a control group, but the groups are not exactly comparable because they were not randomly drawn and ran-

	Time one (Before)	Time two (After)
Experimental group (those in the integrated school)	(1) Segregated	(2) Desegregated
Control group (those in the segregated school)	(3) Segregated	(4) Segregated

Figure 22-1   A four-cell experimental design to determine the effects of integration.

domly assigned to different schools. Sometimes the backgrounds of students were not equivalent or school characteristics differed significantly. Very few studies actually meet the requirements of a solid experimental design.

In this section, we examine studies that measure the effects of school integration on a number of important variables: academic achievement, self-confidence, and student attitudes. Longitudinal, quasi-experimental, and experimental studies will be considered, but greater weight will be given to carefully designed studies.

Effects of Integration on the Academic Achievement of Students

Even after three decades of research, there are no definitive answers to the question, What effect does desegregation have on the academic achievement of white and black students? No large-scale studies meet the requirements of a rigorous experimental design. However, longitudinal and quasi-experimental studies suggest that desegregation did not bring about the instant improvement suggested by the pro-integrationists nor did it cause the academic and social collapse predicted by those opposed to integration. Nancy St. John, in a thorough review of desegregation research up to 1975, concluded that "desegregation rarely lowered academic achievement for either black or white children."[44] Later, Krol reviewed 129 studies of student achievement after integration. Like St. John, he concluded that there was little evidence that integration had a quick, positive effect on student achievement. Where achievement gains were found, they tended to be small and not statistically significant.[45]

More recently, Crain and Mahard reviewed ninety-three studies of the relationship between integration and academic achievement. They eliminated those studies that did not have an adequate research design and were left with forty-five separate studies. They concluded that the best-designed studies showed that integration positively affected black achievement. Forty out of forty-five studies showed achievement gains of almost one grade-year. Crain and Mahard went on to say that their findings were "consistent with the hypothesis that the benefits of [racial] desegregation are the result of socioeconomic desegregation."[46]

Crain and Mahard concluded, further, that desegregation was most effective (had the greatest achievement gains) when 10 to 30 percent of the student population were black and 70 to 90 percent white. Their review of studies of achievement among Hispanic students led them to conclude that students from low socioeconomic backgrounds are likely to benefit from attending schools where the majority of students are from middle-class homes.[47] There is also reason to believe that the beneficial effects of integrating a school will be lost if classes are segregated and students of different races are treated differently by teachers and administrators. It is disturbing that, three decades after the Brown

---

[44] Nancy H. St. John, *School Desegregation: Outcomes for Children* (New York: Wiley, 1975), p. 36.
[45] Ronald A. Krol, "A Meta-analysis of the Effects of Desegregation on Academic Achievement," *The Urban Review*, Vol. 12 (1980), pp. 211–224.
[46] R. L. Crain and R. E. Mahard, *Desegregation Plans that Raise Black Achievement: A Review of the Research* (Santa Monica, CA: Rand Corporation, 1982), p. vi.
[47] Ibid., p. 35.

decision, black children are more than three times as likely to be placed in classes for the mentally retarded than their white schoolmates, but only half as likely to be placed in classes for the gifted.[48] Blacks are suspended from school at a rate three times higher than their white classmates and are twice as likely to drop out of school.

The integration studies reported here do not examine the effects of improved instruction in integrated settings. There is increasing evidence, however, that academic achievement is enhanced when integration is accompanied by instructional improvements.[49] Not enough attention was paid in most studies to the problem of segregating classes within integrated schools. Also, there is reason to believe that the benefits of classroom-level integration are cumulative, yet most of the studies do not look at the long-term effects of integrated education.

Effects of Integration on the Self-Confidence of Students

It is generally assumed, especially by educators, that black students generally have lower self-esteem than white students. There is reason to doubt this belief. Rosenberg and Simmons interviewed nearly 2000 students in twenty-six Baltimore schools and found that blacks scored higher on a validated self-esteem scale than did whites.[50]

Studies of self-esteem are numerous in the desegregation literature. However, few studies meet the research-design criteria described at the beginning of the section. Results of available studies give mixed results. A few studies show a slight rise in self-esteem among black students after integration. The majority of studies, however, show no effect or a slight lowering of self-esteem scores after desegregation. Results are somewhat more positive when long-term results are measured. St. John concludes from her review of the literature that the longer black students remain in integrated schools, the higher their self-concept is likely to be.[51]

More recent research suggests that attitude and performance are enhanced when cooperative teaching methods are employed, when students enjoy equal status, and when they work together in small groups to achieve shared goals. However, students should not be thrown together, given an assignment, and then expected to perform on their own without teacher intervention. Cooperation is a skill and students need instruction and experience in order to master it.[52]

---

[48] Board of Inquiry, National Coalition of Advocates for Students, *Barriers to Excellence* (Boston: Author, 1985), p. 10.

[49] Daniel U. Lavine and Robert Havighurst, *Society and Education,* 6th ed. (Boston: Allyn & Bacon, 1984), p. 434.

[50] Morris Rosenberg and Roberta G. Simmons, *Black and White Self-Esteem: The Urban School Child,* Arnold and Caroline Rose Monograph Series (Washington, DC: American Sociological Association, 1971).

[51] St. John, *School Desegregation,* p. 55.

[52] Mercer, Iadicola, and Moore, "Building Effective Multiethnic Schools," p. 281–304. See also T. A. Weissbach, "Laboratory Controlled Studies of Change of Racial Attitudes," in *Toward the Elimination of Racism,* ed. Phyllis A. Katz (New York: Pergamon Press, 1976), p. 163. Available in paperback.

Long-Term Effects of Integration

In 1972, Christopher Jencks asserted that "the case for . . . desegregation should not be argued in terms of academic achievement. If we want a desegregated society, we should have desegregated schools."[53] His point, of course, is that segregated schools serve to segregate the society and that the opposite is also true. The research supports Jencks's assertion. Without exception, every study listed in a recent review of research into the long-term effects of integration demonstrates that "desegregated schools lead to desegregation in later-life in college, in social situations, and on the job."[54] Some other salient findings include:

- Minority students who have attended integrated public schools are more likely than those who have attended largely segregated schools to attend predominantly white colleges and universities.[55]
- Blacks who attended desegregated schools tended to make better grades in college than blacks who attended segregated schools.[56]
- Black graduates from integrated schools tend to have better employment opportunities than blacks who graduated from segregated schools.[57]
- Black adults who were educated in integrated schools are more likely than their counterparts educated in segregated schools to work in integrated settings.[58]
- Black adults who were educated in integrated schools are more likely than their counterparts to have white friends and to live in integrated neighborhoods.[59]
- Blacks who were educated in segregated schools and later take jobs in integrated settings are more likely than their counterparts educated in integrated schools to have negative feelings about their white supervisors.[60]

---

[53] Christopher Jencks, Marshall Smith, Henry Acland, Mary Jo Bane, David Cohen, Herbert Gintis, Barbara Heyns, and Stephan Michelson, *Inequality: A Reassessment of the Effect of Family and Schooling in America* (New York: Basic Books, 1972), p. 106. Available in paperback.

[54] Jomills Henry Braddock II, Robert L. Crain, and James M. McPartland, "A Long-term View of School Desegregation: Some Recent Studies of Graduates as Adults," *Phi Delta Kappan*, Vol. 66 (1984), pp. 259–264.

[55] Jomills Henry Braddock II, "The Perpetuation of Segregation across Levels of Education: A Behavioral Assessment of the Contact-Hypothesis," *Sociology of Education* (July 1980), pp. 178–186; and Jomills Henry Braddock II and James M. McPartland, "Assessing School Desegregation Effects: New Directions in Research," in *Research in Sociology of Education and Socialization*, Vol. 3, ed. Ronald Corwin (Greenwich, CT: JAI Press, 1982), pp. 259–282.

[56] Kenneth Green, "The Impact of Neighborhood and Secondary School Integration on Educational Attainment and Occupational Attainment of College-Bound Blacks" (doctoral diss., University of California—Los Angeles, 1982).

[57] Reported in Braddock, Crain, and McPartland, "A Long-Term View of School Desegregation," p. 264.

[58] Jomills Henry Braddock II, James M. McPartland, and William Trent, "Desegregated Schools and Desegregated Work Environments," paper presented at the annual meeting of the American Educational Research Association, New Orleans, 1984.

[59] Reported in Braddock, Crain, and McPartland, "A Long-Term View of School Desegregation," p. 261.

[60] Jomills Henry Braddock II and James M. McPartland, *More Evidence on Social-Psychological Processes that Perpetuate Minority Segregation: The Relationship of School Desegregation and Employment Segregation.* Report No. 338 (Baltimore: Center for Social Organization of Schools, Johns Hopkins University, 1983).

Braddock and his colleagues conclude that racial integration improves the long-term life-chances of minority students: It helps break down racial barriers; it helps blacks take advantage of public education; it increases black students' ability to make their way in the American culture; it improves their chances of getting into integrated colleges, performing well in them, and graduating; and it increases the likelihood that, after graduating from school, black students will be employed, hold better-paying jobs, and be happier in their work.

Other Factors Influencing the Achievement of Black Students

Integration, by itself, is not likely to mend the damage inflicted by living in poverty, growing up on welfare, or being raised in a single-parent home; nor will integration eradicate the residual effects of racial prejudice. The research reviewed so far indicates that, on average, integration helps blacks socially and academically and does not harm whites. Nevertheless, some black children do better in schools than others, even when we take into consideration native ability and home background. Reginald Clark undertook research to discover why some disadvantaged black children made more progress in school than others.[61] He examined the home lives of high school students who were doing well in school and the home lives of similar students who were not doing well. One- and two-parent families were included in his sample.

Clark concluded that high-achieving students learned survival skills in the home that served students well in school. The homes of higher achievers were dominated by certain behavioral and psychological patterns that were not found in the homes of lower achievers. For example, two-parent families with higher-achieving children

- had a positive orientation toward education. Parents of higher achievers thought schooling was important and believed that it was their responsibility to see that their children received a good education.
- displayed an internal locus of control and showed no signs of learned helplessness. Parents of higher achievers felt in control of their circumstances and did not feel worn down even though they suffered financial difficulties.
- had a task-oriented family routine. Parents and children spent their leisure time together and enjoyed one another's company. Everyone had assigned tasks that contributed to the family welfare and that were done regularly and without undue complaint.
- had high expectations for their children. Not only was school seen as important, the families of higher achievers communicated to their children that they were expected to work hard in school and to do well. Good performance in school was acknowledged and poor performance was corrected.
- had clear behavioral expectations. Families of higher-achieving students were well controlled, had few discipline problems, and were generally happy. Parents saw the maintenance of the family welfare as a responsibility to be taken seriously.[62]

Clark also examined the behavioral patterns in families of high and low achievers from one-parent homes. He found that certain patterns were domi-

[61] Reginald M. Clark, *Family Life and School Achievement: Why Poor Black Children Succeed or Fail* (Chicago: University of Chicago Press, 1983).
[62] Ibid., pp. 26–60.

nant in the homes of higher-achieving students and were not found in the homes of low-achieving students. For example, in one-parent families with higher-achieving children, the parent

- was willing to place the needs of the child before his or her own needs.
- valued education and thought schooling was important.
- felt responsible for helping in the education of the child.
- held the child responsible and accountable for routinely pursuing knowledge.
- communicated the expectation that the child should pursue some form of post-high school education or training.[63]

Clark only studied ten families. Such studies are good for generating hypotheses that can be used in future research, but they are not intended to give definitive answers to research questions. However, the results of Clark's work are compatible with the findings of *High School and Beyond,* a larger, longitudinal study completed by the National Center for Educational Statistics. In this study, researchers discovered that students who do best in school are those whose parents are most involved in their lives. Eighty-eight percent of A students indicated that they received a high degree of supervision from their parents. Only 66 percent of D students said their parents kept track of where they were and what they were doing. The parents of good students talk with their children more often, monitor their children's activities, pay attention to grades, take some kind of remedial action when grades turn downward, and attend parent–teacher conferences and PTA meetings more frequently than the parents of low-achieving students.[64]

It was pointed out earlier in the chapter that the effects of integration could be enhanced if they were accompanied by good teaching. These effects are likely to be further enhanced if parents value education and monitor their children's progress. Of course, not all parents hold high expectations for their children, monitor their homework, find a place and a time for their children to study, and stay in close communication with teachers. It is apparent, however, that schools can help parents learn these values and skills. The most successful parent–education programs begin when children are young and when schools act as mediating institutions.[65]

Integration and the Push for Equality: What Has Been Achieved?

The effort to end school segregation was just a part of a much larger struggle to eliminate racial discrimination in American society. That is why we included a short history of the civil rights movement in the United States earlier in this

---

[63] Ibid., pp. 61–110.

[64] George Brown, "The Relationship of Parent Involvement to High School Grades," *National Center for Educational Statistics Bulletin* (Washington, DC: United States Department of Education, March 1985). See also Clifton R. Wharton, "Demanding Families and Black Achievement," *Education Week* (October 29, 1986).

[65] Ira Gordon and William Breivogel, *Building Effective Home–School Relationships* (New York: Basic Books, Inc., 1978). See also Susan McAllister Swap, *Enhancing Parent Involvement in Schools* (New York: Teachers College Press, 1987). Robert V. Carlson and Edward R. Ducharme, eds. *School Improvement: Theory and Practice* (Lanham, MD: University Press of America, 1987), pp. 537–676.

chapter. Thus, the effects of school desegregation must be viewed in the light of a broader effort to extend equal rights and opportunities to all citizens, to maintain the self-respect of every individual, to increase the critical intelligence of each citizen and the collective intelligence of the population as a whole, and to make cooperation and civility possible. Here again, we see that the goals of education complement the objectives of democracy. Integration is not, and never was, merely an educational experiment; it was part of a societal effort to improve the life-chances of minority citizens and the future of democracy.

What Has Been Accomplished? (The Glass Is Half Full)

Whether or not we think integration has "worked" depends on whether we are inclined to see half a glass of water as half full or half empty. There is evidence to support both optimistic and pessimistic conclusions regarding integration. From the material reviewed earlier, we see that an education in integrated schools promotes integration in later life. When integration is combined with good instruction, cooperative learning, parental support, and a disciplined atmosphere, gains are made academically and socially. In this section we look at the positive effects of integration. In the next section we will look at the negative evidence.

CHANGING ATTITUDES.   At the same time that schools were becoming more integrated, racial barriers were being lowered in many parts of the country. Attitudes were changing as well. Surveys of white attitudes show a clear trend toward the acceptance of integration in many areas of American life.[66] These attitude changes have had an impact on the lives and experiences of black citizens. In a recent survey, 75 percent of black Americans said they had never suffered discrimination in "getting a quality education," 73 percent said that they had not been discriminated against in "getting decent housing," and 60 percent said that they had never experienced discrimination in "getting a job." Blacks were also asked, "If a young person works hard enough, do you think he or she can get ahead in this country, in spite of prejudice and discrimination . . . ?" Eighty-two percent said they thought black young people can get ahead if they work hard enough.[67] Respondents to the survey thought conditions had improved for them, that discrimination no longer dominated their life experiences, and that the future held promise. Do blacks have reason for such optimism?

GAINS IN EDUCATION.   The rise of high school graduation rates for whites has remained rather stable over the past twenty years, but the rates of graduation for blacks and Hispanics have grown impressively, as can be seen in Figure 22-2. In 1968, only 58 percent of black students graduated from high school, but, by 1985, that rate had climbed to 75 percent. Among Hispanics the climb has been less dramatic, moving from 52 to 62 percent between 1972 and 1985.

During the past two decades, a period when the average academic achievement of white students was declining, the achievement of black pupils moved

---

[66] Howard Schuman, Charlotte Steeh, and Lawrence Bobo, *Racial Attitudes in America.*

[67] William R. Beer, "The Wages of Discrimination," *Public Opinion*, Vol. 10 (July/August 1987), p. 19.

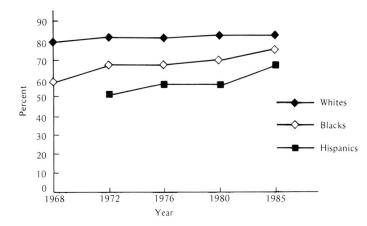

Figure 22-2   High school gradua-tion, 1968–1985. (*Source:* U.S. Bureau of the Census, *Current Population Reports,* Series P-20, Nos. 404 and 409. Note: Rates reflect persons eighteen to twenty-four years old reporting four or more years of high school.)

upward.[68] For example, between 1976 and 1984, the average score for white students taking the Scholastic Aptitude Test declined by twelve points. During the same period the average score of black students increased by 29 points.[69] National assessment examinations measured impressive gains in black and Hispanic students' performance.[70] In all areas, the average scores of black and Hispanic students are considerably lower than the scores of white students. However, progress is being made and in some areas the achievement gap, though still wide, is narrowing.

Higher rates of college graduation and gains in academic achievement have made it possible for increasing numbers of minority students to enter college. Total minority enrollment (blacks, Hispanics, American Indians, and Asians) increased by 22 percent between 1976 and 1984. During the same period, white enrollment increased by only 8 percent.[71] A longitudinal study that followed a sample of the nation's 1980 graduating class revealed that 32 percent of white students and 29 percent of their black classmates went directly into four-year colleges after graduation from high school.[72] Increased access to college and to professional schools has given blacks greater access to middle-class and professional employment.

INCOME GAINS.   Wages for black men have increased over the past three or four decades. Since 1950, for example, wages for black men have increased

[68] It is important to note that the academic achievement of whites declined in both integrated and nonintegrated schools. The achievement troubles of white students do not appear to be related to integration.

[69] These data are for combined scores on the math and verbal portions of the Scholastic Aptitude Test.

[70] National Assessment of Educational Progress, *The Reading Report Card: Progress toward Excellence in Our Schools, Trends in Reading over Four National Assessments, 1971–1984,* NAEP Report No. 15-R-01 (Princeton, NJ: Educational Testing Service, 1984).

[71] James R. Mingle, *Focus on Minorities: Trends in Higher Education Participation and Success* (Denver: Education Commission of the States and State Higher Education Executive Officers, 1987), p. 13.

[72] Ibid., p. 18.

from 55 percent of wages of white men to 73 percent in 1986.[73] Wage differentials still exist, an issue we will discuss in a moment, but the wage gap has diminished significantly. Black women have fared better, especially those holding professional jobs. Black women college graduates earn $1007 dollars for every $1000 dollars earned by white women with the same education.[74] Between 1970 and 1986, the number of black households earning over $50,000 almost doubled, moving from 4.3 percent of black households to 8.8 percent.[75] Families with two working parents living together in the same household have made the greatest income gains.[76]

The economic gains made by blacks were made possible by the relaxation of racial barriers in schools and industry. Increased high school and college graduation rates have opened the way for growing numbers of blacks to enter the middle class. In 1910, only 3 percent of blacks held middle-class jobs, but by 1980, that figure had jumped to 37 percent. Present projections are that, by the year 2000, a majority of black workers will have entered the middle class.[77] The connection between education and economic gains among blacks is clear.

Problems That Persist (The Glass Is Half Empty)

There can be little doubt that discrimination is less powerful today than it was thirty years ago, that educational opportunities open to blacks have improved, that middle-class job opportunities long closed to blacks are slowly opening, and that the quality of life for many blacks has improved. However, there is still much to be done before the dream of equal opportunity will be realized.

ENROLLMENT DISPARITIES IN HIGHER EDUCATION. It was suggested earlier that enrollment in undergraduate and graduate programs by minority students has increased since the 1960s. While this is true, and greater access to higher education has made it possible for growing numbers of blacks to qualify for middle- and high-income jobs, the data reveal some disturbing trends that must be examined. Enrollment in higher education by blacks grew in the 1960s and 1970s, but since 1980, such enrollment figures have been in decline.[78] Enrollment in professional schools by blacks is still low (4 percent in business, 5 percent in law, and 6 percent in medicine) and, in most cases, has also declined since 1980.[79]

The decline in black enrollment in higher education parallels the decline in economic growth in the nation and the availability of student loans and government-sponsored assistance programs. At the same time, in some universities, there has been a slackening commitment of minority students.[80] Higher stan-

[73] Andrew Hacker, "American Apartheid," *New York Review of Books*, Vol. 34 (December 3, 1987), p. 29.
[74] Ibid.
[75] These figures take inflation into account. Ibid., p. 30.
[76] Karl Zinsmeister, "Black Demographics," *Public Opinion*, Vol. 10 (January–February 1988), pp. 41–42.
[77] Bart Landry, *The New Black Middle Class* (Berkeley: University of California Press, 1987).
[78] Scott Jaschik, "Major Changes Seen Needed for Colleges to Attract Minorities," *The Chronicle of Higher Education*, Vol. 34 (November 25, 1987), pp. 1, A31–A32.
[79] Mingle, *Focus on Minorities*, p. 13.
[80] Jaschik, "Major Changes Seen Needed for Colleges to Attract Minorities," pp. 1, A31–A32. See also Robert Wood Johnson Foundation, *Special Report: The Foundation's Minority Medical Training Programs* (Princeton, NJ: Author, 1987), p. 3.

dards for high school graduation and college admission may lower the graduation rates of Hispanic and black students in the future. Taken together, these trends indicate that the educational gains made during the 1970s are now in jeopardy.

ACADEMIC ACHIEVEMENT DECLINES.   We indicated that, on average, academic performance of blacks and Hispanics has improved in recent years. However, other data are more troublesome. In a recent study, conducted at the University of Chicago, schools with high concentrations of minority students were found to have lower average test scores than they did a decade ago. It appears that students in integrated schools are making modest academic gains, but students going to highly segregated inner-city schools are falling further and further behind.[81]

WAGE DISPARITIES.   The wage gap between blacks and whites, though improving in some areas, is still large. When we look at the income distribution of black families (Figure 22-3), we find that it is shaped like a pyramid, with the smallest percentage of households earning the highest incomes and the largest percentage earning the least. As Andrew Hacker has pointed out, the income distribution for whites is "shaped more like a Greek cross, with families earning over $35,000 actually outnumbering those earning less than $20,000."[82]

The income gap depicted in Figure 22-3 is made more dramatic when it is remembered that the number of black families living in poverty has actually increased in recent years, a point discussed in Chapter 17. When calculations are made in constant dollars, so that the effects of inflation are taken into account, we discover that the number of black families making under $10,000 increased by 11 percent between 1970 and 1986. Though 45 percent of black families now earn over $20,000, most still earn less, and 30 percent earn under $10,000 a year. It is becoming clear that the black community is moving in two directions. Some black households are enjoying increasing affluence, while others are falling deeper and deeper into poverty. The reasons for increased af-

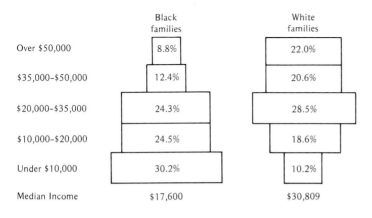

	Black families	White families
Over $50,000	8.8%	22.0%
$35,000–$50,000	12.4%	20.6%
$20,000–$35,000	24.3%	28.5%
$10,000–$20,000	24.5%	18.6%
Under $10,000	30.2%	10.2%
Median Income	$17,600	$30,809

Figure 22-3   Family income of blacks and whites, 1986.   (*Source:* U.S. Bureau of the Census quoted in Andrew Hacker, "American Apartheid," in *New York Review of Books*, Vol. 34 [Dec. 3, 1987].)

[81] See William Julius Wilson, *The Truly Disadvantaged: The Inner City, The Underclass, and Public Policy* (Chicago: University of Chicago Press, 1987).
[82] Ibid., p. 30.

fluence are clear enough; the reasons for increased poverty, as we shall see, are more complex.

CONTINUING DISCRIMINATION.   The battle against prejudice is far from over. Although Americans express greater support for integration in most parts of their lives, they are less enthusiastic about programs designed to implement integration. While they support government and court efforts to enforce the desegregation in public accommodations (theaters, hotels, and restaurants), they are not as supportive of government-enforced remedies such as affirmative action plans, bussing schemes, and welfare programs.[83] Part of this resistance is due to a distrust of government programs and part due to residual prejudice.

Discrimination appears to play a role in the gap between the wages of blacks and whites. Some of that income disparity is due to the facts that blacks hold poorer jobs than whites, have less seniority in the jobs they hold, or have less education than whites. But when these factors are taken into account, so that we are comparing whites and blacks with similar qualifications, wage disparities still exist. For example, black college graduates earn $784 for every $1000 earned by white graduates.[84] A recent study by the United States Commission on Civil Rights concludes that only 30 to 40 percent of the gap in wages between black and white men can be explained by measurable characteristics, such as education and job experience. Blacks and whites with the same education, doing similar work, with similar years of experience, are not being paid equally.[85] Part of the wage disparity is due to residual discrimination. However, other factors influence disparity in the wage gap. We turn now to an examination of those factors.

UNEMPLOYMENT OF BLACKS.   On average, black men who are working earn only 73 percent of the wages earned by white men. However, this figure is somewhat misleading because it does not take into account the high rate of unemployment among blacks. When these figures are calculated into the data, the average wage for all black men is only 60 percent of the wages of all white men. These figures have not changed much over the last twenty years. Unemployment is a growing problem in the black community. In 1954, over 75 percent of black men were gainfully employed. Today, less than 40 percent of black men hold full-time year-round jobs. Competition for jobs once held by black men has increased because women, Hispanics, and Asians have moved into the labor force in large numbers.[86] Black women are faring better than black men in the employment competition because more women graduate from high school and possess the attitudes and skills apparently desired by employers.

SOCIAL ISOLATION AND BLACK POVERTY.   To a degree unprecedented in our history, poor blacks are being raised in urban neighborhoods where only other poor blacks reside.[87] They go to schools with predominantly black stu-

---

[83] Schuman, Steeh, and Bobo, *Racial Attitudes in America.*

[84] Black women graduates, you will remember, have done much better.

[85] The United States Commission on Civil Rights, *The Economic Progress of Black Men in America* (Washington, DC: The United States Commission on Civil Rights, 1987).

[86] Andrew Hacker, "American Apartheid," p. 29.

[87] Reynolds Farley and Walter R. Allen, *The Color Line and the Quality of Life in America* (New York: Russell Sage Foundation, 1987). See also Wilson, *The Truly Disadvantaged.*

dents and live in neighborhoods that are predominantly black and poor. Black men who are young and poor have few economically successful role models in their neighborhoods or in their homes. Increasingly, as we shall discuss shortly, black families are headed by women. Few youngsters have fathers living at home who can act as role models, provide guidance, and help monitor the activities of the young. There are no middle-class men living nearby who can directly and indirectly teach poverty's youth how to escape the urban ghetto.

ANTISCHOOL VALUES.   Black men living in poor neighborhoods do not usually prove themselves by studying hard and taking advantage of the opportunities offered by schools. It is difficult for many inner-city students to believe that schools offer them anything of lasting value. Among their peers, recognition is likely to come from discounting school and the values that encourage academic and employment success.[88] Of course, many whites also grow up in poverty and many of them hold antischool values. However, it appears that poor whites have a greater chance of being exposed to other values as they grow up. The white poor are much more likely than blacks to live in rural communities, have a father present in the home, attend schools with children from other backgrounds, and live in close proximity to other social classes.[89]

Unemployment among black men is the result of many interacting factors that together make it less and less likely that poor men can work their way out of the poverty into which they were born. The legacy of discrimination, inner-city segregation of poor black children, changing factors in black families, poor schools, low aspirations, proliferation of crime, easy access to drugs, severe cutbacks in spending for programs designed to help the poor, and myriad other factors make the problem of black poverty acute, sad, and dangerous.

CHANGING PATTERNS IN THE BLACK FAMILY.   There is no single model for the black family any more than there is one model to which all white, Hispanic, or Asian families conform. Yet, there are trends in black families that should warrant our attention. As Andrew Hacker put it,

> The statistics by themselves are dismaying: currently, more than 60 percent of black infants are born outside of wedlock; almost as many black families are headed by women, and the majority of black children live only with their mothers. These figures are three to five times those for white Americans, and at least three times the statistics for blacks of a generation ago.[90]

Hacker points to other disturbing statistics. One in four black women become mothers by age eighteen and 40 percent are mothers by their early twenties. Fifty-six percent of black single mothers live in poverty and 71 percent of them have more than one child. Eighty percent of black single mothers receive no child support from the father of their children.[91] Interestingly, teenage parenthood is most likely among black girls who attend segregated schools and live in all-black neighborhoods.[92]

---

[88] Jay MacLeod, *Ain't No Makin' It: Leveled Aspirations in a Low-Income Neighborhood* (Boulder: Westview Press, 1987). See also Paul Willis, *Learning to Labor: How Working Class Kids Get Working Class Jobs* (New York: Columbia University Press, 1981). Available in paperback.

[89] Hacker, "American Apartheid," p. 32.

[90] Ibid., p. 26.

[91] Ibid., pp. 26–27.

[92] Cheryl D. Haynes, ed., *Risking the Future: Adolescent Sexuality, Pregnancy, and Childbearing* (Washington, DC: National Academy Press, 1987). See also Wilson, *The Truly Disadvantaged*.

Fathers are taking less and less part in the formal structure of black families. Among men most eligible to play the role of husband and father (those between ages twenty-five and thirty-four), only 39 percent are married and living with their families. This age group is particularly transient, and thus, they are often excluded from government statistics. An estimated 20 percent of this age group were never interviewed during the last census. Of those who were interviewed, fewer than half held full-time jobs.[93]

Present Trends and the Future of Public Education

The issues discussed in this chapter are important in themselves, but also for what they suggest for the future of public education. In this section, we will look at current trends and consider what they tell us about the schools of tomorrow.

Desegregation Trends

Most Americans believe that we have made great progress toward desegregating the nation's schools and that progress continues each year. The facts are quite different. In 1968, 77 percent of black students were enrolled in predominantly black schools. By 1972, that percentage had fallen to 64 percent. Since that time, however, there has been almost no change in these statistics.[94] Today, two out of three black children attend schools with predominantly black students and one in three attend schools where minority students make up 90 percent of the enrollment. Gary Orfield, a professor at the University of Chicago, pointed out that blacks who live in poverty are isolated from other races and from other social classes:

> Whatever may be the roots of the "urban underclass," it is certainly true that its children go to schools that are almost totally segregated by race and class. . . . It may well be that the children being socialized in these underclass schools are even more comprehensively isolated from mainstream middle-class society than were the black children of the South whose problems led to the long battle over segregated education.[95]

The initial progress toward desegregation was the result of court orders and federal enforcement. Most of the progress came in the South in the 1960s and early 1970s. Since that time, the number of court orders has diminished and federal enforcement has become less aggressive. Integration has been further stymied by the fact that, in the 1970s, large numbers of middle-class and affluent whites began leaving the cities to live in the suburbs. Because federal efforts to increase integration have slackened in recent years and because populations

[93] Marian Edelman, *Families in Peril: An Agenda for Social Change* (Cambridge: Harvard University Press, 1987).
[94] Edward Fisk, "Hispanic Pupils' Plight Cited in Study," *New York Times* (July 26, 1987), p. 26.
[95] Quoted in ibid. See also Gary Orfield, *Public School Desegregation in the United States: 1968–1980* (Chicago: Joint Center for Political Studies, 1983).

of minority students are growing in the inner cities, urban segregation is becoming a fact of American life.

Hispanic students are even more likely than blacks to attend segregated schools (schools where minority students constitute the majority of student enrollment). Seventy percent of Hispanic students attend such schools today as compared to 55 percent in 1968.[96] Drop-out rates among Hispanic students are alarming, especially within urban areas. In New York and Chicago, to pick the worst examples, over 70 percent of Hispanic youth drop out of school before graduation.[97]

To sum up, whatever advantages accrue to individuals and the nation through integration will be washed away if a majority of minority students, especially those in poverty, are segregated in run-down schools in poor neighborhoods. The students most in need of, and most likely to benefit from, an integrated educational experience are the ones least likely to attend integrated schools. There is no reason to believe that the academic troubles of these students will be solved by merely raising graduation requirements and requiring that they take more academic courses. While these may be worthwhile goals, black and Hispanic inner-city students will need a great deal of special attention if they are to benefit from such requirements. Without special assistance, higher requirements are simply an invitation for increased levels of failure and student alienation.

Demographic Trends

THE GROWTH OF MINORITY POPULATIONS.   The black and Hispanic population in the United States is growing at a rate much faster than the white population. In 1980, Hispanics made up 6.5 percent of the U.S. population and blacks 11.7 percent. By the year 2005, the Hispanic population will double and the black population will make up 13.2 percent of the population. (See Table 22-1.) Together these two groups will constitute a quarter of the U.S. population and an even greater percentage of the public school population.[98]

Population projections are just that—projections—and events may change present trends. However, we can be reasonably certain that black and Hispanic

TABLE 22-1.   Projected Populations of Black and Hispanic Americans, 1980–2005

	1980	1985	1990	1995	2000	2005
Hispanic	6.5	7.7	9.0	10.3	11.8	12.8
Blacks	11.7	12.2	12.6	13.0	13.4	13.2

SOURCE: Projection of the Hispanic population from data in Oxford Analytica, *America in Perspective* (Boston: Houghton-Mifflin, 1986). Projections for black population from Bureau of the Census data, 1982.

[96] Ibid.
[97] National Commission on Secondary Education for Hispanics, *Make Something Happen: Hispanics and Urban High School Reform* (Washington, DC: Hispanic Policy Development Project, 1985), p. 26.
[98] Calculated from data reported in Oxford Analytica, *America in Perspective* (Boston: Houghton Mifflin, 1986), pp. 51–52.

students, especially those who come from impoverished homes and are at greatest educational risk, are going to make up an increasing percentage of the public school population in the future. It will take a massive educational effort, rivaling that of the Great Society programs of the 1970s, to meet the educational needs of these students. However, requests for greater expenditures for education are going to have to compete with other needs, such as cutting the federal deficit, meeting the medical and social security needs of the elderly (also a growing percentage of the population), maintaining the military, and stimulating economic growth.

ALTERING THE SOCIAL GEOGRAPHY.   Starting in the early part of the century and accelerating after World War II, housing and community patterns in the United States began to shift in significant ways. In preindustrial America, classes lived in close proximity to one another. That meant that as the poor and working classes gained access to public education, they entered schools with children of every class. Children of businessmen sat next to children of shop owners, bookkeepers, artisans, factory workers, domestics, and the poor and unemployed. The policies and programs offered by the school were determined by a heterogeneous public with different interests but with a shared commitment to common schooling.

With the growth of industrialization, urban areas that used to bring citizens of many races and classes into close proximity became instruments of geographical segregation. Neighborhoods within cities became segregated, first by social class and then, increasingly, by race. Beginning in the 1960s, there was a middle- and upper-class exodus to the suburbs that now ring every American city. Businesses have followed the white-collar work force into the suburbs, badly eroding the already weakened tax base of urban areas.

Minorities and low-income whites were left in the city, encapsulated in a faltering economic system that is unable to sustain them. The resettlement of the American population is slowly segregating neighborhoods and schools by class and race. It has recast our political boundaries and reshaped the political debate over education. Common schooling, which was once possible because the poor and the affluent lived in close proximity, is now difficult and sometimes impossible. The ideal of the common school has been undercut. The public forum within communities—where the poor and the affluent once argued matters of policy, curriculum, and educational resources—no longer includes a wide diversity of people and opinion.[99]

Stark inequities now exist among schools that serve different populations, but these inequities are not the result of de jure segregation, as they once were in the South; instead, they are the result of a new social and political geography. One result of the new segregation has been that the education debate increasingly is carried on at the national level. Here, however, officials are far removed from their constituencies. Thus, the course of the debate is not influenced so much by local needs as it is by larger political considerations. Different economic classes are not brought into direct contact; therefore, they are denied

[99] Ira Katznelson and Margaret Weir, *Schooling for All: Class, Race and the Decline of the Democratic Ideal* (New York: Basic Books, 1985), p. 214.

productive debate and the chance to establish a community of purpose.[100] The kind of local decision making promoted in Brown II is impossible when urban and suburban communities become havens of homogeneity. And, if the educational leaders in the federal government adopt a localist perspective and lessen their commitment to integration and educational opportunity, productive debate about educational aims and policies is severely hampered.

Shifts in the nation's social geography change what goes on in schools, change the composition of the student body, alter the educational opportunities open to poor and minority students, affect the life-chances of those same students, change the nature and location of policy debates over education, and ultimately challenge the democratic ideal.

Summary

The American creed extols the virtues of freedom, equality, opportunity, and liberty. Central to this creed has been a commitment to common schooling, where children from all segments of the community are educated together. Educational policies were determined locally in open debate and ultimately were administered by elected officials. The ideology of inclusion brought individuals of different classes into the debate over public education. After a prolonged struggle, blacks won access first to segregated and then to integrated schools. The civil rights movement, the Brown decision, and the Civil Rights Bill of 1964 brought blacks into the public debate over education and gave them a powerful voice.

Prejudice has hindered the educational and economic progress of many black Americans. Some social scientists, those adhering to group *conflict theory*, contend that prejudice results from a battle over scarce resources. Whites are prejudiced toward blacks, these theorists would contend, because discrimination served the interests of the majority. *Social learning theory* contends that prejudices are learned in the course of socialization. Children inherit the prejudices of their parents, of their peer group, and of the culture. *Cognitive processing theories* are interested in how prejudices work in the individual mind. They suggest that schema (organized cognitive structures) help organize our thoughts and perceptions. When schema refer to people and become rigid and difficult to alter, they are called *stereotypes*. *Psychodynamic theories* do not focus on cognitive process but on the personality structure of prejudiced people. The four theories of prejudice are not in conflict; they simply focus on different aspects of prejudice.

Racial prejudices function at many levels and are difficult to alter once they have been established. However, role playing can help some people see the world from the perspective of others and more fully appreciate their situation. Interracial contact, if the conditions promote communication and cooperation, can challenge stereotypes and lessen prejudice. Laws promoting integration were rather successful in lessening prejudices because they promoted greater

---

[100] Some argue that the shifts in social geography have been the result of individual choice and not government policy. That is a debatable assertion. The migration to the suburbs would not have been possible without massive highway construction, subsidies of public transportation, and federal sponsorship of the secondary mortgage market.

interracial contact and because they pointed out the contradiction between the nation's professed belief in equality and its legalized practice of segregation.

Blacks have consistently and courageously worked to achieve full equality in America, and a great deal of that struggle was focused on gaining access to the common school and to the debate over educational policies and aims. Great progress has been made toward that end, but the battle is far from over. It is clear that integration does not harm white achievement as long as an ethos of order and academic purposefulness pervades the school. Integration appears to assist black achievement, especially when classes are integrated, opportunities exist for cooperative learning, middle-class students make up a majority of the student body, teachers employ effective teaching methods, and families support the educational aims of the school. It has also been demonstrated that integration increases the likelihood that blacks will graduate from high school, attend integrated colleges, get better grades in college, work in integrated settings after college, and like their work and their employers.

There is good evidence that racial attitudes are becoming more open and free of prejudice in the United States. We have come a long way in the past forty years. More blacks than ever before are going to and graduating from high school. College attendance rates have turned downward in recent years, but they are still much higher than they were four decades ago. More blacks than ever before are using their education to get middle-class jobs.

Problems persist, however. Black college enrollment fell in the 1980s and increased standards for high school graduation may bring high school graduation figures down in the future. There is also evidence that while middle-class blacks are making social and financial gains, the most impoverished segments of the black population are falling deeper into poverty and becoming more racially isolated than perhaps at any time in our history. Student achievement in schools serving the black urban poor has been dropping for over a decade. Wage disparities between black men and white men and the gap separating the rich from the poor are growing. At the same time, progress toward a more fully integrated school system has come to a standstill. Past progress is being maintained but new initiatives are not being vigorously pursued.

There have been shifts in the family patterns of blacks, especially, but not exclusively, among poor blacks. More than 60 percent of black children today are born to single mothers. A quarter of black women become single mothers by the time they reach eighteen years of age. The majority of black female-headed households fall below the poverty level. Blacks in poverty are increasingly living in urban areas where they come in little contact with other races or other classes. Population growth among the black and Hispanic urban poor is higher than for most other segments of the society. Thus, the number of urban poor people is growing at just the time they are becoming more socially isolated. This new social geography makes integration difficult, if not impossible. It also changes the nature of the common school debate. The interests of different races and different classes are not being represented at the local level because community populations are becoming more homogenous and insular. Conversation about educational aims has been pushed to the national level, where the nature of the debate is quite different. At this level, policy makers are more likely to be influenced by suggestions contained in national reports rather than by the interests of local constituencies. As a result, there has been a proliferation of such reports in recent years. We will examine what those reports have to say in the next chapter.

Suggested Readings

PREJUDICE AND EDUCATION

KATZ, PHYLLIS A., ed. *Toward the Elimination of Racism.* New York: Pergamon Press, 1976.

SCHUMAN, HOWARD, CHARLOTTE STEEH, and LAWRENCE BOBO. *Racial Attitudes in America.* Cambridge: Harvard University Press, 1985.

STEPHAN, WALTER G., and JOE R. FEAGIN, eds. *School Desegregation: Past, Present, and Future.* New York: Plenum Press, 1980.

Society and Education is a journal published by the American Antidefamation League. Printed four times a year, the journal contains articles dealing with discrimination, democracy, and education.

THE HISTORY OF BLACK EDUCATION AND SCHOOL DESEGREGATION

BULLOCK, HENRY ALLEN. *History of Negro Education in the South: From 1619 to the Present.* Cambridge: Harvard University Press, 1967.

LEWIS, ANTHONY. *Portrait of a Decade: The Second American Revolution.* New York: Random House, 1964.

KATZNELSON, IRA and MARGARET WEIR. *Schooling for All: Class, Race and the Decline of the Democratic Ideal.* New York: Basic Books, 1985.

MINGLE, JAMES R. *Focus on Minorities: Trends in Higher Education Participation and Success.* Denver: Education Commission of the States and State Higher Education Executive Officers, 1987.

ORFIELD, GARY. *Public School Desegregation in the United States: 1968–1980.* Chicago: Joint Center for Political Studies, 1983.

RACE, POVERTY, AND EDUCATION

The Center on Budget and Policy Priorities is a nonprofit research and analysis organization that specializes in the study of budget issues. The center takes a special interest in entitlement programs and legislation affecting people in poverty. For information, write Center on Budget and Policy Priorities, 236 Massachusetts Avenue, N. E., Suite 305, Washington, D. C. 20002.

Focus is the monthly newsletter of the Joint Center for Political Studies. Each month it contains brief reviews of research findings and survey results on issues pertaining to race. The subscription cost is low. For more information, write Joint Center for Political Studies, 1426 H Street, N.W., Suite 926, Washington, DC 20005.

Another publication, also titled *Focus,* is published four times a year by the Institute for Research on Poverty at the University of Wisconsin. This newsletter reports on studies done at the institute and supplies information about newly published books. It can be ordered free of charge from the Institute for Research on Poverty, 1180 Observatory Drive, 3412 Social Science Building, University of Wisconsin, Madison, WI 53706.

CLARK, REGINALD M. *Family Life and School Achievement: Why Poor Black Children Succeed or Fail.* Chicago: University of Chicago Press, 1983.

LANDRY, BART. *The New Black Middle Class.* Berkeley: University of California Press, 1987.

LEE, VALARIE. *Access to Higher Education: The Experience of Blacks, Hispanics, and Low Socio-Economic Status Whites*. Washington, DC: American Council on Education, 1985.

MINGLE, JAMES R. *Focus on Minorities: Trends in Higher Education Participation and Success*. Denver: Education Commission of the States and State Higher Education Executive Officers, 1987.

NATIONAL URBAN LEAGUE. *The State of Black America, 1987*. New York: Author, 1987.

U. S. COMMISSION ON CIVIL RIGHTS. *The Economic Progress of Black Men in America*. Washington, DC: U. S. Commission on Civil Rights, 1987.

STUDIES OF FAMILIES IN POVERTY

EDLEMAN, MARIAN WRITE. *Families in Peril: An Agenda for Social Change*. Cambridge: Harvard University Press, 1987.

GARFINKEL, IRWIN, and SARA McLANAHAN. *Single Mothers and Their Children: A New American Dilemma*. Baltimore: Urban Institute Press, 1986.

HAYNES, CHERYL D., ed. *Risking the Future: Adolescent Sexuality, Pregnancy, and Childbearing*. Washington, DC: National Academy Press, 1987.

WILSON, WILLIAM JULIUS. *The Truly Disadvantaged: The Inner City, The Underclass, and Public Policy*. Chicago: University of Chicago Press, 1987.

STUDIES OF SEGREGATION AND HOUSING PATTERNS

FARLEY, REYNOLDS, and WALTER R. ALLEN. *The Color Line and the Quality of Life in America*. New York: Russell Sage Foundation, 1987.

VIDEOCASSETTE

A Class Divided. A video from the "Frontline" series, available from PBS Video, Public Broadcasting Service, 1320 Braddock Place, Alexandria, VA 22314.

Summary of Section V

Americans live in a complex social stratification system. Most understand that such a system exists, but few are fully aware of the powerful part it plays in their lives. There are at least two reasons for our ignorance. First, thinking about social class makes us uncomfortable. We do not like the idea of class because it is fraught with unpleasant connotations of inequality, inherited privilege, arbitrary disadvantage, and social rank. We prefer to think that we live in a just and meritocratic society where all people are essentially equal (equally human and equal before the law) and where a bounteous future is available for the earning. We do not like to believe that the meritocratic society we envision may not be the society we have. Nor do we like to think that we did not fairly earn the position we achieved, or worse, that others have an advantage in life's competition.

The second reason we do not think much about social class is because class is so much a part of our daily lives that we are not conscious of its existence or effects. Most of us spend our time in our social stratum with people with whom we share a vast array of values, tastes, assumptions, and beliefs. Even when we venture into the territory of another class, we don't think in class terms. When we look at a person from another stratum, we don't see "someone in Class II" or "someone in Class IV." Instead, we see "a shiny BMW" or "a shiny polyester suit," and we hear "the opera was marvelous," or "I did real good, irregardless." Teachers do not see Class II or Class IV children; they see children who are "delightful," "stuck up," or "spoiled rotten" or children who are "active," "troubled," or "slow learners." The point is that class differences do not remind us of class itself, but only of beliefs and prejudices that, from the narrow confines of our own class niche, appear only as "good taste" and worthy values.

In Section V, we learned that the United States is a class-bound society in which privilege, power, and prestige are distributed unequally. Social classes are recognizable human groups held together by their own individual sets of cultural characteristics. Those in a specific class are likely to share with others in their class similarities in family background, income, wealth, occupation, education, political and religious affiliations, child-rearing practices and much more. The differences among classes are interesting in themselves, but they have far-reaching consequences in such areas as health, life expectancy, happiness, self-respect, mental health, and how well one is treated by individuals and by institutions.

The United States came into being as a revolt against a feudal system in which class position was inherited and upward and downward mobility were almost impossible. The colonists envisioned a meritocratic society where class position was earned rather than assigned at birth. Conservative and liberal colonists had differences of opinion regarding the proper role of government, the nature of progress, and the causes of inequality and poverty. They agreed, however, on the basic principle of meritocracy: that people (not all people to be sure, but most people) should have the opportunity to compete in an open society for power, privilege, and prestige. It has been the great struggle of meritocratic democracy to make competition increasingly fair and equal and to extend it to all citizens.

Schools play a vital role in the struggle to perfect meritocracy. Today, children of Class II must get a good education if they hope to keep their Class II status as adults. With the exception of the most wealthy individuals, parents cannot simply pass on privilege. Children must earn their own place in society and that work begins in school.

Schools are supposed to be perfectly meritocratic institutions where grades and honors are exactly commensurate with each student's tangible achievements. The scheme is complicated, however, by the fact that a child's readiness to take advantage of what schools offer is greatly helped or hindered by family background. It is further hindered by teachers who consciously or unconsciously stigmatize children from poor families and nurture those from the middle and upper classes.

Data indicate that the United States enjoys a great deal of mobility and that most movement is upward. Historically, America has been a land of opportunity in which the general standard of living has increased rather steadily. However, mobility rates and the distribution of income have remained rather constant. Other nations' mobility rates (and recently their growth rates and standards of living) are as good or better than our own. It appears that when the economy expands, education helps most individuals maintain their class position and assures that some will improve on that position. In economically troubled times, however, education may not have the power to pull large numbers of people up the social-class ladder.

Social scientists have been puzzled by the fact that mobility rates have remained static over the past half century. Hereditarians contend that social class correlates strongly with intelligence and that intelligence is passed on from parent to child through heredity and child-rearing. They argue that mobility rates have not increased because the American class system rewards the meritorious nearly perfectly.

Classical liberals (most Republicans and Democrats) support the meritocratic ideal. They understand that prejudice hinders the life-chances of many children and want those problems eliminated. However, a growing portion of this group worries that the mechanisms designed to improve opportunities for the lower-class and minority groups may violate the very ideal those mechanisms were designed to support. This group argues that affirmative action remedies reward group membership rather than individual talent and achievement and, thus, violate the meritocratic principle. Other classical liberals argue that affirmative action must be taken if competition is ever to become truly meritocratic.

New egalitarians contend that the advantages that accrue to the wealthy and the disadvantages that accrue to the poor are so powerful and so tied to the economic system and social institutions that there simply is no way to assure fair competition in our society. Schools, they claim, tend to reproduce the existing class structure and limit the life-chances of the working class. They conclude that we cannot eliminate poverty indirectly (by improving education and the social services available to the poor), and we must attack the problem directly (by radically redistributing the wealth).

The new egalitarians are doing some interesting research and asking many provocative questions. They have broadened the meritocracy debate, at least within the confines of academe. However, the vast majority of Americans strongly disagree with the new egalitarian conclusions. Most support equality only in the sense of opportunity and not in the sense of guaranteed outcomes. That is to say, they support equality as a means but not as an end. Although Americans are aware that injustices occur and are willing to seek remedies when injustice is uncovered, most adhere to the classical liberal position and believe the class system is basically fair and socially productive.

No known class system is perfectly open. In many societies, an individual's opportunities are limited by such arbitrary factors as race, gender, ethnicity, religion, or political affiliation. In some societies, the opportunities available to particular groups are so limited that group membership becomes a caste from which it is impossible to escape. Caste systems can, and often do, coexist within class systems. That has certainly been the case in the United States. Legislation, court ruling, and schooling have done a great deal to free blacks, Hispanics, American Indians, and other minorities from the shackles of a caste system. Although barriers still exist, educated members of minority groups now stand a better, though not yet equal, chance in the competition for economic success.

The civil rights struggle carried on by blacks since slavery has had common schooling as a central goal. Civil rights groups have argued that schools offer the surest access to the goods and services of American society. Further, they have contended that common schools provide an opportunity for political debate that can reach across the boundaries of race and class.

School integration is now the law of the land. The achievements of blacks since school integration show that the faith black Americans put in education was not misplaced. Minority children who attend integrated schools, get a good education, and go on to college fare comparatively well as adults. Problems persist, however. The numbers of black and Hispanic students attending and completing college declined in the 1980s. Black students from impoverished homes too often languish in segregated, urban schools that offer a poor education and little hope for the future. The accomplishments of integrated education can be read in the growth of the black middle class. The greatest challenge now facing public education is found in the declining quality of schools that serve the growing underclass in our society.

In previous sections, we argued that schools play a vital role in developing individual potential and maintaining democracy. Now we see that schools are intricately connected to the class structure of society. Some claim that schools perpetuate existing inequalities. Others argue that schools are repositories of hope and society's most effective mechanism for the promotion of prosperity and social mobility. We have seen that there is truth in both claims.

R. H. Tawney observed early in the century that the "educational policy of a period reflects its conceptions of human society and the proper object of human endeavor."[1] In the 1960s, schools reflected the nation's concern for equity. Schools were directed to treat all groups fairly and to do what they could to diminish the arbitrary disadvantages of caste and class. The struggle to achieve that goal is far from over, but significant progress has been made. Today, as we shall see in the next section, educators are being asked to shift their focus to quality. The question we must now address is whether equity and excellence are compatible or contradictory aims.

[1] R. H. Tawney, "An Experiment in Democratic Education." Quoted in Ira Katznelson and Margaret Weir, *Schooling for All: Class, Race, and the Decline of the Democratic Ideal* (New York: Basic Books, 1985), p. 222.

Improving Schools: Balancing Quality and Equality

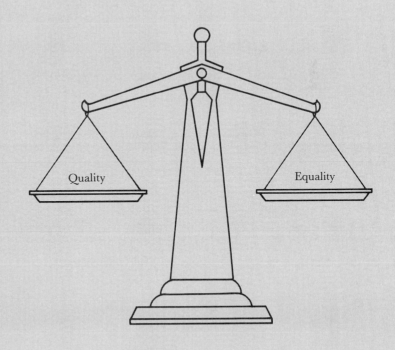

CHAPTER 23

Revising Education: Multiple Calls for Educational Change

Introduction

In 1983, the Commission on Excellence in Education issued its now famous report, *A Nation at Risk*.[1] The commission, made up of college presidents, business leaders, scholars, school and district administrators, school board members, and one teacher, assessed the health of American schools and found it frail. Within three years, over two dozen other major education reports appeared.[2] Each of the studies, known collectively as the *excellence reports*, examined the nation's educational system and proposed reforms. The major reports spawned over 350 smaller investigations by state departments of education, local school districts, and educational associations.[3] The reports differed in significant ways, but were united in the contention that America's schools are in trouble and must be improved.

This chapter begins with a brief history of school reform since World War II. After setting the current collection of excellence reports in a historical context, we review what the major reports have in common. We examine differences among the reports by focusing on the assumptions that undergird them, the educational aims they support, the constituencies they serve, and the recommendations they make for school improvement. The chapter ends with an assessment of where education appears to be headed as we approach the twenty-first century.

---

[1] Commission on Excellence in Education, *A Nation at Risk: The Imperative for Educational Reform* (Washington, D.C., Government Printing Office, 1983). Reprinted in *The Great School Debate: Which Way America Education*, eds. Beatrice Gross and Ronald Gross (New York: Simon and Schuster, 1985), pp. 21–49. Available in paperback.

[2] A list of the major reports appears at the end of the chapter.

[3] Beatrice Gross and Ronald Gross, *The Great School Debate*, p. 17.

The Pendulum of Reform in Education

At any given time in the past half century, one could find critics of education clamoring to attack one or another national problem through school improvement. Whether the issue was racial segregation, underemployment, poor productivity, a space race, an arms race, civil unrest, youth violence, drug abuse, drunk driving, or unwanted pregnancy, the schools were viewed as the best mechanism for social improvement. As a consequence, public schools have had to become highly adaptive institutions, able to change abruptly under some conditions and to resist change under others.[4]

Because the aims of education often are built around the most pressing social crisis of the day, the definition of a good school has changed from one decade to the next. In the 1940s and early 1950s, schools were asked to broaden their functions to include classes in vocational education, family life, and health, and to find ways to excite the interests of working-class students who, in an earlier day, would have quit school to work on farms or in factories. The traditional liberal arts curriculum was altered to make room for learning projects and vocational classes. As Diane Ravitch has pointed out, good schools in this era were considered to be those that had high retention rates and used "progressive methods."[5]

In the mid-1950s, the progressive education movement was attacked by such people as Mortimer Smith (who went on to found the Council for Basic Education), Arthur Bestor (who wrote the scathing and controversial book, *Educational Wastelands),* and Robert Hutchins (chancellor at the University of Chicago). The launching of Sputnik ended both the debate over progressive methods and the progressive era in education. Millions of federal dollars were pumped into the nation's schools to improve the curriculum, especially in the areas of science and mathematics. "Good schools" in the late 1950s were were those that had high academic standards and used newly developed methods for teaching science and mathematics.

By the late 1960s, schools were called on to provide equal opportunities for minority students and to decrease alienation among school-aged youth. The education pendulum swung back toward greater choice and fewer academic requirements. "Good schools" were those that avoided violence, channeled pupil interests in productive directions, and celebrated the exuberance and potential of the young.

By the 1980s, the schools had gone through a number of transformations and the achievements of the system were impressive. Schools were becoming racially integrated. Tests were less biased, and schools were still working to cut racism from the system. The educational attainment levels of minority students had climbed and the income levels of college-educated blacks at last were on a

---

[4] For example, the effort to end racial segregation in the nation's schools was a vast and meaningful reform. On the other hand, the open-spaced school effort was generally subverted by teachers who refashioned traditional classrooms behind bookcases and makeshift partitions.

[5] Diane Ravitch, "The Education Pendulum," *Psychology Today* (October 1983). Reprinted in Fred Schultz, ed., *Education: Annual Editions, 85/86* (Guilford, CT: Dushkin Publishing Group, 1985), pp. 20–23.

par with whites. Special education programs had been expanded, and mainstreaming was accomplished in many school districts. The legal rights of students had been defined with greater clarity, and greater academic opportunities had opened for women.

The achievements of the school system are not often cited in the ongoing public debate over education, because the nation's attention is usually fixed on today's problems rather than yesterday's accomplishments. Recently, national attention has focused on an economy caught in cycles of slow growth and recession. Fluctuating rates of unemployment and inflation have challenged America's preeminent position in the world economy. Smokestack industries have faltered. Today, children of middle-class families cannot depend on equaling the after-inflation income of their parents, and upward mobility is no longer assured. It is in this economic context that the current demands for educational reform have taken shape.

Today's criticisms of education are not like those of the past. In earlier decades, the assumption was that schools were getting better but still needed improvement. Today, educators, legislators, business leaders, students, and the general public agree that the quality of American schools has spiraled downward. Lowering achievement test scores suggest that, for the first time in our history, a generation may grow up less academically competent than their parents.[6] The declining quality in education and the need for school improvement are central themes in every education report issued in the 1980s.

What the Major Commission Reports Have in Common

Public Issues and Private Interests

Commission members are not disinterested observers of the educational scene; they are *interested parties*. They speak from particular points of view and with the interests of specific constituencies in mind. However, their reports are not written in the language of partisanship. Instead, the reports identify the interests of a particular constituency with the well-being of the nation as a whole. We will discuss the specific interests served by the various reports later in the chapter.

Commission reports are political documents[7] and, as such, have several things in common:

1. They are written to verify the public's suspicion that the quality of American education has declined.
2. They are written by nationally known, well-respected leaders from business,

---

[6] Commission on Excellence in Education, *A Nation at Risk,* pp. 27–28.

[7] "At the outset, it should be recognized that these reports are political documents; the case they make takes the form of a polemic, not a reasoned treatise. Rather than carefully marshalling facts to prove their case, they present a litany of charges without examining the veracity of their evidence or its sources. By presenting their material starkly, and often eloquently, the commissions hoped to jar the public into action, and to a great extent they have been successful." Lawrence C. Stedman and Marshall S. Smith, "Weak Arguments, Poor Data, Simplistic Recommendations," in *The Great School Debate,* eds. Beatrice Gross and Ronald Gross, p. 84.

politics, education, and the general public. The varied affiliations and collective prominence of the commissioners lend an air of objectivity to the documents they produce.

3. All make policy recommendations for improving public education. These suggestions generally serve the interests of each commission's funding sources and/or sponsoring organizations.

4. All are designed to galvanize public opinion behind an effort to improve the nation's schools. The reports are written in a passionate and streamlined style. Grim statistics are followed by lists of straightforward, nonradical recommendations. Clear writing, quotable quotes, shocking facts, and manageable recommendations ensure that the reports get maximum media attention.

Documenting the Decline

Most commission reports begin with the assertion that the quality of education is in dangerous decline. For example, the Twentieth Century Fund began its report with the dramatic assertion, "The nation's public schools are in trouble. By almost every measure—the commitment and competency of teachers, student test scores, truancy and dropout rates, crimes of violence—the performance of our schools falls far short of expectations."[8] Ernest Boyer, former United States commissioner of education, began his report for the Carnegie Foundation by documenting the thirty-year decline in Scholastic Aptitude Test (SAT) scores. He pointed out that, between 1952 and 1982, the average score on the verbal portion of the SAT fell by 50 points. Over the same period, a nearly 40 point drop was recorded on the mathematics portion of the test. Some of this decline came about because a larger, more diverse pool of students began taking Scholastic Aptitude Test in the 1960s. Yet, even after these population changes are taken into account, a significant gap remains between the scores of today's academically ambitious students and similar students in the past.[9]

Dropping SAT scores are not the only indication of declining achievement in our nation's schools. According to the National Science Board, "mathematics and science achievement scores of 17-year-olds [have] dropped steadily" over the past twenty years.[10] Other data indicate that students' fundamental political knowledge has fallen, writing and reading scores have declined, and general achievement test scores at every high school grade level have dropped significantly.[11] The National Commission on Excellence listed the following indicators of trouble in the American classroom:

---

[8] Twentieth Century Fund, *Making the Grade: Report of the Twentieth Century Fund Task Force on Federal Elementary and Secondary Education Policy* (New York: Twentieth Century Fund, 1983), p. 3. Available in paperback.

[9] William Turnbull, "Student Change, Program Change: Why SAT Scores Kept Falling," *College Board Report*, No. 85–2 (New York: College Entrance Examination Board, 1985).

[10] National Science Board Commission on Precollege Education in Mathematics, Science and Technology, *Educating America for the 21st Century* (Washington, DC: National Science Foundation, 1983), p. 1.

[11] Ernest L. Boyer, *High School: A Report on Secondary Education in America* (New York: Harper & Row, 1983), pp. 22–35; available in paperback. See also Lee H. Ehman, "The American School in the Political Socialization Process," *Review of Educational Research*, Vol. 50 (Spring 1980), pp. 99–119.

- About 13 percent of all seventeen-year-olds in the United States are functionally illiterate. Functional illiteracy among minority youth may run as high as 40 percent.
- Average achievement of high school students on most standardized tests is now lower than . . . when Sputnik was launched [in 1957].
- Over half the population of gifted students do not match their tested ability with compatible achievement in school.
- Both the number and proportion of students demonstrating superior achievement on the SATs (i.e., those with scores of 650 or higher) have dramatically declined.
- Many seventeen-year-olds do not possess the higher order intellectual skills we should expect of them. Nearly 40 percent cannot draw inferences from written material; only one-fifth can write a persuasive essay; and only one-third can solve a mathematics problem requiring several steps.
- Between 1975 and 1980, remedial mathematics courses in public four-year colleges increased by 72 percent and now constitute one-quarter of all mathematics courses taught in those institutions.
- Average tested achievement of students graduating from college is also lower.[12]

Explaining the Decline

Most reports agree that the decline in academic achievement has occurred because schools expect too little from their students. High school graduation requirements have been lowered,[13] textbooks have been made easier, and less is asked of students in the classroom. The National Commission on Excellence in Education summed up the problem:

> Secondary school curricula have been homogenized, diluted, and diffused to the point that they no longer have a central purpose. In effect we have a cafeteria-style curriculum in which the appetizers and desserts can easily be mistaken for the main courses. Students have migrated from vocational and college preparatory programs to "general track" courses in large numbers. The proportion of students taking a general program of study has increased from 12 percent in 1964 to 42 percent in 1979.[14]

Other reports contend that schools are offering inflated rewards for deflated achievement. They cite studies showing that high school grades have increased over the same period in which scores on standardized achievement tests have fallen dramatically.[15] Social promotion policies have allowed teachers to pass students who are not prepared for the next grade. Students are doing less homework and the decline in assigned homework is greatest among low-achieving students.[16]

---

[12] Commission on Excellence in Education, *A Nation at Risk*, pp. 25–26.

[13] Philip N. Marcus, "Evidence of Decline in Educational Standards," in *Education on Trial: Strategies for the Future*, ed. William O. Johnson (San Francisco: Institute for Contemporary Studies, 1985), pp. 9–26.

[14] Commission on Excellence in Education, *A Nation at Risk*, p. 34.

[15] William Turnbull, "Student Change, Program Change," p. 7.

[16] In 1972, 26 percent of male and 44 percent of female high school seniors reported doing at least five hours of homework a week. By 1980, the corresponding percentages were 20 and 29. In 1972, 47 percent of high-achieving students and 26 percent of low-achieving students spent

In addition to documenting the decline in school quality, many reports assert that the high school requirements are less rigorous in the United States than in many other industrialized nations. For example, only about 40 percent of American high school students take three years of mathematics and under 30 percent take three years of science. In Japan, Russia, and West Germany, however, over 90 percent of secondary students take these subjects for three or more years.[17] Students in these nations devote substantially more time to academic study; they do more homework and stay in schools for more hours per day and for more days per year. The National Science Board calculated that a typical Japanese secondary school graduate spends three times as many hours in science classes than even the most advanced high school students in the United States.[18]

Sounding the Alarm

The findings of the commission reports are disturbing and they are intended to be. The common purpose of the commission reports is to sound an alarm. Most contend that the problem in education is so grave that the future of the nation is "at risk." The Commission on Excellence in Education stated:

> If an unfriendly foreign power had attempted to impose on America the mediocre educational performance that exists today, we might have viewed it as an act of war. We have, in effect, been committing an act of unthinkable, unilateral educational disarmament.
>
> The educational foundations of our society are presently being eroded by a rising tide of mediocrity that threatens our very future as a nation and as a people.[19]

The conclusions of other reports are only slightly less apocalyptic. The Education Commission of the States warns that "a real emergency is upon us," and the Twentieth Century Fund states that "continued failure by the schools to perform their traditional role adequately . . . may have disastrous consequences for this nation."[20]

Common Assumptions

Though the reports offer different policy suggestions, they share common assumptions about the importance of education and the nature of reform. All reports agree that quality education is the fuel that drives the social and economic machinery of the nation. The Education Commission of the States, to cite just one example, argues that "our national defense, our social stability,

---

five or more hours per week on homework in their senior year. In 1980, the corresponding percentages were 42 and 14. A slight recovery in all categories was recorded in 1982. *National Center for Educational Statistics Bulletin*, (September 1985), p. 2.

[17] National Science Board Commission on Precollege Education in Mathematics, Science and Technology, *Educating America for the 21st Century*, p. 19.

[18] Ibid., p. 20. See also Boyer, *High School*, pp. 33–36.

[19] Commission on Excellence in Education, *A Nation at Risk*, p. 23.

[20] Twentieth Century Fund, *Making the Grade*, p. 3.

and our national prosperity . . . will depend on our ability to improve educa-tion."[21] All reports agree that excellent teaching is central to school improve-ment.[22]

Most reports contend that the educational system can be improved by insti-tuting relatively minor changes such as lengthening the school day, instituting merit pay plans, offering fewer "frill" courses, paying more attention to aca-demics, requiring more rigorous testing, and insisting upon greater accounta-bility. These are ambitious changes, but they do not significantly alter the struc-ture of the school system, which is assumed to be fundamentally sound. Perhaps, because the reports wanted to avoid the organized resistance of special interest groups, none of them offered outright sponsorship of controversial proposals such as tax support for private schools, voucher plans, the abolition of tenure, or doing away with colleges of education.[23]

A Common Criticism

As we shall see later in the chapter, the commission reports have been highly praised and heavily criticized. Some critics contend that the commissions only included negative information and avoided positive data. For example, studies of school integration or mainstreaming, two notable accomplishments, were not discussed. Data showing achievement gains in some areas were ignored.[24] While positive data are not plentiful, signs of academic improvement do exist, espe-cially at the elementary level. These data suggest that academic achievement gains were already in the pipeline before the commissions began issuing their reports.

A pamphlet issued by the American Educational Studies Association (AESA) faults the reports for ignoring the accomplishments of public schools and for not adequately examining the consequences their recommendations will have on students. The authors of the AESA pamphlet contend that some report recommendations will exacerbate the problems facing low-achieving students. Raywid and her colleagues point out that the reports do not identify how their recommendations will be funded.[25]

---

[21] Education Commission of the States, *Action for Excellence: Task Force for Education for Economic Growth* (Denver: Author, 1983).

[22] As the National Science Board put it, "The teacher is the key to education—the vital factor in motivating and maintaining student interest." The National Science Board Commission on Precollege Education in Mathematics, Science and Technology, *Educating America for the 21st Century*, p. 27.

[23] The most notable exception to this generalization is found in John I. Goodlad, *A Place Called School: Prospects for the Future* (New York: McGraw-Hill Book Company, 1984).

[24] Paul E. Peterson, "Did the Education Commissions Say Anything?" in *Excellence in Education: Perspectives on Policy and Practice,* eds. Philip G. Altbach, Gail P. Kelly, and Lois Weis (Buffalo, NY: Prometheus Books, 1985), pp. 58–61. Available in paperback.

[25] Mary Anne Raywid, Charles A. Tesconi, Jr., and Donald R. Warren, *Pride and Promise* (West-bury, NY: American Educational Studies Association, 1984), pp. 2–7. For a review of the AESA pamphlet, see Robert R. Sherman, "Dare the Schools Build a New Social Order—Again?" *Educational Theory*, Vol. 36 (Winter 1986), pp. 87–92.

The Commissions and Their Constituencies

The commissions were created and financed by various federal agencies, private foundations, and professional groups. The focus of the commission reports, the data they chose to analyze, the recommendations they made, and the schools they envisioned for the future were generally compatible with the interests and assumptions of their parent agencies. The major reports (the eighteen reports that received the most attention and were commissioned and funded by influential interest groups) can be sorted into four general categories:

1. reports that emphasized economic and technical excellence,
2. reports that focused on academic excellence,
3. reports that envisioned institutional excellence, and
4. reports that emphasized excellence and equity (see Table 23-1).

These four categories do not have clear boundaries, and thus, there are numerous areas of overlapping interest. Nevertheless, these classifications will help us highlight the most significant differences among the reports.

The reports that focus on *economic and technical excellence* are sponsored by business and government interests. These reports contend that the nature of the economy is changing and that schools must prepare individuals for tomorrow's high technology jobs. The *academic excellence* reports were written by scholars and reflect academe's conviction that democracy and education are inseparable and that the fate of individual and social development is determined by the education of the polity. The third category of reports, those that focus on *institutional excellence,* were written by individuals closely connected to the teaching profession. They take a fine-grained look at how schools actually operate and recommend the empowerment and professionalization of teachers. The

TABLE 23-1.   Four Kinds of Commission Reports of the State of American Education

Economic/Technical Excellence	Academic Excellence	Institutional Excellence	Excellence and Equity
A Nation at Risk	The Paideia Proposal	High School	Barriers to Excellence
Action for Excellence	Against Mediocrity	A Place Called School	Make Something Happen
High Schools and the Changing Workplace	An Education of Value	The Good High School	
Making the Grade	Educating America for the 21st Century	The Shopping Mall High School	
America's Competitive Challenge		Horace's Compromise	
		A Nation Prepared	
		Pride and Promise	

Note: Only reports issued between 1982 and 1986 are included in this list.

fourth category of reports were written for organizations dedicated to improving the quality of education offered to minority students and the poor. These reports view education as a mechanism for achieving equity and are suspicious of reforms that threaten to widen the opportunity gap that separates the rich and the poor in America.

We will examine reports in these four categories and review the criticisms that have been leveled against them. At the end of the chapter, we will examine the impact the reports have had and the influence they are likely to have in the future.

Economic and Technical Excellence Reports

The central assumption driving the economic and technical excellence reports is that foreign competition is threatening the military and industrial supremacy of the United States.

> From *A Nation at Risk:*
>
> Our once unchallenged preeminence in commerce, industry, and technological innovation is being overtaken by competitors throughout the world.[26]

> From *Action for Excellence:*
>
> The possibility that other nations may outstrip us in inventiveness and productivity is suddenly troubling Americans.[27]

The economic and technical excellence reports are business oriented. They warn that grave financial problems will overtake the economy unless immediate action is taken to improve the quality of the nation's schools. It is said in these reports that poor schools threaten American prosperity. The nature of the United States economy is shifting from smokestack industry to high technology and from national to international markets. Therefore, the reports say that schools must produce the human capital businesses will need to keep up with "technological change and global competition."[28] The reports suggest that superior schools in Japan and West Germany have given these nations a competitive edge and that inferior schools in the United States have put this nation at a disadvantage.

According to the economic and technical excellence reports (we call them the *business-oriented reports* for short), school curricula must reflect and anticipate the demands of the job market. The reports suggest that students take more courses in science, mathematics, and computing. America will overcome "economic malaise," say the reports, only if "industrial competitiveness" becomes a top priority in education.[29]

The reports contend that schools must serve the needs of business and call for closer links between schools and industry. As one report explained, "We believe especially that businesses, in their role as employers, should be much more deeply involved in the process of setting goals for education in America and in helping our schools reach these goals." The reports promise that the national economy will improve if business has a greater say in setting educa-

[26] Commission on Excellence in Education, *A Nation at Risk*, p. 5.
[27] Education Commission of the States, *Action for Excellence*, p. 13.
[28] Ibid., p. 35.
[29] Business–Higher Education Forum, *America's Competitive Challenge: The Need for a National Response* (Washington, DC: Author, 1983), p. 2.

tional priorities. As one report stated, "If the business community gets more involved in both the design and delivery of education, we are going to be more competitive as an economy."[30]

All the business-oriented reports said that the move to excellence must not be made at the expense of low-achieving students. For example, the Task Force on Education for Economic Growth stated, "We must improve the quality of instruction for all students—not just for an elite, but for all."[31] Other reports contend that substantial progress has been made to help those students "put at a disadvantage by poverty, minority status or both"[32] and that the time is now right for schools to offer *all* young people a rigorous curriculum. The reports contend that there need be no conflict between equality and excellence in education. However, where conflict may exist, the reports recommend that schools not forfeit excellence.

A few reports contend that schools have been harmed by an overemphasis on equality. For example, the Task Force on Elementary and Secondary Education Policy argued that the government's "emphasis on promoting equality of opportunity in the public schools has meant a slighting of its commitment to educational quality."[33]

The reports do not spell out just how their reform recommendations should be implemented. However, all the business task forces suggest that reform be administered from the top. As Clifton Gavin, chairman of the Exxon Corporation, noted, "It is up to us at the senior level to see that the job gets done. . . . Given a clear signal from the top, things will happen."[34]

The business-oriented reports seldom see teachers or teacher organizations as agents of change. In fact, some reports see teachers and their unions as contributing to education's quality decline. The Task Force on Federal Elementary and Secondary Policy states (without supporting evidence) that unions have

> helped transform . . . a noble . . . profession into a craft. . . . The collective bargaining process, moreover, has not only made it difficult to encourage promising teachers or dismiss poor ones, it has forced many of the best to leave teaching for more financially rewarding work. The result is that the quality of teaching suffers.[35]

The schools envisioned by the business task forces are not described in detail. However, enough is said to know that the schools they propose will have high standards, emphasize achievement (especially in science and technology), and will be competitive and receptive to the needs and suggestions of the business community. The schools proposed by the business task forces would help all students achieve but would have a special obligation to sort the "best and the brightest" from the mass of less-talented students. Schools, in the words of the Commission on Excellence, must help students "fix their place and possibilities within the larger societies."[36]

---

[30] Ibid., pp. 3, 18.
[31] Education Commission of the States, *Action for Excellence*.
[32] Ibid.
[33] Twentieth Century Fund, *Making the Grade*, p. 6.
[34] Business–Higher Education Forum, *Corporate and Campus Cooperation: An Action Agenda* (Washington, DC: Author, 1984), p. 27.
[35] Twentieth Century Fund, *Making the Grade*, pp. 5, 9.
[36] Commission on Excellence in Education, *A Nation at Risk*, p. 39.

CRITICISMS OF THE ECONOMIC AND TECHNICAL EXCELLENCE REPORTS. The first and most widespread criticism of the business-oriented reports is that they blame teachers for poor schools and that they assign the task of school improvement almost exclusively to business executives and school administrators. Schools are to be put in service of industry and to work on an industrial model. Teachers are not seen as a resource for change and, therefore, are not included on many of the business-oriented task forces. One critic asked readers to imagine a "public debate on the state of dental health . . . in which the voices of dentists are absent."[37] Other critics contend that the economic and technical excellence reports are so focused on the needs of business that they give scant attention to the complexity of schools or the special problems facing teachers and students.

The business-oriented reports assert that the economy is changing and that schools must prepare students for high-technology jobs. This suggestion is criticized on two grounds. First, some experts contend that the society is *not* undergoing a wholesale transformation to a high-technology economy.[38] Second, our slow shift to high technology is not producing many well-paid, high-skill jobs. In fact, the opposite is the case. Over half of all jobs created between 1979 and 1984 paid less than $7000 a year.[39] Data from the Bureau of Labor Statistics indicate that the fastest growing job opportunities in the 1990s will be for secretaries, word processors, nurses' aides, janitors, sales clerks, and cashiers.[40]

Some critics contend that the business-oriented task forces use education as a "scapegoat" for economic problems caused, not by poor schools, but by failure of management to automate and increase productivity. Joel Spring points out that, between 1960 and 1978, the average annual increase in productivity in the United States was 1.7 percent while in Japan it was a whopping 7.5 percent.[41] The United States has experienced "high unemployment and low productivity," say two other critics, because business leaders have failed "to modernize our industrial plants" and politicians have "mismanaged [the] federal budget."[42] To contend that poor schools have caused the economic downturn, say these critics, diverts public attention away from the real source of our economic troubles.

The business task forces employed a rhetoric of egalitarianism, but according to some critics, they gave little attention to the needs of minorities, the poor, exceptional students, or inner-city youth. Such critics worry that the

---

[37] Eleanor Duckworth, "What Teachers Know: The Best Knowledge Base," *Harvard Educational Review*, Vol. 54 (1984), p. 17.

[38] Stedman and Smith, "Weak Arguments, Poor Data, Simplistic Recommendations," in *The Great School Debate*, p. 92.

[39] Barry Bluestone and Bennett Harrison, in a report of the Joint Economic Committee of the United States Congress, December 10, 1986. Reported in the *Gainesville Sun* (December 10, 1986), p. 3A.

[40] Eleanor Duckworth, "What Teachers Know," p. 16. Similar criticisms are leveled by the Board of Inquiry, National Coalition of Advocates for Students, *Barriers to Excellence* (Boston: Author, 1985).

[41] Joel Spring, "Political and Economic Analysis," in *Excellence in Education: Perspectives on Policy and Practice*, eds. Philip G. Altbach, Gail P. Kelly, and Lois Weis, p. 78.

[42] Stedman and Smith, "Weak Arguments, Poor Data, Simplistic Recommendations," in *The Great School Debate*, pp. 92–93.

"move to excellence" will cause schools to neglect the economically and educationally disadvantaged.[43] If the business task forces' recommendations are followed, asserts Michael Apple, social and economic "inequalities will increase" in the United States. Schools will teach "technical skills and workplace dispositions" and will fail to promote the critical mindedness essential to democracy.[44]

According to Sheila Slaughter, the business-oriented reports "unabashedly put the needs of [corporations] before the needs of people."[45] In the final analysis, the business reports offer little more than a "pedagogy of profit." Their recommendations, say the critics, emphasize technology and materialism and neglect the liberal arts and humane values.[46]

Most critics of the economic and technical excellence report are openly hostile to the interests of business and distrust business motives. Many of their accusations are speculative and are not supported by hard evidence. However, it is safe to say that the business task forces bring a pro-business ideology to their work and that the interests of the business community are well represented in the reports they produced.

Academic Excellence Reports

The academic excellence reports have been written by scholars and reflect the intellectual community's conviction that quality education can "enhance individual freedom and foster democratic communities."[47] Like the business reports, the academic reports contend that we are on the verge of a new era in our national life.[48] However, the academic reports are more concerned with the demands of democracy and intellectual development than with the interests of business and needs of the economy. According to the academic reports, the best medicine for an ailing economy is a well-educated citizenry.

The Paideia Proposal, the most widely read of the academically oriented reports, was written by Mortimer Adler for the Paideia Group.[49] According to the Paideia Group, the nation's two great accomplishments of the twentieth century are compulsory, public education and the extension of universal suffrage:

> The two—universal suffrage and universal schooling—are inextricably bound together. The one without the other is a perilous delusion. Suffrage without school-

---

[43] Ibid., p. 94.

[44] Michael W. Apple, "Educational Reports and Economic Reality," in *Excellence in Education*, p. 102.

[45] Sheila Slaughter, "Main-traveled Road or the Fast Track: The Liberal and Technical in Higher Education Reform," in ibid., p. 117.

[46] Board of Inquiry, National Coalition of Advocates for Students, *Barriers to Excellence*.

[47] Marvin Lazerson, Judith Block McLaughlin, Bruce McPherson, and Stephen K. Bailey, *An Education of Value: The Purposes and Practices of Schools* (Cambridge, England: Cambridge University Press, 1985), p. xvii.

[48] Ibid., especially Chapter 1.

[49] Of the group's twenty-two members, nineteen were from universities or intellectual foundations and three (two superintendents and one principal) were from public education. No public school teachers were members of the Paideia Group. The name *Paideia* indicates the orientation of the group. *Paideia* (pronounced py-dee-a) comes from the Greek words *pais* and *paidos* related to pedagogy, and pediatrics, and refers to the upbringing of children or the general learning that all humans should possess.

ing produces mobocracy, not democracy—not the rule of law, not constitutional government by the people as well as for them.[50]

The next great challenge facing democracy is to offer not only the same quantity of public schooling to all citizens but the same quality. As the system is presently arranged, some students are offered a broad education designed to train their minds, while others take unchallenging courses that lack academic content. Students in the academic track study the humanities, students in the vocational track are trained (albeit poorly) for jobs, and students in the rapidly expanding general track are not prepared for much of anything. These divisions hobble democracy and unfairly determine the academic and social destiny of the young. Adler argues that tracking must be abolished. He faults the present system for assuming that some children are "not educable for the duties of self-governing citizenship" and contends that all but severely injured children are capable of enjoying the most precious products of the human mind.[51] Say the authors of another academically oriented report,

> The shame of American education is that all students are not expected to develop the skills of reason, communication, and literacy and the habits of commitment and participation necessary for full citizenship in a democracy.[52]

The Paideia Proposal argues that schools should have the same three intellectual objectives for all students, without exception:

1. Students must be prepared to carry on learning after graduation from high school. Schooling is the beginning of education and it must prepare students for a life of learning.
2. Schooling must prepare students for full participation in a democratic society. It is not enough that citizens vote; they must possess habits of informed discretion so that they can analyze issues, engage in debate, and vote intelligently.
3. Schools must prepare all citizens to earn a living.[53]

These three objectives are achieved, according to the academic reports, not through specialized study or vocational training, but through a general liberal education. The curriculum of a Paideia school includes courses in the most fundamental branches of knowledge: language, literature, and the fine arts; mathematics and natural science; history, geography, and social studies. Adler insists that "all sidetracks, specialized courses, or elective choices must be eliminated."[54]

The academically oriented reports acknowledge that some students learn faster and easier than others and that some ultimately will learn more than their classmates. Despite these differences, all children share the same "human nature." All are capable of observing, inquiring, learning, thinking, and communicating, and all deserve the opportunity to fully develop these capabilities. Individual differences exist, but these are only differences in degree and not in kind.[55] Schools must acknowledge the common humanity of their students

---

[50] Mortimer J. Adler, *The Paideia Proposal*, p. 3.
[51] Ibid., pp. 5–8, 41–45.
[52] Lazerson, McLaughlin, McPherson, and Bailey, *An Education of Value*, pp. 56–57.
[53] Adler, *The Paideia Proposal*, pp. 15–20.
[54] Ibid., p. 21.
[55] Ibid., pp. 42–43.

TABLE 23-2   The Paideia Proposal's Three Distinct Modes of Teaching and Learning

Column One	*Column Two*	*Column Three*
Acquisition of organized knowledge	Development of intellectual skills and skills of learning	Enlarged understanding of ideas and values
by means of	*by means of*	*by means of*
Didactic instruction, lectures and responses Textbooks and other aids	Coaching exercises and supervised practice	Maieutic or Socratic questioning and active participation
in three areas of	*in the operations of*	*in the*
Subject matter: Language, literature and the fine arts, mathematics and natural science, history, geography, and social studies	Reading, writing, speaking, and listening Calculating and problem solving Observing, measuring, and estimating Exercising critical judgment	Discussion of books (not textbooks) and other works of art and involvement in artistic activities, e.g., music, drama, and the visual arts

SOURCE: Reprinted with permission of Macmillan Publishing Company from *The Paideia Proposal* by Mortimer J. Adler. Copyright © 1982 by The Institute for Philosophical Research.
Note: The three columns do not correspond to separate courses, nor is one kind of teaching and learning necessarily confined to any one course.

by offering the same quality education to all. "There are no unteachable children," Adler asserts, "there are only schools and teachers and parents who fail to teach them."[56]

The reports acknowledge that it will be impossible to provide the same quality basic education to all students if some come to school unprepared for academic learning. Thus, the reports contend, the state must provide one or more years of preschool education for all children who need it. Once in school, children who are still behind must be given whatever special help and attention they need to overcome their academic handicaps. Above all, home background and academic difficulty must not be used as an excuse for withholding an education of intellectual value from any student.

The academic reports do not present research findings; their analysis is philosophical and historical rather than sociological. They spell out the kinds of instruction all students should undergo in all subjects and in all grades. According to Adler and the Paideia group, there are three ways in which the mind can be improved: "(1) by the acquisition of organized knowledge; (2) by the development of intellectual skills; and (3) by the enlargement of understanding, insight, and aesthetic appreciation"[57] (see Table 23-2).

THE ACQUISITION OF ORGANIZED KNOWLEDGE.   Didactic instruction entails "teaching by telling." Students are introduced to organized knowledge through

---

[56] Ibid., p. 8.
[57] Ibid., p. 22.

Even young children benefit from seminars.   (*Source:* National Education Association, Joe Di Dio.)

lectures, laboratory demonstrations, and textbooks.[58] The academic reports emphasize that many students today are not exposed to the rudimentary knowledge necessary to challenge their thinking and improve their minds.

DEVELOPMENT OF SKILLS.   It is not enough that students learn about knowledge, they must acquire the skills of reading, writing, speaking, listening, observing, measuring, estimating, and calculating. These skills are learned and improved, not by listening and reading but by *doing*. Teachers must play the role of a coach when youngsters are practicing academic skills. They must give assignments that involve students and carefully monitor the students' work so that errors can be corrected as they occur. Academic coaching is not unlike athletic coaching in this regard. Students are asked to go through an organized sequence of acts again and again until a measure of perfection is achieved.[59]

A productive coaching relationship requires that teachers work with a few students at a time so all pupils get the attention they need. Didactic instruction and coaching are the backbone of basic education.

ENLARGEMENT OF UNDERSTANDING.   Students must acquire knowledge and skills, but they must do more. If they are to become competent citizens, students must practice the skills of critical intelligence; they must learn to think for themselves. Certain things are required, if teachers are to awaken the creative and inquisitive powers of their pupils. First, students must be introduced

[58] Ibid., pp. 22–25.
[59] Ibid., p. 27.

to *good books* of every kind, not textbooks but "products of human artistry."[60] The books must require that students stretch and struggle. Second, students must have the opportunity to enter conversations that bring life to the ideas and values. Such conversations can occur in any class, but they are most likely to occur in a special kind of class, called a *seminar*. Third, disciplined conversations must be guided by a teacher who knows the material well and who communicates his or her respect for the ideas being discussed. The form of seminar discussions should be Socratic, which means that the teacher must be a skilled listener and a thoughtful questioner.

The topics of seminars should run the full gamut of human artistry. Books, plays, poems, essays, music, and paintings that express important ideas should be discussed in seminars at every grade level. Seminars are not bull sessions but disciplined collective efforts to enlarge students' understanding. It is through discussion that a full appreciation and deep understanding of important ideas are developed. But discussion is not enough. We understand a play best when we act in it, music when we play or sing it, dance when we perform it, and poetry when we read it aloud. All students should have the opportunity to enlarge their understanding of the arts through performance.[61]

The aim of seminars is to improve the reading, speaking, listening, and thinking skills of participants *and* to help them understand the ideas that have shaped our history. For example, the ideas of liberty, equality, freedom, and democracy could be explored through discussions of the Constitution, *Federalist Papers,* "Common Sense," and the Gettysburg Address. Seminars improve the skills of individual students and help them become "culturally literate."[62]

Adler takes pains to point out that the three columns do not represent sequential steps in learning. Students do not first master facts, then master skills and finally develop their critical and imaginative talents. Instead, pupils learn best when all their faculties are challenged and employed. Therefore, all students at all grade levels should be exposed to the three methods of instruction throughout their school careers.

All reports on education published in the 1980s contend that schools must do a better job teaching the basic skills. However, the academic reports insist that basic skills mastery is not sufficient for full participation in democratic society. A person is not fully literate simply because he or she can read and compute at a fifth- or sixth-grade level. True literacy involves critical reasoning.

Reading, when it advances beyond the recognition of words and strings of simple sentences, is an act of analysis. Thoughtful reading entails following a line of thought far enough to know where it came from and where it is going. It involves making inferences, seeing connections, discovering contradictions, and drawing conclusions.[63] The academic reports insist that all citizens must be able to read with insight, compute with accuracy, and write with clarity because words and numbers are the instruments of reason and because reason is the instrument of democracy. Thus, *all students,* not just the academically gifted,

---

[60] Ibid., pp. 28–29.
[61] Ibid., pp. 30–31.
[62] See E. D. Hirsch, Jr., *Cultural Literacy: What Every American Needs to Know* (Boston: Houghton Mifflin Company, 1987).
[63] Lazerson, McLaughlin, McPherson and Bailey, *An Education of Value,* pp. 65–66.

must be given a high-quality education, in which they acquire knowledge, develop skills, exercise imagination, and practice critical thinking.

Only literate teachers can teach literacy and only teachers with informed discretion can help develop the reasoning skills of their students. Teaching, above all else, is an intellectual skill. One prepares for it by developing the intellect. The academic reports contend that the best preparation of the intellect comes from a thorough study of the liberal arts and sciences. The Paideia group suggests that students preparing to be secondary teachers should major in the subject area they plan to teach, not in education. Professional training in pedagogy would be completed after graduation from college.

The business-oriented task forces propose that schools be built on a competitive, business-world model. The academically oriented reports, in contrast, propose that schools be built on a model of academe. Schools are to be communities of scholarship where everyone (administrators, teachers, and students) is actively engaged in learning. The aim of education is to improve the mind.

CRITICISMS OF THE ACADEMIC EXCELLENCE REPORTS.   Of all the academically oriented reports, *The Paideia Proposal* is the most widely read and, perhaps for that reason, the most widely praised and criticized. Some critics belittle Adler's book calling it a "fairy tale proposal."[64] They contend that many children simply do not have the skill or will to benefit from a rigorously academic curriculum. The critics say that Adler's single-track proposal assumes that children who are academically behind can regain lost ground if given special help. The critics are not so hopeful. They point out that today's remedial programs have not significantly closed the gap between high and low achievers and they see no reason to suppose that Adler's special-help programs would be more successful.

Most critics concede that schools are not asking enough of students, but they point out that higher expectations "do not necessarily translate into higher student achievement." They argue that "people learn in different ways, at different rates, and at different times in their lives."[65] Schools, therefore, are justified in teaching different things to different students. The critics also contend that a single-track curriculum is fundamentally undemocratic.[66] Students should be given options and must learn to live with the consequences of their curriculum choices. Giving options, say the critics, makes it more likely that schools will catch the interest of students who come from different backgrounds and have different aspirations. The critics point out that vocational programs were not the invention of educators; they were developed to fill the "growing demand for students . . . trained in specific skill areas."[67]

The academic reports blame teachers when students do not make academic headway but the critics of these reports say students are at fault.[68] For example,

---

[64] Ronald Gwiazda, "The Peter Pan Proposal," *Harvard Educational Review*, Vol. 53 (1983), pp. 384–388; and Floretta Dukes McKenzie, "The Yellow Brick Road of Education," *Harvard Educational Review*, Vol. 53 (1983), pp. 389–392.

[65] Gwiazda, "The Peter Pan Proposal," p. 387.

[66] M. Frances Klein, "The Paideia Proposal Isn't *the* Answer," *Educational Leadership*, Vol. 40 (1983), p. 61.

[67] McKenzie, "The Yellow Brick Road of Education," p. 389–392.

[68] Gwiazda, "The Peter Pan Proposal," p. 387.

Powell, Farrar, and Cohen argue that large numbers of low-achieving students are in school for reasons that have nothing to do with learning.[69] They are there because school is where the action is, where their friends are, where they act out the rituals of adolescence, and where there *is* such a thing as a free lunch. These critics say it makes no sense to increase school standards when so many students are failing to meet today's requirements. Powell does not oppose high academic standards; in fact, he and his colleagues support them. However, he faults Adler for assuming that students will rise miraculously to meet the expectations of their teachers. Powell contends that schools offer a high-quality education to those who want it, but many students have no interest in academics and actively resist the education schools offer. To be credible, says Powell, reform proposals must take student resistance into account and make practical suggestions for overcoming it.

The oddest criticism leveled against the academically oriented reports comes from those who contend that schools cannot and should not transmit organized knowledge to students. These critics claim that the study of "logically organized knowledge" does not promote learning. One critic wrote,

> Most curriculum specialists [agree] that logically organized bodies of content [are] not likely to help students learn how to learn, participate effectively as members of a democratic society, . . . or pursue [their] own unique talents and interests.[70]

More interesting criticisms of the academically oriented reports have come from new egalitarians. Martin Carnoy, for example, argues that Adler has a fundamentally misguided view of the connection between democracy and schooling. He argues that democracy is not an intellectual commodity that has been invented by scholars and passed on to students in public school classrooms. Democracy, says Carnoy, advances when people without power organize themselves into social movements and work for the expansion of rights and freedoms. The democratic cause is best served by public education when intellectuals and teachers openly ally themselves with the democratic aspirations of the least powerful groups in society: women, minorities, immigrants, workers, and the poor.[71] Carnoy does not believe that Adler's single-track curriculum will serve the interests of the powerless and faults Adler for presuming to know what education is best for all children. He suggests that communities must decide for themselves the kind of education they want for their children.[72] For Carnoy (and others on the farther shores of the American left), the purpose of education is not simply to enlighten the mind but to liberate the poor from the unjust consequences of capitalism. Carnoy does not believe that Paideia schools would further this end and suggests that social reform must proceed school reform.

Adler and the Paideia group (unlike the writers of other reports) have an-

[69] Arthur G. Powell, Eleanor Farrar, and David Cohen, *The Shopping Mall High School: Winners and Losers in the Educational Marketplace* (Boston: Houghton-Mifflin Company, 1985), p. 303–304.

[70] Klein, "The Paideia Proposal Isn't *the* Answer," p. 61.

[71] Martin Carnoy, "Education, Democracy, and Social Conflict," *Harvard Educational Review*, Vol. 53 (1983), pp. 401–402.

[72] A similar argument is put forward by Stanley Aronowitz and Henry A. Giroux in *Education under Siege: The Conservative, Liberal and Radical Debate over Schooling* (South Hadley, MA: Bergin & Garvey, 1985).

swered many of their critics.[73] As we might expect, Adler rejects the charge that *The Paideia Proposal* is antidemocratic. He writes, "One might just as well say that requiring children to be vaccinated . . . or requiring them to have balanced diets . . . is authoritarian and antidemocratic."[74] In his view, it is irresponsible to allow uneducated children, in the name of free choice and pluralistic democracy, to make decisions adults know will do lifelong harm. Adler argues that nonacademic courses and tracks do irreparable damage, not only to pupils but to society.

Adler insists that the Paideia program is not as regimented as his critics contend and that individual differences can find expression within the confines of required courses. As students master the basic skills and engage in informed conversations about truly important ideas, Adler says individuality will not only be expressed, it will be enriched. Critical intelligence enhances individuality; it does not repress it.[75]

Adler disagrees with the claim that most students are incapable of serious academic study. He asserts that pupils will rise to the level of their teachers' expectations if assignments are reasonable, challenging, and interesting. If present remedial programs do not help low-achieving students make up their deficiencies, says Adler, then such programs will just have to be improved. Our present willingness to accept high rates of student failure cannot be tolerated in a democratic society.

Adler does not answer the claim that "logically organized bodies of content [are] not likely to help students learn."[76] However, we can imagine Adler asking, "What are schools to teach if not organized knowledge? How exactly do people learn to become members of a democratic society if not through the mastery of organized knowledge and the development of informed discretion? Does anyone seriously think individuals or society would be better off if schools taught disorganized, illogical content?"

To the critics on the left who charge that educational reform will be effective only after social reform has been achieved, Adler says:

> The two sets of changes—the educational changes on the one hand and the social and economic changes on the other—must go forward together and interact with one another. We cannot wait for the social and economic improvements to be fully accomplished before we start on efforts to bring about educational changes. Each set of changes needs the support of the other.[77]

The Institutional Excellence Reports

The institutional excellence reports were written by individuals closely connected to teacher training and the educational establishment. Most bemoan the declining quality of public schools and call for improved instruction and higher academic standards. Most of the reports focus on schooling at the secondary

---

[73] Mortimer J. Adler, *Paideia Problems and Possibilities* (New York: Macmillan, 1983); and Mortimer J. Adler, *The Paideia Program* (New York: Macmillan, 1984).

[74] Adler, *Paideia Problems and Possibilities*, p. 39.

[75] Some critics disagree with Adler's hope that schools can deliver knowledge that liberates the mind. See, for example, Kevin Harris, *Education and Knowledge* (Boston: Routledge & Kegan Paul, 1979).

[76] Klein, "The Paideia Proposal Isn't *the* Answer," p. 61.

[77] Adler, *Paideia Problems and Possibilities*, p. 49.

level and were written after their authors had visited many schools and studied their operations. What sets institutional excellence reports apart from all the rest, however, is the attention they give to the structure of the school, the interior life of that institution, and the problems facing teachers who work in them. Four of the reports (*High School, A Place Called School, Horace's Compromise,* and *The Shopping Mall High School*) study a cross section of American schools. Another report, *The Good High School,* offers a portrait of the character and culture of six excellent schools, both public and private. *A Nation Prepared,* makes specific recommendations for upgrading the teaching profession and improving the structure of schools. Similar recommendations are made in *Pride and Promise.*[78]

The authors of the institutional excellence reports claim that American high schools are routinized, generally quiet, needlessly unproductive, and intellectually dull.

From *A Place Called School:*

How would I react as an adult to [the teaching practices in typical public school classroom]? I would become restless. I would groan audibly over still another seatwork assignment. My mind would wander off soon after the beginning of the lecture. It would be necessary for me to put my mind in some kind of "hold" position. That is what students do. Students turn their minds elsewhere and simply doze.[79]

From *Horace's Compromise:*

[Schools] are not provoking, stimulating places, and their students are not hungry [to learn]. A Hamilton, Ohio, athletic coach is quoted to the effect that schools allow students "to practice stupidity as long as they don't become discipline problems. They get good at dumbness." David Seeley sadly sums up his view: "Education has become a massive process for producing passive minds."[80]

From *High School:*

What occurs in the classroom is often a welter of routine procedures and outside interruptions that come to dominate the life of students and teachers alike and, in the end, restrict learning. Time becomes an end in itself.[81]

From *The Shopping Mall High School:*

[In most classrooms] the only common understanding [between teachers and their students] is that passing, and hence graduation, is contingent on orderly attendance rather than on mastery of anything. The need to hold students for graduation and make them feel happy has the effect of disconnecting mastery from the school's expectations. Learning is . . . profoundly voluntary.[82]

The institutional excellence reports are more descriptive than the rest. They document the test score decline in public education but claim that slipping achievement has been caused not by poor teaching and/or inept administration but by the complexities of the system itself. As Sizer put it, "When one considers the energy, commitment, and quality of so many . . . people working in

[78] Raywid, Tesconi, and Warren, *Pride and Promise.*
[79] Goodlad, *A Place Called School,* p. 233.
[80] Theodore R. Sizer, *Horace's Compromise: The Dilemma of the American High School* (Boston: Houghton-Mifflin, 1984), p. 56.
[81] Boyer, *High School,* p. 141.
[82] Powell, Farrar, and Cohen, *The Shopping Mall High School,* p. 4.

the schools, one must place the blame elsewhere. The people are better than the structure."[83]

All reports claim that schools have lost sight of their primary aims. To be effective, according to Ernest Boyer, schools must have a "clear and vital mission." Teachers, administrators, students, parents, and the public must "share a vision of what, together, they are trying to accomplish." Yet, the institutional excellence reports, say that most schools today have no vision and appear to be adrift.[84] Powell and his colleagues assert that schools will not improve "until there is a much better sense of what is most important to teach, . . . and why."[85]

The institutional excellence reports recommend that schools narrow their focus and concentrate on developing the intellect and character of their students. Schools have tried to ameliorate every social ill and, in the process, have spread themselves so thin that they do not do anything particularly well. The reports advise that schools attempt to do less but do it better.

Of course, Americans have diverse interests and will never agree wholly on the aims of education. However, the public debate over aims has been silenced in recent years because schools have tried to do everything asked of them. Public expectations have risen but the effectiveness of the schools has declined. The institutional excellence reports contend that schools cannot "do it all." They suggest that the debate over aims be reopened so that teachers, once again, can do their work with the guidance of clear goals.[86] The reports suggest that schools return to basic aims: producing students who read with insight and interest, who can write and speak clearly, and who employ critical intelligence. Many of institutional excellence documents advocate a return to a single-track curriculum.[87] Categorizing students by ability and passing them along a path that leads to ignorance and second-class citizenship, Boyer says, "can no longer be defended."[88]

In addition to academic goals, the institutional reports suggest that schools promote decency and civility, what educators in an earlier day called *character*. Here the emphasis is not on socialization (getting people to behave according to group norms) but on helping students think before they act and act with informed discretion.

The institutional excellence reports pay closer attention to the lives of teachers than reports in the other categories. The problems of isolation, anonymity, poor pay, status panic, the lack of career advancement, heavy work loads, large classes, dissatisfaction, and burnout are detailed. The reports assert that teaching will not improve until the quality of teachers' work lives is enhanced.[89] A number of suggestions for improving the workplace were made. We will not detail those suggestions here because they have been discussed earlier in the text (see Chapters 10 and 11).

[83] Sizer, *Horace's Compromise*, p. 209.
[84] Boyer, *High School*, pp. 58, 63, 147, 301.
[85] Powell, Farrar, and Cohen, *The Shopping Mall High School*, p. 306.
[86] Goodlad, *A Place Called School*, pp. 33–60. See also Boyer, *High School*, pp. 43–57; and Raywid, Tesconi, and Warren, *Pride and Promise*, pp. 8–13.
[87] This is not surprising, for both Boyer *(High School)* and Sizer *(Horace's Compromise)* were members of the Paideia group.
[88] Boyer, *High School*, p. 126.
[89] See Raywid, Tesconi, and Warren, *Pride and Promise*, pp. 14–20, for a particularly interesting discussion of this topic.

The institutional excellence reports show how teachers make compromises between what is desirable and what actually can be achieved given limited time, energy, and resources. Everyone (teachers, students, parents, administrators, and the public) has accepted such compromises so that now mediocrity is the norm rather than the exception in public education.

Agreements struck between reluctant students and disheartened teachers have drastically lowered what schools expect of students. Exceptional pupils still get a good education if they are willing to put in the effort, but most teachers and students settle for too little. The institutional excellence reports claim that most classrooms today are orderly but woefully unproductive. "The agreement between teacher and student to exhibit a facade of orderly purposefulness is a *conspiracy for the least,* the least hassles for anyone"[90] (emphasis added). Teachers agree to ask little of their pupils, and students, in return, agree to stay out of trouble and to keep up the pretense that learning is taking place.

Lightfoot's *The Good High School* examines schools that work well and carry out the promise of excellence. She offers portraits of such schools and shows that, though they differ in many ways, all share the following characteristics:

- They have clear, largely academic goals that guide faculty and student decisions and that give the institution a sense of confidence, stability, purpose, and pride;
- They monitor student progress and gather indices of institutional successes and failures;
- They are self-assured, self-monitoring, and willing to engage in self-criticism. They admit when they are not achieving goals they have set for themselves and take steps to remedy problems before trouble gets out of hand. They have clear goals, a mechanism for measuring whether they are achieving those goals, and display a willingness to try new approaches when the old methods no longer work.

Good schools, says Lightfoot, are good communities. They know what they are trying to do and how they are trying to do it. Administrators in good schools adopt styles that fit their own personalities and suit the character and needs of the institution. They monitor the life of the school and work to assure that teachers and students believe that their actions count for something. Good schools "provide a safe and regulated environment" in which students and teachers build friendly and productive relationships.[91] Teachers have high expectations for their pupils and confidence in their own professional ability. They recognize the achievements of their students and good teaching is recognized and rewarded. Good schools are productive communities that allow teachers to be reflective practitioners.[92]

The last of the institutional excellence reports, the Carnegie Forum's *A Nation Prepared,* was discussed in Chapter 10, so we will not detail its content again here. It is enough to say that the report offers a plan for improving the qualifications of teachers, improving the quality of the workplace, and for giving

---

[90] Sizer, *Horace's Compromise,* p. 156.

[91] Sara Lawrence Lightfoot, *The Good High School: Portraits of Character and Culture* (New York: Basic Books, 1983), p. 350.

[92] See Chapter 10 for a discussion of reflective practitioners. See also Donald Schön, *The Reflective Practitioner: How Professionals Think in Action* (New York: Basic Books, 1983).

teachers greater discretion and autonomy. It is suggested that collegial decision making replace top-down administrative practices. Teachers are to be paid more and allowed to advance within the profession without leaving the classroom. The leaders of the National Education Association and the American Federation of Teachers were members of the task force, and the plan was quickly approved by the members of both unions.

CRITICISMS OF THE INSTITUTIONAL EXCELLENCE REPORTS.   This set of reports has received widespread attention but only occasional criticism. There are a few possible explanations for this lack of criticism.

1. The reports are well written and designed to capture the interest of a wide audience.
2. They are based on research, though in most cases specific methodologies are not discussed,[93] and claim to be objective accounts of school life. Further, the descriptions of the interior workings of schools offered by the reports have a "ring of truth" for most educators.
3. Though the reports document severe problems, no group is singled out for blame and no particular constituency is offended. The cost of the recommendations made in these reports was high and may exceed the nation's will (and perhaps ability) to pay. Nevertheless, all groups connected with the present system are promised a part of increased revenues should they ever materialize.
4. The reports deflect the criticisms directed at teachers by the business-oriented reports (and to a lesser extent by the academic reports) and call for improvements in the workplace.

For these reasons, most reviewers have greeted the reports with enthusiasm. There was one notable exception. Reginald Damerell, a former education professor at the University of Massachusetts, claims the institutional excellence reports offer a self-serving and shallow analysis of the problems facing education today. The reports document problems but none traces those problems back to what Damerell says is their primary cause, the failure of colleges of education to adequately prepare teachers for their profession. If, as the reports suggest, teachers and their students plod mechanically through "the material," if the teachers' lectures too often lack clarity and convey incorrect information, if assignments are vapid, if ditto sheets have replaced Socratic questioning in most classrooms, if thousands of veteran teachers have failed basic skills tests that would not overly tax the abilities of an academically attentive sixteen-year-old, if teachers are willing to trade away academic requirements for student cooperation, if the intellectual performance in public schools is declining, if all this is happening even though more teachers than ever hold master's degrees in education, and if all signs point to the fact that teachers are inadequately prepared—then why do the reports systematically avoid criticizing the programs

---

[93] All the reports employ qualitative methodologies. A conspicuous exception to this is Goodlad's *A Place Called School.* However, Goodlad presents his quantitative results in a qualitative format. Findings are intermingled with commentary, history, hunches, and recommendations. The book follows few of the conventions of a research report but all of the conventions of a commission report.

that failed to prepare them? Damerell suggests an answer: The reports were written by people who have a stake in teacher preparation programs.

Some reports call for changes in teacher education, but in Damerell's view the reforms are superficial and require that students take even more methods courses than they have in the past. What is missing in these reports, says Damerell, is a critical examination of the preparation programs themselves. The real problem, he says, is that "the education field is devoid of intellectual content, has no body of knowledge of its own and acts as if bodies of knowledge do not exist in other university departments."[94] Damerell concludes that real reform will not happen in our schools until colleges of education are abolished and teachers are trained in the liberal arts.[95]

Colleges of education have not been deaf to the criticism that they lack rigor and intellectual focus. The National Commission for Excellence in Teacher Education acknowledged that "the quality of teacher education programs has been widely criticized [and that such] criticism is valid."[96] Leaders from many of the nation's largest and best colleges of education formed a group called the Holmes Consortium that set as its first priority making teacher education more intellectually solid. In an early position paper, the consortium insisted that teachers must have a command of the subjects they teach and the skills needed to teach them.[97] Both reports call, albeit cautiously, for increasing admission standards, and for a genuine liberal arts major, or its equivalent, for teacher-training students. Raywid, Tesconi, and Warren argue for high academic standards in teacher education programs but point out that good teaching entails more than knowledge of subject matter. Teachers must also have a knowledge of practice that is based on the solid research findings. Their training must equip them to evaluate research, adapt it for classroom use, and to exercise sound professional judgment.[98]

The Excellence and Equity Reports

Two reports have been issued that deal exclusively with equity and education: *Barriers to Excellence* by the National Coalition of Advocates for Students and *Making Something Happen* by the National Commission on Secondary Education for Hispanics.[99] The reports assess educational trends especially as they relate

---

[94] Reginald G. Damerell, *Education's Smoking Gun: How Teachers Colleges Have Destroyed Education in America* (New York: Freundlich Books, 1985), p. 13.

[95] Others have made similar proposals. Mortimer Adler, when he is speaking for himself and not the Paideia group, and B. F. Skinner have called for the abolition of colleges of education. Richard Mitchell makes a forceful attack on the teachers of teachers in *The Graves of Academe* (Boston: Little, Brown and Company, 1981). For a review of Damerell's book see Clinton B. Allison, "The Gunslinger—A Critical Review of Reginald G. Damerell's *Education's Smoking Gun: How Teachers Colleges Have Destroyed Education in America,*" *Journal of Thought,* Vol. 21 (Winter 1986), pp. 91–98. Damerell responds to this review in the same issue.

[96] The National Commission for Excellence in Teacher Education, *A Call for Change in Teacher Education* (Washington, DC: The American Association of Colleges of Teacher Education, 1985).

[97] The Holmes Consortium, *Tomorrow's Teachers: A Report of the Holmes Group* (East Lansing, MI: Holmes Consortium, 1986), p. 2.

[98] Raywid, Tesconi, and Warren, *Pride and Promise,* pp. 29–38

[99] Board of Inquiry, National Coalition of Advocates for Students, *Barriers to Excellence* (Boston: Author, 1985); National Commission on Secondary Education for Hispanics, *Make Something Happen* (Washington, DC: Hispanic Policy Development Project, 1985).

to minority students and children in poverty. They also critically evaluate the recommendations made by other task forces. The equity-oriented reports contend that the current suggestions for reform will not increase the educational opportunities or academic achievements of poor and minority students.

The equity reports begin by reviewing the literature on discrimination in schools. They make the case that minority students and the poor have not been well served by the nation's educational system. Black and Spanish-speaking children are more likely than other youngsters to go to overcrowded, under-funded schools, learn from inexperienced teachers in dilapidated buildings, suffer poor instruction, and have less expected of them. As a result, these groups are less likely than their white Anglo counterparts to do well academically and more likely to drop out (or be pushed out) of school before graduation.[100] The reports list demographic and achievement data in order to show that poor and minority students have not yet had a fair chance to succeed in school. The reports also cite data to show that these groups want to succeed and, with the proper attention and guidance, can succeed.

The equity reports reject the idea that the social and educational programs of the 1960s and 1970s failed. The reports contend that Great Society programs lifted many people out of poverty and increased high school graduation rates for minority students. Present conditions, the reports say, call for a continuation rather than a diminution of social programs that help the poor. Like all the others, the equity reports say that excellence in education must have a high priority nationally and that today's schools have lost their intellectual focus. They complain that current teaching practices encourage passivity. Teachers lecture and pass out work sheets while students listen (or daydream) and fill in the blanks. Facts are not tied together by concepts, and concepts are not tied to clear educational aims. Thus, course material is merely "covered" and seldom mastered. The curriculum, the reports go on to say, has become fragmented and learning for many students has become an aimless exercise. Schools must recapture their direction and set higher standards.

The reports warn that children of minority groups and the poor must be given assistance or many will never meet new, more rigorous requirements. The drive for excellence in education must include all students and not be used to drive minority children into dead-end nonacademic tracks. Nor should new requirements set insurmountable barriers to graduation. Remedial programs must help students meet higher standards. Bilingual education must be made available to all who need it. Funding from state and federal sources must eradicate funding disparities between the schools that serve affluent communities and those that serve the poor.

The equity reports insist that a push for excellence must take place in an atmosphere of caring. The children of poverty are more likely than their affluent counterparts to live in substandard housing with a single parent. Often unsupervised, such children are more likely to fall victim to drug abuse, pregnancy, crime, and despair. Schools must take these realities into account. Caring institutions, as they are defined by the equity reports, work closely with parents; create an atmosphere of mutual respect among students, teachers, parents, and the community; provide counselors for youngsters needing help

---

[100] National Commission on Secondary Education for Hispanics, *Make Something Happen*, pp. 2–23.

and direction; respect the ethnic heritage of students; and are influenced by community advisory councils.

CRITICISMS OF THE EQUITY AND EXCELLENCE REPORTS.   The equity and excellence reports are the youngest generation of commission products. Aside from an excellent review by David Cohen,[101] the reports have received very little attention. Cohen comments on what the inconsistencies (or, perhaps, a better word would be *tensions*) he found in the documents. He suggests that these inconsistencies exist because liberals have not yet found an adequate response to the growing conservative mood among policy makers in education. It is as if the reports' authors have lost their ideological footing and, in an effort to steady themselves, have grabbed onto any reform ideas that were close at hand.

For example, the equity reports bemoan the fragmentation of the curriculum and say that the proliferation of courses has contributed to the lowering of student achievement. Yet, the reports also call for special remedial programs, more counseling programs, community-based work programs, more bilingual programs, and for greater attention to the cultural heritage of minority students. Many would applaud these proposals, but if adopted, they would add to the very curriculum fragmentation that the reports have criticized.

The equity reports call for higher academic standards, but they are suspicious of using nationally normed tests to see if those standards are being met. The reports point out that it is a common practice for districts or states to create "gates" in the educational system that can only be entered if a student has earned a passing score on a standardized test. This, *by itself*, is not a problem. However, if the test is biased or, more commonly, if certain groups in the school system are given an inferior education and are thereby denied access to the information needed to pass the test, then the process is unfair and hinders the life-chances of children who already suffer a host of disadvantages. The equity reports want higher standards but are not sure how those standards can be fairly measured and equitably enforced.

The equity reports come out against tracking, but mindful that many students need special help, they also call for more and better remedial programs. Tracking and remediation are not necessarily the same thing, but they can be and often are. Tracking is a mechanism for giving different children different kinds of information and different forms of education. Though remediation programs do not necessarily offer a different and inferior curriculum, past experience indicates that remediation programs are often a form of de facto tracking. The equity reports say children must get all the special help they need, but they do not say how to keep remediation programs from turning into separate tracks.

The equity reports criticize the "materialistic motives" of the business-oriented task forces. They contend that greater attention should be paid to the intrinsic and intellectual aims of education. Yet, they also complain that schools are not doing enough to fight unemployment among the youth and call for more and better job training programs within the schools. On the one hand, the reports are offended by the utilitarian claim that the goal for education is to prepare

---

[101] David Cohen, "Greater Expectations," *The Nation*, Vol. 240, No. 20 (May 20, 1985), pp. 16, 18–23.

students for jobs; and, on the other hand, they criticize the present system because it does not prepare minority students for the world of work.

The Future Outlook

Predicting the future is a dangerous exercise in a fast-changing world. The only safe prediction is that schools are likely to change, perhaps significantly, in the near future. The support for reform is growing and it is coming from several different sources. As we have seen, different interest groups are proposing very different reform agendas. They are using the debate over the future of education to guard their own special interests and promote their own objectives. In the early stages of political struggles, various interest groups argue as if their suggestions are the only ones that make sense. They often criticize the proposals of the opposition. We have traced the course of that debate in this chapter. As the debate matures and it becomes obvious that no single group is persuasive enough or powerful enough to get its own way, then compromise becomes inevitable.

There is evidence to suggest that the compromise process is already underway. Unions are relaxing their opposition to teacher testing, businesses are showing a greater willingness to contribute financially to school improvement, state governments are making higher teacher salaries a part of their legislated reform packages, colleges of education are raising their standards and requiring that students take more courses in the liberal arts, and most groups are seriously considering the Carnegie Commission's suggestion that teachers be given a greater say in the administration of their school.

Recent surveys by the Louis Harris organization indicate that Americans are "desperately eager" to improve public education. Of those surveyed, 77 percent said they would pay higher taxes for better schools. In a parallel survey, 64 percent of business executives said they would be willing to see their firms pay higher taxes to support improvements in education. Seventy-nine percent of the public supported giving teachers a real say over what is taught, how materials are used, and how school money is spent. Eighty-two percent said that teachers should be paid on a par with accountants and other professionals, in the range of $20,000 to $60,000 for a full year's work.[102]

All signs indicate that the need for reform is great and the possibility for reform is real. Seldom has there been such a clear agreement that schools are in trouble and must be improved. Neither has there often been such a widespread willingness to make those improvements. People entering the teaching profession today (or entering leadership roles within the profession) have an unprecedented opportunity to contribute to school improvement. Some of the methods for improving schools are discussed in the next chapter.

Summary

Since *A Nation at Risk,* more than two dozen major reports have been published that focus on the state of American education, especially at the high school

---

[102] Associated Press, "Americans Want Improvement in Public Schools," *The Gainesville Sun* (August 27, 1986), p. 9D.

level. The reports shared a number of things. All are partisan documents that advance the interests of their sponsoring agency. They were designed to influence public opinion and the decisions of policy makers. All give evidence that the quality of schooling has declined in recent years, and all make recommendations on how the downward trend should be reversed. Most agreed that schools were asking too little of students and that teachers and students must set higher standards.

The focus of the various reports, the data they included and ignored, and the recommendations they made were compatible with the interests and ideologies of their sponsoring and funding agencies. Eighteen of the most influential and widely read reports have been reviewed in this chapter. These were divided into four categories: those that emphasized economic and technical excellence (sponsored by business interests and conservative politicians), those that focused on academic excellence (written by academics), those that envisioned institutional excellence (written largely by college of education professors and sponsored by professional organizations and political liberal private foundations), and those that dealt directly with excellence and equity (sponsored by organizations representing the interests of minority and poor students).

The economic and technical excellence reports contend that the achievement decline in schools is putting the United States at a competitive disadvantage militarily and in the world economy. They suggest that schools raise their standards and become more attentive to the needs of business. They envision a rigorous, competitive education that gives business a greater say in policy decisions.

Critics contend that the economic and technical excellence reports unfairly blame educators for the nation's economic troubles. They fault the reports for underestimating the inertia of the school system and for overestimating the power of administrators to effect change. Critics say inadequate attention was paid to the problems facing teachers and low-achieving students. The schools proposed by the economic and technical excellence reports were built on a competitive business model, and the aim of education advocated in the reports was narrowly vocational.

The academic excellence reports focus on developing the intellectual potential of all students. The central assumption underlying these reports is that democracy demands an informed citizenry. As Richard Mitchell stated, "If we cannot make ourselves a knowledgeable and thoughtful people—those are the requisites of informed discretion—then we cannot be free."[103] According to these reports, the best way to adjust to a changing economy is to train the intellect through study in the liberal arts and sciences.

The academic reports emphasize that all students are capable of learning and that all deserve exposure to the same high-quality education in the public schools. Disadvantaged students must be given access to free preschool programs and, if need be, additional tutoring throughout their school careers. The reports emphasize the importance of didactic instruction, coaching, and Socratic questioning. The schools envisioned by the academic excellence reports are constructed on a model of the liberal arts college and the aim of education is the development of the intellect.

---

[103] Richard Mitchell, *The Graves of Academe* (Boston: Little, Brown and Company, 1981), p. 17.

Critics contend the proposals of the academic reports are naive and impractical. A single track system would not benefit students who are uninterested in academics. It makes little sense, say these critics, to raise graduation requirements for those pupils who are failing to meet present standards. They also point out that, up to now, remedial programs have had only limited success in raising the achievement of low-achieving students. They suspect that new remedial programs will not adequately prepare students for the one-track curriculum proposed by the academic reports. Carnoy criticizes the Paideia group for not tying its proposals to specific social movements and for not giving the underclasses a chance to frame the reforms affecting their schools.

The institutional excellence reports were written by people closely connected to the teaching profession. These reports analyze problems facing teachers and students and make recommendations on improving the quality of the workplace and the education offered students. Generally, they conclude that instruction in schools has become dull though orderly, that current practices encourage docility not thought, and that teachers are accepting too little from their students. The reports claim that schools have pursued too many objectives and, in the process, have lost track of their primary aims. The reports want to reopen the debate over educational aims and suggest that schools concentrate on the development of critical intelligence, decency, and civic virtue. The curriculum suggestions vary from one report to the next but most do little more than modify the Paideia suggestions.

The institutional excellence reports have been highly praised in education journals. The harshest criticism of the reports is that they do not take adequate account of problems that exist within colleges of education.

The last group of reports, those that address the issue of excellence and equity, examine what the push for excellence might do to and for minority students and the children of the poor. They review the record on discrimination in public schools and the data relating to the disadvantages that plague impoverished students. They argue that the instillation of new requirements carries with it an obligation to help low-achieving students improve their academic performance. They worry that new testing and course requirements would make it impossible for growing numbers of poor and minority students to graduate from high school.

The excellence and equity reports have been praised for bringing the public's attention back to the tensions that exist between excellence and equity. They have been criticized for not making clear recommendations for relieving that tension. The proposals detail the problems of tracking and criticize the proliferation of courses, yet they call for more remedial classes, counseling programs, and bilingual courses. The reports do not explain how these programs could be added (or expanded) without perpetuating the discrimination, tracking systems, lower expectations, and watered-down curriculum the reports quite rightly criticize. Nor is it clear how the school system could enforce higher standards without installing minimum competency "gates" that would keep some students from advancing until they have mastered certain skills.

The calls for reform have sprung from many sources: federal, state and local governments; business; the teaching profession; college professors; minority groups; and the general public. The interests of these groups are not identical and compromises will have to be struck. Those compromises already are under way. Requirements for graduation have been increased in most states, teacher pay is rising after a long period of decline, state legislatures are taking the lead in educational reform, the number of five-year teacher preparation programs is increasing, and there are indications that student achievement is inching upward. The 1990s are likely to be an exciting time to be a teacher.

Suggested Readings

MAJOR REPORTS

ADLER, MORTIMER J. *The Paideia Proposal.* New York: Macmillan, 1982.

ADLER, MORTIMER J. *Paideia Problems and Possibilities: A Consideration of Questions Raised by the Paideia Proposal.* New York: Macmillan, 1983.

ADLER, MORTIMER J. *The Paideia Program: An Educational Syllabus.* New York: Macmillan, 1984.

AMERICAN ASSOCIATION OF SCHOOL ADMINISTRATORS. *The Excellence Report: Using It to Improve Your Schools.* Arlington, VA: American Association of School Administrators, 1983.

BOARD OF INQUIRY, NATIONAL COALITION OF ADVOCATES FOR STUDENTS. *Barriers to Excellence.* Boston: Author, 1985.

BOYER, ERNEST L. *High School: A Report on Secondary Education in America.* New York: Harper & Row, 1983.

BUSINESS–HIGHER EDUCATION FORUM. *America's Competitive Challenge: The Need for a National Response.* Washington, DC: Author, 1983.

BUSINESS–HIGHER EDUCATION FORUM. *Corporate and Campus Cooperation: An Action Agenda.* Washington, DC: Author, May 1984.

COLLEGE BOARD EDUCATIONAL EQUITY PROJECT. *Academic Preparation for College: What Students Need to Know and Be Able to Do.* New York: Author, 1983.

COMMISSION ON INTERNATIONAL EDUCATION. *What We Don't Know Can Hurt Us: The Shortfall in International Competence.* Washington, DC: American Council on Education, 1983.

EDUCATION COMMISSION OF THE STATES. *Action for Excellence: Task Force on Education for Economic Growth.* Denver: Author, 1983.

EDUCATION COMMISSION OF THE STATES. *Action in the States: Progress toward Educational Renewal.* Denver: Author, 1984.

FEISTRITZER, EMILY E. *The Making of a Teacher: A Report on Teacher Education and Certification.* Washington, DC: National Center for Education Information, 1984.

FINN, CHESTER E., JR., DIANE RAVITCH, and ROBERT T. FANCHER, eds. *Against Mediocrity: The Humanities in America's High Schools.* New York: Holmes and Meier, 1984.

GOODLAD, JOHN I. *A Place Called School: Prospects for the Future.* New York: McGraw-Hill Book Company, 1984.

HOLMES GROUP CONSORTIUM. *Tomorrow's Teachers.* East Lansing, MI: Author, 1986.

LAZERSON, MARVIN, JUDITH BLOCK MCLAUGHLIN, BRUCE MCPHERSON, and STEPHEN K. BAILEY. *An Education of Value: The Purposes and Practices of Schools.* Cambridge, England: Cambridge University Press, 1985.

LIGHTFOOT, SARA LAWRENCE. *The Good High School: Portraits of Character and Culture.* New York: Basic Books, 1983.

NATIONAL ACADEMY OF SCIENCES, NATIONAL ACADEMY OF ENGINEERING, INSTITUTE OF MEDICINE, COMMITTEE ON SCIENCE, ENGINEERING AND PUBLIC POLICY. *High Schools and the Changing Workplace: The Employer's View.* Washington, DC: National Academy Press, 1984.

NATIONAL COMMISSION FOR EXCELLENCE IN TEACHER EDUCATION. *A Call for Change in*

Teacher Education. Washington, DC: American Association for Colleges of Teacher Education, 1985.

NATIONAL COMMISSION ON SECONDARY EDUCATION FOR HISPANICS. *Make Something Happen*. Washington, DC: Hispanic Policy Development Project, 1985.

NATIONAL SCIENCE BOARD COMMISSION ON PRECOLLEGE EDUCATION IN MATHEMATICS, SCIENCE AND TECHNOLOGY. *Educating America for the 21st Century*. Washington, DC: Author, 1983.

NEW YORK STATE EDUCATION DEPARTMENT. *Proposed Action Plan to Improve Elementary and Secondary Education Results in New York*. Albany: Author, 1983.

POWELL, ARTHUR G., ELEANOR FARRAR, and DAVID COHEN. *The Shopping Mall High School: Winners and Losers in the Educational Marketplace*. Boston: Houghton-Mifflin, 1985.

RAYWID, MARY ANNE, CHARLES A. TESCONI, JR., and DONALD R. WARREN. *Pride and Promise*. Westbury, NY: American Educational Studies Association, 1984.

SIZER, THEODORE R. *Horace's Compromise: The Dilemma of the American High School*. Boston: Houghton-Mifflin, 1984.

TASK FORCE ON TEACHING AS A PROFESSION. *A Nation Prepared: Teachers for the 21st Century*. New York: Carnegie Forum on Education and the Economy, 1986.

TWENTIETH CENTURY FUND. *Making the Grade: Report of the Twentieth Century Fund Task Force on Federal Elementary and Secondary Education Policy*. New York: Author, 1983.

UNITED STATES DEPARTMENT OF EDUCATION. *Meeting the Challenge: Recent Efforts to Improve Education Across the Nation*. Washington, DC: United States Department of Education, 1983.

UNITED STATES DEPARTMENT OF EDUCATION. *The Nation Responds: Recent Efforts to Improve Education*. Washington, DC: United States Department of Education, 1984.

BOOKS AND ARTICLES THAT ANALYZE THE REPORTS

ALTBACH, PHILIP G., GAIL P. KELLY, and LOIS WEIS, eds. *Excellence in Education: Perspectives on Policy and Practice*. Buffalo, NY: Prometheus Books, 1985.

ARONOWITZ, STANLEY, and HENRY A. GIROUX. *Education under Siege: The Conservative, Liberal and Radical Debate over Schooling*. South Hadley, MA: Bergin and Garvey, 1985.

CARNOY, MARTIN. "Education, Democracy, and Social Conflict," *Harvard Educational Review*, Vol. 53 (1983), pp. 401–402.

COHEN, DAVID. "Greater Expectations," *The Nation*, Vol. 240, No. 20 (May 20, 1985).

DAMERELL, REGINALD G. *Education's Smoking Gun: How Teachers Colleges Have Destroyed Education in America*. New York: Freundlich Books, 1985.

DUCKWORTH, ELEANOR. "What Teachers Know: The Best Knowledge Base," *Harvard Educational Review*, Vol. 54 (1984), pp. 15–20.

GROSS, BEATRICE, and RONALD GROSS, ed. *The Great School Debate: Which Way American Education?* New York: Simon and Schuster, 1985.

GWIAZDA, RONALD. "The Peter Pan Proposal," *Harvard Educational Review*, Vol. 53 (1983), pp. 384–388.

JOHNSTON, WILLIAM J., ed. *Education on Trial: Strategies for the Future*. San Francisco: Institute for Contemporary Studies, 1985.

KLEIN, M. FRANCES. "The Paideia Proposal Isn't *the* Answer," *Educational Leadership*, Vol. 40 (1983).

MCKENZIE, FLORETTA DUKE. "The Yellow Brick Road of Education," *Harvard Educational Review*, Vol. 53 (1983), pp. 389–402.

PRESSEISEN, BARBARA Z. *Unlearned Lessons: Current and Past Reforms for School Improvement*. Philadelphia: Falmer Press, 1985.

RAVITCH, DIANE "The Education Pendulum." In Fred Schultz, ed., *Education: Annual Editions, 85/86*, pp. 20–23. Guilford, CT: Annual editions, 1985.

Making Schools Work

Introduction

Human beings learn from their environment. Consciously and unconsciously, they internalize significant portions of the world around them. Formal education is a process of deliberately ordering a student's environment to facilitate the acquisition of specified habits, skills, and knowledge. The improvement of schooling depends on clarifying the aims of education and determining the teaching methods that achieve them. It is as simple as that.

As is often the case in life, the goals toward which we strive are more easily described than achieved; their simplicity hides vast complexities. As we have already seen, determining warranted education aims is a mind-stretching enterprise. The question of how to achieve our chosen aims is an even more challenging enterprise.

Educational research offers some guidance as to how we might best achieve our stated aims for education. But perhaps a more basic contribution of research, at least at its present stage of development, is that it exposes the multiple arenas in which educators must be active if they are to make schools work.

This chapter examines some of the most significant educational research of the past twenty years. Its purpose is (1) to review pertinent research findings, (2) to clarify the school factors that contribute most to student learning, and (3) to specify some of the things teachers need to do to improve schools. The chapter is descriptive, in that it discusses what research has to say, and prescriptive, in that it makes suggestions regarding future directions for education.

Research in Education

Formal education has been around for thousands of years, but research in teaching is a new enterprise. It was not until the early part of this century that educators began to think of teaching as a natural event with properties that could be investigated and discovered. In a 1920 article, John Dewey called for the scientific study of education. Teachers, said Dewey, must have "a body of verified facts and tested principles which may give intellectual guidance to the practical operating of schools."[1] It was Dewey's contention that effective teaching strategies were neither so obvious that they did not warrant study nor so complex that they could not be verified by science.

By mid-century, research in teaching was well under way. Nate Gage commented in 1960 that teacher effectiveness studies had become so numerous that it was an overwhelming task merely to catalogue (let alone digest and evaluate) what had been written.[2]

Early Research

Early research on teaching was generally of two kinds. The first variety focused on character traits of teachers, and the second kind focused on teaching methods. Neither line of research was particularly productive, but there was something to be learned from the shortcomings of these original endeavors.

Character research assumed that teaching was largely a matter of personality. It supported the still-popular view that good teachers were born not trained. Such studies would typically identify good and bad teachers (often with the aid of school administrators) and compare their characteristics. Research results reported character traits that researchers believed distinguished effective teachers from ineffective ones. Good teachers were found to display such qualities as leadership, flexibility, interest, charisma (sometimes called *magnetism*), and a pleasing appearance.

The flaws of character trait research soon became apparent. Investigators seldom checked to see if the teachers identified as effective did indeed produce greater learning gains in their students. Studies also indicated that the teachers whom administrators identified as the most talented were not necessarily the most effective when judged by the performance of their students.[3] A second problem with this research had to do with its reliability. The traits that researchers identified were vaguely worded and seldom defined specific behaviors; that is, they were "high inference items." The behaviors one researcher saw as signs of leadership or flexibility were not necessarily the behaviors another researcher associated with the same qualities. A third problem of character trait research was related to the second: The research was not useful. It didn't help teachers to improve their performance. For example, the research did not tell teachers how they might become more "magnetic." Even if teachers could determine what the term meant, it hardly seemed to be a trait that one could acquire by will or training.

The failures of character trait studies made it apparent that educational research would have to move in a new direction. One promising new course was charted by researchers engaged in comparative studies of teaching methods. Typically, these investigators would select groups of students matched for ap-

---

[1] John Dewey, "Progressive Education and the Science of Education," in *Dewey on Education*, ed. Martin S. Dworkin (New York: Teachers College Press, 1964), p. 116. Available in paperback.

[2] Quoted in Michael J. Duncan and Bruce J. Biddle, *The Study of Teaching* (New York: Holt, Rinehart and Winston, 1974), pp. 12–13.

[3] Don Medley and H. Mitzel, "Some Behavioral Correlates of Teacher Effectiveness," *Journal of Educational Psychology*, Vol. 50 (1959), pp. 239–246.

titude, socioeconomic status, and other pertinent characteristics. The groups would be exposed to different teaching methods for specific periods of time. Pretests and posttests would measure student achievement and allow researchers to determine which methods produced the greatest gains.

Methodological problems plagued early research in this area, but its major drawback was that it did not produce consistent results. By mid-century, commentators were beginning to voice what was to become a common theme regarding educational research: It simply was not informative. The American Educational Research Association summed up the situation this way:

> The . . . fact of the matter is that, after forty years of research on teacher effectiveness during which a vast number of studies have been carried out, one can point to few outcomes that a superintendent of schools can safely employ in hiring a teacher or granting him tenure, that an agency can employ in certifying teachers, or that a teacher-education faculty can employ in planning or improving teacher-education programs.[4]

Large-Scale Research

Complaints that teacher effectiveness research was unproductive continued into the 1960s. Not only was this research of little use to teachers, it was also uninteresting. It provided neither insights nor surprises. As Charles Silberman remarked sometime later, there is less to educational research than meets the eye.

The urgent quests of integration and the civil rights movement, the hopeful endeavors of the war on poverty, and the new urge to equalize opportunity through education set the stage for new and more ambitious research in the 1960s and 1970s. Although this research, at least in its early stages, did not provide clear guidance on how to improve schools, no one could accuse it of being uninteresting.

In 1964, the United States Congress commissioned a study of the nation's schools. It charged the U.S. Office of Education with determining the extent and consequences of unequal educational opportunity in America. James Coleman was put in charge of the project.

Assembling a team of highly qualified researchers and statisticians, Coleman began one of the most ambitious studies in the history of social science. Working under a two-year deadline, the team designed a massive project involving 645,000 children and 60,000 teachers in roughly 4000 schools across the nation. Students in grades one, three, six, nine and twelve were given a battery of tests designed to measure achievement in reading, writing, calculating, and problem solving. Research results might have been quite different if the investigators had employed tests of intelligence, creativity, moral development, and other factors associated with schooling. Coleman, however, defended the use of achievement tests on the ground that they measured the basic skills necessary for full participation in an increasingly technological world.

We turn now to the complex findings of this research, which will be discussed under the headings "Achievement Scores," "School Characteristics," "The Influence of the Home," "Student Body Characteristics," and "Student Fate Control."

---

[4] American Educational Research Association, "Report of the Committee on Criteria of Teacher Effectiveness," *Journal of Educational Research,* Vol. 46 (1953), p. 657.

ACHIEVEMENT SCORES.   Achievement test results confirmed what had been
known for some time: Minority students generally enter school at an academic
disadvantage. Achievement scores for the *average* American Indian, Mexican-
American, Puerto Rican, or black student were lower than those for the *average*
white or Asian-American student.[5]

A second finding, again confirming the findings of previous research, was
that the gap separating achievement scores of minority and majority students
widened as students progressed through school. This finding brought the accusation from some quarters that the relative decline in minority-student performance had less to do with the pupils' native ability than with the schools'
inability (or unwillingness) to educate them.[6]

Coleman thought he knew the reason for low scores among minority groups.
First, as his study dramatically documented, white and minority students usually attended different schools. Second, he speculated that minority-group schools
would be of poorer quality and that this inferiority would account for their
poor showing on achievement tests. As Coleman explained to an interviewer
midway through the research project:

> The study will show the difference in the quality of schools that the average Negro
> child and the average white child are exposed to. You know yourself that the
> difference is going to be striking. And even though everybody knows there is a
> lot of difference between suburban and inner city schools, once the statistics are
> there in black and white, they will have a lot more impact.[7]

SCHOOL CHARACTERISTICS.   In order to get at the question of school quality,
Coleman and his collaborators collected data on such factors as the age of school
buildings; access to physics, chemistry, and language laboratories; library facilities; number of textbooks; average class size; per-pupil expenditures; and teacher
background characteristics, such as education and test scores. Although differences were found between schools, for blacks and whites, the disparities were
small and not always in the favor of the schools for whites. More significantly,
none of the differences studied by Coleman appeared to explain the disparity
between the achievement test scores of blacks and whites. Surprisingly, class
size, per-pupil expenditures, school facilities, and varied curricular offerings
had virtually no impact on academic achievement. Even the test scores, experience, and family background of teachers had only a modest influence on
student test-score results.

THE INFLUENCE OF THE HOME.   If differences in student achievement could
not be explained by disparities in school quality, where was the explanation to
be found? By Coleman's analysis, the answer lay in the home. "Taking all these
results together," Coleman concluded,

---

[5] It is important to keep in mind that Coleman was reporting average scores. Large numbers of
   minority students outperformed many of their white and Asian-American classmates. Although
   Coleman's findings have group significance, they tell us nothing about the scores of individual
   students.
[6] For an example of this argument, see Kenneth B. Clark, *Dark Ghetto* (New York: Harper &
   Row, Publishers, Inc., Torchbooks, 1967). Available in paperback.
[7] This statement was reported in the *Southern Education Report* (November–December 1965). It is
   quoted in *On Equality of Educational Opportunity*, eds. Frederick Mosteller and Daniel Moynihan
   (New York: Random House, Inc., Vintage Books, 1972), p. 8. Available in paperback.

> One implication stands out above all: that schools bring little influence to bear on the child's achievement that is independent of his background and general social context; and that this very lack of an independent effect means that the inequalities imposed on children by their home, neighborhood, and peer environment are carried along to become the inequalities with which they confront adult life at the end of school. For equality of educational opportunity to the school must imply a strong effect of schools that is independent of the child's immediate social environment, and that strong independent effect is not present in American schools.[8]

Of all the tangled variables that contribute to what a student learns in school, none was found to be more critical than the influence of the home.

The Coleman report did not suggest that schools were without effects. It merely pointed out in stark, unambiguous terms that students come to school with wide differences in academic achievement and that these differences grow wider with each year of school. Schools teach students many things and have enduring effects on their lives and minds. These effects are large and have been well documented.[9]

Coleman was not measuring the absolute effects of schooling, however. He was looking at its comparative effects. To everyone's surprise, the differences among schools were slight at this level of analysis. One school did not appear to be much more able than another to encourage learning or to reduce the gap between low-SES students and their more affluent classmates. Robert Nichols, writing in *Science* magazine shortly after the report appeared, observed that readers

> may find it hard to believe that the $28-billion-a-year public education industry has not produced abundant evidence to show the differential effects of different kinds of schools, but it has not.[10]

STUDENT BODY CHARACTERISTICS.   Some school factors did have a modest impact on student success. The most significant of these was the social-class makeup of the student body. Coleman found that the achievement of low-SES students was adversely affected if they were denied access to affluent higher-achieving classmates. As Coleman put it,

> Attributes of other students accounted for far more variation in the achievement of minority group children than do any attributes of school facilities and slightly more than do attributes of the staff.[11]

The implication of this finding was clear enough; insofar as we segregate our schools racially and socioeconomically, we hinder the academic opportunities of already disadvantaged children.

STUDENT FATE CONTROL.   Another factor that Coleman found to be related to academic progress, especially among black students, was a sense of control over the events of their lives. Coleman asked students to give "agree," "not sure," or "disagree" responses to each of the following questions:

---

[8] James S. Coleman et al., *Equality of Educational Opportunity* (Washington, DC: U.S. Government Printing Office, 1966), p. 325.

[9] For an account of what schools accomplish, see Herbert Hyman, Charles Wright, and John Reed, *The Enduring Effects of Education* (Chicago: University of Chicago Press, 1975).

[10] Robert C. Nichols, "Schools and the Disadvantaged," *Science*, Vol. 154 (December 9, 1966), p. 1314.

[11] Coleman, *Equality of Educational Opportunity*, p. 302.

1. Good luck is more important than hard work for success.
2. Every time I try to get ahead, something or somebody stops me.
3. People like me don't have much of a chance to succeed in life.

Coleman found that disadvantaged students were more likely than their advantaged counterparts to believe that they were unable to affect their environment and that what happened to them was more a matter of luck than a matter of planning and effort. Of all the variables measured in his study (including measures of family background and school quality), Coleman found that positive fate-control attitudes showed the strongest relationship to achievement at the sixth grade and above.[12]

Responses to the Coleman Report

The findings of the Equality of Educational Opportunity study were devastating. Robert C. Nichols described the report as

> literally of revolutionary significance. . . . [U]ntil these findings are clarified by further research, they stand like a spear pointed at the heart of the cherished American belief that equality of educational opportunity will increase the equality of educational achievement.[13]

Charles Silberman, writing in *Fortune* magazine, reiterated this conclusion:

> The Coleman Report suggests forcibly that the public schools do not—and as now constituted cannot—fulfill what has always been considered to be one of their main purposes and justifications: to insure equality of opportunity . . . or, in Horace Mann's phrase, to be "the balance wheel of social machinery."[14]

The Coleman Report generated an interest in education among social scientists, an interest that had been long lacking. A number of investigators reanalyzed Coleman's data, but their findings simply reinforced his basic conclusions.[15] Outside the research community, however, the report was largely ignored. Patrick Moynihan and others attributed this to a resistance among educators to abandon their most cherished myths. As he put it:

> A proposition may thus be asserted: The educational establishment is resistant to research findings on institutional grounds, and will probably remain so unless institutional or professional changes occur which change this disposition.[16]

Doubtless there is some truth in Moynihan's accusation, but he overstates the case. More to the point was that Coleman and his colleagues were unable to explain their own findings. Their report did not show why schools were less effective than had been hoped nor did it spell out what could be done to change the situation.[17]

---

[12] Ibid., p. 319.
[13] Nichols, "Schools and the Disadvantaged," *Science*, p. 1314.
[14] Charles E. Silberman, "A Devastating Report on U.S. Education," *Fortune* (August 1967), p. 181.
[15] Mosteller and Moynihan, eds., *On Equality of Educational Opportunity.*
[16] Daniel P. Moynihan, "Sources of Resistance to the Coleman Report," *Harvard Educational Review,* Vol. 38 (Winter 1968), p. 26.
[17] Moynihan had suggestions, to be sure, as did many other politically active social scientists. It appears that Moynihan was not so much annoyed that educators ignored the findings of Coleman as by the fact that they ignored his own prescriptions for the future of education.

Social scientists were themselves deeply divided on the question of what should be done. Hereditarians, classic liberals, and the new egalitarians (see Chapter 21) had their own explanations for Coleman's bubble-bursting findings. They offered proposals for the future, but no argument was more compelling than the call for further research. It was clear that education would have to change, but one did not yet know enough to make changes wisely.

Process–Product Research

The Coleman Report, along with similar research that generally supported his findings,[18] was hampered by its very size. By looking at the effects of schooling on a district level or school level, investigators missed the finer details of school life. For example, they did not study teacher–student interaction patterns, which, many now contend, are at the heart of the teaching process. About the time that Coleman and his colleagues were engaged in their gargantuan work, a number of other investigators were doggedly pursuing another, more modest avenue of inquiry: process–product studies of teacher effectiveness.

Process–product research attempts to discover correlational links between what teachers do in the classroom (the teaching process) and what students learn (the achievement product). To do process–product research, investigators must observe in classrooms and exhaustively record teacher behaviors. Researchers use one of a variety of instruments that identify and carefully define specific activities. These "low-inference" instruments require little interpretation by the recorder. He or she is instructed to record specific items of behavior every time they occur. Such items might include using praise or criticism, asking high-order or low-order questions, addressing small groups or the total class, and assigning seat work or homework. Pre- and posttest measures are used to ascertain student progress. Measures of academic achievement are most frequently used, but attitudinal changes, problem-solving ability, creativity, and social awareness are sometimes measured as well. When the data collection period is over, information regarding teacher behaviors and student change is tabulated by computer and analyzed using sophisticated statistical techniques. The results of the research are recorded as correlations between specific teacher behaviors and equally specific student gains.

Until quite recently, it was widely assumed that there was too little agreement across studies to make process–product findings useful. The research generated little interest in people other than the process–product investigators themselves. This situation is rapidly changing. Recent reviews of the teacher effectiveness literature have provided a set of specific teacher behaviors that have consistently correlated with student gains on academic achievement tests. Most of this research was conducted in early elementary grades, among low-SES students. The results can be generalized only to similar classrooms.

We cannot discuss all the pertinent research findings here, but some of the most useful and provocative results will be reviewed. Successful teachers in low-

---

[18] John C. Flanagan et al., *Studies of the American High School* (Pittsburgh: Project Talent Office, University of Pittsburgh, 1962); and Harvey Averch et al., *How Effective Is Schooling?* (Englewood Cliffs, NJ: Educational Technology Publications, 1974). See also Christopher Jencks et al., *Inequality: A Reassessment of the Effects of Family and Schooling in America* (New York: Basic Books, 1972); available in paperback.

SES, early elementary classrooms have been found to demonstrate the following behaviors and attitudes:[19]

1. Effective teachers see their jobs primarily in terms of instruction and organize their activities around this aim.

2. They see pupils as capable of learning and do not write off students as unteachable.

3. They see to it that students spend major portions of class time engaged in tasks designed to promote learning.

4. They employ direct instruction. They circulate around the classroom, organize friendly but task-oriented drill sessions and recitation experiences, use sequenced and structured materials, and keep students focused on the learning task. The goals are clear to students, and their performance is monitored.

5. They are likely to ask students low-cognitive-level, straightforward questions. They are careful to fit the difficulty of their inquiries to the capabilities of the student queried. As a result, students of successful teachers have an error rate of under 20 percent. Repetition is used to enforce knowledge, and a slow pace is employed when needed to ensure that instruction does not move faster than the students' understanding.

6. The emotional climate of the classroom is warm, with a conspicuous absence of hostility or harping on the part of the teacher. It is structured but not authoritarian. Effective teachers manage to keep a sharp eye on the class to ensure that students are not the source of emotional or behavioral disruption. Teacher rebukes and discipline maneuvers are held to a minimum.

Moving beyond the process–product data for a moment, we might speculate on how teachers manage to run orderly, friendly classrooms. Classroom rules and routines must be established early in the year, perhaps in collaboration with students. Rules must be simple and sparse enough to ensure that students can understand and remember what is expected of them. Furthermore, it is important that students be given an opportunity to practice the behaviors they are expected to display.

There is evidence that teachers with productive classroom management skills stay aware of what's going on in the class. When misbehaviors occur, successful teachers respond in one of the following ways:

[19] Kern Alexander et al., *Compensatory Education Literature Review* (Gainesville, FL: Institute for Educational Finance, March 1979); Jere E. Brophy, "Advances in Teacher Effectiveness Research" (Paper presented at the meeting of the American Association of Colleges for Teacher Education, March 1, 1979); Wilbur B. Brookover and Jeffrey M. Schneider, "Academic Environments and Elementary School Achievement," *Journal of Research and Development in Education,* Vol. 9 (November 1, 1975), pp. 83–91; Thomas Good, Howard Ebmeier, and Terrill Beckerman, "Teaching Mathematics in High and Low SES Classrooms: An Empirical Comparison," *Journal of Teacher Education,* Vol. 29 (September–October 1978), pp. 85–89; Don Medley, *Teacher Competence and Teacher Effectiveness: A Review of Process–Product Research* (Washington, DC: The American Association of Colleges for Teacher Education, 1977); Barak Rosenshine, "Recent Research on Teacher Behaviors and Student Achievement," *Journal of Teacher Education,* Vol. 27 (Spring 1976), pp. 61–63; Barak Rosenshine, "Content, Time, and Direct Instruction," in *Research on Teaching,* eds. Penelope Peterson and Herbert Walberg (Berkeley, CA: McCutchan Publishing Corporation, 1979), pp. 28–56; Robert Soar and Ruth M. Soar, "Emotional Climate and Management," in *Research on Teaching,* eds. Penelope Peterson and Herbert Walberg (Berkeley, CA: McCutchan Publishing Corporation, 1979), pp. 97–119.

- They spot potential trouble early, dealing with it appropriately and firmly before it gets out of hand and disrupts the flow of the lesson.
- They identify inappropriate activities and suggest more acceptable behaviors.
- They may ask the misbehaving student to identify more appropriate behaviors.
- They may avoid a direct confrontation with a misbehaving student by praising pupils who are behaving appropriately.

7. The bulk of process–product evidence indicates that large-group instruction is more conducive to academic achievement in low-achieving classrooms than independent seat work or small-group activities. Small-group work per se is not ineffective; Robert and Ruth Soar have shown that when students work in adult-supervised groups, there are significant achievement gains. Students are kept on task and benefit from the guidance and rewards the teacher provides. When students work without adult supervision, however, they generally will not learn as much.

The problem with small-group work is simply this: The teacher cannot be everywhere at once. If he or she is working with a group, the rest of the class is left on their own. *The Beginning Teacher Evaluation Study,* a large government-financed research project, found that students working with a teacher were clearly off-task only 4 to 6 percent of the time. When they were working without teacher supervision, they were off-task 16 percent of the time and used another 10 percent of their time moving from one activity to another.[20]

Teachers at best have only three or four hours of instructional time a day. The question becomes How can one use this time most productively? If the class is easily distracted and if the objective is to improve basic skills, then small-group work is probably not the best choice.

8. More and more studies are confirming the importance of teacher wait time. After asking a question, a teacher should give students adequate time to think out an answer and respond. If a child has difficulty with a question, effective teachers rephrase what is being asked, probe, or (as a last resort) ask an easier question. It is probably a poor teaching strategy to move on to another student with the same question. When possible, it is more productive to stay with a pupil until he or she has experienced success. This tactic serves two important functions. First, students come to understand that they are capable and that with effort they can succeed. Second, they learn that the teacher expects success and that they cannot excuse themselves from effort by simply outwaiting the teacher.

Most teachers wait less than a second for a student's response to a question. Mary Budd Rowe has found that extending wait time to three seconds has the following positive consequences:[21]

1. The length of student responses increases significantly (up to 700 percent in some classrooms).
2. Appropriate (but unsolicited) responses increase.

[20] Discussed in Barak Rosenshine, "Content, Time, and Direct Instruction," in *Research on Teaching,* p. 42.
[21] M. B. Rowe, "Wait-time and Rewards as Instructional Variables, Their Influence on Language, Logic and Fate Control," *Journal of Research in Science Education,* Vol. 11 (1974), pp. 81–94.

3. Failure to respond decreases.
4. Students are more likely to respond with confidence rather than with answers that are shaped into questions.
5. Reflective and speculative responses increase.
6. Low-achieving students are more likely to contribute, and their contributions are more likely to be correct.
7. Frequency of student questioning increases.
8. The variety, quality, and number of logical moves by students increase.

Some Cautionary Notes

The process–product research brings the clear message that teachers can make a difference in student achievement. Its findings will certainly expand as time goes on. Although this prediction is good news, a few cautionary notes must be sounded.

1. The research studies reported here are in primary grades among low-SES children. They may not apply to higher grades or to students from other backgrounds.[22]

2. As students progress (become more proficient learners), the behavior of the teacher may need to change. More complex questions can be asked (although they still must be in the range of a student's ability), and the student can be given more responsibility for self-monitoring (although the teacher must still make sure that the student is handling this challenge effectively).[23]

3. It would be a mistake to think that all poor children must be treated one way and that all middle-class children should be treated another. The factor that determines a teacher's methods must be the child and not the child's social class. As educational research becomes more sophisticated, studies will focus on the developmental needs of the child and not on the crude measures of his or her family's financial status. True, many poor children have attributes in common, but this is *not* to say that all such children are alike or that they will all respond to the same teaching methods. Thus, teachers must be careful to monitor a child's development and adjust their teaching methods accordingly.

What should teachers be looking for? For one thing, they should check a child's proficiency level. Children with academic deficiencies seem to benefit from structured instruction more than other students do. Similarly, dependent or highly anxious students appear to learn better in structured situations, whereas independent and less anxious students can accommodate more freedom to explore their own ideas and monitor their own learning.[24]

4. All the research reviewed here measured student outcomes, often math and reading scores, on standardized achievement tests. Although no one would

---

[22] Thomas Good and C. Power, "Designing Successful Classroom Environments for Different Types of Students," *Journal of Curriculum Studies*, Vol. 8 (1976), pp. 45–60.

[23] M. Powell, "Educational Implications of Current Research on Teaching," *Educational Forum*, Vol. 43 (1978), pp. 27–38.

[24] P. Peterson, "Interactive Effects of Student Anxiety, Achievement Orientation, and Teacher Behavior on Student Achievement and Attitude," *Journal of Educational Psychology*, Vol. 69 (1977), pp. 779–792.

suggest that mastery of these skills is unimportant, neither would we want to limit our objectives to such a narrow focus.

Outcomes we might associate with the aim of creative intelligence—cooperativeness, acceptance of responsibility for academic success, independence, high achievement on nonverbal problem solving—were found by Jane Stallings to be associated with more open and flexible educational programs. Stallings's conclusions were drawn from Follow Through research, which was also limited to low-income, early elementary classrooms. Similarly, a review of process–product research by Robert Soar concluded

> In summary . . . the direct instruction model seems to be a very appropriate description of the teaching style which is best adapted to teaching low cognitive level, . . . simple outcomes to low socioeconomic status, lower grade-level children, but the extent to which this model is appropriate for other objectives, other pupils, or other grade levels is questionable. The major danger lies in generalizing this model of teaching past its limits. Research to date suggests that, even for lower grade, low SES children, *this model of teaching risks handicapping children in learning to think.* While learning basic skills is a critical objective—a necessary building block to future education—to teach only in a way which limits extension of those skills to more complex mental operations seems a considerable price to pay, and an unnecessary price, if the complexity of the situation is understood.[25] (emphasis added)

Ethnographic research suggests that direct instruction has consequences in student social behavior that process–product studies are unlikely to pick up. In a small study of third- and fourth-grade classrooms, Bossert found highly structured, recitation-oriented instruction (the type suggested by process–product research) has some negative consequences:

> The structure of recitation allows for individual comparisons and when accompanied by comparative assessments of performance, fosters the development of a competitive status system within the classroom. Status and interpersonal bonding depends on individual performance. This decreases overall group cohesion and reinforces social relationships that support both the pupil's productivity and chances of attaining rewards. In recitation-organized classrooms, children separate into performance-homogeneous friendship groups that remain exclusive and fairly stable throughout the year. By contrast, the structure of multi-task organization does not involve comparative assessment of pupil performance. Status, based on academic achievements, and competitive peer interactions do not develop. Pupils are free to establish a variety of social relations without regard to their instrumental value in obtaining performance recognition. They choose friends and workmates often on the basis of task or hobby interests, changing groups as their interests shift.[26]

Bossert also found that recitation-oriented classrooms inhibit cooperative behavior among students, tend to segregate students into academic ability groups,

---

[25] Robert Soar, "Classroom Environment," Chapter 4, in Kern Alexander et al., *Compensatory Education Literature Review*, p. 170 (Gainesville, FL: Institute for Educational Finance, 1979). See also Penelope Peterson, "Direct Instruction Reconsidered," in *Research on Teaching*, eds. Penelope Peterson and Herbert Walberg (Berkeley, CA: McCutchan Publishing Corporation, 1979), pp. 57–69.

[26] Steven T. Bossert, *Tasks and Social Relationships in Classrooms: A Study of Instructional Organization and Its Consequences* (New York: Cambridge University Press, 1979), p. 83.

force teachers into a role of institutional authority, and increase the likelihood that low-achieving students will be overlooked by teachers.[27]

The negative effects of classroom recitation were, according to Bossart, a product of the teaching method and not of the personality of the teacher who employed it. When teachers changed their teaching style, the social dynamics of the classroom changed as well. In Bossart's view, the recitation mode of instruction virtually guaranteed a total institution atmosphere in the classroom.

The Importance of Aims

Faced with what appear to be contradictory results, we might assume that educational research has led us down another blind alley. This, however, would be a hasty and unwarranted conclusion. The research merely points out that different classroom practices will result in different student outcomes. A closed, tightly regimented, no-nonsense classroom system that emphasizes recitation, drill, and large-group interaction and avoids a negative emotional climate will indeed produce gains in basic skills and low-level cognitive processes (at least among early elementary, low-achieving students).

Well-run, more open classrooms that allow cooperative effort, small-group work, and student choice will produce higher-level thinking and greater cooperation among students. As Soar has stated, if pupils are to learn "complex thinking operations, they need some degree of freedom to work on their own, to follow different modes of attack . . . to apply ideas of their own, and to test alternative approaches." In short, they need some freedom to approach a problem independently. "Apparently pupils do not learn to think best where the entire learning process is prescribed."[28]

Once again, we see the necessity of having clear educational aims. Unless we know what we want to accomplish, research results are of little use. This is not to suggest, however, that we need to choose between teaching basic skills and creative intelligence. It means instead that some blend of these two teaching approaches may be necessary in early grades. Again, quoting Soar,

> The conclusion appears to be that once pupils have mastered the most basic of the basic skills, or perhaps even simultaneous with that learning, some part of the classroom day needs to be given over to a teaching style which fosters more complex objectives.[29]

Teachers in classrooms with low-achieving students may wish to devote a portion of each day to recitation and drill in basic skill areas (learning the alphabet, phonics instruction, memorizing arithmetic facts, and so on). Other portions of the day might be devoted to cooperative activities, although it remains important to keep students on task. A diversification of activities could ameliorate some of the negative consequences of recitation activities. At the same time, diversification could promote the mastery of basic skills, which themselves serve as a stepping stone to higher-level thinking.

---

[27] Ibid., p. 62.
[28] Soar, "Classroom Environment," in *Compensatory Education Literature Review*, p. 160. See also Penelope Peterson, "Direct Instruction Reconsidered," in *Research on Teaching*, p. 67.
[29] Ibid., p. 174.

School Climate Research

Process–product studies offer a strong argument against the claim that the school performance of low-SES students is exclusively controlled by the home and is unrelated to teacher behavior. It is now clear that teachers do make a difference. Another line of research—what we will call *school climate studies*—suggests that other school factors also contribute to student learning.

Wilbur Brookover and a team of researchers at the University of Michigan found a number of schools in low-SES areas where achievement test scores were improving and others where scores were declining. Using interview and observation techniques, the researchers studied the characteristics of the schools. When the results were tabulated and compared, clear differences were found between "improving" and "declining" schools.

Teachers in improving schools had a clear commitment to teach academic material. They expected their students to learn, expected underachieving students to improve, and assumed responsibility for making learning happen. Effective schools had an academically oriented, supportive climate and an atmosphere of academic seriousness and productivity. Students knew that teachers expected them to learn and would keep after them to ensure their academic improvement. Teachers spent most of their class time on instruction. Individual competition was minimized through group activities, although there was competition among groups.

The declining schools, on the other hand, were staffed by teachers who were willing to write off students they saw as unteachable. They held little hope for the immediate improvement of these students' academic skills and predicted that many would not graduate from high school. Brookover found that teachers in ineffective schools used praise in their classrooms but were likely to use it inappropriately (for example, by praising students even when they gave incorrect answers).[30] Students in the declining schools expressed attitudes of academic futility. As Brookover described it, they

> feel they have no control over their success or failure in the school social system, the teachers do not care if they succeed or not, and their fellow students punish them if they do succeed.[31]

The Brookover results find confirmation in three other studies comparing effective and ineffective inner-city schools: one conducted by G. Weber, another by the New York State Office of Education, and a third by J. Madden and his colleagues for the state of California. The reports shared these conclusions:[32]

[30] Wilbur Brookover et al., "Elementary School Social Climate and School Achievement," *American Educational Research Journal,* Vol. 15 (Spring 1978), pp. 301–318. See also Wilbur Brookover, *School Systems and Student Achievement* (New York: Praeger Publishers, 1979), and Wilbur Brookover and Jeffrey Schneider, "Academic Environments and Elementary School Achievement," *Journal of Research and Development in Education,* Vol. 9 (November 1, 1975), pp. 82–91. For a discussion of the harm done by inappropriate reinforcement, see Mary Budd Rowe, "Relation of Wait-time and Rewards to the Development of Language, Logic and Fate Control: Part II—Rewards," *Journal of Research in Science Teaching,* Vol. 11 (1974), pp. 291–308.

[31] Wilbur Brookover et al., "Elementary School Climate and School Achievement," *American Educational Research Journal,* p. 314.

[32] Ronald Edmonds, "Some Schools Work and More Can," in *Education 80–81* (Guilford, CT: Dushkin Publishing Group, 1980), pp. 39–42. See also G. Weber, *Inner-city Children Can Be*

1. Professional personnel in more effective schools believed they could help their students learn. Educators in less effective schools attributed children's problems with the basic skills to factors outside the school's control. It would appear that students in less effective schools failed because they were not expected to succeed.
2. More effective schools had a plan for improving student performance. Teachers and administrators worked to see that the plan was implemented.
3. School policies and administrative practices in the more effective schools were organized to achieve the academic mission of the school.
4. Administrators in effective schools displayed management skills and an understanding of instructional strategies.
5. Teachers in effective schools displayed greater effort; ran orderly, task-oriented classrooms; spent more time on subject matter; and defined professional success in terms of student achievement gains.

Other studies have drawn similar conclusions. A study of the management and organization of twenty-six elementary schools found that staff commitment to academic matters was vital to student achievement. Jean Wellisch and her co-researchers summarized their findings:

> In successful schools, that is, in schools which succeeded in raising student achievement, the administrators: were more concerned with instruction; communicated their views about instruction; took responsibility for discussions relating to instruction; coordinated an instruction program; and emphasized academic standards.
>
> Successful . . . schools were characterized by administrators who felt strongly about instruction and assumed relatively more responsibility for instruction-related tasks such as selecting basic instructional materials and planning and evaluating programs for the entire school. These leadership qualities were recognized and reported by teachers, which no doubt reflected the fact that effective administrators also communicated their views concerning instruction to teachers. One means of communication, especially prevalent in successful schools, was a regular review and discussion with teachers about their classroom performance. Extensively coordinated programs also distinguished successful schools from non-successful ones. Finally, it was found that administrators in successful schools emphasized academic standards by reviewing teacher performance, by opposing the postponement of basic skill instruction, and by requiring students to repeat grades when standards for achievement were not met.[33]

A study of English secondary schools further documented the relationship between academic performance and school climate. A British team of researchers headed by Michael Rutter found that teachers in successful schools had clear academic aims for their pupils and generally believed that their pupils could achieve the high standards they had set for them. The staff worked closely together, and there was a "consensus on the values and aims of the school."[34]

Taught to Read: Four Successful Schools (Washington, DC: Council for Basic Education, 1971); State of New York, Office of Education Performance Review, *School Factors Influencing Reading Achievement: A Case Study of Two Inner-city Schools* (March 1974); and J. V. Madden, D. R. Lawson, and D. Sweet, *School Effectiveness Study: State of California* (Sacramento: 1976).

[33] Jean B. Wellisch, Ann H. MacQueen, Ronald Carriere, and Gary Duck, "School Management and Organization in Successful Schools," *Sociology of Education*, Vol. 51 (July 1978), p. 219.

[34] Michael Rutter et al., *Fifteen Thousand Hours: Secondary Schools and Their Effects on Children* (Cambridge: Harvard University Press, 1979), p. 193.

There was also a strong agreement among teachers as to the norms of student behavior. As Rutter and his colleagues expressed it,

> For there to be an accepted set of norms which apply consistently throughout the school, it is necessary not only to have ways of ensuring that there is joint staff action but also that staff feel part of a group whose values they share.[35]

The British team found that teachers in successful schools set a positive example for students. If pupils were to have high academic achievement and to behave in a socially productive manner, it was necessary for teachers to display these behaviors themselves. Teachers in successful schools were found to be punctual; conscientious about assigning, collecting, and correcting student work; unfailing in their class preparation; efficient in their use of class time (time on task was again found to be a significant variable); accessible to students; and vigilant as well as fair in their monitoring of student behavior. It was also important that teachers genuinely like their pupils.

School Improvement Strategies

Listing the characteristics of effective teachers and effective schools is helpful, but it does not tell us how to make any particular school more effective. For guidance in that area we must turn to another body of research, the school improvement literature. Research in this area is growing rapidly and does not lend itself to quick summation. In this section we will set out some guiding principles of school improvement.

THE SCHOOL AS THE FUNDAMENTAL UNIT OF REFORM.   For years individual teachers were seen as the fundamental unit of educational reform. The idea was that schools and school districts could be only as good as the faculty who teach in them. Therefore, administrators who wanted to improve schools almost always tried to change the behavior of individual teachers. The problem with this approach is that it ignored the many ways individual behavior is influenced by institutional arrangements. Perhaps schools can be no better than the teachers who work in them, but they can be a great deal worse. Therefore, it makes sense to make the school and not the individual the fundamental unit of educational improvement.

SCHOOL IMPROVEMENT TO PROMOTE COLLEGIALITY AND REDUCE TEACHER ISOLATION.   Teachers, as we learned in Chapter 14, are often isolated from one another and seldom interact professionally. In effective schools, however, teachers have many opportunities to share ideas and take part in school-wide decisions. School improvement efforts must promote collegiality among the staff. Teachers must be able to give and receive help from one another, influence school policies, solve school problems, and exercise collective intelligence.

SCHOOL IMPROVEMENT EFFORTS CONTROLLED BY THE STAFF.   If effective schools reduce teacher isolation and promote collegiality, it stands to reason

---

[35] Ibid., p. 194.

that the effective school improvement efforts should promote teacher participation. This is most often accomplished by having a team of teachers, building
and district administrators, parents, and students made responsible for the school
improvement effort. Though many groups are represented on the team, teachers constitute the majority. It is the team's responsibility to conduct a needs
assessment, target areas for improvement, develop improvement plans with the
staff, implement and monitor the plan, evaluate progress, and modify the plan
as needed.

SCHOOL IMPROVEMENT EFFORTS BEGIN MODESTLY AND PROCEED GRAD-
UALLY.   It is important that the first work of the school improvement team
end in success. Therefore, it is wise to begin working on a modest but important problem, for example, reducing misbehavior in the lunch room. Change
efforts often meet with resistance from the staff. If the school improvement
team begins in failure, the chances of eliciting faculty support for future projects will be greatly diminished.

   After the first success, the school improvement team should focus on another small but significant issue. Over time, the problems the team attacks will
be more complex, and their plans will be more ambitious. The team will identify target areas for improvement by studying school effectiveness research.

PROVIDING ASSISTANCE.   Teachers will change their behavior only if they
are convinced that the changes are possible and worthwhile. However, teachers
need clear instructions on what is expected, and they need to practice new
behaviors in a supportive (nonjudgmental) environment. They need constructive feedback and access to reinstruction should they require it.

CONSTRUCTIVE LEADERSHIP.   Effective schools have effective leadership in
the front office. Administrators in effective schools are highly accessible and
involved. There are many effective leadership styles, but the most effective
principals have a clear vision of instructional improvement and communicate
that vision convincingly to the staff. In academically successful schools, effective
principals emphasize student achievement. They help teachers set clear instructional goals and performance standards. They are aware of classroom factors
that enhance and inhibit effective instruction and help teachers maintain comfortable environments for learning. At the same time, effective principals focus
on improving the culture of the school. They promote collegiality, high expectations, civility, and a climate of moral order in the school. They do all they
can to encourage teachers to be reflective practitioners and try to create an
environment in which such reflection can be carried on individually and collectively.

LONG-TERM IMPROVEMENT.   Schools do not become effective and then mag-
ically stay that way. The staff in effective schools are continually monitoring
the events in the institution. When things get a bit off course, adjustments are
made. New ideas are tried and people work together to make good things even
better. In other words, effective schools are self-monitoring. Thus the long-
term goal of any school improvement program is to create a self-monitoring,
self-improving institution.

The Uses of Educational Research

Teaching is not a bag of tricks. It would be a sad misunderstanding of science if we allowed research to reduce the act of teaching to a list of maneuvers. To ask that educational research produce fail-safe recipes for teaching is to ask for more than social science can provide.[36] The aim of science is to guide the art of teaching, not to replace it.[37]

The research reviewed in this chapter does not give a full understanding of how schools work or fail to work, but it does begin to show that many factors contribute to effective schooling. Our purpose in reviewing research findings has not been to set out iron laws for teachers. Half a century ago, John Dewey observed,

> No conclusion of scientific research can be converted into an immediate rule of educational art. For there is no educational practice whatever which is not highly complex; that is to say, which does not contain many other conditions and factors than are included in the scientific findings.[38]

Science can be of use to educators, but educators must understand both its strengths and its limitations.

Scientific research requires a tight methodology, a clear question or problem, and of necessity, a limited vision. All the propensities of research are aimed at limiting and controlling the elements under study. Science cannot investigate much of the world at one time. It must take some narrow slice of the environment and subject it to intense scrutiny. In other words, it must screen out of its vision infinitely more than it can take in. The intent of science is to disentangle the ambiguities alive in a situation, to set carefully controlled variables against one another, and finally to observe the results. When the outcomes are consistent (when they can be reproduced by other scientists), research provides a fuller understanding of some small segment of the world. Science is an exploratory enterprise intent upon achieving a bit-by-bit understanding of reality.

Teaching is quite a different undertaking. It is constructive rather than descriptive. It is a creative enterprise in the sense that it seeks to produce out of available materials something different and more satisfying than was previously there. Like scientists, teachers manipulate variables in an effort to produce results, but teachers cannot limit their vision to some small piece of reality. They must deal with the world as they find it, with all its messy ambiguities and interactive elements; and when their efforts fail, they cannot toss out the botched results and begin again. Educators must continue to work with the products of their mistakes.

If teaching and research are such different kinds of activities, how can the findings of science be of use to educators?

---

[36] John Dewey, *The Sources of a Science of Education* (New York: Liveright, 1929).

[37] Nate L. Gage, *The Scientific Basis of the Art of Teaching* (New York: Teachers College Press, 1978). Available in paperback.

[38] John Dewey, *The Sources of a Science of Education*, p. 19.

Things to Try and Things to Do

Dewey pointed out that the findings of science give educators guidance rather than answers. Research results call a teacher's attention to the influence of subtle and obscure conditions that are easily overlooked. They provide insights into the effects prolonged failure has on students, the subtle powers of wait time, the dangers of inappropriate praise, the benefits and costs of direct instruction, the workings of total institutions, and so on. Science, in Dewey's view, does not provide teachers with rules for overt action but with guides for their teaching. It directs their attention, informs their observations, and helps them more intelligently monitor the events of classroom life. It gives them things to *try* rather than to *do*.[39]

Dewey had something special in mind when he used the word *try*. To try something out implies that we are paying attention to what we are doing. We have a problem, something we want to accomplish, an end in view. We think about our situation, consider alternative courses of action, and decide on the one that appears most likely to succeed. We don't choose activities willy-nilly; we attempt to fit the action to the problem at hand. Science can help a teacher make a wiser (more informed) decision about what to try. This decision doesn't guarantee success, of course; it merely increases the likelihood of a better outcome.

But trying something out involves more than a decision about what to do. It suggests that we stay alert, watch how things are going, *and* pay close attention to how things turn out. We may modify our methods as we go along or after we see that they don't produce quite the results we wanted. The big difference between having things to *try* and being told what to *do* is that in the former case the teacher is intimately involved in the activity: Intelligence is at work; the educative process is being improved. In the latter case, teaching is reduced to routine; the teacher is merely carrying out a mechanical operation.

To ignore science, in Dewey's view, is unwise and irresponsible. However, research results have to be considered in the context of educational aims and the nuts-and-bolts reality of the educational situation. Deciding where and under what conditions research results are applicable in a school or classroom is the responsibility of the teacher not the scientist.

Dewey makes this point directly:

> If you find that what I am telling you, or what another teacher here tells you, gets in the way of your common sense, of your use of your own judgment in an actual school situation, forget what you have learned and rely upon what your own judgment tells you is the best thing to do under the circumstances.[40]

This is an important point, one that is easily misunderstood. Dewey was not claiming, as some others have done, that there is nothing to be known about education that common sense does not supply, nor was he saying that anything that goes on in the classroom is worthwhile as long as it feels right to the teacher. Such ideas are nonsense. He was pointing out that teachers must be students and constant critics of their own enterprise. They should monitor their own

[39] Ibid.
[40] Ibid., pp. 30–31.

activities and stay aware of their results. The benefit of research in education, then, is not that it tells teachers precisely what to do but that it sharpens their powers of observation and analysis so that they can more intelligently judge the course they should take.

What guidance can be derived from the research reviewed in this chapter? Looked at narrowly, the research findings provide teachers with many teaching techniques and classroom arrangements to try out. But, when viewed on a higher level of analysis, the research provides another, and perhaps more fruitful, insight. When taken together, the research findings provide an ecological vision of effective schools. That is to say, successful schools are not just a collection of a few good classrooms and some devoted teachers; they are complex social systems that work at many levels to further the educational undertaking. Each component of the system is interconnected with every other component. Activities at one level of the system reinforce and are reinforced by every other element in the system. The importance of this point cannot be overstated. If educators hope to improve schools, they must improve the system at every level. It will not do merely to change the curriculum, employ a few new techniques, or otherwise tinker with one or another segment of the school.

Let's review some of the material we have covered. Effective schools employ teachers who share a collective vision of the school's educational aims. The administration of the schools devotes itself to the promotion of these aims and provides an environment where teachers are able to pursue them effectively. The organization of classrooms, curriculum, the rules of conduct, classroom work and homework assignments, and the behavioral example set by teachers all work to further these educational aims. Parents are aware of the aims, support them, and work with the school to see that they are accomplished. The social structure of the school enforces a community of effort and encourages frequent interaction and a sharing of problems among teachers. As educational problems become clarified in the school, teachers work in unity to see that they are solved. Students understand the expectations held for them by teachers, their parents, and the community. They understand that the school views them as capable and fully expects them to act on their capabilities.

These are some of the characteristics of effective schools. There is no single way to achieve these ends, no best place to start to work on them, but unless they are seen as objectives of the school, it is unlikely that they will be achieved. And unless teachers and administrators work together to see that these things happen, nothing much will improve in education.

Summary

The 1970s may be remembered as the decade when America lost confidence in itself. We neither abandoned our goals nor lost our courage, but we became less sure that social improvement is possible. This decline in morale was especially apparent in education. As education expenditures soared (to $80 billion a year by the end of the decade), student achievement plummeted. School vandalism increased, along with youth crime and drug abuse. Opinion polls charted the downward course of public confidence in education. Educators heard rumors of research that showed that one school was pretty much as good (or as bad, depending on one's point of view) as another. Slowly, there developed among teachers an idea, more felt than spoken, that perhaps the public was right, the research was right, and their own dreaded suspicions were right as well. Education was in a sorry mess, and was not likely to get any better.

The system was reified in the public mind and, more astonishingly, among educators ranging from kindergarten teachers to college professors. They spoke of "the system," as if it had no connection to human will, as if it had a life and purpose of its own and were out of human control. They spoke as if the activities of education were not their responsibility.

Some teachers left the profession. Others would have liked to do so but were held to their jobs by economic necessity. And still others, the vast majority, merely narrowed their sights: If large change was not possible, perhaps they could make a smaller contribution.

In teachers' lounges around the coffee pot, when old hands and newcomers allowed themselves a moment of reflective conversation, one phrase was repeated over and over again: "Well, if I can just 'get through' to one kid, then I guess it will have been worth it." Such an attitude is more debilitating than it might first appear. Hidden in the rhetoric of altruistic dedication ("My aim is to get through to one student") is the fatalistic acceptance of a more chilling reality ("I'm not going to get through to the other twenty-eight").

John Dewey has said that "the schools, like the nation, are in need of a central purpose which will create new enthusiasm and devotion, and which will unify and guide" their plans for the future.

The research reviewed in this text is important, not because it provides lesson plans for a brighter future, but because its total effect is to show that schools can indeed make a difference. If we can decide on what needs to be done, the research suggest the *kinds* of things we will have to do to make school work. It gives empirical substance to our most democratic convictions. Effective schools are more than collections of isolated individuals. Teachers within such schools must work together, not in isolation. Administrators and teachers must work toward shared goals. Teachers and students must not confront one another in the cool hostility of total institutions but in the warmer (although not lax) climate of personal authority. The school must become a mediating institution.

If we want schools to work, we will have to decide what we want to accomplish. Educators, students, and parents must be united, at least on the broad purposes of education. Schools will then have to organize their activities with these goals in mind.

Suggested Readings

LARGE-SCALE RESEARCH

COLEMAN, JAMES S., et al. *Equality of Educational Opportunity*. Washington, DC: Department of Health, Education, and Welfare, U.S. Office of Education OE 38001, 1966. This study was designed to assess the impact of multiple variables upon student achievement. Data were collected on approximately 60,000 students in grades one, three, six, nine, and twelve in approximately 4000 schools. The findings indicate that achievement variations are strongly related to family background (social class) and that a number of measures of school quality (e.g., teachers' educational background, experience, per-pupil expenditures, number of books in the library) accounted for comparatively small achievement differences between schools.

COLEMAN, JAMES. "Methods and Results in the I.E.A. Studies of Effects of School on Learning," *Review of Educational Research*, Vol. 45, (1975), pp. 355–386. This is an analysis of achievement test data in the areas of literature, reading, and science collected from children between the ages of ten and fourteen in Chile, England, Finland, Italy, Sweden, and the United States. Analyses indicate that home variables have at least as much impact as school variables upon pupil achievement.

HYMAN, HERBERT H., CHARLES R. WRIGHT, and JOHN SHELTON REED. *The Enduring Effects of Education*. Chicago: University of Chicago Press, 1975. This book summarizes the findings of a secondary analysis of more than 300 measures of knowledge. Unlike the Coleman Report, which examined the student population, this report examines results of national surveys among adults, ages twenty-five to seventy-two. The book's conclusion is "Many and varied measures of thousands of adults, drawn from a long series of national samples . . . , lead us to conclude that education produces large, pervasive and enduring effects on knowledge and receptivity to knowledge."

JENCKS, CHRISTOPHER, et al. *Inequality: A Reassessment of the Effects of Family and Schooling in America*. New York: Harper & Row, Publishers, 1972. This book draws on data from various studies to assess the effects of family and schooling on achievement and "success" in adult life. The authors contend that schools make only a modest contribution to student achievement and adult earnings.

LEVINE, DONALD M., and MARY JO BANE. *The Inequality Controversy: Schooling and Distributive Justice*. New York: Basic Books, Inc., Publishers, 1975. This useful collection of essays sums up the argument of the *Inequality* study and the controversy that surrounded it.

MOSTELLER, FREDERICK, and DANIEL P. MOYNIHAN. *On Equality of Educational Opportunity*. New York: Vintage Books, 1972. This is a collection of reports on reanalysis of pupil achievement data from the Coleman Report and other studies. The findings generally support Coleman's conclusion that home variables have as much if not more impact upon pupil achievement as selected school variables.

PROCESS–PRODUCT RESEARCH

ALEXANDER, KERN, et al. *Compensatory Education Literature Review*. Gainesville, FL: Institute for Education Finance, 1979. This is an ambitious review of the pertinent research literature in the areas of administration and organization of schools, home–school relationships, instructional organization procedure, and classroom environment.

GAGE, N. L. *The Scientific Basis for the Art of Teaching*. New York: Teachers College Press, 1978. The author challenges the contention that education does not have a scientific body of knowledge to guide the activities of teaching.

GAGE, N. L., and DAVID C. BERLINER. *Educational Psychology*, 2d ed. Chicago: Rand McNally & Company, 1979. This is probably the best educational psychology textbook in the field. Its section on teaching methods summarizes research findings.

MEDLEY, DON. *Teacher Competence and Teacher Effectiveness: A Review of Process–Product Research*. Washington, DC: American Association of Colleges for Teacher Education, 1977. This is an extensive review of process–product literature, but only studies that meet stringent quality standards are included. The results are classified by pupil socioeconomic status, grade level, and the nature and complexity of outcome measures. Medley's contribution is that he has clarified and explained results that have long appeared inconsistent and confusing.

PETERSON, PENELOPE L., and HERBERT J. WALBERG. *Research on Teaching: Concepts, Findings, and Implications*. Berkeley, CA: McCutchan Publishing Corp., 1979. This is a collection of original chapters that review where research on teaching has been, where it is presently, and where it should go in the future.

ROSENSHINE, B. "Classroom Instruction." In *The Psychology of Teaching Methods*, edited by Nate Gage, pp. 335–371. Chicago: National Society for the Study of Education, 1976. The book draws heavily on large-scale studies (although others are cited) to identify patterns of classroom instruction that prove effective for teaching basic skills for lower-grade, disadvantaged pupils.

SCHOOL CLIMATE/CLASSROOM CLIMATE RESEARCH

BOSSERT, STEVEN T. *Tasks and Social Relationships in Classrooms: A Study of Instructional Organization and Its Consequences.* New York: Cambridge University Press, 1979. This small but suggestive study shows the relationship between instructional style and classroom climate.

BROOKOVER, WILBUR. *School Systems and Student Achievement.* New York: Praeger Publishing Co., 1979. The author studies the difference between low- and high-achieving elementary schools in Michigan.

RUTTER, MICHAEL, et al. *Fifteen Thousand Hours: Secondary Schools and Their Effects on Children.* Cambridge: Harvard University Press, 1979. This is a precedent-setting study of how school climate is related to student outcomes.

SOAR, ROBERT S., and RUTH M. SOAR. "Emotional Climate and Management." In *Research on Teaching*, edited by Penelope Peterson and Herbert Walbert, pp. 97–219. Berkeley, CA: McCutchan Publishing Corp., 1979. This is a thoughtful review of the large-scale studies of teacher effectiveness that the Soars have conducted over the past ten years.

SCHOOL IMPROVEMENT

ASHTON, PATRICIA T., and RODMAN B. WEBB. *Making a Difference: Teachers' Sense of Efficacy and Student Achievement.* New York: Longman, Inc., 1986.

BROOKOVER, WILBER B., C. BEADY, P. FLOOD, J. SCHWEITZER, and J. WISENBACKER. *School Social Systems and Student Achievement: Schools Can Make a Difference.* New York: Praeger Publishing Company, 1979.

BROOKOVER, WILBER B., and L. LEZOTTE. *Changes in School Characteristics Coincident with Changes in Student Achievement.* East Lansing: Michigan State University Press, 1979.

CARLSON, ROBERT V., and E. R. DUCHARME, eds. *School Improvement—Theory and Practice.* Lanham, MD: University Press of America, 1987.

EKHOLM, MATS. "Research on School Improvement in Scandinavia," *International Journal of Qualitative Studies in Education*, Vol. 1 (January–March, 1988), pp. 69–78.

FINN, CHESTER E. "Towards Strategic Independence: Nine Commandments for Enhancing School Effectiveness," *Phi Delta Kappan*, Vol. 65 (1984), pp. 518–524.

GRANT, G. *Education, Character, and American Schools: Are Effective Schools Good Enough?* Syracuse, NY: Syracuse University Press, 1982.

JOYCE, BRUCE R., RICHARD H. HERSH, and MICHAEL McKIBBIN. *The Structure of School Improvement.* New York: Longman, Inc., 1983.

LAUDER, HUGH, and G. I. A. R. KAHN. "Democracy and the Effective Schools Movement in New Zealand," *International Journal of Qualitative Studies in Education*, Vol. 1 (January–March, 1988), pp. 51–68.

LITTLE, JUDITH W. "The Effective Principal," *American Education*, Vol. 18 (August–September, 1982), pp. 38–43.

LOUCKS-HORSLEY, S., and L. F. HERGERT. *An Action Guide to School Improvement.* Alexandria, VA: Association for Supervision and Curriculum Development, 1985.

MILLER, LYNNE, and ANN LIEBERMAN. "School Improvement in the United States: Nuance and Numbers," *International Journal of Qualitative Studies in Education*, Vol. 1 (January–March, 1988), pp. 3–20.

SHIMAHARA, NOBUO. "The College Entrance Examination and Policy Issues in Japan," *International Journal of Qualitative Studies in Education*, Vol. 1 (January–March, 1988), pp. 39–50.

VANDENBERGHE, ROLAND. "School Improvement from a European Perspective," *International Journal of Qualitative Studies in Education*, Vol. 1 (January–March, 1988), pp. 79–90.

VANDENBERGHE, R., and G. E. HALL, eds. *Research on Internal Change Facilitation in Schools*. Leuven, Belgium: Academic Publishing Company, 1987.

WIDEEN, MARVIN. "School Improvement in Canada," *International Journal of Qualitative Studies in Education*, Vol. 1 (January–March 1988), pp. 21–38.

Summary of Section VI

Educators in a democracy must always do their work in contested terrain. Parents, students, legislatures, interest groups, and cranks all want to influence what is taught in the classroom and how it is presented by the teacher. Schools typically respond to reasonable requests, and thus, nearly every social problem is placed at the door of the school for solution. It appears now that schools have promised more than they can deliver, and as a result, faith in public education is declining. A faltering faith in our schools has sparked a major debate over what is wrong in education and what must be done to put things right.

Debates over education are always debates over aims and usually contests between competing goods. Are schools going to serve vocational goals or intellectual aims? Will they serve the group or the individual? Are they going to promote quality or equity? Few would argue against any one of these aims but, faced with limited resources, which of these goals will schools pursue? As we have seen in Section VI, different groups provide different answers to these questions. Business groups want schools to prepare students for the competitive, highly technical world of business. Academic groups want schools to more vigorously pursue an intellectual agenda. Minority interest groups want schools to emphasize equity and provide special assistance to all who are at risk. Teacher interest groups believe that structural changes would help make schools more democratic, caring, and intellectually responsible.

The present debate is useful for many reasons. It has focused public concern about education on the issue of improvement; opened a national conversation about educational aims, a topic that had been ignored for too long; brought a wide array of individuals and groups into this discussion; forced interest groups to consider the views of others; forced compromise; and given teachers hope that the conditions of the workplace will be improved. Perhaps more than anything else, the debate has sparked a national interest in school improvement.

Throughout the text we have tried to help teachers achieve a ridge-rider's perspective on education. We have given a broad view, showing how history, culture, the megastructure, bureaucracy, institutional arrangements, social stratification, the teaching profession, the private sphere, peer groups, and the family all influence the school and affect how teachers teach and how students

611

learn. After seeing the big picture, you may now wonder if schools can be changed at all. So many powerful forces hold the present system in place that it is difficult to contemplate meaningful reform.

Teachers must have a ridge-rider's view in order to understand what education means and what forces promote and inhibit learning. Seeing the big picture can help teachers understand what is going on in their school and classroom. Understanding opens options and, as we learned in Chapter 1, increases individual freedom. However, teachers cannot teach from the ridge; their work must be done in the cultural flat lands where individuals live their lives. Teachers must work with the big picture in mind, but they must be content to work in a very small territory, attending to the "minute particulars" of everyday life. They cannot alter the big picture in a few grand strokes. Huge changes are accomplished because many people (perhaps, generations of people) make pint-sized contributions to giant-sized change.

No one of us is going to make the culture more cooperative, socially intelligent, or capable of nurturing the self-respect of its citizens. But we can, and we must, improve the culture by making these differences in one child at a time. However, our impact as teachers will be increased if other teachers are working in a unified way toward similar goals. For that reason, we believe teachers must work in coordination with parents and colleagues to make schools safe and exciting places in which to teach and learn. The suggestions for school improvement outlined in Section VI do not provide recipes for change. Instead, they offer a means for empowering teachers and administrators so that they can find new and better methods for improving themselves, their teaching, their relationships with students and colleagues, and their schools. The goal is for teachers to become reflective practitioners, working in an hospitable environment toward clear social and intellectual aims.

From the ridge, we can see many problems and many impediments to improvement. However, that vantage point also lets us see that the strength of a people is determined by the quality of their education. The task facing teachers is large, but no work in the world is more important.

Name Index

Subject Index